A Treatise of Legal Philosophy and General Jurisprudence

Volume 6

A History of the Philosophy of Law from the Ancient Greeks to the Scholastics

Second Edition

edited by

Fred D. Miller, Jr.

Bowling Green State University and *University of Arizona, USA*

and

Carrie-Ann Biondi

Marymount Manhattan College, USA

with contributions by

Mahesh Ananth, Thomas M. Banchich, Annabel Brett, Charles E. Butterworth, Janet Coleman, Michael Gagarin, Brad Inwood, Anthony J. Lisska, Roderick T. Long, John Marenbon, Fred D. Miller, Jr., Charles J. Reid, Jr., Richard F. Stalley, Brian Tierney, and Paul Woodruff

Springer

Editors
Fred D. Miller Jr.
Social Philosophy and Policy Foundation
Bowling Green, OH, USA

Carrie-Ann Biondi
Department of Philosophy
and Religious Studies
Marymount Manhattan College
New York, NY, USA

ISBN 978-94-017-7652-3 ISBN 978-94-017-9885-3 (eBook)
DOI 10.1007/978-94-017-9885-3

Springer Dordrecht Heidelberg New York London

Softcover reprint of the hardcover 2nd edition 2015

Printed on acid-free paper

Springer Science+Business Media B.V. Dordrecht is part of Springer Science+Business Media (www.springer.com)

A Treatise of Legal Philosophy and General Jurisprudence

Volume 6

A History of the Philosophy of Law from the Ancient Greeks to the Scholastics

A Treatise of Legal Philosophy and General Jurisprudence

TABLE OF CONTENTS

A NOTE ON THE AUTHORS

MAHESH ANANTH is Associate Professor of Philosophy at Indiana University at South Bend. He is the author of *In Defense of an Evolutionary Concept of Health* (Ashgate, 2008). He was a Lynde and Harry Bradley Fellow at the Social Philosophy and Policy Center, Bowling Green State University.

THOMAS M. BANCHICH is Professor of Classics and History at Canisius College. He is the author of *Cebes' Pinax* (Bryn Mawr Greek Commentaries, 2nd ed., 2002); *Aristotle's Nicomachean Ethics, Book I* (Bryn Mawr Greek Commentaries, 2004); and also of "Julian's School Laws," *Ancient World* (1993); "The Epitomising Tradition in Late Antiquity," in *The Blackwell Companion to Greek and Roman Historiography*, edited by John Marincola (Blackwell, 2007); and, with Eugene N. Lang, of *History of Zonaras from Alexander Severus to the Death of Theodosius the Great*, 2nd ed. (Routledge, 2012).

CARRIE-ANN BIONDI is Associate Professor of Philosophy at Marymount Manhattan College. She is author of "Aristotle's Moral Expert: The *Phronimos*," in *Ethics Expertise* (Springer, 2005) and "Aristotle, Citizenship, and the Common Advantage," *Polis* (2005). She was a Lynde and Harry Bradley Fellow at the Social Philosophy and Policy Center, Bowling Green State University.

ANNABEL BRETT lectures on History at Gonville and Caius College, Cambridge. She is author of *Liberty, Right, and Nature: Individual Rights in Later Scholastic Thought* (Cambridge, 1997) and "Changes of State: Nature and the Limits of the City," in *Early Modern Natural Law* (Princeton, 2011). She has also edited and translated *Marsilius of Padua: The Defender of the Peace* (Cambridge, 2005).

CHARLES E. BUTTERWORTH is Professor Emeritus of Government and Politics at the University of Maryland. He is the author of *Alfarabi, The Political Writings: "Selected Aphorisms" and Other Texts* (Cornell University Press, 2001) and *Averroes' Decisive Treatise and Epistle Dedicatory* (Brigham Young University Press, 2001). He is also coeditor of *Between the State and Islam* (Cambridge University Press, 2001). He has served as president of the American Council for the Study of Islamic Societies and president of the Société Internationale pour l'Étude de l'Histoire de la Philosophie et la Science Arabe et Islamique (SIHSPAI).

JANET COLEMAN is Professor Emeritus of Ancient and Medieval Political Thought in the Department of Government, London School of Economics and Political Science. She is author of *A History of Political Thought: From Ancient Greece to Early Christianity* and *A History of Political Thought: from the Middle Ages to the Renaissance* (Blackwell, 2000). She is the editor of *The Origins of the Modern State in Europe, 13th–18th Centuries* (Oxford University Press, 1996); *Ancient and Medieval Memories: Studies in the Reconstruction of the Past* (Cambridge University Press, 1992); and *Against the State: Studies in Sedition and Rebellion* (BBC and Penguin, 1990, reissued 1995). She is also co-editor of *The History of Political Thought.* She is a Fellow of the Royal Historical Society (FRHS) and has been a Leverhulme Major Research Fellow.

MICHAEL GAGARIN is James R. Dougherty, Jr. Centennial Professor Emeritus of Classics at the University of Texas at Austin. He is author of *Early Greek Law* (University of California Press, 1986) and *Antiphon the Athenian: Oratory, Law, and Justice in the Age of the Sophists* (University of Texas Press, 2002) and editor of *The Cambridge Companion to Ancient Greek Law* (Cambridge University Press, 2005). He is also general editor of a series of new translations of the Greek orators published by the University of Texas Press. He has served as president of the American Philological Association and of the Classical Association of the Middle West and South.

BRAD INWOOD is Professor of Classics and Canada Research Chair in Ancient Philosophy at the University of Toronto. He is author of *Ethics and Human Action in Early Stoicism* (Oxford University Press, 1985), *The Poem of Empedocles*, rev. ed. (University of Toronto Press, 2001), and of *Reading Seneca* (Oxford University Press, 2005); and is coauthor of *Hellenistic Philosophy: Introductory Readings*, 2nd ed. (Hackett, 1997) and *The Epicurus Reader* (Hackett, 1994). He is also editor of *The Cambridge Companion to the Stoics* (Cambridge University Press, 2003) and coeditor of *Assent and Argument: Studies in Cicero's Academic Books* (Brill, 1997) and of *Hellenistic and Early Modern Philosophy* (Cambridge University Press, 2003). He is a Fellow of the Royal Society of Canada.

ANTHONY J. LISSKA is Maria Theresa Barney Professor of Philosophy at Denison University in Granville, Ohio. He is the author of *Aquinas's Theory of Natural Law: An Analytic Reconstruction* (Oxford University Press, 1996). His essays on Aquinas have appeared in *Current Legal Problems* (Oxford University Press, 1998) and *The American Journal of Jurisprudence.* He has received the national Carnegie Professor of the Year Award and the Sears Teaching Award. He has served as president of the American Catholic Philosophical Association.

RODERICK T. LONG is Professor of Philosophy at Auburn University. His publications include *Reason and Value* (The Objectivist Center, 2000), "Aristotle's Conception of Freedom," *Review of Metaphysics* (1996), and "Aristotle's Egalitarian Utopia," *Acts of the Copenhagen Polis Centre* 7 (2005). He has served as president of the Alabama Philosophical Society.

JOHN MARENBON is a Senior Research Fellow of Trinity College, Cambridge. He is author of *Early Medieval Philosophy (480–1150)* (Routledge, 1983, revised 1988), *Later Medieval Philosophy (1150–1350)* (Routledge, 1987, 2nd ed. 1992), *The Philosophy of Peter Abelard* (Cambridge University Press, 1997), *Aristotelian Logic, Platonism, and the Context of Early Medieval Philosophy in the West* (Ashgate, 2000), *Boethius* (Oxford University Press, 2003), and *Le temps, l'éternité et la prescience de Boèce à Thomas d'Aquin* (Vrin, 2005). He is also editor of *The Routledge History of Philosophy, vol. III (The Middle Ages)* (Routledge, 1998); coeditor and translator of *Peter Abelard "Collationes" ("Dialogue between a Christian, a Philosopher and a Jew")* (Oxford Medieval Texts, 2001).

FRED D. MILLER, JR. is Professor Emeritus of Philosophy and Executive Director of the Social Philosophy and Policy Center, Bowling Green State University. He is the author of *Nature, Justice, and Rights in Aristotle's Politics* (Oxford University Press, 1995). He is coeditor, with David Keyt, of *A Companion to Aristotle's Politics* (Blackwell, 1991). He also served as associate editor of *Social Philosophy & Policy*. He has served as president of the Society for Ancient Greek Philosophy from 1998 until 2004.

CHARLES J. REID, JR. is Professor of Law at the University of St. Thomas, Minnesota. He is the author of *Power over the Body, Equality in the Family: Rights and Domestic Relations in Medieval Canon Law* (Eerdmans, 2004), "Thirteenth-Century Canon Law and Rights," *Studia Canonica* (1996), and "The Canonistic Contribution to the Western Rights Tradition," *Boston College Law Review* (1991).

RICHARD F. STALLEY is Professor of Ancient Philosophy at the University of Glasgow. He is the author of *An Introduction to Plato's Laws* (Blackwell, 1983) and editor of *Aristotle, The Politics* (Oxford University Press, 1995).

BRIAN TIERNEY is the Bryce and Edith M. Bowmar Professor in Humanistic Studies Emeritus at Cornell University. His publications include *Foundations of the Conciliar Theory* (Cambridge University Press, 1955), *Medieval*

Poor Law (University of California Press, 1959), *Religion, Law, and the Growth of Constitutional Thought* (Cambridge University Press, 1982), and *The Idea of Natural Rights* (Scholars Press, 1997). He is a corresponding Fellow of the British Academy and a Fellow of the Medieval Academy of America and of the American Academy of Arts and Sciences. He has received honorary doctorates from Uppsala University, Sweden, and from the Catholic University of America, Washington, D.C.

PAUL B. WOODRUFF is Royal Professor in Ethics, at the University of Texas at Austin. He is the author of *Reverence: Renewing a Forgotten Virtue* (Oxford University Press, 2001), editor and translator of *Thucydides: On Justice, Power, and Human Nature* (Hackett, 1993), coeditor of *Early Greek Political Thought from Homer to the Sophists* (Cambridge University Press, 1995), and translator of several Greek tragedies. His latest book is *First Democracy: Facing the Original Ideas* (Oxford University Press, 2005).

GENERAL EDITOR'S PREFACE TO THE HISTORICAL VOLUMES OF THE TREATISE

In the preface to Volume 7 of this Treatise, Andrea Padovani and Peter Stein point out that the volume purposely omits to treat the rationalistic natural-law school of the 17th and 18th centuries, this despite the volume being entitled *The Jurists' Philosophy of Law from Rome to the Seventeenth Century*. This is how they explain why Volume 7 does not, despite its title, discuss Grotius (1583–1645) and the so-called natural-law school:

It is not by any accident that we have omitted to treat [...] the rational school of natural law. True, this school must be credited with affording the best innovation that juristic reflection would see in seventeenth-century Europe. But then an enquiry into the doctrines of the natural-law theorists would take us too far from our main focus, which is the *jurists'* philosophy of law. Now, it is well known that not only the jurists contributed to bringing out the new natural law, but also philosopher-jurists and philosophers tout court. Exemplary in this regard is Hugo Grotius. He was not a philosopher and had no philosophical interests properly so called, *yet he grounded the validity of his thought on a whole series of speculative questions* that cannot be ignored. In short, given any problem, such as defining "just war," the solution for it had to be forged on philosophical grounds, and only then would it find confirmation or validation through the authority of the *ius commune*. This procedure was common to the entire modern school of natural law. [...] The exponents of this scientific movement forsook all interpretive activity (no longer deemed useful) devoting themselves instead to the effort of "discovering" a new law, a law capable of sustaining each nation, and the family of nations, in its future course. The natural-law theorists found that the source of law no longer lay in the *Corpus Iuris Civilis* or the *Corpus Iuris Canonici*, but rather lay in the "nature of things," the only standard, certain and constant, by which to assess human behaviour. Thus, we no longer see in their treatises any mention of the methods of textual interpretation—no *argumenta* or *loci* devoted to that subject—which for three centuries had been the focus of the commentators and their exegesis. And not just anciently, either: most of the modern European jurists who practised law continued to be faithful to the canons of that long tradition. (Volume 7 of this Treatise, XIV–XV; italics added on first and second occurrence; in original everywhere else)

This passage contributes to illustrating the guidelines adopted in planning out the eleven volumes making up this Treatise, and the historical volumes in particular (Volumes 6 through 11). Indeed, in the preface to the theoretical volumes of this Treatise (Volumes 1 through 5), I indicate, on page XXI of Volume 1, that among the distinctions that from the outset served as guiding principles at the meetings held to plan out the Treatise project was the distinction (tracing back to Norberto Bobbio) between the *philosophers'* philosophy of law and the *jurists'* philosophy of law. Accordingly, the first of the historical volumes—Volume 6, entitled *A History of the Philosophy of Law from the Ancient Greeks to the Scholastics*, edited by Fred D. Miller, Jr. and Carrie-Ann Biondi—is dedicated to the *philosophers'* philosophy of law from ancient Greece to the 16th century, and spans from the early Greek thinkers to early modern Scholasticism. And the second of the historical volumes, Volume 7 (entitled *The Jurists' Philosophy of Law from Rome to the Seventeenth Century*, and edited by Andrea Padovani and Peter Stein) is dedicated precisely to the subject stated in its title, namely, the *jurists*' philosophy of law, and as such acts as a complement to Volume 6.

Then, too, there emerges from the previously quoted passage by Padovani and Stein a further kind of philosophy of law which came to bear in planning out the historical volumes of this Treatise. In fact, alongside the *philosophers*' philosophy of law and the *jurists*' philosophy of law, we thought it appropriate to introduce the *legal philosophers*' philosophy of law: the philosophy of law par excellence. Prior to the modern era there was no distinct discipline that could be called "legal philosophy": It was only in the modern age that thinkers began to view themselves as legal philosophers.[1]

For a long time, and in particular in the reaction that German legal positivism mounted against it, the "rational school of natural law" (as Padovani and Stein call the rationalistic natural-law theory of the 17th and 18th centuries) was regarded as *the* philosophy of law, meaning the *legal philosophers*' philosophy of law: It was regarded as the *Rechtsphilosophie* par excellence. (*Rechtsphilosophie* is a German expression that, in the light of what I maintain in Volume 1 of this Treatise, would be better translated to "the philosophy of what is right.") In this sense, the philosophy of law of the rationalistic natural-law school was the first classic instance of what I am calling here the legal philosophers' philosophy of law. Now, there are of course theoretical differences that distinguish these legal philosophers from one another, but then they all laid at the foundation of their doctrines a series of speculative questions from which they derived systems of ethics *ordine geometrico demonstrata* (Benedict de Spinoza, 1632–1677) or systems of natural law *methodo scientifica pertractatum* (Christian Wolff, 1670–1754). In other words, citing the title of a work by Wilhelm Leibniz (1646–1716), one of the fundamental aspects characterising the rationalistic natural-law school is a *nova methodus discendae docendaeque jurisprudentiae*, a new method for learning and teaching legal science, a method that leads to a systematic construction or reconstruction of law.[2]

[1] I am using here a formulation kindly suggested to me by Fred Miller, Jr.

[2] "The *Nova methodus* is aimed at reducing law to systematic unity, this by giving legal material an order that ascends to simple principles from which to obtain exceptionless rules. This material is, again, Roman law [it is so in Leibniz's *Nova methodus*, but not with any of the other exponents of the new natural-law theory], the law which at that time [when Leibniz was writing] was in force in Germany as the *ius commune*, but a *ius commune* reordered on the basis of a new method, a method using which the law can be rationalized and hence endowed with the unity which in the Justinianian system it lacked. The system Leibniz envisioned and put forward must be such that, as a complete whole, it provides a solution for each question, and must do so through precise arguments expressed in a rigorous language, on the model of logical-mathematical procedure" (Fassò 2001, 189; my translation; cf. also ibid., 186).

The rationalistic natural-law school—traditionally made to begin with Grotius—developed in the 17th century and received its classic Enlightenment form in the 18th century: It was the first philosophy of law to be considered a legal philosophy par excellence, the legal philosophers' philosophy of law.

The second classic instance of a legal philosophers' philosophy of law in the history of legal thinking was, ironically, German legal positivism itself, which proclaimed the end of the legal philosophers' philosophy of law as embodied in the rationalistic natural-law theory of the 17th and 18th centuries and replaced it with the *Allgemeine Rechtslehre*, that is, with the general doctrine, or theory, of law.[3]

Hence, from the 17th to the 19th century, the legal philosophers' philosophy of law (understood as legal philosophy par excellence) developed in various forms, and took different names, following a formalistic path and taking as well a strong systematic approach: It runs from the so-called natural-law school to the legal positivism of German inspiration.

This last orientation, in turn, German formalistic and systematic legal positivism, reached its most refined version in the 20th century, with Hans Kelsen (1881–1973), who gave us a very sophisticated representation of *the legal system*—a glorious and fragile representation of *das Recht* ("what is right") *als Rechtsordnung* ("as a system of what is right") that had the strengths and the weaknesses of a daring cathedral of crystal.

In the second half of the 20th century, Kelsen's formalistic legal positivism spread not only in civil-law countries (even outside of Europe: in Latin America, for example), but also, in some measure, in common-law countries, this on account of the influence that Kelsen's work and thought had beginning from the time of his emigration to the United States. Of course, as is well known, there is a native and very important empiricist legal positivism in Anglophone countries that traces back at least to Hobbes and was then developed in the so-called analytical jurisprudence, whose fathers are Jeremy Bentham (1748–1832) and John Austin (1790–1859).[4]

If we go back now to the observations made at the beginning of this preface, we can see that Volumes 6 and 7 bring out the twofold distinction (tracing back to Bobbio) between the philosophers' and the jurists' philosophy of law in a complementary fashion: Volume 6 (edited by Fred D. Miller, Jr. and Carrie-Ann Biondi) is mainly a history of the philosophers' philosophy of law from the early Greek thinkers to the 16th century; and Volume 7 (edited by

[3] Or again, we might call this the "general doctrine of what is right," in keeping with the view I argued in Volume 1 (and in particular in Chapters 1 and 14) of this Treatise.

[4] I just qualified Anglophone legal positivism as "empirical" and did so to stress its difference from the German-inspired legal positivism of Europe, which by contrast is formalistic. I will not enter here into any detail, as into American and Scandinavian legal realism, since these matters I leave to the discussion in Volumes 8 through 11.

Andrea Padovani and Peter Stein) is dedicated to the jurists' philosophy of law from Rome to the 16th century, and as such acts as a complement to Volume 6.

In Volumes 8 through 11, dedicated to the period running from the 17th to the 20th century, the underlying distinction is, instead, the threefold distinction sketched above between the philosophers', the jurists', and the legal philosophers' philosophy of law. These three philosophies of law are present in various forms in these volumes, however much not always in explicit distinction from one another, the reason being that the distinction was meant to be a principle for each author to interpret freely, according to his view of the purposes and contents of his volume. Volume 8 is a history of the philosophy of law in common-law countries from the 17th to the 19th century and, as is observed by its author, Michael Lobban, it is "primarily concerned with jurists' and legal philosophers' understandings of law, rather than with those of philosophers." Volume 9 is a history of the philosophy of law from the 17th to the 19th century in civil-law countries. Volume 10 can be considered in the first instance an ideal continuation of Volume 6, and hence a history of the philosophers' philosophy of law from the 17th to the 20th century, but it also discusses some thinkers, such as Grotius and Pufendorf (1632–1694), whose philosophy of law we might properly describe as a legal philosopher's philosophy of law. Volume 11, the last of the Treatise volumes, is concerned with 20th-century philosophy of law overall, in civil-law and common-law countries alike.

For the background leading up to the Treatise, and for the acknowledgements, I refer the reader to Sections 2 and 3 of the editor's preface to the five theoretical volumes, a preface found in Volume 1. The assistant editor's preface, by Antonino Rotolo, also in Volume 1, presents, instead, the editorial rules on which the Treatise is based.

In fine, I should like to take the opportunity of this preface to note that it would not have been possible to carry through the Treatise project without the care and farsightedness of the people at the publishing house (initially Kluwer, now under Springer). I have fond memories of a meeting I had, in 1995, with Alexander Schimmelpenninck and Hendrik Van Leusen. A word of thanks goes also to those at Springer who have since been entrusted with the Treatise project.

Enrico Pattaro

University of Bologna
CIRSFID and Law Faculty

PREFACE TO VOLUME 6
(SECOND EDITION)

We thank everyone who helped with the creation of this volume, beginning with the authors, who wrote excellent drafts and revised them in response to editorial suggestions. Most of the authors and several discussants convened at two symposia, chaired by Douglas B. Rasmussen, to discuss early drafts and plans for this volume. We gratefully acknowledge the support of the Liberty Fund (and especially Douglas Den Uyl and Emilio Pacheco) for holding these symposia and releasing the copyright of the papers so that they could be published here.

In addition to the authors, the following individuals provided advice and comments on the manuscripts: Kevin Crotty, Richard Epstein, John Haldane, Richard Helmholtz, David Keyt, Louis Lomasky, Phillip Mitsis, Charles Nalls, Gerald Postema, Anthony Preus, Sam Silverman, Stephen Sheppard, Christopher Shields, Leonidas Zelmanovitz, and Michael Zuckert.

Mahesh Ananth compiled the initial bibliography and abbreviations, and Galen Foresman and Pamela Phillips corrected the page proofs. The staff of the Social Philosophy and Policy Foundation provided logistical support for both editions of this volume.

This second edition became necessary after questions arose concerning Chapter 14 of the first edition submitted by Martin Stone. We were informed by the Katholieke Universiteit Leuven that, following an investigation of allegations of plagiarism against the author, it had retracted its affiliation with the publication. The unfortunate affair is documented in an article, "40 Cases of Plagiarism," by M. V. Dougherty, P. Harsting, and R. L. Friedman in *Bulletin de Philosophie Médiêvale* 51 (2009), 350–91. The editors extend their apologies to the authors whose work was inappropriately used and to readers who were misled. We are grateful to Enrico Pattaro and to Springer for making every effort to rectify the problem, including the publication of this replacement volume. We also thank Annabel Brett for contributing a new Chapter 14, which is an excellent original treatment of the later scholastic legal philosophers.

Finally, we again express our admiration and gratitude to Professor Pattaro and his staff at the University of Bologna for expertly orchestrating the monumental Treatise of which this volume is a part.

Fred D. Miller, Jr.
Bowling Green State University and the University of Arizona
Carrie-Ann Biondi
Marymount Manhattan College

ABBREVIATIONS

ACRONYMS FOR MODERN SERIES OR COLLECTIONS OF TEXTS

CC	*Corpus Christianorum Continuatio Mediaevalis*
CSEL	*Corpus Scriptorum Ecclesiasticorum Latinorum* (Vienna and Leipzig)
CTh	*Theodosian Code=Theodosiani Libri XVI* (Mommsen and Meyer 1954/ trans. in Pharr 1952, reproduced 1969).
Diehl	Ernestus Diehl, ed., *Anthologia Lyrica Graeca* (Leipzig: Teubner, 1952)
DK	H. Diels and W. Kranz, *Die Fragmente der Vorsokratiker*, 3 vols., sixth edition (Berlin: Weidmann, 1951–1952)
IC	F. Halbherr, *Inscriptiones Creticae* (Rome: Libreria dello Stato, 1935–)
IG	*Inscriptiones Graecae* (Berlin: G. Reimer, 1873–)
PL	J. P. Migne, ed., *Patrologia Latina* (Paris: Migne, 1854–1856)
POxy.	B. P. Grenfell and A. S. Hunt, eds., *Oxyrhynchus Papyri* (London: Egypt Exploration Fund, 1898).
SVF	J. von Arnim, *Stoicorum Veterum Fragmenta*, 3 vols. (Leipzig: Teubner, 1903–1905)

ABBREVIATIONS FOR ANCIENT AND MEDIEVAL TEXTS

Aeschylus

Eu.	*Eumenides*
Supp.	*Suppliants*

Alcinous

Did.	*Didaskalikos*

Alfarabi

Aphorisms	*Selected Aphorisms*
Virtuous City	*Principles of the Opinions of the Inhabitants of the Virtuous City*

Ambrose of Milan

Off.	*De Officiis Ministrorum*
Ep.	*Epistles*

Anon. Iamb.	*Anonymous Iamblichi*

Aristotle

An. Pr.	*Analytica Priora*
Ath.	*Athênaiôn Politeia*
Cael.	*De Caelo*
Cat.	*Categories*
de An.	*De Anima*
EE	*Eudemian Ethics*
EN	*Nicomachean Ethics*
GA	*De Generatione Animalium*
MA	*De Motu Animalium*
Metaph.	*Metaphysics*
MM	*Magna Moralia*
PA	*De Partibus Animalium*
Phys.	*Physics*
Pol.	*Politics*
Rhet.	*Rhetoric*
Rhet. Al.	*Rhetorica ad Alexandrum*
SE	*Sophistici Elenchi*
Top.	*Topics*

Athenaeus

Deipn.	*Deipnosophistae*

Augustine of Hippo

CD	*De Civitate Dei* (*City of God*)
Conf.	*Confessions*
Lib. Arb.	*De Libero Arbitrio* (*On Free Will*)
Op. Mon.	*De Opere Monachorum*
Enarr. in Psal.	*Enarratione in Psalmos*
Ench.	*Enchiridion*
Ep.	*Epistolae*
Faust.	*Contra Faustum Manichaeum* (*Against Faustus the Manichean*)
Iohann. Evangel.	*Tractatus in Iohannis Evangelium*
Questions	*De Diversis Quaestionibus*

Sermo	*Sermones*
Sol.	*Soliloquia*
Trin.	*De Trinitate*

Averroes (Ibn Rushd)

Republic	*Commentary on Plato's Republic*
Rhetoric	*Middle Commentary on Aristotle's Rhetoric*

Avicenna (Ibn Sīnā)

Epistle	*Epistle on the Divisions of the Intellectual Sciences*

Bible

Cor.	Corinthians
Deut.	Deuteronomy
Exod.	Exodus
Ezek.	Ezekiel
Gal.	Galatians
Gen.	Genesis
Heb.	Hebrews
Jer.	Jeremiah
Lev.	Leviticus
Macc.	Maccabees
Matt.	Matthew
Neh.	Nehemiah
Phil.	Philippians
Rom.	Romans

Calcidius

Tim.	*In Platonis Timaeum* (Commentary on Plato's *Timaeus*)

Cicero

Att.	*Letters to Atticus*
Fin.	*De Finibus* (*On Goals*)
Leg.	*De Legibus* (*On the Laws*)
ND	*De Natura Deorum* (*On the Nature of the Gods*)
Off.	*De Officiis* (*On Duties*)
Rep.	*De Re Publica* (*On the Commonwealth*)
Tusc.	*Tusculan Disputations*

Clement

Strom.	*Stromateis* (*Miscellanies*)

Dio Chrysostom

Or. — *Orationes*

Diogenes Laertius

D.L. — *Vitae Philosophorum*

Diogenes of Oenoanda

New Frag. — *New Fragments*

Duns Scotus, John

Rep. — *Reportatio Parisiensis*

Epictetus

Diss. — *Dissertationes* (*Discourses*)
Ench. — *Encheiridion* (*Handbook*)

Epicurus

KD — *Kuriai Doxai* (*Key Doctrines*)
Nat. — *On Nature*
Sent. Vat. — *Vatican Sentences*

Euripides

Ba. — *Bacchae*
Supp. — *Suppliants*

Gaius

Inst. — *Institutiones*

Gratian

Decr. — *Decretum*

Hesiod

Th. — *Theogony*
WD — *Works and Days*

Homer

Il. — *Iliad*

Irenaeus of Lyons

Haer. — *Adversus Haereses* (*Against Heresies*)

Isidore

Etym.	*Etymologies*
Sent.	*Sentences*

Josephus

Ant.	*Jewish Antiquities*

Justin Martyr

Dial.	*Dialogue with Trypho*

Justinian

Code	*Code* (*Corpus Iuris Civilis, vol.* 2)
Dig.	*Digest*
Inst.	*Institutes* (*Corpus Iuris Civilis, vol.* 1)

Lactantius

Inst.	*Divine Institutes*

Las Casas, Bartolomeo de

De Regia	*De Regia Potestae o Derecho de Autodeterminación*
De Úncio	*Del Úncio Modo de Atraer*

Lucretius

RN	*De Rerum Natura* (*On the Nature of Things*)

Maimonides

Guide	*The Guide of the Perplexed*

Marcus Aurelius

Med.	*Meditations*

Molina, Luis de

Concordia	*Concordia Liberi Arbitrii cum Gratiae Donis, Divinia Praescientia, Providentia, Praedestionatione, et Reprobatione, ad Non Nullus Primae Partis D. Thomae Articulos*
De Iure et Iust.	*De Iure et Iustitia*

Nemesius

Nat. Hom.	*De Natura Hominis* (*On the Nature of Man*)

Origen

Cels.	*Against Celsus*

Philo

Leg.	*Legum Allegoriae*
Mos.	*On the Life of Moses*
Opif.	*De Opificio Mundi*
Prob.	*Quod Omnis Probus Liber Sit*
Spec.	*De Specialibus Legibus*

Philodemus

Acad. Ind.	*Academicorum Index*
Herc.	*Herculanensia Volumina*
Stoic.	*On the Stoics*

Photius

Bibl.	*Bibliotheca*

Plato

Alc.	*Alcibiades*
Ap.	*Apology*
Clit.	*Clitophon*
Crat.	*Cratylus*
Ep.	*Letters*
Erx.	*Eryxias*
Euthd.	*Euthydemus*
Gorg.	*Gorgias*
Hipparch.	*Hipparchus*
Hp. Ma.	*Hippias Major*
Phd.	*Phaedo*
Plt.	*Politicus (Statesman)*
Prot.	*Protagoras*
Rep.	*Republic*
Tim.	*Timaeus*

Plautus

Bacch.	*Bacchides*

Plutarch

Alex. Fort.	*The Luck or Virtue of Alexander*
Contr. Ep. Beat.	*Contra Epicuri Beatitudinem*

Lyc.	*Life of Lycurgus*
Sol.	*Life of Solon*
Stoic. Rep.	*De Stoicis Repugnantiis*
TG	*Life of Tiberius Gracchus*

Porphyry

Abst.	*On Abstinence*

Pseudo-Plutarch

Fat.	*De Fato (On Fate)*

Seneca the younger

Ben.	*De Beneficiis*
Brev. Vit.	*De Brevitate Vitae*
Clem.	*De Clementia*
Cons. Marc.	*Consolatio ad Marciam*
Ep.	*Epistulae Morales (Moral Epistles)*
Nat.	*Naturales Quaestiones*
Otio	*De Otio (On Leisure)*

Salas, Juan De

Tract.	*Tractatus de Legibus*

Sextus Empiricus

M	*Adversus Mathematicos*
PH	*Outlines of Pyrrhonism*

Sophocles

Ant.	*Antigone*
OT	*Oedipus Tyrannus*

Soto, Domingo de

De Iust. et Iure	*De Iustitia et Iure Libri Decem*

Suárez, Francisco

Leg.	*De Legibus sue de Deo Legislature*

Tacitus

Ann.	*Annales*
Dial.	*Dialogus de Oratoribus*

Tertullian

Anim.	*On the Soul*
Jud.	*Against the Jews*
Marc.	*Against Marcion*
Praescrip.	*Prescription of Heretics*

Thomas Aquinas

Comm. Eth.	*Commentary on Aristotle's Nicomachean Ethics*
SCG	*Summa Contra Gentiles*
STh	*Summa Theologiae*

Ulpian

Inst.	*Institutes*

Vázquez, Gabriel

Comm. STh.	*Comentarios a la Summa de Santo Tomas*

Vitoria, Francisco de

Comm. STh.	*Comentarios a la Secunda Secundae de Santo Tomas*
De Ind.	*De Indis*
De Mat.	*De Matrimonio*
De Pot. Civ.	*De Potestae Civile*

William of Ockham

Rep.	*Reportatio*
In I Sent.	*Commentary on the Sentences*

Xenophon

An.	*Anabasis*
Cyr.	*Institutio Cyri* (*Cyropaedia*)
HG	*Historia Graeca* (*Hellenica*)
Hier.	*Hiero*
Lac.	*Respublica Lacedaemoniorum*
Mem.	*Memorabilia*
Oec.	*Oeconomicus*
Smp.	*Symposium*
Vect.	*De Vectigalibus*

Prologue

NEAR EASTERN ANTECEDENTS OF WESTERN LEGAL THOUGHT

by Fred D. Miller, Jr.

Western legal philosophy, like a stream flowing over three millennia, was fed by far-flung tributaries. A major spring was ancient Greek law and legal thought, manifested in a variety of sources, including poets, historians, orators, philosophers, and sophists (see Chapter 1). Greek philosophers made major contributions, including Socrates, Plato, and Aristotle and their followers, as well as the Hellenistic schools of philosophy (see Chapters 2–5). Another wellspring of Western legal philosophy was Roman jurisprudence, presented in a systematic manner by legions of Roman jurists. The combined influence of Greek philosophy and Roman law was evident in the Roman philosophers Cicero, Seneca, Epictetus, and Marcus Aurelius (see Chapter 6). A third important source was ancient Jewish legal thought, arising with the traditional Mosaic code and culminating in the Talmud. Emerging as a Jewish sect, Christianity soon became a separate branch and a distinct and powerful fourth influence on Western European medieval legal philosophers (see Chapter 7). St. Augustine's philosophy of law represented a major confluence of the Greco-Roman and Judeo-Christian streams of thought (see Chapter 8). Another important tradition was Islamic thought, represented by Alfarabi, Avicenna, and Averroes, which directly influenced Jewish philosopher Maimonides and indirectly Catholic philosopher Thomas Aquinas, and presented a fundamental challenge to European philosophers of law in the Middle Ages (see Chapter 9). Finally, the revival of Roman law and the development of Christian canon law, together with the rise of scholastic philosophy in the late Middle Ages, infused new concepts and theories into medieval European law codes and thereby created fertile ground for early modern Western legal philosophy (see Chapters 10–14).

Although Western legal philosophy arose in ancient Greece, the Greeks themselves recognized the existence of far older legal traditions. Aristotle remarks that the Egyptians "are thought to be the most ancient of people, and they have acquired laws and a political order" (*Pol.* VII.16.1329b32–3). The great antiquity of the Egyptian legal system is also accentuated in the story in Plato's *Timaeus* about the visit of Solon of Athens to Saïs in Egypt, where he interrogated priests about early history. The priests told him that "you Greeks are forever children" and "you have in your souls no belief about antiquity handed down by ancient tradition" (*Tim.* 22b4–8). While the Greeks had forgotten their own distant past due to a series of natural catastrophes, the Egyptians, who were sheltered in the Nile valley, retained their history and social arrangement for 8,000 years according to their sacred scriptures. The priests reported that Athens already possessed a constitution 9,000 years before, which resembled the current Egyptian legal system (*Tim.* 23e2–6, 24a2–4; cf. *Laws* II.656d5–657a2).

Later, during the Hellenistic and Roman periods, it was claimed that early Greek statesmen were inspired by Egyptian archetypes. Diodorus Siculus (ca. 80–20 B.C.) mentions reports "in the records of the sacred books of Egyptian priests" that, in addition to Solon, Lycurgus the legislator of Sparta and Plato himself visited Egypt and "incorporated many Egyptian *nomima* (customs or statutes) into their own legislation" (*Library* I.96.1, 98.1). Plutarch (ca. A.D. 45–121) (*Lyc.* 3.6) also cites Egyptian claims, confirmed by some Greek historians, that Lycurgus visited them and copied some of their institutions. On the basis of such texts it has been argued that Greek political and legal philosophy was heavily indebted to Egypt. Whether these events actually occurred, however, is questionable. Lycurgus was a semi-mythical figure about whom little is certain, and there is no early report of him going to Egypt. Solon did visit Egypt, according to Herodotus (490–425 B.C.) (*History* I.29–30), but only after finishing his legislative work in Athens. Herodotus (*History* II.176; cf. Diodorus Siculus, *Library* I.77.5) elsewhere says that Solon copied an Egyptian law against idleness, but this seems to be an error later corrected by Theophrastus (Plutarch, *Sol.* 31.2), who writes that Pisistratus, not Solon, laid down this law. As for Plato, there is no evidence in his own writings or other classical sources that he visited Egypt or had firsthand knowledge of Egyptian laws.[1]

Granted that the claims of direct influence are exaggerated and poorly substantiated, the question remains whether Greek legal thought was stimulated in a subtler, more general way by contact with Near Eastern societies. Greek merchants and mercenaries frequented Egypt by the end of the sixth century, and the Greeks had extensive commercial ties with Asia much earlier than that. Scholars have detected foreign influences in Greek religion, philosophy, and science (e.g., mathematics and astronomy). "In a much broader context, eastern influences helped shape the development of Greek religion, crafts, art and architecture, technology (both civil and military), coinage, and writing. Although more debated, such influences are visible also in social, legal, and political phenomena, such as tyranny, the enactment of written law, and the symposium" (Raaflaub 2000, 51).

[1] Bernal 1987, 53, 103–8, alleges extensive influence based on evidence about Lycurgus and Plato. Lefkowitz 1996, 75–6, 81–2, however, notes problems in Plato's guarded account of Solon in Egypt (which Critias heard from his grandfather, who heard it from his father), questions the historicity of the later anecdotes, argues that such stories of influence become suspiciously more colorful and detailed over time, and concludes that "[t]he idea that early Greek law was inspired by Egyptian law is a historical fiction." See also Vasunia 2001.

The question of Egyptian influence is complicated by the fact that the study of Egyptian law presents serious problems of its own. The legal documents of Egypt, mainly kept on papyrus or ostraca, have largely perished, and what has survived is often incomplete and difficult to interpret (e.g., the fragmentary edict of Horemheb from the nineteenth dynasty, ca. 1300 B.C.). Yet a text from the eighteenth dynasty (thirteenth century B.C.) affirms that "everything is done according to what is specified by law" and refers to recorded legal precedents, and "thousands of legal documents of trials, inheritance, and transfers of real and personal property, attest to the functioning legal system" (Brewer and Teeter 1999, 73; see also Théodoridès 1971; Lorton 1995; Jasnow 2003, 255). But it is debatable whether Egypt had a regular system of law courts following genuine legal codes, in the sense of systems of laws promulgated by a king, during most of the dynastic period. There is also a danger of projecting later legal categories (deriving from the Greeks and Romans) back into Egyptian thought, a process no doubt already underway by the Hellenistic period (Kruchten 2001, 279).[2] Nonetheless, some Egyptian legal terms have been thought to offer parallels to important Greek concepts. One such word *hp*, understood to correspond to "law," is also often used for a "decree," for example, of a pharaoh, although it has a broader meaning of "rule" or "regulation," and can even refer to the regular movement of a planet (Kruchten 2001, 277–8).[3] The legal term *hp* came into common usage during the Middle Kingdom (Jasnow 2003, 255). Another word *ma'at* is often interpreted as "justice" or "truth." In addition to naming a goddess, the word refers to the cosmic order, which holds together the natural world, the kingdom of Egypt, and the individual subject. *Ma'at* has a normative connotation, for the gods placed the pharaoh on earth "forever and ever, judging mankind and propitiating the gods, and setting (*ma'at*) in place of disorder" (Vasunia 2001, 128). In a social context it involves reciprocal justice: "The reward of one who does something lies in something being done for him. This is considered by god as *ma'at*" (Assmann 2002, 128). The extent to which individuals internalize *ma'at* in this life determines their fate in the afterlife (Assmann 1996).[4] *Ma'at* "goes down into the necropolis with him who renders it" (trans. Wilson 1946, 94). In the *Book of the Dead*, during postmortem judgment the deceased's heart is weighed on a scale against an ostrich feather, a hieroglyphic symbol for *ma'at* (see Taylor 2001, 36, fig. 17). The value of impartial justice is assumed in the

[2] By the end of the Ptolemaic dynasty in the late first century B.C., the Egyptians had an elaborate judicial system. "The entire body of the laws was written in eight volumes which lay before the judges," reports Diodorus Siculus (*Library* I.75.3). He also mentions the legend that the laws were initially laid down by the first pharaoh Menes (compared to Lycurgus), who had received them from the god Hermes (i.e., Thoth) (ibid., I.94.1). But these phenomena may well reflect Greco-Macedonian influence.

[3] Nims 1948 discusses the later use of *hp* in demotic.

[4] See Tobin 1987 on *ma'at* in comparison to the Greek term *dikê*.

injunction of the vizier Ptahhotep (probably sixth dynasty, 2345–2181 B.C.) to judges to "hew a straight line [...] do not lean to one side" (as quoted in Brewer and Teeter 1999, 73; cf. similar passages in Wilson 1946, 98–100). Similarly, a Middle Kingdom papyrus states that "partiality is abhorrent in god's eyes" (as quoted in Assmann 2002, 155). The underlying principle of human equality is implied by a pronouncement of the sun god: "I have made each man the same as his neighbor and have prohibited that they do wrong. But their hearts have violated my commands" (as quoted in Assmann 2002, 154).

After the conquest of Egypt (525 B.C.) Darius, king of Persia, ordered his satrap in Egypt to assemble Egyptian sages and compile all the laws of ancient Egypt. Working from 519 until 503 B.C., the commission published a written legal code in Demotic and in Aramaic. There was a basic division into public law, temple law, and private law. This work governed subsequent legal practice in Egypt and may have provided a basis for legislation during the Ptolemaic period including the "code of Hermopolis West" (*POxy.* 3285) from the reign of Ptolemy II Philadelphus (308–246 B.C.) (see Briant 2002, 474; Bowman 1989, 61–6; Mattha 1975).

Ancient Mesopotamia has yielded much more legal evidence preserved on cuneiform tablets and inscriptions on monuments. These include fragmentary records of the law codes of Ur-Nammu, founder of the third dynasty of Ur (ca. 2100 B.C.), Lipit-Ishtar of Isin (ca. 1900 B.C.), Dadusha of Eshnunna (ca. 1770 B.C.), and, most importantly, Hammurabi of Babylon (ca. 1750 B.C.) (Richardson 2000; Driver and Miles 1960; Pritchard 1958, 133–72; Pritchard 1975, 31–41; Kramer 1963, 336–40). The early Mesopotamians had no general word for "law," but the word *di* in Sumerian (*dīnu* in Akkadian) was used for a lawsuit, trial, or decision, and *nì-si-sai (mīšaru* in Akkadian) signified "justice" (Soden 1994, 131; Saggs 1968, chap. 7; Saggs 1989, chap. 8). Justice was upheld throughout the universe by the gods, especially the sun god Utu (Shamash), also god of justice, with the king as his representative. Hammurabi declares, "By the command of Shamash, the almighty judge in heaven and earth, let my justice shine over the land" (E10; as quoted in Richardson 2000, 123). The king was ordained by the gods "to demonstrate justice within the land, to destroy evil and wickedness, and to stop the mighty exploiting the weak, [...] to improve the welfare of my people" (P3; as quoted in Richardson 2000, 30–1; see also Westbrook 2003b, 364). Although ultimately responsible for administering justice, the king could, and generally did, delegate this responsibility to judges who held court in or before temples (Jacobsen 1946, 208–9; Saggs 1989, 170–3; Postgate 1992, chap. 15).[5] Hammurabi proclaimed that his commandments should remain in force unchanged in perpetuity:

[5] Saggs and Postgate reconstruct early Mesopotamian legal procedures. Hammurabi's code is distinctive in adhering strictly to the *lex talionis* (law of retribution) and prescribing very severe punishments.

"May any king appearing in this land at any time at all in the future heed the righteous commands that I have inscribed on this stone. May no one change the justice for the land which I have ordained and the verdicts for the land which I have rendered" (E14; Richardson 2000, 125). Anyone who violated or emended the code would fall under a curse (E19). Hammurabi's code evidently influenced later legal codes, including the Assyrian, Hittite, and Jewish.

Persian legal practices may also have had a direct influence on the Greeks who had numerous contacts with the Persian Empire over several centuries. Plato (*Ep.* VII.332b) remarks that Darius of Persia (522–486 B.C.) "set an example of what a good lawgiver and king should be, for he established laws that have kept the Persian Empire to this day" (cf. Plato, *Laws* III.695c; Xenophon, *Oec.* 14.6). Plato here uses the Greek word *nomos* (law) for the Persian word *dāta*. Olmstead (1948, 120–33) argued that Darius promulgated a code with echoes of Hammurabi's code, so that his legislation might have served as a conduit for much earlier Mesopotamian influence. But later scholars question the existence of a "royal code" of Darius for the entire Persian Empire (see Briant 2002, 510–11, 956–7).

It must be emphasized that even when Greek laws and legal concepts resembled their predecessors', this does not prove influence. Different societies can independently find similar ways to meet similar challenges, as Aristotle observes:

> [O]ne should believe that nearly everything has been discovered often in a great span of time—or rather infinitely often. For need itself is likely to teach the necessary things, and once these are already present, it is reasonable to expect that the things that promote elegance and abundance will increase. And so one should suppose the same to hold for constitutional affairs. And that all such things are ancient is indicated by facts about Egypt. (*Pol.* VII.16.1329b25–32)

Moreover, the Near Eastern view of law was in important respects alien to the later Greek view. The Sumerians and Babylonians (like the Egyptians) viewed "the cosmos as a hierarchically structured state that is ruled, with absolute authority, by the gods under the leadership of the sky god Anu," and the human king was an agent authorized by the gods and charged with the responsibility of maintaining divine order and justice in his domain. These views implied that virtue consisted in unquestioning obedience to political authorities (Raaflaub 2000, 56–7; cf. Jacobsen 1946). Later, Greek thinkers challenged the top-down model of divinely sanctioned oriental despotism.

Further Reading

Westbrook 2003a is a valuable comprehensive history of ancient Near Eastern legal systems with separate chapters by specialists on different periods of Egyptian, Sumerian, Akkadian, Babylonian, Assyrian, Israelite, and international law, including extensive bibliographies and excellent indexes. Early concepts of law are discussed in general histories of the ancient Near East, including Saggs 1989, chap. 9, Soden 1994, and Snell 1997. Frankfort et al. 1946 examines the place of various concepts (including law) in myth before the emergence of Greek philosophy; see Wilson 1946 on Egypt and Jacobsen 1946 on Mesopotamia. Assmann, Janowski, and Welker 1998 includes comparative studies of law and justice in ancient Near Eastern, Egyptian, Jewish, Assyrian, Christian, and Greek traditions. Pritchard 1958 includes translations of some legal documents from Mesopotamia and Egypt.

Breasted 1906–1907 and Lichtheim 1973, 1976, and 1980 are multi-volume collections of translated Egyptian texts, including references to *ma'at* (justice). Sarraf 1984 is an overview of the ancient Egyptian concept of law. Assmann 2002 is a valuable comprehensive study of Egyptian thought including law. Assmann 1996 discusses Egyptian views of justice in relation to the afterlife. Seidl 1942, Théodoridès 1971, Lorton 1995, Brewer and Teeter 1999, chap. 5, Kruchten 2001, and Versteeg 2002 provide concise introductions to ancient Egyptian law. Tyldessley 2000 is an account of crime and punishment in pharaonic courts. Mélèze-Modrzejewski 1995 discusses law and justice in Ptolemaic Egypt. See Bernal 1987, Lefkowitz 1996, and Vasunia 2001 for very different views on the question of whether Greek thinkers were influenced by the ancient Egyptians.

A comprehensive recent source is Roth 1997, containing translations of Sumerian, Babylonian, Assyrian, and Hittite laws. Driver and Miles 1960 offers a transliterated text and translation with commentary on Babylonian laws. Yaron 1988 is an edition of the laws of Eshnunna, and Richardson 2000 is a transliterated text and translation of Hammurabi's code. Brief discussions of Mesopotamian law are found in Kramer 1963, Saggs 1968, Oppenheim 1977, Postgate 1992, chap. 15, and Greengus 1995.

Regarding Assyrian legislation Driver and Miles 1935 offers a transliterated text and translation with commentary. Neufeld 1951 and Hoffner 1997 provide texts and translations of the laws of the Hittites. Gurney 1990 includes discussion of Hittite laws and legal institutions.

On the controversy over the so-called code of Darius of Persia, contrast Olmstead 1948 and Briant 2002.

Chapter 1

EARLY GREEK LEGAL THOUGHT

by Michael Gagarin and Paul Woodruff[1]

1.1. Law and Legal Procedure in Early Greece[2]

To write about early Greek legal thought requires, first, some consideration of what this expression might have meant at the time. "Legal philosophy" in the modern sense did not exist before Plato, but "legal thought," in the sense of thinking about law, undoubtedly did. We find various reflections on law explicitly or implicitly in the writings of many who are now classified separately as poets, philosophers, sophists, or historians, but whom the Greeks would have grouped together under the term *sophoi*—"wise men." In thinking about law, however, the Greeks differed considerably from us in their basic construction of the subject.

This is evident in the first place in the fact that there is no single word or phrase in Greek that conveys the general notion of "law," as, for example, in the expressions "early Greek law" and "Athenian law." The closest equivalent to "law" is *nomos*, which can mean a legal rule or statute and is also broadly used for "custom," "tradition," "social norm," etc., but which never means "law" in the most general sense that the English word can have.[33] *Nomos* does not come to designate a law (or statute) until the fifth century B.C.; earlier Greeks used different words: *thesmos* ("what is laid down"), *rhêtra* ("what is said"), and *graphos*, *grammata* ("what is written"). In fifth-century Athens, the plural of *nomos*—*hoi nomoi*—can designate the entire set of a community's laws, and this is perhaps the closest the Greeks could come to our general sense of "law." But *hoi nomoi* still designates only "the laws" and does not necessarily include that aspect of law we would categorize as the legal process

[1] This paper is the result of a joint effort, with Gagarin writing the first draft of Sections 1.1–3 and Woodruff of 1.4–6; both of us then read and revised all sections. All translations are by the authors unless otherwise indicated. We received much good advice at a meeting in Williamsburg, Virginia, from the authors of other chapters in this volume, and we especially thank Fred Miller for his many useful comments and suggestions as well as his overall stewardship of this project.

[2] Along with archaeological discoveries, poetry is our main source for Greek civilization in the eighth century B.C.; no inscriptional evidence for Greek law is earlier than the seventh century B.C. (see below, Section 1.2). One must exercise care in using poetic sources, of course, since their intent is not historical accuracy; but to the extent that similar features are found in several different sources, we can be more confident that these accurately represent conditions at the time.

[3] On the meaning of *nomos*, see Section 1.4 below. English differs from Latin and many modern languages in using only one word ("law") for both a legal rule and an entire institution (the Law). Contrast Latin (*lex*, *ius*), French (*loi*, *droit*), German (*Gesetz*, *Recht*), etc.

(i.e., courts, trials, etc.). For "legal process," the closest equivalent was *dikê*—"judgment," "settlement," "trial"—which, especially in its later form *dikaiosynê*, comes to mean "justice" with much the same broad range of meaning as the English word.

Early Greek thinkers tended to be concerned with one or the other of two aspects of law: substance and process. The earliest are more concerned about the means of regulating conflict and bringing order to society (process); later there was more interest in the rules and standards that govern the way humans lived their lives (substance). To some extent, however, this change reflects the emergence of self-conscious reflection on theoretical issues that does not appear in our earliest sources, the poets.[4]

The poems of Homer and Hesiod, composed around the end of the eighth century B.C., already indicate the importance the Greeks attached to the rudimentary process they had developed for the peaceful settlement of disputes. In the *Iliad* this is most evident in the trial scene portrayed on Achilles' great shield. On the shield are two cities, one at war, the other at peace. In the latter, there are just two scenes in the town, a trial and a wedding, and one scene in the country, a harvest. The inclusion of a trial in itself conveys the sense that a process for resolving conflict is an essential ingredient of peace and prosperity. The details of Homer's portrayal, moreover, indicate the characteristic features of this process. The scene portrays two litigants who wish to resolve their disputes:

> Meanwhile a crowd gathered in the *agora*, where a dispute
> had arisen: two men contended over the blood price
> for a man who had died. One swore he'd pay everything,
> and made a public declaration. The other refused to accept anything.
> Both were eager to obtain a settlement from a referee.
> People were speaking on both sides, and both had supporters;
> but the heralds restrained them. The old men
> took seats on hewn stones in a sacred circle;
> they held in their hands the scepters of heralds who raise their voices.
> Then the two men rushed before them, and they in turn gave
> their judgments. In the middle there lay two talents of gold
> as a gift for the one among them who would give the straightest judgment. (*Il.* XVIII.497–508, as quoted in Gagarin and Woodruff 1995, 6)

Two men disagree about payment for a man who has been killed. The precise point of disagreement has been much debated and need not concern us here,[5]

[4] This poetry was probably composed and transmitted largely without the help of writing. It is difficult to speak of substantive law before the introduction of writing because rules of all sorts (legal, moral, practical, religious, etc.) tend to be undifferentiated in oral cultures, as in Hesiod's *Works and Days*. Writing provided a means of distinguishing laws from other rules. See further Gagarin 1986, 1–17.

[5] The main possibilities are that the two men disagree about the amount of payment, or

for the procedural details are fairly clear. They seek a resolution and so they have brought their dispute to the *agora*, or central meeting place, where a special gathering of elders will hear the case. A crowd of onlookers and supporters attend the session; they express themselves vocally and have to be restrained by heralds. The litigants plead their case one after the other, after which the elders express their opinions. One of these opinions is eventually determined (probably by consensus) to be "the straightest judgment (*dikê*)," and the elder who gave this opinion is rewarded with a prize. There is much that we are not told (Homer is, of course, not a legal historian), but ideally (we may assume) the litigants accept the "straightest" (fairest, most acceptable, most just) judgment and are reconciled, and the community thus remains at peace.

Already here we see the main features of the Greek concept of procedural justice. First, the process is public; like all large gatherings it takes place in the *agora*, and much of the community is present. A small group of respected members of the community "judge" the case—that is, they seek the best ("straightest") resolution; in other scenes of judgment there is often a single judge, but this variation does not appear to affect the other features. The entire process is oral: Litigants speak their cases, judges speak their settlements, and the members of the crowd voice their feelings. It is a characteristically Greek scene with substantial community participation, turbulent but still orderly. The goal is a settlement that is "straight," the primary metaphor for justice in early poetry.[6] And since there is no mechanism for enforcement of the settlement (and enforcement would be incompatible with the loosely structured society portrayed by Homer), "straightest" must be determined by some sort of consensus, and the outcome must, in the long run at least, have the support of the community.

The importance of this process is also evident in the work of Homer's contemporary Hesiod, who tells us he experienced it directly in the course of a dispute with his brother Perses over the division of their inheritance. In *Works and Days* he complains that Perses has been trying to get more than his fair share of their father's estate and worries that the "gift-devouring kings" who want to judge the case may side with Perses. In a long passage (*WD* 213–85), he urges first Perses, then the kings, then Perses again, not to give way to "crooked" justice, for in the long run crooked justice will result in famine and destruction for the whole community, whereas straight justice will lead to prosperity. Hesiod summarizes his advice in the following conclusion:

whether the agreed sum has been paid, or whether payment must be accepted or may be accepted. See Gagarin 1986, 26–33, with further references.

[6] A "straight" settlement may originally have been a straight boundary line dividing a disputed piece of property, but the metaphor is also often used of speech that is truthful, honest, and unbiased ("straight talk").

This was the way of life (*nomos*) Zeus established for human beings:
for fish and beasts and flying birds he allowed
that one may eat another, since there is no justice (*dikê*) among them;
but to human beings he gave justice, which turns out to be
much better. For if someone is willing to speak justly (*ta dikaia*)
in full knowledge, wide-seeing Zeus makes him prosper;
but if someone lies intentionally under sworn oath
in giving testimony, and so hurts justice, he is incurably ruined.
From that time forth his family will be left in obscurity,
while the family of an oath-keeping man will prosper ever after. (*WD* 276–85, as quoted in Gagarin and Woodruff 1995, 19)

Like Homer, Hesiod understands the importance of the legal process; a corrupt process will lead to ruin, whereas justice leads to prosperity. Hesiod is also aware, like Homer, that justice is an oral process requiring speech that is just, here specifically in the form of truthful testimony and true oaths.

Hesiod also portrays this process for settling disputes in his *Theogony*, where he praises the Muses for the blessings they can give a king:

If the daughters of great Zeus [the Muses] should honor and watch
at the birth of one of the kings who are nourished by Zeus,
then they pour sweet honey on his tongue, and the words
from his mouth flow out in a soothing stream, and all
the people look to him as he works out what is right (*diakrinonta themistas*)
by giving judgments (*dikai*) that are straight: he speaks out faultlessly
and he soon puts an end to a quarrel however large, using his skill.
That's why there are kings with intelligence: so they
can turn things around in the *agora* for people who have suffered
harm, easily, persuading them with gentle words.
As he comes to the hearing, they seek his favor like a god
with respect that is soothing, and he stands out from those assembled. (*Th.* 81–92, as quoted in Gagarin and Woodruff 1995, 19–20)

Here, although there is only a single judge, the process resembles Homer's description in several ways: It takes place in the *agora*, where a crowd is assembled; people come forth to seek a resolution for their dispute or some compensation for injury. The king's success depends in part on his intelligence and his ability to find a straight (fair, just) resolution, but Hesiod's main point is that with the Muses' help the king is also a successful speaker. His honeyed tongue speaks "a soothing stream" of words and he persuades the people (litigants and supporters) "with gentle words." The gifted king, in other words, is able not only to declare a resolution to a dispute that is fair, but to speak it effectively, so that both sides will be satisfied and accept the settlement. Such a king is honored like a god.

These scenes, together with many briefer references to settling disputes,[7] give a good picture of how the Greeks at the time envisioned law in terms of

[7] For a review of these scenes, see Gagarin 1986, 19–50.

an effective process for achieving a fair resolution to conflict. "Straight" justice required in the first place a process for hearing the pleas of both litigants—a requirement summed up in the maxim attributed to Hesiod but perhaps coined at a later time: "Do not judge a case before hearing both sides" (Hesiod, frag. 338, as quoted in Merkelbach and West 1967).[8] The hearing took place in a public setting, open to all members of the community, and a judge or group of judges, who were figures of authority (often kings), heard the pleas and proposed settlements. A straight *dikê* provided adequate compensation for loss and for the most part satisfied the litigants. The entire process was oral: A set of speech acts by litigants and judges (and perhaps by onlookers, too) culminated in the straight settlement persuasively delivered by a judge. As Hesiod's complaints make clear, the process did not always work as envisioned, but straight justice ideally not only resolved conflict between litigants, but also contributed to the general harmony and cohesiveness of the community.[9]

1.2. The Emergence of Written Laws

The poetry of Homer and Hesiod shows that a process for settling disputes was well established in Greece at the beginning of the archaic period (ca. 700–500 B.C.). By this time we can also discern the main features of that characteristic Greek political form, the *polis* ("city-state" or "city"). Greece remained a collection of independent city-states through the classical period (ca. 500–322 B.C.) and beyond, each *polis* being governed by its own set of laws.[10]The political structure of most cities in the archaic period was some form of oligarchy with at least one deliberative body. Democracies developed in some cities by expansion of the franchise beyond the wealthy, and some cities experienced a period of "tyranny," or the illegitimate rule of a single man.[11]

Our evidence for different cities varies widely,[12] but none of it is inconsis-

[8] This fragment is not included in Hesiod, *The Homeric Hymns and Homerica*, edited by Evelyn-White 1914.

[9] We should note that a similar process is found in many early communities in other parts of the world; see, for instance, Köhler 1956.

[10] Of course, there were similarities among many of these independent legal systems, and some small cities may have adopted laws of a larger city with little change, but it remains problematic whether we can usefully speak of "Greek law." For further discussion, see Todd 1993, 15–6, 32–3, and other works cited there.

[11] "Tyranny" reproduces the Greek word *tyrannis*, but many of the tyrants ruled benevolently and did much to promote their city's culture. The Athenian tyrant Pisistratus (sixth century B.C.) ruled "more like a citizen than a tyrant"; he maintained the laws as they had been before him and, when accused of homicide, he even appeared in court, though his accuser did not (Aristotle, *Ath.*16).

[12] For the archaic and classical periods, in addition to poetry and archaeology, our sources include the accounts of later historians and philosophers, which vary widely in reliability, and inscriptions recording laws and other material. Inscriptions have been found, somewhat haphazardly, all over Greece, but they are often incomplete or fragmentary and very difficult to under-

tent with the assumption that the legal process portrayed by the poets formed the basis for the emergence of a more formal legal system based on written laws in many, if not all, Greek cities during the archaic period. As written laws emerged and the *polis* grew in size and authority, there was a general shift toward a more compulsory process and toward some degree of state involvement in the enforcement of settlements, but even in the classical period, litigation and its consequences depended largely on the initiative of individuals. And the basic structure of an oral legal process remained in place through the classical period, long after the use of writing for legal matters became widespread.

Writing was introduced into Greece around 750 B.C.[13] At first it was used only for private matters—dedications to a god, personal sentiments, and other graffiti. More than a century later it began to be used for public matters, and the earliest public inscriptions, beginning sometime after 650 B.C., were predominantly legal in nature. These inscriptions, together with later historical sources, show that during the next century (ca. 650–550 B.C.) cities all over Greece began to use writing to inscribe and publicly display legislation. In some cities early legislation was traced to a few figures who first wrote laws, Zaleucus of Locri (traditionally the first, ca. 650 B.C.), Lycurgus of Sparta (seventh century B.C., but perhaps legendary), and Draco (ca. 620 B.C.) followed by Solon (ca. 590 B.C.) in Athens. Except in Sparta, which had an antipathy to writing, almost all cities wrote laws and inscribed them, often on stones that were displayed in prominent public places such as the *agora* or a religious sanctuary. At this time laws were almost the only public documents that were thus displayed, so that in some cities writing became synonymous with law, and the expression "what is written" became a way of referring to the city's laws.

Writing down laws on relatively permanent materials and displaying them in public had several effects. First, it differentiated certain rules of the community so that they could be identified as laws. Second, it conveyed a sense of the stability and permanence of these rules. Third, it assured that the laws were available to the members of the community—not to all members, given the fairly low degree of literacy at the time, but probably to most of those who commonly participated in public affairs and would be likely to be involved in litigation. Fourth, it conveyed the idea that these were a special set of rules with special authority: the rules that are written (*ta grammata*), or that are laid down (*hoi thesmoi*). Fifth, it implied or affirmed that these rules were backed by the authoritative political body that caused them to be enacted.[14]

stand. Van Effenterre and Ruzé 1994–1995 is a useful collection of most archaic legal inscriptions (with a French translation).

[13] An earlier form of writing Greek, called Linear B, was used in the Bronze Age, but it did not survive the end of that civilization (ca. 1200–1100 B.C.), and the later script we know as Greek was an independent development out of Near-Eastern scripts.

[14] The earliest surviving law from the Cretan city of Dreros (ca. 650–625 B.C.) opens with the statement, "the following was pleasing to the *polis*" (i.e., "the *polis* approved the following").

Thus, writing created the idea of laws as a special class of rules backed by the authority of the *polis*. The stories of the lawgivers, moreover, even if much distorted (and sometimes clearly false), also conveyed the sense that the community's many different laws were a unified set. Even in the fourth century, Athenian litigants spoke of "the laws of Solon" as including all Athenian laws, even though many of them had been enacted long after Solon's time. Lawgivers could easily become idealized, and some were said to have been given their laws by a god (see Section 1.5.2 below), thus adding to the authority of their legislation. In sum, publicly displayed, written legislation conveyed the sense that the community had a coherent collection of fixed norms of behavior backed by the authority of the *polis*, which we would call the city's "law."

From all this we see that during the archaic period, Greek law was developing into a productive combination of fixed, stable, written legislation together with an oral, dynamic process for settling disputes. Although some thinkers focused their attention on one aspect or the other, Solon, who not only wrote an extensive set of laws for Athens but also wrote poems reflecting on his political accomplishments, seems to understand the connection between them when he says, "I wrote laws [*thesmoi*] too, equally for poor and rich, and made justice (*dikê*) that is fit and straight for all" (Solon, frag. 36.18–19, as quoted in Gagarin and Woodruff 1995, 27). Here for the first time we see substantive laws (*thesmoi*) and legal process (*dikê*) put together, suggesting that they are part of a single sphere of human activity, though this thought is not further developed at this time. But Solon's verses suggest that archaic Greeks understood the close connection between written laws and the process of settling disputes, even if they did not have a word for this unified entity.

Other sixth- and fifth-century B.C. thinkers also seem to understand justice (*dikê*) as legal process. For example, the idea of a dynamic process of dispute settlement underlies Anaximander's use of the metaphor of justice to describe the behavior of the cosmos: "they render justice (*dikê*) and retribution (*tisis*) to each other for injustice (*adikia*) according to the assessment of time." Like litigants in court seeking retribution for injuries, the elements may give and take from each other, but over time the universe maintains a stability, which is not inert but is a dynamic process. Justice resides in the process, producing just outcomes in the long run though not necessarily in each case. Similarly, Heraclitus's paradoxical equation (Heraclitus, DK 80, as quoted in Gagarin and Woodruff 1995, 22) of justice (*dikê*) and strife (*eris*) conveys the idea that the essence of justice is not permanence but a dynamic process of adversarial competition. But Heraclitus also sees the importance of substantive law for the survival of the city: "The people must fight for the law (*nomos*) as they would for

The Dreros law can be found in Gagarin 1986, 81–2. See Section 1.3 below for one provision of the law.

the city walls" (Heraclitus, DK 44, as quoted in Gagarin and Woodruff 1995, 7; see further Sections 1.5.1 and 1.6.1 below).

The continuing interest in law as process is evident in the story of Deioces, the first king of the Medes, told by the mid-fifth-century B.C. historian Herodotus, which illustrates the sharp difference between the traditional, oral procedure in Greek law and an oriental legal process using writing (Herodotus, *History* I.96–100, as quoted in Gagarin and Woodruff 1995, 80–1). At first, when the Medes were still living in separate villages, Deioces acted like an archaic Greek judge: He was a prominent citizen to whom people came to have their disputes settled. He gained a reputation in his own village for "practicing justice (*dikaiosynê*)," and soon people in other villages heard of it and began coming to him. In the end they would take their disputes to no one else; Deioces (as we might say) had cornered the market on settling disputes. One day, realizing the power this gave him, he stopped judging cases entirely, saying he needed to tend to his own business. Lawlessness (*anomia*) and disorder immediately ensued. When the situation became intolerable, a group of Medes gathered and decided that they needed to institute a monarchy. Naturally, they chose Deioces as their first king.

Once Deioces was king, his whole approach to justice changed. He built a large new palace and shut himself off from his people, conducting all business through messengers. Specifically with regard to law, Herodotus tells us, Deioces

> became a severe guardian of justice. People had to put their cases in writing and have them sent in to him; then he made his decisions and sent them back. In addition to this procedure for legal disputes, he established others: if he heard of anyone assaulting someone, he would send for him and impose on him a punishment appropriate to the crime, and he had spies and observers throughout the extent of his kingdom. (Herodotus, *History* I.100)

Herodotus presents this story as a historical event, but most scholars consider it fictional. We see it as a discourse contrasting Greek legal procedure, which Deioces follows at first, and an oriental type of justice, which he implements once he becomes king. When Deioces becomes king, law changes from an oral, public procedure open to the whole community to a closed process dependent on writing, in which the king is an absolute judge (presumably not himself subject to the law), dispensing decisions alone and in writing. Law thus is removed from the people and controlled by a single ruler. From this perspective, the story can be seen to illustrate the importance the Greeks attached to maintaining their traditional oral public procedure, thereby keeping law open to the participation of ordinary people.

1.3. Law in the Classical City

In the fifth century, interest in and use of the law increased substantially, especially after 450 B.C. For this period we concentrate on Athens, the political and cultural leader of Greece in the fifth and fourth centuries, where the public inscription of laws and decrees flourished and use of the courts expanded dramatically. Our sources of information for Athenian law far surpass those for other cities; in addition to inscriptions, they include drama, history (especially the *Constitution of the Athenians*, a work attributed to Aristotle but perhaps written by his pupils), and most notably some one hundred speeches written for delivery in actual trials. But before considering Athens, we look briefly at the city of Gortyn in Crete, which, although apparently of little importance at the time, has left us the largest and best preserved Greek legal inscription, the Gortyn Law Code, a set of laws covering especially family and property matters, that runs to twelve columns and some 3,000 words. We know nothing about law at Gortyn besides what can be inferred from this code and a few other separate legal inscriptions, but it is striking that the very first sentence of this document establishes the principle that the process of law must take precedence over extra-legal action: "If anyone wishes to contest the status of a free man or a slave, he is not to seize him before a trial." The provisions that follow set substantial fines for violating this rule and procedures for adjudicating disputed cases. This endorsement of law over an earlier system of self-help is notable, as is the large number of inscribed laws, which go back as early as the late seventh century.

One of the early provisions from Gortyn limits the term in office of the highest official, the *kosmos*, by prescribing a minimum interval of three years between terms; a similar provision at Dreros requires a ten-year interval.[15] These *kosmoi* and other public officials at Gortyn and elsewhere could also be fined if they did not enforce the law properly.[16] Gortyn and some of the other cities where such provisions occur had aristocratic forms of government, but they all seem to share the sense that the highest officials are subject to the law like everyone else.[17] Such provisions, together with other evidence, indicate that all Greeks held to the principle of "the rule of law."

[15] The provision from Gortyn is line 2 of *IC* 4.14.*g-p* (as quoted in Gagarin 1986, 93–4); line 1 has the Gortyn law on fining public officials. For the Dreros law, see Gagarin 1986, 81–2.

[16] See preceding note. It was very common in Greece to fine judicial officials who did not carry out their duties as specified by law, and similar provisions are found in many other cities; see, e.g., van Effenterre and Ruzé 1994–1995, 1: no. 78 (seventh century B.C., from Tiryns), and 2: no. 95, lines 11–3, 48–9 (fifth century B.C., from Thasos).

[17] One of the provisions concerning illegal seizure in the Gortyn Code (col. 1, 51–5; see Arnaoutoglou 1998, 29–30) provides that accusations of illegal seizure involving a *kosmos* as either accuser or accused are to be heard after the *kosmos*'s term of office ends (though any fines are to be calculated from the date of the original seizure)—an ancient precedent the U.S. Supreme Court might have done well to follow when it ruled that President Clinton was subject to private litigation during his term of office.

In general, Athenians placed a similar emphasis on the importance of law. One of the earliest and best-known endorsements comes in Aeschylus's *Oresteia* trilogy, when Orestes and the Furies (his mother's avenging spirits) seek the help of Athena in resolving their dispute over Orestes' responsibility for his mother's death. After hearing their preliminary pleas, Athena sets up a human court, the Areopagus, because the matter is too important for a single god to decide (*Eu.* 470–88). The court's decision and the more general resolution at the end of the play seem to connect the city's peace and prosperity directly to the existence of the legal process.

Support for the legal system in Athens was also assisted by the close connection between law and democracy. Democracy meant not just equal access to the courts—as Pericles says, "we have equality at law for everyone here in private disputes" (Thucydides, *History* II.37, as quoted in Gagarin and Woodruff 1995, 94)—but also popular control of the courts. This association of law and democracy seems to have originated under Solon, among whose "most democratic" reforms, according to the *Constitution of the Athenians* (9.1), were that anyone who wished could bring suit for an injured party and that cases formerly decided by a magistrate could be referred to the popular courts.[18] The popular courts were originally a counterweight to the aristocratic Council of the Areopagus and to the individual magistrates, who at the time were all from the upper class. After Solon, almost all important matters were referred to courts staffed by large numbers of ordinary citizens. Solon also opened up some types of cases to prosecution by any citizen who wished; previously, only victims could bring suits, but Solon realized that some victims would be unable to act for themselves and so he allowed others to act on their behalf. Gradually, this procedure expanded to include many sorts of offenses.[19]

In the fifth century further reforms, by Ephialtes who reduced the power of the Areopagus (ca. 462 B.C.) and by Pericles who first instituted pay for jurors (ca. 450 B.C.), opened up the legal process to anyone who wished to participate. Almost all legal power now resided in the popular courts, where juries numbering in the hundreds and composed of any citizens who wished to participate decided most cases. Also in the fifth century *nomos* ("custom," "convention") became the word for "law," replacing *thesmos* ("enactment"); this was probably intended to convey the sense that the city's laws were not imposed from the outside but were a natural development of the city's customs and traditions. One result of all these reforms was that litigation increased

[18] Elsewhere Aristotle says that Solon "established the democracy by creating courts whose members were drawn from everyone" (Aristotle, *Pol.* II.12.1274a2–3).

[19] This new procedure was called a *graphê* ("writing," perhaps because the charge had to be filed in writing) to distinguish it from the traditional suit called *dikê*. In some ways the distinction between *graphê* and *dikê* mirrors our distinction between criminal and civil actions, respectively, but there are important differences, too, such as the fact that homicide always remained a *dikê* for the Greeks.

substantially during the fifth century, to the point that the comic poet Aristophanes often joked about Athenian litigiousness (see below). The Athenians undertook several reforms, most notably providing that in some cases a plaintiff who did not receive one-fifth of the jurors' votes had to pay a stiff fine. But in general they felt it was more important that people with grievances have their day in court than that the amount of litigation be reduced.

Another important development was that increasingly in the fourth century B.C. political decisions were also made by the popular courts, especially by means of the *graphê paranomôn* or "suit against unlawful (*para-nomos*) decrees." This was a process whereby any citizen could bring suit against a decree of the Assembly on the ground that it violated an existing law. The resulting trial would normally consider both the legality of the decree and the larger issue of its merit. The most famous of such cases was the trial "On the Crown" (ca. 330 B.C.). A certain Ctesiphon proposed a decree awarding Demosthenes a crown for service to Athens. Aeschines, a political opponent of Demosthenes, then brought suit, charging that the decree violated two laws.[20] Demosthenes joins in Ctesiphon's defense and he, like Aeschines, concentrates most of his efforts on defending his own public record and attacking the character and record of his opponent. But although the case clearly turns on a political judgment about the two opponents, both devote some attention to the narrow legal issues,[21] showing that even in a highly political case, litigants felt an obligation to adhere to the city's laws. Such cases also indicate a sense of obligation to uphold "the rule of law," but in other cases litigants sometimes seem largely to ignore the law.[22]

Unlike modern liberal democracies, which to a large degree treat law as an autonomous institution and generally make every effort to keep law and politics separate, the Athenians openly acknowledged the close ties between them. Litigants sometimes addressed jurors as if they were sitting in the Assembly hearing a political debate, and the large number of jurors in important cases, sometimes as many as 1,500, made identification with the Assembly easier, as did the fact that jurors were not expected to have any professional or technical expertise. There were no professional judges, moreover, so that these jurors carried out most of the functions that we today assign to judges together with those of modern jurors. We today consider law to be the province of specifically trained professionals in which amateurs have a limited role. We also tend to think that political concerns ought not to affect legal decisions, although we may admit that in practice they often do. But, to take a modern example, the

[20] One law made it illegal to award a crown in the theater, the other to crown someone who still held office.

[21] Both speakers cite various laws and discuss their meaning and relevance, much as a modern lawyer might do.

[22] See Carey 1996 (with further references), who notes that although litigants may use laws in various ways, no one directly criticizes a law of the city.

U.S. Supreme Court insisted that it decided the 2000 presidential election on legal rather than political grounds; openly to admit that it was moved by political considerations would have been generally condemned (though it might be different if the Court were composed of a thousand randomly selected citizens, as would be the case in Athens, rather than nine trained professionals). In any case, the Athenians were not concerned that political interests might influence legal decisions; law was one of the most important pillars of their democratic form of government, and referring political decisions to the popular courts was only natural and desirable.

Modern critics have often complained about the politicization of Athenian courts, but the complaint is almost never voiced by ancient critics, who focus instead on the litigiousness of Athenians.[23] Aristophanes devotes an entire play, *Wasps*, to satirizing the legal system (the name comes from a chorus of jurors in the form of these insects). The protagonist, Philocleon, is addicted to jury-duty; he loves to vote for harsh sentences and to see litigants grovel before him. And many other plays of Aristophanes poke fun at people's fondness for litigation. Further criticism from the same period comes from an anonymous treatise commonly known as the "Old Oligarch"[24] because of its author's conservative views. He argues that although democracy is a deplorable system of government, the Athenian system does in fact benefit those who control it—the worst people (i.e., the lower classes).[25] He complains that Athens's allies are forced to come to Athens for trials, but he admits that this additional litigation benefits the city in higher fees for the courts (and more pay for jurors) and other sorts of revenue. The system also helps Athens control its allies' affairs (pseudo-Xenophon or Anonymous, *The Constitutions of the Athenians*, 1.16–18).

A more sophisticated critique of the Athenian legal process comes in the papyrus fragments of *Truth* (44B), by the sophist and speechwriter Antiphon (ca. 480–411 B.C.).[26] Since only a small amount of the original work survives, we cannot know what Antiphon's overall view was, but in the text we have he presents several criticisms of the legal system. First, after noting that a person will not suffer any penalty if he disobeys the law when no one sees him, he observes that people who do what the law requires of them are often worse off for it. He continues:

[23] On litigiousness, see further Todd 1993, 147–63.

[24] This treatise, entitled *The Constitution of the Athenians* (not to be confused with Aristotle's work of the same name), is falsely ascribed to Xenophon. It is translated in Gagarin and Woodruff 1995, 133–44.

[25] This anticipates Thrasymachus' view (discussed in Section 1.5.2 below) that law is the advantage of those in power.

[26] The entire text is translated in Gagarin and Woodruff 1995, 244–7. This text is also important for the issue of *nomos* and *phusis* (see Section 1.5.3 below). On the identity of the Antiphon who wrote speeches and the Antiphon who wrote *Truth*, see Gagarin 2002, 38–52.

> If the laws provided some assistance for those who engaged in such behavior [behavior required by law], and some penalty for those who did not but did the opposite, (col. 6) then the tow-rope of the laws would not be without benefit. But in fact it is apparent that the justice (*to dikaion*) derived from law (*nomos*) is not sufficient to assist those who engage in such behavior. First, it permits the victim to suffer and the agent to act, and at the time it did not try to prevent either the victim from suffering or the agent from acting; and when it is applied to the punishment, it does not favor either the victim or the agent; for he must persuade the jurors that he suffered, or else be able to obtain justice by deception. But these means are also available to the agent. (Antiphon, *Truth*, cols. 5–6, as quoted in Gagarin and Woodruff 1995, 246)

Antiphon here contests the traditional view of law's benefits. The legal process, he argues, does not prevent wrongdoing or provide support for victims, who are not compensated unless they can persuade a jury. In other words, the principle of hearing both sides does not ensure justice, since the wrongdoer may be acquitted. This indictment targets not just the legal system in practice but also the system as conceived, for it was not designed to prevent wrongdoing (except by its deterrent value, which Antiphon ignores) or to compensate victims automatically.

Despite these criticisms, some of which are reflected in later court speeches, Antiphon later directed his energy toward working within the legal system, writing speeches for litigants to deliver in court. In these he naturally praises the laws and the legal system, though he can be very critical of the opposing litigant, especially for misusing the legal process. One such passage of criticism seems to suggest that law everywhere grants certain basic rights to Greeks. The defendant, accused of homicide, is arguing that he should not have been imprisoned before trial but allowed to leave and go into exile if he wished: "This rule is common to all, but you have enacted your own private law, trying to deprive me alone of something available to all other Greeks" (Antiphon, *Truth*, 5.13, as quoted in Gagarin and MacDowell 1998, 54). The argument that the law everywhere in Greece grants defendants this right suggests an awareness, at least in embryonic form, that there exist certain basic legal rights that are being violated in this case. This criticism of the way law is used in this particular case, however, also implicitly praises law in general for assuring this right. Indeed, praise of the laws is, not surprisingly, common in forensic oratory of the fifth and fourth centuries B.C.

1.4. The Concept of Law

We now turn to the substantive concept of law in archaic and classical times, concentrating mainly on *nomos* in the sense of statute law. We must distinguish at the outset between what we take to be prevailing views about law, expressed in a wide range of authors, and the critical views that arose within what we call the New Learning. This is the intellectual movement that brought much of Greek traditional thought under critical examination in the later fifth century. The most famous spokesmen of this movement included some of the traveling teachers known after Plato as sophists, but we must keep in mind that not all sophists were critical of tradition, and that not all of the critics were sophists. Scientists, especially those interested in medicine, were especially prominent in the New Learning.

Although criticisms of law as unnatural became strident in the later fifth century, the prevailing view never seems to have abandoned its confidence in law as a bulwark of society, one that was consistent both with nature and with the will of the gods. This is all the more impressive in view of the wide range of usage for the word *nomos*. When not used of statute law, the word could refer to an opinion that is contrary to the truth (see Section 1.4.2), and this usage could give the word an awkward penumbra when it was used of statute law.

The word *nomos* has a range of uses that are distinct in English translation and, indeed, are distinguished by most modern theories. For ancient speakers of Greek, however, the various uses probably resonated with one another in such a way that they could not be sharply separated. Normative and descriptive uses of *nomos*, to begin with, were not clearly distinguished; this reflects the view, common in many unselfconscious cultures, that the laws or customs that are found to obtain among a people are precisely those that are right and were ordained by a god. Experience of different cultures provoked intellectuals in the fifth century to examine the difference between what is and what ought to be, but such examinations were not fundamental to the felt meaning of the word *nomos*. Hence, as we shall see, *nomos* almost always seems to carry some normative weight, and the idea that it is opposed to *phusis* ("nature," "reality") developed fairly late in the fifth century, was not widely accepted, and was unrelated to the earlier history of the words. The opposition of *nomos* to *phusis* is an important development in the history of ideas, however, serving as one of the roots of the ideal of natural, as opposed to conventional, justice.

1.4.1. Way of Life

Nomos is used in many contexts in which modern speakers would not use a word cognate with law. It can refer to a way of life, a procedure for farming (Hesiod, *WD* 388), a manner of making music, a custom for social interaction, and so on (see Ostwald 1969). Still, even these uses of the word are only small shades of meaning away from more familiarly legal ones. Consider this striking passage, from Hesiod's *Works and Days*, the end of which we cited for a different purpose in Section 1.1 above:

[I]t is bad to be a just man
When the greater injustice leads to the better verdict.
But I don't expect that Zeus in his wisdom is quite finished!
But you, Perses, should take this to heart:
Listen to justice, and forget the use of violence altogether.

This was the *nomos* that Zeus established for human beings:
For fish and beasts and flying birds he allowed
That one may eat another, since there is no justice among them;
But to human beings he gave justice, which turns out to be
Much better. (*WD* 271–80, as quoted in Gagarin and Woodruff 1995, 18–9)

The consensus of scholars is that *nomos* "does not here bear the sense of 'law' or 'ordinance' which prescribes a certain behavior but designates the behavior itself," and being god-given is "only incidental" (Ostwald 1969, 21). True, the passage implies that the behavior of birds is their *nomos*, and such behavior hardly counts as a norm—or even as something governed by norms. To speak of the *nomos* of birds would be to use the word descriptively. But in the human case, as line 272 makes clear, Hesiod means that, although the usual behavior of human beings is unjust, the *nomos* of Zeus is such that people will eventually be punished for what they have done unjustly—by a divine judge if not by a human one. And although Hesiod is not appealing to statute law here, he is appealing to *nomos* as the gift of a norm (for human beings, justice) that is enforced by a god and ought to be enforced by human judges. In the end, the distinction between such a gift and divine law is a small one.

1.4.2. Conventional Opinion

Nomos can also be used for merely conventional opinion or the customary manner of speaking as opposed to what can be known to be true. This is the most striking way in which *nomos* departs from the sphere in which we find modern words for law. Empedocles opposes *nomos* to *themis:* It is not right (*themis*) to speak of dissolution as a dreadful fate, but even Empedocles, following custom (*nomos)*, will do so (Empedocles, DK 9, lines 4–5). Democritus opposes *nomos* to truth: "By *nomos* sweet, by *nomos* bitter, by *nomos* hot, by *nomos* cold; but in truth atoms and void" (Democritus, DK 9). The most famous example of this usage is the *Nomos-Basileus* fragment of Pindar:

Nomos, king (*basileus*) of all,
Of mortals and immortals,
Takes up and justifies what is most violent
With a supremely high hand. (Pindar, *Nomos-Basileus* fragment, as quoted in Gagarin and Woodruff 1995, 40–1)

Pindar's example is Heracles' theft of cattle from Geryon and of horses from Diomedes. Interpretation of the passage is vexed, but the prevailing view is that *nomos* here refers to the tradition that Heracles is a hero and that his deeds must be accepted as justified. The poet seems to side with the victims of these two stories, and is therefore impressed by the power of *nomos* to make a crime acceptable to common opinion. The passage was much quoted in antiquity, most famously by Herodotus (*History* III.38, as quoted in Gagarin and

Woodruff 1995, 82) and Callicles in Plato, who does not seem to realize that Pindar's sympathies here are not with the thief (Plato, *Gorg.* 484b, as quoted in Gagarin and Woodruff 1995, 311). *Nomos* as statute law and *nomos* in compounds have much more positive connotations than Pindar's usage would predict; still, the positive usage does not shed the linguistic memory of *nomos* as something that may be artificial and false.

1.4.3. Compounds

Nomos appears in various compounds in which the original meaning was not directly related to statute law[27] (see Ostwald 1969, 62–95): *Eunomia*, good order, came to be used for specific legal systems admired by conservatives in Athens, such as that of Sparta. *Anomia*, lawlessness, ranges from disregard for norms of behavior to absence of law as a process. It is a condition under which human life is impossible—even worse, says an anonymous writer of the period, than living in solitude. *Autonomia* is not exactly independence, but it does not draw its meaning from statute law, since it is attributed to Antigone in virtue of her resistance to Creon (Sophocles, *Ant.* 821), where it seems to mean that she is taking the law into her own hands. Generally, it is the condition of life unfettered by tyranny.

1.4.4. Statutes

The pride that ancient Greeks took in their laws was a significant part of their sense of national and civic identity. Herodotus shows the Spartan Demaratus boasting of his city's laws to Xerxes:

> Although they [the Spartans] are free, they are not free in all things; for they have a master—law—whom they revere more than your people revere you: to remain in battle array and either conquer or be destroyed. (Herodotus, *History* VII.104)

The contrasting speeches by Archidamus and Pericles early in Thucydides' *History* reveal the importance Spartans and Athenians placed on their distinctive laws (Thucydides, *History* I.84, II.36–7). The Hippocratic text *Airs, Waters, Places* 16 (as quoted in Gagarin and Woodruff 1995, 165) represents the view that Greeks were superior to Asians because of their laws, which are inimical to tyranny (cf. Herodotus, *History* VII.104, discussed below). The idea that written statute law is a bulwark against tyranny is sounded again and again in the classical period. According to Thucydides, the Thebans excused their

[27] On *eunomia*, see, e.g., Solon, W 4, as quoted in Gagarin and Woodruff 1995, 25–6. On *anomia* as a condition under which people cannot live, see Anon. Iamb. 6.1, as quoted in Gagarin and Woodruff 1995, 293, and also the story of Deioces summarized in Section 1.2 above. On the value of *autonomia* in contrast to tyranny, see the Hippocratic text *Airs, Waters, Places* 16, as quoted in Gagarin and Woodruff 1995, 165.

actions during the Persian Wars by appealing to the fact that their city at the time was governed not by laws but by a tyrannous clique (Thucydides, *History* III.62). The clearest statement is from Euripides:

> Nothing means more evil to a city than a tyrant.
> First of all there will be no public laws
> But one man will have control by owning the law,
> Himself for himself, and this will not be fair.
> When the laws are written down, then he who is weak
> And he who is rich have equal justice. (Euripides, *Supp.* 429–37, as quoted in Gagarin and Woodruff 1995, 70.18)

1.5. The Origin of Law

The concept of law is partly fleshed out by theories of its source or origin. In the period before Plato, three sources for law were under consideration: Law might be given by gods, invented by human lawgivers, or developed by nature. With each account of origins comes a slightly different concept of law. Ancient thinkers were concerned with the question whether law really is something that is ordained by god or nature, or whether it is something human beings invent. The legitimacy of law seems to depend on the outcome.

Generally, ancient theories about the origin of law seem designed to serve as theories of moral foundation—or the lack of it. Historical origin and moral foundation are not the same, however. If the laws are god-given, it does not follow that their moral foundation lies in their origin, though this is often assumed. The point is most clear for the theory that laws were developed by agreement, which could be used to de-legitimize as well as to legitimize the laws. We need to keep in mind also that early Greek thinking allowed the possibility that an event has concurrent human and divine causes. Similarly, one might believe that laws are a human invention and that they can be supported by an appeal to nature, as we shall see in the case of the Anonymous Iamblichi.

1.5.1. Gift of the Gods

The idea is as old as Homer, and is felt even among the younger sophists. In the *Iliad*, Odysseus speaks of "one king / To whom the clever son of Cronus gave the staff / And the rule of *themis*" (*Il.* II.204–6, as quoted in Gagarin and Woodruff 1995, 4). Thus the basic rules of life, *themis*, are enforced by kings though given by Zeus. Tyrtaeus expresses the Spartan view that their basic law was given to the human lawgiver Lycurgus by Apollo at Delphi (Tyrtaeus, frag. 4, as quoted in Gagarin and Woodruff 1995, 23). The idea is taken up by orators and poets. Gorgias, in his funeral oration, speaks of "the most divine and universal law: to speak, to be silent, and to act as one ought and when one ought" (Gorgias, DK 6, as quoted in Gagarin and Woodruff 1995, 203). We find the idea also in all three of the surviving tragic poets: Aeschylus (in *Supp.* 670–3), as well as Sophocles and Euripides in the following:

Chorus:
Be with me always, Destiny,
And may I ever sustain holy
Reverence in word and deed
according to the Laws on high,
brought to birth in brightest sky
by Heaven, their only father,
the Laws that were not made by men.
Men die, but the Law shall never sleep forgotten;
great among gods, it never ages. (Sophocles, *OT* 863–71)

Ion:
Since you [Apollo] are powerful, strive for virtue.
When anyone who is mortal
is by nature wicked, he is punished by the gods;
so how could it be just for you to write the laws
for us mortals, and then incur a charge of lawlessness
yourselves? (Euripides, *Ion* 439–43, as quoted in Gagarin and Woodruff 1995, 67)

The author of the *Sisyphus Fragment* (either Critias or Euripides, imitating sophists) questions this view, suggesting that a clever man invented fear of the gods, in order that human beings would obey the law in private as well as in public when they are subject to human punishment—but this presupposes that people generally believed that the gods were behind human law (*Sisyphus Fragment*, lines 12–5, as quoted in Gagarin and Woodruff 1995, 261).[28] Antiphon treats human law as parallel to the will of the gods: "whoever kills someone unlawfully sins against the gods and violates the rules of human society" (Antiphon, *Tetralogy* 3.a2, as quoted in Gagarin and Woodruff 1995, 237). Heraclitus mentions a more sophisticated idea, that human law is supported by divine law, using the image of nourishment:

Those who speak with intelligence should strongly defend what is shared by all, as a city does its law, only much more strongly. For all human laws are nourished by one divine law; it controls as much as it wants, it is sufficient for all things, and it prevails. (Heraclitus, DK B 114, as quoted in Gagarin and Woodruff 1995, 152)

1.5.2. Human Invention or Agreement

At least from early classical times, bodies of law were attributed to legendary lawgivers such as Lycurgus for Sparta and Solon for Athens. The antiquity and authority of these figures conferred legitimacy and permanence on the laws

[28] On the provenance of this fragment, see Kahn 1997. Although often attributed to Critias, recent opinion is swinging toward taking this as a fragment from a lost play by Euripides.

associated with them, as well as a sense that the laws of a founding lawgiver formed a kind of unity (see further Section 1.2 above). To speak of the laws of Athens as the laws of Solon is to invite the sort of respect for them that in the modern United States is evoked by mention of its founding fathers. Legends of lawgivers need not exclude divine sources; indeed, the Lycurgus legend, as we have seen, is consistent with a divine source.

In the second half of the fifth century, however, various intellectuals began to argue that law as found in cities was entirely the product of human intelligence and therefore suspect:

Human beings laid down laws for themselves, without knowledge of what they were legislating about, but the gods put the nature of all things in order. (Hippocrates, *de Victu*, DK 22 C 1)

There was a time when human life had no order
But like that of animals was ruled by force;
When there was no reward for the good,
Nor any punishment for the wicked.
And then, I think, men invented laws
For punishment. (*Sisyphus Fragment*, lines 1–6, as quoted in Gagarin and Woodruff 1995, 260)

A similar idea shows up in *Antigone*'s Ode to Man, in which the Chorus say that man "has taught himself speech and windswift thought and *astunomoi orgai* (the character to live in cities under law)" (Sophocles, *Ant.*, line 355, as quoted in Gagarin and Woodruff 1995, 51). They proceed to distinguish "the law of the land" from "the oath-bound justice of the gods," which, however, are supposed to be woven together in harmony. In the broader context of the play, the Chorus seem to be alluding to the power of the state to make law (in this case through its king, Creon) and insisting that the laws made by the city be in accordance with divine justice (as Creon's apparently are not).

Elsewhere, the idea that law is a human invention is held against obedience to law. Plato's Thrasymachus says that justice is nothing other than the advantage of the stronger (Plato, *Rep.* I.338c, as quoted in Gagarin and Woodruff 1995, 255.3 b), meaning that law is made by whoever happens to rule in a city (338e); he goes on to say that it is therefore foolish to pursue justice or (by implication) to obey the law (348c). A similar argument is recorded in Antiphon (see Section 1.3 above).

An analog to modern social contract theory emerged in the fifth century—law by agreement. Although Socrates famously treats his agreement as obliging him to obey the law (Plato, *Crito*), he is not taking agreement to be the foundation of law. The only clear text in which agreement theory occurs before Plato is Antiphon's *Truth*, but Plato's treatment of the theme suggests that the theory was known to many intellectuals. The prevailing theory of this kind seems to have been this: People invented law by an agreement that limited their freedom to harm others while promising to protect them from the harm others might inflict upon them; but if law is merely the product of such an agreement, it has no basis in nature or reality, and therefore no real harm can come from violating it—not, that is, to the one who violates it without being observed. Antiphon's text[29] takes law to be a product of human agreement, contrasting the requirements of law against those of nature (we will return to the theme of nature below). It observes that violations of nature bring true harm on the violator, whereas violations of law damage only the opinion (*doxa*) in which the violator is held—and then only if he is caught (Antiphon, *Truth* 44b, col. 1, as quoted in Gagarin and Woodruff 1995, 245). These two basic ideas—that breaking the law hurts you only if you are caught, and that law is a product of agreement among human beings—are developed more fully in Plato's *Republic* (*Rep.* II.358e3–359b5, as quoted in Gagarin and Woodruff 1995, 309–10), where they are presented in the hope that they will be refuted.

Modern contract theory derives the legitimacy of law from an original or ideal contract, but nothing like this is explicit in early antiquity.[30] The agreement theories that have come down to us are designed to de-legitimize laws, apart from the theory implicit in Socrates' argument of the *Crito*. Generally, in ancient Greece, the analogs of modern contract theory are advanced as arguments against the legitimacy of law—that is, as reasons why an individual has no reason to follow the law that was created by the agreement of other people. Apparently, then, ancient Greeks had the anti-positivist tendency to hold that law is legitimate only insofar as it is actually—and not merely by agreement—in accordance with *dikê*.

1.5.3. Nature

The concept of unwritten law (to which we will turn below) seems to imply commitment to the existence of a law of nature, as Aristotle recognizes:

> For there is something of which we all have an inkling, being a naturally universal right and wrong [...] to which Sophocles' Antigone seems to be referring [by "unwritten laws"]. (Aristotle, *Rhet.* I.13.1373b6–9)

The clearest statement of the idea that law is natural to human beings—even if they invented it—is found in an anonymous fifth-century B.C. text preserved in Iamblichus:

> For if humans were by nature incapable of living alone and therefore joined together, yielding to necessity, and have developed their whole way of life and the skills required for this end [i.e., for living together], and cannot be with each other while living in a state of lawlessness—

[29] The text of his *Truth* is fragmentary and may represent a set of opposing views none of which Antiphon himself espoused. See Gagarin 2002, 63–92.

[30] But see Kahn 1981b, who finds traces of social contract theory very early in Greek thought, most remarkably in early Greek science.

for the penalty of lawlessness is even greater than the penalty for living alone—because of all these constraints, law and justice (*to dikaion*) are king among us and will never be displaced, for their strength is ingrained in our nature. (Anon. Iamb. 6.1, as quoted in Gagarin and Woodruff 1995, 293)

This of course is consistent with the thesis that law was invented differently in different cultures. But justice and law are conceptually linked (as we can see from this passage), and we have abundant evidence that a concept of natural justice was entertained in the fifth century. Because Antiphon's text contrasts law with nature, it has no way of articulating the concept of natural law, but it does seem to allow for the separation of justice from law (Antiphon, *Truth* 44c, col. 1, as quoted in Gagarin and Woodruff 1995, 247), where it appeals to justice in its criticism of legal procedure. In context, the justice appealed to could well be conceived as natural justice. Certainly Callicles, as represented in Plato, contrasts law-based justice against natural justice (Plato, *Gorg.* 483a7–484c3), and this—in view of the close conceptual link between justice and law—could be thought to imply the idea of natural law.

Defenders of traditional law, however, claimed that their law was simply natural. Such claims appear fairly late, so that the idea of nature-based law is probably a response to the criticism of existing law by figures such as Antiphon and Callicles. The Chorus in *Bacchae*, in the larger context, are inveighing against those who take traditional law lightly:

The cost of these beliefs is light:
Power lies
With whatever thing should be divine,
With whatever law stands firm in time
By nature ever-natural. (Euripides, *Ba.* 893–6, trans. Woodruff 1998, 36)

In Antiphon, the contrast between human agreement and nature is parallel to the contrast between opinion and truth: Agreement is a matter of opinion, nature is truth. This builds on the opposition we mentioned above between truth and *nomos* when the latter is used to refer to conventional opinion. But the concept of truth does not exhaust that of nature. What sort of nature, or rather, the nature of what sort of thing, is supposed to underlie natural law or natural justice? Callicles' concept of nature is based on his view of the behavior of beasts of prey (dissolving a distinction between humans and other animals that meant a great deal to most Greeks).[31] The details of Antiphon's view are lost to us, owing to a lacuna in the surviving text, but the outline is clear: Our natural goal is to live and to avoid death; our natural advantage, therefore, lies in whatever supports life and puts off death, whether obtaining that advantage is lawful by convention or not.

[31] Recall Hesiod's distinction between humans and animals, *WD* 271–80 (see Section 4.1 above).

We have tantalizing scraps of evidence for theories of natural law that would challenge custom in more positive ways. Hippias, as Plato represents him, argues that the concept of citizenship divides people unnaturally (Plato, *Prot.* 337d–338b, as quoted in Gagarin and Woodruff 1995, 216.5; cf. Gagarin and Woodruff 1995, 70.17). We have also this striking fragment:

One day showed us all to be one tribe of humans,
Born from one father and mother;
No one is by birth superior to another.
But fate nourishes some of us with misery
And some with prosperity, while others are compelled
To bear the yoke of slavery. (Sophocles, *Tereus* frag. 591 Radt, as quoted in Gagarin and Woodruff 1995, 56.24)

And we can be fairly sure that someone in this era raised the question whether slavery accords with natural justice. The main evidence for this is Aristotle's response to the argument of an unnamed opponent that slavery is unnatural because slaves may not differ from their masters in a way that would justify their situation:

Others think that it is contrary to nature to be a master, because the fact that one man is a slave and another free is by *nomos*, whereas in nature they do not differ at all, which is why it [slavery] is not just either; for it is the result of force. (Aristotle, *Pol.* I.3.1253b20–23)

Certainly some thinkers thought it wrong for Greeks to enslave Greeks, but a human nature theorist should discount the moral relevance of Greekness, as we find in the *Truth* of Antiphon:

We have therefore become foreign to one another, when by nature we are all at birth in all respects equally capable of being both foreigners and Greeks. We can examine the attributes of nature that are necessarily in all men and are provided to all to the same degree, and in these respects none of us is distinguished as foreign or Greek. For we all breathe the air through our mouth and through our nostrils. (Antiphon, *Truth* 44a, col. 2, as quoted in Gagarin and Woodruff 1995, 244)[32]

1.6. The Functions of Law

1.6.1. *Laws of the Polis*

Similar to what is now known as positive law is the law given by the authorities of the city in order to maintain order and preserve the city from internal dissension. The law of the *polis* seems to include what we would call its constitution or system of government,[33] but it is mainly the body of statute law. There

[32] See Ostwald 1990, for commentary on this passage.

[33] See the Tyrtaeus poem quoted above; see also Thucydides, *History* II.37, as quoted in Gagarin and Woodruff 1995, 94: "We have a form of government that does not try to imitate the laws of our neighboring states."

was a broad consensus in early antiquity that the laws of the city—any city—were good in themselves.

The law sustains the *polis*, protecting everyone, and most importantly the common people, from those who would tyrannize over them. Heraclitus recognizes this in saying, "The people (*demos*) must fight for their law as for the city wall" (Heraclitus, DK 44, as quoted in Gagarin and Woodruff 1995, 152). The content of the law does not matter very much for this purpose; Thucydides has Cleon say, in defense of the decision to kill all the men of Mytilene: "A city with inferior laws is better off if they are never relaxed than a city with good laws that have no force" (Thucydides, *History* III.37, as quoted in Gagarin and Woodruff 1995, 109). Elsewhere, Thucydides writes of the dreadful effects of lawlessness on Athens during the plague (ibid., II.53) and on Corcyra during the civil war (ibid., III.81–4).

Civil conflict was what the Greeks of this period most feared from a breakdown of law. Internal tensions, ranging from factionalism to outright rebellion could not only weaken a city's moral fabric (Thucydides' point) but also deliver it to its enemies. Many of the victories of Athens as it expanded its empire were made easy by conflicts within the cities that Athens subdued. In Sophocles' *Antigone*, King Creon expresses the view that he must uphold the law in order to prevent such disasters (Sophocles, *Ant.*, lines 382, 449, 481).

The law of the *polis* is usually understood to consist of written statutes (see Ostwald 1969, 46). The importance of written law is clear in Euripides' *Suppliants*:

> When the laws are written down, then he who is weak,
> And he who is rich have equal justice. (Euripides, *Supp.*, lines 433–4, as quoted in Gagarin and Woodruff 1995, 65)

We find a similar thought implied in Gorgias' *Palamedes*: "written laws, guardians of justice" (Gorgias, *Palamedes*, DK 11a.30, as quoted in Gagarin and Woodruff 1995, 201). In one of Aesop's fables the Frogs ask Zeus for a king; instead, Zeus sets up a piece of wood in their pond—probably meant to stand for a tablet on which laws were written. Not seeing the value of this, they insisted on a real king, and Zeus sent them a snake that devoured them (Aesop, *Fables* 44, as quoted in Gagarin and Woodruff 1995, 146.5).

In the later fifth century B.C., intellectuals came to criticize the laws of the city as artificial and conventional; this apparently did more to add to people's fear of the New Learning than it did to undermine the consensus. Thucydides has the Spartan king, Archidamus, speak to this issue in his first speech: "We [Spartans] have good judgment because our education leaves us too ignorant to look down on the laws" (Thucydides, *History* I.84, as quoted in Woodruff 1993, 28). Fear of the New Learning was very real in Athens; it is given vigorous play in Aristophanes' *Clouds* (which ends with the burning of Socrates' school) and it surely helped the prosecution secure a conviction of Socrates some twenty years later.

1.6.2. *Unwritten Law*

In the funeral oration, Thucydides has Pericles say that Athenians obey "the unwritten laws that bring shame on their transgressors by the agreement of all" (Thucydides, *History* II.37, as quoted in Gagarin and Woodruff 1995, 95). We find a similar expression in Sophocles' *Antigone:*

> What laws? I never heard it was Zeus
> Who made that announcement.
> And it wasn't justice, either. The gods below
> Didn't lay down this law for human use.
> And I never thought your announcements
> Could give you—a mere human being—
> Power to trample the gods' unfailing,
> Unwritten laws. These laws weren't made now
> Or yesterday. They live for all time,
> And no one knows when they came into the light.
> No man could frighten me into taking on
> The gods' penalty for breaking such a law. (Sophocles, *Ant.*, 450–60, trans. Woodruff)

Unwritten law may be understood as either the law of the Greeks or, more generally, the law of nations. The two concepts are not clearly distinguished; an author who seems to write of universal law may have in mind law that is universal among the Greeks. But we must not overlook the tendency of Greek writers before Herodotus to imagine all human societies as following Greek customs, as Homer does in the case of the Trojans.

In any case, the concept of unwritten law as something distinct from the law of the *polis* appears to be new in the mid-fifth century B.C., and may be due to debates about the legitimacy of the *polis* law. Before this period, there seems to have been no need to remind potential lawbreakers of the idea that laws as such are divinely ordained (although both Hesiod and Solon took pains to argue for divine support of justice). The idea of unwritten law may be an artifact of the challenges to the laws of the city by intellectuals such as the sophists.

1.6.3. *The Law of the Greeks*

It is not easy to distinguish references to universal law from references to the laws of the Greeks, meaning laws common to all of the cities and governing the interaction of the cities. Some texts, however, refer fairly clearly to Greek law as such. In Thucydides the Plataeans urge the Spartans not to "violate the common laws of the Greeks" (Thucydides, *History* III.59, as quoted in

Woodruff 1993, 80); in context, these appear to be laws supporting the keeping of sworn promises, as the Spartans had sworn to protect Plataea. The same principle, keeping promises across the boundaries of the cities, is at stake in Herodotus (*History* VI.86). Also in Thucydides we find the Athenians insisting that every power has a right to punish its own allies (inference from Thucydides, *History* III.40; see Woodruff 1993, 70–1)—apparently an appeal to laws of the Greeks governing warfare. To these we should add the passage from Antiphon cited above (Section 1.3), which appeals to a common Greek law protecting defendants from imprisonment before trial (Antiphon, *Truth* 5.13).

We have said that the Greeks of the fifth century took pride in their laws, because they believed that their laws made them superior to other peoples. Herodotus has the Spartan Demaratus say in reply to Xerxes' boasts of Persian power: "Poverty is as familiar to Greece as its nursemaid's child, but virtue we have achieved out of wisdom and strong law" (Herodotus, *History* VII.102.1).

1.6.4. The Law of Nations: Universal Law

A concept of universal law, applying to all peoples (and sometimes even to gods and animals), is well attested for the classical period. Some thinkers, for example, the Athenians on Melos, according to Thucydides, took this universal law to be natural and destructive of conventional laws, whether of the cities or of the Greeks:

> Nature always compels gods (we believe) and men (we are certain) to rule over anyone they can control. We did not make this law, and we were not the first to follow it, but we will take it as we found it and leave it to posterity forever. (Thucydides, *History* V.105, as quoted in Gagarin and Woodruff 1995, 122)

Elsewhere we find the related idea that conventional law is powerless against human nature: "They all have it by nature to do wrong, both men and cities, and there is no law that will prevent it," says Diodotus (Thucydides, *History* III.45, as quoted in Gagarin and Woodruff 1995, 115). Later, in his own persona, Thucydides observes that men bent on revenge "are determined first to destroy without trace the laws that commonly govern such matters." And he goes on to say, "but it is only because of these [laws] that anyone in trouble can hope to be saved, and anyone might be in danger some day and stand in need of such laws" (ibid., III.84, as quoted in Gagarin and Woodruff 1995, 108).[34] Thucydides saw the destruction of law as one of the harmful consequences of

[34] This chapter of Thucydides' *History* III.84, was not known to certain ancient authors who commented on the section to which it belongs, which is on the civil war in Corcyra. It is therefore under suspicion as an addition by a later author. The language and thought, however, are thoroughly Thucydidean, and we may consider it representative of fifth-century thought about law.

civil war; he would not agree with the Athenians or with Diodotus that human nature is always destructive of law. Human nature, he believes, shows itself differently in different circumstances:

Civil war brought many hardships to the cities, such as happen and will happen as long as human nature is the same, although they may be more or less violent or take different forms, depending on the circumstances in each case. In peace and prosperity, cities and private individuals alike are better minded because they are not plunged into the necessity of doing anything against their will; but war is a violent teacher: it gives most people impulses that are as bad as their situation when it takes away the easy supply of what they need for daily life. (Thucydides, *History* III.82, as quoted in Gagarin and Woodruff 1995, 105)

Most commonly, Greeks of this period seem to have believed in a universal law that is not at odds either with nature or with the laws of their cities. Gorgias speaks of "the most divine and universal law: to speak, to be silent, and to act as one ought and when one ought" (Gorgias, *Funeral Oration*, DK 6, as quoted in Gagarin and Woodruff 1995, 203). And Euripides writes that the only law that is common to humans, gods, and animals is the law that parents love their children (Euripides, frag. 334). In Thucydides' debate between Plataeans and Thebans, both sides appeal to universal laws: "The law that holds everywhere: piety allows one to repel an aggressor" (Thucydides, *History* III.56.2, as quoted in Woodruff 1993, 79) and "it is the leaders who break the law, not the followers" (ibid., III.65 as quoted in Woodruff 1993, 84), where the law in question is evidently a universal one.

In some cases, the universal law is represented as divine:

Chorus:
Ingenious, how the gods
keep time's long foot a secret
while hunting down irreverent men.
There's no improvement on the laws,
none we should know or practice.

The cost of these beliefs is light:
power lies
with whatever thing should be divine,
with whatever law stands firm in time
by nature ever-natural. (Euripides, *Ba*. 888–96, trans. Woodruff 1998, 36)

1.7. Conclusion

In the above remarks we have tried to convey something of the range and diversity of early Greek thinking about law and to show the close connection between this and the historical development of early Greek legal systems. These never developed into the kind of autonomous system created by the Romans, nor did the early Greeks ever have a single word, like Latin *ius*, to designate the entire legal system, substance and procedure, together with the expected result, namely, justice. Greeks very early developed a legal (or proto-legal) process before they had civic laws (in the strict sense), and this process (*dikê*, later *to dikaion*, *dikaiosynê*) became synonymous with its proper outcome: justice. Only later, around the end of the seventh century, did they begin to isolate (by means of writing) specific rules that were the city's laws. At this point the difference between their customs, traditions, and ways of behavior, on the one hand, and laws, on the other, was clear from separate terminology: *nomos* versus *thesmos*, *grammata*, *rhêtra*, and related words. In the fifth century, when *nomos* was extended to cover civic law, gradually displacing these other terms, resonance among its wide range of meanings led to new ways of thinking about laws, including new concepts such as "unwritten laws." Some thinkers brought law and justice together conceptually, but *nomos* never expanded to include procedure, nor did it (or any other term) ever come to mean "law" in the most general sense (though some uses, e.g., Heraclitus DK 44, suggest the possibility of such a development). The closest one could come to this expression was to use the plural, *hoi nomoi*, and this expression was thus taken up later by philosophers such as Plato and Theophrastus for the title of their treatises on law, though these still are primarily concerned with substantive rules.

Further Reading

Translations of many of the important passages from the poetry and drama cited in this chapter, as well as the fragments of the sophists, are included in Gagarin and Woodruff 1995. Also relevant are the speeches of the Attic Orators, many of which were written for delivery in law courts. These are mostly from the fourth century, but Antiphon and Andocides wrote in the late fifth century (see Gagarin and MacDowell 1998). A useful selection from other orators is Carey 1997.

For thinking about Greek law in general, an excellent place to begin is with the first study undertaken from a comparative viewpoint by Maine 1861. Many of Maine's major theses (such as the progress "from status to contract") still influence scholarly discourse today. For Greek law in the pre-classical period see Gagarin 1986. Ostwald 1986 is a good political and intellectual history of fifth-century Athens. For the concept of *nomos*, Ostwald 1969 is still the standard work. For historical information about Athenian law, the most important ancient source is *The Athenian Constitution*, attributed to Aristotle but perhaps by members of his school. For specialists, Rhodes 1981 provides an excellent, thorough commentary; non-specialists should consult the notes to his fine 1984 Penguin translation.

The best modern works covering all of Athenian law are MacDowell 1978 and Todd 1993; of these Todd is more theoretical and is more explicit about similarities and differences between Athenian and modern common law. Harrison 1998 is more oriented toward the needs of specialists. Boegehold et al.

1995 has a useful collection of the archeological evidence for Athenian law together with testimony from ancient authors (all of it translated into English).

For more theoretical, and quite controversial, work on Athenian law, see D. Cohen 1991 and 1995. Also theoretical are many of the essays in Boegehold and Scafuro 1994; Cartledge, Millett, and Todd 1990; and Foxhall and Lewis 1996. Among the most recent approaches to Athenian law and litigation are Christ 1998 and Johnstone 1999. For forensic oratory and Athenian ideology, Ober (1989) has been very influential, although the emphasis he and others have placed on citizen ideology has now been strongly challenged by E. Cohen (2000).

Chapter 2

SOCRATES AND EARLY SOCRATIC PHILOSOPHERS OF LAW

by Richard F. Stalley and Roderick T. Long[1]

2.1. The Socratic Movement

Socrates is arguably the most important and elusive figure in the history of moral philosophy. The few known facts about his life are easily told. He was an Athenian citizen, born in 469 B.C., and worked as a sculptor. He served his city bravely in the Peloponnesian War, but did not seek an active role in politics. Nevertheless, he was briefly forced into prominence after the battle of Arginusae when, as one of the presidents of the Assembly, he resisted the clamor to try the generals en masse, which he saw as illegal. During the rule of the Thirty Tyrants (404–403 B.C.) he refused an order to take part in arresting Leon of Salamis. After the restoration of democracy, he was put on trial in 399 for introducing strange gods and corrupting the young.[2] He refused to save himself by opting for exile or by using any of the devices by which defendants usually sought to arouse the sympathy of Athenian juries. As a result, he was condemned and put to death by poisoning.

It is clear that Socrates was an exceptional individual for his intelligence and for his moral character and integrity. He was interested less in questions about the nature of the universe than in what we could call moral questions, above all the question "What sort of life should we lead?" Although he wrote nothing and did not call himself a teacher, he acquired an extensive circle of admirers. These included the notorious Alcibiades, as well as Critias and Charmides, relatives of Plato who both took part in the tyranny of the Thirty. Several of his followers wrote "Socratic" dialogues, but only those by Plato (427–347 B.C.) and Xenophon (ca. 430–355 B.C.) survive in more than a fragmentary form. After Socrates' death, the hedonistic Cyrenaics and the ascetic Cynics both traced their intellectual ancestry to Socrates. All these authors were immensely impressed by Socrates' moral character and mode of argument, but they interpreted these in very different ways. It is therefore better to talk of a "Socratic movement" than a "Socratic school."

[1] In this chapter, Richard F. Stalley is the principal author of Sections 2.1 and 2.2, while Roderick T. Long is the principal author of Sections 2.3 and 2.4. All translations are by the authors unless otherwise indicated.

[2] The precise grounds of these charges are unclear. The involvement of some his pupils in the tyranny of the Thirty may account for the charge of corruption. His own references to a divine "sign" (*daimonion*) may explain the charge of introducing new gods.

According to Plato, Socrates claimed to be wise only in the sense that, unlike most other people, he recognized his own ignorance about the important things of life. He thus did not give lectures or make long speeches, but rather chose to question people reputed to have knowledge. Not surprisingly, those of Plato's dialogues that seem most Socratic in character generally end inconclusively. Socrates leads his interlocutors to appreciate their own ignorance without asserting any view of his own. Nevertheless, some positive doctrines do emerge. The most important of these are that everyone seeks the good and that it is always in our interest to be just. Taken together these imply that anyone who knows what is just will act justly. Unjust behavior must result from ignorance of what is truly good. It follows both that those who do wrong do so unwillingly and that virtue is a kind of knowledge. In many respects, the picture of Socrates offered by Xenophon is similar to Plato's, though Xenophon's Socrates seems less enigmatic than Plato's and is more prone to give positive moral advice.

At one time scholars assumed that Xenophon gives the more historically accurate picture of Socrates, but most now give preference to that of Plato. More recently, many have followed Vlastos (1971, chap. 1; 1991, chap. 2), who claimed that Plato's early dialogues embody "the philosophy of Socrates" and that only in the middle period does Plato begin to speak with his own voice. But this view is now under scholarly attack,[3] as is the practice of dismissing Xenophon's evidence (Morrison 1987; Cooper 1999). Even though Plato seems to have known Socrates well, he is clearly not concerned with historical accuracy as we now understand it. Some scholars conclude that there is no reliable means of disentangling the Socratic and Platonic elements in Plato's work; others defend a "triangulation" strategy, using overlapping evidence from Plato and Xenophon to reconstruct the views of the historical Socrates. Whether or not those facts on which all the sources agree permit us to attribute to Socrates a fully worked out philosophy of law, they are sufficient to confirm his importance for the history of legal thought.

Both Xenophon and Plato agree that Socrates was always obedient to the law of Athens. He showed this most notably in his willingness to accept the verdict of the court that condemned him to death. According to both authors he lived by the principle that one should never behave unjustly. But if Socrates never committed injustice, the legal system that allowed him to be condemned cannot itself have been wholly just. This implies that positive law and justice do not necessarily coincide. Socrates' life thus presents a kind of paradox: We must be just and must obey the law, yet the law itself may be unjust. As we shall see in this chapter, several of Plato's dialogues, particularly the *Euthy-*

[3] This is argued at length by Kahn 1996. Of course, the fact that Plato's dialogues may not give an accurate picture of the historical Socrates does not, in itself, mean that we should rely on Xenophon. Kahn (1996, 393–401) also argues that Xenophon relies on Plato as a source.

phro, *Apology*, and *Crito*, which are all dramatically linked to Socrates' trial, seem to wrestle with this problem.[4] There are similar concerns in certain passages from Xenophon's *Memorabilia*. Socrates' insistence on the importance of justice suggests that justice cannot simply be the product of convention. He must therefore take issue with the sophistic use of the distinction between *nomos* ("law" or "convention") and *phusis* ("nature") to imply that justice is simply a matter of conforming to the customs of one's community.

2.2. Plato's "Trial" Dialogues: *Euthyphro*, *Apology*, *Crito*

Early in the *Euthyphro* we learn that Socrates' interlocutor claims to be an expert in matters of religion. In fact, he is so confident of his expertise that he is prosecuting his own father for impiety.[5] This prompts Socrates to question him about the nature of piety or holiness. In the first phase of the dialogue Euthyphro defines the holy as "what is dear to the gods" (6e–7a). But, since he accepts the traditional tales of quarrels among the gods, especially over matters of right and wrong, he has to admit that what is dear to some gods may be hated by others. So, his definition implies that the same thing may be both holy and unholy (8a). Socrates sets this issue aside by agreeing to investigate the claim that the holy is what is dear to *all* the gods, and then asks Euthyphro whether the holy is holy because it is dear to the gods or whether it is dear to the gods because it is holy (9e–10a). Euthyphro eventually agrees that the fact of the gods loving something is not what makes it holy. Rather, the gods love holy things because they are holy (10d). As we might say, there must be some standard of what is holy that is independent of whether the gods love it.

Plato's Socrates is evidently aware that similar difficulties can be raised for the claim that the just is the lawful.[6] If we take this to mean that any act permitted by a legal system is just and that any act forbidden by a legal system is unjust, then we have to concede that the same act can be both just and unjust, for obviously acts forbidden in one city may be permitted in another. We cannot avoid this difficulty by arguing that to be just is to be in accordance with a law promulgated by the gods, because Socrates would then ask whether the fact that an act is commanded by the gods makes it just or whether the fact that something is just leads the gods to command it. Socrates would certainly opt for the latter view. He believes that what is just is not dependent on the

[4] Most scholars assume that the *Apology* and *Crito* are among Plato's earliest dialogues. The *Euthyphro* is dramatically linked to the others and its brevity and simplicity of construction suggest that it is an early work. Whenever it was written, it seems likely that Plato intended it to be read in conjunction with the other two.

[5] When a slave killed one of his free workmen, Euthyphro's father had the slave bound and left him in the open while he sent to Athens for a religious ruling on what should be done. The slave died, presumably of exposure.

[6] Later in the dialogue it is argued that the holy is part of the just (11e–13e).

will of any agent, human or divine. It follows that human legal systems may include measures that are contrary to true justice. So, if merely being in accordance with some human code is enough to make an act lawful, the just and the lawful need not coincide. Since the gods are wise and good, the requirements of divine law must be the same as those of justice. So, if "lawful" means "in accordance with divine law" Socrates would recognize that the just and the lawful are in fact identical. But he would still insist that justice is prior to lawfulness.

The *Apology* purports to describe the three speeches Socrates made at his trial. Rather than dwelling on the legal niceties of his position, he mainly offers a justification of his life in moral and religious terms. A main element in this justification is the claim that he has a divine mission to subject his fellow citizens to philosophical examination. He first realized this when the Delphic oracle, questioned by his friend Chaerephon, replied that no one was wiser than Socrates (21a). This puzzled him, because he was not conscious of possessing any special wisdom. He therefore began questioning those, such as politicians and poets, who were reputed to be wise, only to find that they really understood nothing about the most important things in life. Socrates then understood the real meaning of the god who spoke through the oracle to be that the wisest human beings are those who recognize that they have no real wisdom (23a–b). Since then he has assisted the god by questioning those who seem to be wise and showing that they are not really so. This activity has naturally made him unpopular.

This account of his mission enables Socrates, later in the defense, to compare his own duty to philosophize with that of a soldier: "[W]herever a man has taken a position that he believes to be best or has been placed by his commander there he must, I think, remain and face danger without a thought of death or any thing else rather than disgrace" (28d). It would be dreadful if Socrates, who during his military service had remained where his commanders posted him, had abandoned the post assigned to him by a god (28e). No one knows whether death is a good or bad thing, but it is certainly wrong to disobey one's betters, whether they be gods or men. So, even if the court offered to release Socrates on condition that he gave up philosophy, he would have to refuse (28e–29d; cf. 37d–e).

The second main theme of Socrates' defense is the overriding importance of being just. In particular, it is more important to be just than to preserve one's life: "You are wrong, sir, if you think that a man who is any good should take into account the risk of life or death; he should look only to this in his actions whether what he does is right or wrong and whether he is acting like a good or a bad man" (28b). In fact, as he claims in his concluding speech, "a good man cannot be harmed" (41d). It is a good thing that he has refrained from political activity, because no one can survive who opposes the populace and prevents it from doing unjust and illegal things (31d–32a).

As evidence that he would rather die than do wrong, Socrates refers to the trial of the generals when he risked his life to be on the side of law and justice. He also cites his refusal to arrest Leon of Salamis as showing his determination to avoid unjust or impious acts (32a–e). In the same vein he refuses to beg the jury for mercy, partly out of a regard for his own reputation, but also because it would be wrong to induce the jurors to decide a case other than in accordance with law (34b–35d, 38d–39b).

The *Apology* certainly gives modern readers the impression that Socrates is much more concerned to show that he has lived justly than to show that he has broken no law. It may be that the vagueness of the charges forced this strategy upon him—we have no real information as to what activities on his part were supposed to have constituted introducing new gods and corrupting the young. But, in any case, most interpreters take his speeches to imply that considerations of what is morally right override those of legality in the sense that they may sometimes justify one in breaking the law. Two passages in particular have been thought to make this point explicit. One refers to the affair of Leon of Salamis. Some scholars have argued that since the Thirty had legal authority at the time, this passage shows that Socrates was prepared to defy the law when it conflicted with justice. Unfortunately, we do not know whether Socrates and the majority of his fellow citizens regarded the Thirty as having valid legal authority. So it is not clear that he or the jury would have seen the incident in this light (Weiss 1998, 14).

In a more important passage Socrates insists that, even if the court were to release him on condition of giving up philosophy, he would not comply with their wishes. This has generally been taken to show that Socrates was willing to defy a legal requirement in order to do what he believed to be just. It certainly looks as though Socrates is envisaging a situation, albeit a purely hypothetical one, in which he would have to disregard a legal requirement in order to carry out his divinely imposed mission. As a matter of fact there was, it seems, no legal basis on which the jury could have imposed such a requirement, so Socrates cannot be seen as announcing an intention to break a requirement that could have been imposed upon him under the law as it stood at the time of his trial. But the passage surely does imply that if the Athenians had passed a law forbidding Socrates from philosophizing, he would have defied it.[7]

[7] According to Brickhouse and Smith 1994, 146, even if the Athenians had introduced such a law, Socrates could have argued that, since he had a divine mission to philosophize, failure to do so would be an act of impiety and, as such, contrary to Athenian law. But it might be argued that to obey the law is not simply to follow one's own interpretation of the laws; it also requires us to obey the commands of duly appointed officials, if they are issued in accordance with the law, and to respect the decisions of properly constituted judicial bodies, if they are reached by correct procedures. Socrates might have argued that a law forbidding him to philosophize would conflict with the laws against impiety, but there would be little likelihood of his convincing his fellow citizens that this was the case. So he would in practice have been faced with a choice of defying the law or abandoning his mission. See Weiss 1998, 12; and Kraut 1984, 14–5.

Hence, there are conceivable circumstances in which he would be willing to break Athenian law.

This is closely linked to the idea that the gods have assigned him the task of philosophizing. If he had argued that divine authority is higher than that of any human legal system, his contemporaries would easily have understood his position. The difficulty for him would be that he has very little evidence to support his claim that his divine mission was imposed on him by the gods. It is not *obviously* implied by the response of the Delphic oracle. Socrates may be relying on his own conviction that he has a moral duty to philosophize and that the gods, being good, want us to do our moral duty. His position would then be very much what we would expect from our reading of the *Euthyphro*. Right and wrong do not depend on the decision of any human or divine agent, though we may be sure that the gods command us to do what is right. Human laws, on the other hand, may be incorrect and inconsistent. We may in the last resort have to break human laws in order to do what is right, but in doing so we can claim the authority of a superior law, namely, that of the gods.

The *Crito* reports a conversation that is supposed to have occurred when Crito visited Socrates in prison a day or two before the latter's execution. Crito, who, in spite of being a close friend of Socrates, seems to have little philosophical insight, urges him to escape. His main point is that if Socrates is put to death he and Socrates' other friends will be seen as having failed him in his hour of need and will thus be disgraced in the eyes of the public. Moreover, by failing to save himself, Socrates will leave his children without a father and create the general impression that he has been totally spineless. In response to these arguments, Socrates points out that he and Crito have always agreed that they should attend not to the views of the ignorant many, but to those of the one who has knowledge. Just as those who undergo physical training follow the advice of the expert trainer, so in matters of right and wrong we should be guided by those with knowledge rather than by public opinion. Given that we think that life with a sick body is not worth living, it would be absurd to allow "that part of us which is improved by justice and spoiled by injustice"—presumably, Socrates means the soul—to become corrupted (47d–e). It is not living as such that matters but living a good life. Thus the question to be addressed is not what the general public will think if Socrates does not escape, but whether it would be just for him to do so. In fact, Socrates goes on to argue, we must never willingly do any kind of unjust act, even when we have been treated unjustly ourselves.[8] He thus insists on the principle that "neither to do wrong nor to return wrong is ever right, not even to injure in return for an injury received" (49d).

[8] Vlastos 1991, chap. 7, suggests that this would have seemed extraordinary to most of Plato's contemporaries. Certainly the idea that we should seek to help friends and harm enemies was central to Greek popular morality. On the other hand, *harming* and *doing injustice* need not be synonymous.

At this point Socrates secures Crito's assent to the claim that one ought always to do what one has agreed to do, provided that it is just.[9] He goes on to suggest that by leaving prison without persuading the city, they would not only be failing to abide by what they agreed to be just, but would also be harming the very thing that they ought least to harm (49e–50a). Socrates' point is clearly that by escaping he would be doing an unjustified harm to the laws of the city; to elucidate his position, Socrates personifies the laws of Athens and imagines them coming to complain that by ignoring the verdict of the court he would be destroying them. The laws present two main reasons why this would be particularly unjust. The first main reason appeals to the principle, which Socrates himself accepts, that we ought to keep our agreements (at least when it is just to do so). Socrates has shown his agreement to live by the laws of Athens by remaining in the city throughout his life, by fathering children there, and by refusing the opportunity to go into exile before his trial when it would have been legal for him to do so. The second main reason is that the laws are in a quasi-parental position. They were responsible for his birth and education, so the obligation he owes to them is stronger even than that which he owes to his parents. In fact, he belongs to the laws as a child or slave and must therefore obey them. Even if Socrates has been unjustly convicted, it is human beings who have wronged him, not the laws themselves (54c).

On a superficial reading, at least, the laws personified appear to maintain that it would always be unjust to disobey them. If this is what they are claiming and if we assume, as most commentators have, that Socrates endorses their view, then there would be a discrepancy between the *Crito* and the *Apology*. Socrates in the *Apology* seems to allow that there are circumstances in which disobedience would be justified, while in the *Crito* he seems to deny it. But the discrepancy between the two dialogues is not the only point that is puzzling. The laws argue that because Socrates has entered into an agreement with them and is, as it were, their child, he has an obligation to obey them. This implies that our obligations to keep agreements and to obey our parents are independent of and prior to positive law. Thus the arguments of the laws themselves seem to imply that there is a distinction between justice and mere lawfulness. If this is right, then there is at least a logical possibility that the laws might require Socrates to do something unjust. Since Socrates also believes that one must never act unjustly, he must recognize that in such circumstances he would be obliged to disobey the law. Indeed, the laws themselves indicate ways in which this might happen. They base their case on the obligations to keep agreements and to obey superiors. These two grounds are distinct and could in principle conflict. For example, a parent, or other superior, might order a child to break an agreement. If we think of the laws as quasi-parental su-

[9] See Kraut 1984. Here we have ignored an ambiguity in the passage, which could perhaps be taken to say "we should keep our agreements because it is just to do so."

periors, we may ask what would happen if they required us to break an agreement. Conversely, if we think of the obligation to obey the law as resting on an agreement, we may ask what would happen if their requirement clashed with those of some superior authority such as the gods. Presumably, in such cases, the commands of the gods would be overriding. Thus if the laws are taken to be demanding unconditional obedience, their arguments seem to undermine themselves.[10]

There are other indications in this dialogue that the arguments of the laws are perhaps not to be taken at their face value. Socrates compares these arguments with what an orator might say (*Crito*, 50b), which suggests that they are not rationally convincing. In this he is arguably right, since the apparent claim of the laws to unconditional obedience seems to go beyond anything they could reasonably justify simply on the basis of their arguments. Ordinary morality, then as now, recognizes that there are cases where it is legitimate to break agreements, and even in ancient Greece parents did not have an unlimited right of control over adult children. Thus neither of the laws' arguments would support a demand for unlimited obedience. It is not surprising therefore that at the end of the laws' speech Socrates does not say that he finds their arguments logically unassailable, but rather that he is overwhelmed by the noise they make: "[T]hese are the words I seem to hear, as the Corybantes seem to hear the music of their flutes, and the echo of these words resounds in me and makes it impossible for me to hear anything else" (54d). Plato may well be hinting here that the laws have overstated their case (Weiss 1998, 134–40).

If we are not supposed to be convinced by the claims of the laws to unconditional obedience, the obvious question is "what are we supposed to believe?" The most useful guide may be the passage at 49e, cited above, where, immediately before introducing the laws, Socrates stipulates that we ought to keep our agreements provided that they are just. The most natural interpretation is that there may be occasions when keeping agreements would be unjust, in which case we ought to break them. Since the obligation to obey the law is seen in part as a matter of keeping agreements, this implies that there may be occasions when it would be unjust to obey the law. This could happen, for example, when obedience to the law would involve the violation of some higher obligation. Socrates would thus have been justified in breaking a law forbidding him to carry out what he saw as his divine mission to engage in philosophy. Similarly, in the circumstances of the *Crito* he would be justified in escaping from prison if remaining there would involve him in violating some higher duty. But no argument presented in the *Crito* suggests that this is the case. So, because he has no superior obligation to escape, it is his duty to obey the law and await his execution.

[10] For more on these points, see Harte 1999.

A somewhat different solution—similar in spirit, but requiring less discounting of the arguments in the *Crito*—is to take Socrates to be distinguishing between laws commanding one to *suffer* injustice and laws commanding one to *commit* injustice, and to be counseling (a) obedience to the former and (b) disobedience to the latter.[11] The *Apology*, as we have seen, is plausibly interpreted as endorsing (b), but Socrates' concern for obeying human authorities when doing so does not clash with obeying divine ones (28d–29d) likewise favors (a). The *Crito* clearly endorses (a), but Socrates' insistence that one should never commit injustice, together with his emphasis on our duty to keep *just* agreements, suggests (b) as well. Hence, the two dialogues would be propounding the same doctrine.

If either of these readings is correct, then we can find a consistent view of the law across the three dialogues we have been considering. According to this view, we must in all things do what is just. Although Socrates claims to be ignorant, he is evidently convinced that there is an absolute standard of justice and that human beings can become clear about this standard through reasoned discussion. By giving a central place to reason, he points forward to Platonic doctrines that will be discussed in the following chapter of this volume. But it is already clear that justice, in Socrates' view, is prior to both the commands of the gods and human laws. Because the gods are wise and good we may be sure that they command only what is just. Thus, to be just is to obey divine law. We have a general obligation to obey human law, but because it is the product of imperfect beings it may sometimes conflict with the requirements of justice and divine law. On such occasions we should break human law in order to do what is just.

2.3. Xenophon

Xenophon (ca. 430–ca. 355 B.C.), like Plato, was one of the young Athenian aristocrats drawn into Socrates' intellectual orbit; and his writings are, like Plato's, among our principal sources of information about Socrates.[12] Unlike Plato, however, Xenophon spent much of his life in exile from Athens, serving as a mercenary soldier in Persia, Sparta, and elsewhere. His writings encompass a variety of topics and genres, but Socratic ideas and values nevertheless inform all his works. As with Plato, we face the usual puzzles about the extent to which the characters in his dialogues represent either Xenophon's views or the views of their historical originals, though from Xenophon at least we do have much that is asserted *in propria persona.* While many readers find Xenophon superficial and conventional, others argue that a more careful reading reveals a subtle and creative mind at work.

[11] Socrates argues at length in Plato's *Gorgias* that suffering injustice is preferable to committing it.

[12] For a defense of Xenophon's reliability as a source, see Cooper 1999.

The two Xenophontic texts that most directly address the nature and status of law are both in the *Memorabilia* (I.2.40–46 and IV.4). In the first, *Mem.* I.2.40–46, Xenophon recounts a (probably fictitious) conversation on the nature of law between the youthful Alcibiades and his guardian, the democratic statesman Pericles. Xenophon's stated purpose in giving us this account is to show how Alcibiades learned the Socratic technique of dialectic simply in order to advance his own political career, but Xenophon may have other purposes as well. In the dialogue, Alcibiades exploits a tension within ordinary Athenian thinking about law; Pericles is torn between a positive conception, identifying law with manmade statutes, and a moralized conception, denying the status of law to statutes that fail to meet certain moral requirements. He does not at first feel this tension when discussing democracy, being a democrat himself, but the tension soon becomes evident when the conversation turns to oligarchy and tyranny, systems of which Pericles disapproves. On the one hand, Pericles feels the pull of the positivist account, according to which whatever is enacted by the supreme power in a state counts as law. But it turns out that, on the other hand, Pericles is still more deeply committed to the conceptual association of *law* with *persuasion*, and of *lawlessness* with *violence*, and so he is driven to conclude that the edicts of tyrannical and oligarchic governments are not laws after all, since they are imposed by force on an unwilling majority rather than emerging from democratic consensus. At this point Pericles does not yet see any conflict between his moralized conception of law and his own political commitments, but is left without an answer when Alcibiades then points out that a democratic government, in forcibly imposing the will of the majority on an unconsenting minority, is departing from lawfulness no less than is a tyrant or a body of oligarchs.

For Cartledge (1997, 5), Alcibiades' argument is a "clever piece of oligarchic pamphleteering" that stigmatizes democracy as "a form of collective tyranny, whereby the ignorant and ill-educated masses ruled despotically over the unwilling and unconsenting elite few." But of course the argument says nothing about the masses being ignorant and ill-educated, and in any case it is just as much an indictment of oligarchy as of democracy. (Indeed, in Roman times Tiberius Gracchus used a similar argument to draw a *democratic* moral: Plutarch *TG* 15; Erskine 1990, 171–80.)

The connection that Alcibiades draws between law and consent surely represents Xenophon's own view, since he likewise attributes to Socrates, with clear approval, the claim that a genuine king is one who rules in accordance with laws (*kata nomous*) over those who consent (*hekontôn*), while he who rules unwilling subjects not by law but by his own will, is a mere tyrant (*Mem.* IV.6.12).[13] Why, then, does Xenophon choose Alcibiades, a character

[13] It is striking that Xenophon thinks that lawfulness depends not just on the *benefit*, but also on the *consent*, of the governed; compare Aristotle, *Pol.* III.14.1285a27–b21, IV.9.1294b34–39,

he portrays negatively, as the spokesman for this view in I.2.40–46? Perhaps he does so because it allows him to state a criticism of Athenian institutions without being in the position of having to endorse it explicitly; both Alcibiades and Socrates state the premises, but only Alcibiades draws the anti-democratic conclusion.[14] Certainly the greater effectiveness of persuasion over coercion is a theme that pervades Xenophon's writings (*Mem.* I.2.10–11, II.6.31; *Oec.* XXI.12; *An.* V.7, VII.7; *HG* II, VI.1.7–8; *Vect.* I.1–2, V.1–10). It is unclear whether Xenophon's case against violence is purely consequentialist (basing the rightness of an act solely on its having beneficial consequences) or whether he also recognizes a deontological aspect (regarding an action as right even apart from its consequences); there is certainly a deontological flavor to Xenophon's defense of justice over expediency in the "trial of the cloaks" passage (*Cyr.* I.3.16–17).[15] There are no grounds for attributing to Xenophon a special concern with *freedom* in its modern sense(s).

If the rule of a majority over an unwilling minority is no less tyrannical than the reverse, it might seem that nothing short of unanimous consent could justify political authority; but perhaps all that is required is that the ruler do his *best* to gain the consent of his subjects, rather than simply imposing arbitrary edicts. At any rate, Xenophon's aversion to forcible rule is not absolute, since he happily endorses paternalism (*Mem.* I.2.49–60, IV.2.14–18; *Lac.* X.4–6; *Hier.* X.2–4; *Oec.* XIII.5–9). Perhaps compulsory measures are not regarded as "violent" or "forcible" in the forbidden sense if they aim to benefit the ruled; after all, if such paternalistic measures succeed in shaping noble characters, the ordinary problem of backlash against violence will be avoided.

This suggests that Xenophon's criteria for legal legitimacy include not only *consent* but also *benefit*; and indeed some indication of this is found in the Alcibiades/Pericles exchange itself, where it is established that all laws state what ought to be done—but on the assumption that good rather than evil is what ought to be done (*Mem.* I.2.42). The implication is that the legitimacy of a law depends not only on the way in which it is imposed, but also on its beneficial content. This may simply be an instance of Xenophon's apparent conviction (IV.2) that ready-made exceptionless rules of just conduct are hard to come by.

In addition to the benefit and consent criteria, Xenophon also invokes a wisdom criterion: The claim to rule must be based on *knowledge* and *virtue*

IV.10.1295a15–24, V.10.1313a5, VII.2.1324b22–36, VII.14.1333b5–1334a10, *EN* IX.5.1167a26–b16; Plato, *Plt.* 276d–277a, but contrast Plato, *Plt.* 291e–293e. Cf. R. Long 1996, 787–98.

[14] The identification of lawfulness with the choice of persuasion over violence was a Greek commonplace (Lysias, *Funeral Oration*, 2.19). Hence it is the (potentially anarchic) conclusion, not the premise, that is controversial.

[15] Young Cyrus is chastised for adjudicating a dispute over cloaks by awarding a cloak to the disputant it fits best, rather than to its rightful owner. It is equally possible to follow Hume in seeing the passage as an endorsement of *indirect* consequentialism (Hume 1751, Appendix III).

(equivalent terms for a Socratic).[16] He has Thrasybulus ask the Thirty what entitles them to rule: Are they more just, more courageous, more wise (*HG* II.4.40–42)? We should no more accept a ruler than we would accept a physician without evidence of his expertise (*Mem.* IV.2.3–7), for "kings and rulers [...] are not those who hold the sceptre, or who are chosen by just anyone, or who are selected by lot, or who use violence or deception, but rather those who possess knowledge of ruling" (III.9.10–11). Here the wisdom and consent criteria appear in combination; the benefit criterion may be implicit as well, if Xenophon assumes that anyone who possesses the art of ruling would want to benefit his subjects, would know how to do it, and would also recognize the greater utility of persuasion than of violent measures.

In yet another passage (*Mem.* IV.3.16), we are told that, when the Athenians asked how they should go about worshipping the gods, the Delphic Oracle replied that they should do so in accordance with the *nomos* ("law," "custom") of the city. Crucially, Xenophon leaves out what happened next, but his audience would certainly know it and could be expected to supply it: We learn from Cicero (*Leg.* II.40) that when the Athenians explained that their traditions contained many competing and conflicting *nomoi* and asked which of these was meant, the oracle answered "whichever is best." The clear implication is that Xenophon's test for whether something is a genuine *nomos* of Athens is the fact that it is best.[17]

This may sound odd to modern ears. When we disapprove of governmental edicts, we generally say that they are bad laws or unjust laws, not that they are not laws at all. But the moralized conception of law (which was in fact the orthodox position in legal philosophy throughout most of European history) can be given some plausibility. What is the difference between a command issued by a legislature and a command issued by a mugger with a gun? Both have the *power* to enforce their demands, but the legislature, unlike the mugger, is presumed to have *authority.* Yet the legislature's authority is conditional, being derived from the people or the constitution. But where do the people, or the constitution, get *their* authority? If the regress terminates in a bare fact of power, all the subsequent links of the chain seem to revert to mere power, not authority; hence, it can be argued, the regress must terminate with something inherently authoritative, and only a *normative* fact could meet this requirement.

[16] Xenophon's much-noted stress on the importance of noncognitive training does not conflict with his commitment to the Socratic thesis that virtue is knowledge, since for Xenophon the role of noncognitive training is not to supply a motivational force that moral knowledge on its own would lack, but to prevent moral knowledge from being lost; cf. Charlton 1988, 13–33; R. Long unpublished.

[17] Xenophon's usage is not entirely consistent, however; an unjust provision that he describes at *Mem.* I.2.31 as being "written into law" he describes at IV.4.3 as being "contrary to law." Presumably "law" has a positive sense in the first passage and a normative sense in the second.

Although the first major passage of Xenophon (the Alcibiades-Pericles dialogue), with related passages, supports a moralized conception of law, the second passage might seem to point to a different view of law. In a conversation between Socrates and Hippias at *Mem.* IV.4, Socrates defines the just as the lawful (IV.4.12; cf. 6.5–6), prompting many commentators to view him as a legal positivist.[18] But Socrates' equation of the just with the lawful does not commit him to a positivist account of *justice* unless he is committed to a positivist account of *law*.[19] Hippias offers such an account (*Mem.* IV.4.13), defining law as a written agreement among citizens concerning what ought and ought not to be done.[20] Hippias disparages Socratic respect for law on the grounds that laws are constantly changing, but Xenophon's Socrates counters that cities first go to war and then later make peace (*Mem.* IV.4.14; cf. Plato, *Minos* 316c); presumably, the idea is that the same principle may issue in different concrete recommendations in different circumstances. Hence, it seems, what is really *nomos* in a city's written agreements is not the concrete applications but the principle they embody.

In his discussion of the passage, Morrison (1995, 334–5) argues that a defender of what he calls "legal idealism" cannot coherently say that "it is just to obey the [positive] law in force, even if that law can and will be changed," because "[i]f the first law is not beneficial, and its later replacement *is* beneficial, on the idealist interpretation the first law was not a law and should not have been obeyed." Now Morrison does admit that "[l]egal idealism can accommodate the idea that different laws are best in different circumstances," so that "when the statutes are changed due to a corresponding change in circumstances, the idealist view can allow that the earlier and later statutes are both 'law'." But Morrison objects that this qualification applies only in a "limited range of cases." Yet Xenophon clearly thinks (as Morrison 1995, 335, sees) that *a general habit of obedience to manmade statutes is beneficial.* So if the state commands something harmful, it is not a law, but if it commands something that is (prior to being commanded) neither beneficial nor harmful, acting as the new statute dictates is *now* beneficial (as an instance of the general habit of obedience) and so is required by natural—that is, nonconventional—justice.

In any case, Hippias, like Pericles before him, finds his commitment to legal positivism undermined by his other beliefs, though in Hippias' case it is

[18] Striker 1996b and Strauss 1972, from very different perspectives, both agree that Xenophon's text endorses positivism. Striker dismisses the argument as evidence of Xenophon's limitations as a thinker; Strauss dismisses the argument as insincere and looks for a coded anti-positivist message buried in the subtext. But as we shall see, both responses are inappropriate, because there is no positivism in the text to dismiss.

[19] Hence it is also no concession to positivism when Xenophon defines holiness (*Mem.* IV.6.2–4) as the knowledge of what is lawful in relation to the gods.

[20] It is not actually clear that even this must be taken as a positivist definition (see the discussion of the *Minos* below, in Chapter 5, Section 5.2), but Hippias probably so intends it.

not the unlawful character of violence but, as Xenophon indicates, the recognition of *unwritten laws* that trips him up.[21] These hold everywhere—and, as Hippias grants, are laid down by the gods. It soon becomes evident, however, that Socrates and Hippias do not have quite the same understanding of what it means for a law to hold everywhere. Hippias thinks that holding everywhere means being *accepted* everywhere, since a law cannot hold where it is not backed up by penalties, and (he assumes) only where people accept a law is it backed up by penalties. But Socrates, in the spirit of an Antiphon moralized,[22] argues (*Mem.* IV.4.19–25) that there are penalties inherent in the natural consequences of human actions. Ingratitude naturally breeds distrust, and no one wants to be distrusted; so even if the unwritten law against ingratitude were not *accepted* everywhere, ingratitude would still be *penalized* everywhere, and so is unlawful. Likewise, Socrates says, the prohibition on incest, though not accepted in every country (and therefore, Hippias initially thinks, not a candidate for an unwritten law), is unlawful everywhere because it has bad consequences everywhere (cf. Plato, *Gorg.* 469d–470b).

This notion of natural law as a set of hypothetical imperatives backed up by natural penalties (cf. Barnett 1998, chap. 1) recurs throughout Xenophon's writings. Those who break their oaths, Xenophon tells us, will be punished by the gods (*An.* II.5, III.2); but he also tells us that those who break their oaths suffer by getting a reputation for being untrustworthy (*An.* VII.7), and it is not clear that there is anything more to the divine punishment than this. A tyrant cannot disregard good advice with impunity, since the automatic penalty is that he ends up doing the wrong thing; nor can he kill the wise man with impunity, since in doing so he loses his most reliable advisor (*Mem.* III.9.12). The god commands us to sow in the autumn (as was the Greek custom) by making that the time when sowing has the best consequences (*Oec.* XVII.1–4). The earth is a teacher of justice because it teaches people that they reap benefits from it in proportion as they serve it (*Oec.* V.12–14). It is against the laws (*thesmoi*) of the gods to reap without having sown or to succeed in battle without having trained, and so it is impious to pray for such things (*Cyr.* I.6.6). In Xenophon's historical writings, accounts of wrongdoing are often immediately followed by a description of the natural penalty the perpetrators eventually paid in consequence (*An.* V.1; *HG* I.7.35, V.7.1; *Lac.* XIV.2–7).

Some may conclude that Xenophon's profession of belief in the gods is disingenuous, and that for him the causal sequences we find in the natural world are all the reality there is to the notion of divine legislation. But reading Xenophon as a crypto-naturalist would do unneeded violence to his text; his religious beliefs are genuine, though unconventional. He argues rather inge-

[21] The appeal to unwritten law was another Greek commonplace; cf. Sophocles, *Ant.* 447–56; Thucydides, *History* II.37. See Chapter 1, Section 1.6.2, of this volume.

[22] On Antiphon, see Chapter 1, Section 1.3, of this volume.

niously (employing a combination of the arguments from design and from consciousness) for the existence of a divine creator (*Mem.* I.4.8–18, IV.3.13–14; cf. DeFilippo and Mitsis 1994); and if nature is the work of a god, the causal sequences embedded in nature must presumably be the god's handiwork as well. (Hence, although Hippias does not challenge the idea that the unwritten laws are of divine origin, Socrates would have had an argument ready, had Hippias done so.) Xenophon also thinks that some of the causal sequences we need to know are too obscure to discover without divine help; hence, he recommends divination for those cases (and *only* those cases) where the natural connection is not manifest (*Mem.* I.1.6–9).

Xenophon's account of natural penalties clarifies his position on law. We have already seen that no unjust statute counts as a genuine law for Xenophon, but this might suggest that the content of true law is restricted to a *subset* of positive law—namely, all those positive laws that meet Xenophon's normative criteria. But now we see that Xenophon also recognizes laws even where no manmade statutes apply. Hence, contra Morrison (1995, 333), the body of true law for Xenophon includes both *less* and *more* than the body of manmade statutes—less, because it excludes the unjust statutes,[23] and more, because it includes divine law. (This of course is likewise the opinion of jurists from Aquinas to Blackstone.) Hence, there can be no clash between nature and law (cf. *Oec.* VII.30).

As further evidence that law for Xenophon includes both divine (or natural) laws and (just) human laws, consider Xenophon's vindication of the justice of Socrates. To prove this justice, Xenophon first points out Socrates' obedience to positive law (*Mem.* IV.4.1), but then describes Socrates' disobedience to commands that were contrary to positive law (IV.4.2–3; cf. *HG* I.7.15),[24] and finally cites Socrates' refusal to employ flattering appeals to the jury on the grounds that such conduct was "contrary to the laws" (*para tous nomous*)—though of course it was at that time contrary to no *positive* law. Hence, Xenophon's Socrates apparently regards the *laws of Athens* (i.e., the laws that hold there, the laws whose violation is penalized there; cf. *Mem.* IV.4.13) as containing requirements not embodied in any manmade Athenian statute.

Xenophon's theory of divine law raises a question analogous to that posed in Plato's *Euthyphro*: Do the gods issue these edicts because they are just and lawful, or are the edicts just and lawful because the gods issue them? The *Euthyphro* suggests a theologically objectivist view: Divine approval is a *response*

[23] The phrase "unjust statute" is not unambiguous. In the light of the discussion in Plato's *Apology* and *Crito*, we should perhaps distinguish between statutes that it is unjust for the legislator to *enact* and statutes that, once passed, it is unjust for the subject to *obey*; arguably it is only the latter that Socrates means to exclude as unlawful.

[24] Significantly, as Xenophon describes the cases, it seems clear that Socrates would have disobeyed the same commands even if they *had* been authorized by positive law, since obeying them would be unjust.

to the non-theologically based property of promoting human welfare. Xenophon's account of divine law might seem to tend in the same direction, since the things the gods forbid are things that naturally tend to have bad results for human beings. But on the other hand, given Xenophon's teleological cosmology, the divine mind *constructed* the natural world. It is not as though, for example, the god saw in his wisdom that jumping off cliffs has bad results, and so he benevolently commanded us not to do it; rather, the god *made* the cliff, and the law of gravity, and the fragile structure of the human body, and his making these things as he did is what his commanding us not to jump off cliffs *amounts* to—so the binding force of these commands is a product of divine will. Hence, Morrison (1995) concludes that the theologically subjectivist reading must be the right one (cf. Striker 1996b).

However, premises drawn from Xenophon's own text show that his own commitments are theologically objectivist:

(1) Nature contains cause-and-effect sequences that count as natural laws backed up by penalties [defended in *Mem.* IV.4 and passim].
(2) The natural world is the product of the Divine Mind [defended in *Mem.* I.4, IV.3.13–14, and to some extent also in IV.4.24–5, as an inference from (1)].
(3) Therefore, the cause-and-effect sequences that count as natural laws backed up by penalties are the product of the Divine Mind [(1), (2)].
(4) The Divine Mind, in constructing the natural world, was guided by a concern to promote human welfare [defended in *Mem.* IV.3].
(5) Therefore, the cause-and-effect sequences that count as natural laws backed up by penalties are designed to promote human welfare [(3), (4)].

Hence, for Xenophon's Socrates as for Plato's, human welfare seems to be an independent standard to which divine law must measure up in order to be authoritative.

Xenophon, like many of his contemporaries, supports the "mixed constitution," a blend of aristocratic and democratic elements (*HG* II.3.48)—which is no great surprise, in the light of his argument that the despotism of the rich over the poor and the despotism of the poor over the rich are equally objectionable (*Mem.* I.2.40–46). Yet Xenophon also gives an impression of sympathizing with the sentiment "For forms of government let fools contest; Whate'er is best administer'd is best." For Xenophon, the welfare of a regime depends primarily on the virtue or vice of its rulers rather than on constitutional structures; Persia did well under Cyrus and badly under his successors, despite the same laws remaining in place (*Cyr.* VIII.1.7–8, 8.1–2; cf. *Vect.* I.1). For the successors found it possible to keep to the letter of the law while distorting its spirit; a written law cannot guarantee its own correct application

(*Cyr.* VIII.8.8–11). Hence, Xenophon concludes that a king is superior to written laws because he is a *law with eyes* (*Cyr.* VIII.1.22; cf. *Oec.* XII.19–20). Thus the first aim of Lycurgus, founder of the Spartan constitution, was not—contrary to popular belief—to instill respect for law in the citizens of Sparta, but rather to secure first the support of the Spartan elite (*Lac.* VIII.1–2); virtuous leaders are more important than laws. Yet at the same time Xenophon has a horror of constitutionally unrestrained factions scorning procedural niceties and disregarding the rule of law, be those factions democratic (*HG* I.7.26–29), oligarchic (*HG* II.3.20–21), or autocratic (*HG* VII.1.43–45).

Xenophon's remarks on governmental administration do not add up to a system; but in other respects Xenophon appears to have a reasonably coherent legal philosophy. Natural law is based on cause-and-effect relationships with a bearing on human welfare; human law derives its authority from natural law. Xenophon's theory of natural law would exercise a profound influence on later developments in legal philosophy, particularly among the Stoics.

2.4. Cyrenaics and Cynics

Apart from Plato and Xenophon, the Socratic thinkers most important for legal philosophy are the Cyrenaics and the Cynics. Each school traced its ancestry to a disciple of Socrates—the Cyrenaics to Aristippus of Cyrene (ca. 435–355 B.C.), whence the name "Cyrenaic," and the Cynics to Antisthenes (ca. 446–366 B.C.).[25] In the case of both movements, however, there is a dispute as to whether the school's founder has been correctly identified. The Cyrenaic doctrine in its systematic form appears to derive not from Aristippus of Cyrene but from his grandson and namesake, Aristippus the Mother-Taught; and while the traditional story that Diogenes of Sinope (ca. 412–ca. 324 B.C.), who gave Cynic doctrine its distinctive shape, was the student of Antisthenes is chronologically possible (barely), it is now thought unlikely.[26] Nonetheless, whatever their personal involvement, Aristippus and Antisthenes incontrovertibly exercised a strong influence on the schools that later claimed them as founders.

The urbane hedonism of the Cyrenaics and the rough asceticism of the Cynics initially seem so different from one another that one might easily wonder in what sense they could be part of the same Socratic movement, but each school could reasonably claim to be developing some aspect of Socrates' lega-

[25] Whether the label "Cynic" first arose because Antisthenes taught at the Cynosarges gymnasium (so D.L. VI.1.13) or because the Cynics were "doglike" (*kunikoi*) in their shamelessness and ferocity, it was for the latter reason that the name stuck.

[26] For a summary of the argument, see A. Long 1996, 45. On the other hand, Goulet-Cazé (1996) argues that Aristotle's reference to *kuôn*, "the Dog," at *Rhet.* III.10.1411a24–5 is probably to Antisthenes (rather than, as is usually thought, Diogenes), which would bolster Antisthenes' claim to be the first Cynic.

cy.[27] In any case, the differences between the two schools are easily exaggerated; hedonism regards pleasure as the highest good, while asceticism embraces self-discipline and self-denial, but the "ascetic" Cynics advised indulging one's sexual desires as freely as animals, while the "hedonistic" Cyrenaics cautioned that pleasures should be pursued only so long as one is not mastered by them but can take them or leave them (D.L. II.8.69, 75). Aristippus endorses the Cynic view that those who lack philosophic wisdom are mere slaves (II.8.72), and both schools emphasize self-mastery and self-construction (cf. Foucault 1985; 1986).

The relevance of the Cyrenaics and Cynics to legal thought lies in their social philosophy. Both Aristippus and Diogenes practice a certain kind of independence and detachment from the world; but for Aristippus this means adapting himself with effortless flexibility to every social circumstance, while for Diogenes it means "defacing the currency" by rejecting social conventions and material comforts, mocking the establishment, and seeking maximal self-sufficiency. Hence, Diogenes throws away his cup as a superfluous luxury upon seeing a child drinking from his hands (D.L. VI.2.37). Aristippus cultivates the social graces and biting wit of a courtier, cajoling favors from tyrants like Dionysius of Syracuse, whereas Diogenes scorns social distinctions and, invited to ask Alexander of Macedon for a favor, tells him to step out of Diogenes' light. Yet Aristippus might well justify his life of luxury with the same reply that Diogenes gives to justify his life of squalor: That sunshine is not sullied when it lands on filth (D.L. VI.2.63). Diogenes refers to Aristippus as a "royal dog" (*basilikon kuôn*; D.L. II.8.66); the epithet is (no doubt deliberately) ambiguous between the complimentary "regal Cynic" and the abusive "king's lapdog," and either judgment could plausibly be defended.[28]

The generally indulgent lifestyle of the elder Aristippus was worked into a comprehensive system by his grandson, Aristippus the Mother-Taught. The new theory was hedonistic and egoistic in ethics and psychology alike; among its implications (II.8.91–3) is the doctrine that "wisdom is good not for itself but on account of its consequences," and so "nothing is just or noble or base by nature, but only by convention [*nomos*] and habit [*ethos*]"; nevertheless, "the virtuous man will do nothing inappropriate, on account of the penalties imposed and on account of reputation [*doxas*]." The latter rationale appears to clash with the elder Aristippus' statement (D.L. II.8.68) that if all laws were abolished, the virtuous man would continue to act in the same way as before.[29]

[27] Plato's Socratic dialogues, for instance, exhibit concerns congenial to each group; see Irwin 1992 and 1997, Rudebusch 1999.

[28] Diogenes and Aristippus are also described as similar in their reliance on gifts and money from friends, but the amounts required were no doubt vastly different.

[29] But similar remarks are attributed to Aristotle (D.L. V.1.20) and Xenocrates (Cicero, *Rep.* I.3), so it may just be a commonplace that has attached itself to Aristippus.

At least one early Cyrenaic, Theodorus (late-fifth century B.C.), maintains (D.L. II.8.98–9) that patriotism is irrational—since a wise man would not risk his life to save a country of fools—and that social conventions exist in order to hold communities together, but only because their citizens lack wisdom; in themselves theft, adultery, sacrilege, and the like are not wrong by nature and should be indulged in when the circumstances call for doing so; and likewise there is nothing wrong with gratifying one's sexual appetites in public, since whatever is appropriate in private is equally appropriate in public. This antinomian attitude is embraced by the Cynics as well; Diogenes endorses theft, adultery, and cannibalism (D.L. VI.2.72–3), and also masturbates in public, saying that he wishes his appetite for food could be satisfied as easily (VI.2.46). The Cynic philosophers Crates (ca. 368–287 B.C.) and his wife Hipparchia likewise have sexual intercourse in public (D.L. VI.7.97). This attitude of indifference to the public is arguably a development of Antisthenes' advice to be concerned solely with virtue and to despise reputation and social convention (VI.1.11), and indeed goes still further back to Socrates' insistence that we should care for no one's opinion but that of the wise, but this antinomian development of the idea appears to have been pioneered by Diogenes.

The Cyrenaics and Cynics are also like-minded in their cosmopolitan rejection of local ties and allegiances. On the Cyrenaic side, we are told (Xenophon, *Mem.* II.1.8–13) that in Aristippus' view, to be a ruler is to take on an unwelcome burden of responsibility, and to be ruled is to be a slave; hence, Aristippus favors a "middle path" that leads "neither through rule nor through slavery but through freedom," avoiding compulsion by not submitting to any regime but being a *xenos* ("stranger," "guest," "foreigner") everywhere. Theodorus calls the cosmos his only homeland (D.L. II.8.99). On the Cynic side, Antisthenes holds (VI.1.12) that to the wise man nothing is foreign (*xenon*), while Diogenes claims to be a "citizen of the cosmos" (*kosmopolitês*; D.L. VI.2.63; cf. 72) and may well have coined the term. Again, Crates claims to be at home in every land (VI.7.98; frag. 15 Diehl), also identifying himself as a "citizen of Diogenes" whose homeland was the Land of Penia (Poverty) and the City of Pera (Knapsack) (VI.5.93; frag. 6 Diehl).

Scholars debate whether these forms of cosmopolitanism are "positive" or "negative"—that is, whether they represent a genuine allegiance to a global community or merely an alienation from all local ones. Cynic cosmopolitanism seems negative in contrast with later, more Stoic forms of cosmopolitanism, which stress participation in human life rather than dropping out. On the other hand, Cynic cosmopolitanism seems more positive than that of the Cyrenaics; the Cyrenaics may practice more outward conformity than the Cynics, but they are less engaged, as is suggested by the difference between the elder Aristippus' advice to be a *xenos* everywhere, and the Cynics' advice to be a citizen everywhere (Diogenes) and a *xenos* nowhere (Antisthenes). (However, among the Cyrenaics, Anniceris and the younger Aristippus, unlike Theodorus, did endorse patriotism.) To be sure, being a citizen of Poverty and the City of Knapsack sounds a bit less positive than being a citizen of the cosmopolis, and may suggest a withdrawal from society, but *kunismos* was a proselytizing faith, and Diogenes presents his mocking attacks on convention as philanthropically motivated: Other dogs bite to harm, but he bites to save (Stobaeus, *Eclogues* III.462).[30]

With Diogenes in particular we see the first steps toward the later Stoic theory of the Cosmopolis.[31] Diogenes is said (D.L. VI.2.72) to have offered the following argument:

(1) Without the polis, the civilized (*asteion*) is of no benefit.
(2) The polis is civilized.
(3) Without law, the polis is of no benefit.[32]
(4) Therefore, law is civilized.

The sense of the argument is elusive. Assuming that Diogenes must have had a negative attitude toward polis, law, and civilization, Schofield (1991, 130–40; 1995, 134) and Moles (1995, 130–1; 1996, 107–8) take *asteion* pejoratively; Goulet-Cazé (1982) by contrast takes *asteion* approvingly, but only to conclude—on the basis of Stoic parallels—that the argument is of Stoic provenance and not attributable to Diogenes at all. Yet Diogenes did not always use *polis* and *politeia* pejoratively, since he spoke approvingly of the cosmos as the true *polis* and *politeia* (D.L. VI.2.63, 72), so why should he not on occasion have drawn a distinction between true and false *nomos* as well?

Proceeding from the assumption that the argument is Diogenes', and that the Stoics got it from him, let us further assume that he meant by *asteion* what they meant by it. We know from Clement (*Strom.* IV.26, as quoted in *SVF* III.327) and Arius Didymus (Stobaeus, *Eclogues* II.103.14–17, as quoted in *SVF* I.587) that the Stoics used *asteion* approvingly, arguing that nothing counts as a genuine polis unless it is *asteion*. We also know from Cicero (*Leg.* II.12–13) that some Stoics argued as follows:

[30] Moles 1996 argues convincingly against a purely negative interpretation of Cynic cosmopolitanism.

[31] Diogenes' own preferences, if he had any, among existing political systems are difficult to discern. According to one story (D.L. VI.2.50) he, unlike Thucydides and Plato, thought highly of Harmodius and Aristogeiton, the tyrannicide heroes of Athenian democracy, whatever that may imply about his political sentiments; yet he was also an admirer of Sparta over Athens (VI.2.27, 59).

[32] Or: Without the polis, law is of no benefit; *nomou de aneu poleôs ouden ophelos* could bear either meaning. But the first reading is more likely if, as seems plausible, Diogenes is consciously echoing Plato's "to whom would a polis be acceptable without laws?" (*tini gar an polis areskoi aneu nomôn*) at *Crito* 53a.

(1) If being without *X* makes the state worthless, then *X* is good.
(2) Being without law makes the state worthless.
(3) Therefore, law is good.
(4) But unjust statutes are not good.
(5) Therefore, unjust statutes are not laws.

Putting Arius Didymus, Clement, and Cicero together, we can reconstruct Diogenes' intended argument as follows, supplying some implicit premises.[33]

(1) [If being without *X* makes a good/civilized thing of no benefit, then *X* is good/civilized.]
(2) Without the polis, the good/civilized is of no benefit.
(3) Therefore, the polis is good/civilized [(1), (2)].
(4) Without law, the polis is of no benefit.
(5) [Therefore, being without law makes a good/civilized thing of no benefit.] [(3), (4)]
(6) Therefore, law is good/civilized [(1), (5)].

Propositions (3) and (6) must mean not that existing cities and laws are good/civilized (a claim that Diogenes would not accept), but, *more stoico*, that nothing counts as a city or a law unless it is good/civilized. Presumably, only the cosmopolis will count as a city, and only the dictates of reason as laws. And perhaps it is in this city that Diogenes will employ his vaunted art of ruling (D.L. VI.2.29, 74); for Diogenes offers the following argument (VI.2.37; cf. I.12) as well:

(1) All things belong to the gods.
(2) Friends share all their belongings in common.
(3) Therefore, all things belong to the friends of the gods [(1), (2)].
(4) The wise are friends of the gods.
(5) Therefore, all things belong to the wise [(3), (4)].

This is presumably one of the arguments Diogenes uses to justify theft (D.L. VI.2.72–73), since if all things belong to the wise, then the wise have the authority to take whatever they can make good use of. But if gods rule the universe, and the wise enjoy a share in all that the gods possess, it would seem to follow that gods and wise men rule the universe together. The Cynics, like Xenophon, thus lay the foundations for the more detailed theories of natural law and cosmopolitanism that will be developed in the Hellenistic era by Stoics

[33] Notice too that (3) below is here treated as an inference from (2) rather than as an independent premise; this reading makes better sense of the argument, and brings out the parallel with Cicero.

and others, while the Cyrenaics, with their stress on the instrumental character of social relationships, lay the foundations for the contractarian approach to law that will be championed by the Epicureans.

Further Reading

Socrates has been the subject of an extensive literature. Scholars have debated the "Socratic problem," that is, the comparative value of Plato, Xenophon, Aristophanes, and other ancient authorities as sources for the views of Socrates. Most scholars have regarded Plato as the most reliable, and *Apology* and *Crito* as especially important sources for Socrates' views about the law. *Apology* is discussed by Brickhouse and Smith 1989, Reeve 1989, and Colaiaco 2001. Brickhouse and Smith 2002 is an excellent collection of translated ancient and modern writings on the trial of Socrates. For Socrates' views on obeying the law in *Crito*, see Woozley 1971 and 1979; Allen 1980; and Kraut 1984. Scholars often consider whether the views attributed to Socrates in *Apology* and *Crito* are consistent, an issue taken up by Santas 1979, chap. 2, and Brickhouse and Smith 1994, chap. 5; 2000, chap. 6.

Some of the best recent research on the early Socratic philosophers is collected in Vander Waerdt 1994b, which includes essays on Plato, Aeschines, Aristippus, Antisthenes, and four on Xenophon. Morrison 1988 has compiled an invaluable compendium of bibliographical information on Xenophon. An influential study of Xenophon is Strauss 1972. Recent defenses of Xenophon as a source for Socrates' views include Morrison 1987 and Cooper 1999. Morrison 1995 argues for a legal-positivist interpretation of Xenophon's *Memorabilia.* Annas 1993, chap. 11, offers a thoughtful discussion of Cyrenaic social philosophy. A rich source of articles on Cynic social philosophy is Branham and Goulet-Cazé 1996.

Chapter 3

PLATONIC PHILOSOPHY OF LAW

by Richard F. Stalley[1]

3.1. Introduction

Plato (427–347 B.C.) belonged to an aristocratic Athenian family and appears to have been a follower of Socrates from an early age.[2] A letter ascribed to him describes how he originally intended a political career but decided after Socrates' death to devote himself to philosophy (*Ep.* VII.324b–326b). To this end he founded a school, known as the Academy, in which he was joined by many pupils including Aristotle. In his later life he made two visits to Syracuse, apparently with the intention of educating the young ruler of the city in the ways of philosophy (*Ep.* VII.342a–e; 345c–352a). This brief involvement in practical politics was totally unsuccessful.[3]

Plato wrote some thirty dialogues. Socrates leads the discussion in most of these and is present in all except the *Laws*. Modern scholars usually assign the dialogues to three periods (Guthrie 1975, 41–54; Lane 2000, 155–60). Those of the early period are mostly quite short, present a lively picture of Socrates, and generally end in uncertainty. Those of the middle period are longer, present a less lively picture of Socrates, and expound a more positive philosophy based on the theory of "Forms."[4] The dialogues of the late period are stylistically distinct from their predecessors but differ considerably from one another in form and content. Most make no overt reference to the theory of Forms as that was understood in middle period dialogues.[5] Whereas the distinction between the late period dialogues and the others is firmly based on stylometric analysis, the distinction between early and middle period dialogues depends on literary and philosophical judgment (Brandwood 1990; 1992). Many scholars have held that Plato's thought developed in important ways over his

[1] All translations are by the author unless otherwise indicated.

[2] For an account of what is known of Plato's biography, see Guthrie 1975, 8–30.

[3] There is considerable disagreement both about the authenticity of *Ep.* VII and about the purposes of Plato's visit to Syracuse; see Schofield 2000a, 298–302.

[4] In the *Republic*, Plato argues that besides the many beautiful things of ordinary experience there is a single "Form" of beauty. The beautiful things of ordinary experience are subject to change and decay and may be found to be ugly from some point of view, but the Form of beauty is unqualifiedly beautiful and does not change or decay. In the same way, Plato claims that there are Forms of justice, equality, and so forth. The Forms are known by reason. The Form of the Good is given a preeminent role as the source of knowledge and being.

[5] The apparent exception is the *Timaeus*. Owen 1953 (criticized by Cherniss 1957) proposed an earlier dating of this dialogue, but this has generally been rejected on stylometric grounds; cf. Brandwood 1990; 1992.

lifetime. It is claimed that in the early period Plato sticks fairly closely to the teaching of Socrates (Vlastos 1988; 1991; criticized by Kahn 1981a; 1997). The middle period dialogues, with their emphasis on the Forms, represent a more distinctively Platonic philosophy, but Plato changed his mind very substantially in the late period when he modified (or perhaps even abandoned) the theory of Forms (Owen 1953; Cherniss 1957). However, other scholars argue that his fundamental views remained essentially unchanged throughout his career, despite important changes in the manner of presentation.[6] This controversy affects our understanding of Plato's legal thought, since many developmentalists would argue that his middle period philosophy allows only a subordinate place for law while his later philosophy gives it much greater prominence (Barker 1918; Klosko 1986; see also Owen 1953).[7]

Five dialogues will be examined in this chapter. Taken together, they provide us with a rich understanding of Plato's views on law. The *Protagoras* and *Gorgias* both depict Socrates in vigorous debate with representative figures of the sophistic movement. Although there is disagreement about the relative dating of these dialogues, virtually all scholars assign them to Plato's early period. The *Republic*, the most celebrated of Plato's works, is assigned to the middle and the *Statesman* to the late period. There is evidence that Plato was still working on the *Laws*, his longest work, when he died.[8]

3.2. Plato's Critique of the Sophists: *Protagoras* and *Gorgias*

If the interpretations offered of the *Euthyphro*, *Apology*, and *Crito* in Chapter 2, Section 2.3 of this volume are correct, Socrates there insists that right and wrong are not simply matters of human decision. He must therefore reject the sophistic view that they are the product of convention (*nomos*) rather than nature (*phusis*) (see Chapter 1, Sections 1.4–5 of this volume). But he does

[6] The traditional view saw the Forms as the center of Plato's thought throughout his life. Dialogues that made no explicit reference to the Forms were read as pointing toward them. The more recent tendency has been to emphasize that Plato's works are dialogues rather than monographs. The dialogue form enabled Plato to approach questions from different points of view without committing himself to a dogmatic position. This more nuanced approach, which pays close attention to the form of Plato's writing, is evident in Schofield 2000c, and Laks 2000.

[7] An alternative view is that differences between the *Republic* and the *Laws* stem from the fact that the former presents an ideal while the latter offers a more practical model. Thus Saunders 1970, 28, sees these two dialogues as "opposite sides of the same coin." Laks 2000 sees the *Laws* as completing and revising the *Republic* while also pointing to the implementation of Plato's views.

[8] Diogenes Laertius (D.L. III.37) reports that Philip of Opus transcribed the *Laws* "from the wax" (i.e., from wax tablets). There are other signs, such as the absence of dialogue in Book V and the presence of inconsistencies and stylistic infelicities, which may indicate that the work did not receive its final polish.

not make this point explicitly. We can now look at two dialogues where Plato brings this issue to the surface.

Early in the *Protagoras* the great sophist, after whom the dialogue is named, defends his claim that virtue or political excellence can be taught, even though there are no recognized experts or teachers in the field (319a–320b). He bases his case on a myth that tells how human beings at first lived in isolation from one another but fell prey to the animals. Zeus then sent them the gifts of justice and respect, which enabled them to band together and form cities (320c–323a).[9] This myth is usually interpreted naturalistically as showing that law and morality are human creations (Taylor 1976, 80).[10] In order to survive, human beings must form communities and agree on common standards of behavior. These agreements determine what counts as virtue. On this basis Protagoras argues that cities, in fact, make great efforts to train citizens in virtue from earliest childhood. Law is essential to this process, for citizens are compelled to learn the laws and to use them as patterns in their everyday lives (326c–d). The use of punishment manifests, particularly clearly, the belief that virtue can be taught, since people are not punished for faults that are due to nature or chance, but for those resulting from poor training: No one punishes for the sake of what is past. That would be to exact blind vengeance like a beast. Punishment is in fact directed to the future. Its purpose is to prevent both the one who undergoes it and those who witness the punishment from repeating the offense (323c–324b; see Saunders 1981; Saunders 1991, 133–6, 162–4; and Stalley 1995b). So, although Protagoras sees justice as resting on laws established by convention, it is still vitally important in his eyes because it is essential to the survival and well-being of society.

Instead of attacking Protagoras' account of virtue directly, Socrates raises the question whether virtue is one thing or many, and proceeds to argue that virtue is knowledge of what is good for us (351b–360c). This, of course, implies that Protagoras' account of law and morality as resting on convention must be rejected. Nevertheless, it leaves untouched several features of Protagoras' account, in particular his view that punishment and training are essential to the acquisition of virtue. As we shall see, Plato came to incorporate similar ideas into his own theories.

The *Gorgias* is ostensibly a discussion of the nature and value of oratory. But several passages bear on the philosophy of law. For example, Socrates argues, against the sophist Polus, that oratory and sophistry are spurious arts be-

[9] Many scholars have supposed that the speech paraphrases or perhaps even quotes from a genuine work of Protagoras, but there is little real evidence for this (see Taylor 1976, 77–84; Kerferd 1982, 125–6; and de Romilly 1991, 196–203).

[10] Given that Protagoras was well known for his agnosticism about the gods, it seems unlikely that Plato would put into his mouth a doctrine that required a literal belief in their existence.

cause they aim merely at pleasure and the appearance of good and can give no rational account of what they do. They are contrasted with the genuine arts of legislation and justice, which seek the good and involve rational understanding. Legislation, in fact, stands to the soul as gymnastics does to the body because it makes us live in ways that promote the well-being of the soul. The administration of justice is like medicine because it restores disordered souls to health (461b–466a). Underlying these arguments are Socrates' claims that it is better to suffer wrong than to do wrong and better to be punished for one's misdeeds than to go unpunished. Vice is, in fact, a disorder or disease of the soul. Just as we take the sick to the doctor for treatment, so we must take the wicked to the judge for punishment. Thus, just punishment cures criminals of their wickedness. The really wretched individual is the criminal who goes unpunished. Oratory should not be used to escape punishment, but to ensure that we and our friends receive the punishment that will cure us of wickedness (472d–481b).

The *Gorgias* offers no explanation of how just punishment might cure criminals.[11] But Plato is certainly serious about the claims that legislation demands a rational understanding of the good, that it is better to suffer wrong than to do wrong, and that wrongdoers benefit from punishment. These claims imply that legislation, properly understood, should not only promote conformity to accepted norms of behavior, but also secure the good of the citizens' souls. Moreover, what counts as good is determined not by the amount of pleasure it produces but by rational judgment.

This view of law and justice is contested by Callicles, who argues that by nature it is right for the stronger to rule.[12] Laws are mere conventions, created by the weak to restrain the strong. The truly admirable man is strong enough to ignore the restraints of law and gratify his desires at will (482c–484c, 488c–492e). Callicles thus agrees with Protagoras that laws are human creations that benefit the community at large, but his attitude toward law thus understood is totally different. According to Protagoras, laws deserve everyone's support because without them life would be intolerable, but according to Callicles, they have no claim on those strong enough to break them with impunity. Only the weak and worthless have a motive for obedience. As the dialogue progresses, Callicles proves unable to defend this ideal of unlimited self-gratification against Socrates' persistent questioning. This leaves the way open for Socrates to reassert his view that the good, which is the object of everything we do, is to be distinguished from pleasure. An orator who genuinely sought the good

[11] In *Gorg.* 504d–505b Socrates claims that if a soul is to be virtuous its unhealthy desires must be restrained. Since the word *kolasis* ("restraint") is standardly used to mean "punishment," there is a suggestion here that just punishment restores the soul to health by disciplining or restraining the desires; see Irwin 1979, 218.

[12] The character of Callicles has been much discussed. He is not known from other sources and may be a Platonic creation. Some have seen him as representing a position Plato himself found seriously attractive in his youth; see Dodds 1959, 12–15.

would aim to create regularity (*taxis*) and order (*kosmos*) in the souls of his audiences. These orderly states of the soul are called "law" (*nomos*) and "lawful" (*nomimos*). Those with souls ordered in this way possess the virtues of justice (*dikaiosunê*) and self-restraint (*sophrosunê*) (503e–504d). They are brought about by restraining the desires of an unhealthy soul. Such restraint is called *kolasis* ("discipline" or "correction").

In this part of the *Gorgias* Socrates identifies law with order and harmony, particularly the order and harmony of the just soul. The same principles, Socrates claims, characterize a healthy body, a well-made artefact, and even the universe at large. In fact, the universe is called *cosmos* ("order") because, according to wise men, "heaven and earth, gods and men are held together by community (*koinonia*) and friendship (*philia*), and orderliness, temperance and justice" (507e–508a). Thus, in the view presented in the *Gorgias*, law is so far from being a purely human creation that it governs the entire universe. Earthly courts and legislative assemblies may, of course, be led astray by orators who pander to the masses, but, Socrates claims in the mythical account of divine judgment that rounds off the dialogue, the just will be rewarded and the wicked punished after death (523a–527e).[13] So, whatever may be the case with the positive laws of existing cities, genuine laws, such as would be enacted by true statesmen, promote the true good of the citizens by creating order and harmony in their souls.

3.3. The Philosophy of Law in Plato's *Republic*

Plato's *Republic* is primarily an investigation of the nature and value of justice, though it also deals with many other questions about morality and society, about the nature of reality, and about the possibility of knowledge. The questions "What is justice?" and "Is it worth our while to be just?" are raised in Book I. There Socrates encounters Cephalus, for whom justice consists simply in the kinds of behavior conventionally regarded as just, such as telling the truth and giving back what one owes, and Polemarchus who sees justice as a matter of helping friends and harming enemies. Socrates shows that neither view can be defended in a coherent way (328b–336a). He is then challenged by a more formidable opponent, the sophist Thrasymachus, who claims that "justice is the interest of the stronger" (338c–339a). His point is that what is commonly called "justice" is simply obedience to the positive laws of one's community. These laws, as a matter of fact, embody the interests of the domi-

[13] There are similar myths of judgment in the *Phaedo* and the *Republic*. The *Phaedrus* and the *Laws* also contain accounts of what happens to the soul after death. The details of these myths vary and their meaning has been much discussed. But Plato certainly seems to believe that the soul survives death and that the universe is so organized that we will eventually suffer for our misdeeds in this life. In this sense, human law derives from and is supported by divine law.

nant party. The implication is that everyone else should ignore considerations of "justice" if they can get away with it.[14] Although he does not appeal explicitly to the sophistic distinction between *nomos* and *phusis*, Thrasymachus is evidently using similar ideas to undermine conventional morality. He goes on to claim that justice is "another person's interest," in other words, that just acts always benefit someone else. So the unjust person always gets the better of the just one. As Thrasymachus sees it, justice is thus mere stupidity; the genuinely wise and admirable person is the one who gets away with injustice. Best of all is the tyrant who exploits the city for his own benefit (343b–344c).

Socrates "refutes" these claims by forcing Thrasymachus to contradict himself. Although his arguments are largely fallacious, they introduce ideas which play an important part in Plato's thought—that the genuine ruler seeks the good of his subjects rather than his own interests (341a–342e), that excellence in anything consists in achieving the correct standard rather than going to excess (349b–351d), that the just city and the just man are genuinely strong (351e–352b), and that to be just is to live well and therefore to be happy (352d–354a).

A new start is made in Book II where Socrates avows that justice is good not only for the rewards and reputation it brings, but also for its own sake (357a–358a). As Glaucon points out, this is not the usual view. Most people think of justice as something like medical treatment, which we reluctantly accept because of its beneficial consequences. According to this view, the ability to injure others if one wants is good, but suffering injury is bad. As a kind of compromise, people therefore agreed not to injure one another. They established "laws and covenants" and called what these laws required "lawful and just." The implication, according to Glaucon, is that only the fear of punishment and disgrace makes people behave justly (359b–360d). Justice has no intrinsic value of its own. To see this we have only to compare a just man who suffers extreme misfortunes with an unjust man who succeeds in everything he does and avoids the punishment and disgrace which are the normal penalties of injustice. No one in his right mind would prefer the life of the just individual who suffers to that of the unjust one who prospers (360e–361d).

The common view of justice, as described in the passage under discussion, is very close to that of Protagoras. So in effect, Plato here shows that conventionalism, for all its apparent plausibility, has serious weaknesses. If justice rests solely on agreements made for mutual self-protection, someone who can commit crimes without fear of detection has no motive to be just. Thus the Protagorean theory collapses into the immoralism of Callicles and Thrasymachus. To defend the claims of justice, one must show that it has some foundation other than positive law.

[14] The exact interpretation of Thrasymachus' position is a matter of dispute. In fact, he seems to change his ground a good deal. At times he seems to be arguing, rather like Callicles, that the strong have a right to rule; see Annas 1981, 34–57.

The reply that Plato puts into the mouth of Socrates is long and complex. He proposes first to look for justice by examining a city coming into being. He argues that a city will function best when each citizen sticks to one task for which he or she is fitted by nature and training. This requires a clear division between the soldier class and that of the farmers, artisans, and traders who engage in economic activities. The soldiers should undergo an elaborate training in poetry, music, and gymnastics in order to develop their characters (II.376c–III.412b). They will live in common having no private property, wives, or families of their own (III.416c–417b). The best of these soldiers will be selected as rulers or "guardians" (412a–414b). These are seen as constituting a third class within the city (414b–415d). Since the city's well-being and survival depend on each of these classes sticking to its own task, this must be what makes the city just. Plato thus comes up with a surprising definition of justice in the city as "doing one's own work and not meddling with what isn't one's own" (IV.433a, trans. Grube). He then gives a similar account of justice in the individual. Our souls have three parts: reason, spirit, and appetite. We are just when each of these does its own work, that is, when reason rules—with the aid of spirit—and appetite obeys reason (441e). Conversely, we are unjust when the order of the soul is subverted and the appetites seize control.

The *Republic*'s account of justice both in the city and in the individual is very different from any ordinary conception of justice. Some commentators have therefore seen a fallacy at the very heart of the dialogue (Sachs 1963; discussed by Vlastos 1971; 1977; Demos 1964; Annas 1981, 118–23, 152–9). Plato claims to show that justice is good for itself as well as for its consequences, but since what he in fact talks about is not justice as ordinarily understood, he has not done what he set out to do. It is impossible here to review the extensive literature on this issue, but two points seem crucial: (a) Plato evidently believes that to define justice he must describe the ideal case. So he is concerned not with what counts as justice in existing imperfect cities, but with the genuine justice of the best possible city. Similarly, he aims to describe the ideally just individual, not someone who might be regarded as just by ordinary opinion. (b) He realizes that justice cannot be defined by giving lists of right and wrong acts. He therefore claims that for the individual to be just is for his or her soul to be constituted in the right way. We may think of acts as just, in a secondary sense, if they approximate to what the truly just individual would do, but the primary concern of a legislator must be to shape the character of the citizens rather than simply to control their outward behavior.

The middle books of the *Republic* explain how a long training in philosophy will enable the rulers ultimately to grasp the Forms of goodness, justice, and the like. Books VIII and IX reinforce the account of justice and injustice by describing inferior kinds of constitution in order of merit, beginning with timarchy, the government of those motivated by military and political ambition, and proceeding though oligarchy and democracy to the ultimate degradation of tyranny. For each of these constitutions, Socrates describes the character of a corresponding individual. He takes these descriptions, particularly that of the tyrannical man whose soul is dominated by an overwhelming lust, to show that the just individual is truly better off than the unjust one (IX.571a–580c). The dialogue ends with a myth, telling how the just are rewarded and the unjust are punished after death, and links this moral order with the visible order of the heavens (X.612a–621d).

According to most interpreters, Plato in the *Republic* holds that a city with genuinely wise rulers will have little or no need for law (Barker 1918, 225–7; Klosko 1986, 134, 190; Annas 1981, 105–7). The rulers will be able to direct the affairs of the city in the best possible way, untrammelled by legislation. On the surface at least, it seems true that the account of the ideal city makes little reference to law. No legislative procedures are described and there is only a brief mention of a judicial system (III.409a–410a). Moreover, a passage in Book IV has been taken to say explicitly that the ideal city has no need for legislation (425b–e). There, Socrates claims that, if the guardians and soldiers are properly educated and have orderly and law-abiding characters, the rest of what is required of them should not prove too difficult. There will be no need to legislate about matters of good manners, such as the behavior of the young toward their elders. Written legislation on such matters is ineffective, while those who have been properly educated need no further inducement to correct behavior. Similarly it is inappropriate to lay down rules about commercial matters such as contracts and market dues, since good and honorable men will easily discover them for themselves (425c–d). They must not waste time making and amending petty regulations, like people who become sick through their own intemperance but refuse to adopt a healthier lifestyle (425d–e).

In considering this passage and the general lack of emphasis on law in the *Republic*, there are a number of points to bear in mind. First, the city of the *Republic* is avowedly an ideal. No doubt citizens of an ideal community would seldom, if ever, take explicit recourse to law. Because they are virtuous and fully accept the principles on which the city is founded they will settle disagreements amicably and will fulfill their obligations without the threat of sanctions. But this ideal is unlikely to be achieved in practice. So Plato ought to recognize the need for law in the world as we know it. The condemnation of democratic cities for openly flouting the laws (VIII.557e–558a) implies that law has an important role at least in nonideal communities.

Second, Plato devotes virtually all his attention to the rulers and soldiers who have received an intensive education focused on the development of character and have no interest in money or property. The farmers, artisans, and traders, who form the largest part of the citizen body, will apparently not receive the same education and will have property and families. Even if the soldiers and rulers could manage without law, it is difficult to see how the economically active people could do so.

Third, Plato frequently describes Socrates and his companions as legislating or making laws (*nomoi*) (e.g., III.409e–410a, 417b; IV.424c–e, 430a; V.458c; VI.501a; VII.530c). The rulers are called "guardians of the laws" (VI.504a; VII.521c; Morrow 1993, 582) and there is even one reference to a law binding on the guardians themselves (VII.519e–520a). This may suggest that the city will have a fairly extensive legal system. Indeed, one might argue that *nomos* is needed to define the functions of the different classes. It thus enables the city to instantiate the form of justice. The difficulty is that the Greek word *nomos* can refer not only to measures promulgated by a government and enforced by courts of law, but also to customs and conventions of an informal kind that are enforced mainly by social pressures. It is not clear whether the *nomoi* of the *Republic* are to be written down or whether there is to be any formal system of adjudication and enforcement. But the claim that there is no need for legislation about good manners (IV.425b) presupposes some distinction between laws and informal customs.[15]

Fourth, the concluding pages of Book IX sum up the moral argument of the *Republic* by stressing that if we are to be truly happy the lower elements in our souls must be subordinate to the divine power of reason. Those who lack this power within themselves must, for their own good, be "enslaved" to those who have it. This is the purpose both of law, which is the "ally" of everyone in the city, and of education, which does not allow children to be free until a "constitution" (*politeia*) has been established within them (590c–e). Whether this passage refers to existing cities or the ideal one, it implies that law is essential as a guideline and means of restraint for those who have yet to develop the power of self-direction.

Read in the light of these points, the critique of petty legislation at IV.425c–e clearly cannot be taken to imply hostility to law as such. There is no need to propose laws about markets and the like because the well-trained rulers of the ideal city can do this for themselves. Similarly, the attack on those who try to improve the life of the citizens by constantly introducing new laws does not imply that there is no need at all for legislation. The point is rather that, if the system is fundamentally sound and if the citizens are well educated, there will be no need to regulate every detail of their lives. If, on the other hand, the system is not sound or the citizens are not well educated, then no amount of legislation will solve the problem.

If this is right then the *Republic*'s account of law is consistent with that of the *Gorgias*. The fundamental aim of the city and of the individual must be

[15] It is not entirely clear how Plato would distinguish matters that require legislation from those which may be left to habit and custom. Evidently, legislation determines the main structures of the state, the educational system, and the methods of procreation (II.380c; III.417b; V.452c, 453d, 457b–c). If these work effectively, the citizens will have good characters and there will be no need for legislation on matters such as dress and deportment (IV.425b–c).

justice. But being just is not, as people generally suppose, simply a matter of conforming to conventional norms. It consists rather in the rule of reason. The soul is just when its rational element rules over its passions and desires. The city is just when it is ruled by the guardian class, but this can come about only when all classes conform to the fundamental laws of its constitution. Laws not only make social life possible but are also the precondition of rational government. However, in a well-ordered city they work through education rather than through sanctions. They provide guidelines for the young and for those without developed powers of reason, which enable them to acquire habits of virtuous behavior. This, in turn, creates order and rational government in their souls.

3.4. Law in Plato's *Statesman*

In the *Statesman* an unnamed "stranger" from Elea leads a search for the definition of the statesman.[16] In conducting this search his key assumption is that the statesman is an expert who possesses the "royal art" of ruling. This leads him to take issue with conventional classifications of constitutions. These are based on factors such as the number of rulers (one, few, or many) and on the manner in which they rule: whether they use force or rely on consent, whether they are rich or poor, and whether they do or do not make use of written laws.[17] The Stranger dismisses such matters as irrelevant to the search for a genuine constitution. All that really matters is whether the ruler (or rulers) possesses the genuine science of government (*Plt.* 292a–293e).

The Stranger defends his claim that the use of law is irrelevant to the classification of governments, by arguing that laws, because they are general, cannot adapt to particular circumstances. They thus resemble "some self-willed and ignorant person," who allows no one to modify or question his instructions (*Plt.* 294b–c). However, the Stranger concedes that laws may in practice be necessary. Just as a gymnastic trainer who cannot give individualized advice to each member of his class has to prescribe what is best for the majority, so lawgivers, who obviously cannot attend to the individual needs of each citizen, give rulings that suit most of them (293e–295b). Moreover, a doctor or trainer who left written instructions for those in his charge before going abroad would not be bound by them, were he to return early. He would gladly modify them in the light of changed circumstances. Similarly, expert rulers should not be

[16] The structure and purpose of the *Statesman* are far from clear. The dialogue is ostensibly a demonstration of philosophical method and the discussion is led by the Stranger rather than by Socrates. It is clearly relevant to Plato's views on politics and law, but it is doubtful whether we should take it as an authoritative exposition of Plato's own view.

[17] On the conventional view there are five forms of government. The lawful form of rule by one man is kingship, while the unlawful form is tyranny; the lawful form of rule by a few is aristocracy, while the unlawful form is oligarchy; and no distinction is made between lawful and unlawful forms of rule by the many (democracy).

bound by anything they have written (295b–296a). It would be even more absurd to subject genuine rulers to laws approved by the populace at large. That would be like compelling doctors, navigators, and the like to carry out their duties in strict accordance with rules laid down by a democratic assembly, leaving no room for professional judgment. However, it would be even worse if a city that had established such laws, after taking advice and persuading a majority to pass them, then allowed officials to dispense with them at will (300b). The upshot is that only rulers with expert knowledge may ignore laws. Others should imitate them not by dispensing with law, but by using as laws the written instructions that the experts would give. In the light of this, the Stranger claims that we should recognize six forms of constitution besides the true one with its expert ruler(s). The city may be ruled by one person, by a few, or by many, and in each case government may be conducted in accordance with law or without law (300b–303c).[18]

Many commentators assume that the expert ruler, who can dispense with law, is the philosopher-king of the *Republic*. By allowing that cities without such a ruler should use laws, the *Statesman*, it is claimed, moves from the unrealistic utopianism of the *Republic* to the more practical ideal of government by law (Klosko 1986, 194–7). However, this interpretation overlooks significant differences between the philosophers of the *Republic* and the expert ruler of the *Statesman*. The knowledge of the philosopher-rulers differs in kind from any other form of expertise. To achieve it they have to undergo a long training that develops their character and enables them to grasp the Form of the Good. This grasp of the good differentiates them from other experts who know how to achieve specific ends but cannot tell whether these are worth pursuing. None of this is mentioned in the *Statesman*, which assimilates the ruler's knowledge to other forms of skill or expertise.

Another difference between the expert ruler of the *Statesman* and the philosophers of the *Republic* is that the latter do not dispense with law. One message of the *Republic* is that a city must have the right institutions. In particular, it needs a system of education and a social structure that will enable philosopher-rulers to emerge, while ensuring that other citizens willingly obey the philosophers' instructions. Laws make these institutions possible and act as guidelines for those without the power of reason. In the *Statesman*, these points are simply ignored. Moreover, its comparison of law with the instructions of a doctor or gymnastic trainer is manifestly flawed. Trainers give general instructions to a whole class only because they cannot give separate instructions to each

[18] Of the lawful forms the most tolerable is the rule of a single individual, and the least tolerable the rule of many, but the order is reversed in the case of the lawless forms. Thus in order of merit we have kingship (the lawful rule of one person), aristocracy (the lawful rule of a few), lawful democracy, lawless democracy, oligarchy (the lawless rule of a few), and finally tyranny (the lawless rule of one individual).

individual, but the generality of law is not merely a regrettable necessity. It is precisely because laws are general that they enable people to coordinate their activities and to establish complex institutions. The *Republic* does not thematize these points, but it is certainly aware of them.

The inadequacy of the *Statesman*'s account of law undermines such arguments as it offers to show that a city governed by laws is the best practical possibility. Moreover, the concessions made to law are extremely grudging. The Stranger, in effect, satirizes the law-governed city by imagining one where medicine and navigation are treated in a totally legalistic way. Although he goes on to the more positive idea that those who make laws may imitate the truth embodied in the rule of the genuine statesman (*Plt.* 300b–e), he does nothing to develop this idea. If Plato had intended to make the case for government by law as the best practical alternative to rule of the expert he could hardly have done so in a less convincing way. The interpretation of the *Statesman* as marking a transition from the ideal of the philosopher-ruler to that of government by law is therefore questionable (see Rowe 1995a, 5–19; 2000, 244–51; Gill 1995, 301–4; Lane 1995; Schofield 1999a; and Laks 2000, 270–3). The passages we have been considering form only part of a dialogue ostensibly devoted to questions of philosophical method. Its primary significance for the philosophy of law may lie in what is not said explicitly, but should be obvious to an intelligent reader: There is a distinction between ruling and other forms of expertise and between laws and professional advice. Because ruling is not just another craft, laws are essential to its very nature.

3.5. Plato's *Laws*

The *Laws* describes the conversation of three old men—an unnamed Athenian, a Spartan named Megillus, and a Cretan named Clinias—who are walking to the cave where, according to legend, Zeus gave laws to King Minos. The Athenian opens the discussion by asking his companions whether the laws of their own cities were the work of a god or of some man. Both claim a divine origin for their own systems, which, they suggest, were designed for success in war (I.624a–626c). But the Athenian shows the inadequacies of this conception. Internal disputes are a greater danger than external wars. So, as well as seeking victory over other cities, the legislator must ensure that the better elements within the city are victorious over the worse. But it is even better to achieve peace and reconciliation so that the worse elements gladly obey the better. Analogous points are made about the individual (626c–628e). Because they sought victory in war, the Cretan and Spartan legislators concentrated on a single virtue, namely, courage. But the legislator ought to aim at virtue as a whole (630d–631a; cf. III.688a–b). He will then make the citizens really happy, for the virtues of wisdom, temperance, justice, and courage are divine goods. Without them, human goods, such as health, beauty, strength, and wealth, are

Plato (427–347 B.C.)

unattainable. The legislator must therefore proclaim that all his commands are directed toward these divine goods, that the human goods are subordinate to them, and that the divine goods themselves are under the leadership of reason. He must direct every aspect of the citizens' lives, from conception to the grave, toward this end. Those who are most obedient to the laws must be honored while the disobedient must be punished. In this way reason will show how legislation is subordinate to virtue rather than to wealth and ambition (I.631a–632c; cf. III.697b–c).

These pages reveal much about the attitude toward legislation that underlies the rest of the dialogue. Genuine law is a divine gift and is likely to be the work of a single inspired legislator who creates an all-embracing system. His ultimate aim is to make the citizens virtuous, but the *Laws* and the *Republic* differ significantly in their understanding of virtue. In the *Republic* it was implied that virtue, in the fullest sense of the word, requires an insight into the good, so only philosophers could be genuinely virtuous. But the *Republic* also seemed to recognize a secondary kind of virtue characteristic of the soldiers or auxiliaries. These have not only learned correct opinions about right or wrong, but have also been trained to live by them no matter what temptations they encounter (III.412b–414a; IV.429e–430c). The kind of virtue envisaged in the *Laws* is much more like the latter, so the object of legislation is to enable citizens to make correct judgments about right and wrong and to harmonize their passions and feelings with these judgments (II.653b–c, 654b–d). They must learn to take pleasure in what is right and hate what is wrong (659d–e). All citizens and not just the philosophers can acquire this virtue.[19]

The implications of this view both for cities and for individuals are explored in the remainder of Books I–III. Then the Cretan suggests that he and his companions should continue their conversation by imagining a constitution and legal code for a new city that is about to be established in Crete (III.702b–e). This occupies the remainder of the dialogue. The fact that a city is to be founded in a specific location gives their discussion practical relevance and enables Plato to emphasize that legislation must be adapted to the circumstances of a particular community (704a–705c). On the other hand, because the three old men are not themselves legislating for the new city, they are free to talk about principles rather than particularities (V.745e–746d).

The city of the *Laws* appears very different from that of the *Republic.* For example, the former has no philosopher-rulers and nothing like the *Republic*'s division of the citizens into three classes. All are to participate in public affairs and to serve as soldiers (753b). Those elected to office have experience,

[19] Most scholars see this as a consequence of the fact that there are no philosopher-rulers in the *Laws*, but Bobonich, in 1994, 1995, and 2002, argues that Plato had changed his view and came to believe that ordinary people are capable of being virtuous. This in turn led to major changes in his political thought.

practical wisdom, and a good moral character, but no specifically philosophical training. However, at the end of the dialogue we hear briefly about a body called "the nocturnal council," which will apparently ensure that there is some philosophical input into government (XII.951c–952d, 961a–968c). Equally the *Laws* abandons the idea that guardians should be without families or private property of their own. Common families and property may be a theoretical ideal, but it could happen only among gods or the children of gods (V.739a–e). All citizens will be required to marry and will have their own farms (739e–741a), though they will not be allowed to engage in trade and manufacturing (VIII.846d–847b).

The key idea underlying the political arrangements is that of the sovereignty of law. Every success comes to cities whose rulers are slaves to the laws, while destruction threatens any city where the laws are overruled (IV.715d). Indeed, cities where different factions wield power in their own interest cannot really be said to have constitutional government (715b). This idea of the sovereignty of law is worked out in two main ways. There must, firstly, be a fixed code of law that is difficult to change (VI.772b–d; XII.957a–b), for if the members of any group within the city could change the law at will then they, and not the laws, would be supreme (IV.712e–715d).[20] Secondly, officials must be subject to law in everything that they do. This is ensured by complex constitutional arrangements.[21] Virtually all who hold office act as members of collegial bodies rather than as individuals, different elements within the constitution act as checks and balances on one another, and the actions of all officials are subject to scrutiny to ensure that they always follow the law (945b–948b; Morrow 1941; Morrow 1993, 219–29, 244–5, 538–40, 550–1; Stalley 1983, chap. 8). Thus no one exercises unrestricted power. This is, of course, very different from what was envisaged in the *Republic*. Even if there was a place for law in that dialogue, its dominant idea was that philosophers should rule. In the *Laws* this is replaced by the rule of law.

Many scholars see this as reflecting a change of mind on Plato's part (Barker 1918, 338–43). Traditionally this has been attributed to Plato's realization, after the unsuccessful visits to Syracuse, that the city of the *Republic* is not a practical possibility. A more plausible suggestion associates it with a change in his view of moral psychology. On this interpretation, Plato abandoned the idea

[20] There is disagreement about how difficult it would be to change the laws. Morrow 1993, 570–1, claims that it is extremely difficult, which is a view followed by Stalley 1983, 82, and Klosko 1986, 323; 1988, 87, but criticized by Bobonich 2002, 395–408.

[21] At V.735a and VI.755a, Plato notes that there are two elements in the formation of a constitution (*politeia*): establishing magistrates and giving laws for those magistrates to enforce. This has been read as indicating a distinction between the constitution and the laws; see Laks 2000, 263. But since both elements are seen as part of the *politeia* and since the word *nomos* (law) is used in describing what we would think of as constitutional measures, Plato does not seem to have a clear distinction between constitutional and other types of law.

that there are distinct reasoning, spirited, and appetitive parts of the soul, and with it the ideal of the philosopher-king. Other scholars maintain that there is a broad consistency between the two dialogues (Saunders 1970, 20–8). The *Republic* uses the figure of the philosopher-king to set out the ideal of rule by reason, but Plato always realized that this ideal was unlikely to be achieved in practice. The closest we can come to it is by submitting to laws which embody the principles of reason (Morrow 1993, 563–9; Stalley 1983, 21, 92–3, 113–5).

From the beginning of the *Laws* it is clear that there are objective standards of right and wrong that can be known by reason and embodied in law. For example, at I.644d–645b, the Athenian compares human beings to "puppets" of the gods who are pulled not only by "hard and steely" strings of the passions and desires, but also by the "pliable golden string" of reasoning, which is called "the common law of the city." At IV.713e–714a, having described an imaginary golden age when the god Cronos ruled directly over mankind, he insists that wherever people have mortals rather than gods as rulers they will have no rest from trouble unless they imitate the rule of the god by ordering their homes and their cities in obedience to "the immortal element within them." The name given to this rational order is "law."

This position is supported by the long and closely argued preamble to the law on atheism in Book X. This is targeted against those who distinguish nature (*phusis*) from convention (*nomos*) and see the latter as the source of all ethical standards (888e–890b). Against this it is argued that the universe is directed by a divine soul (or souls) that is concerned with human affairs (893c–899b, 901d–903c). Thus the universe is ultimately the product of rational design. The legislator must therefore insist that law exists by nature or by "some cause not inferior to nature," since it is "the offspring of reason" (890d). In other words, law is the product of the same divine mind that creates order in the universe.

The task of translating the principles of divine reason into the positive laws of earthly cities ideally belongs to a wise legislator. We learn very little about the qualifications of this legislator, but he seems to rely on natural intelligence, experience, and good character rather than on philosophical training. At several points the wisdom and experience of the old are seen as guides to what is right (I.634d–e; II.659d; IV.715d–e). Insofar as anything provides a philosophical basis for the city, this is the work of the Nocturnal Council. It is required to understand the rational principles underlying the city's laws, but the details of its function are left very unclear. The trust Plato places in the common sense of the old and the borrowings he makes from the legal codes of existing cities (particularly Athens) suggest that conventional wisdom can be an acceptable basis for legislation (Morrow 1993, 295–6, 533–5, 546–8; Saunders 1991, 353). Perhaps the underlying idea is that most individuals have some grasp of the good and that this is, to a considerable extent, reflected in existing codes of law. Experienced people, who have received a good education, who are no longer dominated by the passions of youth, and who can decide matters in a calm and impartial way, will have sufficient understanding of the good to make sound laws. This view may seem preferable to that of the *Republic* in that it does not require us to put all our faith in philosopher-kings. But it is still vulnerable to serious objections. In practice, even the wisest and most experienced people may disagree about what is good. And even those who agree about what sorts of thing are good may differ in the priorities they attach to them. These points could be met only if there is a single objective standard of good. This claim, in turn, may need to be grounded in something like the theory of Forms.

If genuine law is the work of reason, what about the so-called laws of existing states that are not founded on rational principles? Three passages in the Platonic corpus imply that these should not be called laws, but none of these commands much conviction as a statement of Plato's own view.[22] The point is not explicitly raised in the *Laws*. However, the claim that cities whose rulers pursue their own interests have neither constitutions nor correct laws (IV.715b) seems to imply that their "laws" are invalid. On the other hand, Plato could hardly show such respect for traditional wisdom unless he saw the legal codes of existing cities as containing much that is fundamentally sound. Perhaps he holds that these codes may be called "laws" and should be obeyed insofar as they are consistent with the demands of justice. If, however, a ruler lays unjust demands on his subjects, these are not genuine laws and need not be obeyed.

As we have seen, the legislator's task is to inculcate virtue rather than merely to ensure compliance with norms of outward behavior. One implication of this is that the legislator must pay close attention to the education and upbringing of children, since this obviously influences the development of moral character (see, for example, I.643b–644b; VII.804c–d). It also obliges the legislator to concern himself with matters that we might see as belonging to the private sphere or as being best left to social custom. Not surprisingly, in the city of the *Laws* the educational curriculum is as much concerned with character as with knowledge or practical skills. Music, dance, poetry, and even children's games are strictly regulated. The minister of education is deemed to be the most important of all the officials (VI.766e). Much legislation is also designed to strengthen family life, but in this, as in some other areas, Plato allows for what he calls "unwritten laws," that is, customs enforced by social pressure rather than formal sanctions (VII.788a–c, 790a–b).

[22] The passages are *Hp. Ma.* 284d–e, *Crat.* 429a–b, and *Minos* 314–5. Most scholars believe that the *Minos* is spurious, and some take the same view of the *Hippias Major*. In the *Hippias Major* the claim is put into the mouth of Socrates, but in a context where there seems to be a good deal of irony. In the *Cratylus* the argument is attributed to Cratylus and may not represent Plato's own view.

A striking feature of the *Laws* is the idea that government should rely on persuasion rather than force. Most legislators simply issue instructions and impose penalties on those who disobey. But, according to the *Laws*, it is preferable to use persuasion, resorting to penalties only when that has failed. Thus all laws should be preceded by preambles designed to secure voluntary obedience (IV.720e–722c). There is, therefore, a general preamble to the legal code as a whole, as well as individual preambles for specific measures. For example, the law that men should marry by the age of thirty-five begins with the argument that only by marrying and having children can men satisfy their natural desire for immortality. Those who are unconvinced by this and remain unmarried will be punished by a yearly fine and by deprivation of honors (721b–e).

This emphasis on persuasion rather than force is clearly important. No legal system can rely exclusively on the threat of penalties. Moreover, imposing penalties on individuals who do not understand or accept the reasons for them may alienate them and reduce their respect for the law. Persuasive methods also avoid the pain and inconvenience of penalties. But persuasion can have a more sinister side. The institutions of the state cannot inculcate specific opinions and kinds of character if they allow the expression of contrary views. Thus, the use of persuasion is linked to a feature of the *Laws* which most modern readers find distasteful: its hostility to freedom of thought and expression. The most striking indication of this is the provision that persistent atheists should be put to death (X.908e–909a).

Some commentators see the role of persuasion in a more optimistic light, taking it to imply that the legislator must secure the consent of the citizens through rational argument. If this is correct, then there would be a big difference between the *Laws* and the *Republic* where only the philosophers have a rational grasp of right and wrong and where the other classes simply obey (Hall 1981, 93–6; Bobonich 1992; criticized by Stalley 1994). But this cannot be his point. Proposals made elsewhere in the *Laws*, such as those for the tight control of music, poetry, and children's games (II.656d–660a; VII.797a–798e), make it clear that Plato would rely heavily on nonrational methods of persuasion. The same also applies to the preambles. For example, the law on marriage described above does not require that someone should argue in a rational way with bachelors until they see the error of their ways. Rather it simply offers a highly suspect argument for marriage and then imposes a penalty on those who are not persuaded (IV.721b–e). Many other preambles make even less use of rational argument. They are mostly conventional exhortations relying more on prejudice than reason (see, for example, V.741a; VI.772e–773a; VII.823d–824a). The notable exception is the law on impiety with its extended proof of the existence of a god who cares about human affairs. But, although this preamble uses rational argument, it certainly does not respect the right of an individual to make up his or her own mind. The penalty for remaining unconvinced is ultimately death. Thus Plato's emphasis on persuasion rather than force is not as attractive as it initially sounds. He does not expect the legislator to secure the free and informed consent of the citizens, and he certainly does not see the authority of law as resting on that consent.

3.6. Plato on Punishment

In the *Protagoras*, as we saw in Section 2 above, Plato makes the sophist denounce a retributive conception of punishment (324a–b). He insists that it must look to the future and emphasizes its role as a deterrent. In the *Gorgias* Socrates also rejects a purely retributive account. He compares judges with doctors and argues that just punishment cures the criminal's soul of its wickedness in much the same way that medical treatment cures bodies of physical disease (476a–479c). Several passages in the *Republic* suggest a similar view (II.380a–b; III.409e–410a; IV.445a; IX.591a–b). In the *Laws* Plato again denounces purely retributive accounts of punishment and repeats many times that its primary purpose is to cure wrongdoers. But if criminals are so depraved as to be beyond cure, they should be put to death (IX.854d–855a, 862c–863a, 933e–934c; XII.941d, 957e–958a). This will rid the city of their presence while also providing an example to others (IX.862e; XII.942a, 957e–958a). Indeed, these incurable characters will be better off dead than living with their depravity. A few passages also hint at other purposes of punishment. For example, the contrast between the persuasion exercised by preambles and the force involved in penalties suggests a deterrence theory: If persuasion fails, fear of the penalty must force us to obey the law.

The penalties prescribed in the *Laws* vary considerably. Many offenses are punished by fines. In cases such as theft, which involve loss or injury to fellow citizens, the general principle is that the criminal should compensate his victim and pay an additional sum as punishment (IX.857a–b). For other crimes, particularly minor offenses against the state, the penalty involves deprivation of certain civil rights or some form of public disgrace (VI.754e–755a, 762c, 784d). Corporal punishment is sometimes prescribed for slaves or foreigners and very occasionally for citizens (IX.881d). Sentences of exile are mainly used in cases of homicide where, according to traditional religion, the continued presence of the killer in the city would cause pollution (IX.864e, 867c–868e). For a few offenses the penalty is imprisonment, usually for a period of a year (IX.880b–c; XI.919e–920c; XII.954e–955a). The death penalty is used for very serious offenses against individuals, such as deliberate murder, and for public offenses, such as theft from temples, taking bribes, and persistent atheism (IX.854e, 871d, 877b–c; X.910c; XII.955b–d). Most of these proposals have precedents in Athens or in other Greek cities, though the use of imprisonment as a punishment was unusual (Saunders 1991, chaps. 8–14).

These punishments might be effective as deterrents, but it is not clear how they could cure criminals of their wickedness. Indeed, if the aim is to cure the criminal, we may wonder why punishment, understood in the traditional sense as the infliction of something painful or unpleasant, should be applied at all, since there is no obvious reason why it should make people better. Some commentators have concluded that Plato is engaging in wishful thinking (Dodds 1959, 254). He is convinced that punishment could only be justified if it cures the criminal. He cannot contemplate the thought that it is in fact unjustified, so he concludes that it is a cure. T. J. Saunders (1991, 131–95; criticized by Stalley 1996) argues that the physiology of Plato's *Timaeus* would allow him to argue in purely medical terms that the experience of pain helps to bring the soul to order. The main trouble with this argument is that there is no apparent way in which the punishments Plato actually prescribes (few of which involve physical pain) could have this effect. A more plausible explanation may be that Plato is influenced by the view, which seems to have been more or less universal in Greece, that the punishment of children improves their characters by restraining their unruly desires (*Prot.* 225d). Given the generally paternalistic attitude he adopts toward the citizens of the *Republic* and the *Laws*, it would not be surprising if Plato held that this idea could also apply to adults. This would not mean that the punishments imposed in existing cities necessarily benefit those on whom they are inflicted, for Plato is committed only to the idea that *just* punishment improves the soul (*Gorg.* 476d–477a). But he could, perhaps, argue that in an ideal city, where there is every inducement to citizens to identify with their community and to internalize its values, it could be genuinely beneficial (Stalley 1995a).

If the interpretations offered here are correct, there is a substantial continuity in Plato's legal thought. From his earliest writings onward, he argues that there is an objective criterion of what is just and that this is determined neither by an agreement among the citizens nor by the will of a legislator. Because the gods are wise and good their laws are always, as a matter of fact, just. Human laws, on the other hand, may fall short of what is just, so it may sometimes be right to disobey them. In Plato's later works these fundamental claims remain unchallenged, though they are developed and expanded.

Two themes that come to prominence in these writings give Plato's legal thought much of its distinctive character. The first is that the purpose of law is not merely to secure conformity to norms of external behavior, but to make people virtuous, virtue being understood as an orderly and harmonious condition of the soul. This implies that law cannot be neutral between different conceptions of the good, that it must be concerned with all areas of life, and that it is inseparable from education. In these respects Plato's view is very different from that of modern liberals who advocate a state that is neutral between competing conceptions of the good and does not interfere with the private lives of citizens. Indeed, his arguments have something in common with communitarian critics of liberalism.

The second theme, that law is the product of reason, may not in itself seem particularly controversial. After all, rational discussion is necessary if a community is to agree on norms of behavior that are acceptable to its members as a whole, and lawmakers must use reasoning to assess the likely effects of their proposals. But, coupled with the idea that the goal of legislation is virtue, it implies that reason enables legislators to form a correct conception of the good. In the *Republic* this view is underpinned by the theory of Forms and the associated doctrine of the philosopher-ruler. The *Laws* gives the impression that wisdom is the product of natural intelligence combined with experience, but it still assumes an objective criterion of good that is independent of human wishes and desires. The problem of explaining how there can be such a criterion and how it can be known constitutes the greatest difficulty for Plato's theory of law.

Further Reading

The main texts for Plato's philosophy of law are found in his *Protagoras*, *Gorgias*, *Republic* (especially books I–II and IV), *Statesman*, and *Laws*. Although almost every page of *Laws* has some relevance to the topic, books I and IV are particularly important for Plato's conception of law and book IX for his view of punishment. Cooper includes modern translations of the entire Platonic corpus, and translations of most dialogues are also available in separate editions published by Hackett. A translation of *Laws* by Saunders, with helpful notes, is readable but sometimes imprecise. Bury is often more reliable. The translations of *Republic* by Bloom and *Laws* by Pangle may be helpful to Greekless readers who wish to make a careful study of particular passages. The Clarendon Plato series includes literal translations with philosophical commentaries (from an analytic point of view) of *Protagoras* (Taylor) and *Gorgias* (Irwin).

Guthrie (1975 and 1978) provides very useful discussions of the evidence for Plato's biography, of views on the chronology of his works, and of interpretations of each dialogue. Kraut 1992 includes chapters on the dating of Plato's dialogues and on his later political thought. Rowe and Schofield 2000 contains authoritative treatments by leading scholars of Plato's political philosophy, which sheds light on the context of his legal thought. De Romilly (1971) discusses many Platonic passages in the course of the general history of Greek legal thought. Otherwise there is little systematic writing on Plato's philosophy of law. Commentaries on *Republic* pay little attention to questions about law, though all give a central place to its theory of justice (see, e.g., Annas 1981; Santas 2001). Most treatments of Plato's political philosophy assume that Plato became seriously concerned with law only at a late period when he had despaired of making his ideal state a reality (e.g., Barker 1918; Klosko 1986). This style of interpretation is criticized by Kahn 1995 and several other contributors to Rowe 1995b. For other recent treatments of *Statesman* see Rowe 1995a and 2000; Lane 1998; and Schofield 1999a.

Saunders and Brisson 2000 gives a very full bibliography for *Laws*. Morrow 1993 provides an extended account of the institutional proposals of *Laws* and relates them to Greek practice. Stalley 1983 is a philosophical introduction to *Laws*, including questions about the nature of law. Saunders 1992 and Laks 2000 offer overviews of *Laws* from very different perspectives. Laks pays special attention to the form and structure of the dialogue. There are discussions of the relation between *Republic* and *Laws* in Laks 1991a; 1991b; and 1995. In a major new study, Bobonich (2002) argues that Plato's later political philosophy is a radical departure from his earlier views.

The literature on Plato's theory of punishment includes Mackenzie 1981, Saunders 1991, and Stalley 1995a and 1995b.

Chapter 4

ARISTOTLE'S PHILOSOPHY OF LAW

by Fred D. Miller, Jr.[1]

4.1. Life and Writings of Aristotle

Aristotle was born in 384 B.C. at Stagira in northern Greece, the son of Nicomachus, a physician of King Amyntas II of Macedonia. At age seventeen he entered Plato's Academy in Athens, where he studied for nineteen years. In addition to composing a number of dialogues now lost, he may have then begun work on his *Rhetoric*. After Plato's death (348) Aristotle grew alienated from the school and soon after left Athens. He resided at Assos, where he married Pythias, the niece of the philosophically trained tyrant Hermeias, and then lived at Mytilene on Lesbos. In 343 he was invited by King Philip of Macedonia to educate his thirteen-year-old son Alexander. Subsequently, Philip and his successor, Alexander, defeated an alliance of Greek city-states, and most of Greece—including Athens—submitted to Macedonian hegemony while Alexander was conquering the Persian Empire. Aristotle returned to Athens in 335 after the death of Philip and became a metic (resident alien). He founded his school at the Lyceum outside the city and began the most productive stage of his career. He offered lectures on technical philosophy (logic, physics, and metaphysics) in the morning, and on more popular subjects (rhetoric, ethics, and politics) in the evening. He also collected a celebrated library, and with his students compiled descriptions of 158 constitutions. During this period he probably composed most of his greatest treatises, including much of the *Politics*. After his wife's death he took a mistress, Herpyllis of Stagira, who gave birth to Nicomachus, after whom the *Nicomachean Ethics* was named. This work is probably Aristotle's revision of an earlier work, the *Eudemian Ethics*, from which three books were reused (*Eudemian Ethics*, Books IV–VI becoming *Nicomachean Ethics*, Books V–VII).

After Alexander's sudden death, the Athenians rose up against the Macedonians. Aristotle, who was a friend of Alexander's viceroy, Antipater, bore the brunt of anti-Macedonian sentiment. Charged with impiety he left Athens lest she "sin twice against philosophy." Appointing Theophrastus his successor as head of the Lyceum, Aristotle retreated to Chalcis, where he died soon after (322).

According to an ancient tradition, Aristotle's writings were lost after his death and only rediscovered in the first century B.C. Andronicus of Rhodes assembled numerous papyrus scrolls into treatises, which were recopied in man-

[1] All translations are by the author unless otherwise indicated.

uscripts over two millennia. Consequently, the works of Aristotle as we now have them raise many difficulties. This applies to the major works that contain Aristotle's legal philosophy: the *Politics*, the *Nicomachean Ethics*, and the *Rhetoric*. In the case of each of these works, scholars debate over the following questions: Were the parts of this work written at roughly the same time or do they express Aristotle's thought at different stages of his life? Does the organization of the work reflect Aristotle's intention or is it the construction of a later editor (which may be contrary to what Aristotle intended)? Does the work as it now exists express a coherent philosophical position? Moreover, another work that contains material on the law, *Magna Moralia*, may have been written not by Aristotle but by an early member of his school. An early spurious work, *Rhetoric to Alexander*, also contains some relevant material. Finally, Aristotle's 158 constitutions vanished altogether except for scattered quotations, until the rediscovery of a major fragment of the *Constitution of Athens* in the late nineteenth century. This work may also have been written by an early student of Aristotle during his lifetime.

4.2. Overview of Aristotle's Concept of Law

The concept of law is deeply embedded in Aristotle's political philosophy. Although legal terminology occurs frequently in his writings, Aristotle does not himself present a systematic and unitary legal treatise. Not infrequently he quotes (or paraphrases) others and appropriates their remarks, which results in considerable imprecision and apparent inconsistency in his various characterizations of law. He identifies law in different places with reason, with agreement, and with order. A reconstruction of Aristotle's legal philosophy should explain how these different characterizations are interrelated.

Aristotle's main term for "law" is the noun *nomos* (plural *nomoi*). Related expressions are *kata ton nomon*, "according to the law," *nomikos*, "legal," and *nomimos*, "lawful." The noun *nomimon* can also have the sense of "statute." In contrast, *para ton nomon* signifies "against the law," and *paranomos* means "illegal" or "unlawful." The precise meanings of these terms vary with the context. Sometimes Aristotle speaks of written law, in contrast to unwritten custom (*ethos*), for example, that one should honor one's parents, do good to one's friends, and return good to one's benefactors (*Pol.* III.16.1287b5–8; *EN* X.9.1180b4; cf. Pseudo-Aristotle, *Rhet. Al.* 1.1421b35–1422a1). But he also distinguishes between unwritten law and written law (*Pol.* VI.5.1319b40; *EN* X.9.1180a35; *Rhet.* I.10.1368b7, I.13.1373b4). He also uses *nomos* more loosely for "convention," the sense in which *nomos* was opposed to *phusis* ("nature") by the sophists (*SE* 12.173a7–30). Aristotle's term *nomos* can denote either a particular law or the law in an abstract sense.

A particular law is a rule (*kanôn*) prescribing or prohibiting various kinds of actions (see *EN* I.2.1094b5). For example, it commands the citizens not to leave their posts in time of war, not to commit adultery or act abusively, not to hit or slander others, and so forth (see *EN* V.1.1129b19–23). Because they command and prohibit general classes of action, the laws are universal in form: "The law speaks universally" (*EN* V.10.1137b13, 20; cf. 7.1135a5–8). The universality of the laws has an obvious advantage: The citizens can learn what the laws require, adapt their behavior to them, and acquire the habit of obedience.

But because laws are universal, they cannot address unusual cases. For example, the assembly might want to bestow honorary citizenship on a foreign potentate who has come to the aid of the city-state (*polis*). This requires an ad hoc rule. In an authoritarian regime this is called an "edict" (*epitagma*), and in a popular constitution a "decree" (*psêphisma*). Such rules concern individual acts to be done (*EN* VI.8.1141b27–8); they cannot be universal (*Pol.* IV.4.1292a37).

What distinguishes a universal rule *as* a law? This is the question, "What is law?" in the abstract sense, which Aristotle does not address in a systematic fashion in our extant texts, although there is considerable evidence as to how he would answer it: Law is "a sort of order" (*Pol.* VII.4.1326a30; cf. III.16.1287a18; II.5.1263a23). Unfortunately, Aristotle does not explain this claim, but we can gather what it means by considering how he understands order in his metaphysical works. Order is a ratio or proportion of opposites (*Phys.* VIII.1.252a14–15). Aristotle illustrates the concept of order in his discussion of the atomist theorists Democritus and Leucippus, who distinguished order from the relations of position and shape. For example, **A** differs from **N** in shape, **AN** from **NA** in order, and **A** from in position (cf. *Metaph.* I.4.985b17; *Phys.* I.5.188a24). As this illustration indicates, order is a ratio or proportion of prior and posterior elements (cf. *Metaph.* VII.12.1038a33). In a social context the fundamental type of priority is that of ruler to ruled:

> Whenever a thing is established out of a number of things and becomes a single common thing, there always appears in it a ruler and a ruled. (This is true whether it is formed out of continuous or discrete parts.) This [relation of ruler and ruled] is present in living things, but it derives from all of nature. For even in things that do not have a soul there is a sort of rule, for example, of harmony. (*Pol.* I.5.1254a28–33)

According to this principle of rulership, social order must be produced and maintained by a ruling element. This assumption reflects the link between the Greek noun, *taxis*, "order" ("arrangement," "organization," etc.), and the verb, *tassein*, "to order" ("to command," "to arrange," etc.). Similarly, in a living organism the soul is the natural ruler and authority over the body (*de An.* I.5.410b10–15; cf. Plato, *Phd.* 79e–80a). Aristotle also compares the order of the entire cosmos to that of an army; just as military order is due to the general, cosmic order is due to God. In both cases the parts are organized for the sake of a single end (*Metaph.* XII.10.1075a13ff.).

Given that law is a kind of order, where does it come from? Aristotle recognizes two different causes of order: nature and reason. In the physical world, outside of human creation, "nature is everywhere the cause of order" (*Phys.* VIII.1.252a12). Aristotle here understands "nature" (*phusis*) in terms of his teleological theory that entities have natural ends. Nature provides an internal directing principle, which causes a body to move or remain at rest in a regular manner (*Phys.* II.1.192b20–3). For example, an acorn grows by nature into an oak tree. Because of its internal nature the acorn grows in an orderly manner. Hence, "order is the proper nature of perceptible objects" (*Cael.* III.2.301a5–6). That is, orderliness is the natural condition of things (*GA* III.10.760a31), and disorderliness is unnatural (*Cael.* III.2.301a4–5). In the realm of human production, however, it is reason rather than nature that does the ordering (see *EN* III.12.1119b17). For example, a builder conceives of a form of a house and imposes this form upon a heap of bricks, constructing the house through a definite sequence of stages: foundations, walls, roof, etc. If, then, all order is due either to nature or to human reason, which of these is the cause of law?

For Aristotle, the primary source of law is reason embodied in a human legislator. The *Constitution of Athens* describes Solon's legislative activity at the beginning of the sixth century B.C.:

> Next Solon established a constitution and laid down other laws; and they stopped observing the ordinances of Draco, except those relating to murder. They wrote up the laws on the wooden tablets [mounted on pillars revolving on an axis], and set them up in the Stoa (porch) of the Basileus, and everyone swore to observe them. And the nine archons used to swear an oath upon the stone, declaring that they would dedicate a golden statue if they transgressed any law. This is the origin of the oath to that effect which they take to the present day. Solon fixed his laws for a hundred years, and he ordered the constitution in the following manner [...]. (*Ath.* 7.1–2)

Nomothetês, the Greek word for "legislator," derives from *nomos*, "law," and *tithenai*, "to lay (down)." The name "legislator" thus implies that the laws owe their existence to a human producer, who is also compared to a "craftsman" (*dêmiourgos*) of the laws or constitution (*EN* X.9.1180a21–2; *Pol.* II.12.1273b32–3). Like a weaver or shipbuilder, the legislator imposes a certain form on his materials, in particular, on the population of the city-state (*Pol.* VII.4.1325b40–1326a5). The legal order resembles cosmic order caused by God (1326a29–34). Legislators include the founders of constitutions, such as Lycurgus of Sparta and Solon of Athens, as well as assemblies or magistrates who lay down particular laws, unwritten as well as written (*Pol.* IV.1.1289a22, 14.1298a17; VI.5.1319b40; *EN* X.9.1180a35–b1).

Aristotle would have rejected the notion of "spontaneous order" espoused by some modern social scientists. He criticizes the theories of some pre-Socratic philosophers that the order of the cosmos arose by chance from earlier events, because he holds that regular outcomes cannot result from chance events: "chance is a cause in a disorderly or haphazard way" (*MM* II.8.1206b39–1207a1; cf. *Phys.* II.4.196a24–b5, 8.198b34–6, and *Cael.* III.2.301a10). If order does not arise by nature, order can only be due to rational design. Consequently, Aristotle would have dismissed the suggestion that legal order evolves spontaneously through myriad human interactions, as if (but not in fact) "by an invisible hand."

Aristotle also recognizes, however, that the legal order can subsist only if the citizens are law abiding. He thus characterizes law as a kind of common agreement (*homologia*) (*Pol.* I.6.1255a6) and as, "on the whole, a sort of convention [*sunthêkê*]" (*Rhet.* I.15.1376b9–10; cf. *Pol.* III.9.1280b10–11). His point is not that law is *merely* conventional, but that ruling according to law goes hand in hand with being ruled voluntarily (*Pol.* IV.10.1295a15–16). Furthermore, he states: "The law has no power to command obedience except that of habit" (*Pol.* II.8.1269a20–1). Habitual obedience is a precondition of the "compulsive power" of the law (mentioned at *EN* X.9.1180a21). But how is the claim that law results from agreement to be reconciled with the thesis that reason is the source of law? The answer may be sought in Aristotle's distinction between a strict cause and a contributing cause (*sunaition*). For example, he argues that heat is a contributing cause—but not the strict cause—of biological growth, because it does not determine when the process is complete (*de An.* II.4.416a14). Similarly, the laws of Athens required the general agreement of the Athenian citizens if they were to have the force of law. Solon's constitution, in fact, soon failed partly due to the wealthy class's general "dissatisfaction with the constitution because of the great change that had occurred" (*Ath.* 13.3). The contributions of reason and agreement are both recognized in the Aristotelian *Rhetoric to Alexander*: "Law, simply described, is reason [*logos*] defined according to the common agreement [*homologia*] of the city-state, regulating action of every kind" (1.1420a25; cf. 1422a2–3, 2.1424a9–12).

The purpose of law must be understood in relation to the constitution. The following passage makes clear that the study of law is subordinate to constitutional theory:

> The laws ought to be laid down (and everybody does lay them down) with a view to the constitutions, but not the constitutions to the laws. A constitution is the ordering [*taxis*] of offices in city-states: in what way the offices are distributed, what element has authority in the constitution, and what is the end of each community. But the laws which are separate from those revealing the constitution are those according to which the magistrates should rule and guard against violators of them. (*Pol.* IV.1.1289a13–20)

Like law, the constitution (*politeia*) is a sort of "order" (cf. *Pol.* III.1.1274b38), which provides the answer to three questions: (1) How are political offices distributed? (2) What is the sovereign or authoritative element? (3) What is the end of the city-state? Aristotle devotes considerable attention to the first two questions, and, from this viewpoint, the constitution is identified with the government (*politeuma*) (III.6.1278b8–11). Hence, some translators render *politeia* as "regime." But insofar as *politeia* signifies the order or "form" of the city-state (III.2.1276b7), it corresponds to "constitution." Although the Greek city-states did not have written constitutions in the modern sense, the constitutions were often administered by means of written laws, as in the case of Solon. The above passage (IV.1.1289a13–20) distinguishes three kinds of laws: laws that reveal the constitution, that is, laws regarding the orderly selection of officials (cf. III.16.1287a18); laws administered by magistrates, presumably to maintain order among the citizenry; and laws concerning the prevention and punishment of crime. Such laws are necessary: "The salvation of the city-state depends on the laws" (*Rhet.* I.4.1360a19–20; cf. *Pol.* V.9.1310a34–6). And "where the laws have no authority," Aristotle declares, "there is no constitution" (*Pol.* IV.4.1292a32). Yet the laws are subordinate to the constitution, and the constitution is the first concern of the legislator (III.1.1274b37).

The constitution has to do with the end or goal of the city-state. This is correctly defined by the basic principles of Aristotle's political philosophy: First, the city-state exists for the sake of the good life or happiness (*Pol.* I.2.1252b30, III.9.1281a1–2). Hence, the legislator should try to fashion laws that will tend to produce and protect happiness and its components for the political community (see *EN* V.1.1129b17–25). Second, the best life or happiness consists of a life of virtuous activity (*EN* I.7.1098a16; *Pol.* III.9.1281a2–3, VII.1:1323b40–1324a2). Therefore, the highest purpose of the legislator is to make the citizens virtuous (*EN* X.9.1180b23–5). When the laws are "laid down correctly," they command the citizens "to live according to each excellence and [forbid] us to live according to each vice" (V.2.1130b23–4, 1.1129b23–5). From this standpoint the constitution is "the way of life of the city-state" (*Pol.* IV.11.1295a40). Citizens who are habituated under the laws acquire self-ruling souls: that is, they are governed by reason rather than appetite. Having internalized the law, a virtuous individual becomes "a law unto himself" (*EN* IV.8.1128a32; *Pol.* III.13.1284a13).

Just as a doctor accepts as a given that health is his aim, "a statesman does not deliberate about whether he shall produce good law, nor does any one else deliberate about his end" (*EN* III.3.1112b14–15; cf. *EE* I.5.1216b18; cf. *Pol.* III.9.1280b6). Good law (*eunomia*) is defined in normative terms: "[L]aw is a certain order, and good law is good order" (*Pol.* VII.4.1326a29–31). By "good law," however, Aristotle means not merely that the laws are good, but that the city-state is in a good legal condition:

Good law does not consist in laying down good laws, if they are not obeyed. We must therefore suppose that good law in one way consists in the actual obedience to the laws that have been framed, and in another way it consists in the fact that the laws that are actually obeyed are laid down nobly (for laws laid down badly can also be obeyed). (*Pol.* IV.8.1294a3–7; cf. *MA* 10.703a30–4)

A city-state with good law is like a virtuous person who knows the right thing to do and acts accordingly. But it may happen that a legislator frames good laws that the citizens fail to obey. For example, the Athenians did not abide by the constitution of Solon, and the tyrant Pisistratus soon after rose to power (see *Ath.* 13–14). Such an inconstant city-state resembles a morally weak person: "[I]t passes the decrees it should and has excellent laws, but makes no use of them" (*EN* VII.10.1152a20–1).

There is thus a close connection among Aristotle's different characterizations of law as "order," "reason," and "agreement." Laws are general rules that produce a kind of order in the actions and desires of the citizens, which are devised in a rational manner by a legislator, and which are effective only if the governed accept and obey them. Because legislation is a rational activity, it is the appropriate subject for an Aristotelian science.

4.3. Legislative Science

The special science called "legislative" (*nomothetikê*) belongs to the second of the three main Aristotelian divisions of the sciences: contemplative, practical, and productive (*Top.* VI.6.145a15–16; *Metaph.* VI.1.1025b25, XI.7.1064a16–19; *EN* VI.2.1139a26–8). Each has a distinctive aim. The end of contemplative thought (e.g., physics, mathematics, and theology) is knowledge or truth for its own sake; the end of productive thought (e.g., poetry, medicine, and architecture) is the creation of an object distinct from the productive activity; and the end of practical thought is good action for its own sake. "Practical" thought is so called because it aims at action (*praxis*). The excellence of practical thought is practical wisdom or prudence (*phronêsis*), which issues in true judgments about actions that are good or bad for a human being (cf. *EN* VI.5.1140b4–6). This has three subtypes: practical wisdom concerned with the individual, economics (*oikonomikê*) concerned with the household (*oikos*), and political science ("politics" for short) concerned with the city-state. Politics includes legislative science (*nomothetikê*) and politics in a more familiar sense, involving everyday political activities such as deliberation and adjudication (*EN* VI.8.1141b29–33; *EE* I.8.1218b12–14). The latter are concerned with particular circumstances; for example, a judge must determine whether a particular crime was committed or not (*Rhet.* I.1.1354b13–15). Thus, legislative science is a part of politics (*EN* X.9.1180b30–1). Aristotle conjoins the term "legislator" with "statesman" (*politikos*) (*Pol.* III.1.1274b37, IV.1.1288b27, V.9.1309b35; cf. *EN* I.13.1102a7–10), and he likens the laws to "acts [*erga*] of political science" (*EN* X.9.1181a23).

Aristotle views legislative science as the capstone of politics:

> Of the practical wisdom concerned with the city-state, the practical wisdom which plays a controlling role is legislative, while that which is related to this as particulars to their universal is

known by the common name of "political." This is capable of action and deliberation, for a decree is a thing to be carried out in the form of an individual act. That is why the exponents of this art are alone said to take part in politics; for these alone do things as manual laborers do things. (*EN* VI.8.1141b24–9)

Legislative science is thus the "master science" of the human good (*EN* I.2.1094a26–b7). The study of legislation, and in particular constitutional theory, is needed to bring "the philosophy of human affairs" to completion (X.9.1181a12–15).

Aristotle discusses in *Politics* IV.1–2 the tasks of "the legislator and true statesman" (1288b27). Any complete science or craft must study a wide range of issues concerning its subject matter. Political (i.e., legislative) science studies a range of constitutions (1288b21–35): not only the ideal constitution, but also inferior systems. "For it is probably impossible for many persons to attain the best constitution, so that the legislator and true statesman must overlook neither the best constitution without qualification nor the best under the circumstances" (1288b24–7). The legislator must be acquainted with three sorts of constitution: first, the best without qualification, that is, "most according to our prayers with no external impediment" (1288b23–4); second, the best under the circumstances for a given population; third, the constitution that serves the aim a given city-state population happens to have that is best based on a hypothesis:

[F]or [the political scientist] ought to be able to study a given constitution, both how it might originally come to be, and, when it has come to be, in what manner it might be preserved for the longest time; I mean, for example, if a particular city happens neither to be governed by the best constitution, nor to be equipped even with necessary things, nor to be the [best] possible under existing circumstances, but to be a baser sort. (1288b28–33)

This passage has been interpreted in very different ways: Some view Aristotle as endorsing "Machiavellian realism," with the political scientist as a "hired consultant" equipped with "political mechanics employed perhaps for an inferior or even a bad end" (Barker 1931, 164; Irwin 1985, 155). Others note Aristotle's emphasis on constitutional reform (*Pol.* IV.1.1289a3–4) and argue that "constitutional reform presupposes a political ideal" (Keyt 1999, xv; F. Miller 1995, 183–90).

Aristotle chides earlier theorists (including Plato no doubt) for fixating on ideal theory and neglecting practical necessity. The legislator/statesman should try to establish "a constitutional order that people will be easily persuaded to accept and able to participate in," since reforming a constitution is no less a task than setting one up in the first place (*Pol.* IV.1.1288b35–1289a7). This requires a thorough knowledge of constitutions: what kinds there are, how many there are, how they can be combined with each other. "It is with this same practical wisdom that one knows the laws that are best and those that are suited to each constitution. [...] So grasping the varieties and the number of each type of constitution is clearly necessary also for laying down laws" (IV.1.1289a13–22).

Aristotle distinguishes between correct constitutions, which promote the common advantage, from deviant constitutions, which promote the advantage of the rulers, and combines this with the observation that the ruling class may consist of one person, a few, or a multitude. Hence, there are six basic constitutional forms (*Pol.* III.7):

	Correct	*Deviant*
One ruler	KINGSHIP	TYRANNY
Few rulers	ARISTOCRACY	OLIGARCHY
Many rulers	POLITY	DEMOCRACY

The correct constitutions are just and according to nature, and the incorrect constitutions are unjust and unnatural (*Pol.* III.6.1279a18–20, 17.1287b36–41). And since the laws are subordinate to the constitution, "the laws conforming to correct constitutions must be just, but those conforming to deviant constitutions must be unjust" (III.11.1282b10–13).

The above sixfold schema[2] is only the starting point for Aristotle's classification of constitutions, because there are many varieties of each type. A large democracy like Athens might include wealthy landed aristocrats, farmers, craftsmen, merchants, sailors, fishermen, and manual laborers. The character of the democracy would depend upon the relative power of these different classes (IV.3.1290a8). Aristotle distinguishes a range of democratic constitutions that might arise, from a moderate form with a modest property qualification (excluding the "baser" sort of citizen) to an extreme form, which included all freeborn persons no matter how poor and uneducated who were susceptible to demagoguery (IV.4.1291b14–1292a13). In general, "the legislator and statesman ought to know what democratic measures save and what destroy a democracy, and what oligarchic measures save or destroy an oligarchy" (*Pol.* V.9.1309b35). This requires knowledge of the different sorts of constitutions and how these can be combined to become "mixed" constitutions of various sorts (*Pol.* IV–VI). Aristotle's view is, again, open to different interpretations: Should legislators try to bring about genuine reform, making actual democracies or oligarchies more like the ideal constitution? Or should they strive for quasi-reform, making them more stable and viable constitutions of their type, even if they are not more just?

[2] This is adapted from Plato's *Plt.* 300b–303c. See the discussion in this volume, Chapter 3, Section 3.4.

In any case, the legislator for the best constitution must possess broad knowledge of human cultures and be able to adapt the laws to variable social contexts: "[T]he excellent legislator should observe how a city-state or race of men or any other community may participate in a good life and in the happiness that is possible for them." For example, in the case of military affairs, the legislator must obviously take into account the actual threats faced by the city-state: "There will be differences, however, in the statutes that are enacted; and if there are neighbors, legislative science has the task of seeing what sorts of training are needed in relation to what sorts of people, and which measures should be adopted in relation to each sort" (*Pol.* VII.2.1325a7–14). But, as an overriding objective, "the legislator should be more serious about arranging military regulations and other legislation for the sake of leisure and peace" (VII.14.1334a3–5).

Aristotle discusses two distinct but interrelated applications of legislation: laying down laws and educating the citizens (VII.14.1333b9). Let us consider these in turn. The statutes and customs regulate all aspects of conduct, including marriage and family relations, contracts, property, voluntary transactions, and torts; but the most important of these concern the distribution of political power within the city-state. Aristotle argues that every constitution contains three elements: deliberative (e.g., the popular assembly), adjudicative (e.g., jury courts), and offices (e.g., treasurers, wardens, and auditors). The excellent legislator must consider which of these is advantageous for each constitution (IV.14.1297b38). These elements can take very different forms; for example, all the citizens have a right to deliberate (e.g., extreme democracies), or only some may be permitted to deliberate (e.g., oligarchies), or all of them may deliberate about some things (e.g., whether to pass a decree), but not about others (e.g., determining whether a decree is legal), as in moderate democracies and polities. Aristotle provides (*Pol.* IV.14–16) a systematic and almost exhaustive account of the different "modes" or ways these matters are handled; for example, which persons are eligible for office, how are they selected, in what manner, etc.? This systematic and almost exhaustive inventory of modes is the fruit of Aristotle's extensive empirical study of existing city-states. Drawing on such knowledge, the legislator can fashion appropriate statutes for each constitution.

Education is the other major concern of legislative science. For the legislator has not completed his job by merely laying down good laws. As the unfortunate example of Solon shows, the citizens may not be disposed to obey the laws. Threats of punishment are not in Aristotle's view a sufficient guarantee that the citizens and officials will support the constitution and laws (see *Pol.* IV.5.1292b11–17). The laws themselves thus must have an educative function: "Whoever wants to make people, whether many or few, better by his care must try to become capable of legislating, if it is through laws that we can become good" (*EN* X.9.1180b23–5). Aristotle argues as follows: Rational moral arguments involve an appeal to goodness or nobility. People will be motivated only by pleasure or pain unless their souls have first been cultivated "like earth which is to nourish seed," that is, unless they have been taught by habit to love the good and noble and to hate the evil and base (1179b25–6). They will come to recognize the inherent value of virtue only by performing virtuous actions repeatedly, so that they acquire the habit of acting virtuously. Hence, they will not respond to rational moral arguments unless they have first been morally habituated. Further, those who have not yet been morally habituated will only respond to "compulsive power," which commands have only when they are backed by the law (1180a21). Therefore, people can be morally educated only if they are habituated under the laws.

Because legislative science has an important pedagogical function, Aristotle devotes over half of his discussion of the ideal constitution to its educational system (*Pol.* VII–VIII). The legislator must be knowledgeable of human nature and cognizant of the diversities of human lives and actions as he designs a system of education that will promote the development of the citizens' bodies and souls (VII.14.1333a37–41, 15.1334b6–28). There must be a detailed program of prenatal and infant care, physical education, and liberal education, including letters, mathematics, and music. The educational system must be public in view of the fact that the citizens have a single common end, the life of moral virtue, which can be achieved only if every citizen is educated (VII.13.1332a31–6; VIII.1.1337a21–6). But education in civic virtue is also necessary for deviant constitutions. "The most beneficial laws, even though they are ratified by everyone in the government, will be of no benefit, unless the people are habituated and educated in the constitution, democratically, if the laws are democratic, and oligarchically, if the laws are oligarchic" (*Pol.* V.9.1310a14–18).

Even when there is not a system of public education, private citizens should undertake to educate their children and friends, and they will do so more effectively if they are capable of legislating. "For it is clear that public care comes about through laws, and reasonable care through excellent laws. And it would seem to make no difference whether the laws are written or unwritten, nor whether an individual or many persons are educated through them" (*EN* X.9.1180a34–b2). Furthermore, parental statements and habits may have a force in households analogous to that of statutes and habits in city-states, perhaps even more since they are buttressed by natural affection and propensity to obey. Aristotle allows that individualized instruction has an advantage over mass education. The teacher can adapt teaching techniques to the particular needs and circumstances of the individual student, just as a medical doctor can treat the individual patient. But he also notes that just as the doctor requires universal knowledge of what is good for every one or for persons of a specific kind, so also the educator needs universal knowledge: "[H]e who wants to make people, whether many or few, better by his care must try to become capable of legislating, if it is through laws that we can become good" (*EN* X.9.1180b23–5).

4.4. Justice and Law

Law and justice are frequently coupled in Aristotle's thought. "Man when perfected is the best of animals," he maintains, "but when separated from law and justice, he is the worst of all" (*Pol.* I.2.1253a31–3). The close connection between the two concepts is an important theme of his treatise on justice (*EN* V = *EE* IV). Aristotle begins by emphasizing that justice is a moral virtue; justice is "that kind of state which makes people disposed to do just things and makes them act justly and wish for just things" (*EN* V.1.1129a7–9). He remarks that "justice" is spoken of homonymously (i.e., ambiguously), a fact that we recognize more clearly from its opposite "injustice." Sometimes, a person is called unjust in the sense of "unlawful" (*paranomos*), and sometimes in the sense of being "unfair" or "taking too much" (cf. *Pol.* VII.2.1324b27–8). Likewise, "just" has a broad or universal sense of "lawful" (*nomimos*), as well as a narrow or particular sense of "fair." The universal sense of "justice" accordingly presupposes a theory of legislation:

> Since the unlawful person was [seen to be] unjust and the lawful person just, it is clear that all lawful things are in a way just. For the acts that are prescribed by legislative science are lawful, and we say that each of these is just. As they address all affairs the laws aim at the advantage either of everyone in common or at that of the best persons or of those who have authority either based on virtue or on some other basis, so that in one sense we call those acts just that tend to produce and preserve happiness and its components for the political community. (V.1.1129b11–19)[3]

Therefore, a just person (in the universal sense) pursues the same end as the laws, namely, the well-being of the political community (see Kraut 2002, 111–18). Justice in this universal sense is not a particular virtue like courage. Instead, it is the same as complete virtue, not in itself but in relation to other persons. It is complete virtue in the fullest sense, because its possessor can exercise his virtue in relation to other persons and not merely in relation to himself. Similarly, its opposite—universal injustice—is identical with the totality of vice. Universal justice provides the standard by which the legislator can define lawful and unlawful acts:

> By and large most of the lawful acts [*ta nomima*] are those prescribed from a concern with virtue as a whole; for the law commands us to practice every virtue and forbids us to practice any vice.

[3] The text is apparently redundant. Editors propose two solutions: Susemihl's Teubner text deletes *ê tois aristois* ("or at that of the best persons") at 1129b15–16 and reads *ê* before *kat'* at b16. Bywater's Oxford Classical Text deletes *kat' aretên* ("based on virtue") at b16. The two solutions seem equivalent.

And the things that tend to produce virtue as a whole are those lawful acts which have been prescribed with a view to education for the common good. (*EN* V.2.1130b22–6)

This implies that completely virtuous persons have been educated under the laws, and they are thoroughly law-abiding individuals who seek the common advantage of their fellow citizens.

"Justice" can also designate a particular virtue on a par with courage or temperance, and in this case its opposite is the vice of unfairness or taking too much (*pleonexia*), involving an excessive desire for gain. Aristotle distinguishes forms of particular justice, namely, distributive justice, corrective justice, and perhaps also commutative justice.[4]

Distributive justice applies to the distribution of offices, honors, property, or other things that may be divided among the citizens. It implies that people should be treated equally in terms of their merit or desert. This involves a "geometrical" equality, since the parties should receive shares proportional to their merits rather than precisely the same shares. Conflict often results from disagreements over distributive justice: "Although everyone agrees that justice in distributions ought to be according to merit in some sense, they do not call merit the same thing, but democrats call it free birth, advocates of oligarchy wealth, and those of aristocracy virtue" (3.1131a25–9). The constitutional theory in the *Politics* is explicitly based on Aristotle's theory of distributive justice.[5] He holds that constitutions such as democracy and oligarchy are deviant because they are based upon conceptions of distributive justice that fall short of justice in the unqualified sense, in that they have a mistaken standard of merit and ultimately a mistaken hypothesis about the end of the city-state: The democrats think that the end is freedom, and the oligarchs think that it is wealth. The correct conception of justice for Aristotle makes moral virtue, along with freedom and adequate property, the criterion of merit. But the legislator must also be cognizant of the deviant conceptions of justice in framing the constitution and laws of a city-state, or it will be plagued by faction and even revolution.

Corrective justice is concerned with the rectification of past injustices, where the loss may be either voluntary (e.g., loans or sales) or involuntary (e.g., adultery, fraud, murder, or robbery). Unlike distributive justice, which involves "geometric" equality, corrective justice assigns shares to parties based

[4] The place of commutative or "reciprocal" (*antipeponthos*) justice in Aristotle's theory is controversial. At *EN* V.2.1130b30–1131a9, he expressly distinguishes between two types of particular justice: distributive justice and corrective justice (cf. 1131b25). But at 5.1132b31–4, he both recognizes reciprocal justice as a distinct type involved in communities of exchange and emphasizes its importance (cf. *Pol.* II.2.1261a30–1). This discussion assumes that commutative justice has a place in Aristotle's legal thought.

[5] Note that *Pol.* III.9.1280a18 refers to *EN* V.3.1131a14–24, and *Pol.* III.12.1282b20 refers to *EN* V.3.1131a11–14. See Keyt 1991 for an illuminating discussion.

on their relative merits, and so involves an "arithmetical" proportion. It treats the violator and victim as equals: "The law looks only to the distinctive character of the injury, and treats the parties as equal, if one is in the wrong and the other being wronged, and if one inflicted injury and the other received it" (4.1132a4–6). To reach a just verdict the judge must in effect restore equality by transferring from the perpetrator to the victim an amount equivalent to his loss so that he is made whole again. The penalty is thus intended to restore equality. Aristotle argues that this is generally what people have in mind when they go to a law court and seek justice. The judge is a kind of "mediator" who is supposed to arrive at a just settlement consisting in a distribution that is intermediate between an unjust gain and an unjust loss.

Aristotle's account of corrective justice can be viewed as an early explanation of the law of torts. This account plausibly "links the plaintiff's right to compensation to the defendant's duty to compensate" (Gordley 1999, 96). But it seems unsatisfactory as a theory of punishment, since guilty parties merely have to yield up their ill-gotten gains while suffering no real loss for their misdeeds. But Aristotle elsewhere indicates that the law may require punishment apart from mere compensation. For example, the law forbids suicide, even though the person who kills himself has not inflicted a harm on anyone else. Because the person who committed suicide has committed an injustice against the city-state (presumably for failing to carry out his duties as a citizen), the law may punish him, for example, posthumously "dishonoring" him by stripping him of his civil rights (11.1138a9–14). Again, someone who injures an official should not be merely injured to the same degree in return but should also suffer an added punishment (5.1132b29–30). Aristotle also mentions seemingly with approval the doubling of penalties in the case of drunkenness (III.5.1113b31–2). But there is no sign that he sees the need for a theory of punishment over and above his discussion of corrective justice.

Aristotle does however discuss a topic related to punishment, namely, the "difference between a voluntary and an involuntary act" (V.5.1132b30–31). Understanding this distinction is "necessary for investigators of virtue and useful for legislators with a view to assigning honors and punishments" (III.1.1109b34–5; cf. *EE* II.10.1226b36–1227a1). His treatment of voluntariness (*EN* III.1–5; cf. *EE* II.6–11) influenced subsequent theories of legal responsibility. In brief, an occurrence is involuntary if it takes place under compulsion or due to ignorance. "Under compulsion" means that the moving principle is outside the party in question, that is, the person makes no contribution, as in the case of a ship carried somewhere by the wind, or a person transported by kidnappers. "Due to ignorance" means not ignorance of a universal rule, for example, against patricide (one is culpable for this), but of the particular circumstances or objects of an action, for example, killing one's own father in battle thinking that he was an enemy. Conversely, "the voluntary would seem to be that of which the moving principle is in the agent himself, when he knows the particular circumstances of the action" (*EN* III.1.1109b35–1111a24). Although this seems clear-cut, Aristotle mentions several complex cases, which he handles with subtle and controversial distinctions. For example, actions performed under duress (e.g., breaking the law when ordered to by a tyrant who holds one's relatives hostage) or in an emergency (e.g., throwing cargo overboard in a storm) are voluntary in Aristotle's sense. He calls these "mixed" actions (because they are voluntary but nobody would choose to do such acts unless one had to), and suggests that forgiveness may be in order "when one acts wrongly due to factors which exceed human nature and which no one could endure." Aristotle also denies that a crime committed due to drunkenness or rage is involuntary. If a drunken person causes harm without realizing it, he is acting "in ignorance" rather than due to ignorance, because he is responsible for his ignorant condition. Aristotle also denies (rather unpersuasively) that the act is involuntary when the agent subsequently lacks remorse, even when he was nonculpably ignorant of what he was doing, and he classifies this case as "not voluntary."

Commutative or reciprocal justice holds the city-state together (*EN* V.5.1132b33–4), because it ensures that parties to a voluntary exchange each receive a fair or equal outcome. This equality is measured in terms of need (*chreia*), Aristotle says rather obscurely. Money is introduced as a representative of need by convention (*sunthêkê*). It exists not by nature but by law (*nomos*), which is why it is called *nomisma*, "money" (*EN* V.5.1133a25–31; cf. *Pol.* I.9.1257b10–11, *MM* I.34.1194a23). Because Aristotle thinks that exchanges must be equal, he denigrates the use of trade to generate profits: "[F]or it is not natural, but a way of gaining from one another. Usury is very reasonably hated, because it makes wealth out of money itself, and not from the aim for which it was introduced. For money came into existence for the sake of exchange, but interest makes it greater. [...] So of all the modes of acquisition this is the most unnatural" (*Pol.* I.10.1258b1–8). The clear implication is that just laws would prohibit or severely limit commerce and banking.

Having discussed the three particular forms of justice, Aristotle considers the application of justice to the city-state. "Political justice exists among persons who share a way of life with a view to self-sufficiency, who are free and are equal either proportionately or numerically." If these conditions are not satisfied, there is no political justice but only justice in a qualified or analogous sense. For the law and judicial proceedings discriminate between just and unjust acts (*EN* V.6.1134a26–32). Political justice is "according to law" (*kata nomon*), and holds for persons who are naturally able to obey the law. These are the sort of people who are capable of self-government, because they can share equally in ruling and being ruled (1134b13–15).

4.5. Natural Law

The relationship between law and nature is one of the hardest issues in Aristotle's legal philosophy. Especially controversial is his stance on natural law. He has been dubbed "the father of natural law," and he unquestionably exerted a profound influence over later natural law theorists such as Thomas Aquinas (Shellens 1959, 72; cf. Barker 1946, 336; Friedrich 1958, 22–3; Crowe 1977, 19). Yet Aristotle discusses "natural law" explicitly only in his *Rhetoric*, and these discussions seem inconsistent with doctrines expounded in his ethical and political works. Some scholars even deny that Aristotle belongs to the natural law tradition (Ritchie 1895; Kelsen 1957, 128; Yack 1990, 216). This section will summarize the discussion of natural law in the *Rhetoric*. The following section will examine the related topic of natural justice in Aristotle's ethical and political works, and consider to what extent the different discussions can be reconciled.

The idea of natural law is discussed in three different passages.[6] These discussions basically agree on several points: The law is both particular (*idios*) and common (*koinos*) (10.1368b7, 13.1373b4). The common law consists of things agreed upon by all persons (10.1368b7–9, 13.1373b6–9), and it is law according to nature (*kata phusin*, *phusei*) (13.1373b6–7, 10; 15.1375a32). It is tacitly assumed that the common law is equivalent to common or natural justice (13.1373b6–9; 15.1375a27–9, b3–5). The common law is eternal and never changing, because it is natural (13.1373b9–13, 15.1375a31–b2). The common law can come into conflict with the particular law in the sense that the same act can violate natural law but conform with the former. Here Aristotle cites the example of Sophocles' Antigone, who buries her brother Polyneices in defiance of an edict of the tyrant of Thebes (13.1373b9–13; 15.1375a27–9, a33–b2, 7–8).

The three discussions also make distinct but complementary points to the effect that particular law is conventional: Particular law is the law according to which people govern themselves (10.1368b7–8). It is defined by each group in reference to themselves (13.1373b4–5) and is a sort of covenant (15.1376b7–11). Hence, in contrast to the common law, particular written laws often change (15.1375a32–3). His citations from Sophocles and reference to Alcidamus also suggest that natural or common law has a divine origin (13.1373b9–18, 15.1375a33–b2), but it should be emphasized that this claim is not explicitly made in the *Rhetoric*.[7] Nevertheless, Aristotle does state an important implication of the preceding claims: Natural law is the law of all in the sense that if an act is just for some persons it is just for all (13.1373b14–17). That is, common or natural law differs from particular law in that it is abso-

[6] Subsequent references in this section are to *Rhetoric* I unless otherwise indicated.

[7] Alcidamus' condemnation of slavery and Empedocles' denunciation of the killing of animals seem to be familiar invocations of natural law, rather than precepts endorsed by Aristotle.

lute, whereas particular laws are relative to the communities that agree upon their enactment.

So far, these discussions provide an account of natural law which is on the whole coherent, although they do contain some apparent inconsistencies. The most notable of these involves the notion of unwritten law (*agraphos nomos*). Particular law is identified with written law at 10.1368b7–8, whereas particular law is distinguished as unwritten or written at 13.1373b5–6. The most plausible explanation for this inconsistency is that "unwritten law" is not a technical expression with a single fixed meaning for Aristotle, but varies from context to context depending upon what it is contrasted with.[8] In *Rhetoric* I.10 "the unwritten law" is used for the common or natural law, comprised of rules holding for mankind at large, in contrast to the particular or "written law." In *Rhetoric* I.13 "the unwritten law" is used for the portion of the particular law of a community that consists of unwritten customs rather than codified statutes, which might vary between communities, such as burial customs (cf. Pseudo-Aristotle, *Rhet. Al.* 2.1421b35–1422a4).

Apart from minor inconsistencies, the *Rhetoric* offers a coherent account of natural law with noteworthy similarities to the later natural law tradition. A central feature of this account is the claim that natural law is eternal and immutable. Aristotle quotes from Sophocles' *Antigone* 456–7:

> These laws weren't made now
> Or yesterday. They live for all time,
> And no one knows when they came into the light. (Sophocles, *Ant.* 456–7, trans. Woodruff)

This passage illustrates the conflict between natural law and particular law (see especially I.15.1375a25–b25).[9] A persuasive speaker should appeal to natural law in opposition to the written law, on the grounds that natural law embodies eternal and immutable principles of justice. But if the written law supports our case, we should argue that the jurors have a duty to enforce this law. Aristotle's treatment suggests that litigants were more apt to invoke natural law when they had a weak case in regard to written statutes.

4.6. Legal Justice and Natural Justice

Aristotle does not mention "natural law" in his ethical works. Instead, he distinguishes "legal justice" from "natural justice" in *Nicomachean Ethics*.[10]

[8] See Ostwald 1973 on the different uses of *agraphos nomos*. In some contexts "unwritten" is contrasted with "legal" (*kata nomon*), e.g., *EN* VIII.13.1162b21–3, where the issue is whether just claims arise from written or unwritten agreements.

[9] Compare the discussion in this volume, Chapter 1, Section 1.5.3.

[10] This exposition generally follows the *Nicomachean Ethics*, although mention will be made of some important variations in the parallel discussion of this topic in the *Magna Moralia*. Quotations in this section are from *EN* V.7 or *MM* I.33 unless otherwise indicated.

Aristotle distinguishes two forms of political justice: natural and legal (*EN* 1134b18–19; cf. *MM* 1194b30–1). Natural (*phusikon*) justice has everywhere the same force and does not depend on people's thinking that something or other is the case. Legal (*nomikon*) justice is that which is such that at first it does not make a difference whether or not it is the case, but when it has been laid down it does make a difference, for example, that a prisoner's ransom shall be a mina, or in particular cases, to make a sacrifice in honor of Brasidas (1134b20–4; cf. *MM* 1195a4–5). Aristotle's legal justice anticipates the medieval idea of positive law.[11] Aristotle also describes legal justice as based on convention (*sunthêkê*) (1134b30–3, b35–1135a1) and as a human product (1135a3–4). This agrees with the parallel between conventional justice and particular law described in the *Rhetoric.*

The *Nicomachean Ethics* disagrees with the *Rhetoric*, however, in two important ways. The first concerns change and variation in the laws. Although the *Rhetoric* claims that natural law is eternal and immutable, the *Nicomachean Ethics* calls this into question, when it considers an objection against the possibility of natural justice:

> That which exists by nature is unchangeable and everywhere has the same power, as fire burns here and in Persia.
> Just things undergo change. Therefore, there is no natural justice, but all just things are legally just. (1134b24–7)

Aristotle replies that it may be true of the gods that there is no change, but in the human sphere some things may be natural even though they are changeable (1134b27–30; but contrast X.8.1178b10–12). He observes that other things may be natural as well as changeable, for example, the right hand is naturally stronger than the left, although anyone can become ambidextrous through practice (*EN* 1134b30–5; cf. *MM* 1194b33–7). Similarly, the fact that just things are capable of being otherwise does not show that they are not natural.

The *Nicomachean Ethics*' reference to right-handedness is rather opaque. In this case the *Magna Moralia* sheds more light by adding that "what holds for the most part and the greater time is by nature" (1194b37–9). Human beings are for the most part right-handed, although there are exceptions. By analogy, then, what is just for the most part is manifestly just by nature. This gives Aristotle his response to the above objection: Even if things change due to our usage, there is still natural justice (1195a1–4).

There is good reason to take this contribution of the *Magna Moralia* seriously. For the connection between what is natural and what holds always or

[11] On medieval theories of positive law generally, see Ullmann 1975, 62–3; and Van Den Eynde 1949. For discussion of positive law in Abelard, see this volume, Chapter 12, Section 12.3.3; and for discussion of positive law in Aquinas, see Chapter 13, Section 13.5.

for the most part is found often in Aristotle's nonethical treatises.[12] It is tacitly assumed in the *Nicomachean Ethics* itself, in Aristotle's response to the argument that the noble and the just are conventional rather than natural because they are subject to difference and variation. Aristotle concedes this but proceeds:

> We must be content, then, in speaking of such subjects and with such premises to indicate the truth roughly and in outline, and in speaking about things which are only for the most part and with premises of the same kind to reach conclusions that are no better. (I.3.1094b19–22)

This passage presupposes the argument made explicit in the *Magna Moralia*: From the fact that moral propositions about justice hold only for the most part, it does not follow that they are true merely by convention.

This helps to clarify a fundamental difference between "natural law" in the *Rhetoric* and "natural justice" in the *Nicomachean Ethics* and *Magna Moralia*: While the *Rhetoric* regards the natural as eternal and immutable, the ethical works understand nature as consistent with change and what holds for "the most part," as in the biological works. Aristotle doubtless found it necessary to adopt this biological perspective because he had repudiated the metaphysical foundations of Plato's theory of natural law and justice. Plato's *Laws* represents justice and law as "natural" in the sense of having a divine origin (see IV.715e7–716a3, 716c4–6; X.888d7–890d8). Nature in Plato's *Republic* is a transcendent, eternal, and immutable principle involving the theory of Forms (V.501b2; cf. X.597c2, 598a1; also *Phd.* 103b5). Aristotle replaced this Platonic ideal with a notion of nature as a principle of change which is inherent in substances and which, in the sublunary realm at least, holds always or for the most part.[13]

A second important disagreement concerns the relation of nature to human legislation. The previous section noted that the *Rhetoric* emphasizes the possible adversarial relationship between (divine) natural law and (human) written law, a conflict illustrated by Sophocles' *Antigone*. The *Magna Moralia* makes a somewhat similar point, concluding that natural justice is better than legal justice, and then states: "But what we are seeking is political justice; but political justice exists by law, not by nature" (1195a6–8). Although the *Magna Moralia* departs from the *Rhetoric* here by contrasting law with nature, the two seem to agree that there is an opposition between natural justice and political jus-

[12] See *An. Pr.* I.3.25b14, 13.32b5–6; *Phys.* II.8.198b35–6; *PA* III.2.663b28–9; *GA* I.19.727b29–30, IV.4.770b11–13, 8.777a19–21; and even *Rhet.* I.10.1369a35–b2 (cf. *Metaph.* VI.2.1027a8–11).

[13] See Maguire 1947; Morrow 1941; Moser 1952; and this volume, Chapter 3, Section 3.3. The Platonic ideal survives in the pseudo-Aristotelian *De Mundo* (written between 50 B.C. and A.D. 100): "God is to us a law, impartial, admitting not of correction or revision, and better, I believe, and more secure than those which are written up on tablets" (6.400b28–31). On the differences between Aristotle and later natural law theorists, see Striker 1996b.

tice. The paradoxical implications are that although natural justice is superior it plays only a marginal role in legal affairs, and that political justice is conventional rather than natural.

The *Nicomachean Ethics* takes a very different tack: Having defined political justice as the justice found among members of the city-state (see V.6.1134a26–8), it treats the legal and natural as distinct *parts* of political justice, so that natural justice is included in rather than opposed to political justice. There are two ways of understanding this distinction: as a vertical division of political justice into different sets of laws, or as a horizontal distinction whereby each law has a natural and legal (conventional) aspect. The latter seems to be more consistent with Aristotle's approach (see Burns 1998). The natural is thus viewed as penetrating or permeating political justice. This suggests that if one were to examine the constitution, laws, and customs of a just city-state, one would discern some features that were naturally just, and others—such as the example of the amount of a prisoner's ransom—that would be indifferent until they were instituted. When the *Nicomachean Ethics* states that "constitutions are not [the same], though everywhere only one is the best according to nature" (1135a4–5), it implies that constitutions can be evaluated and compared as better or worse on the basis of the extent to which they possess naturally just features.

The claim that political justice has both legal and natural components is bound up with the theory of political naturalism that is defended in Aristotle's *Politics*. This involves the claims that the city-state exists by nature (*Pol.* I.2.1252b30), humans are by nature political animals (1253a2–3), and the city-state is by nature prior to the individual (1253a25–6). But Aristotle conjoins the claim that political association is natural with the recognition that the legislator plays an indispensable role:

> Therefore, there is by nature an impulse for such a community in everyone; but the one who first established it was the cause of the greatest of goods. For just as a human being is the best of the animals when perfected, so also when he is separated from law and justice he is the worst of all. For injustice is harshest when it possesses arms; but a human being is born possessing arms for the use of practical rationality and virtue, which are especially suited the opposite use. Therefore, when he is without virtue he is the most unholy and savage [animal], and the worst concerning sex and food. But justice is political; for the administration of justice [*dikê*] is [the] order [*taxis*] of the political community, and the administration of justice is a judgment regarding what is just.[14] (1253a29–39)

Here Aristotle recognizes human nature and the legislator as joint causes of the city-state: Humans have a natural propensity to join in political life, but the legislator provides the legal order which human beings require to realize their natural human ends (see Barker 1959, 327; F. Miller 1995, chap. 5; Saunders 1995, 63; Burns 1998, 155; for an opposed interpretation see Keyt 1991). Leg-

[14] I read *dikê* at 1253a38 with Dreizehnter and the manuscripts.

islators should follow nature's guidance, taking into account the ways human beings naturally grow and behave (see, e.g., *Pol.* VII.17.1337a1). Yet they must often use their ingenuity to fashion laws suitable for particular city-states. To the extent that the legislator succeeds, the city-state will be in a natural condition—that is, it will have a correct or just constitution.[15]

4.7. The Rule of Law and Legal Change

Aristotle's philosophy of law gives rise to a number of difficulties, some of which he attempted to address. One of these concerns "the rule of law," a generally accepted ideal in classical Greece. According to Aristotle, the best constitution, based upon the correct interpretation of justice, assigns political authority to virtuous individuals (*Pol.* III.9 and 12; see Section 4.4 above). Aristotle notes that "some persons" think that this implies the rule of law:

> [S]ome people think that it is not according to nature for one person to have authority over all the citizens, where the city-state is established out of similar persons. For persons who are similar by nature necessarily have the same right and the same merit according to nature. [...] Consequently, it is just to rule no more than to be ruled, and it is just [to rule and be ruled] by turns. But this is already law; for law is the order [*taxis*] [by which offices are shared]. Hence the rule of law is preferable to that of a single citizen. (III.16.1287a10–14, 16–20)

The statements about the rule of law in *Politics* III.15–16 occur in a context where Aristotle subtly paraphrases interchanges between advocates of absolute kingship and proponents, so this passage needs to be interpreted in a careful manner. Aristotle does however subsequently suggest that he finds the above argument convincing, provided that the citizens are in fact similar and equal (*Pol.* III.17.1287b41–1288a5; cf. *EN* V.6.1139a26–30, b13–15).

Aristotle mentions some of the key elements of the rule of law contrasting it with the rule of an individual or group acting according to mere wish or will. Willful rule occurs when monarchs substitute edicts for laws, or democratic majorities substitute decrees (*Pol.* IV.4.1292a6–7, 18–21). The rule of law is typically found when the citizens take turns in holding offices where statutes define eligibility, selection, review, etc. (III.6.1279a8–13). The rule of law may be enforced by special officials, such as "guardians of the laws" who see to it that assemblies or magistrates do not transgress the laws (see IV.14.1298b26–1299a1).

[15] Kelsen 1957, 128, argues that for Aristotle the correct conception of distributive justice can only be defined by positive law: "Only if it is supposed that the positive law decides the question which rights shall be conferred upon citizens, and which differences between them are relevant, [is] Aristotle's mathematical formula of distributive justice applicable." According to Kelsen (1957, 125) the content of justice can only be determined by the positive law. Kelsen is correct to emphasize legal justice, but he fails to take into account the importance of human natural ends in Aristotle's ethics and politics.

Some of Aristotle's arguments echo Plato (*Laws* IV.714b3–715d6) and others are commonplaces: The law is impartial (*Pol.* III.16.1287a41–b5; cf. *EN* V.6.1134a35–b2). If all political activity were left up to decisions by individuals on a case-by-case basis, there is a danger that they would be influenced by particular factors such as friendship, animosity, and self-interest rather than justice. The process of framing the laws involves considerable deliberation and the legislator can take a broader view of the issues (see *Rhet.* I.1.1354a34–b11; cf. *Pol.* III.9.1280a14–16). Moreover, the law is the embodiment of "thought [*nous*] without desire" (III.16.1287a32; cf. Plato *Laws* IV.714a1–2, and I.644d103, 645a1–2, VIII.835e4–5). The rule of law is therefore superior to the rule of man: "The capacity for passion is not present in the laws, but every human soul necessarily has it" (*Pol.* III.15.1286a18–20). The equation of the law with reason (discussed above in Section 4.2) would be interpreted by Aristotle as the claim that legislation is the product of a legislator endowed with practical wisdom and thus able to frame the best constitution and legal system.

These eloquent arguments have often been quoted in support of the rule of law. Yet Aristotle himself acknowledges a major exception to the principle that "where the laws do not rule, there is no constitution" (IV.4.1292a32). This exception involves the case for absolute kingship. By his own principle of distributive justice Aristotle must admit as a theoretical possibility that if one person (or a small number) is so outstanding in moral virtue and political ability that the others are not even commensurable with him, then the superior person should have complete authority over all. Such a person is like a god on earth, and to deny him complete authority would be unjust and unnatural (III.13.1284a3–11, 17.1288a24–9). Aristotle tries to relieve the problem by remarking that the absolute kings are a law unto themselves (13.1284a13–14, 17.1288a3). Perhaps he means to suggest that such a person acts on his own accord the way an ordinary person would who consistently obeys the laws. Nonetheless, absolute kingship does not qualify as the rule of law in the strict sense (see E. Miller 1979). Aristotle remarks elsewhere that there are no actual candidates for absolute king, so that this is merely a theoretical possibility, and "it is evident due to many causes that everyone must share in ruling and being ruled in turn" (VII.14.1332b23–7). Practically speaking, then, the best constitution involves the rule of law provided there are enough citizens who are at least proportionately equal in virtue (cf. Plato, *Plt.* 301d8–e4; *Laws* IX.875c3–d5). For the principle of distributive justice can justify the rule of the many if the practical wisdom of the multitude (in aggregate) outweighs that of the best man (see Keyt 1991; Waldron 1995).

Aristotle also mentions a problem involving the application of law: "[A] ll law is universal but about some things it is not possible to make a universal statement that is correct" (*EN* V.10.1137b13–14). The legislators try to lay down laws that are almost always correct, and may not realize that exceptional circumstances will occur. Or they recognize that they are "unable to define

Aristotle (384–322 B.C.)

things exactly, and are obliged to legislate universally where matters hold only for the most part; or where it is not easy to be complete owing to the unlimited number of cases that may arise, such as the kinds and sizes of weapons that may be used to inflict wounds—a lifetime would be too short to enumerate these" (*Rhet.* I.13.1374a26–33; cf. *MM* II.1; *Ath.* 9.2). For example, the written law may forbid striking another person with a metal weapon and not specify every exception. If one strikes another while wearing a ring, has he committed a crime? According to the written law he has, but in truth he has not. In order to recognize that this is an exceptional case, we need the virtue of equity (*epieikeia*) rather than justice in the sense of strict lawfulness (*EN* V.10.1137b34–1138a3; *Rhet.* I.13.1364a33–b1). Equity is the correction of a law insofar as it is defective due to its universality. In such a case the equitable decision is just, because it is what the legislator would have decided in these particular circumstances if he had been present. Not all things can be decided according to the laws; in some cases, a decree is needed. Aristotle compares the use of decrees to the use of a Lesbian rule made of soft lead: Just as the rule is not rigid but adapts itself to the shape of the stone, the decree is adapted to particular circumstances (*EN* V.10.1137b26–32). This provides a limitation to the rule of law: "[T]he laws ought to have authority, when they have been correctly laid down; but the ruler, whether one or many, ought to have authority concerning these matters on which laws cannot speak with precision because it is not easy to make a universal declaration about everything" (*Pol.* III.11.1282b1–6; cf. 15.1286a10). Although the laws are indispensable in providing a structure in which the citizens can share authority and seek the good life, they are nevertheless subordinate to the ultimate goal—the survival and well-being of the citizens.

Aristotle grants that legal change may sometimes be warranted: "As in the various crafts, so in the political order, it is impossible that all things should be precisely set down in writing; for it is necessary to write universal [laws], but actions are concerned with particulars. Hence it is evident that some laws should sometimes be changed." But he immediately sounds a note of caution: "When the benefit is small and the habit of casually changing the laws is bad, then some errors of legislators and rulers should be left alone. […] For the law has no power to command obedience except that of habit, and this comes about only through a long time, so that easily changing from old to new laws weakens the power of the law" (*Pol.* II.8.1269a9–12, 14–17, 20–4). Aristotle recognizes the need for legal reform (IV.2.1289a4–5), and he proposes many remedies for existing constitutions (see especially *Pol.* V), but he is conscious that the benefits of change may be outweighed by damage to the respect for law.

Aristotle's philosophy of law is closely bound up with his other views, including his natural science and moral philosophy, and especially his theory of justice. This is a source of both strength and weakness. The advantage is that the meaning and justification of different elements of his legal theory can be found in other parts of his system. The liability is, of course, that when his other doctrines have come under criticism, his legal philosophy has also been called into question. Notwithstanding, his discussions of legal issues are deep and insightful and have continued to influence legal scholars of all persuasions.

4.8. Ancient Greek Conceptions of Rights

By the end of the fourth century B.C. the Greeks possessed a number of locutions to assert and deny claims in legal, political, and other settings. Many translators of classical Greek texts have assumed that such claims are often equivalent to "rights" claims in modern languages. Some scholars, however, agree with MacIntyre (1981, 67) that "[t]here is no expression in any ancient or medieval language correctly translated by our expression 'a right' until near the close of the Middle Ages." Ostwald (1996) also argues that the ancient Greeks thought of citizenship in terms of communalistic "shares" rather than individualistic "rights."[16] Although these scholars generally concede the rough equivalence of some Greek words to the predicate "right," they contend that it is a mistake to translate any Greek term by the substantival expression "*a* right." For, they argue, the ancient terms only refer to an objective condition of justice, such as the correct assignment or relation of things to persons, and thus could not denote a *subjective right*, that is, a right possessed by an individual. To resolve this issue, therefore, it is necessary to explicate the concept of a subjective right, which is difficult in view of the wide assortment of mutually inconsistent modern theories of rights.

The modern jurist Hohfeld's analysis of "rights" locutions (1923) is useful because he relies on minimal assumptions concerning the theoretical underpinnings of rights.[17] Hohfeld distinguishes four senses in which one person *X* might have a "right" against another person *Y*: first, *X* has a *claim* to *A* against *Y*, in which case *Y* has a correlative duty to *X* to do *A* (e.g., the right to repayment of a debt); second, *X* has a *privilege* or *liberty* to do *A* against *Y*, in which case *X* has no duty to *Y* to forbear from doing *A* (e.g., the liberty to consume one's own property); third, *X* has a *power* or *authority* to *A* against *Y*, in which case *Y* has a correlative liability to *X*'s doing *A* (e.g., the authority to arrest someone); and fourth, *X* has an *immunity* against *Y*'s doing *A*, in which case *X* has no liability to *Y*'s doing *A* (e.g., immunity from being required to testify against oneself). Hohfeld sheds valuable light on modern legal discourse by disambiguating the modern term "right." Although the ancient Greeks did

[16] This view is shared by others, such as Strauss 1953 and Villey, e.g., 1996. Villey's thesis that there were no rights in Roman law is also discussed in Chapter 6, Section 6.6, of this volume.

[17] Hohfeld's analysis has been widely accepted by recent legal theorists and philosophers as a basic account of the logical form of rights claims.

not have a single word corresponding to "right," it is noteworthy that they had instead a family of terms that correspond to the conceptions distinguished by Hohfeld:

HOHFELD	GREEK
just claim	*to dikaion*
liberty, privilege	*exeinai*
authority, power	*kurios*
immunity, exemption	*adeia, ateleia*

These expressions will be discussed in turn, considering first some epigraphical evidence, followed by examples drawn from both Aristotle and his contemporary, the orator Demosthenes (384–322 B.C.).

4.8.1. Just Claim (to dikaion)

A just claim, which is at the core of a right, is a claim of justice which a member of a community has against the other members of the community. The most important Greek locution with this sense is *to dikaion* (plural, *ta dikaia*), literally "the just (thing)," the noun phrase formed from the neuter definite article with the neuter form of the adjective meaning "just." Though sometimes equivalent to "justice" (*dikê*, *dikaiosunê*), it often signifies an act required or entitled by justice.

The expression *to dikaion* occurs in connection with rights of pasturage in a law recorded on a bronze plaque from a Locrian community settling new territory (ca. 525–500 B.C.): "Pasturage-rights [*epinomia*] shall belong to parents and son; if no son exists, to an unmarried daughter; if no unmarried daughter exists, to a brother; if no brother exists, by degree of family connection, let a man pasture according to what is just [*ka to dikaion*]" (trans. in Fornara 1977, no. 33; cf. Meiggs and Lewis 1988, no. 13; see also Jeffery 1961, 104f., pl. 14). In this passage the phrase *to dikaion* is equivalent to "justice" (*dikaiosunê*) and has the sense of "objective right." In this context the implication, however, is that the colonists are entitled to pasture in a location, and the entitlement is inherited according to degree of consanguinity as prescribed by the law.[18]

By the fourth century, *to dikaion* has the sense of "subjective right," for example, in an Athenian decree in the archonship of Anticles (325/4 B.C.),

[18] Cf. Tod 1948, no. 174.14–16, which is an Athenian decree (340 B.C.) extending property rights to the citizens of Elaeus, "that the people of Elaeus have their own habitations correctly and justly [*dikaiôs*] along with the people of Athens and Chersonese."

recorded on a marble stele on the Acropolis. The inscription records decrees concerning Heraclides of Salamis, who delivered wheat to Athens for a fair price during a shortage and also contributed 3,000 drachmas toward the purchase of more wheat for the people. The first decree honors him with the titles of *proxenos* and benefactor, and also confers various legal rights (to be discussed below). The second decree mentions that the inhabitants of Heraclea had interfered with Heraclides en route to Athens and seized his sails. The decree authorizes the election of an ambassador "who will go to Dionysius of Heraclea and demand that he return the sails of Heraclides and do no further injustice to those sailing to Athens; and by doing these things he will do just things [*ta dikaia*] and he will not fail to obtain any of the just things [*tôn dikaiôn*] of the people of Athens."[19] The aim of the decree is thus to uphold the just claims of Heraclides who has been robbed, and to protect the just claims of the Athenians and their allies.

The expression *to dikaion* figures prominently in Demosthenes' first oration *Against Aphobus.* Because the defendant has refused to submit to arbitration, Demosthenes is left no option but to try to obtain his just claims (*ta dikaia*) from him in the courtroom (27.1) and he asks the jury to "help me with just claims" (27.3). He elsewhere speaks of the jury deciding the just claims of disputants *against* each other (13.16). That Demosthenes uses *to dikaion* to signify a subjective right is clear from the fact that he treats such claims as belonging to claimants: "*having* this just claim [*to dikaion*] we brought suit for the inheritance with the archon" (44.29). Again, he attaches a possessive pronoun to *to dikaion* contrasting "*our* just claims" with "the just claims *of others*" (3.27; cf. "*your* just claims," 24.3).

This term is also employed by Aristotle, who notes that disputants go to a judge in order to obtain the just (*to dikaion*) (*EN* V.4.1132a19–24). If they think that the judge has correctly resolved the dispute, the disputants "say that they have their own." In this context, *to dikaion* is what one receives in a just settlement of a dispute, that is, that which is "one's own." This is clearly what the claimant has a just claim to (cf. *Pol.* IV.4.1291a39–40). The term also has an important application in the political context in which various parties dispute over who is entitled to hold political office. Those who have an erroneous conception of justice or equality "will have an excess of political just claims [*tôn politikôn dikaiôn*]" (*Pol.* III.12.1282b29). The implication is that only a correct standard of distributive justice will yield a defensible assignment of political rights.

[19] *IG* II^2.360; Schwenk 1985, no. 68.37–42: *outhenos atuchêsei tou dêmou tou Athenaiôn tôn dikaiôn*. For a similar construction, see Xenophon, *HG* III.1.23: *tôn dikaiôn oudenos*.

4.8.2. Liberty or Privilege (exeinai)

Liberties or privileges pertain to acts that individuals *may* perform, that is, they are not obligated to refrain from them. Such rights are typically asserted with the verb *exesti* (infinitive *exeinai* or *exeimen*) or the noun *exousia*. In a legal sphere these rights specify what it is permissible for someone to do, and thus define a sphere of freedom within which the agent is free to choose. This locution occurs in a law inscribed on a bronze plaque by the Hypocnemidian Locrians concerning their colony at Naupactus (ca. 500–475 B.C.?). The term is used to assert a series of civil rights of colonists. For example, a colonist shall "be at liberty [*exeimen*] to share in religious privileges and to make sacrifice as a visitor [*xenos*], when he is present, if he wishes." "If compulsion drives the Hypocnemidian Locrians out of Naupactus, they must be at liberty [*exeimen*] to return, each to his place of origin, without entry fees." "If anyone leaves behind (in Locris) his father and a portion of his property (which he has consigned to his father), when (his father) dies, the colonist shall be at liberty [*exeimen*] to recover his property" (see Fornara 1977, no. 47; Meiggs and Lewis 1988, no. 20.2–3, 8–10, 35–7).

The word *eleuetheros* ("free") can also be used in this sense. For example, a law of Hallicarnassus recorded on a marble stele (465–450 B.C.) states that any citizen of Halicarnassus who has complied with the law is free (*eleutheron einai*) to bring a lawsuit concerning property (Meiggs and Lewis 1988, no. 32; Fornara 1977, no. 70). In addition, the negative form *mê exeinai* is often used for prohibitions, for example: "The people of Athens are not at liberty [*mê exeinai*] to restore the exiles [...]" (Athenian decree concerning Clazomenae, 387 B.C.; see Tod 1948, no. 114).

Demosthenes frequently uses the term *exeinai* to assert a liberty, for example: "Indeed, Callicles, if you have the liberty [*exesti*] to enclose your land, surely we also had the liberty to enclose ours. But if my father did you an injustice by enclosing his land, you also do me an injustice by enclosing yours" (*Against Aphobus* 55.29). The implication is that owners are at liberty to build walls on their property, provided this does not harm others. Especially important is the liberty to name an heir when one has no offspring. For example, in the oration *Against Leptines*, Demosthenes states that "Solon made a law that one had the liberty [*exeinai*] to give his things [i.e., property] to whomever he wishes, if there were no legitimate children" (20.102).

Demosthenes asserts that individuals have a liberty right to defend their property: "Earth and gods! Is it not monstrous, and manifestly contrary to law—I don't mean only contrary to the written law but also contrary to the common [law] of all human beings—that I should not have the liberty [*exeinai*] to defend myself against a person who comes and takes my possessions with force as though I were an enemy?" (23.61). This seems to anticipate modern views that individuals have a natural right to protect their property.

This locution also has an important role in Aristotle's final definition of a citizen: A citizen is "one who has the liberty [*exousia*] to partake in deliberative and judicial office" (*Pol.* III.1.1275b18–19). Different constitutions establish different criteria for assigning this liberty. For example, in a moderate democratic constitution, individuals can meet a low property assessment in order to have the liberty (*exousia*) to hold office (IV.4.1291b40–1). In a moderate oligarchy the assessment is set so high that the majority, who are poor, cannot meet it, but a person who possesses sufficient property has the liberty (*exousia*) to share in the constitution (5.1292a41). Aristotle also uses the negative form of *exousia* for a prohibition: For example, he says, in Plato's *Laws* no citizen has the liberty (*exousia*) to own more than five times the amount of the smallest property holding (*Pol.* II.7.1266b5–7, cf. 5.1265b21–3, on Plato *Laws* V.744d–e).[20]

4.8.3. Authority (kurios)

The term *kurios* signifies that the bearer has the authority to carry out acts in a specific domain. The sphere of authority may vary from narrow to wide, and the authority may be a private individual, group, official, political body, city-state, treaty, contract, will, or the law itself. What distinguishes an authority is its ability to bestow duties and rights on others. The word *kurios* is commonly used for the authority of private persons over their property. An important example of this use, involving the equivalent term *karteros*, is found in the civil laws of Gortyn in Crete (engraved on the inner surface of a circular wall). A section dealing with intestate inheritance begins, "The father has authority [*karteron*] over his children and the division of his property and the mother over her property" (trans. Arnaoutoglou 1998, no. 3; *IG* IV.72; Meiggs and Lewis 1988, no. 41). In this system the father and mother each had legal power over their own property. The wife's property was not merged with her husband's, and women could inherit property in their own right. Neither her husband nor her son could alienate or promise her property. This contrasts with the Athenian system where female "heiresses" were in effect mere conduits for male ownership.

Inscriptions of public decrees understandably contain many political applications of the term *kurios*. In a typical formula the assembly in passing a decree confers discretionary authority to the council to carry it out. For example, in decreeing the dispatch of a colony to the Adriatic (325/4 B.C.), the Athenian assembly directs the council to supervise its implementation, including

[20] Ostwald (1996, p. 60, n. 41) objects that *exousia* in this passage "cannot possibly refer to the 'right' of a citizen to own no more than five times the amount of the smallest property." But here Aristotle clearly means that none of the citizens has the liberty right to own this much. ("Not having the right to own *X*" should not be confused with "having the right to own not-*X*.")

the election of a board of representatives: "If this decree needs anything in addition for the representation, the council is decreed to have authority [*kurian*], but not to nullify anything decreed by the people" (*IG* II^2.1629; Tod 1948, no. 200.262–6; cf. no. 157.35–6).[21] Sometimes the stronger term *autokratôr* is used to indicate that exclusive authority is assigned; for example, in an Athenian decree moved by Callias (434/4 B.C.), the council is said to be the exclusive authority (*autokratôr*) over when the thirty financial officials are to meet (*IG* I^2.91; see Fornara 1977, no. 119; Meiggs and Lewis 1988, no. 58.9).[22]

Demosthenes also uses the term *kurios* to signify that a person has legal authority. For example, a master is *kurios* over a slave, but the slave is not *kurios* even over himself (*Against Aphobus* 37.51, 47.14–15). To be free is to be *kurios* over oneself, in contrast to being a slave (59.46). Demosthenes describes officials and jurors as having authority (27.159, 19.71, 59.12; cf. Isaeus 2.47) and speaks of the assembly delegating authority to the council (literally, making it *kuria*) in some specific domain (19.154). The term *kurios*, in the sense of "sovereign," applies to Philip of Macedonia, who is "*kurios* over everything" (1.4). Ideally, the people of Athens are sovereign: In the good old days, "the people had authority [*kurios*] over everything, and an individual was content to receive from them a share of honor, office, and reward" (13.31; cf. 3.30–1). Demosthenes also applies the adjective *kurios* to laws (20.8, 34; 24.205), decrees (23.96), wills (36.34), and contracts (47.77, 59.46).

Aristotle also uses the term *kurios* in the sense of "sovereign." For example, "Solon seems at any rate to grant the most necessary power to the people, namely, to elect and audit the offices, for if it did not have the authority [*kurios*] over this, the people would be a slave and an enemy [of the constitution]" (*Pol.* II.12.1274a15–18; cf. 10.1272a5).

4.8.4. *Immunity* (adeia) *and Exemption* (ateleia)

A common term for immunity is *adeia*, which implies that one is not subject to the authority of another. This type of legal right is illustrated by the aforementioned decree of Callias, which allocated funds for work on the acropolis of Athens. The decree stipulated that the funds be used for no other purpose: "But for no other purpose shall use be made of the monies unless the people pass a vote of immunity [*adeian*] just as when they pass a vote about property taxes. If anyone proposes or puts to a vote, without a decree granting immu-

[21] Authority is also attributed to a decree, in Tod 1948, no. 162.11, 34, and elsewhere to a law (162.16–17), treaty (142.19), and a city-state generally (114.10, 202.23–4).

[22] In another decree (ca. 445 B.C.) Democlides, governor of the Athenian colony of Brea, is deemed "*autokratôr* in establishing the colony as best he can." The implication is that he has the authority to act on his own discretion without restrictions from the council or assembly; see Meiggs and Lewis 1988, 49.9; cf. Fornara 1977, no. 100.

nity having been passed, that the funds of Athena be utilized, he shall be liable to the same penalty as one proposing to have a property tax or putting this to the vote." Ordinarily, anyone who proposed to divert the funds to another purpose would be subject to prosecution, but this decree provides that the assembly could pass a special decree granting immunity from such prosecution (trans. Fornara 1977, no. 119; *IG* I^2.92; Meiggs and Lewis 1988, 58 B15–19; cf. Meiggs and Lewis 1988, no. 77; cf. Fornara 1977, no. 144).

Demosthenes uses *adeia* for safe conduct granted to foreign troops (*Against Aphobus* 23.159) or an actor on tour (5.6). He declares that only Athens grants immunity (*adeia*) to speak on behalf of its enemies, that is, the Macedonians (8.64). In *Against Timocrates*, Demosthenes addresses the problem of excessive granting of special immunities: Timocrates is prosecuted for proposing an unconstitutional law granting immunity (*adeia*) from punishment to any debtor to the city-state until the ninth prytany of the year if he provided bail (24.103).

Aristotle also recognizes the importance of immunity, observing that law grants immunity (*adeia*) to buy and sell in the marketplace (*EN* V.4.1132b15–16). In a political context *adeia* could also imply "impunity." For example, in a polity (a moderate constitution), the poor should have immunity (*adeia*) from fine if they fail to serve on juries, or they should be subject to smaller penalties than the rich (*Pol.* IV.13.1297a21–4).

A related concept is exemption (*ateleia*) from public burdens, in particular, from taxation. An Eritrean inscription (411 B.C.) grants such an exemption to a foreigner who helped the city-state to rebel from Athens: "Hegelechos of Tarentum shall be proxenos and benefactor, both he himself and his sons, and public maintenance shall be granted to him and his sons when they are in the country, and immunity from public burdens [*ateleia*] and seating privileges at the games, since he joined in the liberation of the city from the Athenians" (trans. Fornara 1977, no. 152; *IG* XII.9.187; Meiggs and Lewis 1988, no. 82; cf. Fornara 1977, no. 199). The Athenians frequently made similar grants, for example, in 338/7 B.C. to Acarnanians who were granted exemption (*atelesi*) from the tax due from resident aliens and equality with citizens in court and in paying special taxes (*IG* II^2.237; Schwenk 1985, no. 1.24–8). These Acarnanians were incidentally also granted *enktesis*, the privilege to acquire and own property. The right of a resident alien to pay taxes at the same rate as a citizen is elsewhere called *isoteleia* (see Schwenk 1985, no. 12.17; *IG* II^2.276).[23]

The grant of *ateleia* is the subject of Demosthenes' first speech, *Against Leptines* (355 B.C.). Leptines had proposed to abolish public grants of *ateleia* from public service: "none shall be exempt from public services" (cf. 20.1–2, 127). Demosthenes defended the right of the people to grant *ateleia* in order

[23] Heracleides (mentioned above) was also granted *enktesis* and *isoteleia*; see *IG* II^2.360; Schwenk 1985, no. 68.19–21.

to protect the polis, and criticized Leptines for assuming a mistaken class envy (20.24). Aristotle mentions an example of exemption in the Spartan constitution: A father of three sons is exempt from military service and a father of four exempt from all burdens of state. Aristotle himself regards this policy as misguided, since it promotes excessive division of property and impoverishment of the citizenry (*Pol.* II.9.1270b1–6).

In conclusion, there is abundant evidence of rights locutions in Greek inscriptions as well as the writings of Demosthenes and Aristotle. The fact that Aristotle and Demosthenes share a common vocabulary of rights is interesting, because they represent polar opposites in the ideological spectrum of the late fourth century B.C. Demosthenes was deeply committed to democratic ideals of equality and liberty, whereas Aristotle favored an aristocracy of virtue. Despite these differences, they and their contemporaries understood legal and political issues in terms of rights, that is, of countervailing claims of justice, liberty, authority, and immunity.[24]

Further Reading

Historical surveys of legal philosophy and of natural law usually devote a chapter to Aristotle. Rowe and Schofield 2000 contains authoritative treatments by leading scholars of Aristotle's political philosophy, which sheds light on the context of his legal thought. A book-length treatment is Hamburger 1951. There are useful articles by Wormuth 1948 (reprinted in 1972) and Schroeder 1981. Aristotle's controversial place in the "natural law" tradition is discussed by Shellens 1959, F. Miller 1991, and Burns 1998 and 2011. Phillips 2013 provides an accurate English translation of a comprehensive collection of literary and epigraphical sources from the first historical trial (late seventh century B.C.) to the fall of the democracy (322 B.C.).

Aristotle's discussions of law are scattered throughout various treatises, most importantly *Nicomachean Ethics*, *Magna Moralia*, *Politics*, and *Rhetoric.* A convenient collection of reliable English translations is Barnes 1984. The relation of law to justice is a major theme in *Nicomachean Ethics* V, including the distinction between legal justice and natural justice, a topic also taken up in *Magna Moralia* I.33. For discussion of justice see Hardie 1980, chap. 10, and Kraut 2002, chap. 4. An illuminating analysis of the relevance of justice to Aristotle's political theory is Keyt 1991. *Nicomachean Ethics* X. 9 discusses the

[24] Ostwald (1996, 55) contends that "there is nothing in [Aristotle's] vocabulary that corresponds exactly to our concept of 'right' in the sense of 'claim' or 'entitlement'." It is evident, however, that the family of terms discussed in this section are parallel to modern terms for legal and political rights, understood as claims or entitlements. And, as Hansen (1996, 96) remarks, "in practice [the Athenians] knew about the privileges and liberties connected with their democratic constitution, and these rights were highly valued and crucial for their belief that democracy was the best constitution."

educative function of law and legislative science, on which see Curren 2000. There are numerous references to law in Aristotle's *Politics*, for which Newman 1887–1902 remains the most important commentary. *Politics* III and IV especially include discussion of constitutions and the rule of law, on which see Robinson 1995. On law in *Politics* generally see Keyt and Miller 1991, F. Miller 1995, and Kraut 2002. *Rhetoric* I contains important discussions of natural law; see the useful commentary of Grimaldi 1980. On *Constitution of Athens* (probably composed under Aristotle's supervision) see the commentary by Rhodes 1981 (revised in 1993) and von Fritz and Kapp 1950.

For recent discussions of whether the ancient Greeks had a concept of "rights," see Ober 2000a and 2000b, Cartledge and Edge 2009, and Miller 2009.

Chapter 5

HELLENISTIC PHILOSOPHERS OF LAW

by Roderick T. Long[1]

5.1. The Hellenistic Era: A New Political Context for Legal Thought

Between 338 and 323 B.C., the entire eastern Mediterranean region—including Greece, Egypt, and most of western Asia (the remains of the Persian Empire)—fell under Macedonian rule. Although the unity of this new empire did not survive the death of its creator, Alexander of Macedon, the various smaller empires into which it had been fragmented continued to dominate the region for centuries to come. This development signaled the end of the independent Greek *polis* ("city-state"); but since the emergent local empires now had Greek overlords, the new era also extended the influence of Greek language and culture, which soon became dominant throughout the area. Alexander's conquests thus mark the end of one age (the Classical) and the beginning of another (the Hellenistic), a turning point conventionally dated from Alexander's death in 323 B.C. The other end of the Hellenistic era is placed by some at the Roman conquest of Greece (146 B.C.), and by others much later, at the Roman conquest of Egypt and western Asia (a gradual process, somewhat arbitrarily fixed around 31–27 B.C.).

The new political conditions of the Hellenistic era naturally had an impact on philosophy in general and on legal philosophy in particular. Unfortunately, few philosophical works from the Hellenistic era have survived intact; as with the Presocratics, Cyrenaics, and Cynics, much of the philosophy of this period is consequently known only through later sources, mostly Roman, and separating the original ideas from their later elaborations (and perhaps distortions) is often difficult—particularly in the case of philosophy of law, where Roman authors might well be particularly prone to introduce, into their discussion of Greek sources, ideas derived from Rome's own distinctive contributions to legal thought. Roman philosophical works also tend to be aimed at a wider, less technical audience than their Greek counterparts, and so to obscure some of the more precise theoretical details of the originals. In addition, Hellenistic philosophers generally proclaim their allegiance to some particular school or tradition, and it is not always clear whether an author is expressing the orthodox consensus of his entire movement or is in a given instance speaking only for himself. Accordingly, the role of guesswork in interpreting and reconstructing Hellenistic thought is inevitably greater than in studying Xenophon, Plato, or Aristotle.

[1] All translations are by the author unless otherwise indicated.

While Hellenistic philosophy of law must be understood within the political context inaugurated by Alexander's conquests, the connection should not be exaggerated. According to a still popular interpretation, for which one influential source is Zeller (1903), Hellenistic thought is above all a response to the new shift of power from *polis* to empire, a shift that leads, on the one hand, to a de-emphasis on political participation (only the imperial dynasties could hope for a share in governance now) in favor of a private, interior life and personal happiness, and on the other hand, to a weakening of local, parochial allegiances in favor of a cosmopolitan identification with the global community. In contrast to Socrates' attachment to Athens, the Hellenistic era sees increased mobility of intellectuals, as scholars migrate to new centers of learning such as Alexandria. The boundaries of concern, formerly aligned with those of the *polis*, simultaneously contract inward to the individual and expand outward to the entire world. The accompanying sense of rootlessness and insecurity allegedly moves Hellenistic thinkers to reject abstract, technical philosophy in favor of pragmatic doctrines offering "self-help" paths to contentment and self-sufficiency. The Hellenistic era is accordingly seen in some respects as an era of intellectual decline. There is *some* truth to this interpretation, but it is more misleading than helpful, for three reasons.

First, the intellectual paths that Hellenistic philosophers followed were not merely an adaptation to social and environmental factors, but were also *theoretically* motivated; in many respects, Hellenistic theories can be seen as responding to and developing themes from within Classical philosophy.[2] This is not to deny that pressures external to philosophy can and do routinely reinforce pressures internal to it; but one-sidedly psychologistic, sociological explanations of philosophical developments are no improvement over one-sidedly ahistorical, decontextualized ones.

Second, the notion of a radical transition from the age of independent city-states to the age of all-engulfing empires is overstated. As Gruen (1993, 341) points out, throughout much of the Classical era itself most Greek cities were already under the hegemony of some empire or other, be it the Athenian, the Spartan, or the Persian, while on the other hand, even during the Hellenistic period most cities still had a fair degree of autonomy. Mobility of intellectuals was nothing new; even in the Classical era, philosophers who kept to their native cities had been the exception, not the rule. Moreover, far from renouncing political participation, many Hellenistic philosophers exercised considerable influence on public policy through their role as advisors to kings and princes.

[2] In any case, the ideals of cosmopolitanism, self-sufficiency, and withdrawal from political participation were already clearly present in the Socratic movement, if not earlier; even Democritus said that the wise are at home everywhere and have the universe as their homeland (DK 68 B 247).

Third, the suggestion that Hellenistic philosophy is less abstract and technical than Classical philosophy is simply untenable. Some of the most complex and sophisticated developments in logic, ethics, and philosophy of language belong to this era; Chrysippus, for example, is easily the match of any Classical thinker in this respect.

While it is a gross distortion to say that the social philosophy of the Classical period had nothing to say about moral relationships beyond the boundaries of the *polis*,[3] it is certainly true that society *within* the polis was the primary object of concern for Classical social philosophy. Hence, the Hellenistic era did see a definite shift in emphasis from one's relationship to one's fellow citizens to one's relationship to humanity in general.

Much of Greek social philosophy turns on the differing senses of the concept of *phusis* ("nature"). This term, in Greek and in English, is ambiguous in (at least) three ways. On the one hand, nature can mean the way things tend to be if nothing is done about them; one might call this nature-as-default. On the other hand, a thing's natural state can be seen as something that has to be *achieved*. (This distinction corresponds roughly to Annas' distinction [1993, 142–58] between nature and *mere* nature.) But nature-as-achievement can, in turn, be seen in two ways: as scouring off all foreign accretions in order to get down to an original, unsullied simplicity (call this nature-as-recovery), or as developing one's innate tendencies in order to achieve one's *telos* ("end"; call this nature-as-completion).[4] From the standpoint of nature-as-default, watering a plant is an artificial intervention that saves the plant from the decay that it would naturally suffer, whereas, from the standpoint of nature-as-completion, watering a plant is working with rather than against the plant's natural tendencies. Perhaps one reason for the disagreement between Aristotle and the sophists concerning whether or not human beings are naturally social and political is that for Aristotle "natural" signifies human beings at their highest potentiality, while for the sophists "natural" signifies the way that people would turn out if it were not for education and law. The Cynics, with their hostility to artificial conventions and abstract theorizing, may in turn be seen as endorsing a lifestyle according to nature-as-recovery; and the transition from Cynicism to Stoicism is arguably a transition from the ideal of nature-as-recovery to a more Aristotelian ideal of nature-as-completion.

[3] Aristotle, for example, though often regarded as particularly parochial in this regard, endorses obligations of both friendship (*EN* 1108a9–28, 1126b19–1127a2, 1155a16–31) and justice (*EN* 1159b34–1160a8, 1161b4–8; *EE* 1242a19–28; *Pol.* 1275a7–10, 1324b22–36, 1333b26–40) to those outside one's polis; cf. R. Long 1996, 783–4.

[4] This distinction has its analogues in ancient Chinese philosophy and early modern European philosophy as well, with Hobbes and Hsün-tzu favoring nature-as-default, Locke and Mencius favoring nature-as-completion, and Rousseau and the Taoists favoring nature-as-recovery.

The emerging cosmopolitanism, particularly in its Cynic-Stoic version, tended not to take a specific institutional form. For example, the cosmopolis of the early Hellenistic philosophers was not yet identified, as it would be later, with any specific earthly community, such as the Roman Empire or the Christian Church. Certainly, it was not intended as ideological support for the Macedonian imperialism; few[5] would have agreed with Plutarch's later claim (at *Alex. Fort.* VI. 329a–c) that Alexander had achieved in action the cosmopolis that philosophers like Zeno had only theorized about. Likewise, the Cynic-Stoic conception of natural law had not yet been brought into connection with actual earthly codes of law (though Xenophon had pointed a way toward the possibility of doing so), and the connection between one's role as a *kosmopolitês* ("citizen of the cosmos") and the specific role in which one finds oneself in the everyday world was not yet clarified. It fell to the practical-minded Romans to work this transformation of Hellenistic philosophy, making Hellenistic views more useful while at the same time depriving them of much of their edge and radicalism.

5.2. Academics

Plato's Academy—so called because of its location in the grove of Hekademos—resembled not only a modern research university, devoted to knowledge for knowledge's sake, but also a public policy institute or "think tank" with the practical aim of influencing legislation and constitutional reform (Klosko 1986, 188). Such an ambition was by no means quixotic; the philosophical schools of Athens boasted princes and statesmen among their graduates, and philosophers were often called upon to play an advisory role in drawing up legal codes. Moreover, the founding of new colonies was a fairly frequent phenomenon in the Greek world, so even the prospect of designing a new political system from scratch was by no means as unrealistic as is often supposed. Unfortunately, after Plato's time little is known of the legal theories of the early Academics; in Diogenes Laertius' catalogue of works by Speusippus and Xenocrates, who were the first leaders of the school, we see such tantalizing titles as *On Legislation*, *On Justice*, *On the Citizen*, *On the Republic*, *On Equity*, and *On the Power of Law* (D.L. IV.2.12), but their contents are unknown.

We do, however, possess four Socratic dialogues from the early Academy that deal with issues of law: *Minos*, *On Justice*, *Sisyphus*, and *Demodocus*. These works have come down to us as part of the Platonic corpus, but (with the possible exception of the *Minos*) they are not the work of Plato.[6]

[5] Among the possible exceptions are Onesicritus, a decidedly heterodox Cynic (see Moles 1995, 144–9), and whoever wrote *To Alexander On Kingship* (see below, Section 5.3).

[6] The *Minos* has the best claim of the four to be regarded as authentic. One argument against its authenticity is an alleged Stoic influence. The doctrines that only just laws are genuine

The *Minos* concerns a conversation between Socrates and an unnamed comrade concerning the definition of law, and is clearly related in some way to Xenophon's treatment of the subject (see Chapter 2, Section 2.3, of this volume).[7] Like Pericles and Hippias in the *Memorabilia*, the comrade is torn between a positivist and a moralized conception of law. The comrade (313b–c) initially defines *nomos*, law, as what is *nomizomenon* ("customarily accepted"); here, the linguistic link between *nomos* as law and *nomos* as custom is being exploited in the service of positivism. But Socrates objects that, just as sight is not what is seen but that *by* which things are seen, so *nomos* must be not what is *nomizomenon* but that *by* which things are *nomizomena*. The comrade's next move is to define law as the judgment of the state; but he, like Pericles, is sensitive to the link between justice and law. Since judgments of the state are sometimes unjust, he is driven to redefine law as the *correct* judgment of the state. In Socrates' words (*Minos* 315a): "[L]aw wishes to be the discovery of what is."[8] But how, in that case, can there be different laws in different places? Socrates' answer is that all these laws agree in one sense and not in another: They all agree in legislating *justice*, but they disagree about which things are just; so they *aim* at agreement even when they fall short of it. It is insofar as they agree, presumably, that they are genuine laws, not insofar as they disagree.

And how can laws change over time? Socrates answers, obscurely, that "being moved like gamepieces they remain the same" (*Minos* 316c). The meaning of this claim is unclear, but is reminiscent of the Xenophontic analogue about war and peace, and is perhaps making a similar point about principles remaining the same when their applications change. Someone might say, "Before I could move my pawn ahead, but now I can't! The rules must have changed!" However, not the rules, but the circumstances—e.g., there is another piece on that square now—have changed. Similarly, all laws, to the extent that they

laws (*Minos* 314d–e, 317c) and that only wise kings are genuine kings (317a–318b) are certainly accepted by the Stoics; but this is a weak argument, since both of these doctrines are likewise found in Plato and Xenophon. For these views on law, see Xenophon, *Mem.* I.2.41–6; Plato, *Hp. Ma.* 284b–285b, *Laws* IV.715b. For these views on kings, see Xenophon, *Mem.* III.9.10–11, IV.6.12; Plato, *Rep.* I.347d, *Euthd.* 292a–c. Moralized definitions of genuine judges (Plato, *Ap.* 39e–40a), work (Xenophon, *Mem.* I.2.56–7), power (Plato, *Gorg.* 466b–470b), friendship (Plato [?], *Alc.* I.126c–127d, *Clit.* 409d–e), beauty (Xenophon, *Mem.* III.8.5–10, *Smp.* V.3–4; Plato, *Gorg.* 474d–475b), and wealth and profit (Xenophon, *Oec.* I.5–13, *Mem.* IV.2.37–9, *Smp.* IV.34–45; Plato [?], *Hipparch.* 230a–231e, *Erx.* 399e–400e) are also found in Plato and Xenophon. Socratic dialogues contain Stoic-looking theses because that is where the Stoics found them in the first place.

[7] If it is not by Plato, then it is probably a response to Xenophon. On the other hand, if it is by Plato then Xenophon might be responding to it, or both authors might be responding to some other thinker—Socrates himself, perhaps.

[8] This might seem counterintuitive, but Hayek 1973 argues that the conception of law as something *discovered* rather than *made* is both older and more defensible than the positivist account; cf. also Leoni 1991.

are laws, embody the same principle; but the applications may differ either through a change in the circumstances or through the ignorance and incompetence of those applying the laws.

True law, the *Minos* argues, is an expression of the art of kingship, which is the knowledge of which laws to pass. Here, the criterion is objectivist rather than subjectivist: Kingship is the art of promoting the welfare of the human soul. Minos, legendary ruler of Crete, accordingly has the best claim to be a true king: First, because his laws are unchanging, which is (some) evidence that they are based on knowledge, since laws based on knowledge do not change (but what about the game pieces?), and second, because he learned them from Zeus (which is presumably evidence that his laws are beneficial). But Minos has a bad reputation in Athens because his version of wisdom comes into conflict with the sort of wisdom claimed by the poets. But until we can discover what, in fact, is best for human souls, we will not fully grasp the essence of kingship. Here the dialogue ends.

The other three dialogues are slighter works. *On Justice* consists mainly of arguments paraphrased from various Platonic dialogues; in its one original contribution (Pseudo-Plato, *On Justice* 373c–e), Socrates claims that when judges determine what is just and what is unjust, they employ *speech* in the same way that weighers and measurers employ scales and measuring sticks to determine what is heavy or light, long or short. Socrates raises (but does not answer) the following question: What sort of thing must justice be, in order for it to be true that speech is the tool for resolving disputes about it?

The *Demodocus* and *Sisyphus* also address the question of how deliberation and debate in assemblies and law courts could be a rational way of settling issues. The worry is that if nobody knows what to do, public discussion is pointless, while if somebody does know what to do, public discussion is superfluous. These arguments could be read either as a critique of democracy or as a *reductio ad absurdum* of strongly individualist approaches to epistemology—and so, indirectly, as a vindication of the necessity of legal institutions of public deliberation (cf. Aristotle, *Pol.* III.11.1281a42–b10; R. Long 2000, 27–9, 101–3, 112–4).

In the third century, the Academy came under the leadership of Arcesilaus (ca. 318–242 B.C.), who moved the Academy in a skeptical direction, interpreting Plato's dialogues as purely aporetic. For the Skeptical Academy, no philosophical questions can be decisively settled, so it is imperative to suspend judgment. It is unclear how far the Skeptical Academics were influenced by the earlier skeptical movement of Pyrrho (ca. 360–270 B.C.), who also advocated suspension of judgment as a way of gaining psychic tranquility.[9] Both

[9] Sedley 1983 argues for, and Decleva Caizzi 1996 against, an influence of Pyrrho on Arcesilaus. The stories that have been handed down about Pyrrho (no doubt exaggerated) suggest Cynic withdrawal and indifference, while the Academics in their social attitudes sound more like Aristippus.

schools of Skeptics practice arguing on both sides of every question, in order to move the mind to a suspension of judgment.

Some Pyrrhonists define law in purely positivist terms,[10] as a written contract among citizens, backed by punishment (Sextus Empiricus, *PH* I.146), maintaining that because of the cultural relativity of laws and customs we cannot say what is right or wrong in itself or by its nature, but only how it appears to us (Sextus, *PH* I.148–63, *M* XI.140; cf. D.L. IX.11.83–4, 101). Hence, nothing is more just than unjust; *nomos* (here meaning "custom") and *ethos* ("habit") govern all human action (D.L. IX.11.61).

The first member of the Skeptical Academy known to have contributed to legal philosophy is Carneades (ca. 213–129 B.C.), who gave two famous speeches in Rome, one in favor of justice and the other against it. It is the speech against justice that excited the most interest, and although it does not survive, numerous reports and paraphrases do. Carneades' speech appears to combine both Pyrrhonist and sophistic arguments. Like the Pyrrhonists, he argues that if justice were a matter of nature rather than convention, all countries and all eras would have the same laws (Cicero, *Rep.* III.818). Like the sophists, he argues that justice clashes with self-interest (Cicero, *Rep.* III.24; Lactantius, *Inst.* V.16–VI.9). Drawing on Glaucon's challenge in Plato (*Rep.* II), he maintains that justice is a mutual nonaggression pact regarded as a poor second-best situation in comparison to the enticing, but excessively risky, alternative of trying to commit injustice with impunity (Cicero, *Rep.* III.23). Thus the vaunted "mixed constitution," recognizing as it does the need to avoid giving any one group too much power, is an open confession that mutual distrust is natural, and so justice is unnatural (Cicero, *Rep.* III.23). Hence, political justice (i.e., acting justly when injustice is punished by law) is mere prudence, not justice, while so-called natural justice (i.e., acting justly when injustice is not punished by law) is folly (Lactantius, *Inst.* V.16).

The anti-Skeptical backlash against the Skeptical Academy was led by Antiochus of Ascalon (ca. 130–ca. 68 B.C.), who attempted to revive the interpretation of Plato as a "dogmatist" (i.e., someone committed to definite doctrines rather than simply suspending judgment), and produced a version of Platonism that borrowed heavily from Stoic and Peripatetic doctrine as well. Cicero (*Leg.* I.23) records an argument that is likely to be of Antiochean provenance:

(1) Reason is shared in common by all rational beings.
(2) For those to whom reason is the same, right reason is also the same.
(3) Therefore, right reason is shared in common by all rational beings [(1), (2)].

[10] Though if pressed they would presumably suspend judgment on whether positivism itself is correct.

(4) Law = right reason.
(5) Therefore, law is shared in common by all rational beings [(3), (4)].
(6) Those who share law in common are fellow citizens.
(7) Therefore, all rational beings are fellow citizens [(5), (6)].

This vision of the cosmopolis is essentially Stoic (it recurs in Marcus Aurelius, *Med.* IV.4), but as Dillon (1977, 80) argues, "it is very likely that the discussion of the Natural Law in Cicero *On the Laws* I is basically Antiochean" because it "contains the characteristic mark of Antiochus' presence, a survey of the doctrines of the old Academy and of Zeno's agreement with it." The argument also fits in well with Antiochus' doctrine that friendship should be extended to the entire human race (Cicero, *Fin.* V.65; Augustine, *CD* XIX.3).

The Academic thinker most important for legal philosophy is Marcus Tullius Cicero (106–43 B.C.). However, in his writings on ethical, social, and political matters, he generally adopts a Stoic position, maintaining that, as an Academic Skeptic rather than a Pyrrhonist, he can accept Stoic doctrines as plausible opinions rather than as knowledge (*Off.* II.7–8). In any case, Cicero, while technically falling into the Hellenistic period (at least under the broader of its two definitions), clearly belongs in the context of Roman thought, and so will be considered in Chapter 6 of this volume.

5.3. Peripatetics

Like its ancestor the Academy, Aristotle's school—the Peripatos (after the *peripatos* or colonnade where the school met) or Lyceum (after the public grove of Apollo Lykeios where the *peripatos* was located)—was *inter alia* a public policy institute that aimed, not without success, at swaying the counsels of state. In addition to Aristotle's own contributions as tutor to Alexander and (allegedly) legislator for Stageira, Theophrastus (ca. 370–286 B.C.), Aristotle's chosen successor as president of the school, was able to exert considerable influence on legislation during the period when Athens was governed by his student Demetrius of Phaleron. Nor did the demand for Peripatetics as political advisors cease with his fall from power; Demetrius, Strato, and Lycon were all invited to foreign courts to serve as political advisors (D.L. V.58, 67–8, 78; Lynch 1972, 151). Concerning Strato's and Lycon's contributions to legal thought, however, we know little; our information about Peripatetic philosophy of law after Aristotle focuses on three figures: Theophrastus, Dicaearchus, and Demetrius.

Among Theophrastus' works on law (which survive only in *fragmenta* and *testimonia*) are the *Laws* (Theophrastus seems to have made collections of laws in the same way that Aristotle made collections of constitutions) and *On Critical Opportunities* (the latter title excellently capturing Theophrastus' focus on the particular situation). Theophrastus criticizes attempts to make laws universally applicable by anticipating every contingency; laws should be framed for situations that occur for the most part, not for those that occur rarely (Justinian, *Dig.* I.3.3, 6, as quoted in Fortenbaugh et al. 1992, 629–30; cf. Fortenbaugh 1993). Accordingly, he advises that one should violate the law, and ordinary moral rules as well, when special circumstances call for it, weighing values carefully against one another, since just as a lot of bronze can outweigh a small amount of gold, so considerations that are usually less important can sometimes outweigh those that are usually more important (Gellius, *Noctes Atticae* I.3, as quoted in Fortenbaugh et al. 1992, 534). This leniency toward exceptions is consistent with Theophrastus' own particularist turn of mind (cf. Sharples 1998, 270).

On Theophrastus' view, good men need fewer laws than bad men (Stobaeus, *Eclogues* III.37.20, as quoted in Fortenbaugh et al. 1992, 628). A useful example of why this is so is his recommendation that the law of contract be reformed to require exceptions for rage and drunkenness (Stobaeus, *Eclogues* IV.2.20, as quoted in Fortenbaugh et al. 1992, 650). Since, on his own view, what happens only occasionally should be ignored, it follows that the law should take rage and drunkenness into account only if these are usual rather than exceptional occurrences; hence, this reform must be intended for a society where rage and drunkenness are frequent occurrences, and so would not be needed in a society where more people were virtuous.

Cicero attributes to Theophrastus, Dicaearchus, and Demetrius a common commitment to the mixed constitution and division of powers (*Leg.* III.14–17). In his treatise *Tripolitikos*, Dicaearchus defended a blend of three principles: democratic, oligarchic, and monarchic (Cicero, *Att.* XIII.32; Athenaeus, *Deipn.* IV.19.141a–c; Photius, *Bibl.* 37; cf. Lintott 1997, 72). Theophrastus seems to have held some version of a cosmopolitan doctrine (Porphyry, *Abst.* II.162.6; cf. III.22, 25); similar concerns are detectable in Dicaearchus' lament that more people die by violence than by natural calamities (Cicero, *Off.* II.5.16–17), and in his nostalgic portrait of a lost golden age free from strife (Porphyry, *Abst.* IV.2.1–9).

Demetrius of Phaleron (ca. 350–280 B.C.) served as governor (some would say dictator) of Athens for ten years, as the result of negotiations between Athens and Macedon, since he was acceptable to both sides;[11] hence, he had maximal opportunity to put his own political theories into practice. Demetrius abolished liturgies and trierarchies (compulsory patronage) in favor of taxation, thus weakening the power of private patronage and centralizing power in the state. He reformed the law courts: Litigation fell sharply under Demetrius because success in the law courts was no longer the path to power and prestige which now depended on external forces (see Gagarin 2000, 361–2; cf. Tacitus,

[11] It was under Demetrius that the metic-controlled Peripatos, the Aristotelian school, finally gained the right to own the land on which it met.

Dial. 40–41). Demetrius also passed sumptuary laws (from which he, notoriously, exempted himself) and assigned officials called *gunaikonomoi* ("regulators of women") to supervise public morals. His *nomophulakes* ("guardians of the law") seem to have had the power to override the decisions of the democratic Assembly. Demetrius' 1,000-drachma requirement for political rights can be seen as a move in an oligarchic direction, if contrasted with the absence of any property qualification under the earlier regime of Polyperchon (Gottschalk 2000, 369), or as a move in a democratic direction if contrasted with the still earlier 2,000-drachma requirement under the regime of Antipater (Tracy 2000, 338–9). In either case it harmonizes well with Aristotle's defense of the "middle constitution."

Issues relevant to philosophy of law are also raised in *Problemata* and *To Alexander on Kingship*, two works which, though traditionally ascribed to Aristotle, are generally thought to derive from the early Peripatos. While the *Problemata* is concerned primarily with issues of natural science, two chapters (29, 30) contain interesting attempts to rationalize common legal practice. The methodology employed is characteristically Aristotelian, starting from the assumption that existing practices are more or less right, and reasoning back to principles that would justify or explain them and solve the puzzles they raise.

The pseudo-Aristotelian letter *To Alexander on Kingship*, preserved only in Arabic, appears to embody both cosmopolitan and anticosmopolitan sentiment. In its cosmopolitan aspect, the letter calls for Alexander to unite all of humankind into a single kingdom (8) and a single city (4), free from strife and devoted to leisure and reflection (8). Less benignly, it seems to reject such notions of universal fellowship by calling for pro-Greek favoritism (6) and an ethnic cleansing of Persians (8).[12]

Stern (1968) inclines to the view that the work is a genuine letter of Aristotle's. Against this is the letter's endorsement (8) of the *lex talionis* (the principle of "eye for an eye") of Rhadamanthys, which Aristotle condemns at *EN* V.5.1132b2–5; but Stern (1968, 32) argues that for Aristotle "what was no justice for the Greeks, could very well be justice for the barbarians." Might Aristotle have favored a cosmopolis ruled by Alexander? Differing historical traditions have cast Aristotle both as a friend and as a foe of his former pupil's imperial aims. The evidence in Aristotle's own writings is equivocal. Aristotle generally rejects empire, both because imperialistic domination is unjust (*Pol.* VII.2.1324b23–1325a8) and because an empire is too large to be a proper political community (VII.4.1326a34–b13). Additionally, his remark that nowa-

[12] Plutarch, *Alex. Fort.* VI.329b, apparently knew of a purportedly Aristotelian letter advising Alexander to treat Greeks as friends but Persians as *animals or vegetables*. This is stronger than anything in *To Alexander on Kingship*. Was Plutarch quoting a different work, now lost? Or was he simply paraphrasing freely? And if he was paraphrasing, might he then simply be paraphrasing the defense of natural slavery in Aristotle's *Politics* rather than a letter?

days all monarchs are tyrants (V.8.1313a4–5) hardly sounds like a ringing endorsement of the Kingdom of Macedon. Still, imperialistic domination might not be unjust when exercised over barbarians; and Aristotle's remark (*Pol.* VII.6.1327b34) that the Greeks could rule the entire human race if they were united in a single *politeia* seems more favorable to Alexander's empire. Despite Stern's inclination to view the letter as authentic, he does acknowledge "some similarity between the phrases of Dicaearchus and those of our passage" (Stern 1968, 60–1). Should Dicaearchus be the letter's author, its cosmopolitan sentiments might stem from his doctrine of a single unitary life force immanent in all of nature (Cicero, *Tusc.* I.21).

5.4. Polybius

While Polybius (ca. 200–ca. 118 B.C.) was primarily a historian and statesman, the constitutional theory adumbrated in his *Histories* is a milestone of legal philosophy. Despite some words of praise (*Histories* II.38, 42) for the democratic policies of the Achaean League (in which he had been politically active), Polybius' favored constitutional order is a blend of monarchical, aristocratic, and democratic elements. The virtue of this system is its division of powers, which provides checks and balances; these are needed because no one is to be trusted with complete independence and unchecked power—not because human nature is inherently corrupt, but because complete independence and unchecked power tend to cause corruption (cf. Plato, *Laws* 694a–695d). Although no constitution can be rendered permanently stable, constitutions with a division of powers tend to outlast those without, because in the latter the ruling party, finding its power unrestrained, begins to abuse its position and so provokes a revolution.[13] The Polybian regime is more flexible: In emergencies, the three powers are able to work together for the common good; in peacetime, when self-serving motivations dominate, the self-interest of each power leads it to restrain the other powers' tendencies toward self-aggrandizement (Polybius, *Histories* VI.18). Polybius identifies Sparta and Rome as examples of his favored system, and sees them as owing their success to that system. They differ primarily in two ways: The Spartan system was established (as Polybius supposes) by a rational plan instituted at a single stroke, while the Roman system evolved through a series of piecemeal adjustments to particular situations (VI.9–10; cf. Cicero, *Rep.* II.2); and Sparta's severe restrictions on commerce weaken its economic power, making it less effective than Rome at maintaining an empire (Polybius, *Histories* VI.48–50).

[13] In Polybius' particular version of the cycle of constitutions, monarchy matures into kingship, degenerates into tyranny, and is replaced by aristocracy, which degenerates into oligarchy and is replaced by democracy, which degenerates into ochlocracy and is replaced once more by monarchy (*Histories* VI.4–9).

To what extent Polybius is relying on earlier thinkers is unclear. His version of the mixed constitution does not fit what we know of the earliest Stoics (there would be no need for a balance of powers in Zeno's community of sages) nor the Epicureans (who never seem terribly interested in questions of constitutional structure),[14] but is more likely to reflect Academic or Peripatetic influence, particularly since Polybius' cycle of constitutions, though not identical with those proposed by Plato or Aristotle, evinces a similarity of approach. Moreover, as Hahm (1995, 16) points out, Polybius' particular version of the constitutional cycle works in terms of the tension between "two elements in the human psyche: (1) a uniquely human, rational element and (2) an element that operates independently of human reason and that human beings share with other animals." This certainly sounds more Academic or Peripatetic than Stoic or Epicurean. Polybius also seems concerned to defend history against Aristotle's charge that history cannot be philosophical because it deals with the particular rather than the universal (*Histories* III.1), which suggests some familiarity with Aristotelian literary theory. Further, as Hahm (1995, 42–5) again points out, Polybius' laws of history take conditional form—the antecedent is not necessary, though once the antecedent is in place, the consequent follows; this suggests familiarity with the Academic doctrine of "legal fate" (Alcinous, *Did.* 26.179.1–20; Pseudo-Plutarch, *Fat.* 569e–570b; Tacitus, *Ann.* VI.22; Calcidius, *Tim.* 150, 179; Nemesius, *Nat. Hom.* 38). Since Dicaearchus in particular is known to have advocated a *trinal* division of powers based on monarchic, oligarchic, and democratic elements (unlike Aristotle's binary division between oligarchic and democratic elements), and since this is the central feature of Polybius' model as well, it seems possible that Dicaearchus influenced him in this respect. Polybius' enthusiasm for the Roman Empire as a kind of universal political order (*Histories* I.1–2, VI.50) may echo Dicaearchus as well.

5.5. Epicureans

In the Classical era, legal thinkers had been divided over whether to regard justice as a conventional agreement, that motivates obedience through sanctions, or as an inward psychic state valuable for its own sake. Epicurus (342–271 B.C.) and his school can be seen as attempting to incorporate aspects of each view into a single account (cf. Mitsis 1988, 59–97; Annas 1993, 293–302): Justice is defined as a contract, yet the wise person behaves justly without being motivated by fear of punishment.

For Epicurus, pleasure is the supreme good; hence, all the virtues have merely instrumental rather than intrinsic value (cf. Diogenes of Oenoanda,

[14] Though Polybius' account of the origin of civilization may owe something to Epicurean speculation.

New Frag. 26.1–3), and justice is no exception. Justice is nothing in its own right, he tells us, but is simply a contract made for mutual benefit, an agreement not to harm or be harmed (Epicurus, *KD* 31, 33); hence, nothing counts as just or unjust conduct among those who are either unable or unwilling to make such contracts (*KD* 32). Justice in general outline is the same universally, but its specific details vary with time and place because the same things are not always useful (*KD* 36–7), and when a law ceases to be useful for social interaction, it ceases to be just (*KD* 37–8).[15]

But what reason do we have to abide by the legal contract? Here our sources seem to differ. According to Epicurus' own words in the *Kuriai Doxai* (*Key Doctrines*), the badness of injustice depends not on anything intrinsic to injustice, but solely on the fear of punishment (*KD* 34). Yet this seems to be contradicted by the testimony of Epicurus' student Hermarchus (ca. 325–ca. 250 B.C.), whose treatise *Against Empedocles*, though lost, is liberally excerpted in Porphyry. In his presentation of the Epicurean account of the origin and justification of law, Hermarchus tells us that wise people obey the law not from fear of punishment but because they recognize its utility; it is only the unwise who need to be motivated by legal punishments. Hence, if all people were wise, no laws would be needed (Porphyry, *Abst.* I.7–12). Our two chief sources of information concerning Epicurean legal thought are the *Kuriai Doxai*, on the one hand, and Hermarchus, on the other. What are we to make of this apparent disagreement between them?

It might seem obvious that as evidence for Epicurus' intentions, the exact language used by Epicurus himself must trump Porphyry's quotations from one of Epicurus' students. But things are not quite so obvious. We possess more material from Epicurus in his own words than from any other early Hellenistic thinker, thanks to Diogenes Laertius' happy decision to transcribe four Epicurean works verbatim in the last book of his *Lives* (D.L. X.35–117, 122–35, 139–54)—the *Kuriai Doxai* is one of these. However, the works that Diogenes preserves for us are abbreviated summaries of a popularizing sort (X.35–6); it is clear from the surviving fragments of Epicurus' *On Nature* that Epicurean theory in its full technical detail was more complex and sophisticated than the summaries suggest. Hence, in reading the *Kuriai Doxai* we must keep in mind that we are probably dealing with a simplified version of a more nuanced theory. Ideally, then, we should try to find an interpretation that makes *KD* 34 come out as being *approximately* right. If the ordinary person's only motivation for obeying the law is fear of punishment, what might the Epicurean sage's motivation be?[16] Something more than punishment, if we are to

[15] There is no suggestion, however, that it ceases to be a *law*.

[16] Epicurus holds that virtue is the one *sine qua non* of pleasure; we can be happy without food, but not without virtue; see D.L. X.138. This is presumably because we can adapt to the absence of food, but not to the absence of virtue, since virtue is what enables us to adapt our

trust Hermarchus, but not something completely unconnected with punishment, lest we do too much violence to *KD* 34.

Epicurus rejects the Cyrenaic version of hedonism, but he had surely considered the views of his hedonistic predecessors seriously, and this may provide a clue concerning his view on obedience and the law. Recall the apparent conflict (Chapter 2, Section 2.4, of this volume) between the elder Aristippus, who said that the wise man would continue to behave rightly if all laws were abolished (D.L. II.8.68), and the younger Aristippus, who said that the wise man behaves rightly "on account of the penalties imposed and on account of reputation" (D.L. II.8.91–3). These views seem contradictory, but may not be. The younger Aristippus gives us *two* reasons to obey the laws: punishment and *doxai* ("reputation"). In the situation contemplated by the elder Aristippus, the abolition of all laws might remove punishment as a concern, but perhaps not reputation.

Why would the Epicurean sage care about his reputation? He would care not in order to win acclaim or renown, of course, but perhaps in order to facilitate relationships of reciprocity. After all, the motivation for making the contract in the first place is not fear of punishment by government officials (since such institutions do not exist prior to the contract), but fear of retaliation by one's neighbors. If I want others to cooperate with me rather than aggress against me, I must convince them that I am a reliable cooperation partner; for if they cannot trust me to behave peacefully, then violence against me will be their only recourse (*Abst.* I.12). Thus it is in my interest to build a reputation as someone who can be trusted to do his part in cooperative interactions; abiding by norms of reciprocity is "useful for mutual association" (*KD* 38; cf. Axelrod 1985). Damaging my own reputation for trustworthiness, and thus increasing the incentive of others to act violently toward me, is what Xenophon would call the *natural* penalty of injustice (Chapter 2, Section 2.3, of this volume).[17] But this natural penalty does not fall upon the wrongdoer at once; the results are gradual and irregular. Hence, the sage will find the natural penalty to be a sufficient deterrent to injustice, but ordinary people tend to be too short-sighted and so need something that is quicker, more certain, and harder to forget or ignore: *legal* penalties.

This is evidently the difference between the motivations of the two groups in Hermarchus. And so *KD* 34 does not turn out to be *exactly* right, since it treats legal penalties as the only reason to avoid injustice.[18] But the fear of be-

desires in the first place. Cf. Plato's doctrine in the *Euthydemus* that virtue is the one tool that cannot be misused because it is the standard of correct use. But this simply pushes us back to a further question: Why is justice a virtue?

[17] Perhaps this is why Epicurus calls justice based on this consideration *natural* justice; see *KD* 31.

[18] *KD* 34's reference to "punishers who are put in charge of such things" (*huper tôn toioutôn ephestêkotas kolastas*) clearly points to an established institution of punishment rather than mere private retaliation.

ing harmed by other people is close enough to the fear of punishment that *KD* 34 can be treated as an over-hasty summary rather than as a decisive repudiation of Hermarchus.[19]

The following dilemma, however, might then be raised for Epicurus: Does the Epicurean mutual nonaggression pact require the sage to renounce or restrain certain desires he has to inflict harm on others? If the answer is yes, then the picture looks too much like Glaucon or Carneades: The sage would ideally like to commit injustice against others but is fearful of the consequences and so settles for justice as the second best. On the other hand, if the answer is no, because the sage lacks the incentive to do harm, then it seems as though the sage is going to have a hard time getting others to enter into a contract with him, since the motive for making such contracts is to avoid being harmed by the other party, and no one is in danger of being harmed by the sage.

Does the sage have motives for harming others? Let us first distinguish between motives for *initiatory* harm and motives for *defensive* harm. Clearly, the sage has motives for engaging in defensive harm, and acts on those motives: The Epicurean community as described by Hermarchus employs violence against both those who break the contract (as when lawbreakers are punished) and those outside the contract (as when dangerous animals are killed).[20] Hence, it would be a mistake to regard the Epicurean sage as a patsy who cooperates no matter how often the other side defects. The contract does not require the sage to renounce his motives for defensive harm; in fact, it assumes their retention.

On the other hand, the sage has no motives for engaging in initiatory harm, since the desire to harm arises from hatred, envy, or low regard (*kataphronêsis*), and the sage is subject to none of these (D.L. X.117).[21] The Epicurean sage shuns the political life and chooses to "live unknown" in simplicity and freedom from disturbance, mastering all unnatural and unnecessary desires. Hence, the justice contract does not require the sage to sacrifice anything he values; its purpose is not to prevent the sage from *committing* harm, but to prevent him from *suffering* it (Stobaeus, *Eclogues* IV.142).

[19] Lucretius (ca. 99–ca. 55 B.C.), the chief Roman expositor of Epicureanism, lends support to this interpretation; see *RN* V.959–1028, where the institution of punishment is clearly intended to be an *additional* incentive, over and above the fear of private retaliation.

[20] Epicurus holds that there are no obligations of justice among "whichever animals" (*hosa tôn zôiôn*) are unable to make contracts (*KD* 32; cf. 39). If the Epicurean requirements for contract are indeed looser and more informal than in traditional social contract theory, it becomes conceivable that some nonhuman animals might meet the entrance requirements for the moral community. Did Epicurus intend this? Some sources (Epicurus, *Nat.* 34.25.22–34; Lucretius, *RN* V.855–77) suggest yes; others (Hermarchus, as quoted in Porphyry, *Abst.* I.12.5–6) suggest no.

[21] Underestimating the extent of retaliatory harm that one's victims might be able to inflict in return would perhaps fall under "low regard."

As Epicurean values spread, then, the need for legal penalties should correspondingly decrease. The Epicurean cosmopolis, unlike its Cynic-Stoic counterpart,[22] is a dream for the future, not a reality for the present; the Epicurean propagandist Diogenes of Oenoanda (*New Frag.* 21.1. 4–14, 2.10–14) looks *forward* to a golden age where justice and friendship will replace laws (cf. Hermarchus) and city walls, and human beings will live "the life of the gods."[23] This is clearly a world in which everybody has become an Epicurean sage, and reliably chooses the benefits of cooperation. But the vision may have implications for the present as well: Diogenes of Oenoanda calls the whole world his homeland (*New Frag.* 25.2.3–11), while Epicurus speaks of friendship dancing around the world (*Sent. Vat.* 52), and is said to have numbered his own friendships by whole cities (D.L. X.9; Cicero, *Fin.* I.65).[24]

To the Roman poet Lucretius (ca. 99–ca. 55 B.C.), Epicurus was "a god indeed, who first discovered the rational system of life that is now called Wisdom, and who by his art moved life from such turbulence and such darkness into such serenity and such light" (*RN* V.9–12). His epic poem *On the Nature of Things* undertakes the daunting task of setting out Epicurus' "rational system of life" in hexameter verse.

Lucretius' brief discussion of law seems to follow Epicurus' contractarian account—particularly in the two-level version related by Hermarchus (Porphyry, *Abst.* I.7–12), where fear of strife motivates the wise to abide by an informal contract, but the unwise need the additional incentive of formal punishment. (Given the scantiness of our sources on Epicurus, the extent of Lucretius' originality is difficult to judge.) In a conjectural history of the beginning of human society, Lucretius tells us that our primitive ancestors, lacking awareness of the mutual benefits of the rule of law, grabbed from one another whatever their strength could win them. However, sexual love eventually gave rise to stable families, which led in turn to a gentling of the human spirit. Now each family, "eager to avoid harming and being harmed," was accordingly motivated to enter a mutual nonaggression pact with its neighbors (*RN* V.959–1028).[25] But as the growth of civilization brought inequalities of status, ambition and conflict arose—until, weary of strife, people were willing to accept a system of

[22] But like that in Pseudo-Aristotle, *To Alexander on Kingship* 8.

[23] The wording suggests Stoic influence. Centuries earlier, we find Cicero—with his Stoic hat on—writing that if human beings ever realize their universal kinship with one another, then they will live "the life of the gods" (*Leg.* I.33, fragment, as quoted in Lactantius, *Inst.* V.8); and Stoics commonly describe the cosmopolis as a common habitation of men and gods.

[24] Why doesn't caring about our friends' welfare impair our self-sufficiency (as per Theodorus the Cyrenaic) by making our happiness vulnerable to the bad luck of our friends? Apparently, this is because Epicurus thinks that we can take as much pleasure in our friends' past or future happiness as in their present happiness (*KD* 19–20, 40, 66; Cicero, *Tusc.* V.95; D.L. X.137; Lucretius, *RN* III.1087–94; Plutarch, *Contr. Ep. Beat.* 1105e).

[25] By contrast with contemporary "hypothetical contract" theories, the Lucretian contract represents an actual (if tacit) accord that we have reason to bring about.

"strict laws and rights" backed up by punishments (1105–61). For Lucretius, formal law is the price humanity pays for its own folly.

5.6. Stoics

The most influential of the various Hellenistic schools was the Stoa (named after the *stoa poikilê*, or "painted colonnade," where the school met), whose founder, Zeno of Citium (ca. 334–ca. 262 B.C.), was a student of Crates the Cynic. The Stoic emphasis on self-mastery and indifference to everything but virtue indicates Stoicism's debt to Cynicism. Since the writings of the early Stoics are lost, it is unclear how much of the Stoa's distinctive doctrines derive from Zeno and how much from the "second founder" of Stoicism, Chrysippus (280–208 B.C.). What is clear, however, is that the early Hellenistic Stoa—the Stoa of Zeno, Cleanthes, and Chrysippus—was much closer to the antinomianism of its Cynic origins than was the more respectable later Hellenistic Stoa that grew up in the shadow of Rome—the Stoa of Diogenes of Babylon, Antipater of Tarsus, Panaetius, Poseidonius, Hecaton, and their successors. The two works that caused the later Stoics the most embarrassment are also the starting point for Stoic legal thought: Zeno's *Republic* and Chrysippus' *On the Republic* (the latter being a commentary on the former).[26]

We are told that in the city advocated by Zeno, only the virtuous are friends or fellow citizens; equality of men and women is established through unisex clothing[27] and the abolition of marriage in favor of open sexual relations based on mutual consent; and temples, law courts, gymnasia, and currency are banned (D.L. VII.1.33). Many of these proposals simply take to their logical extreme the Spartan institutions praised by Xenophon (*Lac.* I.3–4, VI.1–3, VII.3–6). Chrysippus apparently endorsed most of Zeno's program (D.L. VII.1.131), adding a defense of the legitimacy, under the right circumstances, of masturbation, incest, and cannibalism (DL VII.1.121, 188; Plutarch, *Stoic. Rep.* 1044b–1045a; Sextus Empiricus, *PH* III.247–8).

The two clearest influences on the Zeno-Chrysippus *Republic* are the works of the same name by Plato and Diogenes. But is the Stoic republic an independent city-state like Plato's, a utopian blueprint for a community of sages? (Diogenes Laertius' description [D.L. VII.1.33] of Zeno as banning law courts, etc., in the *cities*, plural, might suggest that the envisioned community does not embrace the entire earth.) Or is it a still more utopian blueprint for a worldwide Stoic empire? (Plutarch tells us [*Alex. Fort.* VI.329a–c] that Zeno advocated

[26] Some of the later Stoics found Zeno's *Republic* so embarrassing that they attempted its suppression; cf. D.L. V.1.34; Clement, *Strom.* V.9.58.2.

[27] Presumably following the precedent of the Cynic Hipparchia (D.L. VI.7.96–7), though Plato's female students wore men's clothing as well (D.L. III.46; Philodemus, *Acad. Ind.*, *Herc.* 1021).

replacing local communities with the cosmopolis.) Or is it a description of how the wise should conduct themselves here and now, in the existing universal community, the Cynic cosmopolis? (Thus Zeno began his *Republic* [Philodemus, *Stoic.* 18] with the statement that it was relevant to his own place and time.) But the three interpretations need not be inconsistent. Zeno is describing how the wise will interact; the account will apply equally to a small community of sages living together, or to the entire community of sages scattered throughout the earth, or to a world in which everyone has achieved sagehood.[28] If the sages build their own city, be it a local or a global one, they will not construct any temples or gymnasia; if the sages live among people who do construct such things, they will simply not *treat* any existing structures as temples or gymnasia. Temples are places where conduct that is ordinarily permitted is forbidden (as sacrilege); gymnasia are places where conduct that is ordinarily forbidden (public nudity) is permitted. Zeno is rejecting such artificial divisions; just as the Cynics rejected the idea of different rules of conduct in private and in public, so Zeno is rejecting the ideas of different rules of conduct in different locations.[29] Zeno's rule that there is no part of the body that must always be covered (D.L. VII.1.33) converts the whole world into a gymnasium.

Yet if the rules of the ideal community hold for sages in the here and now, what are we to make of the claim, ascribed to Zeno and Chrysippus (D.L. VII.1.121; Seneca, *Otio* III.2), that the sage will, when circumstances call for it, take part in ordinary civic institutions such as politics and marriage? Perhaps there is a difference between the way a sage interacts with other sages and the way he interacts with ordinary people.[30] The Stoic reverence for both Socrates and Diogenes perhaps required some way of reconciling the marriage and (admittedly limited) political participation of the one with the antinomianism of the other.[31] (As part of the de-Cynicizing of Stoicism, later Stoics would defend

[28] Schofield 1991 argues that the Zenonian republic was an individual community; Erskine 1990 and Vander Waerdt 1994c defend a cosmopolitan interpretation. One of Schofield's arguments (1991, 26) is that we cannot imagine "what it would mean to rule that women are to be held in common" unless Zeno is describing "a community whose members are known to one another and live in more or less close proximity to one another." But Zeno's "community of women" means that sexual liaisons are to be open and based solely on mutual consent; to internationalize this is simply to deny that such freedom of choice stops at national borders. Helen and Paris were practitioners of "community of women" in its internationalized form.

[29] Plutarch (*Stoic. Rep.* 1034b) attributes to Zeno a somewhat different reason for the prohibition on temples, namely, that nothing made by human hands can be sacred. The ban on currency might have a similar motivation.

[30] For example, if community of women holds between sage and sage but not between sage and fool, the sage might commit adultery with Crates' wife Hipparchia, but not with Menelaus' wife Helen.

[31] Seneca offers a different interpretation (*Otio* III.2–3, VIII.1–4). By Zeno's and Chrysippus' rule, a sage will participate in politics unless something prevents him. But, says Seneca, if the state is too corrupt to obey the sage's advice, that will be enough to prevent him. Every state, however, is too corrupt to obey the sage's advice, as the fate of Socrates in Athens (and, by impli-

marriage and political activity as expressions of the natural tendencies of social animals.)

Who are the citizens of the Stoic cosmopolis? Some sources tell us that only the wise are its citizens (D.L. VII.1.33; Philodemus, *Herc.* 1428.7–8; Plutarch, *Lyc.* 31); others extend its citizenship to all rational beings (Cicero, *Off.* I.50–51, *Leg.* I.61; Plutarch, *Alex. Fort.* VI.329a–c). A possible solution is offered by Dio Chrysostom (*Or.* XXXVI.23): Human beings (i.e., unwise ones, actual ones) get counted as citizens of the cosmopolis along with gods in the same way that, in human cities, children get counted as citizens along with adults, because they have a natural potentiality for the functions of citizenship even if they cannot yet exercise that potentiality. Schofield (1991, 78) argues convincingly that Dio's position is likely to have been the orthodox Stoic one. The cosmopolis, then, is both a community of everyone potentially and a community of the wise actually (cf. Obbink 1999).

What are the normative implications of the cosmopolis? According to Cicero (*Leg.* I.61–2), once we recognize our true status as citizens of the cosmos, we will naturally be led to despise ordinary concerns (which sounds Zenonian enough) and to start making orations, enacting legislation, praising the virtuous, protecting the weak, punishing the wicked, and ruling nations—all of which sounds rather more Roman than Zenonian. Knowing where the contributions of Zeno and Chrysippus end and Roman influence begins is accordingly difficult. But we can be reasonably confident that the early Stoics regard the cosmopolis as governed by a moral law that supersedes positive law. Zeno describes the human race as sharing citizenship in common, nurtured by a common law (*Alex. Fort.* VI.329a–c), and Chrysippus identifies law as the supreme ruler, the criterion of justice and injustice, and the standard of correct conduct for political animals (Marcian, *Institutes* I.2.25, as quoted in *SVF* III.314). The only true law—that is, the only rule that has normative authority—is right reason (Cicero, *Leg.* I.23; Marcus Aurelius, *Med.* IV.4). The justice it defines is natural, not conventional (D.L. VII.1.128; Cicero, *Leg.* I.28, 44). It is the same for all times and places, and statutes which deviate from it are not genuine laws but instead have no better status than the dictates of a criminal gang (Cicero, *Leg.* I.17–19, 42, II.8–14; *Rep.* III.33; cf. Augustine, *CD* IV.4). Anyone who does violate the natural law will be punished, even if he escapes all worldly punishments, because the worst penalty of all is to be in violation of one's nature as a rational being (Cicero, *Off.* II.36; Lactantius, *Inst.* VI.8 [cf. V.11]; Epictetus, *Diss.* IV.1.118–22).[32]

cation, Seneca under Nero) shows; so the Zeno-Chrysippus rule in effect rules out political participation entirely. If someone advises "Sail, but not on any sea where storms are likely to occur," that, Seneca concludes, amounts to the advice "Do not sail."

[32] It is interesting to see how the basic Antiphonian idea of natural penalties is developed in a consequentialist direction by Xenophon and Epicurus, and in a nonconsequentialist direction by Plato and the Stoics.

For later natural law thinkers like Aquinas and Locke, obedience to the law of nature involves obedience to certain *rules* that right reason discovers to be appropriate for human beings. This is arguably true for the later Stoics as well—as evidenced by the casuistical debates recorded in Cicero's *On Duties*, and the lists of appropriate Stoic actions in Diogenes Laertius (VII.1.107–9). But is it likewise true of the early Stoics? Vander Waerdt (1994c) argues that the early Stoics have a dispositional rather than a rule-following conception of natural law; the law the sage follows is his own judgment, but his judgment is based on an insight into the requirements of the particular situation, rather than on the application of an abstract rule. By the time of Seneca (*Ep.* 94–5) the official Stoic doctrine was that the wise man will grasp and apply precepts (*praecepta*), but Seneca's discussion shows that the question had once been a matter for debate.[33] Most of the regulations in Zeno's *Republic* might be seen less as rules than as the waiving of rules: One need not treat any one place as special (temples, gymnasia), one need not cover any particular body part, one need not abstain from sexual intercourse with another's spouse—though the prohibition on currency is less easy to fit into this pattern.[34]

Subsequent generations saw a transition from the Cynic-leaning Stoicism of Zeno's and Chrysippus' era to the more Aristotelian Stoicism of Panaetius and his contemporaries. This transition involved two major changes: a shift from an ideal of nature-as-recovery to an ideal of nature-as-completion, and a greater willingness to take our socially assigned roles as well as our natural ones into account in defining that completion. The result was a fuller engagement with the social and legal institutions of the day, and, accordingly, a greater need to sort out the good from the bad in such institutions, rather than simply rejecting them *in toto* in the manner of the Cynics; Diogenes of Babylon, in particular, marks such a turning point. This helps to explain the later Stoa's casuistical turn, and thus the development of a more rule-oriented version of natural law.

What Zeno and Chrysippus had accomplished was to take a way of life—the stern independence of the Cynic—and turn it into a logical system so powerful and rigorous that it quickly placed other schools on the defensive. The Stoics soon came to set the philosophical agenda and terms of debate for the Hellenistic era, so that even those who argued against Stoic doctrine had to use Stoic concepts and terminology. Dazzling dialectical skill in pursuing the implications of an argument to the end, however paradoxical, was the way to win Greek minds. But it was not the way to win Roman minds; the next stage

[33] Seneca's example of an antirule Stoic, however, is Ariston, who is generally so unorthodox that he is dangerous to generalize from. On the whole question of rules versus insight in Stoicism, see Kidd 1979; Inwood 1986; Annas 1993, 96–108; and Striker 1996b.

[34] But it is, of course, a literal application of the Cynic injunction to "deface the currency" of convention.

in the development of ancient philosophy would need a new approach—and it got one. With Diogenes of Babylon, the Stoa begins to turn its face to the West. It is Diogenes who begins the process of bringing the Stoa into engagement with the social and legal institutions that frame and permeate our quotidian practical experience. Significantly, it is also Diogenes who joins the delegation (155 B.C.) that brings Greek philosophy to the Roman world.

The Stoa conquered Greece by learning logic. To conquer Rome, it would learn law.

Further Reading

The writings of the Hellenistic philosophers survive mostly in fragmentary form. An excellent source by Long and Sedley (1987) provides texts and translations of quotations and testimony with valuable interpretive material. Two recent volumes stand out as the indispensable starting point for further study of the philosophy of law in the Hellenistic and Roman periods. The best synoptic account of Hellenistic philosophy is Algra et al. 2000, with separately authored chapters placing the thinkers discussed in this chapter in a wider philosophical context. Rowe and Schofield 2000 contains an extensive section on Hellenistic philosophers, including discussions of Cynicism, Epicureanism, Stoicism, and particular thinkers. An illuminating general study of Hellenistic moral and social thought is Annas 1993. Laks and Schofield 1995 is a helpful collection of essays on Hellenistic social and political philosophy emphasizing themes of justice and generosity. Vander Waerdt 1994b includes articles on the Stoic and Skeptic reception of Socrates. Sorabji 1993, though primarily concerned with the moral status of animals, offers fascinating information and reflections on all aspects of Hellenistic moral and social thought.

The standard collection of *fragmenta* and *testimonia* for Theophrastus (it does not include the works which survive complete) is Fortenbaugh et al. 1992. The collection of essays by van Ophuijsen and van Raalte (1998) is a good introduction to Theophrastus. For other early Peripatetics, text, translation, and commentary for Demetrius of Phalerum is provided in Fortenbaugh and Schütrumpf 2000, and for Dicaearchus of Messana in Fortenbaugh and Schütrumpf 2001. Stern 1968 is a careful study of the "cosmopolitan" passages in the letter *To Alexander on Kingship* attributed to Aristotle.

The best source of Epicurus' writings and testimonia in translation is by Inwood and Gerson 1994. Mitsis 1988 is the definitive study of Epicurus' ethical and social thought. Schofield 1991 is a carefully detailed and persuasive study of the evidence for the political theory of Zeno and the early Stoa. Setting the same evidence in a broader historical and political context, Erskine (1990) defends a more democratic and egalitarian interpretation of the early Stoics. Ierodiakonou 1999 includes useful articles on Stoic social theory. An important discussion of late-Stoic casuistry is Annas 1989.

Chapter 6

LAW IN ROMAN PHILOSOPHY

by Brad Inwood and Fred D. Miller, Jr.[1]

6.1. Historical Overview of Roman Law and Legal Thought

Legal philosophy in late antiquity must be understood in relation to Roman law, a system which continued to evolve from the traditional founding of Rome (753 B.C.) until the fall of the Eastern Roman (or Byzantine) Empire (A.D. 1453). Rome was at first ruled by kings about whom little is certain. A set of laws attributed to them (*leges regiae*) and compiled by Papirius a priest (*pontifex*) were probably statements of customary and religious norms, concerning marriage, family relations, funeral rites, and so forth (Johnson, Coleman-Norton, and Bourne 1961, 3–6). The Roman Republic (509–27 B.C.) was initially threatened by internecine conflict between the patrician and plebeian orders. This was resolved in part through the Twelve Tables (451–450 B.C.), a written public code composed by officials called decemviri, which could not be arbitrarily changed by patrician magistrates. This collection of statutes, which the Roman historian Livy called "the fount of all law, public and private" (*Roman History* 3.34.6, trans. Jones), was lost, although many quotations, paraphrases, and descriptions were preserved by later Roman authors (Johnson, Coleman-Norton, and Bourne 1961, 9–18; Warmington 1967; see also A. Watson 1975).

The republican constitution had three elements: the magistrates, the senate, and the assemblies. The important magistrates (most holding office for a year) included the two consuls, praetors (both of whom held a coercive power termed *imperium*, which entailed a judicial capacity), *aediles* (whose general concern was maintenance of public order through adherence to regulations), quaestors (whose responsibilities were largely financial), and censors (in charge of census and supervision of morals). In emergencies, usually on the advice of the senate, a magistrate with *imperium* could nominate a dictator who, if approved by the senate, would hold supreme *imperium* for at most six months. The senate (literally "council of elders") had a purely advisory role based on *auctoritatas*, a morally binding authority, but it eventually became the dominant political body. Ideally, it had 300 members (later 600) who were mostly former magistrates and had lifelong tenure. Among the vari-

[1] Sections 6.2–5 were written by Brad Inwood, and Sections 6.1 and 6.6 by Fred Miller. Section 6.1 benefited from suggestions by Thomas Banchich and Richard Epstein. Portions of Inwood's discussion appear in an expanded and more fully developed form in Inwood 2003. Sections 6.4 and 6.5 owe a great deal to the assistance of Fred Miller. All translations are by the authors unless otherwise indicated.

ous assemblies, the oldest was the curiate (*comitia curiata*), composed of thirty curiae, which ratified the Twelve Tables but gradually lost importance. The most powerful assembly was the centuriate (*comitia centuriata*), organized into classes based on wealth as an index to military capacity, which elected magistrates such as the consuls with supreme power (*imperium*) and had the right to declare war or ratify treaties. The tribal assembly (*comitia tributa*) elected lower magistrates and adjudicated some non-capital cases. Finally, to help resolve their conflict with the patricians, the plebeians formed their own assembly (*concilium plebis*), presided over by ten tribunes, which gradually became an important legislative body. The tribunes acquired increasing power, including the right to veto the proposals of magistrates and fellow tribunes. These assemblies underwent changes. For example, the patrician and plebeian membership of the tribal assembly gradually melded with the purely plebeian membership of the plebeian assembly, so that the tribal assembly became the dominant legislative and electoral body in republican Rome.

Every adult male citizen was a member of the curiate, centuriate, and tribal assemblies, and every plebeian (the vast majority of citizens) had a right to membership in the plebeian assembly. Although all citizens could vote, their votes were tallied in groups, whether curia, tribe, or century (the last weighted in favor of wealthy citizens who could afford to arm themselves more fully). The Romans recognized different sources for law (*ius*, pl. *iura*). In the Republic, a measure approved by an assembly was called a statute (*lex*, pl. *leges*). The acts of the plebeian assembly (called *plebiscita*) had the force of law binding on all citizens after the enactment of the Hortensian statute of 287 B.C. An assembly's powers were limited, because it could not initiate legislation. It could only approve or reject a measure placed before it by a magistrate, which had been previously discussed and approved by the senate. These resolutions could be vetoed by a tribune or a magistrate with *imperium* before the assembly had the opportunity to act on them. The edicts proclaimed by magistrates were also regarded as laws. In some instances, these edicts served to confirm resolutions of the senate (*senatus consulta*).[2]

Jurists (*iuris consulti* or *prudentes*) also played an important role in the development of Roman law (see Lenel 1889; Frier 1985; Bauman 1971; and Johnston 2000). Originally priests but later normally former magistrates, they were legal experts who advised the praetor as members of his council. Some jurists wrote widely circulated manuals, including Quintus Mucius Scaevola (consul in 95 B.C. and author of an influential treatise on civil law), his pupil Aquilius Gallus (praetor in 66 B.C.), Servius Sulpicius Rufus (consul in 51 B.C.), and Alfenus Varus (interim consul 39 B.C.). There was also a school (*secta* or *schola*) in the senate that discussed legal issues. The jurists wrote an-

[2] Johnson, Coleman-Norton, and Bourne 1961 and Crawford 1996 are collections of laws, edicts, rescripts, and other legal documents. See A. Watson 1974.

swers to legal questions (*responsa prudentium*) concerning the interpretation of laws and official edicts. They also assisted in the drafting of legal documents such as contracts and wills, and they advised judges and disputants in lawsuits. Their opinions were embodied in court decisions which served as precedents for later decisions. The jurists influenced the interpretation of the unwritten (*non scriptum*) law or custom (*mos*, pl. *mores*), which, like the Greeks, the Romans distinguished from written (*scriptum*) law.

The historian Polybius (ca. 200–ca. 118 B.C.) viewed the Roman constitution as the true exemplar of the "mixed constitution," combining monarchical, aristocratic, and democratic elements:

> [I]t was impossible even for a native to pronounce with certainty whether the whole system was aristocratic, democratic, or monarchical. This was indeed only natural. For if one fixed one's eyes on the power of the consuls, the constitution seemed completely monarchical and royal; if on that of the senate it seemed again to be aristocratic; and when one looked at the power of the masses, it seemed clearly to be a democracy. (Polybius, *Histories* VI.11.12, trans. Paton)

Within the Roman Republic, as described by Polybius, each branch has distinct powers: The consuls are the supreme magistrates, especially in matters of war; and they summon assemblies, introduce measures, and preside over the execution of decrees. The senate controls public finance, investigates public crimes such as treason, conspiracy, and assassination, and is in charge of embassies to foreign countries. The popular assemblies have sole constitutional authority (*kurios*) over the imposition of honors and punishments and to bestow offices. Also, writes Polybius, "the people have the power [*kurian*] of approving or rejecting laws [*nomôn*], and what is most important of all, they deliberate on the question of war and peace" (*Histories* VI.14.10, trans. Paton). The three parts of the constitution are each able, if they wish, to counteract and cooperate with the others in various ways. For example, although the people are obliged to be submissive and deferential to the senate (VI.17.1), the assemblies can curb the traditional authority (*exousia*) of the senate and the tribunes can prevent it from acting (VI.16.3–4). Polybius admires the Roman system involving separated powers with checks and balances: "Such being the power that each part has of hampering the others or cooperating with them, their union is adequate to all emergencies, so that it is impossible to find a better political system than this" (*Histories* VI.18.1, trans. Paton).

Polybius was the friend and teacher of Scipio Aemilianus, a powerful politician and the general who destroyed Carthage. Scipio shared Polybius' ideal of the Roman balanced constitution, but feared its eventual decline. This ideal was increasingly jeopardized by the division between the rich and the poor, which was reflected in disputes within the Roman ruling class itself between the so-called *populares* (who tended to rely on tribunes and the tribal and plebeian assemblies) and the so-called *optimates* (who tended to rely on the senate and magistracies). The political order was shaken by a series of crises, including the attempt of the tribune Tiberius Sempronius Gracchus to institute land reform through the plebeian assembly and bypass the senate, leading to his assassination (133 B.C.). His reforms were continued by his brother, Gaius Sempronius Gracchus (d. 121 B.C.), one of whose laws required that juries be selected from the *equites* (cavalry). Although this was meant as a populist measure, it had the unintended consequence of empowering the *publicani* (tax collectors) as an interest group and exacerbating political instability. L. Cornelius Sulla used an army to have himself appointed dictator with unspecified tenure (81–79 B.C.). A succession of violent conflicts among powerful holders of *imperium*, including Marius, Pompey, Julius Caesar, Marc Antony, and others finally brought down the Republic.

Marcus Tullius Cicero (106–43 B.C.) was an influential figure during this tumultuous period. Scion of an affluent but not politically established family, he studied law under the jurist Mucius Scaevola and gained personal influence through his rhetorical skill and successes in the law courts. A supporter of optimate tactics, Cicero defended the Roman Republic as a mixed constitution without parallel. He studied philosophy in Athens, consorted with Greek intellectuals in Rome, and popularized Greek philosophy among his compatriots. Late in life, forced to withdraw from politics, he wrote dialogues dealing with legal philosophy, including *On Duties*, *On the Commonwealth* (with Scipio Aemelianus as an interlocutor), and *On the Laws*, the latter two modeled after Plato's dialogues. He criticized the traditional jurists for concentrating on particular laws, for example, "about water running off roofs or about shared walls," and neglecting questions about the source of law and justice (*Leg.* I.14). (His views are discussed in Section 6.2 below.) After the assassination of Julius Caesar (44 B.C.), Cicero reentered politics only to be killed on order of his nemesis Marc Antony, who was in turn defeated by Caesar's nephew, Octavian, who, as Caesar Augustus, gained constitutional control of the state in 27 B.C. Despite his claim that as "first man" (*princeps*) he had restored the republic, Augustus was in fact the first Roman emperor.

The history of the empire has two main periods: the principate (27 B.C.–A.D. 284) and dominate (A.D. 284–585).[3] During the early principate, legal authority shifted increasingly to the emperor to whom the people had committed its "entire authority and power" (Justinian, *Dig.* I.4.1). Legislation by assembly gave way to imperial enactment (*constitutio*), and the last statute (*lex*) was passed under the emperor Nerva (ruled 96–98). At first the emperor relied on the senate to approve his proposals, but this procedure became increasingly perfunctory and finally ceased. Nevertheless, there was considerable interest in the law during this period. During the reign of Augustus there arose two contending legal schools (intellectual movements, not educational institutions) in the senate: the Proculians and the Sabinians. Since the former school

[3] See Buckland and Stein 1975 and Schulz 1967 for law in the Roman empire.

(founded by Labeo, a critic of Augustus) challenged the more traditional view of the latter (under Capito), there ensued vigorous debate over jurisprudence. Augustus granted certain jurists the right to give answers with the force of law (*ius respondendi*), although this practice died out during the second century A.D. The emperors increasingly relied on edicts, legal decisions, and rescripts (written answers to queries by officials). The power of the jurists in the senate waned under Emperor Hadrian (117–138), but one of his rescripts did establish that the concurrent written opinion of privileged jurists had the force of law, although a judge could use his discretion if the jurists' opinions disagreed.

During the first two centuries of the Roman Empire, Stoic philosophers made important contributions to legal thought. These included, most notably, the statesman and dramatist Seneca (1–65), the freed slave Epictetus (60–140), and the emperor Marcus Aurelius (b. 121, ruled 161–180). (They are discussed in Sections 6.3–5 of this chapter.)

Throughout the course of the Roman Empire, there continued, however, to be considerable scholarly interest in jurisprudence (see Honoré 1994).[4] Many ancient treatises on this subject have unfortunately perished, although numerous excerpts were preserved in Justinian's *Digest* (see Chapter 10, Section 10.1, of this volume). In the first century A.D., Masurius Sabinus published *Three Books on Civil Law*, a collection of opinions of jurists. Like other scholars, he distinguished civil law (*ius civile*), which applied only to Roman citizens, from the law of nations (*ius gentium*), that is, Roman law concerning cases involving foreigners and Romans (as in international commerce). He also distinguished different kinds of civil law—law of succession, law of persons, law of obligations, and law of things—an approach followed by later writers. Many collections of juridical opinions circulated during the first three centuries A.D., including the *Epistulae* of Proculus (mid-first century) and of Neratius Priscus (d. after 133), the *Digesta* of Julian (second century), the *Digesta* and other works of Celsus (second century), the *Enchiridion* of Pomponius (second century), the *Quaestiones* and *Responsa* of the highly revered Papinian (d. 212), the *Institutes* of Marcian (early-third century), and the many works of Paul (d. after 235), fragments of which were later collected in the extant *Sententiae* or *Opinions*. Of special interest to modern legal scholars is the *Institutes* of Gaius (ca. 160), of which a manuscript was discovered in 1816.[5] The only work of a jurist to survive substantially intact, it covers the law of persons, property rights and inheritance, and legal actions. Ulpian (d. 228), perhaps the most influential of the jurists, published a *Digest* and numerous other works with many citations of his predecessors. The extant *Epitome* was a later compilation of excerpts from his

[4] Robinson 1997, chap. 3, gives a valuable overview of critical editions, translations, and studies of the extant texts.

[5] Gordon and Robinson 1988 is a text and translation. Honoré 1962 is a study of Gaius.

writings.[6] The last of the great jurists was Herrenius Modestinus (third century). The *Vatican Fragments* (mid-fourth century) is a valuable extant collection of extracts from Papinian, Paul, and Ulpian, as well as later rescripts and opinions. Also surviving is the *Mosicarum et Romanarum Legum Collatio* (composed between ca. 390–438), which compares Roman law with Mosaic law, quoting legal experts (on Mosaic law see Chapter 7, Section 7.1, of this volume).

These authorities tended to be scholars and editors rather than original legal thinkers. But their works were widely read and often cited in legal decisions. Some of them (e.g., Proculus, Neratius Priscus, Celsus) favored the more rigorously principled Proculian viewpoint, and others (e.g., Masurius Sabinus, Cassius Longinus, Julian, Gaius) favored the more traditional and pragmatic Sabinian position. Their differences in legal philosophy resulted in disagreements on some particular issues, for example, on whether the price of something must be pecuniary (Proculians) or can consist in other goods as in barter (Sabinians) (see Gaius, *Inst.* III.140–1). Some of them, especially Gaius, Paul, and Ulpian, were strongly influenced by the discussions of nature and law in Aristotle and the Stoics, although they understood these concepts differently. For example, Gaius generally follows Aristotle's treatment of law and justice, including his distinction between the natural and the legal. Gaius distinguishes civil law, "which each people makes for itself" and is "peculiar to itself," from the law of nations (*ius gentium*), which is common to all peoples: "The law which natural reason makes for all mankind is applied in the same way everywhere." Gaius here suggests that commonality of legal practice is evidence of its reasonableness. Differences of civil law reflect local conventions that were in effect different ways of implementing general principles (e.g., that promises are binding). Gaius expresses a Roman legal viewpoint that supported toleration of different local legal systems. According to Gaius, natural reason also reveals natural law (as in the case of the right of first acquisition), so that the law of nations is, in effect, equivalent to natural law (*Inst.* I.1, II.65–6; cf. Justinian, *Dig.* I.1.9; see Honoré 1962, chap. 6). Ulpian, in contrast, sharply distinguishes these concepts:

> Private law is tripartite, being derived from principles of natural law, law of nations, or civil law. Natural law is that which nature has taught to all animals; for it is not a law specific to mankind but is common to all animals [...]. Out of this comes the union of man and woman which we call marriage, and the procreation of children, and their rearing [...]. The law of nations is that which all human beings observe. That it is not co-extensive with natural law can be grasped easily, since this latter is common to all animals whereas the law of nations is common only to human beings among themselves. (Ulpian, *Inst.* I *ap.* Justinian *Dig.* I.1.1)

Using this distinction, Ulpian reasons, for example, that slavery and consequently manumission belong to the law of nations, "since, of course, everyone

[6] Translated by Muirhead 1880.

would be born free by the natural law" (Ulpian, *Inst.* I *ap.* Justinian *Dig.* I.1.4; cf. 3–4). Ulpian agrees here with other jurists such as Tryphoninus (*Disputations* VII *ap.* Justinian *Dig.* XII.6.64) and Florentinus (*Institutes* XII *ap.* Justinian *Dig.* I.5.4) (see Carlyle 1936, vol. 1: 39). Unfortunately, the crucial distinction between natural law and the law of nations is not further clarified in the surviving texts of the jurists. Nor do they explain their use of the term "natural," which seems to be used for what they regard as normal or reasonable (Levy 1949, 7; Kelly 1992, 57–63).

Concerning the concept of law, the jurists drew on Greek orators and philosophers in an eclectic way. Marcian quotes Demosthenes and Chrysippus. Drawing on Demosthenes, he mentions three reasons why everyone ought to obey law: "It is a discovery and a gift of god"; "it is a resolution of wise men, a correction of misdeeds both voluntary and involuntary"; and "it is the common agreement [*sunthêkê*] of the *polis* according to whose terms all who live in the *polis* ought to live." Papinian echoes this view, when he defines a statute (*lex*) as a "resolution of wise men" and "a communal covenant of the state" (*Definitions* I *ap.* Justinian *Dig.* I.3.1). Marcian also appeals to Chrysippus, "a philosopher of supreme Stoic wisdom": "Law is king over all divine and human affairs. It ought to be the controller, ruler, and guide of good and bad men alike, and in this way to be a standard of justice and injustice and, for beings political, by nature a prescription of what ought to be done and a proscription of what ought not to be done" (Marcian, *Institutes ap.* Justinian *Dig.* I.3.2, trans. Watson). Ulpian expresses a similar view, closely connecting law (*ius*) and justice (*iustitia*): Legal wisdom (*iuris prudentia*) "is an awareness of God's and men's affairs, knowledge of justice and injustice" (*Rules* I *ap.* Justinian *Dig.* I.1.10). Ulpian also remarks, somewhat obscurely, that civil law neither follows wholly nor diverges entirely from natural law or the law of nations, and that it is made by adding to or taking away from the common law (*Inst.* I *ap.* Justinian *Dig.* I.1.6). The surviving writings of the jurists have little else to say concerning the nature of law.

During the dominate (starting A.D. 284) the emperors wielded absolute political power. The later empire came to resemble an oriental despotism with the emperor as a god or, after the triumph of Christianity, God's representative on earth. Deprived of independent authority, the jurists devolved into mere advisors to the emperor who possessed the ultimate legislative authority. Nonetheless, the emperors and citizens alike recognized the lack of, and pressing need for, a comprehensive and consistent system of laws that would apply throughout the empire. At the beginning of this period, the Gregorian Code (ca. 291) and the Hermogenian Code (ca. 295), named after two officials of the Emperor Diocletian (reigned 284–305), undertook to systematize the rescripts of emperors.[7] In an effort to resolve the many inconsistencies in the

[7] The word "code" translates *codex*, which indicates that the works were published as books with pages rather than as rolls.

extant legal literature, Emperor Theodosius II laid down the Law of Citations (426), which involved the following decision procedure: Follow the writings of Papinian, Paul, Ulpian, Modestinus, and Gaius; and secondarily follow other jurists cited by them. If these five disagree, follow the majority. If there is no majority, follow Papinian. If Papinian says nothing on the issue, the judge may use his own discretion. Finding this procedure insufficient, the emperor promulgated the Theodosian Code (438), which sought to combine the previous codes, laws, and juridical opinions into a consistent statement of public law (see Mommsen and Meyer 2002–2005; Pharr 1952; Harries and Wood 1993; Harries 1999). Laws were dated, with later laws given precedence. The law of citations was retained for citations of the jurists. The code itself was divided into sixteen books, of which the last eleven have survived in manuscripts. Material from the other books was preserved in later works, especially the Justinian Code (528–555), the *Lex Romana Visigothorum* (506), and other legal codes of the Germanic barbarians. After the end of direct Roman rule in much of western Europe, the history of Roman legal thought continued in Constantinople, the New Rome.[8]

6.2. Cicero

There is little original philosophy of law in ancient Roman thought, if "philosophy of law" is understood in a narrow sense to designate a field distinct from political philosophy. But, for whatever reason, legal concepts enjoyed an extensive and vital use in the philosophical discourse of this era. The exploitation of "law" and various legal concepts is especially associated with Stoicism. This is not without reason, although Platonism had a very important influence on Roman legal thought (as did, to a lesser extent, Aristotelianism and Epicureanism).[9] The authors most characteristic of Roman legal philosophy—Cicero, Seneca, Epictetus, and Marcus Aurelius—will be the focus of the rest of this chapter. Particular attention shall be paid to what is regarded as their most important contribution to legal philosophy: the idea of natural law.[10]

In the philosophical tradition it was Plato who first brought "law" and "nature" into fruitful philosophical contact (see Chapter 3 of this volume). Early Stoicism pushed these ideas even further, in ways that remain controversial among scholars (see Inwood 1999; Vander Waerdt 1994c; and Chapter 5, Sec-

[8] See Volume 7 of this Treatise, Chapter 1, for fuller discussion of the Roman jurists' conception of law. See Chapter 10, Section 10.1, of this volume for further discussion of the Justinian code and its historical importance.

[9] Although Lucretius (99–55 B.C.) lived during this period, his thought is more closely related to the Epicureans (and is discussed in Chapter 5, Section 5.5, of this volume) than to other Roman thinkers.

[10] See also Colish 1985, chap. 6, for the issue of the impact of Stoicism on Roman law. More generally, see Johnston 2000, 622–3, 630–3.

tion 5.6 of this volume).[11] Natural law (or the "common law," *koinos nomos*, the better attested term for early Stoics) is the perfected rationality of Zeus and the sage, giving orders about what is to be done and what is not to be done, orders whose content is one of two sorts. First, the common law commands that rational agents act virtuously, in accordance with their perfected reason and nature. These commands are immune to exception when left at this level of generality, but they are not definitively action-guiding since the virtuous thing to do is often to be determined by variable circumstances. Second, this law also provides more concrete guidance about how one should act by specifying the kinds of things one should do in particular circumstances. But once it does this, it loses the immunity from exception that characterizes the broad injunctions to act virtuously. A natural law, then, is always imperatival; but if universal it will be to some extent vague, and if definite enough to be action-guiding it will admit of exceptions (cf. Inwood 1999). This is a perfectly reasonable application of a conception of law to philosophical thinking: It reflects a general truth about the relationship between laws or rules and moral behavior (a truth which Aristotle recognized when discussing equity in its relationship to laws), namely, by their very nature laws have a vagueness that demands flexible interpretation if the underlying purpose of attaining justice is to be achieved.

These Stoic ideas influenced Cicero (b. 106 B.C.), the Roman statesman and philosopher whose career spanned the most turbulent years of the late republic. He was first elected to public office in 75 B.C., won the consulship in 63 B.C., and was preoccupied with the constantly decaying condition of the republic until his murder in 43 B.C. by the minions of Marc Antony. His early education included a thorough study of Greek philosophy, and he continued to read and write philosophical works throughout his life. The two works of Cicero that matter most to the present discussion are *On the Commonwealth* and *On the Laws*, which were composed during the 50s B.C. when Cicero was effectively deprived of political power yet constantly yearning to preserve the old Roman Republic of his ideals, one characterized by the enlightened leadership of a stable elite and by a high degree of social cohesion.[12] These works were part of a Ciceronian project to emulate Plato in a Roman context; Plato's

[11] Contrast the views of Striker 1996b; Mitsis 1993; Mitsis 1994, who have argued with great vigor for a conception of natural law that is markedly at variance with that advanced by Vander Waerdt 1994c and Inwood 1999. For the purposes of this chapter it is reasonable to maintain a rather minimalist view about early Stoicism.

[12] In the dialogue *On the Orator*, a no less Platonic work composed at this period, Cicero shows enormous respect for the intellectual resources and integrity of Roman law and jurisconsults—this forms an important contrast to the relative dismissal of it in *Leg.* I.14–17. In his philosophical treatments of law, Cicero is more concerned to argue for the central importance of the Twelve Tables, which are the foundational documents of the Roman legal tradition, than he is to grapple realistically with the actual state of law in his own day (see Section 6.1). Like the unphilosophical orators of *On the Orator*, unphilosophical lawyers offered little to the vitality of Rome's intellectual culture.

Republic and *Laws* were the obvious models for Cicero when he conceived these works.[13]

These are the first works of distinctively Roman philosophy of law which demand our attention. In *On the Commonwealth* Cicero presents us with a wide-ranging debate about the best constitution, arguing that the traditional Roman manner of organizing a state is the closest to an ideal that one can achieve. In this debate a spokesman for Academic skepticism is the foil for both Stoic natural law theory (which argues that justice has a uniform foundation in nature) and Epicurean conventionalism (which holds that justice is a function of utility in varied human societies). Cicero's sympathy for the natural law position is manifest.[14] But we must also take notice of the fact that at least in *On the Laws* the Stoic character of the theory is ambivalent. No matter how much sympathy Cicero had for Stoicism and despite his use of characters whose persona is Stoic, these works are emulations of Plato, and Cicero is himself an Academic by inclination as well as by choice. One of his teachers in the Academy, Antiochus of Ascalon, argued for the essential harmony of early Academic, Peripatetic, and Stoic philosophy, and Cicero could not avoid being influenced by this view—though it is a position which most members of those schools would have vigorously rejected.

The Stoic influence on Cicero can be seen in his inclusion of a translation of the famous proem to *On Law* by Chrysippus in his own *On the Laws* I.18, though it is highly significant that throughout this work Cicero attributes Stoic ideas not to the school nor even to philosophers, but to "learned men." Where Stoics are explicitly mentioned, it is in a discussion of the demarcation disputes between various Socratic schools and the importance of focusing on their common ground (*Leg.* I.53–6).[15] Overall, the flavor of the books is heavily Platonic (as witnessed by the allusion to recollection at I.25) and for whatever reason Cicero has chosen to conceal the level of Stoic influence (see Inwood 2003).[16]

[13] A consideration of the impact of Cicero's *On the Laws* and *On the Commonwealth* on the development of Roman jurisprudence is included in Vander Waerdt 1994a. See Atkins 2000, sec. 5, for an excellent general account of these two works.

[14] *On the Commonwealth* III contains a defense of the view that justice is natural, based on the famous reply of Diogenes the Stoic to Carneades. Hence, the Stoic credentials of that defense may well be more secure than the theory of *On the Laws* I.

[15] See also *Leg.* I.38, where in an Antiochean spirit Cicero emphasizes that differences between Stoics and Academics are merely verbal.

[16] This issue cannot be discussed at length here, but for now one small observation might be made. The contrast between natural law and positive law is made in *Off.* III.68–9. In this book Cicero is most self-consciously speaking in his own Academic voice, having noted that his Stoic source, Panaetius, left him little to work with. Hence, the Platonic metaphors applied to natural law at the end of *Off.* III.69 (*umbra*, "shadow"; *imagines*, "images") strongly confirm what we also see in *On the Laws*, namely, that Cicero associates what is natural in a normative sense with Platonic idealism and not necessarily with anything characteristically Stoic. On this and related issues, see also Ferrary 1995.

Hence, it is difficult to distinguish with confidence the Ciceronian themes we can claim for the Stoics and those which we cannot—except where there is independent evidence that a given idea is Stoic (as indeed there is on many points). This indeterminacy with regard to the filiation of much of the argument, as well as the sketchy nature of what Cicero says here, help explain why these works have played a less prominent role in the large and well-aired debates about the nature of natural law in Stoic thought.

It may seem peculiar to claim that *On the Laws* gives us a sketchy account of natural law, but this claim can be substantiated by looking at the text. First, though, the following general assessment made by Vander Waerdt should be invoked: Cicero's twin goals in *On the Laws* were to "reformulate Stoic doctrine on natural law so as to make it practically useful, and to reformulate the [Roman] *ius civile* so as to bring it into conformity with this modified Stoic theory" (Vander Waerdt 1994a, 4867). He also maintains that this project was unique and uniquely uninfluential. Vander Waerdt's concern is to show that the Ciceronian project was uninfluential with regard to Roman jurisprudence, but it is just as true that it remained relatively unimportant in later ancient philosophy whether written in Latin or Greek. While the now fragmentary *On the Commonwealth* had a powerful impact in antiquity, just the opposite is the case for *On the Laws*. Zetzel's suggestion (1999, xxi; see also Atkins 2000) is surely right: Cicero never completed the latter book, left off work on it in 51 B.C., and did not think it appropriate to publish it during his lifetime. Left incomplete—in part because changing political circumstances sapped his motivation and in part because he was likely unable to solve serious problems with the consistency and intellectual cohesion of the work as it stood in 51 (cf. Atkins 2000, 501–2)—the work was published posthumously and left to relative neglect for centuries.

In both *On the Commonwealth* and *On the Laws* the central idea is not that "law" in any narrow or well-defined sense is grounded in nature. What matters far more to Cicero is the claim that justice is natural. This is certainly the central point that emerges from *On the Commonwealth*, where Cicero explains what natural law offers us in contrast to human law:

> [The wise man] alone can truly claim all things as his own, not under the law of the Roman people but under the law of the philosophers; not by civil ownership but by the common law of nature, which forbids anything to belong to anyone except someone who knows how to employ and use it. (I.27)

This is a clear reflection of one of the Stoic paradoxes—that all things belong to the wise man, or that only the wise man is wealthy—and we should conclude that one purpose of the Stoic postulation of an ideal cosmopolis is to provide a city in which the paradoxical claims about the wise man are true. Later in the book (I.48–9) Cicero repeats the traditional idea that law is the bond that holds a society together, and suggests that the necessary condition for an ideally stable society is equality under the law. These themes are familiar from earlier Stoic and Cynic thought and ultimately stem, no doubt, from Plato's *Republic*.

The claim that justice exists by nature rather than by potentially variable human convention is explored at greatest length in *On the Commonwealth* III, and it is this idea which we associate most readily with Cicero's treatment of natural law.[17] The principal philosophical claim, as far as philosophy of law is concerned, is that the naturalness and objectivity of moral virtues, including justice, follows from some law-like feature of the natural order of things. The debate played out in Book III is important for political philosophy, but it seems that almost nothing in it turns on any conception of *law*. As with the earlier Stoics and with Plato, Cicero adorns an argument for natural justice in terms of "law" language; but the dress is paper thin.

The more definite claim that there is a natural foundation for specific laws (as opposed to the general institutions of justice) is distinct and far more difficult to defend. It is this claim which comes to the fore in *On the Laws*, especially in Book II. This is a hard position to defend, in part because of the commitment Cicero makes to connect his broad claims about the virtue of justice and a "utopian" natural law (expressed in Stoic terms) with the specific constitutional arrangements of the state sketched in *On the Commonwealth*. That he does take on this commitment in *On the Laws* is indicated by the following:

> Then since we want to preserve and protect that form of the commonwealth which Scipio showed was the best in the six books of *On the Commonwealth*, and since all the laws must be fitted to that type of state, and since morals must be planted and we should not rely on the sanctions of written laws, I will seek the roots of justice in nature, under whose leadership our entire discussion must unfold. (I.20, trans. Zetzel)

Moreover, the exposition of particular laws in *On the Laws* II–III is prefaced by a recapitulation of the utopian conception of natural law as nothing but the perfected practical rationality (in the commanding rather than the theoretical mode) of the wise person or the gods, buttressed by a repetition of the claim that any law which is subject to amendment or abrogation is *eo ipso* not a law at all.

The claim that there is a natural law, then, in contrast to the much more general and less challenging claim that there is a natural foundation for jus-

[17] Cicero does, however, provide a very clear statement of the Chrysippean notion of natural law in a fragment of *On the Laws* III preserved by Lactantius, *Inst.* VI.8.7–9. It begins: "Indeed, true law is right reason in agreement with nature, distributed among all people, consistent, and eternal; it summons to appropriate action by commanding, and by forbidding it deters from wrong-doing." Compare the translation of Chrysippus' *On Law* in Cicero, *Leg.* I.18, which concludes that the natural law in question is the virtue of practical wisdom (*prudentia*). This kind of law is said to have the same features of irrevocability and independence of temporal and spatial contingencies that characterize the utopian natural law of Cicero's *On the Laws* (see below).

tice (and other virtues, too, as a result—see *Leg.* I.42–3) is one of two things. Either it is the claim that there is a divine law which is the perfected rationality of the gods, Zeus, or a perfected human mind (I.18–19, 21–7)—what we might call a Chrysippean conception of natural law, since Cicero is clearly translating the proem to Chrysippus' *On Law* and drawing on Stoic definitions when he identifies law with *recta ratio* (*orthos logos*, "right reason")—or it is the claim that there are laws found in and constitutive of a polity that are grounded in nature via their relationship to the perfect divine law of gods and sages.

To see how sketchy the notion of natural law is in this text, we should consider the options more closely. If by the natural law we mean the perfected rationality of Zeus commanding what ought to be done and forbidding what ought not to be done—that is, the Chrysippean notion of natural law—then we discover in the course of *On the Laws* I and the proem to Book II that its content seems to consist in the virtues and the pursuit of true Socratic utility by perfection of our rational nature and harmonization of it with the divine nature of the cosmos. Hence, its commands would be the sorts of injunctions to act virtuously which are insufficiently action-guiding and hence, from the point of view of *legal* requirements, more or less vacuous.[18] But if we mean by natural law the detailed and contentful specific arrangements given in the rest of *On the Laws*, which are indeed laws that would fit nicely with the kind of state sketched in *On the Commonwealth*, then the problem for Cicero is acute. Are any of the laws which he gives in those books the sorts of permanent, invariant, unamendable, and irrevocable laws which he claims any law must be, on pain of not being any sort of law at all (*Leg.* II.13–14), antedating any written or even conventional instantiation in society (II.8, 10–11, I.19)? No one reading the "laws" of Cicero will claim that these provisions for the idealized republic of Cicero's historical imagination meet this standard.

What we get, then, in *On the Laws* is a powerful and important argument for the natural foundations of justice. It begins in I.16 when Cicero announces that the origin of law and justice will be found in an understanding of human nature, especially our mind, our function, and our natural kinship and unity with other people.[19] By I.21–35 Cicero is arguing for the divine origin of an immutable law which grounds all other laws; it is in itself a feature of the divine mind, but is binding on us humans and our society because we share our nature with the divine. It is only human defects that limit the actualization of

[18] See Inwood 1999. At best, its content will be (as Vander Waerdt 1994c has argued) "appropriate actions" (*kathêkonta*) subject to situational exceptions, but not necessarily fixed and irrevocable "laws" in the sense used in *On the Laws*.

[19] This is, of course, not an idea original to Cicero or even to the Stoics. Yet it recurs consistently in Stoic social and political thought and turns up as being of fundamental importance in Cicero's *On Duties*, written a decade after *On the Laws*.

our godlike potential, so that striving to emulate divine law is something natural for us as humans. Human perfection in virtue is our natural goal, so that the perfection of divine reason has lawlike authority for us, at least if we wish to perfect ourselves and live according to our true nature.

From this broad philosophical argument about the naturalness of human virtue and its kinship with the divine emerges the broadly Chrysippean claim about natural law, that it is perfected reason, human and divine, functioning as the basis and criterion for all normative claims about human behavior. This claim is a common inheritance of the entire Socratic moral tradition (I.37–9).

In the balance of *On the Laws* I Cicero argues for the naturalness of justice, as he did in *On the Commonwealth* III, although the book does end with a rhetorical conclusion that emphasizes our divine origins and the importance of our divine nature. But there is apparently nothing in either work which shows that the facts of nature which ground justice are themselves lawlike; there are only arguments against basing justice on utility and in favor of basing it on permanent and invariable facts of human and divine nature (including natural human sociability). What is divine, wise, perfectly rational, and so forth is genuinely "useful" to human beings and human societies, and just behavior is part of that usefulness.

In *On the Laws*, then, we find a straightforward identification of perfected practical reason and all the virtues that flow from it with "law" in the Chrysippean sense, supported by a splendid exposition of those features of human nature which dictate this perfection.[20] But the lawlike character of this moral and rational perfection seems to be exhausted by the imperatival and authoritative nature of the reason. Nothing else at this level is particularly lawlike; there is no derivation of a code of specific moral rules from this abstract natural law.[21] Where the lawlike features come in is in Books II and III with the specific features of an ideal state. The problem for Cicero is to connect these two kinds of natural law to each other in the way that he claims is the case. But he utterly fails to do so, and the emphasis with which he announces the connection merely underlines this failure. He does not provide even one example of a substantive law that meets the divine utopian criteria that he himself sets out.

In short, Cicero leaves himself in the same dilemma in which many modern students of Stoic natural law seem to find themselves: He can have utopian law, which is equivalent to perfected rationality, or he can have substantial law,

[20] The central features of divine or natural law are recapitulated in the early chapters of Book II.

[21] This is also the view of Schofield 1999b, 767, esp. n. 54: "The idea of natural law is sometimes taken to imply a code of moral rules [...]. But although *kathêkonta* seem to form a system, the fact that they do is not connected in the sources with natural law, whose range of connotations is as indicated above" in *Leg.* I.18–19.

which inevitably fails to meet the demanding and inflexible standard that any perfection will have to manifest. It may be that modern critics of Stoic natural law are in the Ciceronian bind because of direct or indirect Ciceronian influence. It is tempting to guess that Cicero abandoned the project of *On the Laws* in part because he came to see its ultimate incoherence. Cicero perhaps realized that you could not have substantive natural laws without equivocating on the term "law."

It is, however, true that Cicero makes further and significant use of legal concepts in his moral philosophy. The most important example is perhaps the notion that moral decision making should be thought of (to some extent) on the model of legal determinations by a judge who deliberates about the right course of action in a legal case in light of a *formula* ("rule of procedure") for the case in hand. Several passages of *On Duties* III reflect this notion (in particular, III.19–22, 50–53; see Inwood 1999, 120–6). The crucial fact to note in the present context is that this application of legal concepts is both quite independent of the idea of natural law and, it can be argued, more philosophically rewarding than the proposals of *On the Laws*.

6.3. Seneca

Most of Seneca the Younger's life (ca. 4 B.C.–A.D. 65) was spent both in public activities and in studying and writing. He had been tutor to Nero, and after Nero assumed the throne, Seneca shared power with Burrus for several years. After Burrus' death Seneca fell from favor and went into voluntary retirement. Subsequently he was accused of involvement in a conspiracy to kill the emperor, and ordered to commit suicide. One of the most gifted writers of his generation—known for his tragedies as well as for the prose works that are of greatest interest to historians of ideas—he was the next Roman thinker to make a significant contribution to the philosophical use of ideas drawn from the law. Unlike Cicero, Seneca was a professed Stoic, but this did not make him an unreflective transmitter of traditional Stoic arguments and doctrines. He was consistently ready to disagree with his own school and to think through philosophical problems in an independent-minded manner that he thought would be of interest to his Roman readers (see Inwood 1995). Throughout his works he employed various aspects of legal thinking in just this spirit. For Seneca was, like Cicero, educated as an orator in a culture where this in part involved extensive legal training; and he was also a politically active philosopher, though under the markedly different conditions of the Julio-Claudian age.

In some instances, Seneca understands law in a "real world" or narrow sense, that is, the ordinances and conventions of his own time. In the treatise *On Anger*, for example, Seneca consistently presents the law as a sober and unemotional force, able to punish, but doing so without the loss of control and partiality characteristic of an angry man (I.16.5–6). This is an unremarkable connotation for "law." Also familiar is the idea that laws are inflexible and often fall short of the subtlety needed to guide moral deliberations and evaluation.[22] Throughout the treatise *On Favors*, especially in Book III, Seneca acknowledges this point as he argues that the morally significant relationship between willing donor and grateful recipient cannot be legislated. And, again in *On Anger*, Seneca emphasizes that law often has an excessively narrow focus:

> Who is there who can claim that he is innocent under all the laws? And suppose that he can: what a narrow form of innocence it is to be "good" for legal purposes alone! The guidelines for appropriate action extend so much wider than those of the law. Piety, decency, generosity, justice, and honor demand so much, all of which lies beyond the scope of publicly promulgated law [*publicae tabulae*]. (II.28.2)

More interestingly, Seneca makes broad and creative use of various legal ideas. In particular, he exploits the Stoic notion of a natural law in a range of applications that have not often been discussed.[23] This is almost certainly because he does not usually tackle the "problem" of natural law in the form which Cicero's unsuccessful experiment made canonical for the Latin tradition. Augustine and Lactantius looked to Cicero rather than to Seneca for their reflections on the relationship between the realms of divine and human law. It is perhaps not surprising that Christian authors should have turned to the explicitly Platonizing Cicero rather than to the more clearly Stoic Seneca, since the Platonic account of transcendent values fits better with the demands of their theology. The popularity of the "Dream of Scipio"—the conclusion of Book VI of Cicero's *On the Commonwealth*—among Christian readers shows that it was content and not just classical prose style that enabled Cicero to make the mark he did on later authors.

When Seneca writes about natural law, he does so in a way that reflects his distinctive philosophical strengths and weaknesses. Hence, there is little formal system in his use of the concept of natural law; unlike Cicero, he does not even try to use it as a solution to a formally stated philosophical problem. But he does think through several important philosophical issues in terms of various creative applications of the idea of a natural law. These applications are, of course, interconnected, but they can be classified into five uses, outlined as follows: (1) The basic principles of Stoic ethics are thought of as "natural" laws for life. (2) The fundamental sociability of human nature is a special case of this kind of natural law, one that is rooted in our biological nature more obviously than are the principles of Stoic value theory. (3) The basic uniform operations of the physical world are also treated as "laws"; and so too (4) is the

[22] This point is, of course, made by both Plato and Aristotle.

[23] A fuller account of this is given in Inwood 2003. The neglect of Seneca in discussions of natural law is puzzling, given his importance as an author in the Stoic tradition. G. Watson 1971, for example, virtually ignores him. But see Düll 1972, which confirms the realism and legal accuracy of Seneca's handling of legal concepts.

entire system of divinely ordained fate, which is providentially organized for the benefit of all rational animals. But for Seneca, the key sense of natural law emerges as (5) the natural and inevitable fact of human mortality, a sense of natural law which draws on all of the other senses of the term.

(1) In one of Seneca's most important works, *Moral Epistles*, he applies the idea of law to moral concepts in a more direct way, one which transforms the notion of law into a philosophical tool for thinking about the overall governance of our lives. "What, then? Is philosophy not a law for life [*vitae lex*]?" (*Ep.* 94.39). Here he obviously is not using the term "law" (*lex*) in its literal sense. The claim that philosophy is a kind of "law for life" calls to mind the traditional definition of philosophy as an "art of life" (*technê tou biou*), and so yields an ethically important sense of "natural law." Seneca often employs similar language in his description of general moral principles. For example, in the final book of *On Favors*, Seneca is outlining the great invariant moral principles which those making moral progress, the *proficientes*, must cling to and use as a reference point in all of their practical decisions[24]:

> Let him know that nothing is bad except what is shameful and that nothing is good except what is honorable. Let him allot the duties of life by reference to this standard; let him undertake and complete all his duties in accordance with this law, and let him judge to be the most wretched of mortals those who, no matter how great and splendid their wealth may be, are devoted to greed and lust and whose minds lie around in sluggish inactivity. (VII.2.2)

These are the "moral laws" that determine the basic values of things, and so make up the set of *leges totius vitae* ("laws for all of life") (*Ep.* 95.57)[25] and

[24] But it is important to remember that such laws are general, and that they do not dictate to the sage what he ought to do in specific cases. Consider *Ben.* II.18.4 (cf. *Brev. Vit.* XV.5): "Let me remind you repeatedly that I am not talking about sages, who take pleasure in whatever they ought to do and who have control over their own minds and who declare for themselves any law that they want and obey the law they declare [...]." The self-imposed law of sages will, clearly, be in accord with the law of nature. But they do not experience it as an imposition from outside, dictated by a theory they happen to ascribe to. Rather, the law just is their own decision about what to do in the case at hand. In this passage, Seneca is considering choices about who to receive a favor from, an example of the kind of particular moral decision which people must make on a daily basis. But despite the fact that the law is a self-imposed decision, it is no doubt just as deeply rooted in the natural principles that underlie all of the passages considered so far. So too in Letter 70. A wise man, then, lives as long as he ought to, not as long as he can, and the factors which go into deciding how long one ought to live are the kinds of situational particulars with which we are familiar from Aristotle's account of morally sensitive deliberation in the *Nicomachean Ethics*: "He will see where he is to live, in what manner, and what he is to do. He always thinks about the quality of life and not about its length" (*Ep.* 70.4–5). Sometimes circumstances indicate a rapid acquiescence to threatening circumstances (70.5–7), sometimes a delay (70.8–10). There is a particularistic variability in how this kind of situation should be approached. Hence Seneca generalizes: "And so you couldn't make a universal pronouncement on the question of whether, when some external force announces 'death,' one should anticipate it or just wait for it. For there are many considerations which can pull you in either direction" (70.11).

[25] This may be the use of "law" that we see at *Nat.* 3 Pref. 16: "This makes one free not un-

vivendi iura ("laws for living") (*Ep.* 119.15). This kind of "law" can be used to guide character development (*Ep.* 108.6). It also serves to set a limit on the role that wealth and pleasure play in our lives, even on Epicurean principles,[26] and functions as a standard to which we refer when making choices.[27]

(2) The application of legal ideas to moral principles also turns up elsewhere. One of the principles (*Ep.* 95.51–3) asserts the fundamental community of all human beings (cf. Cicero, *Off.* III.20–22). Nature, he says, has made us all blood relatives (*cognati*) and instilled in us a love for our fellow humans, so that the basic moral principle which asserts our fundamental social bond to our fellow man is also a law of nature. This moral principle is regularly referred to with the language of law, especially in *On Favors*. At III.18.2 the "law of humanity" (*ius humanum*) is an assertion of the common humanity of all, slave and free alike, and at VII.18–19 Seneca invokes the "bond of the law of humanity" (*societas iuris humani*), which is broken by the actions of the bloodthirsty tyrant[28]; the same kind of basic bond is referred to as a law of nature (*lex naturae*) at *On Favors* IV.17.3 (see also *Clem.* I.18.2, 19.1–2).[29] The idea that the natural social bonds between humans are like laws relates directly to the idea of a cosmopolis, a universal polity of reason. This idea, which has its roots in Cynic claims and was adopted by both Zeno and Chrysippus among earlier Stoics as well as by Cicero in his *On the Laws* (especially in II.5), turns up in Seneca as well. Although it plays an important role in the fragmentary treatise *On the Private Life*, Seneca's version of Stoic political thought[30] does

der civic law [the *ius Quiritum*] but under the law of nature." Cf. *Ep.* 65.20–22 on the freedom that we have under the law of nature. In both of these cases it is our ability to see the minimal value of life, and so to part with it readily, that constitutes our freedom under natural law. But this assessment of the value of life is precisely one of the basic axiological claims of Stoic ethics. Similarly for the law of death at *Ep.* 70.14–15: The eternal law makes it easy for us to die, a fact emphasized in its relation to human autonomy at *Ben.* VI.3.1.

[26] See *Ep.* 4.10, 25.4, 27.9, where *lex naturae* is used to refer to the limits imposed by nature in Epicurean ethics.

[27] Law as a *kanôn* (or "standard" to refer to) appears in the proem to Chrysippus' *On Law* (*SVF* 3.314); see also Cicero, *Leg.* I.18.

[28] This is again comparable to the view Cicero takes of Caesar's tyranny in *On Duties*.

[29] At *Ep.* 48.2–3 such bonds are called "the common law of mankind."

[30] Seneca's own original reflections on political philosophy are perhaps best represented in his *On Clemency*, a now fragmentary treatise, addressed to the emperor Nero, which (in a striking departure from Roman political traditions) explicitly recasts the role of *princeps* ("first citizen") in the tradition of Hellenistic monarchical regimes. Although this work shows the influence of earlier and Greek theories of monarchy, and although it stands out as an early example of the *speculum principis* ("mirror of princes") genre of political writing, there is little about the philosophy of law (as opposed to political thought) in the work. In *Clem.* I.19, however, the idea of natural law is invoked to reinforce the claim that clemency is the regal virtue *par excellence*, and in the course of this discussion he advances the important but scarcely original argument that kingship is natural based on the analogy with the animal kingdom. The "king" bee is a model for human kings both in the natural legitimacy of his authority and in his mildness in the use of that authority: "the king himself has no stinger." Setting aside the

not otherwise make extensive use of the idea of a universal commonwealth of reason:

We must grasp that there are two public realms, two commonwealths. One is great and truly common to all, where gods as well as men are included, where we look not to this corner or that, but measure its bounds with the sun. The other is that in which we are enrolled by the accident of birth—I mean Athens or Carthage or some other city that belongs not to all men but only a limited number. Some devote themselves at the same time to both commonwealths, the greater and the lesser, some only to one or the other. (IV.1)

(3) Seneca also uses legal language and ideas to express the familiar notion of a natural law as a uniform natural process or the principles which determine it. The underlying notions are fixity and nonarbitrariness, and therefore reliability. For example, in *On Anger* Seneca emphasizes the irrationality of projecting onto the gods and the natural world the kind of vengeful mentality humans are capable of:

And so it is madmen and those who are ignorant of the truth who blame the gods for the sea's cruelty, for torrential rains, and for a stubbornly prolonged winter, while all the time none of the things which harm or help us are directed specifically at us. For *we* are not the motivation for the cosmos to bring back summer or winter; they have their own laws, laws by which divine matters are worked out. We think too highly of ourselves if we think that we are worthy objects of such great activities. Therefore none of these things is done to hurt us, rather they are done to help us. (II.27.2)[31]

(4) Seneca does not restrict the language of law to individual phenomena that occur in an orderly, predictable, and stable way. In fact, he more often uses the language of law to refer to larger and more comprehensive patterns of events in the cosmos, often making it explicit that this is the same as fate. This is clear in *On Providence*:

I am not compelled and I suffer nothing against my will. It is not that I am a slave to god; I give him my assent, all the more so because I know that everything proceeds in accordance with a law [*lege*] which is certain and proclaimed for all eternity. The fates lead us and the first hour of our birth determines how much time remains for each person. (V.6–7)

This lawlike stability and predictability can also be expressed as a feature of the gods' rationality (*Nat.* I Pref. 3; cf. II.35ff.). At one point he says, "consider too that external pressures do not compel the gods. Rather, their own will is an eternal law for them" (*On Favors* VI.23.1). In making a law for themselves by their rational decision, the gods provide us humans with the most reliable framework for our own lives, since they cannot change away from what is already determined to be the best possible arrangement: "Nor do they persist

obvious defects of ancient entomology, this rhetorical argument for regal clemency has little philosophical force.

[31] Cf. *On Providence* I.2; *Ep.* 65.19, 117.19; and frequently throughout the *Natural Questiones* (e.g., *Nat.* III.15–16, VI.1.12).

because of any weakness, but because they do not choose to deviate from what is best and because they had resolved on taking this path" (VI.23.2). This lawlike divine decree has built into it a consideration of the best interests of mankind.[32]

Of course, it is one thing to know that the events of fate are governed by a lawlike rationality and quite another to know the details of what is to come. In Letter 101.5 Seneca says, "To be sure, time does proceed by a 'fixed law' [*rata lege*], but amidst obscurity. However, what is it to me if nature is certain about what I am uncertain about?" Seneca elsewhere argues that it is useful to know *that* whatever happens proceeds from a fixed law; and because it is a divine law, he elsewhere maintains that this knowledge is a crucial component of piety toward the gods (*Ep.* 76.23). Not to see and accept that such unpleasant eventualities as our own death are governed by this law (stable, predictable, part of a benevolent plan) is folly. Daily uncertainty about such prospects is a source of wretchedness; the rational solution is to live each day as though it were our last (*Ep.* 101.7–8).

(5) Seneca concentrates heavily on the inevitability of the transitions and changes dictated by nature as part of what makes nature's functioning lawlike. His interest in this feature of the general laws of nature is so strong that it makes sense to think of it as a distinct application of the metaphor, and to label it the "law of mortality" (*lex mortalitatis*) (see *de Ira* II.28.4; cf. *de Vita Beata* XV.5; *Nat.* VI.32.12; *Ep.* 94.7, 123.16). It is, of course, prominent in consolatory contexts. In *To His Mother Helvia* VI.8 Seneca refers to the "law and necessity of nature" (*lex et naturae necessitas*) that governs people's comings and goings, and later in the same work (XIII.2) he explicitly claims that if we regard death not as a penalty but rather as a law of nature we will be able to conquer the fear of death. In the *Consolation to Marcia* Seneca (sec. 10, esp. 10.3, 10.5) refers to the law governing human life. The "law of birth" (*lex nascendi*) is that we are mortal and transient beings; being born under the terms and conditions of this law, we cannot reasonably complain about it when the inevitable occurs. Of course, this idea also turns up elsewhere. In Letter 77.12 Seneca emphasizes again features of the law of mortality into which we are all born: It is fixed and established, necessary, predictable and comprehensible, uniformly applicable to all. Death is a law for humans because it represents the impartial and fair terms under which we all live. Like any just legal regime in the human sphere, nature treats all its subjects alike (*Ep.* 30.11).

Nature's law has the same features as a good human law, and it is for this reason that it commands our rational allegiance. Just as Socrates in the *Crito* submitted to the laws of Athens because of his agreement to live under them as a fair bargain,[33] so too the Stoic envisaged in *Cons. Marc.* 17–18 faces the

[32] Similar considerations lie behind the language of law at *Ep.* 16.5–6.

[33] Alluded to at *Ep.* 70.9: "Socrates could have ended his life by starving himself and could

perils of life and death with tranquility and resolution just because those risks are part of what he or she chose as part of the overall bargain of life, and because those terms and conditions were, Seneca suggests in section 17, disclosed fully and honestly ("I deceive no one"). Complaint against misfortune would, in the circumstances, be unreasonable: "After the promulgation of these laws [*leges*], if you raise children you exempt the gods from any resentment, for the gods have promised you nothing for certain" (17.7). The seemingly harsh facts of life, elsewhere called the law of mortality, are presented to us by nature in a speech that is honest and frank. There are facts of nature that we all know—or are deemed to know—and these are public and impersonal, known to all, like laws posted on public display. Anything one undertakes in the light of these laws is done on one's own responsibility. It is either unfair or irrational to complain about the application of laws to which one has willingly bound oneself. In a similar vein, at Letter 91.15, Seneca considers our proper reaction to the often unpredictable power of *fortuna* ("fate"):

> None of this is grounds for outrage. We have come into a world where life is governed by these laws. If it suits you, obey. If not, leave however you like. Be outraged if any unfair conditions have been set down for you in particular; but if the same necessity binds the mighty and humble, then be reconciled with fate, by which all things are settled.

Even in this very brief discussion (see also Inwood 2003), it is clear that Seneca exploits the concept of law in a sophisticated philosophical way. Similar lessons can be drawn about his use of the idea of judgment (*iudicium*) or judging (*iudicare*), which is drawn quite concretely from the legal realm (see Inwood 2004). Just as Cicero drew on the procedures of the praetorian tribunal in his account of how moral decision making might best be undertaken (see previous section and Inwood 1999), Seneca developed a range of valuable philosophical and moral ideas using the language and concepts of law.

6.4. Epictetus

Both Epictetus and Marcus Aurelius, the other Stoics of the Roman empire whose works survive *in extenso*, make a similar and quite limited contribution to the philosophy of law in antiquity. This contribution is closely tied to the Stoic tradition of natural law theory and virtually devoid of the kind of independent developments so visible in Seneca.

Epictetus was an ethnic Greek educated in Rome, with the greater part of his philosophical training coming from his study with the Roman knight Mu-

have died by lack of food rather than by poison. Nevertheless he passed thirty days in jail, waiting for death, not in the belief that 'anything could happen and that such a long time gave grounds for many hopes.' Rather, [he stayed] in order to submit to the laws [*ut praeberet se legibus*] and to make available to his friends Socrates in his final days."

sonius Rufus.[34] He was for some time a slave of Epaphroditus, a powerful figure at Nero's court, and after the expulsion from Italy of philosophers under the Flavians he operated a Stoic school in Nicopolis across the Adriatic Sea. As one might expect, his works reflect the full range of Stoic ideas about natural law and the lawlike quality of moral norms. But two features distinguish him from Seneca. First, he is far more interested in the Cynic heritage of Stoic thought than Seneca was, which comes out in his adoption of cosmopolitan theory. And second, he is less prone than Seneca (and Cicero) to use legal ideas in a creative way to forge new philosophical insights.

What Epictetus gives is, for the most part, an embroidered restatement of the early Stoic idea of natural law rather than any new theory. But it would be unfair to leave it at that, for with respect to the notion of "freedom" Epictetus develops earlier Stoic thought with a new emphasis. Like other Stoics, and like Seneca, Epictetus appreciates the limitations of legal institutions in contrast with moral realities. In *Discourses* II.1.21–8 he contrasts merely legal freedom with the moral autonomy that philosophical education can bring. In I.12 and elsewhere (in particular, *Diss.* IV.1, entitled "On Freedom") Epictetus reveals his own particular interest in the idea of "freedom," transferred from the political and legal sphere, as a leading notion in moral reflection. Bobzien (1998, chap. 7) has demonstrated Epictetus' originality on this point. Epictetus makes distinctive and creative use of a broadly legal concept; however, the relevance of the *legal* content is quite limited.

Where Epictetus stays closer to the Stoic tradition, the idea of laws plays a more obvious role. He thus tends to regard moral principles as being lawlike, an idea crystallized in the *Enchiridion* 50–51, where he urges that we regard moral resolutions as inviolable laws. Following nature, the Stoic ideal, is regarded as obedience to a law (*Diss.* I.26.1–2) and such moral norms are frequently treated as divine law (I.29.13, 19; II.16.28; III.17.6)—in accordance with the Stoic equation of god and nature (cf. IV.12.11).

Another traditional Stoic application of natural law is the claim that human social bonds are embedded in nature, and Epictetus accepts this enthusiastically. As rational animals (III.7.33–5) and as "children of Zeus" (I.13.4) all humans are brothers who are bound together in a natural community of social relations (II.10.14; IV.11.1), which (in a polemical spirit) Epictetus thinks that even an Epicurean would have to recognize (I.23.1). It is a mark of divine care for humans, and our own proper benefit is interdependent with the common benefit for the entire polity. This nexus of ideas does draw on natural law, but here the original contribution of Epictetus lies with his development of the idea that all rational animals are "children of Zeus" (see Inwood 1996) rather than with his exploitation of legal concepts.

[34] For the most recent and authoritative general account of Epictetus' philosophical character, see A. Long 2002.

The Stoic claim that we have a natural connection to each other qua rational beings has from the beginning found expression in the idea that we are all citizens of one universal commonwealth, an idea which Cicero and Seneca touch on but which Epictetus uses repeatedly. Thus *Discourses* I.9 contrasts at some length local citizenship, such as Athenian or Corinthian, with cosmopolitan bonds, and does so in a manner reminiscent of Cicero and Seneca. It is very much in character for Epictetus to emphasize the Socratic roots of this idea, as he does here. However, although this idea is widespread in Epictetus' works (II.5.26, 15.10; III.22.84–5, 24.66), there is little that is novel in his development of it. As a "cosmopolite" one has the rationality to understand the divine ordering of the world (II.10.3) of which one is a part (I.9.4–5, 12.7, 29.29)—a contributing part, to be sure, but still a mere part whose value is derived from the superior value of the whole (II.10.5). Epictetus applies rather than develops the familiar idea that rational beings are citizens of a single cosmic city (III.24.10) whose ruler is god (II.14.26–7).

Just as Seneca occasionally reflected on the philosopher's obligations with regard to the laws of his own real-world state, so too did Epictetus, characteristically looking to Socrates as a role model. But Socrates is a complex character, committed to the civic laws in the *Crito* and strong in his defiance of temporal authority in the anecdote about Leon of Salamis in the *Apology*. Epictetus reflects this complexity (III.24.107; IV.1.160, 7.30). In general, the standard Stoic balance between one's social commitments to the laws and mores of society and one's higher moral and philosophical commitments as a rational agent is reflected in Epictetus. We have social duties as family members and citizens (III.2.4, 3.8, 7.21). But in every case our highest duty is to philosophical values, since even these will bring the most genuine service to our society (*Ench.* 24.4). Ultimately, and *only* in cases of conflict between them, we obey the laws of god and not man, following the example of Socrates. The jurisconsults mentioned in *Discourses* IV.3.12 cannot obligate a rational agent to obey when their laws conflict with those of god. *Discourses* I.13.5 is brutal: Laws and conventions that are in conflict with divine law are "the laws of corpses." One could have no clearer or more forceful statement of the priority of cosmic and divine values, thought of as laws of nature, over the merely temporal values of our civic and political lives. It is a powerful expression indeed, but an expression of a traditional idea in the Platonic and Stoic tradition. Epictetus' contribution lies primarily in this expressive power and not in the creative development of new ways to think about moral philosophy using legal concepts and language.

6.5. Marcus Aurelius

The same might fairly be said of Marcus Aurelius Antoninus, who was emperor from A.D. 161 until his death in 180. Though deeply influenced by Epictetus and manifestly Stoic in his basic sympathies, Marcus was not a Stoic in the narrow sense that comes with official school membership or working as a teacher of Stoic philosophy. But he did not present himself as a member of another school, as did the Academic Cicero. Like Seneca (though even more so) he was a member of the ruling elite of the empire, with an education in rhetoric and law as well as in philosophy. So it would not be at all surprising if he had developed creative applications of legal concepts in his philosophical reflection. But for all the interest and insight of his one small book, *To Himself*, it must be said that this work lacks originality on this point.

Nevertheless, the full range of familiar themes involving law and politics is evident in this poignant philosophical diary. He treats the imperatives of reason as "laws" of nature and regards them as being like the law code of a cosmic city governed by rational principles. Even the most unpleasant aspect of nature, our inevitable death, must be regarded as a responsibility to be embraced in a spirit of tranquil rationality. Our fulfillment as rational beings comes through following nature in the traditional Stoic sense, and the foundations of political and social life lie in a natural sociability that it is our duty to cultivate in the practical sphere.

The continuity of Marcus' thought on these matters with that of the early Stoic school is evident from the similarity between what he says in *Meditations* IV.4 (cf. III.2) and the views of Chrysippus:

> If the capacity to think is common to us all, then so too is the reason in virtue of which we are rational. And if this is common, then the reason which commands what ought to be done and what not is also common. And if this is so, then law is common. And if this is so, then we are citizens. And if this is so, then we participate in a political community. And if this is so, then the cosmos is, as it were, a city-state. For in what other political community can one say that the entire human race participates on a common basis? It is from that source, this common cosmic city, that we derive our capacity for thought, our capacity for reason, and our capacity for law.

This cosmic reason lays down rational requirements for our behavior (III.11.3), which we obey as a kind of law grounded in our reason—the fulfillment of which is an expression of our own end (II.16). Our obedience to such a law is, then, an act of human fulfillment as well as an obedience to forces greater and more valuable than we possess. This is in large measure because being rational involves being social (V.30; cf. VI.40, VIII.54), especially on the cosmic scale, and the society to which our rationality gives us access is hierarchical and organized around a single, all-embracing value:

> All things are intertwined and the bond which unites them is sacred. Virtually nothing is alien to anything else, for all things are organized in one whole and together they make up one cosmos. For there is but one cosmos made up of all things, and one god permeating all things, one substance, and one law, which is the reason common to all animals with the capacity to think. (VII.9)

As Cicero claimed in *On the Laws*, this shared rationality is grounded in the divine and in a cosmic law. We find ourselves fulfilled as individuals by playing our role in the hierarchy of nature (*Med.* IX.9; II.9; VII.5) and in respecting the sociability which comes from sharing in a rational nature with our fellow human beings (XI.1.2), working to promote a common good even through our misfortunes (V.8.3, 7.5). This fundamentally social commitment does not alienate us from ourselves, because its sociability is rooted in our own rational nature, living according to which constitutes a pious life (I.17.5; II.9, 5.3, 9.1, 10.2). The general picture is that human rationality, sociability, and naturalness all converge in a kind of character and way of life that is ultimately *right* for us as individuals and also binds us to the universe and our fellow man (V.29; VII.11).

This kind of life according to nature is cosmopolitan in the original Stoic sense (X.15), and this cosmic nature is the foundation for our basic moral and political responsibilities (VIII.12; IX.23, 2; XI.10). Not only does Marcus claim, following his Stoic predecessors, that we should understand our relationship to fundamental moral values on the model of political and legal ideas, but also that our own social nature is itself rooted in (if not an imitation of) the social order of the universe as such.

These ideas are found throughout Marcus' book, and they are expressed with a passion and literary flair that (as far as we can tell) far exceeds that of his predecessors. In many passages he expresses these ideas in a way that suggests the influence of Platonism as well as Stoicism—something which should not surprise us, given both the integration of Stoic and Platonic ideas evident already in Cicero's work and the striking growth of Platonic sentiments in philosophy under the Roman empire. But as with Epictetus, there is relatively little, if any, creative application of distinctively legal ideas or concepts to philosophical purposes.

6.6. Ancient Roman Conceptions of Rights

"Justice is an unswerving and perpetual determination to acknowledge all men's rights [*ius*]." This pronouncement, attributed to Ulpian (*Rules* I *ap.* Justinian *Dig.* I.1.10 pr.), which is the opening sentence of Justinian's *Institutes* (I.1 pr.), implies that the law, insofar as it is just, protects human rights.[35] Indeed, the three parts of Roman law—of persons, of things, and of actions (*Inst.* I.2.12)—each seem to be concerned with rights. For example, the law of persons involves rights "such as the rights of a father over his children or the right of freedom itself" (Nicholas 1962, 98). It also includes the right to own, and to grant freedom to, slaves (*Inst.* I.3–8).

The Roman law of things corresponds to modern property rights. A thing (*res*) may be corporeal (e.g., land, slaves, gold, etc.) or incorporeal. The latter "consist of legal rights—inheritance, usufruct, obligations however con-

[35] All translations of Justinian's *Institutes* in this section are from Birks and McLeod 1987.

tracted." Even though what one inherits may be corporeal (e.g., a house), "the actual right of inheritance is incorporeal, as is the actual right to the use and fruits of a thing, and the right inherent in an obligation" (*Inst.* II.2.2). Roman law distinguished between ownership of property and mere possession (*Inst.* IV.6.1; cf. Ulpian *ap.* Justinian *Dig.* XLI.2.12). It also identified "lesser real rights," which were "universally applicable" and "protected by remedies available against the world at large. The rights in question were 'lesser' in the sense that their scope was less than that of ownership," but they "had the common feature of placing a limitation upon the right of ownership from which they were abstracted" (D. Miller 1998, 65). Usufruct is such a lesser right: Thus, a person may leave to his heir the bare ownership of an orchard, but to someone else a usufruct, the right to the use and fruits of the orchard (*Inst.* II.4.1).

Modern readers are especially disposed to understand the law of actions in terms of juridical rights. "An action is nothing but a right [*ius*] to go to court to get one's due" (*Inst.* IV.6). The Roman jurists made an important distinction between two kinds of action: *in personam*, against a particular individual who is obligated to the plaintiff as a result of a contract or a tort (e.g., a claim of repayment of a debt), and *in rem*, against a defendant who is not under any kind of obligation to the plaintiff but is involved in a dispute with him over a thing (e.g., a suit over ownership of a house). It is apparent to the modern reader that such actions imply disputes over legal rights. Nicholas (1962, 100) remarks, "The Romans think in terms of actions not of rights, but in substance one action [i.e., *in rem*] asserts a right over a thing, the other [i.e., *in personam*] a right against a person, and hence comes the modern dichotomy between rights *in rem* and rights *in personam*." When a *ius* is based on a contract or delict, it corresponds to a right in the sense of a claim that entails a correlative duty (see Hohfeld 1923).

Aside from legal rights in the narrow sense, Post (1973, 687) sees in Roman law "a real concern for human rights. Influenced by the ideals of Stoicism, Ulpian and other great jurisconsults of the Golden Age of the Empire subjected all laws, private and public, to the natural law as a universal reason that should be observed in legislation and in all judicial decisions of courts." Bauman (2000, 8–9) argues "that the notion of human rights was well understood in Ancient Rome," and "that the Roman model was the ancestor of modern human rights." Mitsis (1999, 155) focuses on the Stoic philosophers, who "offer an account in which natural rights are bounded by natural law and grounded in a particular conception of a natural human *telos* and a natural impulse to community and social solidarity."

A number of Latin locutions correspond to the different senses of "rights" distinguished by Hohfeld (1923)[36]:

[36] See the discussion of Hohfeld and of corresponding Greek "rights" locutions in Chapter 4, Section 4.8, of this volume.

Hohfeld	Latin
just claim	*ius*
liberty, privilege	*libera potestas, facultas*
authority	*dominius, auctoritas*
immunity, exemption	*immunitas*

Some of these locutions occur in the so-called "Edict of Milan" (313), whereby the Emperors Constantine and Licinius granted religious liberty to Christians and pagans alike. In addition to its historical importance, this edict is of interest because the original Latin text was preserved by Lactantius (ca. 240–ca. 320) in *De Mortibus Persecutorum* 48, and a Greek translation by Eusebius (ca. 260–ca. 339) in his *Ecclesiastical History* X.5.1–14, thus providing evidence of parallels between Roman and Greek legal terminology in the fourth century. The emperors "grant both to Christians and to all men free power [*libera potestas* = *eleuthera hairesis*] to follow whatever religion each one wished." The emperors decided that "no one was to be denied the liberty [*facultas* = *exousia*] to follow the Christian worship or that religion which he felt to be suited to himself." The emperors granted Christians "the free and unconditional power" (*libera atque absoluta potestas* = *eleuthera kai apolelumenê exousia*) of religion. Others, too, have been granted this opportunity (*facultas* = *exousia*), so that "each individual may have the free 'opportunity' [*libera facultas* = *exousia*] to choose and practice whatever form of worship he wishes." They also recognize that property belongs by right (*ius* = *to dikaion*) to Christian congregations and command restoration of such property to these bodies. To be sure, these rights of religious freedom were conferred by an imperial rescript and were not asserted as natural rights against the Roman state. Constantine himself later issued decrees prohibiting pagan rituals and declared Christian heresy to be, in principle, illegal (Eusebius, *Life of Constantine* II.45.1, III.64–5; see Barnes 1981, 209–10, 224–5).

In spite of the foregoing arguments, a number of scholars have resisted the thesis that the ancient Romans grasped the concept of rights (for references, see Tierney 1997, 15, n. 11). It may be helpful to distinguish two questions: Is there a counterpart to "a right" in Roman legal reasoning? And did Roman philosophers and jurists anticipate the modern doctrine of human rights? Regarding the first question, Nicholas (1962, 100, quoted above) cautions, "The Romans think in terms of actions not of rights." In contrast, for the modern jurist, "rights rather than actions have become the primary concept," so that strict Roman distinctions tend to become blurred. For example, a typical Roman action *in rem* would involve ownership, whereas an action *in personam* would seek restitution for injury to one's property. On the modern rights view, however, the plaintiff's right to compensation presupposes a prior right against injury by the defendant, which implies that the right *in rem* to property involves a bundle of rights *in personam.*

Villey issues a more radical challenge, arguing that rights are alien to Roman law.[37] In Ulpian's above-cited pronouncement that "[j]ustice is an unswerving and perpetual determination to acknowledge all men's rights," the phrase "all men's rights" translates *ius suum cuique*, literally, "to each his own right." Villey begins with the observation that *ius* or "right" has two different senses: In the *objective* sense, it means that a state of affairs is right or just; and in the *subjective* sense, it means *a right* which belongs to an individual subject. In some cases the former sense is clearly meant, for example, "written *ius* is law [*lex*], etc." (*Inst.* I.2.3). Villey argues that the word *ius* did not have the subjective sense for the ancient Romans, because the word acquired this meaning—that is, a licit power—only in the later Middle Ages, in particular in the writings of William of Ockham. Villey (1946, 217) points out that in some instances *ius* does not correspond to a right, for example, when Gaius (*Inst.* II.14) refers to the *ius* of a homeowner to take the overflow from a neighbor's gutter through his own property.[38] In this case, according to Villey, *ius* refers to the entire rightful relationship, which moderns construe in terms of rights and duties of the respective parties. Villey (1946, 219; 1953–1954, 173) also argues that the concept of *dominium* does not entail rights, a fact implied, for example, in the distinction between ownership and usufruct. Ulpian, for example, says, "The only person who can claim at law that he has a right [*ius*] to use and enjoy property is the man who has the usufruct of it. The owner [*dominus*] of the estate cannot do so, as a man who has the ownership does not have a separate right [*ius*] of use and enjoyment" (*Edict* XVII *ap.* Justinian *Dig.* VII.6.5 pr.).

A number of scholars have responded that, while Villey is correct that "Roman jurists did not conceive of the legal order as essentially a structure of individual rights in the manner of some modern ones" (Tierney 1997, 18), he goes too far in banishing individual rights altogether from Roman law. Pugliese (1954) objects that the mere fact that Latin terms like *ius* do not correspond exactly to modern "rights" locutions does not prove that the Romans lacked the concept of a subjective right. Kaser points out that, although *ius* has an objective character, it can also be used in a subjective sense, as in *meum ius*, "my right": When *ius* is subjectively interpreted as someone's entitlement, "the *objective* meaning of *ius* is also intended at the same time, because it defines the basis, the content and the limits of the entitlement" (Kaser 1996). Zuckert

[37] Villey's case is set forth in a series of influential essays, three volumes of collected essays, and several books: see the bibliography. For clear and concise summaries of his argument, see Tuck 1979, 7–13; Tierney 1997, 15–22.

[38] However, the translation of Gordon and Robinson 1988 glosses "a right of streams or run-offs," as "that a neighbor receive a stream or run-off to his buildings or his site."

(1989, 74) also notes "the easy migration of meaning from objective to subjective right: if one begins with right in the objective sense of 'the right or just thing in itself,' that is, the correct assignment or relation of things to person, then the 'part' in that distribution that pertains to each readily becomes the basis for the assertion of a claim of the subjective right sort. From being 'in the right' it is easy to move to 'having a right' [...]" (cf. Tierney 1997, 33). Furthermore, in Roman law, "[o]ur authority [*potestas*] over our children is a right [*ius*] which only Roman citizens have" (Justinian, *Inst.* I.9.2). This treats a right as an authorized exercise of a power (*potestas*), which Villey views as Ockham's innovation. Finally, scholars question Villey's dichotomy between *dominium* and *ius*. For example, Gaius says that although "slaves are in the power [*potestas*] of their owners [*dominorum*] [...] we ought not to abuse our rights [*nostre iure*]" (*Inst.* I.52). Tierney (1997, 17) remarks, "It is hard not to see here an assertion of the subjective *right* of the master consisting in his *power* over the slave who was under his *dominium*."

Aside from legal rights, there is the thorny issue of whether the Romans anticipated "natural rights" or "human rights" in the modern sense. Mitsis contends that Stoicism was a philosophical source for natural rights. On his interpretation, all human beings belong to a cosmic state governed by natural law, which, according to Chrysippus, is the "standard of right and wrong, prescribing to animals whose nature is political what they should do, and prohibiting them from what they should not do" (Marcian, *Institutes* I = *SVF* III.314, trans. Long and Sedley 67R). Just as the law of a particular city defines the rights and duties of each of its citizens, so natural law defines the moral rights and duties of each citizen of the cosmos (*kosmopolitês*) (see Mitsis 1999, 162–3). But this interpretation faces serious objections.

First, it is objected that the Stoics subscribed to an ethics of duty rather than a theory of rights (see Sorabji 1993, 134–57). That is, the Stoics are concerned with achieving a good life, through acting virtuously and living according to nature, rather than with recognizing the rights of others. A Stoic practices the virtue of friendship because he wants to be virtuous not because he is concerned about his friend's well-being.

Against this objection, Mitsis (1999, 168) points out that the Stoics distinguished between the motive for an action and its end or object. "A Stoic may be motivated to help someone by recognizing that such an action conforms to a duty enjoined by nature's law. But the object of that action is the benefit of the individual needing help" (see Seneca, *Ben.* VI.13.3). Insofar as they view the interests of others as the object of their moral duties, the Stoics may be able to cross the divide between duty and rights. Bauman (2000) also argues along similar lines, claiming that the Roman idea of *ius humanum* ("human right") is based on a general principle of *humanitas* (benevolence) and *clementia* (clemency). He finds this ideal expressed by Seneca, who speaks of a society (*societas*), "which makes us mingle as humans with our fellow humans and judges that the human race has certain rights [*ius*] in common" (*Ep.* 48.3).[39] Seneca lays down the following rule or principle (*formula*) concerning our duties toward other human beings:

> Everything that you see, both divine and human, is one; we are the parts of one great body. Nature created us as relatives, for she created us from the same source and for the same end. She has endowed us with mutual love and sociability. She fashioned fairness and justice. According to her regulation it is worse to suffer than to inflict harm. Through her authority let our hands be prepared for what needs help. Let this verse be in your hearts and on your lips: "I am human; I regard nothing human as foreign to me" (Terence, *Heautontimorumenos* 77). Let us have common ownership; our birth is in common. (*Ep.* 95.52–3; see Bauman 2000, 97)

According to Bauman, this principle of *humanitas* was combined with the ideal of *Pax Romana*, a Roman empire that embraced the civilized world and extended clemency even to defeated barbarians, resulting in a moral universalism that prepared the way for the modern doctrine of human rights.

Second, it is objected that the principle of human rights seems to conflict with the brutal realities of Roman law, especially slavery. Ulpian's principle that justice acknowledges all men's rights sounds to moderns like "a resounding [...] affirmation of the sanctity of human rights," but it "must be given a very much more limited scope in view of the fact that among the rights secured by justice in Roman law was that which permitted one person to hold another as a slave" (MacCormack 1998, 1). Ulpian himself says that everyone would be born free by the natural law (*Inst.* I *ap.* Justinian *Dig.* I.1.3) and that "as far as concerns the natural law all men are equal" (Sabinus XLIII *ap.* Justinian *Dig.* L.17.32); and Florentinus also calls slavery "against nature" (*Institutes* IX *ap.* Justinian *Dig.* I.5.4; cf. Justinian *Inst.* I.3.12). Nonetheless, the Roman jurists did not condemn slavery on these grounds (Johnston 2000, 621).

It should be noted, however, that modern proponents of rights, including the American founders, have condoned slavery. Arguably, some Roman philosophers implicitly undermined the moral foundations of slavery. Mitsis (1999, 102) remarks that "the Stoics are the first thinkers in antiquity to develop a view of rights that is natural in the stronger sense of being naturally attached to individuals by the mere fact that they are human beings and, as such, members of a natural human community." Seneca counseled, "Remember that he whom you call your slave sprang from the same stock and breathes, lives, and dies under the same skies as you. Treat your slaves as you would be treated by your superiors. Live mercifully and humanely with your slave, allow him to talk with you, plan with you, live with you" (*Ep.* 47.1–13, as quoted in Bauman 2000, 116). The Romans did in fact make reforms to ameliorate slavery (see Bauman 2000, 115–200). The Stoic emperor Antoninus Pius (161–180) insti-

[39] See the discussion of *ius humanum* in connection with Seneca's use (2) of "natural law" in Section 6.3 above.

tuted legal curbs on cruelty to slaves, making "a man who kills his own slave without good grounds liable to the same punishment as one who kills someone else's slave," and compelling cruel masters to sell their slaves (Justinian, *Inst.* I.8.2). The Romans never abolished the institution, but their philosophers and jurists, by theorizing about natural law and rights, helped pave the way for the moral condemnation of slavery.

Finally, the Romans possessed no document like a modern bill of rights, which delineated citizens' rights and circumscribed the powers of government. However, some scholars argue that Roman citizens possessed various legal rights that foreshadowed the rights enumerated in the U.S. Bill of Rights, including the right of free speech; the right against unreasonable arrest, search, and seizure; the right of the accused to receive due process and a trial by jury, and to be confronted with the witnesses against him (see Wiltshire 1992; Plescia 1995; and Herrmann and Speer 1994). Although it would be an anachronism to attribute a developed theory of human rights to the ancient Romans, the doctrine had roots in ancient Roman thought.

Our interest in this chapter has been in the creative application of ideas drawn from the law in Roman philosophy rather than in those aspects of the traditional Stoic or Stoic-Platonic theory of natural law that were merely reproduced by Roman thinkers. Epictetus and Marcus, working in a Roman milieu but writing in Greek, show surprisingly little innovation in this regard. The Stoic and Platonic ideas expressed in legal-philosophical terms are by and large the familiar ideas from the early generations of the Stoic school. With Cicero we do see more innovation, though to some extent we also see a difficult struggle to maintain consistency within his project of rethinking Roman political ideas along more philosophical lines. The most creative work—on natural law and, indirectly, on human rights—was done, it seems, by Seneca, and arguably the reason for this has a good deal to do with his freshness of approach. For Seneca, more than for Epictetus and Marcus, legal ideas were a part of his apparatus for thinking through independent philosophical questions. Fresh questions and independent thinking about them produce results that a mere reworking of the tradition cannot achieve. This is as true in the philosophy of law and politics as it is elsewhere. On a topic that is so burdened by the unreflective replication of traditional views as is the natural law tradition, such boldness is particularly welcome.

Further Reading

Brief histories of Roman law include Wolff 1951, Tellegen-Couperus 1993 (with a chronological table and bibliography), and Riggsby 2010 (with annotated bibliography). Jolowicz and Nicholas 1972 is a more comprehensive historical introduction to Roman law. Robinson 1997 is a helpful introduction to the sources, and Buckland 1931, Schulz 1992 (orig. 1951), and Nicholas 1962 offer overviews of legal institutions. Buckland 1939 and Bürge 1999 discuss Roman private law. Borkowski and du Plessis 2005 is a useful textbook on Roman civil law. Stein 1988 also offers essays on Roman civil law. Birks 1989 contains essays on the law of property. Crook 1967 and Daube 1969 discuss Roman law in its social and economic context. Watson has published numerous books on Roman law; see Watson 1995a for a summation of his views.

Useful collections of ancient Roman statutes include Johnson, Coleman-Norton, and Bourne 1961 (with English translation, commentary, and glossary), Crawford 1996 (epigraphic and other material with English translation and commentary), Flach 1994 (text with commentary of laws from the early Republic), and Elster 2003 (German translation with commentary of laws from the middle Republic: 366–134 B.C.).

The main source for the jurists is Justinian's *Digest*. Watson published in 1985 a valuable 4 volume edition with Latin text and English translation; there is a convenient paper reprint in 1998 (2 volumes) with the English translation only. On the rise of the early jurists see Frier 1985. Gordon and Robinson 1988 provide a Latin text and English translation to Gaius' *Institutes* with a useful glossary. Honoré 1962 is a study of Gaius, Honoré 1982 of Ulpian, and Honoré 1994 a general history of the role of lawyers in the Roman empire. Pharr 1952 is an English translation of the Theodosian Code, which is discussed in Harries and Wood 1993, Harries 1999, and Matthews 2000. See Volume 7, Chapter 1 of this Treatise, for fuller discussion of the Roman jurists.

For the philosophy of law in the Roman period, Rowe and Schofield 2000 is an indispensable starting point: Part II contains a historical overview of the period and detailed treatments of constitutional theory, Cicero, the historians, Pliny, Seneca, Platonic and Pythagorean theory, Josephus, Imperial Stoics, the Roman jurists, and Christian writers. Algra, Barnes, and Mansfeld 2000 provides valuable background, especially a splendid chapter by Schofield on Hellenistic social and political thought. Schofield 1991 is also a groundbreaking study; no general claims about Stoic political and legal theory or about natural law theory in the ancient world can be made until this book has been mastered.

The most important works of Cicero are *On the Commonwealth* and *On the Laws*, translated with introduction and notes by Zetzel, and *On Duties*, translated by Griffin and Atkins. Cicero's philosophical works are introduced by MacKendrick and Singh 1989. There are many books on Cicero's life and thought. Rawson 1975 is still very helpful, but more recent perspectives are reflected in Powell 1995. A number of relevant works by Seneca are translated in Cooper and Procopé 1995. The best general introductions to Seneca's philosophy and political career are by Griffin 1976 and Maurach 1991. The first thing to read on Epictetus' philosophy is now A. Long 2002. For Marcus Aurelius see Birley 1966 and 1987 and Rutherford 1989.

Inwood 1999 offers an overview of two main trends in recent scholarship about Stoic natural law theory. The "minimalist" tradition, represented by Vander Waerdt 1994a and 2003 and Inwood 2003, argues that natural law has very little to say about substantive social or political matters; Striker 1996b and Mitsis 1994, 1999, 2003 defend the more traditional view that Stoic natural law consists of substantive moral and social norms. On the tensions between these two traditions see Brown 2009. Recent discussions of whether the Stoics recognized "human rights" include Banateanu 2001, Long 2006, Mitsis 2011, and Bett 2012. Various aspects of Roman legal and political philosophy are addressed in articles in collections edited by Griffin and Barnes 1989 and 1997 and Laks and Schofield 1995. Temporini and Haase 1972, vol. 2, has a number of articles relevant to the theme of this chapter.

For an overview of the influence of Roman law throughout European legal history see Stein 1999.

Chapter 7

EARLY JEWISH AND CHRISTIAN LEGAL THOUGHT

by Fred D. Miller, Jr.[1]

7.1. Historical Overview of Ancient Jewish Legal Thought

In addition to Greek and Roman legal thought, the other major ancient source for Western legal philosophy is the Judeo-Christian tradition. Jewish law took shape over two millennia, from the legendary Mosaic code (as early as the thirteenth century B.C.) until the completion of the *Talmud* (seventh century A.D.). After emerging as a Jewish sect (first century A.D.), Christianity soon became a separate religion and developed a view of law in explicit and sharp contrast with Judaism. This chapter offers a brief overview of early Jewish and Christian legal thought, which is indispensable for an understanding of the subsequent history of medieval philosophy of law.

The Jewish legal tradition has its source in the Tanakh—the Hebrew Bible, known to Christians as the Old Testament—and especially, the Pentateuch, the first five books, called the Torah in Hebrew.[2] According to tradition the five books of the Pentateuch—Genesis, Exodus, Leviticus, Numbers, and Deuteronomy—were written by Moses, except for the final verses describing Moses' death. But most modern biblical scholars regard the Pentateuch as a later redaction from earlier texts composed by different authors at different times (see Segal 1967). Four main strata are generally distinguished: J (where God is called Yahweh or Jehovah), E (where God is called Elohim), D (Deuteronomy), and P (reflecting the viewpoint of priests).[3] Exodus recounts the liberation of the Israelites from bondage in Egypt and the establishment of their legal system (perhaps late thirteenth century B.C.). After delivering the ten commandments (Decalogue) orally to Moses on Mount Sinai, God inscribed them on two stone tablets (Exod. 24:12, 32:15–16, 34:28; Deut. 4:13,

[1] Louis Lomasky and Charles Butterworth provided very helpful comments and criticisms of an earlier draft. In this chapter quotations from the Hebrew Bible (or Old Testament) are taken from *Tanakh: The Holy Scriptures*. Philadelphia: The Jewish Publication Society, 1985; and the quotations from The New Testament and from Apocrypha are from *The Revised English Bible*. Oxford: Oxford University Press, 1989. All other translations are by the author unless otherwise indicated.

[2] In common usage, "Jewish" refers to religious belief, "Hebrew" to language, and "Israelite" to racial origin, but the terms are often used interchangeably. "Gentiles" (Greek *ethnê*) refers to non-Jews (later to non-Christians), and "pagans" to believers in polytheistic religions such as the Greek and Roman.

[3] On the historicity of the Pentateuch, see Eissfeldt 1975b.

5:22), and Moses also wrote down all the laws given to him in the book of the covenant (Exod. 24:4, 34:27). The commandments are recorded in Exodus 20:2–17 (cf. Deut. 5:6–21), and other regulations are found in the rest of Exodus as well as in Leviticus (see Stamm and Andrew 1967). Moses may be compared to Asian kings like Hammurabi when he is said to "represent the people before God" (Exod. 18:19), but it is noteworthy that the laws are presented as part of a covenant (*berit*) of God with the Israelites: "If you will obey me faithfully and keep my covenant, you shall be my treasured possession among all the peoples. Indeed all the earth is mine, but you shall be to me a kingdom of priests and a holy nation" (Exod. 19:5–6). The Israelites collectively swore an oath to abide by the agreement (24:3–8). The obligation to obey the laws of Moses thus seems to rest on a form of social contract theory: The laws of Moses have authority over the Israelites because they have explicitly consented to obey them. Deuteronomy 29:14–15 makes explicit that the parties to the original covenant also bound their descendants.[4]

The Mosaic code encompassed not only civil laws ("You shall not murder," "You shall not commit adultery," "You shall not steal," "You shall not bear false witness against your neighbor"; see Exod. 20:13), but also many religious regulations ("You must have no other gods besides me," "Remember the sabbath day and keep it holy"; see 20:3, 8), dietary rules ("You shall not boil a kid in its mother's milk"; see 23:19), and so forth. Many crimes carried severe punishments including religious offenses: "Whoever sacrifices to a god other than the Lord alone shall be proscribed" (22:19; cf. Lev. 17:29). "Whoever does work on the sabbath day shall be put to death" (Exod. 31:15). Jewish law was distinctive in its requirement that all male babies be circumcised on the eighth day after birth (Lev. 12:3).

Scholars have noted many similarities between the Mosaic code, especially Exodus 20:22–23:13, and the laws of the Sumerians, Babylonians, Assyrians, and Hittites (see the Prologue to this volume). "It is generally agreed that Israel took over the laws in question from their neighbors in the ancient Oriental world, and it is natural to regard the Canaanites as intermediaries passing on the regulations which are common to the laws of Israel and those of their neighbors" (Eissfeldt 1975a, 563; cf. Smith 1960).[5] Like the code of Hammurabi, Mosaic law affirms the *lex talionis* (law of retaliation): "[T]he penalty shall be life for life, eye for eye, tooth for tooth, hand for hand, foot for foot, burn for burn, wound for wound, bruise for bruise" (Exod. 21:23–4; cf. Lev. 24:17–20). It is, however, disputed whether early Jewish law ever adhered strictly to the principle that perpetrators must suffer the same harms they had inflicted on others. The two sacred tablets were deposited in the ark of the

[4] See Weinfeld 1991, 6–9, on Hittite and Assyrian parallels to these covenants.

[5] See Assmann 1997 on the more controversial claim that Mosaic laws had an "Egyptian origin."

pact or testimony and kept in the holy of holies within the tabernacle (Exod. 16:34, 25:16; cf. 31:18). Finally, the tribe of Levites were ordained as a priestly caste responsible for enforcing the laws (32:25–9).

A loose federation of Israelite tribes invaded Palestine and fought with difficulty against the Canaanites and Philistines, until the establishment of a monarchy that reached its apogee early with Kings David (1013–973 B.C.) and Solomon (973–933 B.C.). God promised to David that his family and kingdom would be established forever, and his throne would endure for all time (2 Sam 7:10). Solomon is extolled for his "divine wisdom to execute justice." The anecdote in which he judges the claims of two women to be mother of the same child recalls the judicial role of Mesopotamian kings (1 Kings 3:16–28, 4:29–34, 10:23–4). But even Solomon succumbed to pagan gods through the wiles of his many foreign wives. A major theme throughout the Hebrew Bible is the struggle against intermarriage with non-Israelites and against heathen practices such as idol worship and child sacrifice. After his death, Solomon's kingdom split into two: Israel in the north was annihilated in 722 by the Assyrians, and Judah in the south fell in 586 to the Neo-Babylonian Empire. During this period of division and decline, a series of prophets—including Isaiah, Jeremiah, and Ezekial—advocated social justice and religious reform. Jeremiah complains that the priests, "the guardians of the teaching [*torah*]," ignored God (Jer. 2:8).

King Josiah (ruled ca. 640–609) instituted religious reforms in an effort to save the kingdom of Judah. After "a scroll of the teaching [*torah*]" was rediscovered in the temple (2 Kings 22:8), Josiah read it to the assembled population and "solemnized the covenant before the Lord: that they would follow the Lord and observe his commandments, his injunctions, and his laws with all their heart and soul; that they would fulfill all the terms of this covenant written upon the scroll. All the people entered into the covenant" (23:3). Passover was celebrated according to the scroll of the covenant, idols were banned, worship was centralized in the temple, and Josiah followed "the teaching [*torah*] of Moses" (23:25). Many scholars believe that Deuteronomy, the fifth book of the Pentateuch, was written, or substantially redacted, at this time (Driver 1902; Weinfeld 1991; Mitchell 1991). Deuteronomy (Greek for "second law") contains the first use of the word *torah* for an entire book rather than for a specific ritual or statute, for example, "When he is seated on his royal throne, he shall have a copy of this teaching [*torah*] written for him on a scroll by the levitical priests" (Deut. 17:18; contrast Lev. 6:2, 7; 7:1, and passim). This passage incidentally contains a reference to kingship (Deut. 17:14–15), which some scholars regard as anachronistic because the kingship was not established until two centuries after Moses. Deuteronomy 12–26 listed many commandments and statutes that were added to the Mosaic code. One noteworthy development is the injunction, "Parents shall not be put to death for children, nor children be put to death for parents: A person shall be put to death only for his own crime" (Deut. 24:16; cf. 2 Kings 14:6). This seems to be at variance with the principle of inherited or collective guilt implied by Exodus 20:5: "I the Lord your God am an impassioned God, visiting the guilt of the parents upon the children, upon the third and fourth generations of those who reject me." In spite of Josiah's reforms, Judah was conquered soon after by Nebuchadrezzar of Babylon, who forcibly relocated many of the Jews. During the Babylonian captivity (586–538) the Jewish community preserved its cultural identity through strict adherence to the Torah. After the Persian conquest of Babylon (538), the Jews were permitted to return and rebuild the temple in Jerusalem, although the Jews remained under Persian rule (538–332).

In 444 B.C. the Persian king Artaxerxes granted legal authority to Ezra, a Jewish scribe living in Babylon, who "had dedicated himself to study the teaching [*torah*] of the Lord so as to observe it, and to teach laws and rules to Israel" (Ezra 7:6, 10). Ezra was permitted to return to Judea and to "appoint magistrates and judges to judge all the people in the province of Beyond the River who know the laws of your God, and to teach those who do not know them" (7:25). Ezra and his Levite colleagues read and interpreted the Torah to an assembled multitude (Neh. 8:1–3, 7–8). They said that God had handed the Israelites over to foreign conquerors to punish them for rebelling against Mosaic law. God kept his covenant, even though the Israelites had done injustice (9:26–33). The chastened people concluded that their survival hinged on strict conformity to the teaching of Moses, and they swore an oath to obey the law of Moses and fulfill all the commandments, rules, and statutes of God (10:29). The story of Ezra implies an ongoing tradition of judicial interpretation (*midrash halakhah*) by scholars or scribes (*soferim*). Such interpretation was necessary because the ancient laws had to be respected, but often they seemed inconsistent or unclear in application. For example, Exodus 21:5–7 states that if a slave denies that he wants to be free, he will be a slave for life; but Leviticus 25:40 states that a slave will work for his master only until the jubilee year (which occurs every forty-ninth year). Although these two statements seem contradictory, the interpreters tried to harmonize them: "the slave [...] was to be offered his freedom on the seventh year" (Zohar 1998, 205). According to tradition, the oral Torah was transmitted from Moses to Joshua to the elders to the prophets and finally to the Great Assembly (*keneset ha-Gedolah*) of teachers, which was founded by Ezra and continued until the time of Simeon the Just (d. ca. 270 B.C.). The tasks of the assembly were to "be deliberate in judgment, raise up many disciples, and make a fence around the Torah" (Tractate *Avot* 1.1–2, as cited in A. Cohen 1995, xxxvii).

Palestine was conquered by Alexander the Great in 332 B.C. and ruled successively by the Ptolemies (301–200 B.C.) and Seleucids (200–168 B.C.). At first the Israelites enjoyed some autonomy, and King Antiochus III (ca. 198 B.C.) permitted the Jews to govern by their own laws and establish a senate (*sanhedrin*), which became like a supreme court presided over by the high priest. But there were increasing conflicts between Hellenizing and orthodox Jews, until King Antiochus IV (ruled 175–163 B.C.) issued an edict requiring the Jews to abandon their customs and religious practices such as circumcision "and so to forget the law and change all their statutes" (1 Macc. 1:49). Called upon to be "zealous for the law and stand by the covenant" (2:27), the Jews rebelled under Maccabean leadership in 168 and achieved freedom until the Roman conquest in 63 B.C. Throughout this period Jewish society was supported and unified by the "three pillars of ancient Judaism—the one God, the one Torah and the one Temple" (Schwartz 2001, 49). But two major factions disagreed over the Torah: the Sadducees (named after Zadok, a Levite priest; see Ezek. 40:46), who were associated with the wealthy and established priestly class, and the more populist Pharisees, who arose from the class of scribes. The Sadducees insisted on strict adherence to the written Torah, whereas the populist Pharisees accepted the oral Torah along with the written law. The Pharisees were also receptive to ideas such as the resurrection of the dead and postmortem reward and punishment determined by one's conformity during life to the law of Moses—ideas which were repudiated by the literalist Sadducees. The Pharisees were influenced by Greek ideas, although the extent of this influence is debated by scholars. During the third and second centuries B.C. in Alexandria, first the Hebrew Tanakh was translated into Greek as the Septuagint, then the rest of the scripture. This required a Greek reconstruction of Jewish concepts. For example, the Hebrew word *torah* was rendered as *nomos* in Greek. In the second century B.C. Aristobulus, an Alexandrian Jew, wrote a Greek commentary on the Pentateuch, arguing that Moses was a source for Greek philosophy.

Later Philo (Judaeus) of Alexandria (15? B.C.–A.D. 50?) wrote extensive treatises in Greek on Jewish religion and Mosaic law. He was deeply steeped in the writings of Plato, whom he called "that sweetest of all writers" (*Prob.*13). Yet he praises Moses as "the most admirable of all the lawgivers who have ever lived in any country either among the Greeks or among the barbarians [...]. [H]is are the most admirable of all laws, and truly divine, omitting no one particular which they ought to comprehend" (*Mos.* II.12). Philo views Moses as a philosopher, king, and prophet rolled into one (*Mos.* II.2–3). Moses was the living law (*empsuchos nomos*) (I.162, II.4). Philo upholds the Mosaic principle that "one must not add anything to, or take anything from the law [...], for there is nothing which has been omitted by the wise lawgiver which can enable a man to partake of entire and perfect justice" (*Spec.* IV.143). But he also argues that the law must often be interpreted in an allegorical sense (*Leg.* III.236). Moses began the Torah with the creation of the world, "under the idea that the law corresponds to the world and the world to the law, and the man who is obedient to the law, being by so doing, a citizen of the world [*kosmopolitês*], arranges his actions with reference to the intention of nature, in harmony with which the whole universal world is regulated" (*Opif.* 3). This view of law presupposes the Hellenistic Stoic view of the world (*kosmos*) as a city (*polis*) (*Opif.* 143; cf. Clement, *Strom.* 6.172 = *SVF* III.327). The cosmic city possesses a constitution, which Philo calls "the right reason [*orthos logos*] of nature, which in more appropriate language is denominated law, being a divine arrangement in accordance with which everything suitable and appropriate is assigned to every individual" (*Opif.* 143). Philo thus expresses the notion of natural law in terms of his own idea of divine reason (*logos*):

> The unerring law is right reason; not an ordinance made by this or that mortal, a corruptible and perishable law, a lifeless law written on lifeless parchment or engraved on lifeless columns; but one imperishable, and stamped by immortal nature on the immortal mind. (*Prob.* 46)[6]

This concept of law had a profound impact on early Christian philosophers (cf. *Opif.* 20; see Goodenough 1933 and 1940; Tobin 1983; Runia 2001, 142–3; Najman 1999 and 2003).

During the Babylonian exile began the Diaspora, the dispersion of Jews throughout the world. Scattered Jewish communities tried to preserve their religious and cultural identity through a careful study of the Torah. This was also a period of remarkable ferment during which many sects sprang up, including the Essenes, who were mystics and ascetics who regarded matter as evil. The most successful movement, Christianity, hailed Jesus of Nazareth as the lord and long awaited messiah ("anointed one" and deliverer, the successor of King David) (see Matt. 16:16). Jesus acted as a teacher (rabbi) and healer. Although his professed aim was to fulfill the Mosaic law, his followers hailed him as the Son of God and the founder of a new religion that would transform or supplant Judaism, although some continued to comply with the Torah (see the following section). An influential faction, the Zealots, refused to pay taxes to the Romans and led a revolt that resulted in disastrous defeat and the destruction of the temple in Jerusalem (A.D. 70). After putting down further rebellions under self-proclaimed messiahs in the second century, the Romans expelled the Jews from Jerusalem and for a time even prohibited the practice of Judaism. Flavius Josephus (37–95?) reported the foregoing events in the *Jewish Antiquities* and the *Jewish War*. Although his writings contain valuable information, Josephus can be unreliable because he wanted to make the Torah palatable to his Greco-Roman readership. Following Philo, Josephus depicted Moses as a legislator in the Platonic mold:

[6] There is a striking parallel with Cicero's statement that "true law is right reason, consonant with nature, spread through all people. It is constant and eternal [...]" (*On the Commonwealth* III.33, trans. Zetzel). See Horsley 1978 and the discussion in Chapter 6, Section 6.2, of this volume.

He believed that it was above all necessary for one who manages his own life nobly and to legislate for others, first to study the nature of God and then having contemplated His works with his reason [*nous*] to imitate as far as possible that best model [*paradeigma*] of all and to try to follow it [...]. In legislating he did not start with contracts and mutual rights of the citizens; rather, when he led their thoughts up to God and the construction of the world and convinced them that we humans are the finest of God's works on earth, and after he had obtained their pious obedience, he easily persuaded them of everything else. (*Ant.* I.19, 21; cf. Philo, *Opif.* 3, *Mos.* II.48)

Thus Josephus explains why the Torah begins with Genesis, Moses' account of God's creation.

After the suppression of the temple priests and traditional political elites, the rabbis, who were spiritual heirs of the Pharisees, became the dominant force within Jewish society.[7] As scholars and teachers of sacred scripture, the rabbis increasingly provided spiritual leadership for their communities and presided over weddings and other rites. They had at their disposal the *midrash*, commentary preserved since the Babylonian captivity. The oral tradition had been continued under a succession of *zugot* or "pairs of leaders," from the early second century B.C. until the early first century A.D., when Hillel as patriarch founded a school and propounded seven rules of midrashic exegesis, thus initiating the age of the sages (*tannaim*) which lasted through the second century A.D. (see Elon 1994, vol. 3: chap. 28). The Romans permitted Jewish sages such as Johanan ben Zakkai to establish rabbinical schools and thus preserve the Torah. These ensured a period of revitalization of Jewish religion, culture, and law. In order to establish a comprehensive and consistent set of laws, the patriarch Judah ha-Nasi, "the Prince" (135–217 A.D.), commissioned the sages to compile a code of laws called the *Mishnah* (Moore 1927–1930). There were already several oral mishnayos in existence, and the new *Mishnah* presented these in a more concise, written form. The *Mishnah* was organized in six sections dealing with agricultural laws, the sabbath and festivals, family law, torts and financial laws, rules for sacrifices, and dietary laws. This incorporated the oral Torah, comprised of explanations given by God to Moses of the written Torah and supplementary interpretations of later sages and teachers. The Mishnah recognizes different sorts of rule: a commandment contained in the Torah (*mitzvah*, e.g., do not work on the sabbath), a rabbinical decree on how to apply a commandment (*gezeirah*, e.g., do not touch a tool on the sabbath), or a rabbinical enactment not based on the Torah (*takkanah*, e.g., the wife is to light a candle on the sabbath). The commandments of the Torah were more binding in principle, but they often needed to be interpreted or qualified.

[7] Traditionally, historians held that the rabbis quickly filled the leadership vacuum in the second century A.D. Schwartz 2001 argues that the rabbis were at first a peripheral group and only very gradually acquired authority. See also Schäfer 2003, 133–5.

The Mishnah (completed ca. 200) along with the Tosefta ("supplement," completed ca. 250) became the subject of extensive commentary (*gemara*) by exegetes (*amoraim*) that was collected in the Jerusalem (or Palestinian) *Talmud* (ca. 400) and the more extensive and authoritative Babylonian *Talmud* (ca. 500, redacted until ca. 650) (see Ginzberg 1941; Goodblatt 1979; Elon 1994, vol. 3: chap. 29). The term *talmud* ("learning") was originally applied narrowly to the commentaries, but the entire collection of the Mishnah, the commentary, and other writings is called the *Talmud*. It included the *halakhah*, which contained laws and ordinances with many additions to the Pentateuch, and the *haggadah*, which contained anecdotes, parables, and other material. The word *halakhah* ("the way") came to refer generally to Jewish law. The *Talmud* also included the *baraisos*, excerpts from the sages (*tannaim*) that were not in the Mishnah. According to tradition, the *Talmud* represented the opinions of sages belonging to an unbroken oral tradition reaching back to Moses. But the *Talmud* often preserved discrepant interpretations without reaching a clear conclusion, thus encouraging further deliberation. The Babylonian *Talmud* recounts an argument between two rabbis. When a voice from heaven declares that the law accords with the one rabbi's position under all circumstances, the other retorts, "It is not in heaven!" A later rabbi explained, "The Torah has already been given from Mount Sinai, so we do not pay attention to echoes, since you have already written in the Torah at Mount Sinai, 'After the majority you are to incline'" (*Bava Mesia* chap. 4, 59b; cf. Elon 1994, vol. 3: 1068). As the culmination of two millennia of reflections on the Torah, the *Talmud* became the foundation for subsequent Jewish legal thought (see Strack and Stemberger 1992).

7.2. Paul on Christianity and the Law

St. Paul was the first Christian to theorize about the law. Born as Saul to Jewish parents at Tarsus in Asia Minor (A.D. 5?), he became a zealous Pharisee in Jerusalem (Acts 23:6; Phil. 3:5).[8] He helped to lead the opposition against the nascent Christian sect, including the execution of St. Stephen for speaking against the law (Acts 6:13; cf. 8:3). On the road to Damascus, where he intended to persecute other Christians, he had a vision of Christ that resulted in his conversion (9:1–19). He proselytized to the Gentiles, who called him Paul, and conducted major missions throughout the eastern Roman Empire. Finally, he was attacked by a Jewish mob in the temple in Jerusalem, and arrested by

[8] Paul's claim that he was "according to the law a Pharisee" has been questioned on the grounds "that he appears to have read the scriptures, not in Hebrew, as any rabbinic scholar would have done, but in the Greek translation known as the Septuagint" (see Wilson 1997, 30–1). The issue is complicated, however, by the fact, noted in the previous section, that other hellenized Jews including Philo seemed unfamiliar with Hebraic writings.

the Romans. At his hearing he denied that he had offended against the Jewish law or the Roman emperor (25:8). As a citizen he appealed his conviction (25:11–12) and was sent to Rome where he was exonerated after preaching for two years. He was arrested again however and ultimately executed (A.D. ca. 67).

Paul's letters to churches and individual Christians were early accepted in the canon of sacred writings and comprise over a quarter of the New Testament. Although the authorship of some letters is disputed, scholars generally regard as genuine those to the Galatians and Romans, which contain important discussions of law. Textual interpretation turns on thorny issues concerning the historical context, the views of his antagonists, Paul's biography, and Jewish and Greco-Roman culture, in addition to broader questions of theology (see Sanders 1977 and 1983; Richardson and Westerholm 1991). Paul employs techniques of oral speeches and legal argument, so that individual passages must be understood within a wider context. Paul's style is distinguished by the vivid personification of abstract ideas: for example, "Love is patient and kind" (1 Cor. 13:4). Law is sometimes treated as a character in a spiritual drama: "The law entered, in order that the offence might increase. But where sin increased, grace increased all the more, so that, just sin reigned in death, so also grace might reign through righteousness to bring eternal life through Jesus Christ our Lord" (Rom. 5:20–21, trans. by author).

Paul's legal thought was influenced by two main factors. First, Jesus and the early Christians, including Paul himself, were accused of violating Mosaic law because Jesus was presented as the Messiah and the Son of God who openly flouted traditional laws, for example, against working on the sabbath. Jesus retorted, "The sabbath was made for man, not man for the sabbath" (Mark 2:27). But he also stated, "Do not suppose that I have come to abolish the law or the prophets; I did not come to abolish, but to complete" (Matt. 5:17). Later, in response to the Pharisees' question of what is the greatest commandment in the law, Jesus answered, "Love the Lord your God with all your heart, with all your soul, and with all your mind [...]. Love your neighbor as yourself [...]. Everything in the law and the prophets hangs on these two commandments" (22:36–40). Second, Paul himself was involved in an early controversy in the Christian church. He opposed other former Pharisees who maintained that Gentiles who wished to become Christians must become circumcised and follow the law of Moses (Acts 15:5; cf. Gal. 2:3, 6:15). Against this, Paul maintained, human beings are justified by faith apart from works of the law (Rom. 3:28).

In order to understand Paul's writings on law, it should be kept in mind that he uses the Greek word *nomos*, which is usually translated "law," in different senses (see Cranfield 1970, 148–9; Fitzmyer 1993, 131–2): (1) narrowly, for the law of Moses (Rom. 5:13–14, 10:5); (2) more broadly, for moral rules grasped even by Gentiles (2:14–15); (3) in the sense of a principle, for example, of faith (3:27); and (4) in the sense of a commandment (Gal. 5:14). Consequently, the precise meaning of *nomos* ("law") is often in dispute.

Paul's harshest criticisms of law are aimed at the "foolish Galatians" for insisting that pagan converts to Christianity submit to being "under the law," especially through circumcision (Gal. 3:1, 6:12–13). Here "law" clearly refers to the Mosaic code. Paul declares that "no one [i.e. neither Jew nor Gentile] is ever justified by doing what the law requires, but only through faith in Christ Jesus" (2:16). He adds that "those who rely on obedience to the law are under a curse" (3:10). God put the law "in charge of us until Christ should come, when we should be justified by faith; and now that faith has come, its charge is at hand. It is through faith that you are all sons of God in union with Christ Jesus" (3:24–6). There can be no salvation under the law, because even if one is circumcised, he is "under obligation to keep the entire law" (5:3). Paul argues that "if you are led by the spirit, you are not subject to law [...]. The harvest of the spirit is love, joy, peace, patience, kindness, goodness, fidelity, gentleness, and self-control" (5:18, 22). He concludes that the old law, given to Moses, has been superseded by a new law: "The whole law is summed up in a single [commandment]: 'Love your neighbor as yourself'" (5:14). "Carry one another's burdens, and in this way you will fulfil the law of Christ" (6:2). This implies that the law criticized in Paul's letter to the Galatians is the old law of Moses, which has been supplanted by a new Christian law (see Martyn 1997, 548–58).

Paul has been criticized for overlooking a major doctrine of Jewish religion, that a loving God may allow sincerely repentant sinners to atone for their sins. This idea is celebrated in the Jewish Day of Atonement (*yom kippur*; see Exod. 30:10; Lev. 23:27, 25:9). Leviticus prescribes a ritual in which the high priest was to lay his hands on the head of a scapegoat, confess all the sins of the Israelites, and then cast out the creature: "The goat shall carry on it all their iniquities to an inaccessible region" (Lev. 16:22). Although it is widely agreed that Paul's omission of repentance and atonement resulted in an incomplete and inaccurate picture of Jewish religion and law, the explanation for this oversight is debated by scholars (see Sanders 1977). Perhaps it was due to his Pharisaic education, or perhaps his own anti-legalism led him to dismiss atonement, in its traditional form, as an ineffective palliative. In any case Paul claimed that atonement could be achieved only through the ultimate sacrifice of Jesus Christ and that it could be effective only through faith (Rom. 3:25; cf. Heb. 9:25–6).

Although Galatians emphasizes the special burden imposed by the Torah, Paul's letter to the Romans adds that Gentiles as well as Jews are liable to punishment:

> Those who have sinned outside the pale of the law will perish outside the law, and all who have sinned under that law will be judged by it [...]. When Gentiles who do not possess the law carry

out its precepts by the light of nature [*phusei*], then, although they have not law, they are their own law; they show what the law requires is inscribed on their hearts [...]. (Rom. 2:12, 14–15)

This sounds like the idea of natural law in Cicero and the Stoics: All humans in their conscience understand the law's requirements (see Dodd 1953; Martin 1974; McKenzie 1964; Troeltsch 1960, 1: 80). Because pagans also know that their acts are unlawful, they—like the Jews—are condemned to punishment. "No human being can be justified in the sight of God by keeping the law: law brings only the consciousness of sin" (Rom. 3:20). Paul's legal theory is founded on the doctrine of original sin, that as a result of Adam's sin all men are condemned: "It was through one man that sin entered the world, and through sin death, and thus death pervaded the whole human race, inasmuch as all have sinned. For sin was already in the world before there was law [...]" (5:12–13). Although the law reveals to humans their sinful condition, they are incapable of obeying it. Law has the paradoxical effect of prompting even more sin (see 5:20–1 quoted above). We can be saved from the punishment we justly deserve only through the intercession of Christ, the Son of God, who died for our sakes. "If, by the wrongdoing of one man, death established its reign through that one man, much more shall those who in far greater measure receive grace and the gift of righteousness live and reign through the one man Jesus Christ" (5:17).

The foregoing reflections lead Paul to ask whether the law is sin. Although he denies this, he observes that "had it not been for the law I should never have become acquainted with sin" (7:7–8). The law, for example, "You shall not covet," prompts me to covet the forbidden fruit. Our inability to obey the law results from an inner conflict: "In my inner man I delight in the law of God, but I see another law in my members fighting against the law of my mind and making me a prisoner of the law of sin which is in my members" (7:22–3, trans. by author). But even though our bodies are dead because of sin, our spirit is enlivened through the presence in us of Christ and the Holy Spirit (8:10–11). The Spirit strengthens us and enables us to follow the commandment to love your neighbor as yourself. This he calls "the law of the spirit of life" (Rom. 6:2; cf. Gal. 6:2; 1 Cor. 9:21).

In two other influential passages Paul explains the practical implications of the Christian understanding of law. In the first passage, he asserts, "Every person must submit to the authorities in power" (Rom. 13:1). He is expatiating on the dictum of Jesus that one should give to God what is God's and to Caesar what is Caesar's (Mark 12:17). Paul's premise is that "all authority comes from God." Hence, the ruler is a "minister of God" for the good of his subjects and an agent of punishment for wrath to wrongdoers. Paul thus presents a moral argument for obedience to the ruler based upon conscience (Rom. 13:1–5). One has an obligation to pay taxes to the government, and more generally to act justly: "Discharge your obligations to everyone: pay tax and levy, reverence and respect, to whom they are due" (13:7). Paul observes that this is spelled out in the Ten Commandments, but that every commandment "is summed up in the one rule: Love your neighbor as yourself. Love cannot wrong a neighbor; therefore love is the fulfillment of the law" (13:9–10). Thus, according to Paul, the obligation to obey political authorities, and by implication the laws of the land, follows from the principle of Jesus Christ that one should love one's neighbor as oneself.

The second passage explains how Paul understands one's neighbor. Paul declares that, among Christians, "there is no such thing as Jew and Greek, slave and freeman, male and female; for you are all one person in Christ Jesus" (Gal. 3:28; cf. 1 Cor. 12:13). This view, which helped to motivate Paul's energetic proselytizing to the Gentiles, is a striking departure from the view that the Israelites were a chosen people, and the view that Greeks were by nature superior to barbarians. Although God establishes men in authority over women, free men over slaves, and rulers over subjects, these authorities are, as noted above, "ministers" of God whose authority derives from God rather than their innate superiority. Paul's view implies that all human beings are fundamentally equal under God's law.

Paul's considered view of law has been interpreted in very different ways. For example, his statement, "Christ is the end [*telos*] of the law" (Rom. 10:4) is ambiguous, because the word *telos* in Greek can be translated as "terminus" or as "goal." Emphasizing the first reading, some expositors view Paul as an antinomian, that is, a thoroughgoing opponent of the law. This is suggested by Ephesians 2:15: "he annulled the law with its rules and regulations, so as to create out of the two a single new humanity in himself." When Paul speaks of "the law of Christ," he means that we should follow the spirit of the law rather than the strict letter, because Christians "serve God in a new way, the way of the spirit in contrast to the old way of a written code" (Rom. 7:6). Early adversaries of Paul accused him of this view, while Marcion, a Gnostic heretic (d. ca. 160), sought support from this interpretation. Tertullian (ca. 160–ca. 220) criticized Marcion for separating the law and the gospel; and Irenaeus (140?–ca. 203) accused Marcion of mutilating Paul's writings by claiming that Christ "rendered null and void the prophets and the law." Similarly, Nietzsche hyperbolically calls Paul "the apostle of the annihilation of the Law," and further states, "The Law was the Cross on which he felt himself crucified. How he hated it! What a grudge he owed it" (*The Dawn of Day* aph. 68).

Diametrically opposed is the interpretation that Paul means "the law of Christ" literally and understands Christ as the goal (*telos*) of the law. On this view, Paul intends to distinguish a moral law distilled by Christ from the old Mosaic code. The apostle James, along these lines, speaks of "the sovereign law laid down in scripture: Love your neighbor as yourself" (James 2:8; cf. Lev. 19:18). Tertullian argues that a "new law" and a "new circumcision" had replaced the old. Justin Martyr (ca. 100–ca. 165) and Origen (185?–ca. 254) call Christ "the new lawgiver" (Pelikan 1971–1978, 16–8, 38–9). On this interpretation "gospel and law are essentially one" (Cranfield 1970, 169). During the Middle Ages, scholastic philosophers, including Abelard, developed this "new law" interpretation in a more systematic way (see Chapter 11 of this volume).

On a third interpretation, Paul's ambivalence toward the law derives from his view of human nature (see Fitzmyer 1981). St. Augustine (in *On Grace and Free Will*) draws on this interpretation of Paul to criticize the doctrine of Pelagius that human beings have a free will but Christ gave humans grace in the form of the law to help them avoid sin. Augustine objects that the human will has been so impaired by original sin that humans are incapable of following God's law on their own. The Augustinian interpretation was defended and elaborated in Martin Luther's *Lectures on Romans*. Rejecting the scholastic view that the gospel was a "new law" and that Christ was a legislator comparable to Moses, Luther (1961, 199) followed Augustine's interpretation of Pauline psychology. Paul describes an inner conflict between the law of God and sin, for example, when one covets a neighbor's property contrary to the law (Rom. 7:22–3). Paul says, "The good which I want to do, I fail to do; but what I do is the wrong which is against my will; and if what I do is against my will, clearly it is no longer I who am the agent, but the sin that has its dwelling in me" (7:19–20). According to Luther, the "I" that wants or does not want is the mind or spirit, and the "I" that does or does not act is the flesh. Luther (204) explains, "Because one and the same man as a whole consists of flesh and spirit, he attributes to the whole man both of the opposites that come from the opposite parts of him." This recalls Plato's division in the *Phaedo* between the soul and the body, which are described as in conflict with each other. But Luther (213) denies that Paul means that the spirit and flesh are "two separate entities," which Luther dismisses as "a silly and crazy fiction" contrived by "metaphysical theologians." When Paul says, "I myself with the mind serve the law of God, but with the flesh the law of sin" (7:25), he means literally that "one and the same man serves both the law of God and the law of sin, that he is righteous and at the same time he sins" (208). Even "saints in being righteous are at the same time sinners." Humans are inherently sinful and can be saved only through the grace of God and the mediation of Christ. Paradoxically, the spirit will enable us to fulfill God's law, but because of "our corrupted nature" the law itself is unable to bring this about (223–4).

Paul's tortuous discussions about the difficult relationship between law and justification by grace have influenced Christian legal thinkers of all stripes. However, a modern scholar remarks that Paul's "statements are more radical than the church has ever, except in rare moments of crisis, been willing to admit" (Meeks 1972, 441).

7.3. Early Christian Legal Thinkers

The Pauline critique of Jewish law was perpetuated by early Christian apologists such as Justin Martyr (ca. 100–ca. 165) in his *Dialogue with Trypho* (a Jewish philosopher). To the question whether those who have regulated their lives according to Mosaic law would be rewarded with life after death, Justin replied that the Jews who did what was "naturally [*phusei*] good, holy, and just"—that is, "things that are universally, naturally, and eternally good"—would be saved (*Dial.* 45.3–4), implying that the part of Moses' law which conformed to natural law took precedence over the rest. But Justin tells Trypho that there is a "final law and covenant which has authority over all persons." The Mosaic law "is already obsolete and was for you [Jews] only, whereas the [final] law is without qualification for all persons [...]. An everlasting and final law, Christ Himself, has been given to us [...]" (*Dial.* 11.2). Similarly, Origen (ca. 185–254) maintained that "the [divine] providence which long ago gave the law [of Moses], but now has given the gospel of Jesus Christ, did not wish that the practices of the Jews should continue [...]. In the same way it increased the success of the Christians [...]" (*Cels.* VII.26). Irenaeus of Lyons (140?–ca. 203) also asserted the superiority of the gospel to Jewish law: Christ "did not abolish, but extend and fulfill, the natural precepts of the law, by which man is justified." "The Lord himself spoke the words of the Decalogue alike to all: and so they abide equally with us, receiving extension and argumentation, but not abolition, but his coming in the flesh" (*Haer.* IV.13.1, 16.4). There was, however, a tendency toward a new legalism, inspired by Paul's reference to "the law of Christ" (Gal. 6:2). Christ was described as our "new lawgiver" by Justin (*Dial.* 18.3) and as "the lawgiver of the Christians" by Origen (*Cels.* III.7). Thus, Tertullian (ca. 160–ca. 220) contended that a "new law" and a "new circumcision" had replaced the old law, which was only meant as a sign to come (*Jud.* III.8). Tertullian refuted the heresy of Marcion (d. ca. 160) whose "primary and principal work" was the "separation of law and gospel" (*Marc.* I.19.4; see Section 7.1 above). Pelikan (1971, 17–8) observes, "[A]s moralism and legalism manifested themselves in Christian theology, much of the edge was removed from the argument of Christian apologetics against what was taken to be the 'Pharisaical' conception of the law."

Early Christian apologists also answered pagan critics by appropriating the classical idea of natural law (see Troeltsch 1960, 158–61). When the pagan Celsus proclaimed that "Pindar seems to me to have been right when he said that law is king of all," Origen retorted, "We Christians recognize that law is by nature king of all when it is the same as the law of god" (*Cels.* V.40). Origen argued that "where the law of nature, that is of God, enjoins precepts contradictory to the written laws," one ought to obey the divine lawgiver "even if in doing this he must endure dangers and countless trouble and deaths and shame."

In particular, one ought to disobey laws requiring the worship of pagan gods (V.37, trans. Chadwick). Origen was following the tradition of Antigone (see Chapter 1, Section 1.6.2, of this volume), although, among Christians, he was "apparently the first to justify the right to resist tyranny by appealing to natural law" (Chadwick 1953, 7 n.). The Christian rhetorician Lactantius (ca. 240–ca. 320) quoted with approval Cicero's definition of true law as "right reason in agreement with nature" of which God is the author, promulgator, and enforcing judge (Lactantius, *Inst.* VI.8 = Cicero, *Rep.* III.22). Tertullian also compared nature to a teacher in the service of God: "Nature is the teacher; the soul is the pupil. Whatever either the one has taught or the other has learned has come from God, that is, the teacher of the teacher" (*Anim.* 5). Tertullian was a severe critic of pagan philosophy: "What is there in common between Athens and Jerusalem?" (*Praescrip.* 7). Even if philosophers hit upon the truth occasionally, it is by sheer chance: "Most of our ideas about nature, however, are suggested by a kind of common sense with which God has endowed the soul of Man" (2.1). Other Christian thinkers, in particular Clement of Alexandria (ca. 150–ca. 215), took a more favorable view of philosophy: "Philosophy was schoolmaster to bring the Greek mind to Christ, as the law brought the Hebrews" (*Strom.* I.5.28; cf. Paul, Gal. 3:23).

The Christians who accepted the classical concept of natural law had to explain its relation to the law of Moses. St. Ambrose (ca. 340–397) argued that the Mosaic law was given to human beings because they were unable to obey the natural law. He interpreted the apostle Paul as teaching "that there is a natural law [*lex naturale*] written in our hearts [...]. This law is not written, but inborn; it is not perceived by reading, but is expressed in each person as from the flowing font of nature, and is taken in by human minds" (*Ep.* 73.2; cf. Rom. 2:14–15).[9] Ambrose converted and baptized St. Augustine, who gave a similar account of natural law: "Natural law [*natura ius*] is not produced by opinion, but a certain innate force has implanted it" (*Questions* 31.3). Ambrose was the scion of a noble family, a Roman official, and finally bishop of Milan, where he exerted powerful influence over political as well as religious affairs. His *De Officiis Ministrorum* was modeled after *De Officiis* of Cicero, and just as Cicero succeeded in popularizing Greek philosophy among his fellow Romans, "Ambrose reinterpreted Ciceronian Stoicism for a Christian public" (Markus 1988, 97). Following Cicero he described natural law as a moral principle obligating individuals to all humanity, to treat one another like parts of a single body (Ambrose, *Off.* III.17–18; cf. Cicero, *Off.* III.21–2). Ambrose, however, gives Cicero's simile a Christian interpretation: "The church should be the model of how human beings ought to relate"

[9] See Carlyle 1936, 1: 105, who notes similar interpretations in Ambrose, *De Jacob et Vita Beata* VI; in St. Hillary of Poitiers (d. 367), *Tractatus On Psalms* 118.119; and Augustine, *Faust.* XIX.2. On this passage (Rom. 2:14–15), see Section 7.2 above.

(Davidson 2001, 2: 818). Ambrose also emphasizes the universal scope of natural law: "If there really is one law of nature [*lex naturae*] for all, clearly there must be one standard of what is beneficial for all, and clearly we are bound to consider the interests of all. It cannot then be right for a man who wishes to follow nature's norm and consider the interests of his neighbor to transgress the law of nature by doing him harm" (Ambrose, *Off.* III.25; cf. Cicero, *Off.* III.27).

Political justice is to be understood in terms of this concept of natural law. For Ambrose agreed with classical philosophers that "justice is the basis of the association and community of the human race" (*Off.* I.28), and that "equity strengthens governments, and injustice destroys them" (II.19). But Ambrose rejected the pagan philosopher's understanding of justice, as doing no harm except in return for harm done, and as distinguishing private property from public. According to Ambrose's conception of natural law, God ordained the law of universal generation so that the earth is a kind of common possession. Private right was the result of human greed (I.28), that is, an inevitable consequence of original sin. Although Ambrose held that the authorities should comply with justice and law, he also contended that legal justice should defer to divine law. In a debate with the pagan prefect Symmachus (ca. 345–ca. 402), who argued that justice required the restoration of the altar of Victory in the Senate house (Symmachus, *Relationes* III.18), Ambrose wrote in a letter in 384 to the Christian Emperor Valentinian that "injustice is done to no one, over whom almighty God is given precedence" (*Ep.* 17.7).

In waging war on two fronts against Jewish and pagan adversaries, Christian philosophers developed a theory of three laws: the natural law given to Adam and Eve and consequently to all nations, the old law of Moses given to the Jews, and the new law of Jesus Christ. This tripartite view of law is found in a commentary on Romans by "Ambrosiaster" (ca. 380), the unknown author of commentaries mistakenly attributed to Ambrose who received his nickname from Erasmus. He remarks that natural law "which was partly reformed by Moses, and partly supported by his authority in preventing offenses, makes one aware of sin" (*Exposition of Romans* III.20). Augustine (*Faust.* XIX.2) attributes the same threefold distinction to Paul:

> There are three kinds of law: One is that of the Hebrews, which Paul says belongs to sin and death. Another truly belongs to the Gentiles, which he calls natural [citing Rom. 2:14–15] [...]. The third kind of law is truth, which the apostle signifies in the same way, and says, "The law of the spirit of life in Christ Jesus freed you from the law of sin and death." (Rom. 8:2)

The idea of the three laws was later a major theme of Abelard's *Dialogue between a Philosopher, a Jew, and a Christian* (see Chapter 11, Section 11.3, of this volume).

Isidore, archbishop of Seville (ca. 560–636), who oversaw important religious reforms in Spain, also contributed mightily to the transmission of ancient legal concepts. He was an associate of Sisebut, the Visigothic king, who commissioned his *Etymologies*, a widely used desk encyclopedia, with derivations and explanations of important terms. Book V.1–27 discusses legal terminology, beginning with a survey of the first legislators: "Moses of the Hebrew race was the first to publish divine laws in sacred writings" (*Etym.* V.1). He is followed by Egyptian, Greek, and Roman lawgivers. Isidore then briefly sketches the history of Roman legislation down to the Theodosian Code (with no mention of the Justinian Code). This summation suggests a confluence of Jewish, Christian, and pagan legal traditions. He distinguishes human laws from divine laws, which are established by nature (V.2). He treats *lex* ("law") as a species of *ius* ("right"), which he relates to *iustum* ("righteous," "just"). "The word *lex* comes from *legere* (to read) because law is written." But law is also related to reason: "[*L*]*ex* may be considered as everything that is based on reason [*ratio*], provided it is compatible with religion, appropriate to discipline, beneficial for welfare" (V.3). He follows the tripartite analysis of the Roman jurists: "Right [*ius*] is either natural or civil or of the nations" (V.4). He explains natural right as follows:

> Natural right [*ius naturale*] is common to all nations, and consists of what is universally held by natural instinct, not by constitution, e.g., the mating of male and female, the succession and education of children, universal common possession, universal liberty, the acquisition by hunting whatever may be caught in the sky, on land, and at sea. Again: the restoration of a deposit or of money lent; the offering of forcible resistance to violence. All this (and anything like it) is never unjust, but is held to be natural and equitable [*aequum*]. (V.5)

The tripartite account resembles Ulpian's, but Isidore does not adopt Ulpian's assertion that natural law is "not specific to human beings but is common to all animals" (Ulpian, *Inst.* I *ap.* Justinian *Dig.* I.1.1). His view of natural law seems closer to that of the Stoics and of the earlier Christian thinkers for whom natural law was written in human hearts: for the equation of the natural and the equitable is evidence of moral conscience rather than brute instinct. His account suggests some ambivalence about property: The reference to "universal common possession" seems to refer to a state of nature (i.e., prior to the Fall of Adam) in which there was no private property but the earth was owned in common by all human beings, but "the acquisition by hunting" may imply a natural right of original acquisition of private property.[10] Further, the mention of "universal liberty" seems to imply that in the state of nature there were no slaves but everyone is free. It is not clear how common ownership is supposed to cohere with the acquisition of private property. "There is an obvious problem, moreover, in reconciling 'common possession of everything' with rights in deposits and loans" (King 1988, 141). Perhaps he was uncon-

[10] "The right to acquire" for *adquisitrio* in O'Donovan and O'Donovan 1999, 210, is an interpretation rather than a translation.

sciously combining two different notions of natural law: one governing Adam and Eve's innocence before the original sin, and another regulating human beings afterward. Isidore defines civil law (*ius civile*) as "what each people or civil community has established for itself in matters human and divine" (V.5), which closely follows the definition of the jurists (cf. Gaius, *Inst.* I.1; cf. Justinian, *Inst.* I.2.1), as does his definition of the law of nations (see Carlyle 1936, 1: 42–3, 106–10).

The right of nations [*ius gentium*] is the occupation of sites, the construction of buildings, armament, war, captivity, enslavement, the right of return to one's home, peace treaties, truces, the sacrosanct inviolability of ambassadors, the prohibition of mixed-race marriages. It is called the right of nations since all nations, more or less, observe it. (V.6; cf. Gaius, *Inst.* I.1; Justinian, *Inst.* I.2.1)

Finally, Isidore follows the classical principle that the law, properly understood, is just and honest, and "will serve no private interest but the common welfare of the citizens" (V.21). In keeping with this, in the *Sentences* Isidore claims that kings (*reges*) are so called from acting rightly (*recte*): "[T]he title of king, then, is retained by doing right, forfeited by doing wrong" (*Sent.* III.48). Further, a prince should conform to the rule of law: "Princes are bound by their own laws, and may not disallow in their own case laws which they uphold for their subjects. Justly does their voice command authority when they grant no license to themselves which they refuse to their people." He adds, however, that the secular prince has a religious duty: "Secular powers are subject to the discipline of religion. Though invested with the highest sovereignty, they are bound by the chains of faith, to proclaim the Christian faith by their laws and to protect its proclamation by good conduct." Additionally, "secular princes often hold the highest position of power within the church, that they may use that power to reinforce church discipline" (III.51).

Although not a very deep or innovative thinker, Isidore preserved fundamental elements of Roman legal thought, integrated them with Christian belief, and made this blend accessible to a wide readership. "His definitions were finally embodied, in the twelfth century, in Gratian's Decretum" (Carlyle 1936, 106). For example, Gratian cites Isidore's distinction between divine and human laws, his threefold distinction of law, and so forth (*Decr.* D1.1, 6 passim). Isidore thus had a profound impact on the development of canon law and the whole course of medieval philosophy of law.

Further Reading

Elon 1994 is a comprehensive work on the entire tradition of Jewish law—its history, sources, and principles; in particular, vol. 3 contains valuable information concerning the literary sources for the period discussed in this chapter. General discussions of ancient Jewish law include Patrick 1985, Daube 1981,

Neusner 1981, Greenstein 1984, Noth 1984, and Avalos 1995. Phillips 1970 considers the criminal law in the Decalogue. Robinson and Oesterley 1937 and Neusner 1981 discuss the place of law in the wider context of ancient Judaism. Boecker 1980 and Avalos 1995 survey law and legal and social institutions in ancient Israel. Zohar 1998 treats of the philosophical dimension of *halakhah*. On the authorship of the Pentateuch see Segal 1967, and on Deuteronomy in particular, see Driver 1902 and Weinfeld 1991. Moore 1927–1930 is a history of the age of the *tannaim*. Strack and Stemberger 1992 give an introduction to the *Midrash* and *Talmud*. See Ginzberg 1941 on the Palestinian *Talmud*, and Goodblatt 1971 on the Babylonian *Talmud*.

Schäfer 2003 is a detailed history of the Jews in the Greco-Roman world. Richardson and Westerholm 1991 give a general account of the debate over the law between Jews and early Christians in the period of the Roman Empire. Watson 1996 is a general discussion of Jesus and the law. For different perspectives on the place of natural law in the New Testament, see Dodd 1953, Derrett 1970, Martin 1974, and McKenzie 1964. Wolterstorff 2008 contains chapters on antecedents of modern notions of "justice" and "rights" in ancient Jewish and Christian thought; see also Miller 2009. Sanders 1977 and 1983 examine the relationship of the apostle Paul to Palestinian Judaism and Jewish law. Cranfield 1970 and Fitzmyer 1981 give divergent interpretations of Paul's view of law. Wilson 1983 discusses the problem that Paul's legal thought presents for Luke in the Acts of the Apostles. See also A. Watson 1995b for a discussion of Jesus and the Pharisaical tradition according to the apostle John.

Pelikan 1971–1978 is a historical overview of the entire Christian tradition including legal doctrines: Vol. 1 deals with the early Catholic tradition (A.D. 100–600), vol. 2 the emergence of Eastern orthodoxy (600–1700), and vol. 3 medieval theology (600–1300). Carlyle and Carlyle 1936 contains valuable discussion of legal philosophy in the context of medieval political theory; vol. 1 in particular covers early Christian thought from the second to the ninth centuries. Burns 1988 also contains valuable discussions of law in medieval political thought from the fourth to the fifteenth centuries. O'Donovan and O'Donovan 1999 is a valuable sourcebook with readings (in English translation) in Christian political thought from the second century through the Reformation era, with introductions and further reading suggestions.

Chapter 8

THE PHILOSOPHY OF LAW IN THE WRITINGS OF AUGUSTINE

by Janet Coleman[1]

8.1. Life and Writings of Augustine

The Christian theologian and bishop of Hippo, Augustine (Aurelius Augustinus), was born in A.D. 354 to a non-Christian father and a Christian mother in that part of Roman North Africa that is today Algeria. Despite his mother's efforts Augustine initially found her religion uncongenial and intellectually unsophisticated. He received an education typical of ambitious, provincial Romans, becoming a student of Latin rhetoric in Carthage before he left for Rome in 383, whereafter he became a teacher of rhetoric in Milan. As had been the case during the last century of the Roman Republic, to be skilled in oratory with its uses in legal practice and local governance could lead to a civil service posting. During the late Roman Empire Augustine had considered such a career option. He had friends and contemporaries with whom he corresponded throughout his life who had chosen this path. As this chapter will show, Augustine's familiarity with the intricacies of contemporary Roman law had important consequences for his own political theory where he expressed his views not only on what politics was for but also on the compatibility of Christianity and politics.

Augustine harnessed a developing Christian doctrine to a set of distinctly imperial Roman discourses and realities in order to present, in his magisterial *City of God*, an image of two cities, the earthly and the heavenly, and their respective citizens. This considered perspective on history and politics, and the role of positive civil law in the lives of men, would be formulated rather later in his turbulent life lived in turbulent times. It would achieve its most mature form in the *City of God* XIX. What we may call his moral philosophy, however, began earlier in his increasing dissatisfaction with the legacies of ancient philosophy and the explanations philosophers had offered about human nature, self-knowledge, the respective roles of reason and will in determining moral responsibility, and on the nature of moral evil (see Evans 1982). Augustine's contribution to a Christian philosophy of law, then, may be said to fall into two successive but overlapping chronological periods, that of his own spiritual autobiography and his debt to ancient philosophy, and that of his reflection on Rome's history, not least as a consequence of the empire

[1] All translations are by the author unless otherwise indicated.

having adopted Christianity as the state religion (380) during his own lifetime. The development of his moral philosophy took on new dimensions as he came to explore Roman and world history in the light of scripture and the role of the contemporary, institutional church. Thereafter, it gave rise to what may be called his political theory where he explained the role of any state's law in men's lives. Augustine's thinking about law has philosophical, theological, and historical dimensions.[2]

Augustine experienced a series of intellectual and spiritual conversions throughout his life and recounted these in his *Confessions* and in numerous letters to friends. He tells his readers that his training in rhetoric was meant to lead to a profession in the law and thence to a post as governor (*Conf.* VI.11.19). But his youthful enthusiasms drew him instead to philosophy after having read Cicero's *Hortensius*. It was to the skepticism of the New Academy as he found it largely in Cicero's other writings that he next turned.[3] He had learned much of what he knew of the classical and Hellenistic Greek philosophers from Cicero, his master in rhetoric, and from Cicero's contemporary, the encyclopedic polymath M. Terentius Varro.[4] Thereafter, he became familiar with Plotinus and some unknown Platonist writings, most likely in recent Latin translations, and it is through these works that he met a platonizing interpretation of Christianity. Despite his appropriation of an amalgam of ancient philosophical positions whose principal ingredient was Platonism, Augustine's own acquaintance with Plato's writings seems to have been largely secondhand and notably through Cicero (e.g., *Tusculan Disputations*, *de Finibus*, etc.).[5] These were supplemented by his experience of hearing the bishop of Milan, Ambrose, preach a version of Christianity that demonstrated his sophisticated familiarity with Greek Christian theology of the first to fourth centuries A.D., along with pagan, Jewish, and Christian Greek neo-Platonism and its Latin derivatives.[6]

The historical development of Christianity itself, and especially its ethical and political doctrines during its first centuries, was a process of continuous "translation" of its sources stretching back to pre-Christian Stoicism and Hel-

[2] See Coleman 2000, vol. 1: 292–340, for a fuller account of the precursors to Augustine's thinking on philosophy and politics and their influence on his evolving perspectives in the context of his late imperial Roman times.

[3] On Cicero's own incomplete return to skepticism in later years, see Glucker 1988.

[4] Varro (116–27 B.C.) wrote a survey of Roman religion, *Antiquitates Rerum Divinarum*, in 41 books and *De Philosophia* that provided an account of all the possible ethical positions taught by Antiochus of Ascalon, an eclectic Platonist and the anti-skeptical heir to Carneades' skeptical Academy. Augustine targets Varro in *CD* VI, VII, and XIX.2f. For a brief discussion of Varro, see Schofield 2000b. On Antiochus, see Chapter 5 of this volume.

[5] For one of the best discussions of Augustine's debts to ancient philosophy, see Rist 1994. In general, see Bonner 1986.

[6] See esp. Brown 1989, chap. 17, for Ambrose's views and influences. Also see Brown 1972.

lenistic Judaism.[7] Ambrose in particular had read the works of Philo, Origen, and Plotinus, absorbing the fundamental antithesis between soul and body. He identified Paul's war between the flesh and spirit (Rom. 7:23) with the Platonist opposition between body and mind. Augustine heard him argue that man's mind is superior to his body, which is a mere "veil," indeed, a "perilous mudslick" that entices the will to slip. But because Christ sits in the inner person, having come to humanity in human flesh and thereby mediating the antithesis between heaven and earth, man can, even in this life, but with Christ's help through baptism, still the body's instincts. Ambrose emphasized far less than did the ancient philosophical tradition any long purification of the soul through spiritual *paideia* ("education"). Swift baptism secures the required transformation. Ambrose also defended the Old Testament against Manichaeism, a sect to which Augustine had been attracted while in North Africa and to which he maintained a somewhat troubled allegiance. In contrast to the dualism of Manichaeism, which proposed a doctrine of two cosmic forces of spiritual good and material evil in perpetual combat and which thereby limited the omnipotence of God, Ambrose urged his Christian congregation to think of God and the soul as distinct from material reality altogether. He further raised the possibility that belief was the prerequisite for understanding. Augustine was thus forced to confront a contemporary philosophical and cultural world that was constituted primarily by eclectic mixtures of Stoicism and varieties of Platonism. Under the influence of prominent Christians in Milan, notably the priest and Christian Platonist Simplicianus, he converted to Catholic Christianity and was baptized in 387. He returned to North Africa to live the monastic life, and was ordained as a priest in 391.

Nothing survives of Augustine's pre-conversion writings. His *Confessions* were written in 399, almost thirteen years after he converted to Christianity. The influence of Platonism endured throughout his life, even as his "philosophical models" became increasingly theological hypotheses learned out of scripture, notably from a re-examination of Paul's epistles, developed in his rejection of Manichaeism and Porphyry's tract *Against the Christians*, and were elaborated in debates with schismatic and heretical groups such as Donatists and Pelagians within the North African church where he had been elevated to bishop in 396 (see Coleman 1994). Insofar as all the writings we possess of Augustine are Christian, they are the work of a controversialist. They grew out of his arguments with his pre-Christian self, on the one hand, and with views current among his contemporaries both within North Africa (especially as he dealt with the pastoral burdens of being a bishop) and throughout the wider

[7] See Chapter 7 of this volume. The literature here is enormous. For a recent discussion of the ethical and political implications of early Christianity, see Young 2000. Also see the contributions by Chadwick, Nicol, and Markus in Burns 1988. Coleman 2000, vol. 1: 292–310, briefly treats the development of early Christian and Jewish philosophical theology.

world of the late Roman Empire, on the other. He remained in North Africa for almost 35 years until his death in 430.[8]

8.2. Augustinian Ethics

Most analyses of Augustine's writings attempt to place his thought within the various legacies of Hellenistic philosophy (e.g., Kent 2001). His philosophical milieu was the practical, eudaimonistic framework of Greek philosophy during the Hellenistic period (e.g., Epicurean, skeptic, and Stoic), which became more pronounced under the Roman Empire. Pagan philosophy, and especially neo-Platonism, moved closer to religion, indeed to a distinctive, increasingly ascetic Latin Roman version of religion for that "western" part of Rome which was Augustine's fourth- and early-fifth-century milieu.

Augustine was to reuse topics dealing with the virtuous life selected from the agenda of ancient ethical theory. He, too, would focus on the question of happiness and examine the various educational and spiritual exercises recommended for seeking the truth in this mortal life. He believed that all men wish to be happy and the thing signified by the word "happiness" somehow lies in men's memory. In *Confessions* (X.20–23) he asks where or when he had any experience of happiness that he should remember, love, and long for it again. Have we at some time in the past been happy, individually or through Adam, and now know that we have lost this but remember enough to know what we have lost? Is there a natural appetite to learn of happiness as something utterly unknown, or is it somehow known and preserved but obscured in the memory?[9] Augustine equates seeking God with seeking happiness, and he speaks of all men's desire to have joy in truth—not in the seeking but in the finding, in being united with God, in living with God (*Conf.* X.28). But this cannot occur in this life. If God is either truth or something higher than truth, then the standard (*regula*) which is called truth is higher than the human mind and beyond our mortal experiences.[10] Until approximately 411 Augustine accepted that all men have a natural desire for God (see Burns 1980). Thereafter, the natural desire was replaced with a divine gift of charity—grace—which alone provides man's orientation to true happiness. But he always viewed man's life on earth as a trial without intermission, shifting between adversity and fear of future adversity. It is framed by various offices that require the officeholder to be loved and feared by men, men seeking to be praised and their power feared, not for any truth in their intentions or acts but rather relying on deceitful judgments of their fellows.[11] Augustine calls this a fellowship of

[8] There are numerous biographies of Augustine, including Brown 1967.

[9] See Coleman 1992, chaps. 6 and 7, for a discussion of Augustine on memory.

[10] This is a neo-Platonic claim. Cf. Plotinus, *Ennead* V.5.

[11] Cf. Cicero, *Tusc.* III.2.3: "We come to think that there is no higher ambition than civil of-

like punishment (*Conf.* X.36). To escape it, he thought that there was some hope in a monastic setting, and he wrote to his friend Nebridius in 389–390 that he was experiencing a kind of deification through self-disciplined Christian philosophy. This, too, would be rejected, and thirty years later he would see "deification" as a tolerable thought only when considered as God's salvific justification after death (*CD* XIX.22).

From his own experiences of himself and others as ethical agents in the world, Augustine gradually came to the conclusion that men, including those reputed to be wise, are not now capable of giving absolute priority to the moral good or to seeing this as consistent with their nature. Rather, all men show themselves to be massively inconsistent and irrational agents who are forever frustrated in their search to understand whether or not their nature is conducive to the practice of virtue. He concluded that any correlation between a person's state of moral development and his understanding of his own nature is impossible to achieve autonomously and is meaningless without God's help. The only kind of person who can be relied on to look to the general interest of others and see that other-related virtue is natural must be someone who has been prepared and aided by God's grace in the achievement of this ethical state. There is no philosophical method to enable one to do this on one's own and with success. The power of autonomous human reason is incapable of changing a man's desires: No unaided mental process can enable any individual to arrive at the true grasp of the good so that he might live in accordance with the real. Through the power of introspection humans *can* to some degree reach a vision of truth or God within themselves. But if, as the Stoics had it, the beginning of understanding is in a pre-rational impulse that starts from an animal's or infant's love of self and self-awareness,[12] then for Augustine we can go no further. Introspection only

fice, military command, and popular glory. Men seek not true honor but a shadowy phantom of glory."

[12] Stoic *oikeiosis* ("self-awareness") is discussed as a mental process by which a human being will, if things go rightly, arrive at the true grasp of the good, namely, living in accordance with nature (*convenientia naturae*) or "in accordance with the real." The Stoic account of *oikeiosis* has two stages, the first of which provides an account of pre-rational action in animals and infants, which they thought of as a pre-rational impulse (*hormê*). This is followed by an account of a change in understanding of the goals of action that comes with reason, whereafter what is truly good is grasped. The pre-rational stage where actions are governed by impulse starts from an animal's love of self, so that the impulse is explained in terms of the animal's awareness of things in the world either belonging to or being alien to the self of whose "constitution" or structure the animal or child has some instinctive awareness. Underlying the logical starting point of self-love was another relation to the self: self-awareness (Cicero's *sensus sui*; see his *Fin.* III.5.16). Stoics, therefore, worked with a triadic logic of being aware of oneself, seeing oneself as belonging to oneself (*ipsum sibi conciliari*: Cicero, *Fin.* III.5.16), and loving oneself. Cicero had observed that animals could not feel desire toward anything unless they possessed self-awareness and consequently felt love for themselves. These are pre-rational impulses, generic desires, the purely subjective point of view. Augustine adopts something similar but does not take the next Stoic step,

provides a recognition of the existence of the truth within ourselves that is God; it does not provide an understanding of either our own or the divine nature.[13]

Augustine's reflection on and absorption of themes in ancient skepticism (principally from Cicero's *Academica*) led him to make claims about the importance of belief as distinct from knowledge, even before he developed his ideas concerning human dependence on God for the possibility of any moral behavior. He shows in his *Against the Academics* (*Contra Academicos*) how seriously he takes radical ancient skepticism and, likewise, how seriously he is seeking answers to counter it.[14] He concludes that human certitude exists but that it is limited. He argues that one cannot believe falsely, that is, be mistaken in one's belief that one exists (*Trin.* XV.12.21; *CD* XI.26, XIX.18). He also believes that through introspection we can come to recognize the existence, though not the nature, of God. But the result of this introspection—self-awareness, self-love, and self-concern—is insufficient and, therefore, is incapable of leading either to self-understanding or to being extended to other-regarding intentions or acts. Even self-awareness can be diminished by carnal habits. The limits on self-understanding result in a recognition of unfulfilled desires. The dissatisfaction with one's search for truth is replaced with the necessity of the belief in one's dependence on an outside, unmerited redirection of willed attention. The necessity of belief and our dependence, for the plausibility of that belief, on the credibility of the authority that provides it were essential to Augustine's perspective on the conduct of human life. Authority is always followed when humans cannot have firsthand experiences, notably of the past, and most of our understanding of the past relies on the plausible testimonies of others (*Conf.* VI.5.7).[15] Humans necessarily take things on trust; they trust the authoritative community within which they acquire conventional languages and habits, traditions, and laws, and they weigh the plausible positions of authorities in order to settle disputes. Humans should not be characterized as knowers but as believers.

which presumes that reason changes the goals of pre-rational action to eradicate pure impulsive subjectivity in order to arrive at "the good for man" with rationality as a determining constituent of human selves (*hêgemonikon*). See Engberg-Pedersen 1990, esp. 119–23; Striker 1983; generally the various contributions to Schofield and Striker 1986; Inwood 1985; Rist 1979; and Nussbaum 1994.

[13] See Augustine, *Enarr. in Psal.* 42 (41) 13, for: we do not know our own hearts, which are an abyss; *The Nature and Origin of the Soul*, 4.7.10, for: the power of my understanding is actually unknown to me; and *The Usefulness of Belief*, 10.24, for: practically no one understands his capacities.

[14] See Rist 1994, chap. 3, for a good discussion of Augustine's skepticism, and passim for the overriding influence of Stoicism on his thought. On ancient and modern skepticism and the difference between them, see Burnyeat 1984.

[15] See Coleman 1992, 80–111, for a discussion of Augustine's views on epistemology, the problem of language, memory, the presentness of the past, belief, and self-knowledge.

Furthermore, where Stoics argued that what matters is whether the morally right act is performed for the right reason and intention, that motives are to be in accord with right reason for them to be virtuous, Augustine also focused on moral intention rather than on the act, but instead insisted that to perform the good act in the right spirit requires God's grace. This is because man is good not because of what he knows or does but because of what he loves (*CD* XI.28). Without God's aid humans cannot assent to what is truly to be loved, because they experience a divided will with its competing loves and what they love inordinately is themselves rather than God. (The will is now a set of loves accepted and confirmed. We are what we love.)

Augustine came to see the human condition as tragic, a consequence of the Fall following Adam's first disobedience as told in the Old Testament book of Genesis. Augustine provides an account of the post-lapsarian man in *On Free Will* (ca. 395) as both invincibly ignorant of what is of supreme importance to us and morally weak in the ancient philosophical sense of *akrasia* ("weakness of will") (see Kahn 1988). Men struggle and fail to do what they wish to do, although they know what they ought to do (Rom. 7:14–23). Later, he would give an account of pre-lapsarian Adam: Before the Fall Adam was able to decide between good and evil, knowing the difference and being able to exercise a "lesser virtue" of making the right choice. According to Augustine's views (after 411), Adam was in the position of knowing what is evil and being able to choose it. In Paradise he enjoyed divine grace as a "help without which" he could not choose the good or even avoid evil. But divine grace for Adam in Paradise was a necessary, although insufficient, condition of his free choice of the good. It did not render him incapable of sin, but it ensured that he had the means for choosing the good.[16] Freedom of choice on its own was not the sufficient condition of doing good; only free choice coupled with divine grace suffices for doing good.[17] After the Fall, without divine assistance, man is no longer able to choose the good, and he is now motivated by his desires certainly to choose evil. His free choice is a decision already directed by his present incapacity to be motivated by pure love in any of his acts. Without God's intervention he will now choose what is wrong *because* of what he loves, namely, his own private goods, his own autonomy, his self-sufficiency, and his domination of others.

These views are central to Augustine's justification of law in the societies of men whereby their distorted loves will be regulated to secure peace and order.

[16] For a discussion of the changes in Augustine's notion of the will, see O'Daly 1989.

[17] See *CD* XIII in general on the Fall and its consequences, esp. XIII.13–15, XIV.26. Rist 1994, 131, observes: "[The] account of unfallen Adam is odder than it looks," and he notes: "Even if his understanding of the shattered identity of fallen man constitutes some kind of a defense of the free will of the elect, it raises the question of why we are not all elect—as Augustine certainly held—in a very acute form" (ibid., 135).

Men need to be freed from their fallen "free choice." The capacity to choose, of itself, is not man's excellence. Nor is man's will the kind of deliberated desire that can be used as a means to achieve his moral end. In *On Free Will* he has a concept of the will after the Fall as a middle good that is neutral and can be used either rightly or wrongly. From the will as an indifferent instrument, he moves on to a concept of will as good or evil depending on the value of what is willed (*Conf.* VIII.8.19–9.21). He would later[18] see that the will is either good or evil and that a good will is from God; the only way the human will may be moved from being an evil to a good will is through grace (*On Grace and Free Will* XX.41).[19] It is grace that attracts the will to what is true and good. In his later works the will is the human psyche in its role as a moral agent: goal-directed, active to some purpose, desirous of its objects (see Rist 1969). Grace transforms and activates this will. Hence, after the Fall man's will is more closely connected to a set of short-term, habituated wants. Man retains a power of free choice, but his freedom is merely the freedom or power to sin. What he wants needs to be transformed so that he loves what is truly to be loved: God. Man, therefore, needs God's preparation of his will and to have his free will restored by grace in the sense of being released from its corrupt, delusive mutation that we are free to do "what we like" (*Ep.* 157.2.10). He goes further and says that it needs not only preparation by God, but God also eternally and timelessly foreknows that it will be so for both the saved and the damned, without that foreknowledge determining events in men's lives (*On the Predestination of the Saints* III.7; *Iohann. Evangel.* CXXIV.48.4.6, CVII.7, CXI.5).[20]

But in this life no one can be completely freed from his fallen freedom and no one has a "right" to be freed. Even the (unknown) elect cannot be rewarded for something for which they are not responsible: God's gift of salvific grace to some and not others. Augustine's final view in the *City of God* XIII was to deny that man even tries to do what he wishes to do and to know what he ought to do: He does not try at all and he certainly fails.[21] It is this irrational and unintelligible nature that, in the end, requires the kind of punitive law of

[18] In *On the Deserts and Remission of Sin* (*De Peccatorum Meritis et Remissione*), against Pelagius.

[19] For a wide-ranging discussion of Augustine on free will, see Stump 2001, 124–47.

[20] Many have observed a "paradox" in this freedom by noting a determinism that obscures what could be voluntary in willing. See Kenny 1975; and O'Daly 1989, especially 90–7, where he writes that Augustine's defense of a notion of freedom of will is not possible: It is a "glorious and influential failure." See also the remarkable analysis of Connolly 1993.

[21] *CD* XIII.14 describes a permanent condition, a "genetic" covetousness *concupiscentia*: "From the misuse of free will there started a chain of disasters: mankind is led from that original perversion, a kind of corruption at the root, right up to the disaster of the second death which has no end. Only those who are set free through God's grace escape from this calamitous sequence."

states that Augustine would outline elsewhere in the *City of God*.[22] Our condition here is penal. Man's behavior is determined not by reasoning but by the set of his will, which is a morass of habitual loves and hates (*83 Questions*, 40). Augustine had earlier discussed how bad habits can only be broken by suffering not only at the hands of men and their law, but also in the schoolroom: He describes how he was driven with threats and savage punishments to learn Greek (*Conf.* I.14.23). Later in life he saw man as needing to be continuously driven to correction, by the church's unwelcome discipline, by the father's punitive discipline in the home, and by the state's punitive discipline through enforced law and the executioner. If it is not in our power to reform ourselves, it is also not in our power to reform underlying evils that structure secular society: We can only vary them fatalistically. Augustine's final view was that the kind of man who needs God's grace is a man who requires utter transformation. It is the transformation of Saul into St. Paul. The transformation that is promised only to those predestined to salvation—not all are saved (*CD* XIII.23; *Ench.* XXVII.103)—is not a return to the original, Adamic moral self before the Fall, but rather, the gift of a self better than Adam (*CD* XIII.24; XXII.30).

In opposition to the philosophical tradition, men are now unable to achieve their drive toward perfection, wholeness, fulfillment, and peace. Like Paul, Augustine came to deny that the order that leads through all things to God is to be found in human affairs or revealed either in human philosophy or human law (Rom. 3:28). The possibility of securing happiness through the government of the wise, through following the rigors of outward legal precepts, or through men perfectly dedicated either to philosophy or to what they conceive of as God, is, in the end, an illusion. Since human society is irremediably rooted in disordered and tension-ridden history the only resolution of ultimate desires must be eschatological. Consequently, the itinerary to perfection involves finding rather than seeking the truth. Hence, Augustine explained what the *immortal* happy *next* life consists in. He criticized what he took to be pagan philosophy's false accounts of happiness and their bad advice on how to achieve it, changing his own mind as he moved further away from his youthful "Hellenistic" perspectives to a reliance on the Bible, Paul, and the teachings of an increasingly unified, institutional church. He sought, as did philosophers, a moral philosophy—but one based in scripture—that would reveal what has intrinsic, as opposed to instrumental, worth for us. Once this was clarified, he would show how politics should be seen as merely useful rather than as something having intrinsic worth.

We can draw the contrast between ancient and Christian ethics as follows. The answer to the question concerning the scope of human responsibility and

[22] Cf. Cicero, *Tusc.* II, on pain as an evil to be endured or conquered, as well as the various philosophical schools' views on this issue.

free will, for much of ancient ethics as a whole and, in particular, for Stoic ethics, came in their refusal to consider any impulses or desires as inaccessible to rational guidance and discourse. But by the early-fifth century, and especially for Augustine, ancient ethics was seen as part of a perverse human fantasy of self-perfection, self-sufficient omnipotence, and self-dependent authority. The whole philosophical tradition exemplified, for Augustine, man's original sin, that of pride which rejoices in private goods and a perverse self-love. Augustine argued that for man's will to be free it cannot be understood as autonomous. Without Christian revelation we are nothing more than bundles of competing selves, with no sages in our midst. Where ancient ethics focused on man's ability to know himself and his responsibility either for self-perfection in the creation of a unified moral self or for successfully crafting his character to suit his circumstances, Augustine insisted that we can only be inwardly certain of self-existence. Humans may desire, but through their own efforts can never achieve, tranquility and moral wholeness.

Human autonomy is, then, a delusion of self-determination. Politics is no more than a symptom of the multiplicity of fallen man's partial and often competing loves. Augustine's answer to the question concerning the degree to which it is possible to treat man as having a measure of rational control over his political environment or even over his conscious moral intentions is that it is exceedingly limited. Here he absorbs aspects of ancient skepticism. But to this he adds the necessity of receiving God's unmerited grace so that a man's nature might be prepared and repaired if he is to experience moral development at all.

8.3. Augustine on Law and Order

At the basis of Augustine's conception of law and order is the "eternal law" (*lex aeterna*), that eternal plan of the world, reason, and the divine will, where the divine order respects the divinely created natural order and is inscribed in the human soul as the "natural law" (*lex naturalis*).[23] Each conscience, including a pagan's, is constrained by this natural law, and for this reason pagans are also able to formulate "the most useful of precepts" (*praecepta utilissima*). At first Augustine thought that human law could contribute substantially to man's itinerary toward perfection, in that it reflects the eternal law, and as a principle in nature is accessible to men through reason. The order of nature and the order expressed in human choices and enacted in human action could, thereby, constitute two streams of divine providence in the world. He observed that Christianity provides a new orientation in that it posits that the natural law (*lex naturalis*) is anterior to both Mosaic and New Testament

[23] See *Conf.* I.18.29; II.4.9, where such impressed rules are themselves unjudgeable. See also Rom. 2:14–16.

law. But Christianity also insists that God has his law written down so as to prevent men from invoking the excuse of ignorance of its precepts (*Enarr. in Psal.* 57.1 [= *PL* 36.673]). Augustine came to deny the unaided capacity for good in man, and he also refused to accept the philosophical position that a few, wise men have such a capacity and that having this capacity is all that matters. The written Mosaic and New Testament law is there for all and, having been written, it is understood by a weakened but still flickering light of reason. But corrupt wills can, in practice, ignore its light. Where the moral law of the Old Testament is in substance identical with the natural law, Christian law perfects it. Its object is to go beyond the Ten Commandments and provide guidance to prevent one from doing to others what one would not wish done to oneself (*Ep.* 157.3.15 [= *CSEL* 44.463]; *Enarr. in Psal.* 118; *Sermo* 25.4 [= *PL* 37.1574]). The natural law (*lex naturalis*) is, then, the source and measure of human positive law, and the human legislator's mission is to follow its prescriptions. But the legislator need not order everything that the natural law prescribes nor forbid everything it forbids. Augustine saw the legislator's mission as realizing on earth the order that is necessary for human society to attain its temporal and spiritual ends. Hence, legislators are engaged in adapting the eternal law to the varieties of peoples and their social relations at a given time. Eternal law is the unwritten plan of everything, expressive of the divine will as divine order. It is larger than but pervades the created natural order. In man, as part of the created order, it is inscribed as *lex* in his soul, and written down in Old and New Testament law as commandments which constitute the divine law whose precepts should be recapitulated in the positive law of societies to fix men's obligations to one another. Legislators take into account the conditions of the times and the characters of the people being governed; it is the conformity to divine law's precepts that gives human law its obligatory force. But fallible human legislators achieve their end of legislating in conformity with the eternal law by means of historically and temporally judged forms of punitive constraint.

Augustine later defined human law (*ius humanum*)—both secular imperial law and human ecclesiastical law—as it was developing in his own time in *opposition* to divine law. His view of moral evil and his increasing focus on the disordered will in fallen men entailed not only that it is impossible to construct an institutional or legal utopia in this life, but that peace and order on earth also require utilitarian strategies to "do good" to a man against his will in order to secure temporary peace and concord in society. Acculturation to moral norms is to be achieved through infliction of pain throughout the whole of men's lives because both psychological and physical pain are, for him, the essential and enduring conditions of living a fallen, human life (see Rom. 5:3–4; cf. Cicero, *Tusc.* II). He came to argue that the state and its laws cannot make men good or even capable of performing any good act with the right intentions. Rather, it is punishment that constrains us to obey the law. The law does not and cannot reeducate us. Augustine's mature conception of the state is that it is a temporal power that rightly has the monopoly of coercive force. This is so, regardless of any attempts by legislators or philosophers to justify by moral principle either the state's foundations or the means employed to secure its end. Augustine thereby argued not for the moral but for the functional "reason of state": The state and its absolute sovereign authority is the power that is ordained by an inscrutable but loving God; the state has the sole authority to define the terms of justice in this world in order to secure peace and order, even if this definition appears to man to be unjust. We shall see that Augustine argued that there is no legitimate individual resistance to political authority, even when it appears unjust, so long as it serves the end of securing peace and order and, thereby, ensuring men's conformity to the natural law.

8.4. Augustine the Roman in His Times

The half century from around 380 to approximately 430 marked a watershed in the cultural and religious history of western Europe (see Markus 1990; Herrin 1987; Fox 1986; Brown 1972; Coleman 2000, vol. 1; Hunt 1993). The last great controversy over the Altar of Victory in the Roman Senate (382–4)—a conflict between aristocratic pagan Romans with an allegiance to Roman traditions of government and a history of successful expansion and domination, on the one hand, and the Christian regime of emperor Theodosius I in the 390s, on the other—had been preceded by a long preparation for Christianity's triumph. In the late-third century Christians had begun to penetrate every level of Roman society and to assimilate the cultural lifestyles and education of Roman townsmen. Emperor Constantine's conversion to Christianity in 312 and the subsequent flow of imperial favor brought an increase in Christian respectability, prestige, and wealth. By 350 there was very little that seemed to separate a Christian from his pagan counterpart. If Christianity began as a religion attracting the lower classes, by the mid-fourth century the conversion of the upper classes was well underway and their roles in the Senate and civil service expanded. Roman government and education were running down in the western provinces, since Constantine had shifted the bureaucratic center of the empire eastward to Constantinople. Rome was seen by some as a traditionalist backwater. In Rome's social structure and governmental administrative functions, there was a growing prominence of the military and the Christian clergy with their more clerically orientated and scriptural culture. The western part of the empire experienced the spread of an ascetic mentality with its heightened attention to questions concerning Christian identity: What is it to be a Christian? Is being a Christian a special way of being a Jew? How much of the Jewish law is to be applied and how much to be dismissed as of no religious importance? Where does religion end and secular traditions, especially as enshrined in Roman law, custom, and history, begin? To what degree is religion attached to the manners of the inner or outer man? This was the Pauline agenda, penetrated by Stoic and neo-Platonist insights.

It has often been noted by historians that in the pagan polytheistic world, notably of Rome, religion touched everything. A Roman's religion and his civic contribution to the preservation of the "state" were intertwined, since morality and religion were public expressions. Early Christians, however, were regarded, like Jews, with suspicion and as teaching a private religion, caring little for the survival of Roman institutions, customs, and values. They were seen as dedicated to an apocalyptic vision of a united society after Rome and history, and underwent, as a consequence, waves of persecution by Roman authorities and local communities. But by the late-fourth century, the mass Christianization of Roman society was depriving Christians of a discernible identity clearly separable from their pagan neighbors, since Christians could now take for granted the recognition of their church and relegate to the past the collective experience of persecution and martyrdom. But insofar as there was little—other than his religion—to distinguish an educated Christian in this late-Roman world from his educated non-Christian counterpart, intellectuals (not least Augustine) at first found it easy to pass from Stoicism and neo-Platonism to Christianity, because of pagan philosophy's instruction on the soul's access to another, more real world, its return to the One and the soul's own origin, and to truth. In the *Confessions*, Augustine describes his conversion to Christianity by means of his prior conversion to Platonism with its rational control of the body and an ascetic morality of detachment as a means to inner freedom. Indeed, he spent the first months after his conversion in the company of Christian friends in philosophical retirement, linking, as he then saw it, his unbroken progression from philosophical conversion to his adoption of a monastic and contemplative mode of life at Cassiciacum: He was living the "Christian life of leisure/reflection" (*Christianae vitae otium*). This prepared him for his attempt to set up a monastic community in North Africa where he could use his reading in leisurely fashion as an instrument to attain God. He would be living a lifestyle of detached simplicity, emancipated from wants properly regarded as indifferent, which was training in virtue. This was the Christian way to achieve philosophical self-mastery and a freedom from the passions that were thought to disturb the pursuits of the truly educated mind. Although the Stoic parallels are numerous, this monastic life was also consciously modeled on the first apostolic community, living in concord, sharing all property, where the root of all sin was private, self-enclosure that would be banished in this monastic republic (*res publica*) of God (*Op. Mon.* 25.32). The Stoic ideal of unspoiled human relationships and loving friendship would be fulfilled in that Christian monastic setting where men seek their own souls and God in concord together (*Sol.* I.12.20).

But Augustine thereafter recounts in the *Confessions* how he came to realize that the transition from being a Latin rhetor and a Platonist to being a

Christian is not an easy transition at all. It has to be a complete and revolutionary break. The values of his monastic community can only be realized eschatologically in the post-historical city that is the city of God.[24] Gradually, Augustine refused to treat the Roman empire as an "evangelical preparation" (*praeparatio evangelica*) for the evangelical phase of history, coming instead to insist on the homogeneity of redemption history between the Incarnation and the Parousia—the whole period since Christ to the last days—with the consequent lack of significance to sacred history of one or another historical and political regime. He came to see the Christianization of the Roman Empire as accidental to the history of salvation and, furthermore, as reversible: Rome could not be accorded any religious meaning. Indeed, no events after the Incarnation had any sacred significance and, therefore, could not affect the history of salvation. From having originally found scripture unsophisticated and primitive, Augustine came to believe that outside the narrow bounds of the scriptural canon accepted by his contemporary church, no one could have authoritative access to God's intentions in the past, present, or future of the world's history (*Contra Epistulam Fundamenti* V.6; *Faust.* XXV.1.5.6).

Although there were Epicurean, skeptic, and especially Stoic precursors to some of Augustine's views, his final perspectives on an ordered and peaceful life in a human community show him to have been very much a Roman of his times. Roman imperial law in a newly Christian empire exercised a strong influence on his thinking about the earthly city as seen from his vantage point as a bishop in North Africa. His philosophy of law, when applied to historically contingent political regimes, reveals him to be an heir less to pagan Rome and its Latin renderings of Greek philosophy than to imperial reformulations of post-classical Roman law from the Christian Empire beginning with Emperor Constantine (see Gaudemet 1957). His views on the city and its citizens are more easily understood as deriving from, but crucially breaking with, the ancient philosophical tradition. By interpreting Augustine's thought within the social and intellectual context that helped produce it, we can see how much he is a fourth- and early-fifth century North African Roman with a standard and unquestioned view about hierarchies of power from the emperor to the army, government, oligarchies, families, masters, and servants. He believed without question that women should serve men, children their parents, animals their human owners, and slaves their masters (see, e.g., *Sermo* 332.4.4). His vision implies an almost nonexistent power of ordinary

[24] Many of his Christian contemporaries looked upon the post-Constantinian and Theodosian times as progressive, a perpetual Roman peace (*pax Romana*) in which the Christian Empire could now be seen as a special place in God's providential plan of universal history. Mankind was now united under the rule of Remus so that, as Prudentius (*Peristephanon* II.425–34 [= *CC* 126] as quoted in Markus 1970, 51) had written, "customs once diverse now agree in speech and thought" and "this was destined in order that the authority [*ius*] of the Christian name might bind with one tie all that is anywhere on earth."

citizens. Neither Plato, Aristotle, nor Cicero held to such an empty notion of citizenship, or to such a strong view of uncritical faith in, and obedience to, authority. But Augustine's late imperial North African and Roman world under a *princeps* or emperor was not theirs. He accepted the late imperial Roman conditions of dominance and subservience as the very framework of all authority, even if he was also aware of abuses of power. He was unusually outspoken about the degree to which no person escapes, in this life, that kind of verbal and social conditioning to which he is subjected by authorities. This emerges from his theological hypothesis, the Fall of Adam, whereafter a desire to dominate, through speech or otherwise, and the attempt to satisfy this desire, constitute the characteristic features of fallen society. Having rejected obedience to God's authority at the Fall, the sons of Adam are always trying to reconstitute it.

8.5. Contemporary Roman Law and Augustine

Augustine's increasing awareness of political and social instability from 410 onward helped to shift his views on the relationship between the individual and society. Recognizing pervasive human wickedness and folly, he denied that civic institutions could be educational. Peace has always been, and only can be, achieved through force. Under Emperor Theodosius I (d. 395), the western part of the now Christianized empire comprised Italy, Africa, Gaul, Spain, and Britain. In 380 Theodosius issued an edict that defined the apostolic tradition from St. Peter as the *religio* of tradition (*CTh* 16.1.2), and this was meant to bring the language of Christian doctrine into the realms of Roman law. There is scholarly controversy over whether Christian doctrine influenced the laws of Constantine and his imperial successors,[25] but it is certain that the social structure reflected in the laws and the nature of the penalties are evidence of an increasing penetration of civil law into the private realm. The (incomplete) Theodosian Code was compiled by emperor Theodosius II and his advisers beginning in the 420s and finally published in 438. This code rationalized current legislation and legal opinions, assembling imperial constitutions from 312 onward,[26] and gives us a view of the last expression of Roman imperial unity as Augustine himself would have known it.

[25] See the various contributions to Harries and Wood 1993; Matthews 2000; Honoré 1981. On the role of the Catholic Church in North Africa during the later Roman empire of the fifth century, see Courtois 1985; Gaudemet 1958; Gaudemet 1957, 135–212. Gaudemet (1957, 143) states: "The considerable innovation of Constantine would have consisted in transforming the canons of church councils into civil laws and obliging their acknowledgment upon pain of secular sanction. While councils had the power of imposition, the secular law's recapitulations did not provide any new force to such prescriptions *as conciliar* decisions."

[26] The Theodosian Code was meant to be a successor to earlier (late-third-century) codes of Gregorius and Hermogenianus. See Chapter 6, Section 6.1, of this volume for further discussion.

The Theodosian Code contains numerous Constantinian laws, approximately 25 percent of which deal in some way with the family and sexual relations (see Gaudemet 1983; Grubbs 1993). Constantine had repealed laws that previously penalized celibacy and childlessness. This was part of his wide-ranging program designed to facilitate inheritance procedures, especially for the wealthier classes, defending traditional Roman marriage and morality (see Clark 1993, especially chap. 1). Subsequent laws took into consideration the enthusiasm for Christian asceticism and celibacy among Roman senatorial families, and there were sumptuary laws issued in the 390s that forbade actresses to dress like nuns (*CTh* XV.7.11–12) and regulations for prohibiting ascetic women who had cut their hair short from entering churches (*CTh* XVI.2.17.1). Constantine had also toughened up the law on betrothal (*CTh* III.5.4, 5, 332). There is also evidence in the Theodosian Code XVI.10.11, 391, of a legal distinction between *religio* and (pagan, heretical, and Jewish) *superstitio*.[27] The view articulated here (XVI.2.25) is that true Catholic *religio* claims that the heretic commits sacrilege not merely in the bureaucratic sense of refusing imperial orders, but also in the religious sense of challenging the true faith that issues from the emperor. What issued from the emperor was not so much an expression of imperial whim, but was, rather, a reflection of the decisions of a network of episcopal politics and church councils where conclusions of councils were incorporated into imperial legal responses. By 421 this reflected the recognition of the institutional church's privileged place in the eyes of the state (see Hunt 1993, 148–51). Stringent laws were passed against heresy, notably to bring schismatic Christians, such as the Donatists, within their scope (*CTh* XVI.6.4 pr.). The Christian Roman state had not only become intolerant of any other religious allegiances and practices, but also sought to forge a unity of Christians under the law. Increasingly what was taken to be *religio* became a defined set of beliefs derived from the apostles (and the council of Nicaea) now "spoken" by imperial lips. Augustine's familiarity with this Roman law is especially revealed in his ethico-religious concerns regarding his pastoral duties, as reflected in his numerous letters and sermons. He had views on all of these issues concerning betrothal, marriage, celibacy, inheritance, a unified *religio*, and the role of the emperor in enforcing religious discipline and unity.[28]

Late Roman law was presented in the form of the emperor speaking to his people—often in the corporate "we" form of address or sometimes "iuxta stat-

[27] See Lactantius, *Inst.* IV.28.11 and 3, on the etymological origins of *religio*, compared with Cicero, *ND* II.72.

[28] On the relation between law and religious change, see Brown 1972, 301–31. On Augustine's familiarity with Roman law as well as his ethico-religious concerns regarding his pastoral duties, see De Salvo 1993. On Augustine's recourse to secular law in Hippo, see Brown 1967, 192–8; Getty 1931.

utum legis meae"—with the emperor portrayed as a severe but loving *paterfamilias* ("master of the house") responding to questions, threatening penalties, and explaining why changes in the law are necessary, most notably in family law. The Theodosian Code was to be valid for all lawsuits and legal transactions, while jurisprudence was acknowledged as a separate discipline where "judges" (*iudices*) had no authority to interpret or make law themselves. The aim was to communicate the will and the character of the emperor to his subjects. The wording of the emperor's pronouncements from the fourth century was owed to the imperial quaestors as legal advisors who drafted his laws, the topics often coming from "proposals" (*suggestiones*) on the running of the empire sent from praetorian prefects, those authorities to which provincial governors and "local officials" (*vicarii*) looked. Such officials were among Augustine's correspondents.[29] Augustine was in Milan when Valentinian II issued the law permitting the free assembly of Arian Christian congregations (*CTh* XVI.1.4; see also *Conf.* IX.7).[30] This rather pointedly opposed Ambrose's attempts to prevent any congregations other than Catholic ones; Augustine speaks of Ambrose being persecuted for his exclusionist views.

Significantly, from Constantine onward, bishops as one increasingly influential section of the community could approach the emperor without fear. Although internal church discipline was regulated by canons of church councils, bishops often found it convenient to request the backing of the secular arm to enforce ecclesiastical rule. The praetorian prefects were given the task of keeping the peace in cities across the empire, responding to wide-ranging or even local proposals of the clergy. In this milieu Augustine practiced his own ministry in Hippo, and even from his earlier days in Rome and Milan he was acquainted with men of high rank who administered the law.[31] By hearing the law announced in public places and reading it when posted on notice boards, usually in ephemeral form, the populations of the Empire were expected to have knowledge of it, and legal authorities were to take note by making copies of imperial enactments. It is significant that the Theodosian Code I.27.1 (A.D. 318) speaks of a bishop's judgment as "sacred" and final. The *locus classicus*

[29] In earlier years before he became Rome's *praefectus urbi* ("prefect of the city") (417–418) and Italy's *praefectus praetoria* ("praetorian prefect") under Valentinian III (428–429), the senator Rufius Antonius Agrypnius Volusianus (d. 438) had been a correspondent of Augustine: *Ep.* 135.2. He was later baptized and, while on an embassy to attend the wedding of Valentinian III and Theodosius II's daughter, he heard Theodosius' announcement of his compendium of imperial law. On Volusianus and Augustine, see Brown 1967, 300–3; Matthews 1993, especially 20, and Matthews 2000.

[30] The law warned that those who refused other Christians from gathering would be regarded as authors of sedition and as disturbers of the peace of the church and shall, in consequence of their provoking agitation against the regulation of the imperial tranquility, and as authors of sedition and disturbers of the peace of the church, pay the penalty of high treason with their life and blood.

[31] See *Conf.* VI.8, 10, on his friend Alypius' legal career.

is Constantine's reply to the Christian praetorian prefect Ablabius' enquiry on the status of episcopal judgments (*sententiae episcoporum*): "[T]he authority of holy religion searches out and reveals many things which the ensnaring bonds of legal technicality do not allow to be produced in court" (*Sirmondian Constitutions* I.5 [A.D. 333] as quoted in Seeck 1919). In both criminal and civil cases episcopal judgments are said to last forever and without possibility of review. A bishop's word is said to be necessarily true and incorruptible, issuing as it does from a holy man "in consciousness of an undefiled mind"; hence, their verdicts are held to be inviolable and sacrosanct. After Constantine there were efforts to enforce separate spheres of secular and episcopal jurisdiction so that in cases involving religion it was seen as appropriate to trouble bishops, but matters having to do with ordinary judges and the public law were to be heard in accordance with the laws (*CTh* XVI.11.1 [A.D. 399]; *CTh* XVI.2.23 [A.D. 376]). Augustine, as bishop of Hippo, had to have recourse to both secular law and ecclesiastical law in his ministry. There was no generally accepted canon law available for consultation at this time, and church discipline varied over time and place just as did secular law, with the consequence that local magistrates and bishops had considerable discretion in applying the law. The codification of canon law probably did not begin until 545 when the emperor Justinian decreed that the canons of the councils of Nicaea, Constantinople, Ephesus, and Chalcedon had the status of law. In Augustine's time, scope was allowed for the standards of local communities and for the discretion of local magistrates and clergy across the empire (see Clark 1993; Gaudemet 1957, 171, n. 5).

Augustine presents us with a distinction between the normative order of Christian imperial Roman culture, on the one hand, and the varied experiences and individual choices of daily, provincial social life, on the other, interweaving his particular ethical and political perspectives. While accepting late-imperial Roman conditions of dominance and subservience, he also argues that the church on earth is a mixed community of the predestined saved and damned. But he believes that the church, as an authority, backed by its interpretation of scripture which is never wrong (*Contra Epistulam Fundamenti* V.6; *Faust.* XXV.1.5.6), still is able to discern when to take severe measures, even against those who may be innocent, for the greater good of peace and order, since no one is ever truly innocent of sin. This parallels his view of the role of the Roman magistrate and judge, whose knowledge is not infallible but whose duty it is to take severe action, even against the innocent, in order to secure peace and order (*CD* XIX.6). He argues that humans always do and, indeed, must operate within and under authority. Authority is necessarily of a certain kind in this life precisely because of what human nature now is; hence, it determines what politics and unified church discipline necessarily are for. His focus on our need to have faith in authority is a consequence not only of his "reading" of human nature through pagan philosophy, history, and scripture, but also of his having been a late-imperial Roman expressing widely shared views on state authority, coercion, and the utility of paternalistic government for the good of its citizens even against their wills. Augustine grafted his version of why Christians hold paternalism to be permissible onto a Roman imperial argument concerning what law was for and how it operated in citizens' lives.

Law as punitive constraint—where the citizens' liberty is defined by the space carved out by the silence of the authoritative, positive law—was already emphasized by Roman imperial rule of Augustine's time. As he sees it, the space carved out by the silence of the law is filled with acts proceeding from man's now corrupted free choice to follow his divided loves and misconstrued self-interest. Where Augustine argued for Christ's interior teaching, prepared for in each Christian by the authoritative teaching of the unified church, Roman imperial law proliferated to fill that space of silence to regulate those private behaviors seen as potentially disruptive of public order. For Augustine and fellow clergy, Christians were to live by a higher standard than the human law issued by emperors, but they were also to live by imperial law.[32] Constantine had already altered Roman law on divorce with a list of penalties[33] in order to make it more difficult to secure, but he did not limit the reasons for divorce to the wife's adultery as did some Christians. There is some evidence for a Christian influence on this toughening of divorce law, which was generally much harsher on women than on men (see Volterra 1958).[34] But most Christians would not have thought that Constantine's law differed significantly from their own beliefs. Augustine (*CD* XV.16) also discusses the principle by which marriage partners are to be selected, which reflects the law of Theodosius I forbidding marriage of the children of two brothers or the children of two sisters, in contrast to practices in the Christian Greek and near eastern parts of the empire.[35] The growth in imperial constraints on individual liberty, then, served as a partial model for Augustine's understanding of the scope of temporal authority and coercive sanction and the changes in the law reflected the kind of "earthly city" in which Augustine lived his life. It was the general governance of the "earthly city,"

[32] In *On the Good Marriage* VII [*PL* 40.378], Augustine goes beyond contemporary Roman law by insisting not only on restraint from divorce and remarriage, but also by arguing that even if a Christian man divorces his wife for adultery he is forbidden to remarry before her death.

[33] See *CTh* III.16.1. (A.D. 331), which was revived in modified form in *CTh* III.16.2 (A.D. 421).

[34] This is modified by Grubbs 1993, 127–9. For the view that divorce by consent was more readily available in the eastern empire than in the western, see Bagnall 1987.

[35] See Clark 1993, 42–6, on the persistent Roman attempt to end eastern endogamy; also see Saller 1994, 71. On the frequency of pre-Christian Roman divorce, see Crook 1967; Treggiari 1991. Marriage was seen as a continuing contract entered into by consent and, therefore, when consent came to an end the marriage ended (Justinian, *Code* VIII.38.2 [A.D. 223]). Hence, there was less interest in fault, but under Augustus there were strict penalties for the adultery of either spouse, on which see Johnston 1999, 34–7.

and not any historical manifestation of it, that enabled him to craft a vision of secular authority as coercive and useful to all. Imperial legislation and administration thereby allowed him selectively to ignore what was once, in Roman republican theory at least, the recognition of a simultaneous capacity in each citizen to evaluate, rationally and critically, just as opposed to unjust authority, and to act on this evaluation. This is not to say that he does not distinguish between better (Christian) and worse governments, but his point is that no government can be truly satisfying because none can satisfy men's desire for happiness as an intrinsic good.

The increasing inscrutability of imperial authority, brought to a kind of absolutism in the Greek-speaking Christian Byzantine east, would eventually provide the Latin west with the eastern Emperor Justinian's sixth-century codification of Roman law, the *Corpus Iuris Civilis*, which incorporated but went beyond the Theodosian Code. Justinian's Code[36] was to be appealed to by anyone, from the twelfth century when it was revived, who was interested in a centralized theocratic theory and practice of imperial Rome. They would find that it asserts that imperial authority derives from God; medieval commentators interpreted this to mean that the emperor was "ruler of the world" (*dominus mundi*). But where the theory of the theocratic state in the Byzantine east with its emphasis on imperial power, entrusted to the Christian emperor and derived directly from God's command, enabled the imperial law to be regarded as sacred, Augustine stopped short of endorsing this utopian unity of church and state. Instead, he argued for the less than perfect natures of the historical church and state. He transferred the sacred cause of imperial inscrutability away from the state and to God's power working in, and over and beyond, history. For religious purposes—ultimately, the individual's salvation—Augustine held the state to be neutral in the sense of morally and salvifically indifferent rather than sacred. But for secular purposes, necessary and arbitrary constraints by state authority are themselves determined by the needs of the times. Christian rulers and officials, he believed, owe service to God in their public capacities. When they act in the interest of the church, they do so as Christians who happen to have secular authority rather than as officials of the Christian Roman state. The church, then, uses the state to further Christian interests (as these are interpreted by church authority) in order to establish at least the conditions for the morally good act to be performed upon the hoped-for, but not guaranteed, reception of grace. Pastoral expediency, however, was part of Augustine's larger conviction based on his understanding of men's need to believe in authority *tout court.* The need for curbing violence and the sins that men will commit became paramount for him, so that temporal government must do what it can even if God does the rest. It is this vision that emerged in its final form in the *City of God.*

[36] See Coleman 2000, vol. 2: 33–8; also see Chapter 10, Section 10.1, of this volume.

Imperial Rome fostered the image of the civil community as *useful* for maintaining peace and order. In having construed the image of the city and the citizen in this light, the imperial experience in the fourth and fifth centuries de-emphasized that aspect of the vision of the ancient philosophers which saw the *civitas* ("city" as law-governed political community) not only as securing peace and order, but, more importantly, as the setting for the self-motivated achievement of the human good—man's *eudaimonia* ("happiness")—his fulfillment through educated and self-directed moral choice and autonomy. Roman imperial reality and its law, however, highlighted as never before the notion that force can be justified in securing assent when the consequences of dissent for the peace and order of society are grave; more generally, it highlighted that an infinite harm needs only to be minimally probable in order to be worth avoiding through coercion. The utility theory of the state, found in Cicero's *On Duties* and his *On the Commonwealth* (see Coleman 2000, vol. 1: 251–66), was elaborated in late-imperial Christian Roman practice, but without what Cicero had provided as a Stoic balance to this: the reconciliation of the *utile* ("the useful act") with the *honestum* ("the good act in itself"). This utility theory and practice of imperial Rome constituted Augustine's milieu.

Augustine's version of this utility theory of the state is that so long as law serves the end of securing peace and order, and thereby ensures men's conformity to the natural law by preventing them from doing to others what they would not wish done to themselves, law achieves its purpose by being determined by the times and the peoples governed. By definition, human law, including human ecclesiastical law, is both mutable and fallible. Authorities can and do modify or dispense with the law for reasons of necessity and utility. This is not to say that Augustine is unconcerned with the injustice of certain human laws, an injustice that was often the product of the minds of fallen men. Indeed, he insists that human law and certain customs are unjust when they go against religious teaching, morality, and discipline. Local customs, even those not directly "against the faith" (*contra fidem*) are to be rejected if they cannot be shown to be in conformity with scripture and the councils and customs of the universal church (*Ep.* 54.2, 55.34 [= *CSEL* 34, 160, 208]). For him, the public authority suited to interpreting the exact meaning of scripture, church councils, and universal customs is the apostolic Catholic Church (*Faust.* XI.2 [= *PL* 42.246]; *De Vera Religione* 50.99 [= *PL* 34, 166]). The public authority suited to interpreting imperial law is the secular magistrate following imperial will. No separation of the two powers is implied: They are to work in collaboration for peace and order in the earthly city, sharing a concern for man's temporal and supernatural destiny. Secular authority in its juridical and coercive manifestation is to be used for religious ends, most notably in the battle against heresy, which, from the state's point of view, threatened the unity of the empire. The privately acknowledged injustice of human imperial law could not, therefore, authorize rebellion; only a passive resistance to its unjust precepts, even to the point of martyrdom, could be legitimate (*CD* VIII.19). "As for this mortal life, which ends after a few days' course, what does it matter under whose rule a man lives, being so soon we die, provided that rulers do not force him to impious and wicked acts?" (*CD* V.17).

8.6. Augustine on Roman History and the Lessons for Politics

Augustine read about the history of republican Rome during this late imperial period, just before and just after the empire's adoption of Christianity as the state religion, and his political theory emerged from his reading of history. It has become fashionable to say that Augustine does not, strictly speaking, have a political theory. He does not, of course, have a notion of political theory as found in modern university departments of politics, but he has a much more enduring notion of history, which from ancient times was the study of war and politics, so that his political theory is precisely a consequence of this reading of the historical evidence men left of their (usually misguided) motivations to achieve worldly virtue and power. Certain assumptions about second- and first-century B.C. social coherence during the republican period remained dominant in the late fourth century A.D., but were somewhat differently construed (see Shaw 1987; Saller 1994). The Roman theory of governance and Rome's practice of rule by an inner circle of nobles influenced Augustine's view of paternalistic state authority. He insists that men must and do follow authorities, always seeking understanding on the basis of the trusted testimony of others, which is a form of belief rather than certain knowledge. Even the use of conventional language requires a coherent and trusted social context that allows for stable conventions of communication. Belief that is based on the authority of others is a necessary condition of human life in the family and society.

The model of the Roman *civitas* that Augustine accepts is one of a hierarchical society of patrons, who are heads of prominent families with a large clientele and are obliged by religiously sanctioned custom (*fides*) to protect their clients whether or not the clients are economically dependent on the patrons. Clients are obliged by a social and moral duty and by religious sanction to support their patron's political will (*obsequium*). Augustine's notion of authority parallels this Roman model in which the custom of the patron and the support of the clients created strong vertical links within a pyramid structure of society. This is not simply an image of the legal construct of the severe, all-powerful father, but an ideal of mutual allegiances and dutiful affections. The strong coherence within this pyramid, whose structure was based on social power and influence, had two important effects. First, in the republican period there emerged a kind of small state within a state, which relied on the power and patronage used by the *paterfamilias* to rule his kin and clients in order to help safeguard discipline and social order in the state at large. The locus of his dealings with his public was his "private home" (*domus*). Second, the *paterfamilias* did not have the discretion to shape law and order arbitrarily, even in this small state within the state. Rather, moral values and a general code of conduct were forged and adopted by an elite of nobles. A consensus about moral behavior among a few nobles at the top of the social pyramid, who met in political groups or officially in the Senate thereafter, permeated downward to the citizen body. The consequence of this was that the opinion of the few at the top became the obligatory consensus of the much greater number of citizens at the bottom (see Eder 1991).

This top-down creation of an obligatory consensus was related to the conception of citizenship in Rome. Unlike the ancient Greek understanding of the citizen of the *polis*, citizenship for the Roman was an acquired civic right, but as such it did not entail the right to participate in power or self-governance. Indeed, citizenship was not a means to political participation, even in the republican period, unless it was supported by wealth, status, and residence in the capital, Rome. It was the common task of the elite group of citizens, as magistrates in the Senate, to anticipate social violence and destabilizations by taking into consideration the various interests of all Romans through compromises and reconciliations between competing classes or status-groups, a balancing that it was the duty of this elite to secure, which was described by Cicero as their achievement of a "concord of the orders" (*concordia ordinum*; *Off.* II.84).

Augustine finds in Cicero's and Sallust's analyses[37] the story of what happened when this elite no longer saw it as their common task to achieve consensus. Negotiations supposedly were left individually to various heads of the small states within the state, and an upper class elite consensus disintegrated. It was this tendency to a privatization of power that typified the end of the republic, and Augustine sees it as a tendency typical of the human social condition generally when there is no overriding authority to keep such privatized and willful men in awe through punitive means. It is then that Cicero had advised the need for a single rector or a new elite of leaders to bring republican Rome back from corruption to health, by which he meant the re-establishment of a senatorial elite with its confirmed and historical traditions founded in frugality, a disdain for personal luxury and material greed, and commitment to internal civic concord combined with external glory through conquest.

Augustine, the imperial Roman, maintains the need for authoritative elites, but he has much less confidence in them than does Cicero. He sees them not as ideals but as *de facto* necessities in history, in whose authority men believe

[37] Augustine uses Sallust's *War with Catiline* and *War with Jurgurtha* extensively, along with Cicero's *On the Commonwealth*, in many of his writings. See esp. *CD* V.12–15. In fact, all moralizing Roman historians and playwrights, e.g., Plautus, *Bacch.* 410, use the recurrent motif of moral rhetoric to complain of a decline from some prehistoric age of virtue.

because their existence is justified by an even firmer belief in God's authority and the church's authority in interpreting God's will. The historical church and state elites are separately but relatedly provided with written law that enjoins concord, with the state serving the church in order to secure obedience to it. The authoritative elite in the unified church is enjoined to disdain luxury and wealth, and to follow scriptural authority in order to pursue voluntary poverty, continence, benevolence, and the just concord of piety, since "heavenly authority arrived into this filthy confluence for the sake of unity in the earthly city and also for everlasting well-being and the heavenly and divine republic whose peoples are everlasting" (*Ep.* 138, as quoted in Tkacz and Kries 1994, 211). The authoritative elite of the earthly city has a mission, like that of Cicero's Rome, which is coercively to subdue the irrational throughout the world—that is, those who are ignorant of what they ought to will—and to "civilize" them under one law.

Early in his Christian career Augustine wrote against the Manichean Faustus: "God is not the author of sin; nevertheless he is the governor even of it. Thus sins, which would not be sins if they were not against nature, are judged and governed and given the places and conditions they deserve in order that they might not be permitted to disrupt and disfigure the nature of the universe" (see Tkacz and Kries 1994, 227). This reflects Augustine's more optimistic early views where divine law is the divine order, inscribed in the human soul. It prescribes that men respect the natural order and is not yet opposed to the purely human law of civil or ecclesiastical society. The influence of ancient thought is evident, evoking the highest reason inherent in all things of which Cicero had spoken (*Off.* I.11). The primary characteristics of divine law are its universalism and immutability. It is superior, but not here seen in contrast, to human law since there exists a hierarchy of juridical rules comparable to the hierarchy of authorities.

But at the end of his career, Augustine acknowledged more explicitly the horrors of the violence incurred during Rome's imperial outreach to "civilize" men and make them bow to the Latin language and Roman law (*CD* XIX.7). The mature Augustine recognizes that it is the tragedy of human life that requires that something similar will need to occur through the fighting of just wars if men are to be unified in one church and one belief, and in relatively peaceful and orderly earthly cities, preparing them for the selective future salvation in the city of God. Unlike Cicero and Sallust, he thinks that the correct attitudes—instilling a patriotic caring for one's country, holding oneself to principles of frugality and continence, maintaining fidelity to the marriage bond, and remaining chaste, upright, and honorable in one's behavior—are all to be taught by and learned in the one and unified church where the true and truthful God is worshipped (*Ep.* 91 as quoted in Tkacz and Kries 1994, 204). Rejecting Cicero's view that the model for proper moral behavior is the traditional Roman elite of "honorable" men, Augustine says that character formation is taught by Christ dwelling within as the teacher. The correct model for civic behavior is the *Christian* citizen. Augustine insists that there is a compatibility of the Christian religion and politics, against those who think that Christians have no interest in the purposes of the law-governed state. Since the republic is rightly defined both by Cicero and Sallust as "the affair of the people," Augustine argues not only that a city is a multitude of human beings joined in a certain bond of concord but also that Christians are especially concerned to secure it. However, only the Christian recognizes that discord must be mitigated through precepts of concord that are written by divine authority and preached in Christian churches (*Ep*. 138 as quoted in Tkacz and Kries 1994, 206) rather than through rules of concord imagined by and modeled on a dubious elite of fallen men (*CD* XIX.21, 24).

The Roman republican concept of the unity of the state related not to some abstract idea of "the State," but rather, to a unity and consensus within an upper class (the republic was specifically not a democracy), and censors had been given the role to watch over the private and public conduct of this elite. Through the sanctions of censors, members of the senatorial elite were found guilty of deviant behavior and were rendered politically ineffective, thereby enforcing conformity of conduct and holding in check abuses of power. Augustine, in Christian imperial times, gives the role of the censor to church authorities. It is also of significance that in the Roman Republic once a magistrate took up his office he could not be directly controlled either by the people or the Senate; instead, he was supervised by colleagues of equal rank in office or by the aristocratic tribunes of the plebs. The magistrate was not, even in the republic, accountable to his voters. The mass of the Roman people were never allowed to engage actively in the deliberative formulation of public opinion and were, instead, orientated toward high-ranking persons as patrons, successful military leaders, or ambitious tribunes. It is not surprising, therefore, to find Augustine in late-imperial Rome comfortable with the idea and practice of "a people" never being autonomous agents defining the political agenda.

The overriding lesson Augustine learned from republican Roman history was the problem of the control of the nobles by the nobles. It was an illusion to trust in a so-called virtuous elite in order to maintain honest behavior, consensus, and a concern for fairness and concord amongst all members of the society. When this control of nobles by nobles failed, help was sought from the rector or *princeps*. Thus, in actual history, the republic failed and was absorbed into the principate of Emperor Caesar Augustus. Even Cicero's observation (*Leg*. I.19) that law for the people must be written as commands and prohibitions but for the rulers it is the highest reason implanted and developed in their minds (and such minds serve as standards by which justice and injustice are measured), was a terrible mistake, according to the mature, more pessimistic Augustine. Republican Rome had not been Christian and, therefore, none of its rulers could possibly have had access to highest reason and true justice, that is, God. It was no surprise to Augustine to find that, with the increasingly egoistic and irresponsible conduct of a noncohesive elite, at the end of the republic Rome became a society increasingly dominated by legislation. Indeed, social harmony in Rome was originally based less on written laws and more on a general agreement that order was to be regulated and upheld by the personal authority of the *paterfamilias* and the *patronus*. The Romans both in practice and in the ideal republic as fictionalized in Cicero's *On the Commonwealth* saw no need to give the rule of written law priority over the power of almost divine persons like Scipio Aemilianus, especially in times of crisis.[38] During the period in which Rome fell away from its ideals (second century B.C.), it became clear that to keep control over its changing society Rome needed to substitute written laws for moral consensus. The Roman criminal justice system established permanent courts to deal with offenses in Cicero's own lifetime. Rome thereafter reached its juristic high point in what is known as the classical age of the second and early third centuries A.D.—well after the republic was replaced by the principate. And during the principate and the subsequent post-classical imperial period, the rule of law came to take precedence as a juridical ideal.[39] In Augustine's vision of the earthly city, whether it be situated at Rome or anywhere else where men gather together to attempt to live in an unstable peace and harmony, the rule of law is the paramount principle. No Christian should think that law, in principle, is incompatible with his Christian faith.

In some of his letters and sermons Augustine frequently returns to interpret Christ's injunction not to return evil for evil and to turn the other cheek. He does not believe that Christ was espousing pacifism or quietism. While the individual may well turn the other cheek to an evildoer, thereby displaying patience and forbearance rather than revenge, Augustine does not think that this denies the need for laws and precepts backed by coercion of both the church and state. Private acts of vengeance no, but public acts of benevolent punishment, yes and always. And turning the other cheek to one who strikes one is not an acceptance of evil, but rather, a way of forbidding the one who

[38] Cicero, *Rep.* I.2.3 claims that the leading citizen who compels all men by the authority of magistrates and the penalties imposed by law to follow the rules whose principles philosophers have also discovered but could never enforce, is superior to the philosophers who have come up with the principles alone.

[39] Ulpian (d. A.D. 233) includes the much-quoted extract from his *Institutes* in his *Digest*: "Whatever the *princeps* decides has the force of law [*legis habet vigorem*]"; "pronouncements by the *princeps* are admitted to be law" (*ap.* Justinian *Dig.* I.4.1.1). See also Ste. Croix 1981, 378–408. See Stein 1999, 24—and more extensively, Matthews 2000, 104–8—on the introduction of the *cognitio* procedure with state-appointed professional judges, copied by the church in its own administration, replacing the earlier formulary procedure (*in iure* ["in law"] and then *apud iudicem* ["according to the judge"]).

has done this from increasing his wrongdoing. Augustine interprets the act of turning the cheek as a command to another, in effect, the scriptural injunction fixing the natural law precept not to do to another what one would not wish done to oneself. He enjoins men to maintain patience and forbearance in their hearts, but not in their acts. "The precepts of concord, written by divine authority, refer to a disposition of the heart within oneself, rather than to a deed," he writes to Marcellinus in 413 (*Ep.* 138 as quoted in Tkacz and Kries 1994, 208–9). But "with respect to those who, contrary to their own will, need to be set straight, many things must be done with a certain benevolent harshness. Their welfare rather than their wishes must be considered." Augustine observes that even Romans praised this kind of benevolent punishment and emphasized that the one with this duty to act with benevolent harshness is the ruler of the city. The image of the city's ruler is drawn in terms of the Roman *paterfamilias*, but we note that the ruler is one man, a father to his people, a paternal imperial persona:

> In correcting a son, however severely, paternal love is surely never lost sight of. What is not wanted and what is painful is, nevertheless, done to one who appears to require healing through pain, even against his will. Accordingly, if this earthly republic kept to Christian precepts, wars themselves would not be waged without benevolence, so that, for the sake of the peaceful union of piety and justice, the welfare of the conquered would be more readily considered. He whose license for wrongdoing is wrested away is usefully conquered.[40]

Because Augustine believes that wars are found in the order of human affairs, "that very order justly constrains men either to command or obey with respect to such affairs [...]. Wars, then, would always be waged by the good so that by taming unbridled desires they would destroy these vices which ought to have been rooted out and subdued by just rule" (*Faust.* XXII.73–9 as quoted in

[40] In *CD* XIX.15 Augustine says that everyone who commits sin is sin's slave; this is a standard Hellenistic position (that the good man, even if he happens to be enslaved, is really free, while the bad man who is worthless and senseless is always really a slave). Weithman 2001, 239, argues that in *CD* XIX.15 (actually XIX.16), Augustine suggests that, had original sin not been committed, human groups would have been guided by paternal authority akin to that exercised by a Roman *paterfamilias* or a biblical patriarch. On the contrary, however, Augustine argues that a true and just *paterfamilias*, *post*-lapsarian but guided by Christian principles, "has an equal affection for all the members of his family, especially in respect of the worship and service of God, all praying that they may come to the heavenly home and *there alone* will it not be a necessary duty to give orders to men because it will no longer be a necessary duty to be concerned for the welfare of those who are already in the felicity of that immortal state." There is no *paterfamilias* prior to original sin or in the City of God. According to Augustine, original sin does not destroy the naturalness of human sociability, but that sociability is permanently threatened by human quarrelsomeness and conflict, thereby requiring coercion, that is, restraint by force or its threat. Hence, in an *unfallen* condition humans within the family would not have required the coercive control of their actions even by a loving Roman *paterfamilias*. The model for Augustine's *paterfamilias* in the earthly city is something along the lines of what Saller 1994, chaps. 5 and 6, has described.

Tkacz and Kries 1994, 222). For this reason, Augustine argues that Christians do not condemn all wars and they are not prohibited from serving as soldiers. Hence, they benefit the earthly republic rather than being a detriment to it. Soldiers act as the instruments of legitimate state authority, punishing without private vengeance. In *Against Faustus*, Augustine notes that soldiers are not acting on their own desires, but as ministers of the law; they are not avengers of their own injuries, but defenders of public well-being. In the natural order where the peace of mortal things is aimed at, Augustine insists that an authority is required for deliberations and concerning war in order to secure civic peace.

Augustine's earlier thinking on the purpose of the state's law is continuous with what he says, though in a much more developed and vehement form, in the *City of God*. In his dialogue with his friend Evodius in *On Free Will* (I.5.11–6.15 as quoted in Tkacz and Kries 1994, 214–5), Augustine has Evodius ask whether the positive law of the state that allows one to kill in self-defense in order to avoid being killed is just. Evodius argues that the law gives license to lesser wrongdoings so that greater wrongdoings might not be committed: The killing of an unjust aggressor in self-defense is a lesser evil than being killed by an unjust aggressor. (In *Ep*. 47.5, Augustine opposes killing by private individuals even in self-defense, believing this to be the role of punishment by public authority on behalf of all individuals in society. See also *CD* I.17, where Augustine argues that no individual has a private right to kill even a guilty man.) He says that the principle behind this positive law is that no human should be violated against his will. Evodius also claims that in killing an enemy a soldier acts as an agent of the state and its law and can, therefore, fulfill his duty without the "unbridled desire" (*libido*) for vengeance or dominance. The state's guiding mandate from God's eternal justice, that is, to protect the people, requires that it enact law for the people's protection and such a law cannot be accused of unbridled desire. But even if the law itself is blameless, are people who act under it and kill others similarly blameless? The law only gives them a license to kill, but does not oblige them to act on this license. Augustine agrees that human law deals with crimes that require punishment if peace is to be maintained among ignorant humans, to the extent that such matters can be regulated by men. Other sins have other penalties, however, from which God's wisdom alone can free us. Augustine concludes, "It seems to you that the law enacted for the governance of cities makes many concessions and leaves many things unpunished that are nevertheless punished by divine providence and rightly so. Just because it does not achieve everything, what it does achieve should not be condemned" (*CD* I.17 as quoted in Tkacz and Kries 1994, 215).

How far, Augustine asks, should wrongdoing be avenged by the law that restrains people in this life? Because humans are changeable and subject to time, Augustine proposes two scenarios. In the first case, if a people is moderate and serious and a diligent guardian of the common utility, thinking less of private good than public good, then it is right to enact a law permitting this people to choose for itself the magistrates through whom its affairs, that is, its *republic*, are to be administered. In the second case, if this same people, having become depraved little by little, preferring private to public good, sells its votes, is corrupted by those who covet honors, and turns the regime over to shameful and villainous people, then it is right that if some good and most capable man is to be found, he can remove from the people the power to bestow honors and hand it over to a few good men or even one. Augustine, therefore, sees the law as temporal; it can—indeed, must—change depending on the character of the people it governs. With an iniquitous people, the law suited to them must suit their depraved character. He seems to be invoking that very Roman legal principle of rights as civic acquisitions that are themselves changeable—they are not absolute, natural rights. Roman liberty was itself an acquired civic right resting on positive laws; it was not an innate right of man. But Augustine uses this notion to extraordinary effect. The principle of positive law that no human should be violated against his will, as mentioned by Evodius, is, therefore, changeable according to Augustine, just as are those human rights conferred by temporal authority. Depraved wills can and must be violated both for their own good and that of the peace and security of the social whole.

So, too, Augustine the Roman observes that property rights do not have foundations in rights established directly by God, but rather, in human rights distributed to men differentially by state authority (*Iohann. Evangel.* VI.25–6 as quoted in Tkacz and Kries 1994, 249).[41] He goes on to say that even those who acquire or use their property unjustly are still protected by positive law. This is because the purpose of this law is to minimize disorder; regulating even unjust use and acquisition is necessary if even greater harm would occur should it not be regulated (*Ep.* 153).[42] The use of force as a principle on

[41] For Augustine, before the Fall the law of nature would have been sufficient to guide human life, and like Ambrose (*Off.* I.28; see also *Commentary on Psalms* 118.8.22) Augustine argues that the world would have been held as the common property of all men. Augustine explains to what we owe the rights that we enjoy over our property: Property rights arise and are maintained by the law of emperors and kings, and everything we have depends on the authority of earthly rulers. God has distributed to mankind these human rights through emperors and kings. It is by a right derived from the emperor that one possesses the land. By human law alone can we claim anything as our own. But Augustine does not go on to advise extreme poverty, asceticism, or a renunciation of possessions. Money and property are simply not unconditional goods (they are the Stoic "preferred indifferents") and should be put to good use. In *Ep.* 153.6.26, he says: "[I]n this life the wrong of evil possessors is endured and among them certain laws are established which are called civil laws, not because they bring men to make good use of their wealth, but because those who make bad use of it are thereby made less injurious."

[42] This appears to reflect the post-classical lack of distinction between ownership and posses-

which earthly government necessarily operates to preserve unity and order is ultimately justified, even with respect to religious belief, as a particular instance of the necessity for forceful correction of corrupted wills. The Theodosian Code itself, in its recognition of an orthodox Catholic clergy charged with the conduct of the approved *religio*, contains laws of the late-fourth and early-fifth centuries that deprived heretics of the right of assembly, imposed restrictions on their testamentary wills, confiscated their property, and excluded them from civic life (*CTh* XVI.5.24, 8, 14, 66; 6.4 *pr.*).[43] Augustine believes that such men would in no way have considered changing for the better unless they had been terrorized into considering the truth. The weight of habit and unconsidered traditions, he says, prevent them from self-correction. Both the state and the church must, therefore, be engaged in salutary teaching joined to fear, with the power of fear alone being that which breaks the evil chains of custom. God not only teaches us but also frightens us continually for our own well-being (*Ep.* 93 as quoted in Tkacz and Kries 1994, 233).[44] Concord and unity are ultimately to be achieved in this life through men being compelled to justice.[45]

Augustine's philosophy of law has decisive consequences, notably in what he takes to be the Christian's attitude to civil law as it plays its role in the maintenance of an uncertain peace and order. Augustine perhaps best reveals this perspective when he discusses the civil magistrate and his necessary and onerous duties. In an acceptance of the way imperial Roman law necessarily operated, Augustine sorrowfully reflects in the *City of God* XIX.6:

sion, speaking as Augustine does of acquisition and use alone. "Vulgar" Roman law in the west as practiced in the provinces simplified concepts: The notion of *possessio* ("possession") replaced *dominium* ("lordship," "complete ownership"); *possessio* became a right and they opposed *iure possidere*, which designates property, to *corpore possidere*, which designates the possession. Property, possession, and *iura in re aliena* ("rights in an alienable thing") are no longer rigorously distinguished. See Levy 1951; Gaudemet 1957, 123–31.

[43] There is much evidence in imperial Roman law from the times of Ulpian onward that flogging and torture, once reserved for slaves, was increasingly exercised on citizens of humble condition, and Justinian's *Digest* XXII.5.21.2 (third century A.D.) shows that the application of torture in court to accused persons had been extended even to freemen witnesses. The Theodosian Code XII.1.39, 47 (A.D. 349–59) even allows the use of the *plumbata*, the leaded scourge, on all except the leading decurions (*decemprimi*).

[44] Hunt 1993, 156, observes: "The drawing of the boundary around legitimate religion has almost ceased to be metaphorical: The laws envisage a Roman world the borders of which are coextensive with Christian orthodoxy, and which harbors no corner of refuge for the dissenting."

[45] Augustine claims that "it must be a sin to desire what the law of God forbids and to abstain merely from fear of punishment and not for love of righteousness" (*CD* XIV.10). This reflects the twofold purposes of church and state in historical time: to conjoin teaching with fear, and never one without the other. Fear of punishment need not be limited to physical chastisement. It can also include social embarrassment or degradation, and religiously, includes a fear of sin itself and not simply fear of burning in hell. See *Ep.* 145.4.

And so they [judges] are often compelled to seek the truth by torturing innocent witnesses [...]. [I]t is the fact that the judge tortures the accused for the sole purpose of avoiding the execution, in ignorance, of an innocent man [...]. He has tortured an innocent man to get to the truth and has killed him while still in ignorance. In view of this darkness that attends the life of human society, will our wise man take his seat on the judge's bench or will he not have the heart to do so? Obviously he will sit; for the claims of human society constrain him and draw him to this duty [...]. [H]ere we have what I call the wretchedness of man's situation [...] in his judicial capacity.

8.7. Conclusion

If we place Augustine's views in their contemporary context, we find him reflecting, often in detailed ways, on the set of institutions and laws that collectively administered imperial Rome's political affairs. He examines, in short, private legal remedies and what he believes to be the rightful interference in private affairs by local representatives of both the imperial government and the church.[46] No part of society is exempt from the Fall; both *loci* of control—familial and public—must now be regarded as the sites of "unnatural," but necessary, remedies for the Fall. Only eschatologically, after history and in the city of God, will it no longer be a necessary duty to give orders to men, because it will no longer be a necessary duty to be concerned for the welfare of those, formerly in families and in political societies, who have achieved, through God's election, the felicity of that immortal state. But in historical time, and in accordance with the characters of fallen, willful men, it is law backed by punitive sanction that must coerce men's wills to justice.

Much later, and despite his own intentions, Augustine would be recognized as having erected the signposts to the eventual secularization of history and politics. The sphere of politics, construed as belonging irrevocably to the realm infected by sin, would come to be understood by some as capable of mastery only by absolute authority. It would be argued that the only reasonable solution to the tragedy of the human condition, played out in the acts of misguided and destructively competitive wills in a fallen "state of nature," is to renounce and transfer any claims to self-governance to an overarching authoritative third party, namely, a Hobbesian sovereign. Technically, there is no law that Hobbes's sovereign may make that can be unjust and no claim that a subject can make against the sovereign's injustice. The state would come to be seen as the contractual construction of willful individuals, using their reason instrumentally to secure their shifting desires, engaged as they were in self-preserving bargaining. It would take Hobbes, in seventeenth-century conditions of civil war, to recognize what Augustine had already discovered in his own time: That there is no possibility of morality by rational agreement, only

[46] See Weithman (2001), who arrives at a range of interpretations that differ from those presented here, largely due to ignoring the context in which Augustine lived.

by authoritative imposition. To arrive at this conclusion, however, many of the indigenous practices and theories of the medieval city-state—with its corporate governance and collective attempts to secure, through law, the common good—would have to be, and were, either forgotten or misconstrued. Republican Rome and Cicero's idealization of honorable men would come to appear as unrealistic or uncongenial to many in the early modern period as they had appeared to Augustine in late imperial Rome (see Coleman 2000, vol. 2: 272–6).

Further Reading

Although there is a very extensive literature on Augustine, scholars generally have not situated him decisively within his North African, late Roman imperial context. Harries (1999) is perhaps unique in having appropriately placed Augustine in his times, showing him to be a serious player in her detailed and important historical narrative. Similarly, the articles in Harries and Wood 1993 treating various aspects of the Theodosian Code reveal the contemporary backdrop to Augustine's familiarity with the law. Also useful and bold is the work of Matthews 2000.

Tkacz and Kries 1994 contains excerpts from the *City of God* and Augustine's other writings on politics and law. Atkins and Dodaro 2001 brings together thirty-five letters and several sermons that deal with political and legal matters.

The works of Markus are still, by far, the most detailed and sensitive readings of Augustine's philosophy, theology, political, and pastoral concerns; see especially Markus 1970; 1972; and 1990. His works, along with those of Brown 1967; 1972; and 1989, must be read as supplements, and sometimes as correctives, to the essays in Stump and Kretzmann 2001.

Rist 1994 is perhaps the most philosophically informed about what Augustine took and altered from the various legacies of classical philosophy; similarly, O'Daly 1989 and Kenny 1975.

Coleman 1992 discusses what Augustine inherited from his Platonist and Aristotelian forebears, and changed, in order to arrive at an epistemology, a theory of the workings of memory, and a revised conception of history, each of which would influence the future medieval centuries. Coleman 2000, vol. 1, treats more directly Augustine's political theory. Coleman 2000, vol. 2, observes the revival of some of Augustine's most important insights on the role of authority and positive law in all men's lives as the middle ages, more directly influenced by Ciceronian and Aristotelian thinking on the relation of reason, law, and constitution-building, gave way to a different agenda during the early modern period of European political theorizing. Rowe and Schofield 2000 reflects some of the most recent scholarship and bibliography on this formative period.

Chapter 9

PHILOSOPHY OF LAW IN MEDIEVAL JUDAISM AND ISLAM

by Charles E. Butterworth[1]

9.1. Introduction

Properly speaking, there is no philosophy of law in medieval Judaism and Islam. In its place is jurisprudence, that is, the art or science that seeks to explain what the revealed law of either tradition means with respect to one particular situation or another and how it is to be applied. Similarly, jurisprudence entails moving from what is explicitly spoken of by the particular revealed law to what is not—extending that law to new phenomena or new applications. But philosophy of law understood as "philosophical reflections upon the general foundation of law [...] derived from an existing philosophical position" or leading "to such a position" (Friedrich 1958, 3) is not to be found in either one of these traditions; nor is it desired.[2] The reason is quite simple: Law in medieval (and contemporary) Judaism and Islam is Law with a capital "L." It is divine law handed down to a particular religious community by a divinely inspired lawgiver, a prophet or a messenger of the Almighty.

Consequently, those who accept this Law and believe in it do not speculate about it in the sense of asking where it came from or how it has evolved over the ages. They are asked to accept that it has been revealed by the creator and is the same now as when first revealed to the prophet or lawgiver. One need only consult the Law itself, as it is set forth in the scripture particular to each tradition, to see that it is not to be trifled with and certainly not to be subjected to scrutiny about its origins or evolution. Such an undertaking would be tantamount to casting doubt on the Law and on the claims of the particular religious community about its unique character.

This view concerning Law was recognized, although not emphasized, by Friedrich (1958, 8ff.), who, even as he noted that the Hebrew scriptures were part of the heritage to which current understandings of law lay claim or which "played a decisive role in shaping the origins of Western concepts of law," passed over those scriptures and that heritage to focus first on the philosophy of pagan Greece and then on the modern adaptation of both classical philos-

[1] All translations are by the author unless otherwise indicated.

[2] Even less to be embraced is philosophy of law as a pursuit that helps the individual become more aware of how human opinions affect law or as something that "provides clarity, intellectual order and structure, and standards of rational (often moral) criticism and evaluation"; see Murphy and Coleman 1990, xi.

ophy and scriptural revelation to more pressing concerns. Similarly, Murphy and Coleman take their bearings from modern Western sources, yet ignore the religious traditions to which early Western jurists looked for inspiration or from which they sought liberation. Murphy and Coleman are completely silent about the history of jurisprudence in medieval times, Friedrich only about its medieval Jewish and Islamic manifestations. Witting or not, such silence is well-founded.

Indeed, the history of jurisprudence in both traditions is fraught with technicalities—numbing technicalities, more often than not. It entails the drawing of minute distinctions based on the sense given to a particular word or its linguistic antecedents and leads to heated argument about what should be done or not done under a vast array of real and hypothetical circumstances. For the most part, the discussion centers on actions to be performed or not, but it can also reach to opinions. In the latter case, action plays a certain role as well, insofar as primary emphasis is placed on what the members of the community are to believe concerning God, the world, and so on—this on the basis of what has been revealed in divine law.

Given the preeminence of the divine law, theology comes into being as a means of defending the actions and opinions promulgated by that law. Alfarabi provides an excellent summary account of dialectical theology or *kalām*, that is, the art of theology practiced in Islam:

> The art of dialectical theology is a disposition by which a human being is able to defend the specific opinions and actions that the founder of the religion declared and to refute by arguments whatever opposes it. This art is also divided into two parts: a part with respect to opinions and a part with respect to actions.
>
> It is different from jurisprudence in that the jurist takes the opinions and actions declared by the founder of the religion as given and sets them down as fundamentals from which he infers the things that necessarily follow from them, whereas the dialectical theologian defends the things the jurist uses as fundamentals without inferring other things from them. If it happens that there is a certain human being who has the ability to do both matters, he is a jurist and a dialectical theologian. He defends them insofar as he is a dialectical theologian, and he infers them insofar as he is a jurist. (*Enumeration of the Sciences*, V.5)

Those engaged in it draw upon the premises of philosophy, to be sure. They also have recourse to the arts of logic—especially sophistry. But these are weapons to be unsheathed in battle rather than handmaidens employed in the service of learning. The theologians of medieval Islam most often attacked the philosophers, even while making use of their premises. And no less an authority on Judaism than Maimonides (see Section 9.6 below) has recourse to the doctrines of Muslim dialectical theologians (the *mutakallimūn*) when he wants to illustrate important errors concerning the opinions that people hold about God. He does so, apparently, because to dwell on such matters would detract from the attention one ought to accord Jewish law, and understanding it is the supreme concern (*Guide*, I.71–6, especially 71 beginning [93b]).

These general observations need to be amplified in order to distinguish the place of law and reflection upon law in medieval Judaism and Islam from what occurs in medieval Christianity. Once such distinctions have been drawn, it will be easier to explain why philosophical speculation in medieval Islam takes the form it does and how such speculation affects, and is reflected in, the philosophical inquiry proper to medieval Judaism. Moreover, it will be possible to account for the guiding role that medieval Islamic culture takes in such inquiries, a role that appears unusual given the slight claim Islamic culture makes upon our attention today.

9.2. Law and Revelation in the Prophetic Religions

For philosophers belonging to the medieval Jewish tradition, only divine law is deemed worthy of investigation and commentary. Dispersed throughout the different lands of medieval Islam and tolerated, along with Christians and other peoples whose beliefs approximated those of the monotheistic or Abrahamic faiths,[3] Jewish thinkers in medieval times had no reason to dwell on questions related to secular or day-to-day political law. Except in rare circumstances, it was not their task to make such law or pronounce on its administration. Here, too, Maimonides provides an extraordinarily apt account of the world around him.

> Political science is divided into four parts. The first is the individual's governance of himself; the second is the governance of the household; the third is the governance of the city; and the fourth is the governance of the large nation or of the nations [...]. The governance of the city is a science which provides its inhabitants with the knowledge of true happiness along with the way of striving to attain it; the knowledge of true misery along with the way of striving to keep it away; and the way of training their moral habits to reject the presumed kinds of happiness so that they do not take delight in them or covet them. It explains the presumed kinds of misery to them so that they do not suffer from them or dread them. Similarly, it prescribes laws of justice for them by which they can order their communities. The learned men of past communities, each according to his perfection, used to fashion regimes and rules[4] by which their kings would govern the subjects. They called them *nomoi*, and the nations used to be governed by those *nomoi*. The philosophers have many books about all of these things which have already been translated into Arabic. Those that have not been translated are perhaps even more numerous. In these times all that—I mean, the regimes and the *nomoi*—has been dispensed with, and people are governed by divine commands. (*Treatise on the Art of Logic*, XIV)

Maimonides' use of the term "divine commandments" (*al-awāmir al-ilāhiyya*) here is a deliciously indirect way of pointing to the Islamic *sharīʿa* as sole

[3] See Quran 2:62: "Indeed, those who believe, and those who are Jewish, and the Christians and the Sabians, anyone who believes in God and the last day and does what is correct, they will have their reward from their Lord; they have nothing to fear, nor are they to be sad."

[4] The Arabic term translated here as "rules" might more literally be rendered as "canons," for it is *qawānīn* (sing. *qānūn*).

law (or, more accurately perhaps, Law) of the land. Lest the indirectness be missed, he reminds the reader that Arabic culture and language so dominate the thought and learning of his age that almost all of the important learning from the past has been translated into Arabic. Moreover, the learned Jews to whom Maimonides addresses himself here would have been all too aware of this cultural domination because they would have read these words of his first in Arabic—Arabic written in Hebrew script.

Two other aspects of this succinct statement are also deserving of further reflection. First, its whole tone is reminiscent of Maimonides' famous Arab predecessor Alfarabi (see Section 9.3 below), whom Maimonides held in such high esteem as to claim that his thoughts were finer than finely sifted flour (see Marx 1935, 378–80).[5] In *Selected Aphorisms*, for example, Alfarabi moves from a discussion of the way the individual soul is to be disciplined to reflection on the household and its governance, then the city and its governance, and ultimately arrives at the regime and its governance. When speaking of the latter, he notes that it can be a city, a nation, or a group of nations (aph. 95; see also aphs. 25, 26, 28, 38, 39, 42). Similarly, in *Political Regime*, Alfarabi distinguishes between perfect and imperfect political associations:

> Human beings are of the species that cannot complete its necessary affairs nor gain its most excellent state except by coming together as many associations in a single dwelling-place. Some human associations are large, some medium, and some small. The large association is an association of many nations coming together and helping one another. The medium is the nation. And the small are those the city has mastery over. These three are the perfect associations.
>
> Thus the city is first in the rankings of perfections. Associations in villages, quarters, streets, and houses are defective associations. Of these, one is very defective, namely, the household association. It is part of the association in the street, and the association in the street is part of the association in the quarter. And this latter association is part of the civic association. The associations in quarters and the associations in villages are both for the sake of the city. However, the difference between them is that quarters are parts of the city, while villages serve the city. The civic association is part of the nation, and the nation is divided into cities. The unqualifiedly perfect human association is divided into nations. (*Political Regime*, sec. 64)

Imperfect political associations are those smaller than the city, namely, households, associations comprised of those dwelling on particular streets or in a particular residential quarter, and villages. Perfect political associations, on the other hand, are those that are at least the size of the city. It, as well as the nation and even a group of nations that come together and assist one another, constitute the best or most complete—and, in this sense, the most perfect—kind of political association. They are complete or perfect in that they are self-sufficient and able to guide their inhabitants toward happiness.

[5] The additional judgments by Maimonides on figures in the history of philosophy, especially as they reflect on Alfarabi, Avicenna, and Averroes, as cited by Pines in Maimonides, *The Guide of the Perplexed* (1963), lix-lx, are worth considering.

In both treatises, Alfarabi does speak of law. Indeed, in *Selected Aphorisms*, he speaks of traditional law (*sunna*), conventional law or nomos (*nāmūs*), and divine law (*sharī'a*). The existence of the first two in cities is assumed, and Alfarabi is more concerned with the standards for conduct they provide or how they are misused by some rulers in order to achieve their own base goals than with explaining how they come about (see *Aphorisms*, aphs. 14, 15, 31, 58, 92). That is to say, traditional, conventional, and divine laws are spoken of as though their presence were clearly to be expected, but not as anything to whose elaboration attention ought to be given. The emphasis, rather, is on inculcating opinions—especially correct ones—about the soul, virtues, and nonlegal constituents of the well-governed city or regime.

In *Political Regime*, Alfarabi speaks of divine law, traditional law, and a lawgiver who posits traditional law (*wāḍi' al-sunna*). But the term *nomos* never occurs (see secs. 82, 102, 106, 113, 122). As in *Selected Aphorisms*, so here the assumption is that laws exist and that people guide themselves more or less with respect to them. But Alfarabi does not dwell on—indeed, he never turns his attention to—what makes laws or Laws good nor to how they come about. His perspective is more limited: His discussion of the best or virtuous city emphasizes that it alone aspires to bring about true happiness for its citizens, whereas his discussion of the other cities—the ignorant cities, of which he enumerates and explores six kinds—focuses on the goals they pursue that keep them from being virtuous. Not laws or Laws, but ends, are Alfarabi's sole focus in this work.

Yet, to return to the major point, whatever Maimonides may have learned from Alfarabi about the division of political science into four parts, that is subservient here to his dismay over inquiry into politics now being moribund. Anything he might have been able to learn from Alfarabi about regimes, their characteristics, and the qualities that make them sound or unsound is no longer of value. Similarly, what he might have learned about *nomoi* (notice that Maimonides does not speak here of traditional laws) is not now to be pursued. All this has now been superseded by "divine commands."

Second, the term translated as "communities" at the beginning of the above cited passage by Maimonides should properly be understood as "religious communities," the Arabic term being *milal* (sing. *milla*). For Maimonides, as for Alfarabi, political communities work best when they are organized around a religion common to the citizens. Maimonides does not dwell on the question here, but it is clearly central to the way he analyzes politics.

While those representative of medieval Jewish thought dwell on the religious law simply because they have access to no other law or can influence and interpret no other law, another consideration prompts thinkers within the medieval Islamic tradition to do the same. Though freer to explore other avenues as members of the dominant class, they are equally subject to the central tenet of the medieval Islamic tradition which holds that there is no law other than the Islamic *sharīʿa*. Everything within that tradition points to the idea that rule can be exercised only by God's vicegerent, the caliph (*khalīfa*), and his designated subordinates.[6] The prophet Muhammad (ca. 570–632) was the first legitimate ruler of the Islamic community, and all subsequent rulers are legitimate only insofar as they are his genuine successors.[7] More important, their exercise of rulership is legitimate only to the extent that their decrees conform to the letter of the Islamic *sharīʿa*. Such, at least, is the theory, however much actual practice may have differed.

As a result, attention is focused on how to understand and apply the divine law, and political inquiry is limited to the study of this law, that is, to jurisprudence. Alfarabi explains the situation succinctly:

> The art of jurisprudence is that by which a human being is able to infer, from the things the lawgiver declared specifically and determinately, the determination of each of the things he did not specifically declare. And he is able to aspire to a verification of that on the basis of the purpose of the lawgiver in the religion he legislated with respect to the nation for which it was legislated.
>
> Every religion has opinions and actions. The opinions are like the opinions that are legislated with respect to God, how He is to be described, the world, and other things. The actions are like the actions by which God is praised and the actions by which there are mutual dealings in cities. Therefore the science of jurisprudence has two parts: a part with respect to opinions and a part with respect to actions. (*Enumeration of the Sciences*, V.4)

Yet differences about these opinions and actions arise, and they sometimes become so fixed as to be insurmountable. In medieval Islam, this phenomenon gave rise to schools or disciplines of law; these have prevailed through the ages and remain vibrant even now.

The differences concerning opinions and actions have to do, above all, with the way the Quran should be interpreted, that is, the extent to which it is permissible to rely upon analogical reasoning (*qiyās*) and independent or personal opinion (*ra'y*), as well as about how much authority is to be accorded to the sayings and deeds of the prophet—the *ḥadīth* and *sunna*[8]—as opposed to the Quran itself. In Sunni (sometimes called Orthodox) Islam, there are four schools. The Ḥanīfī school, named after Abū Ḥanīfa al-Nuʿmān ibn Thābit (d. 767), is and always was most open both to analogical and independent reason-

[6] The idea of a vicegerent or representative of God on earth goes back to the Quranic account of God first honoring Adam with this role, then David, and—by inference—Muhammad as well as his successors; see Quran 2:30–34, 38:26; see also 6:165; 7:69, 74; 10:14, 73; 27:62; and 35:39.

[7] Quranic verses that confirm this judgment abound, but note these from 2:2–4: "This is the book; there is no doubt about its being a guide for those in awe [of God]; those who believe in what is absent, stand fast in prayer, and spend from what We have provided them; those who believe in what was sent down to thee." The addressee ("thee") is the prophet Muhammad.

[8] A *ḥadīth* is a report or record about one of the Prophet's deeds or sayings; *sunna* is the traditional or customary law based upon these deeds and sayings.

ing. Indeed, the procedure of thinking through and interpreting the divine law in order to reach juridical decisions—what later came to be known as *ijtihād*—was especially developed in the Ḥanīfi school. By contrast, the Mālikī school founded by Mālik ibn Anas (d. 795), gives greater weight to the deeds and sayings of the Prophet, especially to Mālik's own collection of them. The writings of Muḥammad Ibn Idrīs al-Shāfi'ī (767–820) testify to his great reliance on analogical reasoning, and the school that bears his name (Shāfi'ī) promotes that tendency. Finally, Aḥmad ibn Ḥanbal (d. 855) and the school named after him (Ḥanbalī) allow little leeway in interpreting the Quran. It is the most literalist of these schools and frowns upon any kind of analogical or personal reasoning, preferring to privilege the deeds and sayings of the Prophet. In all important respects, the Wahhābī school, named after Muḥammad Ibn 'Abd al-Wahhāb (1703–1792) and dominant in contemporary Saudi Arabia, is the modern successor of Ḥanbalī doctrine.

Disagreement over who should succeed the fourth caliph 'Alī following his murder in 661 prompted a major rupture within the fledgling Muslim community. Demands that the caliphate pass to the heirs of 'Alī rather than to Mu'āwiyya, who became the first caliph of the Umayyad dynasty (and reigned from 661–680), led the partisans of 'Alī to form their own distinct group. Their eventual repudiation of the first three successors to Muhammad as usurpers formed part of other doctrinal differences with the now-dominant Sunni group, and the original designation of them as adherents or partisans of 'Alī (*shī'at 'Alī*) took on a life of its own insofar as they became known simply as the Shi'a, as opposed to the Sunni branch of Islam (or as Shi'i as opposed to Sunni Muslims). Almost eleven hundred years later (that is, around the middle of the eighteenth century), in order to work out a compromise of sorts, the legal school devoted to Ja'far al-Ṣādiq (d. 765) was recognized by Sunni Islam as comprising the fifth acceptable school of Islamic jurisprudence. It stands today as the school representative of Shi'i Islam.[9]

The salient point with respect to these distinctions is that they concern various schools of jurisprudence, which differ over particular approaches to the interpretation of the law. The schools, their adherents, and their doctrines start from the premise that the law is to be accepted as it has come down. No question is to be raised about the status of revealed law or its relationship to conventional and natural law. In fact, there is no discussion of such topics. Nor is any attempt made to inquire into revelation, that is, its character and genesis or its relation to the imaginative faculty of the soul. These are schools of law whose goal is, as Alfarabi so aptly puts it, "to infer, from the things the lawgiver declared specifically and determinately, the determination of each of the things he did not specifically declare." By privileging one approach to the

[9] Further details may be found in Gibb 1955, 72–98; Rahman 1968, 75–95, 203–19; and al-Shāfi'ī 1961, 3–16. See also Corbin 1964, 13–30; and Lewis 1960, 36–98.

divine law or another, the schools "aspire to a verification of that [determination] on the basis of the purpose of the lawgiver in the religion he legislated with respect to the nation for which it was legislated." They are not schools of philosophy.

To be sure, it is sorely tempting to collapse the two and seek in the legal speculations and "mirror of princes" treatises of the jurists some insight into the political theory and political philosophy of medieval Islam. The problem is that inquiries into the principles that explain and justify the imamate, caliphate, sultanate, and wizirate and into how the divine law provides criteria for distinguishing good ones from bad do little to sharpen our understanding of state and government, not to speak of law as a subject of inquiry.[10] One way to illustrate how misleading reliance on the jurists can be is to turn to one, for example, the highly respected Takī al-Dīn Aḥmad Ibn Taimiyya (1263–1328). He has an especially compelling claim to our attention because he is the jurist who most influenced Muḥammad Ibn 'Abd al-Wahhāb. In Ibn Taimiyya's famous attack upon the Greek philosophers, he strives mightily to show that the divine law is sufficient for all the needs of the community. Basically, his argument is that nothing is to be learned either from the logical teaching set forth by the philosophers and logicians or from those jurists and theologians who have been misguided enough to seek to appropriate that teaching. All that an observant Muslim needs to know about logic or about the rules for thinking is clearly expounded in the Quran. Moreover, the teaching of the philosophers and logicians is unduly complicated and involved; the Quran is more direct. Nor is that all. Aware that individuals he deems intelligent, not to mention the philosophers, differ among themselves about the principles of logic, Ibn Taimiyya sees no reason for entering into their debates. Most important, the logic of the philosophers and logicians, in particular the syllogism they praise so highly, adds nothing to human knowledge of the beings or of the creator and the prophets; only the signs or verses (*āyāt*) of the Quran provide such knowledge.[11]

9.3. Alfarabi

Three individuals stand out in the tradition of medieval Islamic philosophy for the light they shed on what constitutes a well-ordered polity: Alfarabi, Avicenna (Ibn Sīnā), and Averroes (Ibn Rushd). Alkindi (d. 866), known as the phi-

[10] For recent examples of such attempts, see Black 2001 and Lambton 1981. Black's book is far more ambitious than Lambton's, both in its historical scope and its geographic purview, but, by his own admission, it suffers from his having no grasp of any of the languages in which these authors wrote.

[11] See Ibn Taimiyya, *Abridgement of the Counsel to the People of the Faith Concerning the Response to the Logic of the Greeks*, 94:17–96:6, 153:4–14, 194:13–195:12, 217:5–218:8, 234:12–235:18; see also Ibn Taimiyya, *Against the Greek Logicians*, secs. 29–30, 125, 207–8, 253–5, 286–9.

losopher of the Arabs, focused his attention primarily on metaphysics and had nothing to say about politics. Alfarabi's near contemporary and sometime fellow resident of Baghdad, Alrazi (864–925), was especially concerned with ethics and medicine, but sometimes also delved into metaphysical speculations. A book on the philosophic life, in which he compares himself to Socrates and speaks of something resembling Socrates' second sailing notwithstanding, he is quite similar to Alkindi in the way he ignores political subjects. Averroes' two illustrious predecessors and fellow Andalusians, Ibn Bājjah (d. 1138) and Ibn Ṭufayl (ca. 1110–1185), did turn their thoughts to political matters from time to time; in their writings, however, they say nothing with respect to law. Although Alfarabi is for the most part also silent about the law, even his silences prompt further reflection.

Widely referred to as "the second teacher," that is, second after Aristotle, Alfarabi (Abū Naṣr Muḥammad Ibn Muḥammad Ibn Ṭarkhān Ibn Awzalagh al-Fārābī) (ca. 870–950) is widely recognized as the most important philosopher within the medieval Islamic tradition. Born in the village of Farab in Turkestan, he resided in Bukhara, Marv, Ḥarrān, Baghdad, and perhaps in Constantinople, as well as in Aleppo, Cairo, and finally Damascus, where he died. Alfarabi first studied Islamic jurisprudence and music in Bukhara, then moved to Marv, where he began to study logic with a Nestorian Christian monk. While in his early twenties, Alfarabi left for Baghdad, where he continued to study logic and philosophy as well as to improve his grasp of Arabic. After a decade or so in Baghdad, Alfarabi went to Byzantium for about eight years to study Greek sciences and philosophy, then returned to Baghdad and concentrated on teaching and writing for the next quarter of a century when the political upheavals of 942 forced him to seek refuge in Damascus. Two or three years later, political turmoil there drove him to Egypt, where he stayed until returning to Damascus in 948 or 949, a little over a year before his death.

Alfarabi's writings address all of the sciences and embrace every part of philosophy. He composed commentaries on Euclid's *Elements*, Ptolemy's *Almagest*, and Plato's *Laws*; wrote several pieces on the history and theory of music; and provided an account of Plato's and Aristotle's philosophy. Alfarabi also wrote numerous commentaries on Aristotle's logical writings and an extensive commentary on the *Nicomachean Ethics*, but the latter is no longer extant. His inquiries into the challenge to traditional philosophy presented by revealed religion, especially its claims that the creator provides for human well-being by means of an inspired prophet-legislator, are central to his attempts to formulate a new political science that combines theoretical and practical sciences along with prudence and thus to political philosophy within Islam. All this has come to light only in recent years as heretofore unknown writings have been recovered.

In *Selected Aphorisms* and the trilogy known as *Philosophy of Plato and Aristotle*, especially in its first part, *Attainment of Happiness*, Alfarabi constantly points to knowledge as the key to sound rulership. Neither Alfarabi's Plato nor his Socrates looks to law when investigating political matters. Rather, they focus on cities and their ways of life, as well as on how different civic regimes lead their citizens to happiness or fail to do so. For Alfarabi, Plato "presented in the *Laws* the virtuous ways of life that the inhabitants of this city [i.e., the city that 'had been rendered perfect in speech' in the *Republic*] should be made to follow." Paying no attention whatsoever to the speeches of the Athenian Stranger about laws and their preludes or to the efforts of Clinias to lead the Athenian Stranger and Megillus to set down a body of law for the colony that Clinias has been charged by his own city with establishing, Alfarabi's Plato focuses solely on virtuous ways of life. Then, after explaining "what distinguishes the human perfection achieved by him who combines the theoretical sciences and the political and practical sciences, and what ought to be his rank in this city," in the *Critias*, *Timaeus*, and *Laws*, his Plato focuses on what is needed "to have this city realized in deed." Though this brings him closer to laws and lawmaking, insofar as he recognizes that "this is accomplished only by the legislator of this city," Alfarabi's Plato does not go further. As Alfarabi notes, "therefore he afterwards investigated how the legislator ought to be" and "that is to be found in his book that he called the *Epinomis*" (*Philosophy of Plato*, secs. 30–35).

Alfarabi's Aristotle does not focus on law either. Indeed, convinced that it is necessary to go back beyond Plato's starting point in order to investigate human perfection, Alfarabi's Aristotle starts from the perception that all human beings pursue four things "from the outset" and deem these things "desirable and good," namely, the soundness of the human body, the senses, the capacity to discern what leads to these two, and the faculty to bring that soundness about. Investigation into what kind of knowledge is needed to realize or establish these four things leads him to note that there is a difference between knowledge or science that is useful with respect to them and another kind that is "beyond the merely useful knowledge and that is desired for itself and not for anything else." Differently stated, Aristotle comes to recognize the difference between practical and theoretical science (*Philosophy of Aristotle*, secs. 1–2).

Alfarabi's account of Aristotle's subsequent investigations says nothing, however, of what the Stagirite learned about practical science. Indeed, it focuses exclusively on the way Aristotle founds the logical arts or sciences so as to gain a better understanding of what wisdom is and how it is acquired, as well as to discern the order of the theoretical arts. This shows him why wisdom is prior in rank and provides him with awareness of the way first premises are used in each of the arts of logic. Along the way Aristotle learns, moreover, what theoretical argument is and how it is to be carried out soundly (*Philosophy of Aristotle*, secs. 4, 7–11). After working his way through such inquiries and pausing momentarily to reflect on how rhetoric and poetics provide a means of instructing those not competent to engage in the other logical arts and of giving persuasive images in speech of things discerned through stringent reasoning, his Aristotle sets about investigating the world around him—the things perceived by the senses and their distinctions with respect to essence and accident, true and false reasoning about being and change, the relationship between matter and form, and the way things both come into being through an agent as well as have specific ends or goals (*Philosophy of Aristotle*, secs. 15–16, 17–23). This investigation of nature leads Alfarabi's Aristotle to recognize that such inquiry is inadequate for his purposes, that he must go beyond the study of nature to what is beyond nature. His metaphysical investigations permit Alfarabi's Aristotle to arrive at a correct understanding of human existence, especially of the human soul's longings.

Although Alfarabi's explanation of Aristotle's philosophical quest ends without any account of how he views practical science, he now speaks in his own voice to emphasize what became apparent to Aristotle "from the preceding," that is, from the inquiry as a whole and not simply from metaphysics. According to Alfarabi, "it has become evident from the preceding that it is necessary to investigate, and to inquire into, the intelligibles that cannot be utilized for the soundness of human bodies and the soundness of the senses." Such necessary knowledge stands in opposition to another, more human, kind of knowledge, namely, awareness of "the causes of visible things." Though the soul longs for or desires the latter, the former is necessary.

But Alfarabi has also learned that it is necessary precisely to obtain the latter. We seek the former "for the sake of" (*li-ajl*) the latter. Indeed, "the awareness we formerly supposed to be superfluous is not so, but is what is necessary for a human being to become substantial or to reach his ultimate perfection." This is a reversal so striking that Alfarabi adds immediately:

> And it has become evident that the knowledge he [Aristotle] investigated at the outset just because he loved to and inspected so as to settle upon the truth about the above-mentioned pursuits has turned out to be necessary for attaining the political activity for the sake of which the human being has come into being. (*Philosophy of Aristotle*, sec. 99)

Now, then, it is imperative that Aristotle or those who have grasped what Alfarabi has said of his pursuits turn to practical science. To remove any doubt about its importance, Alfarabi goes on to explain—still in his own name—how the knowledge or science "that comes next is investigated for two purposes, one is to perfect the human activity for the sake of which the human being has come into being and the other is to perfect what we lack with respect to natural science." The reason for such a lack or deficit is that "we do not possess metaphysical science."

If this is Alfarabi's final word, it would appear that all of Aristotle's investigations have come to nought. Everything we learned about knowledge and the ways to it, plus the many things we learned about the world around us, seem inconsequential and petty so long as we cannot attain the knowledge we now discern to be "necessary for a human being to become substantial or to reach his ultimate perfection." At this point, namely, the conclusion of Alfarabi's *Philosophy of Aristotle*, it is worth recalling its opening words with their sense of promise:

Aristotle sees the perfection of man as Plato sees it and more. However, because man's perfection is not self-evident or easy to explain by a demonstration leading to certainty, he saw fit to start from a position anterior to that from which Plato had started. (*Philosophy of Aristotle*, sec. 1)[12]

The point is that while we are aware of what we need to know and of its importance, we are equally aware that we do not have this requisite knowledge. This is precisely why Alfarabi notes in conclusion "therefore philosophy must necessarily come into being in every man in the way possible for him." Having admitted to a lacuna or deficiency in our knowledge of metaphysics, we are now obliged to wonder about the sufficiency of law, even revealed law, and to take it upon ourselves to consider lawgiving from the beginning.

Before turning to Alfarabi's otherwise questionable attempts to identify knowledge as virtue and as what alone permits sound rule in *Selected Aphorisms*, it is important to return momentarily to the discussion of philosophy that launched him on his curious account of Plato's and Aristotle's philosophy, that is, to the closing words of the *Attainment of Happiness*. The reason is quite simple: Alfarabi's attempt there, first to identify and then to explain "the human things through which nations and citizens of cities attain earthly happiness in this life and supreme happiness in the life beyond," brought him to discern the intimate relationship between philosophy and religion. As he puts it, "according to the ancients," both philosophy and religion

comprise the same subjects and both give an account of the ultimate principles of the beings. For both supply knowledge about the first principle and cause of the beings, and both give an account of the ultimate end for the sake of which man is made—that is, supreme happiness—and the ultimate end of every one of the other beings. In everything of which philosophy gives an account based on intellectual perception or conception, religion gives an account based on imagination [...]. Also, in everything of which philosophy gives an account that is demonstrative and certain, religion gives an account based on persuasive arguments. (*Attainment of Happiness*, secs. 1, 55)

Prior to this insight, Alfarabi had discovered that it is not sufficient to have an intellectual perception of supreme happiness or even of what constitutes it. No, in addition, it is necessary to know how to bring it about, to have a grasp of practical philosophy. By means of practical philosophy, we are able to bring

[12] All of the other passages cited in this and the preceding two paragraphs are from sec. 99. In three places, I have altered the published translation slightly so as to achieve greater clarity.

into existence the things that depend on the will, providing, of course, that we have a clear grasp of them by means of theoretical philosophy.

Now, then, building on the clear importance of practical philosophy and the close relationship between religion and theoretical philosophy, Alfarabi notes that once the person who is intent upon bringing these voluntary matters into existence actually succeeds in doing so by stipulating the conditions needed, he then recasts these stipulations as laws. This line of reasoning leads him to speak less about the particular laws now brought into being than about the character of the person who sets them down:

> Therefore the legislator is he who, by the excellence of his deliberation, has the capacity to find the conditions required for the actual existence of voluntary intelligibles in such a way as to lead to the achievement of supreme happiness. It is also evident that only after perceiving them by his intellect should the legislator seek to discover their conditions, and he cannot find their conditions that enable him to guide others toward supreme happiness without having perceived supreme happiness with his intellect. Nor can these things become intelligible (and the legislative craft thereby hold the supreme office) without his having beforehand acquired philosophy. Therefore, if he intends to possess a craft that is authoritative rather than subservient, the legislator must be a philosopher. (*Attainment of Happiness*, sec. 56)

The laws in question are identified not as divine laws (*sharīʿa*, sing. *sharāʿa*), but as conventional ones (*nawāmīs*, sing. *nāmūs*)—this being the usual way to render in Arabic the Greek term *nomoi* (sing. *nomos*). Similarly, the person referred to here as the "legislator" is more properly the "one who sets down the *nomoi*" (*wāḍiʿ al-nawāmīs*). And the term translated as "legislative craft" is, literally, the "craft of setting down conventions" (*mihna waḍʿ al-nawāmīs*).

In and of itself, such terminology is not striking. Only the context makes it so. A few lines earlier, Alfarabi linked philosophy with religion insofar as both provide the same account of things, philosophy on the basis of an intellectual perception and religion on the basis of an imaginative one. Now, having established that practical philosophy allows one to bring voluntary things into existence and set them down as laws, Alfarabi brings religion together with both theoretical and practical philosophy by affirming "it follows, then, that the idea of Imam, Philosopher, and Legislator is a single idea" and then goes on to insist:

> However, the name *philosopher* signifies primarily theoretical virtue. But if it be determined that the theoretical virtue reaches its ultimate perfection in every respect, it follows necessarily that he must possess all the other faculties as well. *Legislator* signifies excellence of knowledge concerning the conditions of practical intelligibles, the faculty for finding them, and the faculty for bringing them about in nations and cities. (*Attainment of Happiness*, sec. 57)

In other words, the laws that a spiritual leader, an *imam*, or even a prophet, enunciates on the basis of insight gained through religion or revelation are the same ones a philosopher-legislator would.

There is yet another step to this reasoning. Alfarabi continues his explanation as follows:

When it is determined that they be brought into existence on the basis of knowledge, it will follow that the theoretical virtue must precede the others—the existence of the inferior presupposes the existence of the higher. The name *king* signifies sovereignty and ability. To be completely able, one has to possess the power of the greatest ability. His ability to do a thing must not result only from external things; he himself must possess great ability because his art, skill, and virtue are of exceedingly great power. This is not possible except by great power of knowledge, great power of deliberation, and great power of [moral] virtue and art. Otherwise he is neither truly able nor sovereign. (*Attainment of Happiness*, sec. 57)

Syllogisms such as these allow Alfarabi to link seemingly disparate pursuits or activities more intimately and thus to declare: "So let it be clear to you that the idea of the Philosopher, Supreme Ruler, King, Legislator, and *Imam* is but a single idea." Indeed, were we to pause and reflect upon our speech, we would readily assent to the accuracy of the conclusion:

No matter which one of these words you take, if you proceed to look at what each of them signifies among the majority of those who speak our language, you will find that they all finally agree by signifying one and the same idea. (*Attainment of Happiness*, sec. 58, with slight modifications to the translation)

Now, then, to digress for a moment, we may begin to appreciate Avicenna's enigmatic explanation of the political philosophy attributed to Plato and Aristotle, especially the importance he claims they attached to the idea of law. In a small treatise entitled *Epistle on the Divisions of the Intellectual Sciences* (*Risāla fī Aqsām al-'Ulūm al-'Aqliyya*), presented as a response to someone who requested a concise, complete, clear, truthful, easily understood, well-arranged, and well-ordered account of the intellectual or rational sciences, Avicenna provides a general account of what constitutes wisdom (*ḥikma*). It is noteworthy that he substitutes this term for the more usual one of philosophy (*falsafa*). Although Avicenna himself says nothing about the substitution, it is evident that by using the term *ḥikma* as the equivalent of *falsafa*—which for all practical purposes it is—he speaks in a distinctly Arab or even Islamic voice and avoids any suggestion that the intellectual virtue in question is somehow dependent on Greek or pagan learning.

As presented in this small treatise, wisdom is the art of reflection needed for a human being to ennoble and perfect his soul and thus be prepared for acquiring ultimate happiness in the life to come (*Epistle*, 104:13–105:3). Like philosophy, wisdom admits of two divisions: theoretical and practical. Noting that there are three subdivisions to practical wisdom—one focuses on the human being as an individual, another on the household community, and the third on civic community—Avicenna identifies the aim of each, as well as the particular writings that shed greater light on what each is about. The subdivision focusing on the individual human being makes known what this individual's moral habits and actions should be so that he will have a happy life both here and in the world to come; Avicenna pauses to note that Aristotle's *Nicomachean Ethics* encompasses this subject. The second subdivision makes known how a human being ought to govern his household so that his relations with his wife, children, and servants will be ordered in such a manner as to lead to the acquisition of happiness. Citing here Bryson's *On the Governance of the Household*, Avicenna notes that many others have also written on this subject. He does not suggest, however, that the proper management of the household has anything to do with leading a happy life in the world to come; its purview is uniquely limited to concerns of this world (*Epistle*, 107:5–15). The third subdivision identifies the different sorts of virtuous and vicious regimes, rulerships, and civic communities, as well as how to bring each one about; it also explains the cause of each one ceasing to exist and the way each is transformed.

Considerably narrowing the inquiry he has just set forth to the theme of kingship for a moment, Avicenna mentions that this topic is discussed in Plato's and Aristotle's books about politics (107:15–108:2). The reference, presumably, is to Plato's *Republic* and Aristotle's *Politics*, even though it is generally accepted that the latter work was never transmitted to the Arabs. He then adds, as though this will suffice for the rest of the inquiry into political science, that with respect to prophecy (*al-nubūwa*) and divine law (*al-sharī'a*), Plato and Aristotle each have another book about conventional laws (*al-nawāmīs*). In other words, Avicenna places divine law on an equal footing with conventional law. What Alfarabi implies through equivocal use of terminology in the *Attainment of Happiness*, Avicenna makes explicit (*Epistle*, 108:2–3). Moreover, although the reference to Plato's *Laws* is evident, the book by Aristotle he has in mind is by no means clear.

Avicenna apparently understands happiness to be even less a concern of political science than of household management, for he says nothing at all here about it leading to happiness—not in this world nor in the one to come. He seems, instead, to consider that the main subjects of political science can be summarized as kingship, prophecy, and divine law. Indeed, he subordinates further explanation of what constitutes political science to his development of a thought related to this mention of books by Plato and Aristotle about conventional laws (*nomoi*). He is intent, above all, on explaining what the philosophers mean by *nomoi* and how that relates to revelation:

> By *nomos*, the philosophers do not mean what the vulgar suppose, namely, that the *nomos* is a trick and deception. Rather, according to them, the *nomos* is traditional law, established and fixed example, and the coming-down of revelation. The Arabs, too, call the angel that comes down with the revelation a *nomos*. (*Epistle*, 108:3–6)[13]

[13] To highlight the nuances in Avicenna's explanation here, I have translated the Arabic term *nāmūs* as *nomos* throughout the passage instead of as "law"; the Arabic term translated as "traditional law" is *sunna*.

Avicenna contends here, then, that the philosophers—and the context allows him to be thinking only of the pagan philosophers Plato and Aristotle—understand *nomos* in the same way as the Arabs—that is, the Muslim Arabs—understand it. Moreover, his assertion that these pagan philosophers view the *nomos* as traditional law (*al-sunna*) strengthens the appearance of harmonious understanding he seeks to create between them and those who have received revelation.

In the rest of the passage, Avicenna emphasizes the affinity even more:

This part of practical wisdom makes known the existence of prophecy and the need the human species has of the divine law for its existence, preservation, and life to come. It makes known the wisdom in the universal penalties common to [all] divine laws and in those [penalties] particular to one divine law or another, according to one people or another and one time or another. And it makes known the difference between divine prophecy and all of the false claims to it. (108:6–10)

When a comparison is made between this account of what the part of practical wisdom having to do with the larger human community—that is, political science—makes known and what Avicenna has to say shortly hereafter about what metaphysics makes known, the two appear to have many common concerns (see 112:12–114:8, 114:9–116:9). Though he does not explicitly set forth here how political science prepares one for human happiness, reflection suggests that it must do so insofar as it apprises us of the need we have for law, whether it be conventional law or revealed, that is, divine law.

Like Alfarabi, then, and here we return to the point from which we digressed, Avicenna clearly wishes to insist upon the harmony, unity of purpose, or ultimate affinity between philosophy, including its pagan manifestations, and religion. For both, however, the argument in favor of such a relationship between philosophy and religion is based on reasoning whose premises are by no means evident. The same holds for what both have to say about the purview of political science. Still, it is recognition of this problem or impasse that leads them to investigate the teaching of Plato and Aristotle more closely.

Having reached the point of discerning what characterizes true philosophy and the true philosopher, Alfarabi is nonetheless aware that what may be true in theory does not necessarily hold in practice. The problem he now faces is gaining recognition for his new understanding of the philosopher as both a political ruler and a spiritual guide, as a king and an imam. An equally, if not more, important issue—what to do when no use is made of this philosopher who epitomizes the highest grasp we have of what philosophy is all about—troubles him less. Nay, it troubles him not at all:

If after reaching this stage no use is made of him, the fact that he is of no use to others is not his fault but the fault of those who either do not listen or are not of the opinion that they should listen to him. Therefore the king or the imam is king and imam by virtue of his skill and art, regardless of whether or not anyone acknowledges him, whether or not he is obeyed, whether or not he is supported in his purpose by any group; just as the physician is physician by virtue of his skill and his ability to heal the sick, whether or not there are sick men for him to heal, whether or not he finds tools to use in his activity, whether he is prosperous or poor—not having any of these things does not do away with his being a physician. (*Attainment of Happiness*, sec. 62, with slight modifications to the translation)[14]

In this passage, blame is clearly placed upon those who fail to recognize the merits of the philosopher who would also be king and *imam*. And Alfarabi has an explanation for their shortcoming: They do not understand what true philosophy is, that is, the philosophy he has so painstakingly set forth in this first part of the trilogy (*Attainment of Happiness*, sec. 63).

Alfarabi's goal in the two subsequent parts of the trilogy was, as we have seen, to present an account of philosophy as provided by Plato and Aristotle and also of the ways they set forth for its pursuit. We have now discerned that Alfarabi's portrait of the philosophy of the one as well as of the other culminates in a call for their quest to be continued, a call based on acknowledgment that knowledge about the most important things has not yet been acquired. But that is not the issue of most concern to us. Nor is Plato or Aristotle—at any rate, not Alfarabi's Plato or Aristotle—of any help to us for this more pressing inquiry, namely, gaining a better understanding of law and the way it is treated in the medieval Islamic philosophic tradition. For Plato and Aristotle, or at least for Alfarabi's vision of them, and thus for him certainly, law is subordinated to educating or training the citizens. Instilling good habits, the ones that derive from good dispositions and lead to good actions, is the key political goal. Though it is served by law, reflection on, or investigation of, law is secondary. This, at any rate, is the message that appears from these public or political writings by Alfarabi.

Before turning to Avicenna and Averroes, it seems necessary to cast an eye on how Alfarabi addresses the issue of law in his other political works. The only time reference is made to law in *Enumeration of the Sciences* V, it has to do with the definition of jurisprudence cited above. Even then, at issue are two mentions of the term lawgiver—or, more precisely, divine lawgiver (*wāḍiʿ al-sharīʿa*)—as part of the larger explanation of what characterizes the jurist and how his tasks depend upon the preliminary work of the lawgiver. The jurist accepts as valid what the lawgiver has set down, without questioning its origin or validity. His goal is simply to explain how what the lawgiver has already stipulated applies in particular cases and, on rare occasions, to infer how it might be extended to issues the lawgiver did not address.

Even in *Book of Religion*, a small treatise in which Alfarabi explores the multiple similarities between religion and political science and then proposes an entirely novel approach to both, his references to traditional law (*sunna*), divine law (*sharīʿa*), and the lawgiver (*wāḍiʿ al-sharīʿa*) are in keeping with

[14] See also *Aphorisms*, aph. 32, for a similar, albeit slightly stronger, account.

what he says in *Enumeration*, *Philosophy of Plato and Aristotle*, *Selected Aphorisms*, and *Political Regime*. He urges that *sharīʿa* and *sunna* are "almost synonymous" and that they "most often [...] apply to the determined actions in [...] religion" (*Book of Religion*, sec. 4). Indeed, in the rest of the exposition, Alfarabi treats the two terms as largely synonymous (secs. 5, 7, 10).[15] The only hint of a distinction between the two has to do primarily with a matter of degree or nuance. It centers on the way Alfarabi draws attention to the role of the first ruler, that is, to the one presented in the opening words of the treatise as founding the religion:

Religion is opinions and actions, determined and restricted with stipulations and prescribed for a community by their first ruler who seeks to obtain through their practicing it a specific purpose with respect to them or by means of them. (Sec. 1)

To differentiate between this first ruler or founder and those who follow him and apply the opinions and actions—the laws (*sharāʾiʿ*)—he has set down, Alfarabi speaks of the latter as kings of tradition or of traditional law. Their rule may well be virtuous, but it continues what has already been established rather than bringing about something new.

[Political science explains] that virtuous rulership is of two types: a first rulership and a rulership dependent on it. First rulership is the one that first establishes the virtuous ways of life and dispositions in the city or nation without their having existed among the people before that, and it converts them from the ignorant ways of life to the virtuous ways of life. The person undertaking this rulership is the first ruler.

The rulership dependent on the first is the one that follows in the steps of the first rulership with regard to its actions. The one who undertakes this rulership is called ruler of the tradition and king of the tradition. His rulership is based on an existing tradition. (Sec. 14b)[16]

Alfarabi's *Virtuous City* or, more literally, *Principles of the Opinions of the Inhabitants of the Virtuous City*, serves the same basic purpose and covers many of the same subjects as his *Political Regime* (also known as *Principles of the Beings*). In fact, there are numerous instances of parallel passages in the two

[15] In sections 9 and 10, Alfarabi's discussion of the art of jurisprudence and explanation of how the jurist approaches the law (*sharīʿa*) set down by the lawgiver (*wāḍiʿ al-sharīʿa*) are in perfect harmony with what he says about the subject in *Enumeration of the Sciences* V.

[16] The rest of this section reads: "The first virtuous kingly craft consists of cognizance of all the actions that facilitate establishing the virtuous ways of life and dispositions in cities and nations, preserving them for the people, and guarding and keeping them from the inroad of something from the ignorant ways of life—all of those being sicknesses that befall the virtuous cities. In this sense, it is like the medical craft; for the latter consists of cognizance of all the actions that establish health in a human being, preserve it for him, and guard it from any sickness that might occur." Similarly, in Section 18, when setting forth "political science that is a part of philosophy" and its features (as distinct from political science that is not a part of philosophy, discussed in Sections 11–14d), Alfarabi explains the account it gives of "the first virtuous kingly craft," then adds: "The one dependent on it, whose rulership is based on tradition, does not by nature need philosophy."

treatises. For this reason, perhaps, Alfarabi's discussion of law in the *Virtuous City* is highly similar to his discussion of it in the *Political Regime*, even to the point that in the *Virtuous City*, as in the *Political Regime*, he speaks only of divine and traditional law and makes no mention of *nomos*. Laws, divine or traditional, exist. They are eagerly followed by the good rulers in the virtuous city, but adamantly contested by different groups of citizens in the ignorant cities (*Virtuous City* 250:4–6 and 282:6–9, Arabic text; 251:4–8 and 283: 11–16, English).

Finally, almost in desperation, we turn to Alfarabi's *Summary of Plato's Laws* fully expecting to find in this work a detailed examination of law in all its various aspects. Alfarabi does, to be sure, speak frequently here of laws, especially conventional laws or *nomoi*, this term being reflected in the Arabic title of the work. And at times, when reflecting on the laws attributed to the gods by the Athenian stranger or his interlocutors, Alfarabi contrasts *nomoi* to divine laws and even to traditional laws. At most, his analysis of Plato's dialogue confirms the suspicion formed earlier that *nomoi* for Alfarabi are equivalent to the ways of life, moral habits, and states of character that he sees political science striving to develop among the citizens. Consider, for example, this observation:

Then the extended discourse on wars led him to mention many aspects of the advantages of the law: it enables a person to control oneself, to pursue the power to suppress evil things (both those in the soul and the external ones), and to pursue what is just. Moreover, he explained in this connection what is the virtuous city and who is the virtuous person. He mentioned that they are the city and the person that conquer by virtue of truth and rightness. He explained also the true need for a judge, the obligation to obey him, and how this promotes common interests. He described who is the agreeable judge, how he ought to conduct himself in suppressing the evil ones and protecting people from wars by gentleness and good administration, and that he should begin with what is most needed, namely, the lowest. He explained the true need of people for avoiding wars among themselves and the intensity of their inclination to avoid wars because this promotes their well-being. But this is impossible without adhering to the law and applying its statutes. When the law commands waging wars, it does so in the pursuit of peace, not in the pursuit of war—just as someone may be commanded to do something offensive because its final consequence is desirable. (*Summary of Plato's Laws* I.6)

Only the remark "then he mentioned that not everyone who wishes to legislate is a true lawgiver, but only the one whom God creates and equips for this purpose" stands out (I.14).[17] Even this, however, is perfectly in keeping with the explanation Alfarabi provides of the first ruler in the opening section of the *Book of Religion*:

If the first ruler is virtuous and his rulership truly virtuous, then in what he prescribes he seeks only to obtain, for himself and for everyone under his rulership, the ultimate happiness that is

[17] The Arabic term translated here as "lawgiver" is *wāḍiʿ al-nawāmīs*, as distinct from *wāḍiʿ al-sharīʿa* or *wāḍiʿ al-sunna*.

truly happiness; and that religion will be virtuous religion [...]. Now the craft of the virtuous first ruler is kingly and joined with revelation from God. Indeed, he determines the actions and opinions in the virtuous religion by means of revelation. (*Book of Religion*, sec. 1)

Lest such an explanation alienate the reader, Alfarabi quickly goes on to explain what he means by revelation and how it comes about:

This occurs in one or both of two ways: one is that they are all revealed to him as determined; the second is that he determines them by means of the faculty he acquires from revelation and from the Revealer, may He be exalted, so that the stipulations with which he determines the virtuous opinions and actions are disclosed to him by means of it. Or some come about in the first way and some in the second way. It has already been explained in theoretical science how the revelation of God, may He be exalted, to the human being receiving the revelation comes about and how the faculty acquired from revelation and from the Revealer occurs in a human being. (Ibid.)

Differently stated, whether we think that the lawgiver receives a precise image of the laws that he then enunciates or a general idea that he himself refines, we call the process revelation. A fuller explanation of the process belongs to a different inquiry, one not open to most people.

9.4. Avicenna

Avicenna (Abū ʻAlī al-Ḥusayn Ibn Sīnā) (980–1037) was born in Afshanah, in what is now Uzbekistan, and his family soon moved to nearby Bukhara where he began his studies. Having proved himself in the study of the Quran and related works of literature by the age of ten, he turned to Indian mathematics and Islamic jurisprudence, then to the study of philosophy. Afterward, he read Porphyry's *Isagoge*, logic in general, Euclid, Ptolemy's *Almagest*, and eventually undertook the natural sciences and metaphysics. For the latter two pursuits, he claims to have read both the original texts—presumably Aristotle—and the commentaries. At the age of eighteen, he became a physician to the ailing ruler of Bukhara and gained access to his well-stocked library.

Avicenna composed his numerous works under unusually trying circumstances at an intense, almost frenetic, pace and used his medical knowledge to push his body beyond normal limits. After his father's death, Avicenna accepted an administrative post from this same ruler, then moved to other locales where he served as a jurist or practiced the art of politics in service to different minor rulers. Occasionally, he also managed the affairs of the widows of rulers and eventually came to serve as physician to Shams al-Dawlah, the Buyid prince of Hamadhan and Qirmisin. On two separate occasions he was named chief minister (vizier) to Shams al-Dawla. Avicenna is most noted for his multivolume *Book of Healing* (*Kitāb al-Shifāʼ*), a massive exposition of all of the sciences that acknowledges, but does not depend upon, Aristotle. Toward the end of his life, he became a companion and learned advisor to ʻAlāʼ al-Dawla in Isfahan and died in Hamadhan.

Apart from the reflections on law set forth in the short *Epistle on the Divisions of the Intellectual Sciences* already alluded to, Avicenna's most extensive statement about law and political science occurs in Book Ten of his *Metaphysics* at the very end of his major compilation, *Book of Healing*. Taking a cue of sorts from Alfarabi's *Enumeration of the Sciences*, Avicenna postpones his inquiry into politics until after having set forth an account of all of the other sciences, especially natural science and its sequel—metaphysics or divine science. This account in Book Ten of the *Metaphysics* consists of five chapters, and Avicenna's political teaching may be divided into three parts. In the first part, set forth in chapter one, he explains the unique qualities of the prophet and addresses indirectly the all-important question of why it is appropriate to subordinate politics to prophecy. In the following two chapters, he explains how the prophet sets forth a traditional law (*sunna*) containing precepts about God and the afterlife that are needed for a people to come together in communal association. Then in the final two chapters, he enumerates and defends the actual laws a prophet-lawgiver might make in order to regulate a community and prepare its citizens for happiness, both here and in the world to come.

Avicenna begins by noting that just as there is a hierarchy among the things existing in the world and among the beings, with human beings occupying the highest rank or representing what is best among the beings, so, too, is there a hierarchy among human beings. The best or most virtuous of human beings is he who has so perfected his soul as to become fully rational and acquire the practical moral habits permitting him to manage his own affairs in an excellent manner. Among those who reach this level of accomplishment, the prophet is the best (*Metaphysics*, 435:6–16). Having established this hierarchy, Avicenna turns to consider why human beings have to live in communities at all. Simply stated, we cannot survive, much less strive for virtue, when isolated from one another or even when associated in small groupings such as families. Merely to feed and clothe ourselves, we must enter into exchange relationships with other individuals.

To perpetuate such relationships and give them structure, we form cities and communities. It is then necessary for these larger associations to be regulated and for there to exist a standard on which exchange is based, in other words, for there to be law and justice. The law at issue is traditional law (*sunna*), and Avicenna uses an active participle of this term to identify the one who sets it down (*sānnin*). Identifying this individual as a prophet, Avicenna emphasizes that he must exist for the affairs of human beings to be properly ordered (441:3–12, 441:13–442:6). The prophet-lawgiver seeks to teach the citizens about the existence of God and what He is like, as well as about the need for them to obey Him in order to merit happiness in the life to come. As Avicenna puts it, this individual understands how exceptional he is and how unlikely it is that another like him will come along in the near future. Throughout this exposition, Avicenna shows himself to be especially attentive to the immediate needs of human beings. Having started his explanation from the most basic consideration, association in order to provide for physical survival, he now notes that the prophet-lawgiver's provision for acts of worship contributes both to the preservation of his laws and to the well-being of the people. Struggle (*jihād*) against others in defense of the laws and travel to distant places or pilgrimage (*ḥajj*) are also conducive to the worldly concerns of the citizens (see 442:8–443:9, 455:1–13; also 443:16–444:14, especially 444:13–14; see also Avicenna, *The Soul*, 181:5–19, 183:4–17).

In the course of this exposition, Avicenna alters his terminology. The prophet-lawgiver is no longer merely a *sānnin*, that is, one who brings traditional law (*sunna*). Indeed, he has now become one who brings divine law (*sharī'a*), that is, a *shāri'* (*Metaphysics*, 444:17 with 441:13; see also 443:18). In keeping with such a change, the size of his potential community has imperceptibly increased: No longer concerned with mere cities and communities, his focus is now upon a nation (*umma*)—one of such a size that people may have to migrate or travel long distances in order to reach the spot designated as his abode. Even the time for which he wishes to preserve his laws and teaching has expanded. He now thinks it important for the people to remember these things for more than a century or two. Finally, he has also become aware of the need to differentiate between the vulgar or common people (*al-'āmma*) and the select or elite (*al-khāṣṣa*) in his laws and teaching. With respect to the former, he intends merely that the formal aspects of prayer help them remember God and the afterlife so that they continue to obey the traditional and divine laws. With the latter, however, it is the way these acts of worship help them train their souls for happiness in the afterlife that dominates his concerns. These acts help the select develop moral habits and positive dispositions that allow them to purify their souls, that is, gird their souls against desire for the bodily things preventing happiness in the life to come (444:16–445:1, 445:9–10, 445:7–446:7). In this respect, the prophet-lawgiver's teaching becomes so predominantly moral or ethical as to eclipse both its political and its religious content.

Avicenna returns to political considerations in the last two chapters of the *Metaphysics*. Though not presented in a rigidly systematic manner, the subjects seem to fall under ten major groupings. The first—provision for the city being divided into three parts or groups—and the last—a discussion of the moral habits and character traits that lead to justice—echo themes addressed by Plato and Aristotle, while those falling in between evoke Muhammad's early legislation and its development among the first caliphs. Throughout this discussion, Avicenna speaks consistently of the prophet-lawgiver as a traditional lawgiver—that is, as a *sānnin*—and only once uses the term that denotes a bringer of divine laws—that is, a *shāri'* (447:4, 451:13, 454:14; see also 450:7). In this latter instance, even though he clearly means to praise the prophet Muhammad, he uses the term in the plural sense. He has no difficulty in acknowledging that more than one prophet has brought divine laws, but he insists Muhammad is the best of all who have done so. A similar kind of exchange occurs between the term for traditional law, *sunna*, and that for divine law, *sharīʿa*, with the latter being restricted to the community having the best kind of laws. In fact, at the risk of contradicting himself, Avicenna speaks of the possibility for there to be many different systems of traditional laws in effect at a given time, but implies there can be only one divine law or *sharīʿa* (cf. *Metaphysics*, 453:10–454:1 with *Epistle*, 108:6–10).

What this means is that even though Avicenna recognizes a plurality of traditional and divine laws, he insists on the existence of a hierarchy among them—and explicitly among the traditional laws. The prophet-lawgiver identifies the best traditional law with the divine law. That commonality or identity allows him to incite his own followers against those who cling to any other traditional law. For such people, it is better to perish than to live in thrall to a misguided law. Avicenna passes quickly over this consequence, but precision would not be amiss here: For him, adherence to a traditional law that resembles a divine one—a *sharīʿa*—goes beyond the political, as does the bringer of divine laws (*sharīʿ*). In other words, Avicenna does not deem political life, even excellent political life, the highest human good.

Avicenna begins his account of the prophet-lawgiver's political ordering by noting that his first objective is to provide the city with three classes or orders: administrators, artisans, and guardians. Reminiscent as such an ordering is of Plato's *Republic*, Avicenna does not elaborate. Apart from explaining that the prophet-lawgiver also provides for a hierarchy of rulership within each group—without, however, establishing a hierarchical arrangement between these three groups—he says nothing more about them or the duties each is to perform. The major purpose of the ordering appears to be just that, ordering. To ensure that each citizen has an employment, a determined place, and a use in the city, the prophet-lawgiver imposes a rigid hierarchy. This, too, echoes a theme from the *Republic*, namely, that justice consists in each person having one job. Again, however, Avicenna lets the parallel stand without comment.

Nor does Avicenna discuss the kind of regime established by the prophet-lawgiver. This individual himself begins by providing for the needs of the community in his own person and has sufficient foresight to establish conditions for determining the rightful successor and his successors. He does not entertain the possibility that rule by a few virtuous individuals or even by the majority of the citizens might be preferable, for his goal is to preserve the traditional and divine laws that he first set down. The regime, then, is that of rule by one in accordance with the established law. Nonetheless, the law itself is very general. Here, with respect to practical matters, as earlier with respect to theoretical, Avicenna insists that the prophet-lawgiver confine himself to general rules or prescriptions and leave the details to those who come after him (*Metaphysics*, 447:4–5, 454:2–14).

Avicenna concludes his account of political science by insisting that the lawgiver (*sānnin*) must set down traditional laws about the moral habits and character traits leading to justice. He presents justice as a mean, and further explains that a mean is likewise sought with respect to moral habits and character traits. It is sought either to break the hold of the passions so that the soul may be purified and liberated from the body or to use the passions to pursue appropriate worldly goals. Passing over in silence the issue of breaking the hold of the passions—perhaps because it has been adequately treated in *Metaphysics*, Book Nine—Avicenna concentrates on how moderation and courage help human beings function well in this world in that they, along with practical wisdom, lead to justice. Unlike theoretical wisdom, which never admits of a mean, practical wisdom consists in achieving a mean or a balance with respect to worldly affairs; its selfish pursuit to attain for oneself things one would thereby deny to others is denounced strongly. Although theoretical wisdom has nothing to do with justice according to this presentation, happiness cannot be acquired without it. In other words, as important as justice is for the proper conduct of human affairs, it is not the end. More intent on presenting the fullest view of human accomplishment here, Avicenna does not pronounce on whether theoretical wisdom without justice is sufficient to acquire happiness. He concludes by affirming the lofty status of the human being who manages "to win, in addition, the prophetic qualities," for "he becomes almost a human god." Clearly, it is he we should seek as our ruler.

9.5. Averroes

Averroes (Abū al-Walīd Ibn Rushd) (1126–1198) was an accomplished commentator on Plato and Aristotle, physician, practicing judge, jurist, princely advisor, and spokesman for theoretical and practical problems of his day. His great intelligence and profound accomplishments in jurisprudence, medicine, poetry, philosophy, natural science, and theology were recognized by fellow Muslims as well as by the Jews and Christians who first translated his writings into Hebrew and Latin.

Born in Cordoba, Spain, the son and grandson of noted judges, Averroes was educated in jurisprudence, medicine, theology, and the natural sciences. Known above all for his commentaries on the works of Aristotle—commentaries that range across the whole of Aristotle's corpus—Averroes also wrote a commentary on Plato's *Republic*. In his commentaries on Aristotle, he demonstrates a remarkable awareness of Aristotle's vocabulary as well as the Greek tradition of commentary. Yet he knew no Greek and frequently complained about the poor quality of the Arabic translations at his disposal. Moreover, he composed treatises on topics of more immediate concern to fellow Muslims:

The *Decisive Treatise* on the relationship between philosophy and the divine law and the *Incoherence of the Incoherence*, which is an extensive refutation of Alghazali's attack upon the philosophers.

Averroes had a very close relationship with the Almohad rulers, serving them as cadi, supreme cadi of Seville as well as of Cordoba, and as personal physician and trusted advisor in Marrakesh. Nonetheless, in 1195, he was punished, along with other notable scholars, for being overly occupied with philosophy and "the sciences of the ancients" and banished to Lucena, a small town near Cordoba, for two years. Returning afterward to the court in Marrakesh, he died the next year.

In the manner of Alfarabi, Averroes strives to prove the importance of understanding Plato and Aristotle for the pursuit of philosophy, and of philosophy itself for sound political life. In the manner of Maimonides, he alternates between writing as a philosopher and as a learned follower of a revealed religion. To gain some appreciation of the way he understands law, we must turn to each kind of writing. His *Commentary on Plato's Republic* and *Middle Commentary on Aristotle's Rhetoric* are especially representative of the first, while hardly anything could be more pertinent for the second than his famous *Book of the Decisive Treatise: Determining the Connection Between the Law and Wisdom.*

Because the *Commentary on Plato's Republic* has come down to us only in Hebrew translation, on which the medieval Latin version was based, it is better to begin by considering what Averroes has to say about law in the *Middle Commentary on Aristotle's Rhetoric.* For him, rhetoric is an art used to find the possible means of persuasion about any given subject and is addressed most frequently to a multitude or to those who have neither the time nor ability to follow a lengthy or complicated chain of reasoning. Consequently, the extent to which rhetoric can exhaustively investigate any given subject is limited. There are frequent allusions to the idea that rhetoric cannot delve more deeply into the subject at hand, or that in a particular discussion he has actually gone beyond the limits of rhetoric and begun an investigation proper to another art (*Rhetoric*, 33:1–14, 33:17–34:1, 39:8–9, 67:15–19, 71:5–7). Moreover, precisely because rhetoric is usually addressed to those too hurried or not able to follow lengthy and complicated arguments, it is closely linked with the political art.

Patterning the formal structure of his *Middle Commentary on Aristotle's Rhetoric* on Aristotle's *Rhetoric*, Averroes devotes an entire chapter to an inquiry into political regimes. He introduces the chapter by declaring the importance of considering the different kinds of regimes, and speaks about the relationship between laws (*sunan*) and justice in two kinds of regime: The regime of force (*siyāsat al-taghallub*) and democracy (*siyāsat al-ḥurriyya*) (*Rhetoric*, 67:21–68:13). He then enumerates and examines the different kinds of regimes, explores the various laws that can be set down, identifies the ends of each regime, inserts an explanation to the effect that existing regimes are in reality mixed regimes, suggests the importance of knowledge about the moral qualities and characters for rhetorical discourse, and concludes—almost in contradiction to what has preceded—by noting that a fuller examination of these matters is to be found in political discussions.

Within the context of discussing aristocracy, literally, the regime of good dominion (*siyāsa jūdat al-tasalluṭ*), Averroes explains why it is excellent:

> Aristocracy is dominion that takes place in accordance with education about, and imitation of, what is prescribed by law. Thus those who advise according to what law prescribes are the ones who have aristocratic dominion. This is the dominion by which the well-being of the citizens and human happiness is attained. Therefore, these [rulers] possess virtue and are capable of the actions that improve the city; and they possess discernment and are wary of whatever might corrupt the city from without or from within. (*Rhetoric*, 69:7–12; see also Aristotle, *Rhet.* I.8.1365b22–1366a22)

Averroes' comments expand upon Aristotle's observation that authority in an aristocracy is in the hands of those who possess a certain education and who follow the prescriptions of the law. But he does not go beyond the sense of law as Aristotle uses it here.[18]

Later, when commenting upon Aristotle's classification of just and unjust actions according to particular and common laws, Averroes is very assiduous about the divisions. He speaks of law particular to one group or another within the city as opposed to those common to all within the city. And, like Aristotle, he speaks also of written and unwritten laws, characterizing the latter as "those that are natural to all" (*Rhetoric*, 107:16–19). Here, too, the term Averroes uses is *sunna*.

In the *Commentary on Plato's Republic*, Averroes refers to several kinds of law, including divine law (Hebrew *tōrah*, clearly for an original Arabic *sharī'a*) (26:16).[19] Most interesting, however, is his reference on at least two occasions to something called human law or, more literally, human divine laws (*tōrōth enūshiyōth*, that is, *sharā'i' insāniyya*) (*Republic*, 26:16, 63:1). This human law seems to be something like basic natural law and is distinct from both conventional law (*nomos*) and divine law. Traditional law is never discussed, not even as an equivalent for *nomos*. Since the totally unprecedented human law or human divine law is presented with so little fanfare, it may be no more than the Hebrew translator's attempt to find an equivalent for *sunna*, that is, traditional law.

The only law Averroes is concerned with in *Decisive Treatise* is divine law (*sharī'a*). From the subtitle of the work, as well as from the opening words, it

[18] What Aristotle denotes here as *nomos*, Averroes refers to as *sunna*. This is in keeping with the way the Arabic translation of Aristotle's *Rhetoric* renders the Greek *nomos*; see Aristotle, *Rhetoric*, ed. Badawī 1959, 36–8.

[19] Page and line references are to the edition of the Hebrew text, the Arabic not being extant; see the translation by Rosenthal 1956.

is manifest that he seeks to plead here the case of philosophy before the tribunal of the divine law:

Now the goal of this statement is for us to investigate, from the perspective of Law-based reflection, whether reflection upon philosophy and the sciences of logic is permitted, prohibited, or commanded—and this as a recommendation or as an obligation—by the Law. (*Decisive Treatise*, sec. 1)[20]

The first part of this treatise is devoted to that task, the second to explicating the intention of the divine law. To emphasize how much importance he attaches to this latter task, Averroes begins by declaring, for the first and only time in the *Decisive Treatise*, that here is something "you ought to know" (sec. 38), namely, that "what is intended by the Law is only to teach true science and true practice." Defining true science as "cognizance of God," of "all the existing things as they are," and of "happiness [...] and of misery in the hereafter," he presents the Law as providing the all-important cognizance of the hereafter that philosophy has not been shown to provide. Moreover, insofar as the Law makes us acquainted with true practice, it brings about (or at least intends to bring about) unity between knowledge and action.

Addressed to all and intended to teach true science and practice to all, the Law contains different methods for achieving these ends. Too often, the primary intention of the Law—namely, "taking care of the greater number without neglecting to alert the select [few]"—is neglected (sec. 40). Given such disparity among the natural capacities of people, and thus the impossibility of all having the same degree of understanding or being open to the same methods of instruction, the Law must have different ways to speak to these dissimilar interlocutors. That is, the Law must admit of interpretation.

Why Averroes places such emphasis on the intention of the Law and the way it speaks to all the people comes to light once he begins to point out how those who fail to discern this intention and use the wrong kind of speech in speaking to the multitude actually lead them astray—that is, to unbelief—and that leading others to unbelief is itself a form of unbelief. Lest his goal here be misunderstood, Averroes resorts to a rhetorical image or parable of his own: He who declares interpretations to those not apt to receive them is like the one who dissuades people from following a physician; whereas the physician urges them to adopt actions for preserving health and avoiding sickness, this other person causes them to become sick. Like the physician, the Lawgiver seeks the health of the people, that is, the health of their souls. Hence to claim that what

[20] In his justly famous manual of law, Averroes explains that the jurists acknowledge the judgments of the divine Law to fall into five categories: obligatory (*wājib*), recommended (*mandūb*), prohibited (*maḥẓūr*), reprehensible (*makrūh*), and permitted (*mubāḥ*). Here, however, he groups the first two under a more comprehensive category of "commanded" (*ma'mūr*) and—perhaps since it is not applicable to the present question—passes over "reprehensible" in silence; see *Bidāyat al-Mujtahid*, 1: 17–18.

he says is not true on the surface and can be interpreted amounts to dissuading the people from pursuing the health of their souls. Because those who make this claim neglect to add that only certain people under certain conditions may seek to interpret the Law, they lead the many into sickness. Part of their error is their failure to consider the intention of the Lawgiver. Putting their own intention first and failing to ask about that of the Lawgiver, they lead astray even when their interpretation and intention are sound. When these are unsound, they risk leading the people to doubt whether there is health or sickness, even whether there are things conducive to health and such as to avert sickness (*Decisive Treatise*, secs. 48–9).

Averroes insists that his image or parable is very accurate, even certain (sec. 50). What gives it this status is the link between the physician and the Lawgiver, for the health of souls to which the Lawgiver aspires is piety, namely, the piety that is linked with true practice, the teaching of which is said to be intended by the Law. How philosophy provides the best understanding of the intention of the Law and the Lawgiver, and ensures that it will be followed by the people, has now been shown. In addition, the critics of philosophy have been revealed to be incapable both of discerning this intention and of furthering it. Averroes now brings the argument full circle by affirming that knowledge of the health intended by the Lawgiver is precisely what is needed for happiness in the hereafter. As is now perfectly evident, only the philosopher proves himself able to speak to such happiness and to urge the many to seek it in accordance with the intention of the Lawgiver and the Law. And, according to Averroes, only the philosopher is capable of sound interpretation, that is, of "the deposit mankind was charged with holding and held" (*Decisive Treatise*, sec. 51; see Quran 33:22).

9.6. Maimonides

With this account of the lawgiver as physician of the soul and divine law as its medicine, Averroes brings us back to the suggestion made by Alfarabi in *Selected Aphorisms* that the true physician of the soul is the statesman or king and that for either to perform this task it is necessary to have philosophy. It is an account or suggestion with which Maimonides is in full agreement, but on which he does not dwell.

Moses Maimonides (Moshe Ben Maimon) (1135–1204) was a legal scholar, community leader, philosopher, and physician. Born in Cordoba, Spain, Maimonides and his family moved to Morocco and then Cairo, Egypt, to escape the harsh rule of the zealous Almohads. In Cairo, Maimonides became attached to the Sultan's court as a physician and divided his time between medical duties, scholarly pursuits, and tending to the Jewish community.

He is best known for his commentary on a rabbinic law code, the *Mishnah*; his codification of the whole of Jewish law, the *Mishneh Torah*; and his extraordinarily complex and richly philosophical explanation of scripture and theology, *Guide of the Perplexed*, addressed to one of his favorite students. In addition, he is known for *Treatise on the Art of Logic*, based on Aristotelian premises, and for several epistles written in response to particular requests. These, like the *Mishnah* and the *Guide*, were written in Arabic. But since it was an Arabic composed in Hebrew letters, Maimonides' works were closed to Arabic readers who did not also know Hebrew. Though he was a highly accomplished student and exegete of Aristotle, he wrote no commentaries on Aristotelian works.

Maimonides' goal, both in *Guide of the Perplexed* and *Eight Chapters*, is to dispel the doubts arising from the study of philosophy that trouble the more thoughtful of his students. Its pursuit obliges Maimonides to interpret scripture as well as to point out the errors of his predecessors. Thus, Maimonides considers the philosophic teaching that the virtuous man is better than the continent man insofar as the latter "does good things while craving and strongly desiring to perform bad actions" or "does good things while being troubled at doing them" ("The Sixth Chapter," in *Eight Chapters*, 78–80). Though this agrees with what one finds in the divine law, it is questioned by some of the sages in the Jewish tradition. Thus, in contrast to the Biblical "a joy to the righteous is the doing of justice, but dismay to evil-doers" (ibid.), is the Rabbinic saying that "the reward is according to the pain." Indeed, the Rabbis go further and forbid any believer to claim not to want to commit a transgression. Following the precepts of the faith is burdensome and is to be considered as such. The reward of the pious is proportionate to the pain he endures for the sake of his piety.

To resolve the conflict, Maimonides points to the difference between the actions deemed bad by the philosophers—namely, the things "generally accepted by all the people as bad" (ibid.)—and those deemed bad by the rabbis—namely, the traditional laws. Of the former, it may be said "if they were not written down, they would deserve to be written down." The latter, however, concern matters that people of the faith deem themselves bound to obey, for example, religious statutes such as not eating meat with milk. Of these, the rabbis say that "statutes which I have prescribed for you, you have no permission to investigate," that is, to question. It is difficult to observe statutes like these, and there is no wrong in wanting to do what they forbid. On the other hand, it is wrong to want to murder another person, steal from him, hurt an innocent person, be disrespectful to parents, and so forth.

This explanation allows Maimonides to criticize those who call the generally accepted things (*al-mashhūrāt*) rational or intellectual laws (*sharā'i' al-'aqliyya*), on the grounds that they unduly confuse matters by such terminology. These are not rational or intellectual laws, says Maimonides. Rather, the statutes or commandments set forth in scripture are properly rational laws. Of note here is that the constant term used by Maimonides for "laws" is *al-sharā'i'*, even when something like traditional laws (*sunan*) would be more appropriate. The term he does use for traditional laws, and which would not correspond to what rational laws signify, is *al-sharā'i' al-sam'iyya*, literally, "heard divine laws" or "aural divine laws."

For the reasons noted above with respect to Jewish philosophers in general, Maimonides stands apart from the Arab philosophers in that he has little to say about law and its relationship to political rule. In the introductions to the *Guide*, he is at pains to indicate that the work has two purposes and is directed toward a particular kind of addressee. It is, above all, a book the learned can use to overcome perplexity. Yet its goal is not to present the simply right view of the divine law, nor to reveal Maimonides' own personal views about it.

The first or primary purpose of the treatise is to provide an "explanation of the meanings of the names that occur in the books of prophecy." Such an explanation is not meant for everyone, but only for the kind of person whose faith is settled in his soul. About this Maimonides is adamant:

> [T]he purpose of this treatise is to give an indication to a man of religion for whom the soundness of our Law has humbled his soul and been attained in his belief, he being perfect in his religion and moral habits and having speculated about the philosophical sciences and come to know their meanings. (*Guide* 2b–3a)

In other words, not "knowledge of the Law in truth," but something that points to the soundness of the divine law, perhaps because the former is too massive a goal. And it points to the soundness of the divine law for someone who has become perplexed about its superficial aspects, someone for whom there must be a deeper or hidden meaning. Problems arising from a surface reading will cause such a person to lose his faith if they are not corrected.

The second purpose of the work is "to explain exceedingly concealed examples occurring in the books of the prophets" (*Guide* 3a). The emphasis is on the books of the prophets as distinct from other parts of scripture because Maimonides has as his goal taking the thoughtful individual beyond the perplexity arising from superficial interpretation of these perplexing works. The Guide will attempt to remove most, but not all, of the difficulties in scripture, especially those concerning the account of the beginning, which has to do eventually with natural science, and the account of the chariot, which is divine science (*Guide* 3b–6a).

The discourse or discussion in the *Guide* is directed to "someone who engages in philosophy" and who "knows true sciences while believing in the matters of the Law and is perplexed about the meanings leading to perplexity with respect to the equivocal nouns and the examples" (*Guide* 6a). In other words, belief in the divine law is a basic condition for Maimonides' intended reader. This is not a book for philosophers as such, but for believers whose awareness of philosophy and the sciences leads to doubts about things they would otherwise accept without question in the faith. At no point does Maimonides reach beyond society to polity. He is concerned with the things that he can influence, and politics is not one of them.

When Maimonides turns to the Book of Job, for example, he sees the story as "a parable to make clear the opinions of the people with respect to providence" (*Guide* 44b). For Maimonides, the story shows that moral virtue is not sufficient; wisdom is needed to understand the ways of the Lord. Job mistakenly equates piety with wisdom and righteousness with understanding. Righteousness, however, is not enough; rather, Job—and we—must come to the recognition that God does what He wills. Period. We must recognize the great disparity between us and God. From Maimonides' explanation, it appears that the whole purpose of the Book of Job is to explain how God's knowledge and providence differ from our knowledge and providence, yet to do so by arguing from natural phenomena (*Guide* 51a–b). In the end, then, the wisdom Job learns is not to question God or God's ways. He comes to see how insignificant he is in comparison to God and, more important, how little he can discern God's purposes. This explanation, like so many other passages in the *Guide*, sets Maimonides apart from all of his Arab predecessors with the possible exception of Averroes, just as it sets Hobbes and Melville apart from Maimonides. Indeed, insofar as they both try to tame Leviathan, to be his master, they have an entirely different—a completely modern—view of politics and law. For Maimonides, political power is out of reach for faithful Jews. Speculation on law, natural or conventional, is less important than understanding the basic law—divine law as given to the Jewish people at Sinai.

9.7. Conclusion

This examination of what jurists and philosophers within the medieval Jewish and Islamic traditions have to say about the philosophy of law shows that, for the most part, whatever term is used to denote law, it stands in for what ancient Greek philosophers termed *nomos*. The divine law is not questioned, not even by the philosophers. Rather, every attempt is made to understand what its purpose or goal is, that is, what the intention of the lawgiver might be. And the inquiry usually points to the conclusion that all lawgivers—those who claim to have divine inspiration as well as those who seem to be philosophically inspired—intend the same thing by their laws: the health of the soul.

Further Reading

For English readers, Lerner and Mahdi 1963 is far and away the best single source for excellent translations of texts by the philosophers in the Jewish and Islamic traditions. It is now supplemented by the translations of Alfarabi's *Philosophy of Plato and Aristotle* by Mahdi (2002) and political writings by Butterworth (2001 and forthcoming), of Averroes' *Decisive Treatise* by Butterworth (2001) and *Averroes on Plato's "Republic"* by Lerner (1974), and of a number of ethical writings by Maimonides by Weiss and Butterworth (1975). The best translation of Maimonides' justly famous *Guide of the Perplexed* is by Pines (1963), and the introductions by both Pines and Strauss are invaluable.

Thanks to the careful work of Anawati (1952), Druart (1998), Mahdi (1968 and 1971), and Najjar (1971), and Najjar and Mallet (1999), excellent editions of the political writings of Alfarabi and Avicenna are now available. Atāy's painstaking 1974 Arabic edition of Maimonides' *Guide* is also an invaluable tool.

If any single individual is responsible for focusing learned attention on Alfarabi's importance as the founder of political philosophy within the Islamic tradition, it must be Strauss with his pathbreaking 1935; 1936a; and 1936b German and French studies, and with his rephrasing of the *Farabi's Plato* 1945 study and further exploration of the theme in 1952. The English translation of Strauss 1935 now permits a wider audience to judge the merit of those earlier insights. The recent study of Alfarabi by Mahdi 2001, the fruit of five decades of scholarly endeavor, makes evident Alfarabi's importance.

Hallaq (1993) and Khadduri (1961) have provided yeoman service through their translations of the juridic texts of Ibn Taimiyya and al-Shāfi'ī, respectively, as has Twersky (1980) with his introduction to Maimonides' compilation of the Law. To study Islamic jurisprudence with any hope of success, one must begin with Schacht 1964 and Coulson 1964, then move to Rahman 1968. The study by Lambton (1981) of the political thought set forth by the jurists is also of some value, and that by Black (2001) is less reliable.

Gibb 1955 and Lewis 1960 remain ever reliable preliminary informants, but it is to Hodgson 1974 and Hourani 1991 that we must eventually turn for the fullest and most complete account of the all too elusive medieval Islamic world, as well as for the place of Jews and Jewish authors within it.

Chapter 10

THE REVIVAL OF ROMAN LAW AND CANON LAW

by Thomas M. Banchich, John Marenbon, and Charles J. Reid, Jr.[1]

10.1. The *Digest* of the Emperor Justinian

The *Digest* (or *Pandects*), promulgated at Constantinople on December 16, 533, by the Roman emperor Justinian (527–565, born ca. 482), is perhaps the most influential text in the history of Western legal thought. Together with Justinian's *Code* (promulgated on April 7, 529, with a second edition in 534), and his *Institutes* (533), it constituted what in the sixteenth century came to be known in Western Europe as the *Corpus of Civil Law* (*Corpus Iuris Civilis*). Justinian's *Novels* (or *New Constitutions*)—imperial pronouncements from 535, supplemented by post-Justinianic directives from as late as 575—together with the *Digest* and *Code* are our principal sources for the philosophical underpinnings of Justinian's conceptualization of his legislative activity; for the philosophy of law that animated Tribonian, architect of the actual codification; and for the philosophy of law implicit in the finished text of the *Digest* itself.

An appreciation of the first of these interrelated concerns requires the setting of Justinian's legislation within the framework of his reign. For about a decade before he became sole emperor in 527, Justinian was able to contemplate with reasonable certainty the prospect of his eventual rule, to identify what to him seemed to be the major challenges he would face, and to formulate responses to those challenges, all with a self-assurance based on the financial and military strength of the empire that would be his and on the conviction that the empire of Rome was an integral part of a Christian cosmic order (Browning 1971, 87–9). Once emperor, Justinian not only knew what the moment required, but knew that what was required was, in fact, possible (Honoré 1978, 20). Furthermore, Justinian believed that the impetus for his military and diplomatic policies, his push to define and impose an empire-wide Christian orthodoxy, and his activity with respect to law all derived equally from the Christian God (*Dig.*, *Const. Deo Auctore* 2; *Const. Tanta*; *Const. Dedôken*, Prologue).[2] In all three instances, Justinian viewed himself as God's agent.

[1] Section 10.1 of this chapter was written by Thomas M. Banchich; Sections 10.2–4 by John Marenbon; and Section 10.5 by Charles J. Reid, Jr. All translations are by the authors unless otherwise indicated.

[2] These constitutions, each traditionally referred to by its opening words—*Deo Auctore*, *Omnem*, and *Tanta*, the third also in a Greek version, the initial word of which is *Dedôken*—precede Book I of the *Digest*. For translations, see *The Digest of Justinian*, ed. Watson 1998, vol. 1: xliii–lxxi.

But if such was the case, was the will of the emperor, linked as it was to God's will, to be presented as superior to existing law and as the font of future legislation? Was the emperor—God's legislator—to be above the law? Justinian's answer was to maintain that his legislative capacity rested not only on God's favor but also on Roman legal tradition itself, and that the former trumped any trace of dissent in the latter. Indeed, whatever authority resided in the writings of classical Roman jurists was now the result of imperial fiat, part of the *raison d'être* of the *Digest* itself being the arrogation of its contents to the will of Justinian. This had obvious implications, too, for the interpretation of law, future disagreements about which the emperor would resolve. *Codex Justinianus* I.14.12 (as quoted in Dvornik 1966, vol. 2: 720–1) of October 30, 529, is the earliest espousal of this position; *Novels* 105.2.4 is the pointed declaration of its logical correlate that God has dispensed the sovereign—or, in the prolix verbiage of the constitution, "the fortune of the sovereign"—to men as "law animate."[3] The emperor's legislative function was of necessity ongoing, for, while justice might be unchanging, laws, which were only approximations of justice, had to have their application in the realm of becoming, of change both contingent on historical processes and, indeed, inherent in nature itself.

Now things divine are entirely perfect, but the character of human law is to hasten onward, and there is nothing in it which can abide forever, since nature is eager to produce new forms. We therefore do not cease to expect that matters will henceforth arise that are not secured in legal bonds. Consequently, if any such case arises, let a remedy be sought from the Augustus, since in truth God has set the imperial function over human affairs, so that it should be able, whenever a new contingency arises, to correct and settle it and to subject it to suitable procedures and regulations. (*Const. Tanta* 18)

New imperial constitutions would be the vehicles for such changes. The *Digest*—"a handsome work, consecrating as it were a fitting and most holy temple of justice" (*Const. Deo Auctore* 5)—was to be sacrosanct. There were to be penalties for any alteration of its text, a prohibition extended even to the use of ligatures and sigla. Though allowance was made for literal translation from Latin to Greek, commentaries were forbidden (*Const. Deo Auctore* 12–13; *Const. Tanta* 21–2/*Dedôken* 21–2). Once created, the *Digest* was to remain "a single beautiful form" (*Const. Dedôken*, Prologue: "*mian … kallous idean*"), its multiple copies identical, its mandated number of fifty books reflective of perfection, its propaedeutic the *Institutes* (*Const. Omnem*).

Tribonian (d. ca. 542)—Justinian's "minister for legislation and propaganda" (Honoré 1978, 69) and who, as a devotee of the cultured Gaius and Ulpian, considered these classical jurists to be repositories of legal wisdom—

[3] *Nomos empsychos* in the Greek version, see *Novels*, 507, lines 9–10; *lex animata* in the Latin, see *Novels*, 507, lines 7–8. For comment and translation, see Dvornik 1966, vol. 2: 722. On the history of the concept of a ruler as law animate, see Steinwenter and the references under *nomos empsychos* at Dvornik 1966, vol. 2: 965.

determined much of the selection and form of the *Digest's* content. In the process, he ensured the status of the law as an object of intellectual reflection, in consequence of which one could become *learned*, rather than simply *trained*, in law. The authority of Tribonian and his associates derived from Justinian's command, just as the command of former emperors had empowered earlier jurists to compose and interpret laws (*Const. Deo Auctore* 4 and 6). Part of Tribonian's charge was to formulate a canon of juristic authorities. Material in their texts which was "incorrectly written" (*non recte scriptum*) was to be emended and the emended text treated as though it was what had originally been written (*Const. Deo Auctore* 7). Though the stated motive was the removal of contradiction and ambiguity, evidence from the *Novels* suggests that Tribonian's editorial decisions were sometimes calculated to benefit his sovereign, and the degree to which this is so betrays a conception of law as a means of historical legitimization of a rule that, in reality, was based on wealth, privilege, and power (Maas 1986, 17–28). Tribonian's intellectualism may also lie behind a concern, most evident in the *Digest* and *Novels*, for the relationship between legislation as a reflection of eternal verities and the practical application of law in the mutable realm of becoming (Lanata 1984, 165–245; Maas 1986, 28–31).

Finally, the *Digest*, as text, gave to those who consulted and still consult it some intimations of its own about the meaning of law. Its Latin, in sixth-century Constantinople no less than today, afforded striking testimony of a conception of the formulation of law not so much as visionary progress, which leaves the past in its wake, as a backward-looking process: law is conservative. Furthermore, as reflected in the then-striking attention to chirography within each volume and between each copy, law is internally consistent. Yet this expectation created a problem; for, despite Justinian's injunction that there was to be "no antinomy [...], but [...] total concord, total consistency, with no one raising any opposition" (*Const. Deo Auctore* 8), real or simply perceived inconsistencies in the *Digest* remained. Most famously, there seemed to be two different views of the relationship between nature and law—that of Ulpian, for whom "natural law" (*ius naturale*) was "common to all animals" but "law of nations" (*ius gentium*) "only to human beings among themselves" (*Dig.* I.1.1), and that of Gaius, for whom *ius gentium* was "that law which natural reason [*naturalis ratio*] has established among all human beings [and is] among all observed in equal measure" (*Dig.* I.1.9). Likewise, though Justinian may have been convinced of his position with regard to law, the *Digest* preserved the notion of a consensual relationship between ruler and ruled (*Dig.* I.4.1). If one extrapolated from the *Digest* and accepted the principle that law should not admit of contradiction, some explanation was in order. One might, upon reflection, appeal to God's legislator; however, with the end in Western Europe of an *imperium* centered in Constantinople, the identification of that figure came to involve philosophical problems of its own. On the other hand, if contradiction within the *Digest* was illusory, one might expose underlying concord through study and argumentation, a process upon which a broad range of interpretative approaches—for example, philological or historical—could be brought to bear. Whatever the reactions, whatever their results, they sprang partly from the contemplation of the *Digest* as text.

But all this was in the future. When, in 533, Justinian promulgated the *Digest*, he saw mirrored in its pages a Roman *imperium* situated more securely than ever in a divine cosmos and for which he, as sovereign, legislated as God's agent.

10.2. The Varieties of Medieval Law

During the early Middle Ages, especially the twelfth century, the study of law developed, changed, and grew so rapidly that some writers have spoken, with only slight exaggeration, of a "legal revolution." Legal historians have often been keen to find links between this rapid development of law and the philosophy and theology of the time; Peter Abelard (1079–1142), in particular, is frequently mentioned. Yet this attention to the early medieval philosophers has been focused on their role as influences and sources, or even as examples of a "mentality," that underlay the legal developments (Boureau 1992). The main aim here, by contrast, is to set these philosophical developments into the context of legal developments by looking at the different varieties of law in the period.[4]

When, from the fifth century onward, Germanic tribes took control of large parts of the Western Roman Empire and settled there, they brought with them their own customary laws, largely concerned with avoiding feuds by prescribing monetary compensations for injuries. At first, the application of these laws was personal: The Goths or Franks, for example, were subject to Gothic or Frankish law, but the Gallo-Roman inhabitants of an area would be judged according to Roman law. Indeed, the Burgundian and Visigothic kings in Gaul issued collections of Roman law, based on earlier Roman materials, such as the *Lex Romana Visigothorum* ("Breviary of Alaric") of 506, for their Roman subjects (Stein 1999, 30–2). By the end of the ninth century (in many places far earlier), law had become territorial, rather than personal: usually a version of customary law, more or less influenced by its contact with Roman law. Roman law continued to apply to Rome itself and Ravenna.

Customary law tended to be unwritten and local. But some rulers in the earliest medieval centuries had the laws of their people set down in writing: For example, the edict of Euric, king of the Visigoths (ca. 475), influenced by Roman models; the *Lex Salica* (ca. 500) and Charlemagne's revision of it nearly 300 years later; and the *Lex Barbara Visigothorum* of the mid-seventh century.

[4] See Chapter 11 of this volume for the philosophical developments that took place in this legal context.

These codes were by no means systems of law. They were mainly concerned to list in minute detail the different monetary penalties for various sorts of harm done to different types of person. Between the late-ninth century and the late-twelfth century, little codification of customary laws took place in most of Europe. It was not until the later-twelfth century that, influenced by the developments in Roman law and canon law (see Sections 10.3 and 10.4 below), rulers began to see themselves, as they had not during the preceding centuries, as lawgivers. Codes of law for many countries and cities of Europe were subsequently issued in the thirteenth century; the first, large-scale example was Frederick II's codification of the laws of Sicily, the *Liber Augustalis* of 1231 (Wolf 1973; 1983).

Lombardy and England are, in different ways, exceptions to the general pattern. In the eleventh century there was a law school at Pavia, dedicated to glossing, often with reference to Roman law, the Lombard and Frankish capitularies contained in the eleventh century *Book of Pavia* (*Liber Papiensis*) (Weimar 1973, 165; Stein 1999, 45). England had a continuous tradition of written law, stretching back at least to the reign of Alfred (871–901). In 1066, upon conquering England, the Normans thus found a system of law vastly more sophisticated than their own. The conquerors' laws did not displace those of the Anglo-Saxons; rather, the two systems meshed (Lyon 1980, 180–99). The early Anglo-Norman kings were not great legislators, but during the reign of the Angevin Henry II (1154–1189), English customary law underwent a remarkable development, directed by the king and his advisers. As well as introducing new laws, in order to deal with unjust seizure of property and with succession, Henry instituted a system of regular visiting royal justices and introduced the system of returnable writs, which enabled any freeman to have access to the king's courts. He is also credited with establishing the jury system. In 1179, he ordered that defendants in cases involving property rights might opt for trial by jury rather than trial by battle. By the end of Henry's reign there existed the beginnings of English common law, deriving from customary law but subjected to central, royal authority (Pollock and Maitland 1923, 136–68; Stenton 1964, 22–87; Milsom 1981, 11–36).

Alongside the relicts of vulgar Roman law, customary law, and royal law, there was also feudal law. In the years after 900, in the absence of central power after the break-up of the Carolingian Empire, there grew up a system of land-holding that, centuries later, was called "feudalism." It was characteristic of France, but also applied to parts of Italy, Spain, and Germany (and, though differently, to post-conquest England). Under feudalism, knights would hold land and certain powers as "fiefs" of a lord and be his "vassals." A vassal had to do military service for his lord, attend his court, and pay him money in emergencies. A vassal's descendant inherited the fief only on payment of a considerable sum to the lord. This pattern of relationships was repeated at a higher level, between the great lords and the king, but (outside England) in a merely symbolic manner. Kings had little real control over the lords. Feudalism had its own laws, and these were codified (drawing on the Lombard legal tradition) in the *Libri Feudorum* (*Books of Fiefs*). The *Libri Feudorum* reached their vulgate form around 1250, but the original version was produced around 1150 in Milan (Weimar 1973, 166–7).

10.3. The Revival of Roman Law

The history of medieval, and indeed modern, law was profoundly influenced by the ambitious legislative project of Justinian (discussed in Section 10.1 above). Although his court was Greek-speaking, and his lands mainly (despite his reconquest of parts of Italy and North Africa) in Greece and the East, Justinian decided to revive Roman law not in the degenerate form in which it survived in areas of the West, but rather much as it had been in the third century, when great jurists such as Papinian, Paul, and Ulpian were writing.

Parts of the *Corpus of Civil Law* (*Corpus Iuris Civilis*)—the *Institutes*, most of the *Code*, and a Latin abbreviation of the *Novels*—were known in Italy throughout the early Middle Ages. But it was the *Digest* alone that, by transmitting a large body of the best Roman jurisprudence, was able to transform medieval thinking about law and make law into an academic discipline. The story of the rediscovery of the *Digest* is complicated and, in some respects, uncertain. There are occasional references to the earlier parts of the *Digest* (what came to be called the *Digestum Vetus*) in charters and legal sources from 1076 onward; there are citations from the later part of the *Digest* (the *Digestum Novum*) in a canonical text, Gregory of St. Grisogono's *Polycarpus* (ca. 1111–1113) (Müller 1990). By the middle of the twelfth century, the glosses and texts by Bulgarus show a detailed and sophisticated grasp of the *Digest*. Bulgarus is one of the "four doctors" (along with Martinus, Jacobus, and Hugo)—traditionally, the second generation of Bolognese scholars of Roman law.

Credit for introducing and mastering the *Digest*, and for beginning the tradition of teaching at Bologna based in it, is usually given to a figure traditionally called Irnerius (really Wernerius or Guarnerius), who appears in documents between 1112 and 1125. Recent, critical scrutiny of the evidence suggests, however, that Irnerius was a practicing lawyer, not a teacher (Southern 1995, 274–82), and it has even been argued that many of his supposed glosses to the *Digest* have been misattributed (Winroth 2000, 164–8).

Knowledge of Roman law, even in Bologna, may have been far more rudimentary early in the twelfth century than was once supposed. By the end of that century, however, scholarship on Roman law was flourishing. Bologna had become, and remained, the foremost legal university in Europe, but the teaching of Roman law had spread to France, Catalonia, and England, where the Lombard Vacarius in the late twelfth century produced an abbreviation of *Digest* and *Code* known as the *Paupers' Book* (*Liber Pauperum*) (that is, for those who could not afford the complete texts) (Southern 2001, 155–66). Masters not only glossed the *Corpus* in detail; on the basis of their glosses, they also produced various other forms of legal writing by summarizing their findings, collecting the glosses on particular subjects, and presenting the disagreements between different teachers. They also tried to identify the general principles (or "brocards") underlying the discussion of individual cases, not restricting themselves to the list of general rules given in the *Digest* itself (Stein 1999). Between 1220 and 1240, Accursius at Bologna compiled what became a standard gloss to the whole *Corpus*.[5]

In one sense, Roman law (as found in the *Corpus*) occupied a position in medieval life and culture almost exactly antithetical to that of the customary or royal laws of individual lands. The customary and royal laws were never the objects of study in the universities (though the feudal law of the *Libri Feudorum* was appended to the *Corpus* and glossed by Accursius), while Roman law, as codified by Justinian and expounded by the medieval legal scholars, though widely influential on legal codes, was not straightforwardly adopted as the law of any particular medieval country. But Roman law had a profound effect on attitudes toward law in general and on the development of law in different lands—not surprisingly, since legal experts tended to be those who had been trained in Roman law. The example of Roman law moved rulers to codify the laws of their own countries and, more broadly, it encouraged them and their advisers to see law as a rational, coherent system that is built on underlying general principles.[6]

It is impossible to understand the development of medieval law without taking into account the rediscovery of Roman law and its transformation into an academic subject. By the mid-thirteenth century, Roman law would affect how philosophers and theologians thought about law (see Chapter 11 of this volume). Before then, however, its influence on them seems not to have been great.

10.4. Theoretical Foundations of Canon Law: Gratian's *Decretum*

From the early days of their religion, Christian communities had compiled sets of rules (canons) for their members, and soon papal decretals and the canons of church councils provided ample material for collections of church law, such as that made by Dionysius Exiguus, probably in the first half of the

[5] The glossators and legal commentators made extensive use of ancient and medieval philosophers. On metaphysical thought in late medieval jurisprudence see the essay by Andrea Padovani in Volume 7 of this Treatise, and on the use of logic and metaphysics see the essay by Andrea Errera in the same volume.

[6] For fuller discussion of politics in western medieval jurisprudence see the essay by Kenneth Pennington in Volume 7 of this Treatise.

sixth century. By the early eleventh century, the canonist Burchard of Worms had compiled a twenty-book *Decretum*, containing canons ranging in their subject-matter from the procedure for church assemblies and church services, the sacraments, monastic life, fasts, homicide, the procedure in church courts, and a variety of theological topics. The Gregorian reform in the later part of the eleventh century also gave a new impetus and direction to canonical collections.

But canon law, as an academic subject studied from the twelfth century onward, was founded on another *Decretum*, the work of Gratian. The material in this *Decretum* is, for the most part, drawn from just a few older collections (Winroth 2000, 15–7). The novelty and importance of the work lies in how the canons are arranged and treated. As its proper title, *A Harmony of Conflicting Canons* (*Concordia Discordantium Canonum*) indicates, the *Decretum* is concerned to bring together apparently conflicting texts and to show how they can be reconciled. To this end, Gratian adds his own comments (*dicta*) to bring out an underlying train of argument from the texts he cites.

As a person, Gratian is only a little less mysterious than Irnerius. He used to be described as a Camaldolese monk, who taught at a monastery in Bologna. Modern research (Noonan 1979) has shown this identification to be groundless, and the only strong piece of documentary evidence names him as a wise man consulted by the papal legate on a case in Venice in 1143. Internal evidence, however, suggests that—*pace* Southern (1995, 303–4)—Gratian taught law, although he may well have been a practicing lawyer too (Winroth 2000, 7–8). Modern scholarship has also queried whether the *Decretum*, attributed to Gratian from the 1160s onward, was really all his own work, and whether the traditional dating to approximately 1140 is correct. Particular attention has been paid to the passages showing a knowledge of Roman law beyond that contained in the canonical collections used as sources, since they do not seem to fit into the original plan of the work (Vetulani 1946–1947; 1955). According to the most recent hypothesis (Winroth 2000), the *Decretum* exists in two recensions, both produced in Bologna. The first, which can be reconstructed from manuscripts, was indeed written by Gratian and completed around 1140. It contains only about half the number of canons found in the received text, and is without the final section *On Consecration* (*De Consecratione*). The *dicta* are more prominent in the first recension, and the argument is easier to follow. The second recension, the basis for the received text, was ready by 1158 at the latest; the additions, which show, among other things, a much more sophisticated grasp of Roman law than in the first version, were probably not due to Gratian himself.

Soon after the *Decretum* began to circulate, it was commented on. Two of the outstanding later-twelfth-century Bolognese "decretists" (as these commentators are called) are Rufinus and Huguccio, Stephen of Tournai was commenting on the *Decretum* in Paris in the late-twelfth century, and decretists were also at work in the Rhineland and Oxford. From the thirteenth century onward, the study of canon law flourished not only in the university at Bologna, but also at those of Paris and Oxford. Unlike Roman law, canon law was not a fixed, finished body, and the *Decretum*, although always remaining authoritative, quickly became outdated, especially since, from the late-twelfth century onward, the popes were energetic makers of new laws through their decretals. These decretals, gathered together into collections such as Bernard of Pavia's *Breviarium Extravagantium* (*Abridgement of the New Decretals*) (1188–1192) and the *Liber Extra* (*Book of New Material*) (1234), provided fresh material for commentary. In another respect, too, the position of canon law differed from that of Roman law. Canon law was real, contemporary law. Certain classes of persons—principally clerics, crusaders, students, the poor, widows, orphans, Jews, and travellers—and certain areas—for example, the sacraments (including marriage), oaths, and wills—fell under the jurisdiction of canon law (Trusen 1973, 483–7), and there was an elaborate, hierarchical system of canonical courts and papal judges (Brundage 1995, 120–53).

The connections between canon law and the legal thinking of philosophers and theologians were close. For example, the earliest known user of the *Decretum* in its final form was Peter the Lombard, when in the late 1150s he composed the *Sentences*—a work which would become the standard university textbook of theology. Through the *Sentences*, aspects of the *Decretum* would become familiar to every trained university theologian. And one of the earliest commentators on the *Decretum*, Rolandus—not, as once thought, the Rolandus who became Pope Alexander III (Noonan 1977)—was also the author of a set of theological *Sentences* that was influenced by Peter Abelard. Nonetheless, claims about particular influences, especially that of Abelard on Gratian, need to be treated with caution (see Chapter 11, Section 11.3.5, in this volume for further discussion of this point).

10.5. Medieval Canon Law and Rights

The systematic study of canon law properly commenced around the year 1140 with the appearance of Gratian's *Decretum*. The sixty years following its appearance witnessed the emergence of a group of commentators, the "decretists," who made it their business to analyze the strengths and weaknesses of Gratian's work. The middle and later decades of the twelfth century also witnessed the issuance of massive numbers of decretal letters by the reigning popes, a process that continued throughout the thirteenth century. During the thirteenth century, these letters, whose combination of fact-specificity and articulation of general principle can be compared to the kind of judicial legislation found in a case like *Miranda v. Arizona* (384 U.S. 436 [1966]), came to be gathered into collections, which received their own band of commentators known as "decretalists." The great creative impulse represented by decretists and decretalists continued through the mid-fourteenth century and has come to be known as the "classic age of canon law" (Brundage 1995).

It is in this classic age that one witnesses the first systematic association of the idea of an individual right with the Latin word *ius* (see Chapter 6, Section 6.6, of this volume for earlier uses). *Ius* is a notoriously difficult word to translate. In general terms, however, one can distinguish between an objective meaning, in which the term refers to a system of law or transcendent principles of justice, and a subjective meaning of individual right or power. This subjective understanding of *ius* also came to be seen as arising from a natural law foundation. Indeed, it has been demonstrated that the first usages of *ius naturale* (typically, "natural law") to signify a natural right of individuals can be traced to the decretist Rufinus, writing twenty years or so after the appearance of the *Decretum* (Tierney 1989, 615, 632–6; Tierney 1992).

The thirteenth-century decretalists explained this subjective right in terms of the capacities and powers of the human person, and thus associated the term *ius* with a wide variety of synonyms that brought it within a developing vocabulary of subjectivity. Consequently, the word *ius* sometimes came to be associated with "faculty" (*facultas*), sometimes with "power" (*potestas*), sometimes with "liberty" (*libertas*), and sometimes with "immunity" (*immunitas*) (Reid 1996, 295, 312–31).

The decretalists also distinguished between active and passive forms of rights. Bernard of Parma and Hostiensis, two of the most important of the thir-teenth-century decretalists, distinguished between passive and active "rights of voting" (the *ius eligendi passive* and the *ius eligendi active*). The former was a right to stand for election while the latter was the actual right to vote with the attendant freedom that the exercise of such a right entailed (Reid 1996, 307–12). Tuck (1979, 13–5) claims that the canonistic rights system was built around the notion of a passive right. In fact, however, it is clear that the canonists were capable of making use of both active and passive aspects of rights in order to describe a wide range of juridic situations.

Canonistic rights usages can also be analyzed in terms of the categories and correlatives developed by Hohfeld (1923, 23–64). An example of the correlative between a duty and a right is the close correlation the canonists proposed between the obligation in Christian charity to provide for the needs of the poor and the right of the poor, in dire necessity, to take what was necessary to sustain life. The privilege/no right correlation can be illustrated by looking at canonistic election law, which conferred substantial protections on those who enjoyed the right to vote and rigorously excluded from participation those who lacked such a right. The power/liability correlative is seen in the development of agency law, in which the master (*dominus*) would cede certain rights to his representative, the proctor, whose choices and decisions would then bind the principal. The immunity/disability relation can be found in the grants of exemption conferred by the papacy on local monasteries. An exemption from local control allowed monasteries to flourish under the patronage of the papacy, and were called variously a "right" or "liberty" (Reid 1991, 37, 59–72).

Rights were not a vague or subordinate concept for the canonists. Rather, they were a central organizing principle of large parts of the law. The scope and influence of the canonistic rights vocabulary can be identified in areas associated traditionally with both public and private law. Three examples illustrate this point: (1) elections, (2) the power to make war, and (3) domestic relations.

(1) Elections had been a part of ecclesiastical life from earliest times. The Acts of the Apostles (6:1–6) records that the primitive Christian community at Jerusalem elected deacons to minister to its Greek-speaking members. The election of bishops remained a prominent part of the life of the patristic church of the third through fifth centuries. St. Cyprian (d. 258) wrote that the choice of bishops required the participation of the people, a process he termed *suffragium* ("suffrage"), borrowing his choice of words from the practice of the voting assemblies of the Roman Republic (Reid 1998, 150, 154–5).

Popular participation could sometimes be quite vigorous, as in the case of the election of St. Martin as bishop of Tours. Martin was a holy man who enjoyed the reputation of being a miracle worker, and he resided in the environs around Tours. At a time of episcopal vacancy, around the years 370–372, he was lured into the city, whereupon he was proclaimed bishop in a kind of popular uprising. His biographer recounts that "an incredible multitude, not only from that city, but from surrounding communities, converged to bestow on him their *suffragia*" (Reid 1998, 150, 154–5). Through direct, popular participation, Martin was made bishop of Tours.

What is missing from both Cyprian's writing and the account of Martin's election, however, is any notion of an actual right to participate in elections. Elections might take the form of popular uprisings, but there is no evidence in the sources that persons were considered as enjoying an individualized right to vote. This changed dramatically in the twelfth and thirteenth centuries, when the theological requirement that bishops be elected merged with the emerging rights vocabulary to produce a juridically articulated "right to vote" (*ius eligendi*).

The community that enjoyed the exercise of this right came to be drastically narrowed. It now embraced not the community at large, but specialized collegial bodies within the church—the college of cardinals, which enjoyed the right to elect the pope, and the cathedral chapter, which enjoyed the right to elect bishops. But while the community came to be greatly constricted, the right itself came to be hedged in with all sorts of procedural safeguards, in the form of notice requirements and the requirement that electors be free of any kind of force or fear. Violence, and even, for that matter, intimidation, was sufficient to invalidate an election (Reid 1998, 160–9).

At the Council of Constance (1414–1418), convoked to repair the Great Schism, which had witnessed the rise of three competing claimants to the papal throne, at least one theorist looked to the right to vote as a means of resolving the crisis. Pierre d'Ailly, a cardinal and former professor of theology at Paris, confronting a situation in which there were not only competing popes but also competing colleges of cardinals, so that no one knew who had the right to vote for pope, proposed that in the final analysis this right rested variously with the Roman people and the universal church. The Council, acting under the inspiration of the Holy Spirit and as a representative of the entire church, then proceeded to elect the new pope. In this way, the canonistic right to vote came to be associated with developing theories of representation and consent (Reid 1998, 169–74).

(2) The juristic conception of the power to make war went through a similar transformation. Augustine had taught that there was fundamentally no right of personal self-defense. Violence, he maintained, involved *libido* (best translated as passionate, sinful desire), and should be strictly prohibited to individuals since we should prefer transcendent spiritual goods over the things of this world, even including our own lives. Augustine, however, allowed the public taking of life by reference to the principles of Christian charity: Government officials, moved by love of neighbor and the need to keep public order, might authorize killing in war, so as to restrain greater sinfulness. But war, on this "just war" account, was tragic necessity, not righteous or praiseworthy conduct (see Chapter 8, Section 8.6, of this volume).

The medieval jurists borrowed heavily from Augustine's analysis of just war principles, but the canonists, especially the decretists, synthesized his theology with a concept of a right of self-defense, which they had developed on the basis of Roman law jurisprudence. The authority to wage war itself came to be denominated a right— variously the "right of the sword" (*ius gladii*), the "right of waging war" (*ius inferendi bellum*), or the "right to war" (*ius ad bellum*).

The thirteenth-century decretalists used the category of rights to propose means of limiting warfare. Pope Innocent IV (1243–1254) attempted to restrict the right of war to princes without a feudal superior, thus prohibiting countless local feudal lords from taking up arms against one another (Russell 1976, 383, 386–8). Hostiensis, for his part, contended that the whole of European Christendom was bound together juridically by a certain right or law of familial relations (*ius cognationis*), and that individual princes lacked the capacity to renounce this right. Hence, on his account, it was forbidden generally to European princes to engage in fratricidal conflict without committing *diffidatio*, the feudal crime of disloyalty (*Summa* I.4), although some forms of warfare remained permissible, especially "Roman War," namely, crusades led by Rome, the "seat of faith" (*caput fidei*) against the faithless (*infideles*).[7]

[7] See Hostiensis 1581, *De homicidio voluntario* c. 1, v. *diffidatus*.

As the reference to Roman war suggests, however, reliance on rights language also led to the justification of war as an affirmative good, not as a tragic necessity. This sort of rights-based thinking about war deeply colored subsequent analysis and contributed to a view of war as righteous conduct. Johannes de Legnano (ca. 1320–1383), the author of the first real treatise on the law of war, proposed that the right of waging war was given by God to humankind to serve certain affirmative goods, such as keeping the peace and punishing the wicked (Brundage 1995, 218). In this way, the right of war was consonant with both the divine plan and the natural law, in that it allowed society to purge itself of an excess of insurrection and discord. Indeed, Legnano even endorsed the idea that the ailments of society might be cured by "the medicine of an eradicative and exterminative war against evil-doers" (*De Bello, De Represaliis, et De Duello*, 85–6).

(3) The concept of rights also played an important part in the development of canonistic private law. One can take the example of domestic relations. According to canon law, the father was the "head" of his wife and enjoyed the right to govern his household, an authority called the "right of paternal power" (*ius patria potestatis*). The possession of this right, however, did not mean that the father was entitled to rule autocratically. He was constrained by countervailing claims of right on the part of his children and his spouse. Children, fundamentally, had a right of sustenance. They might not be set out in the elements to die (as was allowed under classical Roman law). They had a right, furthermore, to share, in some measure, in the division of their father's estate, a right that was spoken of as arising from nature (*ex natura*).

And while, in most respects, the divine plan called for the husband to be the master of his house and the loving but firm guardian and governor of his wife, an important exception was made where the conjugal debt was concerned. Paul, writing to the Christian community at Corinth, declared: "Let the husband render to the wife her due, and likewise the wife to the husband. The wife has no authority over her body, but the husband; the husband likewise has no authority over his body, but the wife" (1 Cor. 7:3–4).

Paul used the Greek term *opheile* ("obligation") to describe the conjugal debt owed by each of the parties. The *Vulgate* preserved this sense in translating the term as *debitum* ("debt"). The twelfth- and thirteenth-century canonists, however, transformed this moral obligation into a right (*ius coniugale*) and made this right a foundation-stone of their analysis of marital relations (Reid 2002, 471, 499–511).

The canonists disputed when this right came into being. In the process, they inquired whether there was a right forcibly to consummate a marriage. Formal equality, on this analysis, led to extremely one-sided and cruel results. Some canonists answered this question affirmatively, although Aquinas, borrowing juridical language, responded negatively. "Did forcible consummation amount to marital rape?" Aquinas asked. After all, a betrothed seems to have some kind of right (*aliquod ius*) to his spouse. Aquinas ultimately concluded that such a husband sinned mortally by forcing himself on his spouse, but that recourse was before God's throne, not an earthly tribunal (Reid 2002, 501–5).

In other circumstances, however, the canonists understood the *ius coniugale* as conferring on husband and wife a radical equality in the sexual relationship. Husband and wife could demand sexual satisfaction from the other party, and the other party was not free to say no. Third parties, such as feudal lords, were forbidden to interfere with this right. Because the *ius coniugale* was a natural right that endured as long as the sacramental bond of marriage itself, it could not be lost, even where one of the spouses contracted leprosy. Indeed, the healthy spouse was obliged to see to the ill spouse's needs (Reid 2002, 505–11).

Rights served as a central organizing principle throughout much of the rest of medieval canon law. Infidels had a right of self-governance, according to some canonists. The whole ecclesiology of the church—its corporate structure of pope, bishops, abbeys, monasteries, confraternities, parishes, and so forth—was really a web of interlocking rights and duties. Much of the law of private economic dealings, from providing for the poor to agreeing to contracts of purchase and sale, lease, or usufruct, was also analyzed in terms of rights. The ways in which these concepts were deployed, and the patterns of argument that were laid down, would come to have enormous influence on the entire subsequent shape of the Western rights tradition.

Further Reading

The *Corpus Iuris Civilis* has often been reprinted: Volume 1 consists of Krueger's edition of the *Institutiones* and Mommsen and Krueger's edition of the *Digesta*; Volume 2 contains Krueger's edition of the *Codex Iustinianus*; Volume 3 contains Schoell and Kroll's edition of the *Novellae*. There are excellent translations of the *Institutes* by Birks and McLeod (with Latin text) and of the *Digest* by Watson (4 volumes with Latin text; 2 volumes without Latin text). Translations of the *Code* and *Novels* by Scott, while the only readily available English versions, are often unreliable. In addition, because Scott employs consecutive numeration but sometimes omits translation of Greek material, his numbering does not always correspond to the numbering of the Berlin edition.

Dvornik 1966 is a classic survey of early-Christian and Byzantine political philosophy. For the history of Roman law see Jolowicz and Nicholas 1972 and the further reading suggestions for chapter 6. There is much of value on late-Roman and on Byzantine law in Haldon 1997, 254–80, Liebs 2000, Nicol 1988, Pieler 1978, Scheltema 1967, and numerous entries in Kazhdan and Talbot 1991.

Lanata 1984 is a learned and provocative study of Justinian's code. For reservations, see Waldstein 1994. The wide-ranging account of *nomos empsychos* by Steinwenter 1946 is excellent. Browning 1971 provides an authoritative and entertaining account of Justinian and his age. Honoré 1978 is a brilliant, groundbreaking study of Tribonian and of the entire Justinianic legislative corpus. Maas (1986) demonstrates the use of law for Justinian's own ends and discusses the relationship between Justinian's legislation and Christian thought with respect to nature. On these matters and more, Humfress 2005 and Pazdernik 2005 repay careful reading.

On the varieties of medieval law, a comprehensive survey, quite technical, of the period after ca. 1100 is given in Coing 1973. Berman 1983 is more readable and wide-ranging, but is too concerned to present its thesis to offer a balanced, introductory account. On England, Pollock and Maitland 1923 is still valuable. Stein 1999 gives an authoritative and concise survey of Roman law. Kuttner 1982 offers a very short but masterly overview of Roman and canon law in the twelfth century. Brundage 1995 provides a good, short survey of canon law, and Gaudemet 1993 offers an excellent and convenient introduction to the sources and the latest bibliography. For the content of canon law, Le Bras, Lefebvre, and Rambaud 1965 remains the best general account. Winroth 2000 puts forward an important revisionary thesis about Gratian's *Decretum*. Rashdall 1936, vol. 1, chap. 4 describes the revival of jurisprudence at Bologna and other universities.

See Volume 7 of this Treatise for fuller discussion of topics touched on in this chapter: Peter Stein on the Roman jurists' conception of law, Andrea Padovani on the metaphysical thought of late-medieval jurisprudence, Andrea Errera on the role of logic in the legal science of the glossators and commentators, and Kenneth Pennington on politics in western medieval jurisprudence.

Chapter 11

THE RISE OF SCHOLASTIC LEGAL PHILOSOPHY

by John Marenbon[1]

11.1. Intellectual Sources of the Scholastic Tradition

11.1.1. The Main Sources for Philosophy and Theology: A Sketch

The main sources for medieval philosophy and theology fall into two groups: those which were in use by the twelfth century and, in most cases, had been available since 800 or earlier (I shall call these the "old sources"), and those which became available in the years from approximately 1130 to 1280 (I shall call these the "new sources").

The bulkiest part of the old sources consisted of the works of the church fathers (and, of course, the Bible). The writings of most of the Latin Fathers, and of some of the Greek Fathers in Latin translation, were widely copied from the beginning of the Middle Ages. Augustine, in particular, was studied carefully and had an enormous, though varied, influence. Patristic works, however, were not used as school textbooks. Rather, the school curriculum in the period up to the twelfth century was based on the late-ancient model of the seven liberal arts: the three verbal arts of the "trivium" (grammar, logic, and rhetoric), and the four mathematical arts of the "quadrivium" (arithmetic, geometry, music, and astronomy). In one of the most popular textbooks, the allegorical *prosimetrum On the Marriage of Mercury and Philology* (*De Nuptiis Mercurii et Philologiae*), written by a fifth-century pagan, Martianus Capella, each of these arts is briefly expounded. For the most part, however, the emphasis in the schools right through to the end of the twelfth century was on the trivium. Each of the three verbal arts had its very restricted number of ancient or late-ancient textbooks. For grammar, there were the works of Donatus and Priscian; rhetoric was studied on the basis of Cicero's *On Invention* (*De Inventione*) and the pseudo-Ciceronian *Rhetoric to Herennius* (*Rhetorica ad Herennium*). For logic, there were Porphyry's *Introduction* (*Isagoge*) and Aristotle's *Categories* and *On Interpretation*, translated by Boethius (d. ca. 524), along with Boethius' commentaries and his own logical textbooks. In addition, there were three philosophical texts that were often studied (along with the work of classical poets) as part of instruction in grammar: part of Plato's *Timaeus* in the translation by Calcidius and with his commentary, Boethius' *Consolation of Philosophy*, and Macrobius' commentary on Cicero's *Dream of Scipio*. All three works were important in transmitting Platonic doctrines: Macrobius was

[1] All translations are by the author unless otherwise indicated.

influenced by Plotinus; and Boethius, although a Christian, writes in a manner which, at least superficially, could be that of a pagan Platonist.

Theology was not studied as such before 1100, although commentaries were written on the Bible, and doctrinal controversies (including one example discussed in Section 11.2 below) stimulated thinking about theological issues. Early in the twelfth century, scholars working at Laon and then at Paris began thinking more systematically about Christian doctrine. Beginning from the apparently contradictory texts in the Bible, they began to debate over the underlying doctrinal issues and to arrange their teaching systematically. By the later-twelfth century, theological questions were being discussed with immense logical sophistication; and although, in one sense, the Bible was the textbook for theology, some thinkers also turned to Boethius' short theological treatises as their guide.

The earliest of the new sources were the remaining logical works (*logica nova*) of Aristotle, which began to be read from around 1130 onward. Gradually, almost all the rest of Aristotle's works became available in Latin translation. The increasing availability of these new texts coincided with the development of the loosely arranged schools of Paris into a university, where students began in the arts faculty and then a few went on to a higher faculty: theology, (canon) law, or medicine. Oxford, the other great university north of the Alps in the thirteenth century, had a broadly similar structure. Although there were bans on the study of Aristotle's non-logical works in the arts faculty of Paris in the early-thirteenth century, by the middle of the century an Aristotelian curriculum had been adopted there and in Oxford. Linked to the newly available Aristotelian texts were Latin translations of the commentaries produced by the two greatest Aristotelians of the Islamic world: the eleventh-century Persian Avicenna, and the twelfth-century Cordoban Averroes (see Chapter 9 of this volume). Aristotle's non-logical works had been available in the Arab world long before they were known in the Latin West and, while the translations of some Aristotelian texts from the Arabic were soon replaced by versions from the Greek, Avicenna and Averroes were central influences on how Aristotle was understood. Indeed, in the early-thirteenth century, readers of Aristotle were far more prone to reflect Avicennian views than anything authentically Aristotelian. By contrast, there was little interest in any Arab philosophical works other than commentaries (or texts related to commentary); but the Jewish philosopher Maimonides' *Guide of the Perplexed* (written in Arabic) was translated and read by Latin theologians. Knowledge of Plato's work hardly progressed beyond the *Timaeus*, but some new neo-Platonic material became available, such as the *Book on Causes* (*Liber de Causis*), an adapted version of the beginning of Proclus' *Elements of Theology*, which was being read even in the late-twelfth century.

Christian doctrine was studied in the theology faculties by students who had already completed an arts course or its equivalent. There were two textbooks: the Bible and the *Sentences*, which Peter of Lombard wrote around 1155–1158. The *Sentences* drew together the work of the early Parisian theological schools and produced an orthodox and systematic discussion of all the main points of doctrine, based on extracts from the church fathers.

11.1.2. Sources for the Philosophy of Law

In this array there are not, as it turns out, many obvious sources for the philosophy of law. Among the old sources, there are some passages in the Bible and in the works of Augustine, Jerome, Ambrose, and other church fathers (cf. Section 11.3.2 below). The *Etymologiae*, a dictionary/encyclopedia by one of the latest Fathers, the seventh-century Isidore, Bishop of Seville, contains a section on law (V.1–27), although it was used far more by canon lawyers, especially Gratian, than philosophers or theologians. A passing comment in Calcidius' commentary on the *Timaeus* (see Section 11.3.3 below) would prove important. Some manuscripts of Cicero's work, including *On the Laws* and *On Duties*, date back to the early Middle Ages, but writers of the time were much more likely to be influenced by his brief discussion of law in *On Invention* (II.53.160–62).

Among the new sources were Aristotle's *Nicomachean Ethics*, *Rhetoric*, and *Politics*, all of which contain comments on law. But the *Politics*, probably the most important for this subject, was one of the latest of Aristotle's works to be translated into Latin, by William of Moerbeke in 1260–64. In general, Aristotelian influence on theories of law was only just beginning to be felt in the middle of the thirteenth century (see Section 11.5 below).

11.2. John Scottus Eriugena and the Idea of Law

John Scottus (or "Eriugena" as he called himself) gives his most interesting discussion of law in *On Divine Predestination*, a work written in the early 850s, before he encountered and developed the Greek Christian neo-Platonic thought that gives his later masterpiece, the *Periphyseon*, its distinctive character.

On Divine Predestination was written at the invitation of Hincmar, Archbishop of Rheims. Influenced by a reading of some of Augustine's late writings, a monk called Gottschalk was insisting that divine predestination is dual: of the blessed to heaven and of sinners to damnation. To Hincmar this view seemed heretical, but many churchmen remained unconvinced by his efforts to explain why. In 851 he asked Eriugena, who seems to have been a court intellectual who was teaching the liberal arts, to attack Gottschalk's position. Eriugena did so, but argued so vigorously against Gottschalk's oppressively deterministic picture that his treatise was found by many to be more objectionable than the writings it assailed.

Quite early on in *On Divine Predestination*, Eriugena introduces ideas about law (Cristiani 1976, 104–5). He asks Gottschalk what justice is, and Gottschalk replies, using a classic Roman definition that he probably took from Augustine (*Lib. Arb.* I.13, 27), that it is "to give to each his due." Gottschalk's view, he goes on to argue, would make God unjust since he would be rewarding people when they had no reward due to them. For how would a reward be due when they were unable to sin? What would have been the point of God's prohibiting sin when a "law of nature" made it impossible for them to sin in any case (*On Divine Predestination* V.8; 39:171–195)?

By this remark, Eriugena suggests that he is thinking of a law not as an imperative that should be obeyed but can be disobeyed, but rather as a constraining force that cannot be opposed (like a law of physics). But how can this idea be compatible with the other one he puts forward at the same time, namely, that justice requires freedom of choice for those being judged? At the end of his work (*On Divine Predestination* 18, 6–9; 114:109–17:223; cf. Cristiani 1976, 109–14), Eriugena manages with extraordinary deftness to reconcile these two ideas. God, he says, gives every being a nature that has certain bounds. Non-rational things neither are able nor wish to go beyond these bounds. Of creatures that have reason and intellect, some wish to stay within these bounds, and some do not wish to stay within them. But no one *can* go beyond them. The wicked wish to withdraw so far from God, the supreme essence, that they entirely cease to be and become nothing. But God's laws have set up a measure that prevents the wicked from realizing their wish. The eternal punishment of the wicked lies in their inability to gain what they want. They are unwillingly circumscribed by laws—the very same laws which, for the blessed, bring happiness. There is, Eriugena concludes, "one and the same law which disposes the republic in the justest order, as it brings life to those who wish to live well and death to those who desire to live badly," just as the same food tastes sweet to a healthy person and bitter to a sick one (*On Divine Predestination* 117:215–21). Precisely because eternal law, in Eriugena's view, cannot be disobeyed except in will, it not only sets down norms but also by its very existence inflicts punishments—or, rather, it is the instrument by which the wicked punish themselves. Although Eriugena uses the language of predestination, he does not think that God is actively involved in it; rather, having set up his law, God lets the free will of rational creatures bring about their own reward or punishment.

11.3. Abelard on Law and Punishment

11.3.1. Abelard and His Theological Project

Despite the sophistication and breadth of other thinkers of his time, such as William of Conches and Gilbert of Poitiers (see Dronke 1988), and his own debts to predecessors he claims to have despised, such as Anselm of Laon and William of Champeaux, Peter Abelard (1079–1142) was the only twelfth-century thinker to develop a wide-ranging theory of law and punishment. The reason why he did so lies not just in his power and originality as a constructive thinker (Marenbon 1996, 332–49), but also in the nature of the theological project that dominated the second half of his working life.

Abelard had become a famous teacher of logic as a young man in the early 1100s. Over the next two decades his efforts went into thinking about formal logic and (on the basis of logical texts) about metaphysics. When, in 1117, his marriage to Heloise was ended by his castration and he entered the monastery of St. Denis, he did not give up logic. However, he became increasingly interested in Christian doctrine and, although not a rationalist in the way that Michelet and some nineteenth-century historians believed, he tried to give a rationally coherent, ethically centered explanation of the main elements of Christian belief, even at the cost of stretching and adapting dogma beyond what churchmen such as Bernard of Clairvaux thought acceptable. The idea of law, especially natural law, was central to this project in two ways (which the next subsection will clarify). First, Abelard saw the rationality of Christian belief as guaranteed by the way in which, even without revelation, pagan philosophers had anticipated much of it through reasoning, and he discussed this relationship in terms of laws—natural law and the old and new revealed laws. Second, he needed natural law to give a foundation to his ethical theory, which, without it, would have collapsed into an unsustainable subjectivism.

11.3.2. Natural Law, Old Law, and New Law

Abelard's starting point for his ideas about law was the thinking of Anselm of Laon (d. 1117), William of Champeaux (ca. 1070–1121), and their pupils in the School of Laon at the beginning of the twelfth century (Marenbon 1992, 608–12; 1996, 267–9). As Biblical exegetes, the masters of the School of Laon would have had constantly before them the distinction between the two revealed Biblical laws: the Old Testament and the New Testament. Study of scripture also posed a question that made them look more deeply into the idea of law. The early chapters of Genesis tell of men, such as Abel, who led virtuous lives and whose sacrifices were acceptable to God, and yet lived after the Fall, but before God had given Moses the Ten Commandments and even before he had commanded Abraham to circumcise himself and his male descendants—that is to say, before the old law. In order to explain how such morally good lives were possible, Anselm and William turned to the idea of natural law. The basis for their notion was provided by St. Paul (Rom. 2:14–15): "For since the Gentiles, who have no law, do naturally the things which are of the law, they themselves are in this way a law for themselves—they who show the work of the law written in their hearts."

Ambrose, Jerome, Origen, and Augustine had all discussed Paul's remark, and their discussions were systematized in the School of Laon. Three periods of sacred history, each with its own law, were distinguished: the period of natural law, which lasted until God gave special precepts to the Jews (circumcision, and then the Ten Commandments); the period of the old law; and the period of the new law, preached by Christ. The old law repeated natural law in its moral precepts (as, indeed, did the new law), but it also contained figural commandments (circumcision and the dietary laws, for instance) and promises (such as the prophecies of Christ's coming). Natural law and the old law did not just enable people to live good lives; these laws also allowed them to be saved (even if they had to wait until the Crucifixion to be allowed to enter heaven). Just as original sin could be remedied for Christians through baptism, so natural law (by its gifts and sacrifices to God) and the old law (through circumcision) contained the remedies needed to make people fit to be saved. The faith in Christ that a person also requires for salvation need be only, they added, a general ("implicit") faith in God as a just judge who will reward the good and punish the evil.

Abelard adopted his basic structure of thinking about law from the School of Laon. He too thought of each of the laws as providing a way of living well and being saved, and in the *Problemata Heloissae* (*Problems Raised by Heloise*) (no. 15; *PL* 703A–C) he speaks of the division between the moral precepts of the old law and its figural commandments. But the way he used this structure was affected by his unusual attitude toward pagan antiquity. Abelard held, following Augustine, that the pagan philosophers of ancient Greece had come to an understanding of God and his triunity by using their reason, and that they were therefore important witnesses to the doctrine of the trinity. When he was attacked for using pagan writers to support Christian teaching, Abelard replied (*Theologia Christiana* II, ca. 1126; cf. Marenbon 1996, 304–7) by claiming that the philosophers lived in an austere and virtuous manner by following the natural law, which should act as an example to the monks of his own day. The writers of the School of Laon had not been at all concerned with Greek antiquity in their discussion of natural law. For Abelard, by contrast, the Greek philosophers are the most important followers of this law. Consequently, natural law is no longer restricted to a particular chronological period, that is, to the time before the old law. Abelard's point of view emphasizes the idea, already expressed by Anselm of Laon, that the old law, even in the time before Christ, applied only to the Jews. And, instead of seeing a development from natural law to old law and then to new law, as his predecessors had done, Abelard suggests by his lavish praise for the virtues of the ancient philosophers that natural law is nearly on the level of the new law, and far better as a guide to living well than the old law, which the Jews followed slavishly from fear rather than from love (see, e.g., *Sermon* 5; *PL* 424AB).

The form and argument of the *Collationes* (*Comparisons* or *Dialogue between a Philosopher, a Jew, and a Christian*), written probably around 1130 (Marenbon and Orlandi 2001, xxvii–xxxii), bring out clearly these special features of Abelard's thought about law. In a dream, Abelard meets three figures, each of them a worshipper of the one God, but of different faiths: a Jew, a Christian, and a "Philosopher," who is a figure based on the pagan philosophers of ancient Greece (Marenbon and Orlandi 2001, l–liv)—but note that Abelard himself was called the *philosophus* by his close followers. Abelard is asked to act as a judge in their discussions, but in the work as it stands he delivers no verdict. There are two dialogues. In the first, the Philosopher argues with the Jew that the old law adds nothing of value to what he, the Philosopher, has from natural law. In the second, the Philosopher discusses with the Christian what is the highest good and the greatest evil. The immediate impression is that the Philosopher wins his case against the Jew, whereas in his more cooperative dialogue with the Christian, he is gradually brought to accept the Christian's positions, because they are more in accord with reason than his own. It may be, though, that a subtler view is intended, and the Jew is not so clearly defeated as it may seem (Marenbon and Orlandi 2001, lx–lxiii).

Abelard's ideas about natural law were closely integrated into the account of ethical action that he developed, especially in the 1130s (Marenbon 1996, 265–81). Abelard holds that sin consists in contempt for God. We show contempt for God, he says, by acting or intending to act in a way that we believe is forbidden by God. In *Scito Teipsum* (*Know Yourself*), sometimes called the *Ethics*, written around 1138, Abelard explained this intending in terms of "consent" (see, e.g., *Ethica* 10:241–4; cf. *Peter Abelard's Ethics* 16:6–8).[2] Such an analysis of sin raises an immediate problem. Sin, it seems, lies in the disparity between what a person does and what he *believes* God commands. Abelard must keep the word "believes" in this formulation, if he is to retain his fundamental idea that sin consists in contempt. (I show my contempt for you if my surprise birthday present is a night at *Parsifal* and I believe that you loathe Wagner, even if in fact you adore him; it would not be showing contempt if you did hate Wagner, but I did not believe you did.) But then Abelard must allow that whether I sin or not depends on what I happen to believe about God's commands. Abelard does indeed accept this consequence, but his notion of natural law makes it harmless. As a result of natural law, every mentally capable adult knows the fundamental moral laws that are laid down by God. No one, for instance, could murder, steal, or commit adultery and claim, except mendaciously, that he believed he was not doing what God has forbidden.

[2] For *Scito Teipsum*, I give references both to the new edition in *CC* and to the older critical edition with translation and fuller notes.

Given this position, Abelard might have been expected to hold that natural law is derivable from some simple principle. Augustine had tried to derive the different precepts of natural law from the golden rule known in antiquity and cited both in Old Testament apocrypha and in the New Testament: "Do to others what you would have them do to you." The theologians of the School of Laon followed Augustine's lead, but Abelard thought differently (see *Problemata Heloissae*, no. XX; *PL* 708BC; *Commentary on Romans*, 291:180–201; cf. Marenbon 1992, 612–4). He saw that a person's wishes about what should be done to himself may be immoral, and so he thought that the golden rule needed qualifying. He seemed to be willing to assume that the basic moral commands are known, without trying to derive them from any more fundamental principle. He also assumes that there will be no conflict between them and the precepts of the new law, although he does leave unresolved problems about the relations between natural law and other religious laws (Marenbon, 1997, 271–2).

11.3.3. Positive Law

There is a passage on law in the *Collationes* that needs to be quoted in full in order to understand Abelard's views on positive law. It is the Philosopher in the dialogue who is speaking:

> So far as justice is concerned, it is not just the bounds of natural justice, but also those of positive justice that ought not to be crossed. One sort of law is called "natural," the other "positive." Natural law is what the reason naturally innate in all people urges should be put into effect, and therefore remains the same among all people: such as, to worship God, to love one's parents, to punish the wicked, and to do whatever is necessary in the sense that without them no other merits whatever will be sufficient. To positive justice, however, belongs what is set up by humans so as to preserve usefulness and worth more safely and increase them. It rests either on custom alone or on written authority. An example of positive justice is provided by the sort of punishments given in retribution and the procedures of judges in examining accusations which have been made. Among some, there is trial by combat or hot irons are used, among others an oath puts an end to all dispute and everything in contention is put to witnesses. It is for this reason that, when we have to live among whoever it may be, we hold the laws they have set up (as I mentioned) just as we hold natural laws. The laws which you call divine—the Old Testament and the New Testament—also pass down some commands which are, as it were, natural (you call them "moral commands"), such as to love God and your neighbour, not to commit adultery, not to steal, not to murder; and some commands which belong, as it were, to positive justice. These commands apply to certain people at a certain time, like circumcision for the Jews and baptism for you and many other commands which you describe as "figural." Moreover, the Roman pontiffs and the church councils issue new decrees every day or dispense various indulgences, according to which, you say, what used to be lawful becomes illicit and vice versa—as if God put it in their power to make things good or evil which were not previously by their decrees and indulgences, and their authority could pass judgment on the law of nature. (Secs. 133–5; 145–7)

The end of this passage seems to anticipate the enormous growth in papal law-making that would take place later in the twelfth century. From the Philosopher's point of view, papal decretals and church councils go beyond their authority in claiming to change the law of nature. The beginning of the passage has been cited (Kuttner 1936, 729–30; Marenbon and Orlandi 2001, lxxix) as the first use of the term "positive law,"[3] as the canonists would employ it, to distinguish laws set up by humans in particular times and places from natural law. Abelard almost certainly took the term from Calcidius' commentary to the *Timaeus*, where—with the sense of "positive" as "imposed" or "instituted" in mind—Calcidius used it in a broader sense to refer to any sort of human justice (as opposed to the ordering of the cosmos). Abelard had used it in this wider sense in his *Theologia Christiana* (*Christian Theology*). But Abelard was not alone—and very probably not the first—in adapting the term. In the prologue to his commentary on the *Timaeus* (139:11–16), probably written before 1125 (Dutton 1991 suggests 1100–1115), Bernard of Chartres identifies positive justice with Isidore of Seville's customary law (*Etymologiae* V.3.3). In his commentary on Cicero's *On Invention* (probably from the 1130s), Thierry of Chartres (*Commentary on Cicero's On Invention* 189:1–4) talks of positive law in much the same way, while in his commentary on the *Rhetoric to Herennius* (275:91) he puts it into the context of Roman law, saying that it embraces both civil law and the law of nations.[4]

Abelard's Philosopher is distinctive, however, in making "positive law" refer to the particular ways in which the general precepts of natural law are put into practice. It is part of natural law to put suspected criminals on trial and punish those who are found guilty, but *how* they are tried and punished is a matter of positive law. Positive law, then, is binding over people in a particular place, living under a particular set of laws; they must follow it, just as they must follow natural law, but their particular positive law does not bind those who are not living under it. The Philosopher's extension of his discussion to the sacrament of baptism and to circumcision (which was often considered to be an Old Testament sacrament) is, therefore, understandable. These are, in his view, examples of positive law that just apply to certain people at certain times. Abelard and his fellow Christians might have been willing to agree with this judgment of circumcision, but they could hardly have accepted it with regard to baptism. The attitude of Abelard, as author, to the figure of the Philosopher in his dialogue is, in general, a subtle one. It is probably over simple to think that any ideas put forward by the Philosopher that are not explicitly argued against by the Christian are ones that Abelard himself would endorse. Abelard may have expected his readers to do some more thinking for them-

[3] The Philosopher talks of *iustitia positiva* ("positive justice") rather that *ius positivum* ("positive law"). But Kuttner was right to think that, in this context, *iustitia* is close enough in meaning to *ius* for the usage to have counted as the first, were it not for the contemporary or earlier examples cited below.

[4] I am grateful to Irène Rosier for pointing out this reference to me.

selves, and this passage may be one of the instances where the Philosopher is made to develop his ideas in a way that Christian readers are not supposed to accept (Marenbon and Orlandi 2001, liii–liv). Still, given Abelard's own views on baptism and salvation (Marenbon 1996, 327), perhaps Christian readers are also not supposed to reject them *outright*.

11.3.4. A Theory of Punishment

As mentioned above (Section 11.3.2), Abelard defined sin in terms of an internal state (contempt for God). Such a view of morality would seem to favor a theory of punishment where penalties are meted out carefully in accord with the degree of evil intended by an agent. But Abelard's thinking takes a quite different direction. Already, in his *Commentary on Romans* (172:622–30), he had raised as an analogy the case of a judge being forced to condemn a man he knows to be innocent because he cannot show that the witnesses brought against him are lying. In *Scito Teipsum*, Abelard repeats this example and adds another one:

> Here is some poor woman. She has a baby who is suckling, and she does not have enough clothes for both herself and for the little one in his cradle. So, moved by pity for the baby, she takes him to herself so as to keep him warm too with her own clothes, and at length in her weakness overcome by the force of nature, she is made to smother the baby she is embracing with the greatest love. Augustine says: "Have charity and do what you will." Yet when she comes before the bishop for penitence, a severe punishment is imposed on her, not for a fault she has committed, but so that in future she and other women will take more care to anticipate such things. (*Scito Teipsum*, 25:65 –26:668; cf. *Peter Abelard's Ethics*, 39:13–22)

Both examples are used by Abelard to show that justice as practiced by humans should *not* aim to give punishment in accord with the guilt of the wrongdoer. Since the measure of sinfulness (which, for Abelard, is guilt in the proper sense) is internal, it is pointless, he believes, for humans to try to determine it. Instead, he advocates what, from the very few details given, seems to be a strictly consequentialist theory of punishment. By giving a severe punishment to the woman who, without any bad intention, but with a lack of due caution, smothers her child, the good consequence will be achieved that in the future women in the same position will take greater care to avoid such an accident. And, presumably, by condemning the innocent man who is proven guilty by due legal procedure, a judge upholds the institution of law in a way that serves generally to promote good behavior. Since Abelard is sure that God will recognize true guilt and innocence, and that the rewards and punishments of the life to come are incomparably greater than those on earth, he does not think that such a procedure does outrageous injustice to individuals. From a modern perspective, such a resort to the afterlife to solve—or rather dismiss—serious problems about earthly justice can seem peremptory (and at variance with

Abelard's usual eagerness for thinking through rational solutions). And medieval legal thinkers themselves preferred to follow a different approach (see the following subsection).

11.3.5. Abelard and Canon Law

Abelard is often mentioned in discussions of medieval law, not so much as a philosopher of law in his own right, but as an important influence on the development of canon law in general, and on Gratian in particular. How close, though, were the connections?

Abelard had completed almost all his work by around 1140, the earliest date thought possible for the first recension of the *Decretum*, and so influence is certainly chronologically possible (and even more so for the second recension). One of Abelard's works is his *Yes and No* (*Sic et Non*), a collection of passages mostly from the Fathers, arranged so as to show how, on one doctrinal question after another, some support one and others the opposite response (hence the title). The similarity to Gratian's method is striking, and even skeptical scholars mention a link as being possible (Winroth 2000, 17). But a careful study (Luscombe 1970, 214–22) has failed to find any passages in the *Decretum* that are clearly based on Abelard. Indeed, the resemblance between the *Decretum* and *Yes and No* may be rather superficial. Abelard does not add any *dicta* as Gratian does, probably because his book was designed, unlike Gratian's, as a resource for Abelard himself rather than as a textbook for general use.

Abelard did have an influence on some of Gratian's commentators (Luscombe 1970, 222–3). But, as emerges from Kuttner's great study (1935, especially 1–62) of canonistic teaching on guilt in the later-twelfth and early-thirteenth centuries, it was a strangely distorted influence. In his ethical theory, Abelard thought very carefully about guilt in terms of intention and, in his later work, consent. Yet, as explained in the previous subsection, he insisted that this type of assessment of guilt should play no part in human judgment and infliction of punishment, which should be based on the obvious, external features of acts. The canonists turned to Abelard's thinking about ethical acts in order precisely to refine their theory about the judgments to be given by human judges in clerical courts. Perhaps, as lawyers, they had a less brutal view of the processes of earthly justice than Abelard had come to hold. Or perhaps they learned about Abelard's ethical theory through his pupils and the collections of his *Sentences* (*Sententie*) (cf. Mews 1986), which circulated quite widely, but never knew of Abelard's distinctive views on judgment and punishment, which are put forward only in *Scito Teipsum*, a rarely copied work.

11.4. Natural Law in Early Scholasticism: William of Auxerre

11.4.1. The Background in Canon Law

The difference between the philosophical discussions of law in the work of early scholastics—the thinkers of the first half of the thirteenth century—and those of Abelard and his contemporaries has much more to do with these theologians' familiarity with the work of canon lawyers than with the new sources (see Section 11.1 above) that were then becoming available. The new sources would, however, also have their effect by the middle of the century (see Section 11.5 below).

Gratian took his account (dist. I.C.7) of natural law from Isidore of Seville's *Etymologies* (*Etymologiae*) V.4, where it is presented as an instinct that is common to all peoples. It includes not just the coupling of men and women and the upbringing of children, but also "the common possession of all things" and "one liberty for all." In his opening *dicta*, Gratian says that natural law is found in the Old Testament law and in the Gospels, and—like the writers of the School of Laon—he alludes to the golden rule. Commentators on Gratian in the later-twelfth century gave more complex discussions of natural law. They were aware of the treatment at the beginning of the *Digest* (I.2), according to which natural law is common to all animals, and not peculiar to humans. For example, Rufinus (*De Summa Decretorum*, 6–7) says that, although this is the view of the "legal tradition," "we" restrict natural law to the human race. Basing himself perhaps on Hugh of St Victor's distinction (*De Sacramentis* XI.7; *PL* 347A) between good deeds that must never be omitted, bad deeds that are always prohibited, and middle ones that "may be done or omitted, depending on the time and the place," Rufinus distinguishes orders, prohibitions, and "demonstrations." Some parts of natural law, such as the injunction to hold all things in common and one liberty for all, are demonstrations that have now been altered. By the early-thirteenth century, commentators such as John the German were trying to sort out the various ways in which natural law had been discussed by distinguishing various senses of the term (cf. Lottin 1948, 74–5).

11.4.2. William of Auxerre's Summa Aurea (Golden Textbook)

William of Auxerre (d. 1231) was one of the early masters of theology at Paris University. His most important work is the *Summa Aurea*, written between 1215 and 1229. He begins his treatment of natural law there (*Summa Aurea* III.18) by making a distinction (*Summa Aurea* 369:16–23)[5] in line with canon law tradition between Ulpian's "broader" definition of natural law as applying

[5] All subsequent references are to this edition.

to all animals and the "narrower" view held by Gaius and Isidore and repeated by Gratian that restricts it to humans: "what natural reason without any or great deliberation dictates should be done, such as that God should be loved and similar things" (ibid.). It is the narrower sense of natural law that concerns William. He solves the difficulty posed by Isidore's view that, by natural law, all things should be held in common by using the canon lawyers' distinction between the commands and prohibitions of natural law, on the one hand, and its demonstrations, on the other (370:2–371:49). The injunction to hold all things in common is a demonstration, because it applies to the time before the Fall. Given man's corrupt nature after the Fall, neither is it nor should it be a command, because were it followed "the republic would be dissolved and the human race would perish as people slaughtered one another." Surprisingly, however, William (373:106–10) does maintain that common ownership is nonetheless an injunction that binds people at all times. The difference is in *how* it binds: In the state of innocence it was binding for all actions always; now it binds only "in time of necessity." Those who first had private property, William (374:23–8) goes on to explain, did not sin by doing so if they held it not out of greed, but because they saw that it would be harmful for everything to be in common once human nature had been corrupted by the Fall.

William then turns to the distinction between divine and natural commands. Unlike Gratian, but like most of the subsequent canonists, William is unwilling to identify natural law with divine law. He (376:44–5) does, however, say that the two laws are the same materially, that is, they do not differ in the particular contents of their commands. Divine law is distinguished from natural law because of a general requirement about how its commands are to be performed. People must follow divine law from charity, because divine law is given in order to allow humans to gain merit, and merit is gained only by acting from charity.

There is, though, an important objection (375:10–14) to this view that William needs to answer. Although it may be within our power to obey God's laws, it is not under our control whether we do so from charity or not. God would not command what it is impossible for us to fulfill, and so we cannot be required to follow divine laws out of charity. Consequently, there is no difference between divine law and natural law. William (376:46–55) replies by saying that it *is* within our power to act from charity, since charity—that is, God's grace—is offered to us. True, we cannot of ourselves act from charity; we need God to give it to us. But this does not mean that acting from charity is not possible for us. William compares our position to that of a boy who wants an apple that is too high on a tree for him to reach. He cannot *have* the apple *by himself*, but he can *have* it, because his father can reach up and hand it to him. William does not make it clear whether, as this line of reply would require in order to be convincing, God's grace is always available to anyone who wants it.

What, then, is the purpose of natural law, if following it does not gain merit? William (377:63–8) explains that it does, indirectly, lead us to merit, by helping us to cultivate the "political virtues." A distinction between political and higher virtues, going back to Plotinus, was transmitted by Macrobius, and had been long familiar among writers on ethics. By means of the political virtues, natural law leads us on to the theological virtues, including charity.

William (377:69–74) distinguishes two general rules (*regulae*) of natural law, from which the particular commands are derived. One is the golden rule, which he cites in its negative form: Do not do to others what you do not wish to be done to you. The other is the rule that you should love God. As Abelard had done, William realizes that the golden rule faces logical objections (378:94–101). If you are a thief, you do not wish to be hanged. Therefore, you are bound not to hang thieves, which cannot be right, since unless evildoers are punished, the republic will be destroyed. Moreover, we all wish what we seek to be granted to us by others, so do we not all transgress natural law if we do not give everybody what they request of us? The first objection forces William to qualify the golden rule so that it reads (in the positive version): "Whatever you *reasonably* wish should be done to you, do to others" (378:111–12). William first suggests that the second objection can be overcome by saying (most implausibly) that "if we seek something and we do not need it, then we do not wish it to be given to us" (378:114–15). But he (378:115–379:126) goes on to make the important point that commands to act (as opposed to prohibitions) do not oblige on every occasion; for example, I am not bound to give what someone in need requests, since I may be saving it for someone who is more in need or who belongs to my family or neighborhood. Indeed, it is not a matter of skill (*ars*) but rather charity to decide when to accede to a request or not. Charity will enable us to weigh up the different circumstances, says William, and he supports himself with not only a biblical quotation but also a comment from Aristotle's *Nicomachean Ethics*: "virtue is more certain and better than any skill [*ars*]" (II.6.1106b14–15). This out-of-context citation is the only reference William makes to Aristotle in this whole discussion, and a sign of how little Aristotle has influenced him here.

Further evidence of William's distance from the Aristotelian considerations that would guide speculation about natural law just a few decades later is provided by his discussion of how we know natural law: In what sense is it "written in the heart of man"? William's far from clear answer (*Summa Aurea* 381:44–54) is based on the idea that, because the rational soul is an image of God's essence, people can look into themselves and see God. When the soul sees God, it is delighted, and the good is that the apprehension of which gives delight, and so the soul is seeing "the first goodness in itself, according to the way in which it is the first goodness." The soul also sees that the first good is good from itself, not from anything else, and that it most greatly hates evil and so punishes it; and in seeing this, the soul sees "the first justice."

11.5. Legal Conceptions of Early Scholastics: The *Summa Fratris Alexandri*

The *Summa Fratris Alexandri* (*Brother Alexander's Textbook*) is a compilation, begun by 1236 and completed by 1245 (except for Book IV, added later), based in part on the work of Alexander of Hales (ca. 1185–1245), the secular master of theology at Paris who became a Franciscan and inaugurated the tradition of Franciscan theology at Paris University. Alexander may well have been involved in putting it together, but the redactor of Book III, where law is discussed, was Alexander's pupil John of La Rochelle. The discussion on law is based on earlier material that might itself have been Alexander's work or John's (Father of the College of St. Bonaventure 1948, ccxx–ccxxii, ccclvi–cclxx). (For convenience, I shall refer to the writer of the treatise on law [*Summa Fratris Alexandri* III.2] as "John.") This treatise is comprehensive and vast (amounting to nearly half a million words). John begins by looking at eternal law and natural law. There is a very extensive treatment of the old (or, as he calls it, "Mosaic") law and a slightly shorter treatment of the new ("evangelical") law, and between them a long discussion of the practice of law and judgment: judges, advocates, legal procedure, sentences, and punishments. This central part on legal practice shows a full familiarity with the writings of the canonists and also knowledge of Roman law. The opening section is more theoretical (*Summa Fratris Alexandri* III.2.1–2; 314–64).[6]

Most of the areas discussed by William of Auxerre are also considered here (except for questions about grace and charity, which are treated elsewhere in the *Summa*). For instance, the question of whether natural law extends to all animals, not just rational ones, is raised on several occasions and eventually dealt with by a distinction between natural law as innate (*nativum*), human, and divine (350). And there is a discussion about whether natural law requires all things to be held in common (362–3), where one of the solutions given limits this requirement, as William does, to the time before the Fall, "otherwise the good would be in need and human society would not stand, because the wicked would snatch everything." These topics are, however, incidental to the thrust of John's argument. Whereas William allowed his agenda to be set by the canonists, John—who clearly knows well the work of both civil and canon lawyers—has his own scheme and priorities.

John begins not by discussing natural law and considering to whom it applies and its relation to other sorts of law, but by looking at eternal law. He (314–15) shows that there is an eternal law (315–16) above the human mind, a notion of which is impressed on the mind. John gives three definitions of eternal law (316–19), all taken from Augustine, each of which shows it from a different perspective. Insofar as it concerns good and bad things in general, it is "that by which it is just that all things be ordained." Insofar as it con-

[6] All subsequent references are to this edition.

cerns good things in general, it is "the law of all skills [*artes*] and the law of the omnipotent artificer." Insofar as it concerns the goods of rational creatures alone, the law is "the highest reason, to which everything is to be submitted, through which the evil merit a wretched life and the good a good life, through which what belongs to temporal life is rightly tolerated and rightly changed." All laws, both human laws, insofar as they are just and legitimate, and natural law, are derived from eternal law, "just as what is good in a creature is drawn from the first goodness and what is true from the first truth" (327).

The most striking aspect of John's whole discussion is his explanation of how natural law is innate in rational creatures, and its relation to conscience. John writes that the natural law is

> in a rational creature. For just as the cognitive faculty has innate within it the principles of the true and the notion of them, as for example, "Every whole is greater than its parts" and "Of anything it is true either to affirm or deny that it is so," so the motive faculty has an innate rule, by which it is guided to the good, and this we call "natural law." (339)

In place of the golden rule (which plays only a minor part in his discussion) and William's ideas about humans finding God within their souls, John has a way of thinking about self-evident first principles that is clearly influenced by Aristotle, although Aristotle would not have thought of them as innate in the way John envisages. A little further on in his treatment (344–5), John explains in more detail how people come to act in accord with natural law. He draws on the thinking about conscience and *synderesis* ("spark of conscience"). The term *synderesis*, originally used by Jerome, had been introduced into theological and canonistic discussions in the second half of the twelfth century and, by the mid-thirteenth century, theologians such as Philip the Chancellor and William of Auxerre were giving detailed accounts of its relation to conscience (Lottin 1948, 103–349). John, however, is one of the first writers to use *synderesis* in a discussion of natural law. Natural law, he says, provides the rule about what should or should not be done. It is what principally regulates the motions of a rational creature with regard to what ought to be done, in the way that the weight of heavy thing guides its motion (*Summa Fratris Alexandri* 343). Conscience is formed as a result of natural law (345), when the person begins to reason and judge what should be done. Although John's discussion is not completely explicit, he suggests that natural law merely tells a person that "good is to be done and evil avoided," and so it is left to conscience to work out what course of action is good. *Synderesis* is what incites the will to perform the good action on which the conscience has decided.

11.6. Conclusion

From the ninth to the mid-thirteenth centuries (and especially from around 1100 onward), not only was law established as a discipline in medieval schools with the rediscovery of the *Digest* and the work of Gratian and his followers in canon law, but also many of the important concepts of medieval legal philosophy were first fully developed, and some of the central arguments first explored. In particular, building on patristic foundations, Abelard and his successors investigated the relations between natural law and the revealed laws of the Old and New Testaments, while Abelard and his contemporaries were the first to use the notion of positive law. A very important development in the thirteenth century was the notion of *synderesis*, and its links with conscience and natural law. By the mid-thirteenth century, the discussion of *synderesis* was already being seen in terms of Aristotle's theory of knowledge—an indication, perhaps, of the direction that one important strand of legal thinking would take in the following decades.

Further Reading

Marenbon 1988 provides a general introduction with detailed bibliography to early medieval philosophy (480–1150) and Marenbon 1987 to the later period (1150–1350). See also Glauche 1970 for the early period, Dronke 1988 for the twelfth century, and Dod 1982 for the thirteenth century.

General studies of John Scottus Eriugena's contribution to the controversy on predestination include Schrimpf 1982 and Marenbon 1990. Cristiani 1976 looks in detail not only at Eriugena's ideas about law, but also at those of the other parties to the dispute. For general background on Abelard, see Marenbon 1996 and (with a strong emphasis on Abelard's philosophical importance and interest for contemporary philosophers) Brower and Guilfoy 2004. A fine, recent biography is Clanchy 1996. A very good study of Abelard's discussion of law is De Gandillac 1975. On the wider background to the notion of positive law, and the implications of the idea, see Gagnér 1960.

A general guide to the editions and manuscripts of early scholastic theological treatises is provided in Landgraf 1973. Natural law in medieval thought, including this period, is studied in Chroust 1946, and in more detail for the twelfth and early-thirteenth century in Lottin 1924 on the canonists and Lottin 1948, 71–100, on the theologians. Useful shorter background studies, going on to consider later medieval developments, are provided in Luscombe 1982 on natural law and Potts 1982 on conscience and *synderesis*.

Chapter 12

THE PHILOSOPHY OF LAW OF THOMAS AQUINAS

by Anthony J. Lisska[1]

12.1. Life and Work

The great thirteenth-century philosopher and theologian Thomas Aquinas (ca. 1226–1274) played a pivotal role in the history and development of Western jurisprudence. During his productive but short life, Aquinas wrote extensively on moral matters, and as a corollary, on topics in political and legal philosophy. His exposition in *Summa Theologiae* on matters of law is often referred to as the classical canon of natural law theory.

Aquinas was born in 1226[2] of Italian noble parents of the family of Aquino. His birthplace was Roccasecca, which was not far from Naples in south central Italy. At an early age, while a beginning student at the University of Naples, he aspired to join the then newly formed mendicant friars known as the Order of Preachers or, more popularly, the Dominicans after their founder, Dominic de Guzman. Aquinas embarked upon this religious life voyage against his parents' wishes—for they had visions of their son becoming the reigning abbot of the wealthy monastery of Monte Casino near their ancestral home. Nonetheless, young Aquinas persevered in his decision to join the Dominicans. Sent first to Paris and then to Cologne in order to study under the Dominican friar Albert the Great, Aquinas soon showed great intellectual promise.

The Dominicans saw themselves above all else as preachers and teachers. Moving away from the pastoral conditions of the countryside, which traditionally had served as the setting for most Western religious orders, the Dominicans established priories in the large European cities, usually associating themselves with major universities. Under the tutelage of Albert the Great, Aquinas' intellectual star shone brightly. In fact, Albert accurately predicted that Aquinas would reach stellar intellectual achievements—the "bellow" of the "dumb ox" (as his fellow students at Cologne called him) would be heard around the world! He taught at the University of Paris on two distinct occasions; this institution was the leading center of academic and intellectual work in the thirteenth century. Albert the Great called it "a city of philoso-

[1] All translations are by the author unless otherwise indicated.

[2] The exact year of Aquinas' birth has been contested for centuries. Tugwell (1988, 291–2) seems right in asserting that there is now sufficient evidence to assign 1226 as the correct year. Some documents state that Aquinas was forty-eight when he died in 1274. Torrell 1996 argues that 1225 is the appropriate year of Aquinas' birth.

phers." Aquinas was also assigned to Rome and to Naples at various times during his life.

Aquinas' principal contribution to Western thought was his attempt to reconcile Aristotelian science and philosophy with the tenets of Western Christianity. He was a prolific writer; Kenny (1993, 10–1) claims that when one considers only the works generally acknowledged to be authentic, Aquinas' *omnia opera* total over eight and one half million words. Including the texts of questionable authenticity increases the number of words to eleven and one half million. Aquinas wrote several commentaries on Aristotle's texts, including his *Commentary on the Nicomachean Ethics* (*In X Libros Ethicorum*), which is important in the development of his own moral theory. Yet his greatest achievement was the composition, organization, and writing of his monumental *Summa Theologiae*.[3] While it is correct to say that Aquinas never wrote a specific, "stand alone" treatise devoted to law, one finds what is often referred to as his "Treatise on Law," which comprises Questions 90–97 of the *Prima Secundae* of the *Summa Theologiae*. He wrote the *Summa Theologiae* during the last few years of his scholarly life. It remained incomplete at the time of his death. Aquinas died at the premature age of forty-eight, probably due to a stroke. Tugwell (1988, 261) claims that today we would probably call Aquinas a "workaholic."

This section concludes with a brief overview of Aquinas' legal writings and their historical antecedents. McNabb (1929) traces many of the influences on Aquinas' work in legal matters, and he also discusses the influence that Aquinas' writings in turn had in the development of Western jurisprudence.[4] McNabb (ibid., 1048) writes that Aquinas rethought the ethical system of Aristotle, and even argues boldly that the *Nicomachean Ethics* "is so enriched in form and matter by Aquinas that it might be well disputed who is the real founder of Ethics as a Science." Aquinas' texts indicate that he undertook reflective studies on law throughout his scholarly life. His early *Commentary on the Sentences of Peter Lombard* demonstrates that the "Law of the Decalogue" was foremost in his mind. Even at this early date in his intellectual career, Aquinas refers often to Aristotle's *Nicomachean Ethics* and *Metaphysics*. Both

[3] The *Summa Theologiae* is divided into three major parts, with the second part divided further into two sections. Hence, there is the *Prima Pars* (The First Part), the *Prima Secundae* (the First Section of the Second Part), the *Secunda Secundae* (the Second Section of the Second Part), and the *Tertia Pars* (the Third Part). There is also the *Supplementum*, which contains the final sections of this work, compiled from assorted earlier writings after Aquinas' death. The *Prima Pars* deals with God and the set of creatures that come from God. The *Prima Secundae* deals with human actions, moral theory, and law. The *Secunda Secundae* concerns the virtues in some detail. The *Tertia Pars* treats Jesus as the sacramental vehicle for human beings to return to God. The *Tertia Pars* is principally theology, then, while the other two parts are essentially philosophical approaches to questions about the human condition.

[4] Several historical references used in this analysis of Aquinas on natural law are dependent upon this thoughtful article by McNabb.

of these treatises influenced Aquinas' own construction of natural law moral and legal theory. His *Summa Contra Gentiles*, which was written five years after the commentary on Lombard, bears witness to the continued development of his legal insights. Nonetheless, his mature consideration on the nature and scope of law, *De Lege*, which is often translated as "The Treatise on Law," is found in the *Prima Secundae* of *Summa Theologiae*, where Aquinas discusses human action. Aquinas' references resemble a listing of the "Great Books" of ancient and medieval philosophy—the works of Plato, Aristotle, Cicero, Ulpian, John Chrysostom, Hilary, Jerome, the Pseudo-Dionysius, Augustine, Boethius, Isidore, and Moses Maimonides, among others. Aristotle the pagan philosopher, Augustine the Christian philosopher, and Moses Maimonides the Jewish philosopher are quoted most often. McNabb (ibid., 1055) notes that Maimonides served as a special influence on Aquinas' understanding of the nature and scope of law: "[H]ad Moses Maimonides not written his famous book, *Guide of the Perplexed*, there would never have been written a still more famous book, St. Thomas's treatise on Law."

Aquinas also discusses references to law in the Bible. His treatment of the "old law" and the "new law" is in *Summa Theologiae*, QQ. 98 to 114, where the *Prima Secundae* ends. For example, Aquinas considers the Torah in the following manner:

> We must, therefore, distinguish three kinds of precepts in the old law: a) moral precepts, which are dictated by the natural law; b) ceremonial precepts, which are determinations of the divine worship; and c) judicial precepts, which are determinations of the justice to be maintained among human persons. (*STh* IaIIae.99.a.4)

In addition to the analysis of law in the *Summa Theologiae*, Aquinas wrote several political documents, one of which is his unfinished *Commentary on Aristotle's Politics*. He also authored selected notes on political leadership to the King of Cyprus, *On Kingship* (*De Regimine Principum*),[5] and a brief letter on political theory to the Duchess of Brabant.[6]

[5] There is serious scholarly debate over the structure and content of this opusculum of Aquinas. Early manuscript collections conflate two texts; the first was Aquinas' *De Regno: Ad Regem Cypri* and the other *De Regimine Principum*, often attributed to Aquinas' confrere, Tolomeo of Lucca. See Aquinas *On Kingship*, ed. Eschmann 1982 for further discussion of this debate.

[6] *Epistola ad Ducissam Brabantiae*. Parts of this letter are translated in Bourke 1960, 248–51. Torrell 1996, 335, explains the importance and structure of this document, written at Paris in 1271. The letter responds to queries concerning the financial administration of the subjects of a prince. In this text, Aquinas justifies collecting taxes on the principle of the public good. Torrell notes that recent research suggests that the letter was written for Margaret of Constantinople, the countess of Flanders, and daughter of Baldwin, the Count of Flanders and the first Latin emperor of Constantinople.

12.2. The Treatise on Law

Aquinas' discussion on law is a component of his substantive treatise on human action, which is the topic of the *Prima Secundae*. His philosophy of law must accordingly be viewed as part of a more comprehensive philosophy of action. His analysis of law covers eight questions in the *Summa Theologiae*, and includes significant discussion of many topics germane to the study of Western jurisprudence:

Question 90: Considerations on Law
Question 91: The Different Kinds of Law
Question 92: The Effects of Law
Question 93: The Eternal Law
Question 94: The Natural Law
Question 95: Considering Human Law in and of Itself
Question 96: Concerning the Power of Human Law
Question 97: Concerning the Possibility of Changing the Law

Aquinas defines law in the following way: "Law of its very nature is an ordinance of reason for the common good, which is made by the person who has care of the community, and this rule is promulgated" (*STh* IaIIae.90.a.4). A suitable reading, as Finnis (1998, 226) suggests, for "common good" is the "public good." In his *Summa Contra Gentiles*, Aquinas writes that "in human affairs, there is a common good that is, in fact, the good of the state [*civitas* or *polis*]" (*SCG* III.80, no. 14). In many respects, what Aquinas meant by *civitas* is similar structurally to the Greek concept of *polis*.

Aquinas uses his definition of law for the four categories of law he discusses: eternal law, natural law, positive or human law, and divine law. It is necessary to pay careful attention to the distinctions between these four kinds of law. In particular, one must not conflate eternal law with divine law, a practice that happens frequently in discussions of Aquinas on law. Moreover, one must not equate natural law with divine law in Aquinas, even though these two categories of law are coextensive in several medieval treatises on law. The first three divisions of law—eternal, natural, and human or positive—are all interrelated yet distinct; all three are the result of a fairly rigorous philosophical analysis. Divine law, to the contrary, is in a class by itself and is entirely a matter of theological investigation.

12.3. Eternal Law

One issue that contemporary students of natural law must confront is the role that eternal law plays in Aquinas' general theory of natural law. Aquinas writes that the natural law in some way participates in the eternal law: "Hence, it is obvious that the natural law is nothing other than the participation of the eternal law in the rational creature or human being" (*STh* IaIIae.91.a.2). Many commentators assume that, according to Aquinas in *Summa Theologiae*, the existence of God is a necessary condition for understanding natural law. D'Entreves, for example, writes:

> Now it seems to me that in our divided world the first and most serious stumbling block to the Thomist conception of natural law lies precisely in its premise [...] of a divine order of the world, which St. Thomas recalls at the very beginning of his theory of law, and from which he infers, with unimpeachable logic, the most detailed and specific consequences: *supposito quod mundus divina providentia regatur, ut in primo habitum est* [it is assumed that the world is ruled by divine providence, as we demonstrated in the first part of *Summa Theologiae*]. Once that premise is granted, the whole majestic edifice of laws can be established on it: eternal law, the natural law, human law, and divine law. All are ultimately based on and justified through the existence of a supreme benevolent being. (D'Entreves 1970, 153–4)

In addition, O'Connor (1967, 60) writes that "the nature of law depends upon establishing the existence of a provident God who planned and guides the universe. St. Thomas, of course, believed that he had done this"; and A. Ryan (1985, 180) argues that "a secular natural law theory is simply incoherent." The argument set forth in this chapter claims, to the contrary, that the eternal law is reducible to a Platonic archetype in the divine mind, which renders the objections articulated by D'Entreves, O'Connor, and A. Ryan, among others, moot.

Plato's analogy of the Demiurge in his *Timaeus* provides an instructive paradigm for understanding the function of eternal law. A consistent analysis elucidates the concept of eternal law as the set of divine ideas in the divine mind. One idea in this set is the archetype for human nature. Following Plato's suggestion offered in the *Phaedrus*, the archetypes in the divine mind "divide nature at its joints" (Plato, *Phaedrus* 265e). Aquinas uses this Platonic insight in rendering an interpretation of the following scriptural passage: "Let us make mankind in our image and likeness" (Gen. 1:26–8; New Catholic Edition). Aquinas argues that human nature is what it is, that is, the *quidditas* ("quiddity") or set of essential properties determined by *materia prima* ("prime matter") and *forma substantialis* ("substantial form"), because it is a reflection of the archetype of human nature in the divine mind. Working in a manner generally familiar to most medieval philosophers, Aquinas adopts insights from what he understood to be Platonic philosophy. In many ways, his was the received interpretation of Plato, which asserted that a subsistent world of the Forms existed in a transcendental realm. Aquinas situates these forms, which Plato articulated as freestanding, eternal, unchangeable essences, in the divine mind; most early medieval philosophers and theologians did likewise. Hence, a Platonic Form functions as a divine idea or archetype. This appropriation of Platonic Forms, which is rooted in Plotinus and Augustine, is accepted by most of the early medieval philosophers and theologians.

This Platonic schema serves as the philosophical basis for what Aquinas refers to as eternal law. The Renaissance philosopher Domingo de Soto (1494–1560) of early modern Scholasticism[7] at Salamanca in Spain, commenting on Aquinas' account of law, explained the role of eternal law in some detail. De Soto explains that the eternal law is the *ratio* ("explanatory principle") for understanding the order of the created world. Eternal law, as a formal cause, exists causally in the divine mind. A formal cause is that which provides the structure or organization for a natural object. For Aristotle and Aquinas, it refers more to a principle of explanation than to source of movement. De Soto writes:

> God [...] out of eternity conceived in his mind the order and dispensation and rule of the universe of things, in the likeness of which conception all laws are to be constituted: that ordainment and commandment therefore is called the eternal law in accord with its nature. (*De Iust. et Iure* I.3, Ad. 1 as quoted in Brett 1997, 142)

Since Aquinas writes that the natural law "participates" in the eternal law, many commentators (e.g., D'Entreves 1970) claim that the natural law depends on the eternal law. It would follow then that any understanding of the natural law requires the existence of God. This account entails a theological definist position for Aquinas (i.e., a metaethical position that defines the basic rightness or wrongness of an action by means of theological principles alone). Hence, in principle, it is in opposition to a natural law position, where the moral qualities of actions are determined by their connection with human nature rather than God. Such a position suggests the following puzzle: Must one understand the eternal law prior to coming to terms with the natural law?

There are two possible responses to this query, one metaphysical and the other epistemological. The metaphysical position articulated by Aquinas is that the archetype of human nature in the divine mind is the metaphysical principle after which all humans in the terrestrial realm are patterned. This is, to be sure, a rather rarefied ontological position, and the foundation for what the medievals often called "the truth in things," also referred to as "ontological truth." However, a human knower is able to determine the set of necessary properties that constitute an essence without understanding that this essence fundamentally is a copy of the archetype in the divine mind. In other words, one can understand the set of necessary properties that make up the content of human nature as just that—an essence of human nature—without realizing that this essence is patterned after the archetype in the divine mind. Now, how might this be explained? We must look to Aquinas' epistemological position to answer this question.

The epistemological position depends upon insights gleaned from Aquinas' philosophy of mind. Through the use of abstraction via the *intellectus*

[7] This early modern or "second" scholasticism is discussed in Chapter 14 of this volume.

agens ("agent intellect"), a knower can determine the content of a human essence totally within the human sphere of awareness. One need not know that this essence depends on a divine archetype in order to flesh out the set of synthetic necessary properties that comprise the content of a human essence. Aquinas claims that human beings never have *propter quid* ("essential knowledge") of God but only *secundum quid* ("incidental knowledge"). To assert or imply that a human being needs to know the eternal law, which is an archetype in the divine mind, in order to understand the natural law is inconsistent with Aquinas' philosophy of mind, natural theology, and epistemology. The archetype of human nature is, to be sure, the foundation of human nature, which in turn is the foundation of natural law. Nonetheless, it is possible to understand the content of human nature without realizing its dependence on the divine archetype. This is an important point that Aquinas appropriated from Aristotle's doctrine of abstraction and used in his own philosophy of mind. Hence, what Aquinas needs for his theory of natural law is a theory of natural kinds rather than the existence of God. (This issue will be discussed further in the next section.)

12.4. The Natural Law

Recently, modern historians have advanced the theory that a revived sense of the study of nature occurred in the twelfth century in several cathedral schools, especially Chartres. This renewed interest in the natural world accompanied the introduction of a systematic order into the matters of learning inherited from an earlier time (Southern 1995, 4–5; Haskins 1927, 303–40 *passim*). Consequently, as the universities began to blossom in the early-thirteenth century, full sets of lectures on the philosophy of nature became part of the curriculum.

Given this renewed interest in the study of nature, philosophical and theological discussions ensued within the context of a better understanding of the natural world. These new studies demonstrated a rationale for the intelligibility of the natural world and advocated the intrinsic goodness of the realm of nature. As Porter (1999, chaps. 1 and 2) argues, nature and revelation, under the direction of reason, worked in tandem during the formative stages of the development of natural law theory.[8] Working with Albert the Great, Aquinas became immersed in these new studies, arguing that the development of a natural law theory in the Aristotelian mode followed coherently from the emerging studies in the philosophy of nature. Aquinas, furthermore, offered an interpretation of nature using the Aristotelian categories of matter and form. "Matter" refers to the material substratum or underlying "stuff" that is

[8] Porter's analysis here of the formative stages of natural law theory provides a useful guide to this topic.

organized by the "form." "Form" is the principle of organization much like the "blueprint" for a building. Any individual natural thing in the world is made up of matter and form; neither exists separately by itself. In order to explain the causal structures of nature, Aquinas argues for the existence of natural kinds, which is a metaphysical theory of essence that claims that there is a set of properties that renders an individual a member of a class or natural kind. A substantial form is a set of dispositional properties that determines the content of a natural kind. A dispositional property is a "capacity" that something has to become more developed or brought to fruition. In *De Anima*, Aristotle writes that the soul, which is nothing more than the substantial form of a living organism, is "the first act of a body with the potency of life" (*de An.* 415b5–10). Using the categories of contemporary analytic philosophy, we might suggest that this set of dispositional properties is a synthetic necessary set. It is necessary because it determines the essence—in all possible worlds, one might argue—and it is synthetic because it has a referent beyond the use of language.[9] This synthetic necessary set is *de re*, or about the nature of things, and not *de dicto*, or only about the use of language. Aquinas' realist ontology is apparent in his discussion of the philosophy of nature.

The concept of human nature is a necessary condition for Aquinas' account of natural law to cohere consistently. What Aquinas needs, in turn, to account for his theory of human nature is a metaphysics of natural kinds. As noted above, human nature as elucidated by Aquinas is best analyzed as a natural kind. It follows that what Aquinas needs in order to explicate his account of natural law is the concept of a natural kind. The natural kind of human nature is defined as a certain set of dispositional properties.

In the latter part of the *Prima Secundae* of the *Summa Theologiae*, Aquinas delineates his exposition of the three generic categories of dispositional properties that determine what human nature is:

> Insofar as good has the intelligibility of end and evil has the intelligibility of contrary to end, it follows that reason grasps naturally as goods (accordingly, as things to be pursued by work, and their opposites as evils and thus things to be avoided) all the objects which follow from the

[9] Nelson (1967) refers to synthetic necessary properties as the means to distinguish what he takes to be "nomic universal propositions" from "accidental universal propositions." A nomic universal proposition is a general claim that will stand up under a counterfactual conditional: for example, "All water is H_20." An accidental universal proposition, on the other hand, is the random assortment of things under a class term: for example, "All the chairs in this room are blue." A counter-example is used in the following way. It is true to say about a liquid that "If this were water, then it would be H_20." This would indicate that there is a natural kind of water, which is interpreted as a set of essential properties that define the essence. On the other hand, it is not true to say of a blue chair, "If there were a chair in this room, then it must be blue." The contrary to fact conditional does not hold of accidental universal claims; however, it does hold in the area of essential properties determining a natural kind. See also Lisska forthcoming.

Thomas Aquinas (ca. 1226–1274)
Detail of Beato Angelico, *Virgin and Child Enthroned with Angels and St. Thomas Aquinas, St. Barnabas, St. Dominic, and St. Peter Martyr* (ca. 1422), San Domenico, Fiesole, Italy

> natural inclinations central to the concept of human nature. First, there is in human beings an inclination based upon the aspect of human nature which is shared with all living things; this is that everything according to its own nature tends to preserve its own being. In accord with this inclination or natural tendency, those things (actions, events, processes) by which human life is preserved and by which threats to human life are met fall under the natural law. Second, there are in human beings inclinations toward more restricted goods which are based upon the fact that human nature has common properties with other animals. In accord with this inclination, those things are said to be in agreement with the natural law (which nature teaches all animals) among which are the sexual union of male and female, the care of children, and so forth. Third, there is in human beings an inclination to those goods based upon the rational properties of human nature. These goods are uniquely related to human beings. For example, human beings have a natural inclination to know the true propositions both about God and those necessities required for living in a human society. In accord with this inclination arise elements of the natural law. For example, human beings should avoid ignorance and should not offend those persons among whom they must live in social units, and so on. (*STh* IaIIae.94.a.2)

Human nature as a generic set of dispositional properties might be rendered in the following manner: (1) The set of *living* dispositions (which humans share with plants), (2) the set of *sensitive* dispositions (which humans share with animals), and (3) the set of *rational* dispositions (which makes humans unique in the material world). Aquinas' analysis of human nature is dependent on philosophical claims found in Aristotle's *Nicomachean Ethics*, *Metaphysics*, and *De Anima*.

A living disposition is the capacity, active potency, or drive that all living beings possess that enables them to continue in existence. Had humans evolved or been created differently, there might be a different set of dispositions that comprise their set of essential properties. This living disposition is similar structurally to what Hart (1961, 190) calls the natural necessity of "survival." In a similar fashion, one of the rational dispositions is the capacity that humans exhibit to know, which is best described as an innate curiosity. Aquinas was familiar with the opening passage in Aristotle's *Metaphysics* indicating that "[a]ll human beings, by nature, desire to know" (*Metaph.* 980a25). Aquinas argues that this rational disposition is only developed when a human knows what is true. This "rational curiosity" is analogous to what Fuller (1964, 185) calls "communication."[10] Finnis (1998, 81) describes this structure in the following way: "The order Aquinas here has in mind is a metaphysical stratification: [1] what we have in common with all substances, [2] what, more specifically, we have in common with other animals, and [3] what is peculiar to us as human beings." C. Ryan (1965, 28) writes that these three general aspects of the human person are "the good of individual survival, biological good, and the good of human communication."[11] Golding (1974, 242–3)

[10] In this part of his account of natural law, Fuller refers explicitly to Aquinas' *Summa Theologiae*.

[11] C. Ryan's analysis is one of the best overall succinct accounts of natural law theory, explicating many concepts in the writings of Aquinas.

refers to the living dispositions as the "basic requirements of human life," the sensitive dispositions as the basic requirements for the "furtherance of the human species," and the rational dispositions as the basic requirements for the "promotion of (a human person's) good as a rational and social being." The purpose of Aquinas' argument here is to elucidate and understand in a general fashion those dispositional properties that are central to the concept of a human being.[12]

Metaphysical realism, as Simon (1965, 7–8) argues so well, is a necessary condition for an adequate theory of natural law. Aquinas' account of natural kind is similar to what Kripke (1971, 144–6) calls the "metaphysically necessary," which is a truth that is dependent on reality. This concept is not a mere convention of human language. Hence, the "metaphysically necessary" is coextensive with "synthetic necessity" (as discussed above). Kripke argues that the proposition "Water is H_2O" is a metaphysically necessary truth because something would not be water if it were not H_2O. This is the essence, or what Kripke calls the natural kind, of water. This structure is the nature of the kind of thing water is, and it is, Kripke argues, true in all possible worlds. Kripke's concept of the metaphysically necessary seems commensurate with what Aquinas holds.[13]

This account of a natural kind reflects Aquinas' claim that all human persons possess the quiddity of human nature, that is, they share the same set of fundamental properties that constitute human nature. This would hold, in principle, in all possible worlds. To help elucidate this claim, one might explain, for instance, how Aquinas refutes the Latin Averroists on the structure of human nature regarding the separated agent intellect. Aquinas argues that whatever we name by human intelligence—what Kripke would say we "rigidly designate"—is not part of what we name by a separated agent intellect. Of course, human knowers might be mistaken in their attempts to understand the specific set of properties that determine a natural kind. Aquinas often remarks about the difficulties encountered in this epistemological enterprise. That this is a difficult enterprise is, however, a different question in the philosophy of mind; it does not diminish the need for a set of causal properties in reality that serve as the foundation for the natural kind. In this regard, Aquinas is an essentialist in his theory of natural kinds. This is what underlies the

[12] Nussbaum (1993, 263–4) offers eight properties that she claims "we can nonetheless identify [as] certain features of our common humanity, closely related to Aristotle's [and Aquinas'] original list"; they are mortality, the body, pleasure and pain, cognitive capability, practical reason, early infant development, affiliation or a sense of fellowship with other human beings, and humor.

[13] Cf. Ayers 1981, 248, who argues that Kripke's view "is not at all unlike Aristotelian doctrine." For Aquinas, like Aristotle, an account of a human essence is more than a modal necessity. Aquinas intends a *de re* (about things) necessity and not a *de dicto* (about language) necessity, which entails that this is a synthetic necessary claim about the nature of reality.

frequently made claim that Aquinas is a "moderate realist" in his theory of essences.[14]

Aquinas' account of natural law requires as a necessary condition an ontological theory of natural kinds because he must account for the regularity of the world. He accomplishes this through his theory of essence, which in turn is rooted in his account of substantial form (or formal cause). Once Aquinas has provided his theory of essence, he has the blocks in place needed to develop his moral theory of natural law. This suggests that Aquinas views moral theory as a "second order inquiry." It is second order because it follows from the primary ontological theory of the natural kind of human nature.

Natural law for Aquinas is thus best understood as rooted in the set of dispositional properties that comprise human nature. Following in the footsteps of British empiricism, most analytic philosophers consider a disposition to be a property like "fragility," understood as a fixed, closed set of mathematical properties. A disposition for Aquinas is more than this, though; it is a built-in property that tends toward the completion of its development in some way or other. It is not reducible to the capacity to be "acted upon." A disposition in the human essence is an Aristotelian "active potency" or an "active power." A biological disposition would be, for example, the built-in tendency of an acorn to grow into an oak tree. If certain material conditions are present, the thing will do *X*, which is to develop in a structured manner toward a certain end. In the case of a passive power like solubility, on the other hand, an external cause determines whether or not the thing does *X* (that is, dissolves).

When the set of dispositional properties has developed properly in human persons, this results in *eudaimonia*, *felicitas*, or *beatitudo*, all of which mean "happiness," "functioning well," or "flourishing."[15] Nonetheless, with any dispositional natural kind, to function well is to develop the dispositions or capacities according to the nature that it has. Using the hylomorphism concepts (i.e., concepts using matter and form as fundamental principles) common to Aristotelian texts, the development of the dispositional properties of the substantial form, which is the formal cause, is to reach the final cause.[16] In the case of human nature, the moral agent attains flourishing when the supreme set of dispositional properties determining the human essence—that is, the living, the sensitive, and the rational dispositions—is developed in a harmonious,

[14] For example, Copleston (1957, 151–4) provides an illuminating discussion of these issues dealing with the problem of universals in medieval philosophy.

[15] In contemporary discussions of Aristotle's moral theory, Anscombe 1958 and Foot 1978 began writing about Aristotelian *eudaimonia*, which they called "flourishing." Finnis 1998, 115, uses "integral human fulfillment" to elucidate a more contemporary reading of *eudaimonia*.

[16] Hochberg 2001 claims that the modern analytic philosopher Gustav Bergmann, near the end of his academic career, considered claims similar to the hylomorphic concepts found in Aristotle and Aquinas.

self-actualized manner. This Aristotelian account of flourishing, in turn, is the very foundation of Aquinas' natural law theory of morality.

Aquinas' metaphysics and philosophy of mind are such that a human knower can determine, theoretically at least, the concept of an essence without any appeal to God's existence or God's providence. Knowers are aware of the content of a human essence just as they know any other natural kind, which is through the process of abstraction from phantasms[17] by means of the "active intellect" (*intellectus agens*). Finnis (1982, 400) offers a similar position on this issue: "For Aquinas, there is nothing extraordinary about man's grasp of the natural law; it is simply one application of man's ordinary power of understanding."[18] The important point is this: Knowing an essence is, in principle, a human activity undertaken in the normal human ways of knowing.[19]

Natural law is the foundation for moral development in Aquinas. Like Aristotle, Aquinas assumes that flourishing means that a human's nature has reached the development of the basic dispositional properties by which it is defined. It is this set of dispositional properties that comprise the basis for natural law. Natural law for Aquinas thus is not an unwritten set of commands built into the human conscience; it is not the unwritten law in the mind of God as Antigone seems to imply (see Chapter 1, Section 1.6.2 of this volume); nor is it the understanding of right reason articulated by the Stoics.

Because morality, for Aquinas, depends upon the development of these dispositional properties, the first principle of practical reason is "good is to be done and pursued, and evil avoided." Following Aristotle, Aquinas argues that the good by definition is defined in terms of an end. In *On the Nature of Truth* (*De Veritate*), Aquinas writes: "All things found to have the criterion of an end at the same time meet the criterion of a good" (21, I). Hence, the end, which is the good, is the development of the dispositional properties. There are as many goods as there are ends. Aquinas adopts a set of goods that are incommensurable, which means that one good or end is not reducible to another.

[17] Often "phantasm" is rendered as "image." However, a consistent analysis of the concept of phantasm is more complicated. Each of the three internal sense faculties in Aquinas' philosophy of mind has its own unique phantasm. For further discussion, see Lisska forthcoming.

[18] In commenting on Finnis' work, Covell (1992, 222–3) writes: "In *Natural Law and Natural Rights*, [Finnis] claimed that the principles of natural law admitted of an entirely secular derivation, which involved no metaphysical assumptions regarding the existence, nature or will of God."

[19] While Finnis would agree on the role of God in Aquinas' account of natural law as developed in this chapter, nonetheless he would not accept the totality of the account of human essence and its relation to natural law theory articulated here. Finnis rejects basing natural law theory on what he calls "philosophical anthropology." Resolving this debate, however, is beyond the limits of this inquiry. For a complete analysis of these meta-philosophical differences in reading Aquinas on natural law, see Lisska 1996, chaps. 6–7; an earlier version of this argument is found in Lisska 1991. McInerny 1998 refers to Finnis' position as "doing natural law without nature."

Aquinas' analysis thus does not require that the good be defined in terms of a single natural property. This incommensurable character of goods is a necessary condition for understanding Aquinas' natural law theory.

Once Aquinas has determined the justification for his theory of natural kinds, two additional questions arise: (1) Is an instance of a natural kind itself self-explanatory and totally independent, or, in the ontological order, is it a dependent being? (2) How does one introduce a theory of obligation into what is a theory of ethical naturalism?

In response to the first question, what if a philosopher who adopted a theory of natural kinds accepted an evolutionary theory and offered the following retort: "Well, natural kinds are what they are through some evolutionary process, and we really cannot say anything more; they are just there!" At this particular juncture, Aquinas and the evolutionist philosopher are on the same level. Both could, eventually in response to the second question, articulate a theory of natural duties based on the developmental properties of a natural kind. The evolutionist philosopher, like Aristotle, believes that the development of a moral theory from his metaphysics is the best that one can do.

What does Aquinas do now? Aquinas, to use a favorite metaphor of Copleston (1965), must get the evolutionist philosopher on the metaphysical chessboard. Aquinas must convince the evolutionist philosopher that an analysis of human nature, even as a natural kind, requires that a human person is a dependent being. This requires the "essence/existence" distinction.[20] The essence/existence distinction requires that there is a radical difference between the set of defining properties of an instance of a natural kind—the essence—and the question of whether an individual with such an essence actually exists. Hence, there is a real distinction, Aquinas believes, between determining "what" a thing is and ascertaining "that" the thing exists. Here Aquinas must argue cogently that a dependent being, or "contingent being" in cosmological argument circles, requires a real relation with an independent, necessary being. God as the *actus purus* ("pure act of existence itself") provides a response to the dependency question. Aquinas would recommend that the evolutionist philosopher consider the "Third Way" in the *Prima Pars* of the *Summa Theologiae*, which is the argument that contingent beings entail a necessary being (*STh* Ia.2.a.3). Only at this juncture in Aquinas' metaphysical scheme does God enter the analysis. God, as a necessary being whose essence is existence, provides the response to this further question about the dependent character of individuals of natural kinds.

Any philosopher—theist, atheist, or agnostic—could still construct a theory of natural law based on natural kind theory rooted in dispositional properties.

[20] This is a distinction that Aristotle did not make. For a discussion of the difference between Aquinas and Aristotle on the essence/existence distinction, see Owens 1993. See also Wippel 2000.

What Aquinas provides additionally is an explanation rooted in the concept of dependency. The moral theory proposed by the evolutionist philosopher would be similar structurally to the moral theory that Aristotle articulated in *Nicomachean Ethics*. Aquinas would remark that this theory is not a false moral theory but an incomplete one. Ultimately, the concept of essence depends for a complete metaphysical explanation on the archetype of human nature—the foundation for the natural kind—that subsists in the divine mind. If one asks about an interpretation of scriptural passages concerning human beings made in the image and likeness of God, Aquinas borrows the archetype language acquired from Augustine and Plato. If one asks the dependency question, then Aquinas introduces the essence/existence distinction. Both of these points go beyond the direct development of natural law theory based fundamentally on Aristotelian eudaimonism.

The second question Aquinas must address concerns the justification of a theory of obligation within the context of this account of ethical naturalism. The "metaphysics of finality" (see Gauthier 1959, 47–8; Veatch 1985, chaps. 1–2) claims that the concept of obligation can be derived from the very structure of a dispositional view of essence. The teleological analysis developed in Aquinas differs radically from any teleological analysis found in either nineteenth-century utilitarianism or twentieth-century naturalism rooted in utilitarianism. Utilitarianism is the moral theory that argues that an action is right if it produces the greatest amount of pleasure for the greatest number of people. Naturalism refers to the claim that moral values are reducible or definable in terms of naturally occurring qualities or properties. Bentham (1843) dismisses natural law and natural rights theory, claiming that it is "rhetorical nonsense—nonsense on stilts." For Aquinas, the "end" is built into the very ontological structure of the disposition. This is why a dispositional theory of essence is necessary for Aquinas' theory of natural law. The end to be attained is not a subjective desire or wish on the part of the agent; rather, it is determined ontologically by the dispositional property. It is the final cause determined by the formal cause. The human essence as a set of dispositional properties determines the ends to be attained. The ends are not determined by the arbitrary, subjective preferences or aspirations of the agent. The "final cause" in Aristotelian theory is determined by the metaphysics of human nature, which is based on the dispositional structure of the formal cause. The result is a natural law theory "without stilts."

An objection common in twentieth-century analytic philosophy (see Moore 1903, 13–20) to all forms of ethical naturalism is the so-called "naturalistic fallacy." This mistake allegedly occurs whenever one tries to derive a value statement (or an "ought" statement) from a factual statement (or an "is" statement), for example, "*X* is pleasant, therefore *X* is good." The assumption here is that any form of ethical naturalism is ensnared in this fallacy. In response, one must consider the structure of this purported fallacy, which is rooted in the ontological and moral theories of Moore. Moore's ontological analysis of an object is reducible to a collection of simple properties. Given that the foundation is a simple natural property, a value property must be "added onto" this simple natural property—like a layer of paint put on a chair. Moore concludes that this "addition" is, by definition, fallacious.

The natural law response to Moore is that the fundamental properties are not simple but dispositional. Hence, the end—what Aquinas calls the final cause—is the development of the properties in the essence—what Aquinas calls the formal cause. Given this analysis, the end, which is the good, is not an additional property but the development or completion of an entity's dispositional property. The charge of the naturalistic fallacy brought against Aquinas's metaethics is thus met.

12.5. Human or Positive Law

Once Aquinas' view of natural law has been understood, articulating his account of positive or human law is a simple extrapolation from natural law. Positive law is the formulation and promulgation of statutes that "ensure the smooth running of the commonwealth" (*Comm. Eth.* V.2). Aquinas adopts Aristotle's concept of the common or public good, for he agrees with Aristotle that all humans are by nature political or social beings. The purpose of positive law is to establish and to enhance the general conditions that make the common or public good possible. In *On Kingship* I, Aquinas writes that "if by nature, human persons are to live together, then the community they form must needs be ruled [...]. Any organism would disintegrate were there no unifying force working for the common good of all the members" (Aquinas, *On Kingship*, I.1 no. 8). Hence, positive law is the set of prescriptions made, articulated, and promulgated by the person or persons in authority for the smooth functioning of the community for the common or public good.

What interested Aquinas is what we call criminal law; he is less concerned about procedural law. Aquinas appears to have no concept of what Hart (1961, 91–6) refers to as secondary rules of law. A secondary rule is a rule of procedure that helps eliminate problems in what Hart calls the primary—or moral—rules of a society. According to Hart, law is the union of primary and secondary rules, where the secondary rules are the rules of (1) recognition (to identify a law as a law), (2) change (to provide for an orderly process of change in the laws), and (3) adjudication (to remedy the problem of inefficiency in the legal system by conferring powers or abilities on a person in charge).

In matters regarding the extent and pervasiveness of the legal system, Aquinas is probably best categorized as a legal conservative. Sigmund (1993, 230) notes that "Lord Acton described Aquinas as 'the First Whig' or believer in the limitation of governmental power." Aquinas, quoting Isidore, writes that the primary purpose of law is to protect the innocent:

We remember what Isidore once wrote: "Human laws have been made so that human audacity might be held in check by their threat, and also so that the innocent might be protected from those exerting evil; and among those capable of doing evil, the dread of punishment might prevent them from undertaking harm." It should be noted, however, that these matters are most important and necessary for human beings. Therefore it is necessary that human laws should be made. (*STh* IaIIae.95.a.1, *sed contra*)

Hence, Aquinas does not appear to accept that the role of a legal system is to foster social change, or other more modern conceptions of the legal enterprise.

Although Aquinas maintains that laws should promote the common good, as a legal conservative he believes that they should have limited scope: "[H]uman law does not forbid all vices, from which virtuous persons keep themselves, but only the more serious vices, which the majority can avoid, and principally those that harm others, and which must be prohibited in order for human society to survive" (*STh* IaIIae.96.a.2). He also notes that "human law cannot forbid all and everything that is against virtue; it is sufficient that it forbids actions that go against community life" (*STh* IIaIIae.77.a.1, ad 1). These passages indicate, furthermore, that Aquinas would not accept a position of moral perfectionism in the law.[21] Note the following passage from *Summa Theologiae*:

So also in human government, it is right for those who are in authority to tolerate some evil actions so as not to hinder other goods or to prevent some worse evil from occurring. As Augustine writes in *On Ordination* (II. 4): "If one suppresses all prostitution, then the world will be torn apart by lust." (*STh* IIaIIae.10.a.11)

In addition, Aquinas agrees with Augustine that an "unjust law is no law at all":

A law is unjust when it is contrary to the human good and contrary to the things we have discussed above: Either from the end as when a person presiding imposes a law with undue burdens or prescribes a law which does not pertain to the commonweal of the society but rather to his own proper desires and glories. Or even on the part of the author, as when someone makes a law beyond the power commissioned to him. Or also from the very form, for example, as when burdens are dispensed unequally upon members for the community, even if they are ordained to the common good. Cases like this are more like acts of violence than laws, because, as Augustine writes, "A law that is not seen as just is no law at all." Hence, such laws do not oblige in the matter of conscience except perhaps in order to avoid scandal or a disturbance. (*STh* IaIIae.96.a.4)

This is the passage to which Martin Luther King, Jr. (1963) refers in his *A Letter from a Birmingham Jail*. Aquinas argues that if a positive law hinders the development of human flourishing, then that law basically is unjust. It follows

[21] Commenting on these issues, Finnis (1998, 228) writes: "Aquinas's position remains firmly outlined [...]: Those vices of disposition and conduct which have no significant relationship, direct or indirect, to justice and peace are not the concern of state government or law. The position is not readily distinguishable from the 'grand simple principle' [...] of John Stuart Mill's *On Liberty*."

that an unjust law fails to meet the criteria for justification as articulated by the natural law. Nonetheless, while Aquinas did propose that an unjust law is no law at all, given his conservative bent, he argues that conditions must be extreme before even an unjust law ought to be overturned. In *On Kingship*, he writes the following about tyranny:

> Finally, provision must be made for facing the situation should the king stray into tyranny. Indeed, if there be not an excess of tyranny, it is more expedient to tolerate the milder tyranny for a while than, by acting against the tyrant, to become involved in many perils more grievous than the tyranny itself [...]. This is wont to happen in tyranny, namely, that the second becomes more grievous than the one preceding, inasmuch as, without abandoning the previous oppressions, he himself thinks up fresh ones from the malice of his heart. (Aquinas, *On Kingship*, I.4 nos. 43 and 44)

12.6. Divine Law

In Aquinas' analysis of law, divine law and eternal law are neither identical nor coextensive. Divine law primarily reduces to the commandments of God, which are the prescriptive propositions found in the scriptures. This is part of what Aquinas would call "revelation." For Aquinas, like many medieval philosophers and theologians, faith is fundamentally propositional; part of what is meant by revelation consists in the set of propositions found in the scriptures. The passages in the scriptures are statements that are to be accepted and believed on the word of God. Faith is not reducible to a commitment, which is an understanding of faith that has pervaded religious discussions since the time of the Reformation.

Given this account, the role of divine law, as manifested in the propositions found in the scriptures, is conceived as a cognitive and prescriptive divine process by which God assists human beings to live morally appropriate lives. An analogy in Aquinas for the role of divine law is his requirement that God provide revelation—that is, scriptural passages—indicating his own existence. When discussing the proofs for the existence of God, Aquinas argues that there is a moral necessity on God's part for divine revelation (*STh* Ia.1.a.1), because the sustained philosophical analysis required to establish the existence of God is a difficult enterprise. Hence, those demonstrations can be mastered by only a few, only after much time and effort, with a genuine possibility of making serious conceptual mistakes in the process of developing a sophisticated metaphysical demonstration. Since it is immensely difficult to apprehend a metaphysical proof for the existence of God, Aquinas argues that revelation from God is morally necessary for nearly everyone because knowing that God exists is a necessary condition for human beatitude.

A similar argument holds for the role of divine law concerning the moral maxims that are necessary for embarking on the process of a complete moral life. Aquinas argues:

> Because there is always an unclarity and lack of certitude in human judgments, especially on contingent and particular matters, it follows that different human beings will make different judgments about different kinds of actions; it sometimes happens that not only diverse but sometimes contrary laws come about. Therefore, so that a human person might be free from all doubt about that which must be done and that which must be avoided, it is necessary that in the matter of right actions, a human being should be directed by being given a divine law, from which law one is not able to go astray. (*STh* IaIIae.91.a.4)

Developing a moral system that is rooted in Aristotle's naturalistic philosophy would also require difficult and controversial arguments drawing on metaphysics, philosophy of mind, action theory, and philosophical anthropology. Hence, Aquinas proposes that the Ten Commandments are God's way of assisting limited human beings to understand the role and content of moral law. These moral maxims are necessary conditions for human well-being. From this analysis, it follows that Aquinas differs from several earlier medieval philosophers who suggested that the divine law and the natural law are co-extensive. For example, canonist Huguccio (d. 1210) writes: "Likewise, in a fourth sense, the divine law, that is, what is contained in the law of Moses and the evangelical law, is said to be a natural law" (Huguccio, as quoted in Porter 1999, 133). Aquinas rejects Huguccio's interpretation of natural law.

From the fact that the divine law helps illuminate what the natural law prescribes, it is impossible for divine law—or any form of theological definism—to be in opposition to natural law. In his metaethics of moral maxims, Aquinas is not an advocate of divine prescriptivism (i.e., a theory that asserts that an action is right by the very fact that God commands or prescribes such an action to be undertaken). Since human nature is a copy of the divine archetype in the divine mind, the maxims of natural law follow from this essence. If God were to command a moral maxim in opposition to the content of the human essence, this would render God an inconsistent being. What Aquinas suggests, furthermore, in opposition to an argument made by William of Ockham (*Rep.* IV.Q9, E–F), is that God, as a rational being, cannot command human beings to undertake actions that are in opposition to the precepts of the natural law. There are indications that ultimately Ockham is a proponent of divine prescriptivism in justifying the moral law.[22] If Ockham is a proponent of a form of divine prescriptivism, then moral prescriptions are justified principally from the will of God. If the foundation of a moral theory is the very prescription or command uttered by God, then it follows that it is the will of God commanding that provides the final metaethical justification for an act's moral quality. Hence, some form of voluntarism follows from prescriptivism, because prescriptivism removes any cognitive content that might serve as a foundation for a moral judgment. Aquinas would not accept this position because, for him, human nature plays the necessary cognitive role. At root level, a fundamental

[22] A more thorough discussion of Ockham's position on moral theory is found in Chapter 13.

voluntarism runs through the Franciscan tradition, which Ockham upholds, that is in opposition to the preeminence of the intellectualist tradition to which Dominicans such as Aquinas adhere.

While Aquinas was a member of theology faculties most of his scholarly life, he was also a sophisticated philosopher in the Aristotelian tradition. One can structure a philosophical argument of natural law independently of Aquinas' system of theology (see Veatch 1971, 4; Lisska 1996, chap. 5). This is not, of course, to deny that there are theological elements in Aquinas' account of natural law. However, what one needs to do is develop the structure of the philosophical argument as far as possible in conceptual isolation from the theology. This entails that Aquinas' account of natural law, while certainly profiting from the theological milieu of the late-twelfth and thirteenth centuries, nonetheless can be held accountable on philosophical grounds. In addition, Aquinas always argued that theology complements philosophy. An important maxim he affirms is that "grace perfects nature." Hence, the natural order must be in a suitable condition before grace can have any application. That this concept is opposed by reformation theologians is not to be denied. In this dimension of what later historians would call the "faith/reason" problem, the thirteenth century philosophy of Aquinas is distinct categorically from Reformation theology.[23]

A puzzling item connecting Aquinas' theology and philosophy concerns the role of "natural" happiness in his system. There are two parts to this issue. First, Aquinas, as a theologian, postulates that full human happiness—what he calls "perfect happiness"—occurs only in the afterlife when the human intellect exercises a direct intuitive relationship with the Godhead (*STh* IaIae.3.a.6, 8). He argues, however, that this perfect happiness is not achieved without supernatural grace, which he calls "the light of glory." This is, to be sure, a theo-

[23] Some recent scholarship on the writings of Aquinas proposes that Aquinas adopted more of a theological principle than a philosophical one. Jordan 1993 affirms this interpretation. Wippel 2000, to the contrary, argues that one can articulate independently and consistently a philosophical position, especially in metaphysics, from Aquinas' texts. Tugwell (1988, 257–8) provides probably the best succinct analysis of this issue: "Gauthier argues that Thomas' concern was always theological, even in his 'philosophical' writings, but his critics have pointed plausibly enough to signs that Thomas did have a serious philosophical purpose and that he was interested in clarifying Aristotelian philosophy in its own right. Probably there is no real contradiction between the two positions. As we have seen, Thomas' own theology drove him to recognize the importance of philosophy as a distinct discipline, if only because philosophical errors that might threaten faith need to be tackled philosophically. But his philosophical interests were not just apologetic. He was surely sincere in believing that the theological attempt to understand faith is essentially at one with the universal human attempt to understand reality. In his last years, as we have noted, the philosophers seem to have been more enthusiastic about Thomas than many of his fellow theologians were; it is quite likely that he in return found the philosophers more congenial than some of the theologians. He believed that the best way to discover the truth is to have a good argument, and in this he was being true to the tradition of Albert and indeed St. Dominic."

logical dimension beyond the philosophy of Aquinas' system. What Aquinas argues is that the natural law has limits, but that, like any philosophical theory, it can be judged satisfactory or not from a philosophical perspective. Second, even Aristotle (*EN* II.8.1101a19) argues that it is difficult for human agents to attain a complete degree of happiness in this life, which is the only life that Aristotle understood. Commentators like McInerny (1992, 39, 173–7) argue that Aristotle's position on happiness entails that human happiness is at best episodic. Aquinas considers this position when he argues that the complete happiness of a human person can be attained only in the afterlife. However, Aristotle also suggests in Book I of the *Nicomachean Ethics* that his system of moral theory is the best that one could do. Aquinas follows Aristotle in these judgments. Nonetheless, in this life, humans can attain only incomplete or imperfect happiness; only in the afterlife is complete or perfect happiness possible. Aquinas would be in full agreement with Adler, who proclaims: "Aristotle's *Nicomachean Ethics* is the only sound, practical and undogmatic moral philosophy in the whole Western tradition" (Adler 1990, 254).

12.7. Punishment

While many medieval philosophers appear to adopt some form of a retributivist theory of punishment, several texts indicate that Aquinas argues more for a consequentialist justification of punishment. A consequentialist theory of punishment bases the justification for punishment in some manner on the consequences of punishment. A retributive theory of punishment, on the other hand, bases the justification for punishment on the need to atone for the guilt arising from committing an immoral or illegal act. Aquinas considers the nature of punishment while elucidating his general account of the virtue of justice in *Summa Theologiae*, but writes sparingly about the nature and conditions of justice. Nonetheless, in considering divine justice, he adopts a retributivist position, suggesting that because a sin has been committed against God, it must be rectified through the bestowing of punishment by God. Yet when Aquinas considers punishment in the human legal sphere, he appears to adopt more of a consequentialist position. He is more interested in the effects that punishment will have. At times, he is interested in the reformation of the evildoer; at other times, punishment seems to be justified by appealing to the effectiveness of deterrence. Yet the consequentialist dimension always appears to require that the party to whom the punishment is administered is guilty. Hence, it would seem that Aquinas, in the matter of temporal punishment, adopts a mixed theory of punishment, which would be a middle ground between a strict consequentialist and a strict retributivist position.

Aquinas upholds capital punishment, and he appeals, strangely enough, to a sort of consequentialist utilitarian argument in defending it. His argument appears to be that criminals who undertake heinous crimes have violated the conditions for the public good and have thus forfeited their rights to be members of the society. In the later sections of the *Summa Theologiae*, Aquinas writes: “In this life, there is no punishment for punishment’s sake. The time of the last judgment has not yet come. The value of punishment is medicinal and insofar as it promotes public security or the cure of the criminal” (*STh* IaIIae.68.a.1). In “Letter to the Duchess of Brabant,” Aquinas also writes, “In cases of extortion you should indeed punish severely, in order to deter others from undertaking such actions in the future” (*Letter to the Duchess of Brabant*, XIII).

These passages indicate that in matters of temporal human punishment, as opposed to divine punishment, Aquinas adopts a consequentialist model of justification. He maintains, though, what contemporary philosophers of law would consider a “mixed” consequentialist position. First, he appears to accept a general deterrence model of justification for punishment. In discussing the structure of human law, Aquinas notes that the fear of punishment is a motivation for obedience to the law, especially among the young. Punishment will deter others from undertaking criminal actions. Second, he adopts what we might call a reformative theory of punishment. In this case, punishment is to be administered so that the criminal might be “cured” and “reformed.” The justification for imposing punishment on the guilty person is in terms of the end result, whether it be the deterrence of future criminal actions or the reform and rehabilitation of criminals. These determinations are matters of human law, for Aquinas writes that “to specify a punishment according to the condition of the person and his offense belongs to the province of positive law” (*STh* Suppl. 52, ad 3).

Even though Aquinas adopts a consequentialist form of justification, because of his concept of human nature and the requirement of guilt, it would never occur to him to justify what Rawls (1955, 9) calls “telishment,” which is the punishment of an innocent person in order to achieve some social good. Aquinas argues that punishment is in some sense a part of the natural law. He writes that “the natural law decrees that a punishment should be inflicted for every offense, and furthermore it decrees that no one who is innocent should be punished” (*STh* Suppl. 52, ad 3).

12.8. The Virtue of Justice

Aquinas’ treatment of *ius*, which is often translated as “right,” begins in the *Secunda Secundae* of the *Summa Theologiae*, Question 57. This question immediately precedes the general discussion of justice (*iustitia*). The term *iustitia* is derived from *ius*, which suggests that justice is a derivative of the term for right. Thus, *ius* is rendered as “the just thing.” Hence, a *ius* is a “right thing” that occurs among persons or between persons and things; in other words, it is the right thing that takes place in various human situations. Moreover, as

Villey (1983), McInerny (1992, 212), and Tierney (1997, 23) note, Aquinas' account of *ius* is more understandable in relation to Roman law than it is in the context of modern rights theory. Roman law, and its ecclesiastical expression found in canon law, exerted a significant influence on Aquinas' treatment of legal matters.

Aquinas writes that "it is proper to justice, in comparison with the other virtues, to direct human persons in their relations with others; this is true because justice denotes a kind of equality" (*STh* IIaIIae.57.1). In the second article of Question 57, Aquinas asks whether there is a *ius* that is natural and a *ius* that is positive. He responds affirmatively to both queries. A natural *ius* comes about by the very nature of the case, whereas a positive *ius* arises because of common consent either between private individuals or between the community and its citizens. Hence, a *ius* refers to an objective, relational state of affairs. This sense of *ius* is different from the account of a human right as articulated by late medieval canon lawyers and by several late medieval and Renaissance philosophers. Many of these lawyers and philosophers began to use the term *ius* for "a right" in the modern subjective sense. For example, Suárez (1548–1617) reports that "according to its strict signification *ius* is called a kind of moral power [*facultas*] which anyone has concerning his own property or something due to him. So the owner of a thing is said to have a right in the thing and a workman is said to have a right to his wages" (Suárez, *Leg.* I.1.2.5, 24, as translated in Tierney 1997, 50).[24]

Aquinas, it appears, no more than hints that from these natural properties rooted in human nature there might be developed what later philosophers would call natural rights. While Aquinas does not articulate a theory of natural rights, nonetheless one might propose a derivative theory; in this derivation, a right might be that which protects the development of dispositional properties. For instance, Aquinas argues that a principal living disposition is the sense of continuing in existence. This requires, so Aquinas writes, that it is immoral for one to engage in arbitrary killing. Hence, life is to be protected. This is what C. Ryan (1965, 28) calls the "biological good." It follows that killing is to be avoided not because it is a divine commandment, but because killing frustrates or hinders the continual development of the natural dispositional property to continue in existence. This is similar structurally to Hart's concept of "survival" as a "natural necessity" (1961, 190–5). This natural law analysis entails that evil—in this sense, a metaphysical evil—is the repression of a natural

[24] The historical development of the modern concept of rights is controversial, but there seems to be a scholarly consensus that the concept of a subjective natural right was developed by canon lawyers, philosophers, and theologians during the later middle ages. See Chapter 10, Section 10.5, of this volume on medieval canon law and rights; Chapter 13, Section 13.4, on Ockham and natural rights; and Chapter 14 *passim* for early modern scholasticism and rights. See also Chapter 4, Section 4.8, and Chapter 6, Section 6.6, respectively, for controversies over possible ancient Greek and Roman antecedents of rights concepts.

dispositional property. The same holds for the development of sensitive and rational dispositions and their opposing repressions. Nonetheless, Aquinas did not himself develop a theory of individual human rights. While Aquinas contrasted a "natural right" (*ius naturale*) with a "positive right" (*ius positivum*), a natural right in the modern sense is either absent from his thought or present only in an inchoate way.[25]

Finnis (1998, 187–8) notes that Aquinas adopts almost identically the conceptual schema for justice as found in Aristotle's *Nicomachean Ethics*. Finnis further reflects on this situation, indicating that Aquinas' account of justice is limited because he tries to fit every aspect of the virtue of justice into the Aristotelian schema. Agreeing with Aristotle, Aquinas writes that justice "is a habit whereby a human person renders to each one what is due by a constant and perpetual will" (*STh* IIaIIae.58.a.1). Aquinas argues that justice, by its very name and function, implies equality. Hence, justice entails a relation to another, for anything is equal never to itself, but always to another. Justice is twofold: universal and particular. First, universal legal justice is the virtue that directs human persons immediately to the common good or the public interest of the community. In addition, there is a second category of justice, namely, particular justice, which directs the human person immediately in matters relating to particular goods and particular persons. In Question 61, Aquinas delineates two categories of particular justice: commutative justice and distributive justice. Commutative justice deals with the mutual dealings between two persons. Distributive justice deals with the relations between the community itself and the persons in the community. In effect, this part of the virtue of justice oversees the distribution of the common goods of the community proportionately to its citizens. Commenting on Aquinas' exposition of the virtue of justice, Gilby writes about universal legal justice (*iustitia generalis*) and the two subsets of justice—commutative and distributive:

[25] While Aquinas does not consider the concept of natural right directly, nonetheless, contemporary natural law philosophers like Veatch and Finnis, among others, argue that a philosophical derivation of rights from Aquinas' moral theory of natural law is possible: see Veatch 1985; Finnis 1982 and 1998. According to Veatch, one determines a concept of "duty" based on the set of dispositions. A natural right becomes the "protection" of the duties that are derived from the natural kind of the human person. This proposed derivation, so Veatch suggests, limits the present debate on the nature and scope of rights. One source of contention in Veatch's analysis, however, is the discussion of positive and negative rights. Veatch argues that a theory of natural law can provide an analysis only of what he calls negative rights. A negative right is a protection (e.g., rights to property, life, and liberty). These are, Veatch writes, the "rights simply *not* to be interfered with" (Veatch 1990, 315). Positive rights, on the other hand, are entitlements (e.g., rights to education, health care, retirement benefits, and so forth). One might respond that Aquinas' account based on the fundamental dispositions of the human person could justify a limited set of positive human rights. Space constraints limit the explication of this argument here, but see Lisska 1996, chap. 9.

Justice is an analogical value pitched at various levels according as it renders what is due for the common good of the political community (*justitia generalis*), to one private person from another (*justitia commutativa*), and to one person from the political group (*justitia distributiva*). (Gilby, intro. to *STh*, xv)

Aquinas sounds a bit like Rawls (1971, 85–6) in suggesting that justice is primarily the fair dealings of the members of the society with one another and the fair dealing of the society itself with the members of the society. In some ways, Aquinas was ahead of his time in his rather sophisticated analysis of the virtue of justice as fairness.

A corollary of his account of justice is Aquinas' discussion of the criteria for a "just war." Aquinas writes on warfare in the Western Christian tradition, following in particular the insights of Augustine. Aquinas was never a pacifist, although he argues that waging war must be a last resort. In *Summa Theologiae*, Aquinas puts forward his influential writing on what has become known as his just war theory; interestingly enough, the title of this question asks whether engaging in a war is always a matter of sinfulness:

There are three conditions for a just war. First of all, the ruler under whom the war is to be engaged must have the authority to carry out the war [...]. Secondly, a just cause is required—this is necessary so that those against whom the war is waged deserve such a response because of some offense on their part [...]. The third condition of a just war necessitates that those in charge of the community have a right intention in this matter, which is to achieve some good or to avoid some evil. (*STh* IIaIIae.40.a.1)

On this account, war may be carried out, to be sure, but one must make it perfectly clear that the war is purely defensive. Aquinas' analysis seems to provide a retributive justification of war rather than a teleological justification.[26]

Aquinas was a thoroughgoing philosophical realist.[27] His moral and political theories depend necessarily on the essential properties that comprise natures and essences of things in the external world. The theory of natural law as developed by Aquinas is thus principally a second-order inquiry, which is dependent upon his analysis of Aristotle's theory of the human person. Knowing the structure of a human essence and developing a moral theory of natural law on this human essence demonstrates Aquinas' commitment to an intellectualist account of moral theory. His theory of natural law often serves as the paradigm for an ontological theory of natural law moral and legal theory. Not only

[26] See Chapter 14 of this volume for discussion of further developments of just war theory by Vitoria and Suárez.

[27] One should note that in their analysis of Aquinas' account of truth, Milbank and Pickstock 1999 argue for a noncognitivist account of truth in Aquinas. In fact, Pickstock writes: "How should one respond to the death of realism, the death of the idea that thoughts in our minds can represent to us the way things actually are in the world? For such a death seems to be widely proclaimed by contemporary philosophers" (Pickstock 2000, 308). For a critical response to this postmodern interpretation of Aquinas' concept of truth, see Kenny 2001.

have scholars in jurisprudence recently re-discovered the texts and insights of Aquinas' account of natural law, but the late-twentieth century also witnessed the revival of what has been called "virtue ethics," and Aquinas' moral theory based on Aristotle's *Nicomachean Ethics* is a central part of those discussions. This adaptation of Aquinas' moral realism has been used to respond to some versions of postmodernism, which reject any possibility of a legitimate rational inquiry into moral and legal matters. Aquinas is a bulwark of ethical naturalism based on an ontological theory of human nature.[28]

Further Reading

The authoritative English translation (with Latin text, footnotes, and generally excellent appendices) of Thomas Aquinas' *Summa Theologiae* is the Blackfriars edition under the editorship of Gilby in sixty volumes (1964–1980). An earlier translation by Shapcote has been reissued often. Lisska 1996 includes a translation of Questions 90–97, without the objections and responses. A critical Latin edition of *Summa Theologiae*, with the commentary of Cajetan, was published by the Leonine Commission. The Leonine edition of Aquinas' *Commentary on the Nicomachean Ethics* appeared under the direction of Gauthier; the most recent English translation is by Litzinger (1964). The best shorter biography of Aquinas is Tugwell 1988. Two more thorough biographical accounts are Torrell 1996 and Weisheipl 1983. Finnis 1998 (chap. 1) is a short but reliable biographical narrative.

There is an extensive literature on Aquinas' philosophy of law and especially his theory of natural law. Two periodicals, *The American Journal of Jurisprudence* (formerly called *Natural Law Forum*) and *Vera Lex*, have published many articles on natural law moral and political theory. Important articles on Aquinas' approach to natural law theory are by C. Ryan (1965), Hittinger (1993), and George (1992). Golding 1974 discusses the jurisprudential dimensions of Aquinas' theory. Donagan 1982 and Finnis 1998 are good accounts of the theory of action underlying Aquinas' legal philosophy. Mitsis 2003 discusses Aquinas in relation to the Stoics on virtue and natural law.

Earlier interpretations of Thomistic natural law theory are Maritain 1951, Simon 1965, and D'Entreves 1970. Sigmund 1988 contains thoughtful commentaries together with a collection of twentieth-century analyses of Aquinas on natural law. Sigmund 1993 is a useful introduction to Aquinas and political thought.

The last half of the twentieth century saw a resurgence of interest in natural law moral theory and jurisprudence in English-speaking countries. Anscombe 1958 challenges analytic philosophers to reconsider natural law theory in both Aristotle and Aquinas. MacIntyre 1984, 1988, and 1990 contain a reformula-

[28] The author is grateful to Marianne Lisska for excellent proofreading assistance.

tion of Aristotelian and Thomistic moral theory. Hart (1961) contributes to this general revival of natural law jurisprudence with his claim about the "core of good sense in natural law jurisprudence" and his discussion of natural necessities. Fuller 1964 introduced the concept of "procedural" natural law.

Two opposing approaches to natural law emerged in the latter part of the twentieth century. Veatch 1971, 1985, and 1990 defend a more traditional Aristotelian account, and McInerny 1992 and 1998 similarly offer a neo-scholastic account of natural law. This approach is defended by Lisska 1996 and Hittinger 1993. Opposed is the "new natural law theory," articulated by Finnis 1982, 1983, and 1998, drawing on the insights of Grisez (1965) who reformulated the notion of practical reason. The essays in George 1993 bring natural law theory into discussion with Rawls, Dworkin, and other American liberal theorists. George 1999 is a systematic defense of the new natural law theory with a reply to critics who favor the traditional approach. The debate between these two camps has encouraged a deeper examination of the natural law tradition and Aquinas' place in it.

Porter 1999 and Trainia 1999 bring together Aquinas' natural law theory with contemporary feminist philosophy. Dewan 2002 articulates some reservations about Porter's rendition of Aquinas.

Chapter 13

PHILOSOPHY OF LAW IN THE LATER MIDDLE AGES

by Anthony J. Lisska and Brian Tierney[1]

13.1. Roger Bacon and John Duns Scotus

This chapter has a twofold purpose. First of all, it considers the development of natural law moral theory and jurisprudence in the work of certain philosophers who followed Thomas Aquinas (ca. 1226–1274), including Roger Bacon (1214–1294), John Duns Scotus (1274–1308), John of Paris (d. 1306), Marsilius of Padua (1280–1342), and William of Ockham (1280–1347). Second, there follows an elucidation of the development of natural human rights theory. This deals with recent work in the history of human rights theory, arguing that subjective human rights have an earlier appearance in Western jurisprudence than previous scholarship suggested.

Roger Bacon, possibly the most brilliant and independent of the Franciscan philosophers of the Middle Ages, is sometimes referred to as *Doctor Mirabilis* (the "Wonderful, or Marvelous, Doctor"). Greatly interested in the rise of natural philosophy occurring at this time,[2] Bacon developed several philosophical themes that influenced his later Franciscan brothers. Bacon endorsed the primacy of theology in matters of philosophy. He argued that metaphysics should be placed under moral theory, and that moral theory was subsumed under theology. The moral philosophy of Aristotle was inadequate, and moral theory was only rendered sufficient within the context of Christian theology. Theological issues thus became directive for philosophical matters, a position later Franciscans would also find attractive to a greater or lesser degree. One theological proposition concerns Adam's Fall through original sin; Bacon believed that the Fall so impaired human understanding that genuine philosophical knowledge in the Aristotelian sense was nearly impossible to attain (Sinkler 1998, 634). His principal work, the *Opus Maius* (*The Major Work*), was an encyclopedia of science.

[1] Sections 13.1–3 and 13.5–6 were written by Anthony J. Lisska, and Section 13.4 was written by Brian Tierney. All translations are by the authors unless otherwise indicated.

[2] The important work of Moody 1975a, among others, offers original insights into the rise of science in the late-thirteenth and early-fourteenth centuries. There is some historical evidence that the condemnations in 1270 and 1277 by Bishop Stephen Tempier, the Archbishop of Paris, brought a chill to metaphysical and philosophy of religion efforts. He issued a set of prohibitions against holding certain philosophical propositions. While directed principally at various current interpretations of Aristotle, nonetheless several positions affirmed by Aquinas were included in this list. This less-than-friendly attitude toward ontological speculation forced philosophers to move toward empirical investigations of nature.

Duns Scotus is, to be sure, the most serious metaphysical philosopher of the three. Born in Scotland, Scotus, often called the *Doctor Subtilis* (the "Subtle Doctor") by historians of philosophy, exhibited such complicated arguments that most scholars agree that this appellation is by no means unmerited. Unlike Aquinas, Scotus did not write a commentary on the *Politics* of Aristotle. Scotus' ethical writings are scattered among his other works, and he appears not to have written any lasting treatises dedicated to political issues.

In Scotus' system, God's will is preeminent. The will is the source of love, and hence divine love is the important principle in Scotus' moral system. Given this, the first moral principle is that "God is to be loved" rather than "Good is to be done and evil avoided" (the latter of which Aquinas appropriated from Aristotle). The first two commandments of the Decalogue—and possibly the third commandment as well—are exemplifications of how divine love is to be followed by human persons. This is referred to by Scotus as the first tablet (*tabula*) of moral precepts. The metaphor here is the tablets on which Moses brought back the Ten Commandments from the mountaintop. Scotus argues that there is a category difference between the first three commandments on the one side of the tablet and the remaining seven, which he argues are on the second tablet. While the second tablet considers those actions that govern the actions of human beings among one another, the first tablet concerns a human person's relationship and obligations to God. These commandments on the second tablet, hence, have a different justification than do those on the first tablet.

As Scotus sees the function of natural law, the role of love or will is paramount, and the role of reason is secondary.[3] The first tablet, according to Scotus, followed necessarily from the fact that God exists. These precepts are independent of any divine command and cannot be changed or altered. The divine commandments in the second tablet are not self-evident (*per se nota*) to reason in the manner that the natural law principles of practical reason are in Aquinas' account in his *Summa Theologiae*. On the contrary, their necessity follows from the fact that God commands them. Hence, this appears to be the beginning of a late medieval theory of divine prescriptivism, which holds that the validity of a moral precept depends fundamentally on the issuance of the command by God. Scotus is concerned about how much of the Decalogue is contained within a philosophical analysis of the natural law. He offers a distinction between those commandments that pertain strictly to the natural law and those that pertain to the natural law only in an extended fashion. In *Ordinatio III* (*A Prescription III*), Scotus writes:

[3] The scholarly debate on the exact nature of voluntarism in Scotus is beyond the scope of this analysis. Nonetheless, Cross 1999, 89–95, argues that Scotus is not a divine command theorist. Williams 1998, 214, on the other hand, holds that in some sense Scotus' moral theory is rooted in the voluntarism of a divine command theory. Ingham 1993, 128, notes that "the intricate dynamic between reason and willing constitutes the core of Scotist ethics."

First of all, we deny that all the commandments of the second table pertain strictly to the law of nature. Secondly, we admit that the first two commandments belong strictly to the law of nature. Thirdly, there is some doubt about the third commandment of the first table. Fourthly, we concede that all the commandments fall under the law of nature, but speaking broadly and in an extended sense. (*Ordinatio III* dist. 44; 294)

Scotus and Aquinas differ over which precepts found in the Decalogue pertain directly to the natural law and which precepts do not. For Aquinas, unlike Scotus, all of the commandments of the Decalogue pertain necessarily to the natural law, either in a self-evident manner or through a process of derivation by practical reason. Aquinas thinks that the commandments, as moral prescriptions, follow directly from a rational analysis of the content of human nature. Scotus, however, thinks that the rational analysis common to Aquinas' rendition of moral principles is never a sufficient condition to justify the philosophical content of natural law prescriptions.

A biblical issue prompted much if not all of this discussion. Scotus understood the Old Testament texts to report occasions when God commanded persons to undertake actions directly at variance with one or more of the commandments. God's command to Abraham to offer his only son, Isaac, as a sacrifice to God, is probably the best known of these cases, although other Old Testament passages that worried medieval theologians involved the polygamy of some of the Patriarchs and the fornication of Hosea (*Ordinatio III* Suppl. dist. 37; 198–9). Given Scotus' analysis, God could grant dispensations to the commandments contained on the second tablet. In addition, those commandments prescribing moral duties and obligations to one's neighbor have obligatory or moral force only because God prescribes them. The prescriptions are not based upon any dispositional property or relation found in human nature, which differs radically from the Aristotelian analysis put forward by Aquinas in his *Summa Theologiae* (see Chapter 12, Section 12.4, of this volume). For on Aquinas' account, the moral obligations found in the second tablet are derived necessarily from human nature. Just as God could not create a human person without the set of dispositional properties found in the human essence, so too God could not create a human person for whom moral obligations based on natural law do not apply. For Aquinas, good Aristotelian that he was, a dispensation from a moral rule could occur only when the circumstances had become altered to such a degree that the commandment did not apply. Scotus, on the other hand, denies that the only case for altering a moral command would be a change of circumstances. This position would apply to the precepts subsumed under the second tablet.

The difference between Scotus and Aquinas concerning the commandments is founded on the differing role of the intellect and the role of the will in their respective positions. In the *Prima Secundae* of *Summa Theologiae*, Aquinas writes as follows about the preeminence of the intellect:

It needs to be noted that, in the acts of the soul, the act that is essentially of one potency or habit, receives the form and species from the higher potency or habit; this is so because the inferior is ordained by the superior. Now it is obvious that, in a way, reason precedes the will, and reason ordains the act of the will: namely, insofar as the will tends to its object according to the order of reason, since the apprehensive power presents the object to the appetite. Therefore, the act by which the will tends toward some object or other that is proposed as good, in that it is ordained to the end by reason, is materially an act of the will, but formally is an act of the reason. (*STh* IaIIae.13.a.1)

While the importance of this distinction between the intellectualist and the voluntarist traditions has been downplayed in recent analysis of late medieval moral theory, nonetheless it appears that it is this distinction that forces Scotus to limit inclusion of the second tablet's commandments into his theory of natural law strictly considered. Scotus writes that "the divine will, which is the primary rule of everything that is to be undertaken and of all actions, and the action of the divine will, from which is the primary or first rule for action, are the principal source of moral rectitude" (*Rep.* IV, d.46, q.4, n. 8). Ultimately, an act is right and an object is good by the very fact that God wills the act to be right or the object to be good. Scotus writes that "the divine will is the cause of good objects and therefore by the very fact that something is willed by God, that very object is good [*ipsum est bonum*]" (*Rep.* I, d.48, q.unica). Scotus appeals to *recta ratio* ("right reason"), but right reason appears to be an awareness that something is reasonable because God wills it.

As a Franciscan friar, Scotus was interested in a proper analysis of the right to property and how such rights fit in with the vow of poverty that Francis of Assisi considered important for his friars. From these writings by Scotus and others emerged a more modern position on individual rights theory. Two questions direct the analysis that Scotus provides in *Ordinatio IV*: What is the justification for a person acquiring property in the first place? How can property, once obtained, be given or transferred to another person?

Scotus developed a response to the first query in the form of six conclusions. Developing a philosophical rationale for the requirements of poverty advocated by his spiritual father, Francis of Assisi, Scotus argued that in the state of original justice, which was before the Fall of Adam and Eve, no one held any property whatsoever.[4] On this matter, Scotus writes the following to support his first conclusion: "In the state of innocence, neither divine nor natural law provided for distinct ownership of property; on the contrary, everything was common" (*Ordinatio IV*, 220). In the *Acts of the Apostles*, one reads that "no one of them claimed anything as his own; rather, all things were held in common" (Acts 4:32). Scotus puts forward his second conclusion: "Our sec-

[4] Scotus refers often in these discussions to Augustine. This illustrates a common thread in historical discussions of Franciscan philosophers that they were much taken with the philosophical and theological analyses put forward by Augustine.

ond conclusion is that after the Fall of man, this law of nature of holding all things in common was revoked" (*Ordinatio IV*, 220). Scotus then proceeds with the third conclusion: "Once this natural law precept of having all in common was revoked, and thus permission was given to appropriate and divide up what had been common, there was still no actual division imposed by either divine or natural law" (ibid., 221). He next argues that the following fourth conclusion is entailed by the third: "It would follow from this that the first division of property was brought about by some positive legislation. To see why this division was just, therefore, we must look at why such a positive law would be just" (*Ordinatio IV* dist. 15, q. 2; 221). Scotus then articulates for his fifth conclusion what we might take to be a form of a consent theory of the origin of political authority:

> Political authority, however, which is exercised over those outside [the family], whether it resides in one person or in a community, can be just by common consent and election on the part of the community [...]. [This] has to do with those who live together, even though there is no consanguinity or close relationship between them. Thus, if some outsiders banded together to build a city or live in one, seeing that they could not be well governed without some form of authority, they could have amicably agreed to commit their community to one person or to a group, and if to one person, to him alone and to a successor who would be chosen as he was, or to him and his posterity. And both of these forms of political authority are just, because one person can justly submit himself to another or to a community in those things which are not against the law of God and as regards which he can be guided better by the person or persons to whom he has submitted or subjected himself than he could by himself. Hence, we have here all that is required to pass a just law, because it would be promulgated by one who possesses prudence either in himself or in his counselors and enjoys authority in one of the several ways mentioned in this conclusion. (*Ordinatio IV* dist. 15, q. 2; 221–2)

This fifth conclusion is important in understanding Scotus' political theory and his justification for positive law. His analysis of a "just law" upholds procedural rather than substantive natural law; a law is just only if a prudent person in power exercises due authority and promulgates the ruling.[5] Scotus' sixth conclusion is: "The first division of ownership could have been just by reason of some just positive law passed by the father or the regent ruling justly or by a community ruling or regulating justly, and this is probably how it was done" (*Ordinatio IV* dist. 15, q. 2; 222).

The fifth conclusion concerning political authority expounded by Scotus is justly famous in the development of Western political theory. Harris argues:

[5] Fuller 1964 distinguishes between procedural and substantive natural law. The former indicates the process by which a law is determined and promulgated by the person in authority. Fuller lists eight "rational principles" that a ruler must follow in order to pass a just and reasonable law. Substantive natural law, on the other hand, is the claim that a law is just only if it is in accord with the moral principles determined by human nature. This is often called the requirement for a "thick" rather than a "thin" theory of human nature. Aquinas' account, discussed in Chapter 12 of this volume, is a substantive theory of natural law.

Scotus is important in the history of political science as one of the pioneers of modern social theory. His doctrines bear a strong resemblance to the later teaching of Locke. Scotus' account of the social contract is a philosophic analysis of the origin of society. Society, he held, was naturally organized into family groups; but when paternal authority was unable to enforce order, political authority was constituted by the people. Accordingly all political authority is derived from the consent of the governed. (Harris 1937, 282)

Scotus next responds to his second query, which concerns the legitimate transfer of property. In opposition to Aquinas, Scotus holds that private property is not a matter of natural law but is dependent on positive law. Transfer of property is thus reducible to someone having the proper authority to carry out such an activity. This analysis also upholds procedural natural law. Harris provides the following account of the importance of Scotus' treatment of property issues:

Concern for the public welfare is the basis of Scotus' economic doctrines. He regarded private property as a product of positive rather than natural law and insisted that property must not be administered in a way detrimental to the community. He formulated principles for the equitable employment of various commercial contracts, and while he accepted the current concept of a just price he recognized the social importance of a merchant class. (Ibid., 75)

Scotus argues that the question of happiness is determined ultimately by a divine principle. This is in opposition to the Aristotelian analysis adopted by Aquinas that happiness—*eudaimonia*—results in the fully functioning person developing the dispositional human properties. In effect, Scotus is moving beyond what he takes to be the philosophical rationalism in moral theory expounded by Aquinas; Scotus emphasizes the role of divine love and divine will. This emphasis is further developed by his Franciscan successor William of Ockham (see Sections 13.3 and 13.4 below).

13.2. John of Paris and Marsilius of Padua

Brief mention should be made of the Dominican friar John of Paris (d. 1306), who developed the concepts of his religious brother Aquinas. John of Paris can be regarded as a Dominican respondent to the early claims in the poverty debates mustered by the Franciscans.[6] It is unclear historically how any rivalry between the Dominicans and the Franciscans contributed to these sometimes heated discussions. Certainly the respective founders of these two highly regarded mendicant orders of friars in the early thirteenth century, Dominic de Guzman and Francis of Assisi, knew and respected one another. Furthermore, Aquinas and Bonaventure, while often offering differing theological positions, held academic chairs at the University of Paris and teamed together in the

[6] For an extended discussion of the importance of John of Paris in the development of political theory, see Coleman 2000, vol. 2, chap. 3.

seemingly constant battles with secularists and with the faculty of arts at Paris. Whatever the state of these intramural debates, John of Paris wrote a series of essays entitled *On Royal and Papal Power* (ca. 1302) that exerted some degree of influence in the murky political and legal situations of the time, especially those dealing with debates between the papacy and various European monarchs.

John of Paris developed what has become known as the "Dominican position" regarding matters of poverty and rights to ownership and use of property. These concepts as spelled out by John are rooted in the texts of Aquinas. In his *Summa Theologiae*, Aquinas argued that the private ownership of a modicum of material things beyond the barest necessities is part of the natural law in the present temporal circumstances. Ownership is not reducible only to a positive right as Scotus claimed. Since Aquinas adopted the theological maxim that "grace perfects nature," his analysis of the natural world was always that it is a good, especially since it results from the creative forces of an all good God. There was, for Aquinas, a "truth in things," which is called "ontological truth." This means that things correspond to divine ideas in God's mind. Since Aquinas argued that "Truth, Being, and Goodness" are convertible—that is, they are reducible to each other—he believed that the material world possesses an innate dimension of goodness because it had an innate dimension of truth and being. Given this account of the material world and its contents, it is not surprising that Aquinas would hold that it is natural for human beings to own and use a modicum of these contents and that a proper use is a reflection of the glory of divine wisdom. It is here that the Dominicans and the Franciscans parted company on the issues of the ownership and use of property.

John of Paris defended Aquinas' view on property. Like Aquinas, John argued in *On Royal and Papal Power* that the interpretation of absolute poverty defended by the Franciscans was at least muddled conceptually if not outrightly false. John based his analysis of private property on the Aristotelian theory of matter and form as the fundamental principles determining things in the external world. Simply put, matter, as the Aristotelian principle of potentiality, is brought into act by form. What is true of the natural world, John argues, also applies to the world of human labor. Hence, material elements that are potentially products of manufacture or artifacts, only become artifacts by the agency of human persons. The importance of human agency in exercising a craft—what Aquinas called an art, or "productive reason"—justifies the ownership by the craftsperson of the object produced.[7] Hence, there is a "natural" reason and justification why one attains ownership over material things in the world.

[7] Aquinas argued that practical reason is "ordained to do something" (*quae ordinatur ad opus*). This "something" is either the undertaking of an action, which is morality, or the producing of an object or artifact, which is the exercise of an art or a craft.

In the first quarter of the fourteenth century, Pope John XXII, in his battle with the Franciscans in general and William of Ockham in particular, sided with the Dominican position as articulated by John of Paris. One might surmise a bit of self-interest on the part of Pope John in his resolution of these issues. If the radical Franciscan position was correct and if a necessary condition for Christian perfection and purity was to emulate both Jesus (*imitatio Christi*) and the apostles in the renunciation of property ownership, then if the Franciscans attributed the ownership of their material goods to the pope, by definition the pope was a religious inferior.[8] It is not difficult to see why an argumentative pontiff on the papal throne, as John XXII certainly was, would disagree vehemently with the Franciscans and side with the Dominicans.

In addition, John, following Aquinas, claims that the common or public good has its source in the natural law and that human persons are, by nature, social beings. It follows, then, that living in community is prior to any common agreement among members of a community either about living together in community or in the establishment of rights and duties. Thus, for John of Paris, the role of the community and the public good, as derivable from the natural law and not dependent wholly on the positive law, are aspects of a theory of ethical naturalism (i.e., the metaethical theory holding that moral terms are reducible to some natural fact in the world), as they were for his philosophical forebears Aristotle and Aquinas.

An important legal and political theorist of the early-fourteenth century, Marsilius of Padua (1280–1342), often referred to as "Marsiglio," is best known for his *The Defender of the Peace* (*Defensor Pacis*), published in 1324. Educated both at Padua and Paris, Marsilius appears not to have been a religious cleric, although he was a canon of the Cathedral at Padua. First studying medicine, Marsilius journeyed to Paris and studied with the faculty of arts where he became interested in the pressing philosophical and theological issues connected with political problems. There is some evidence that Marsilius served briefly as rector of the University of Paris. Along with John of Jandun (1285–1328), Marsilius became a member of the court of Ludwig of Bavaria (d. 1347), who had himself crowned as the Holy Roman Emperor in direct opposition to the wishes of the Pope John XXII. Pope John was in extended conflict with both Marsilius and John of Paris, and later with William of Ockham. All three, as well as the emperor, were excommunicated. A theme that runs through the writings of Marsilius is the placing of limits on papal power; he argued that papal power is subject to and derived from the secular power rooted in the body politic.

[8] All property comes from God through the act of creation. As Vicar of Christ on earth, by default the pope is the owner of all material goods. The pope permits the Franciscans to use property. That there appears to be a conceptual problem here with the pope being Vicar of Christ yet not being able to engage fully in the imitation of Jesus taught by Francis is not to be denied.

The concrete political situation of the early-fourteenth-century Italian city-states appears to be the backdrop against which Marsilius wrote *The Defender of the Peace*. Early in this text, he writes, "the fruits of peace or tranquility, then, are the greatest goods" (*The Defender of the Peace*, *Discourse* I.1; 5). Appalled with the lack of peace and concord then extant in the city-states, Marsilius judged that papal interference contributed causally to this political unrest. Hence, his disquisition is a bold attempt to place limits on what he perceived to be the theoretical and practical excesses of papal sovereignty.[9] It is highly probable that Marsilius deemed the structure of republican Rome to be the best of all possible political worlds, and his theory was an attempt to resurrect these ideals from what he perceived to be the muddled sea of scholastic church/state relations. Skinner (1978, 56) notes that for Marsilius, among others, "the attainment of peace and concord, *pax et concordia*, represents the highest value in political life."

The Defender of the Peace, which some critics suggest is a forerunner of the Protestant reformation, exhibits strong Aristotelian influences. Marsilius no doubt studied Aristotle's work while he was a Paris student; he quotes Aristotle's *Politics* extensively and much of the early sections of *The Defender of the Peace* reads like an Aristotelian commentary. William of Moerbeke translated Aristotle's *Nicomachean Ethics* and *Politics* in the 1260s; both treatises were well-known in Western university circles, and the Aristotelian passages in Marsilius' text are from Moerbeke. Referring to Aristotle's *Politics*, Marsilius discusses three forms of government: knightly monarchy, aristocracy, and the polity or city-state (*The Defender of the Peace*, I.8; 28). Marsilius, who appears worried about the Augustinian theory about the role of the church in state affairs, most notably present in Augustine's *City of God*, attempts to dissociate and redirect the Aristotelian concept of polity from any dependence on ecclesiastical control or influence. He does this through placing the legislative power for governing bodies directly in the hands of the people, which is an early account of a theory of "popular sovereignty." Marsilius notes that the issues of papal sovereignty were not part of Aristotle's political purview, and hence an expanded political theory derived from Aristotle was necessary.

The Defender of the Peace is divided into three sections or "discourses." The first discourse, based on Aristotle with a passing glance at Cicero, is a somewhat diffuse account of political sovereignty resting in the members of the polity, which included the male citizens. Using insights from Aristotle and Cicero, Marsilius argues that the state is a perfect polity that exists for the common good of its citizens. The ruler is in charge only by the authority of the body politic. The second discourse, based principally on the scriptures and the writings of the church fathers, is a bold exposition of a theory of ecclesiastical

[9] Skinner 1990, 401, writes that Marsilius discussed this negative critique of papal power "with a boldness that won him instant excommunication and lasting notoriety."

power that is derived from the will of the people. Here Marsilius argues for a conciliar theory of papal rule with the power vested in the members of the church polity. Yet it is derived ultimately from the civil authority. Marsilius, by using New Testament passages like "My kingdom is not of this world," and "Render to Caesar the things that are Caesar's, and to God the things that are God's," and Paul's claim that "[n]o soldier of God entangles himself with secular affairs," argues that the person on the papal throne ought not be a temporal ruler but only a spiritual ruler. The church, while necessary for morals and education, should be under the secular ruler, who is in power through the will of the people. Of course, this account is directly opposed to the strong popes of the thirteenth century. The third discourse, which is a list of forty-two propositions, is a concise summary of the positions articulated in the first two discourses. The 1327 papal bull of John XXII condemned outright five of these propositions as heretical and referred to Marsilius as a "son of perdition."

In Chapter 10 of the first discourse, Marsilius defines law as "an ordinance made by political prudence, concerning matters of justice and benefit and their opposites, and having 'coercive force'" (*The Defender of the Peace*, I.10.36). Hence, a law requires a command conjoined with a sanction. However, right reason and justice are also necessary conditions for law, so this is not a reductionist version of legal positivism. (Reductionism entails that a term or proposition can be placed into a prior category on which it ultimately depends. Legal positivism is the theory that all law is fundamentally the articulation of commands by the person in power, who has the force or sanction to enforce the imperative.) Furthermore, "the human authority to make laws belongs to the whole body of the citizens or to the weightier part thereof" (ibid., 46).

Marsilius' "extraordinary tract" (Coleman 2000, vol. 2: 134) indeed exerted significant influence on late medieval and renaissance political theory. For example, Thomas Cromwell (1485–1540) supported the translation into English (1535) of Marsilius' treatise during Henry VIII's squabbles with Rome on church-state issues. Yet scholarly debate is vibrant on the exact nature of that influence, with interpretations ranging from ultramontane criticisms found in early-twentieth-century Roman Catholic writers to secular theorists suggesting that republican democracy and modern constitutionalism are rooted in this treatise. While the accounts rendered by several reformation theologians are structurally similar to Marsilius' work, nonetheless it is another question articulating the direct causal influence.

Marsilius of Padua's treatise certainly indicates that the late middle ages were more diverse theoretically than the typical "age of faith" label suggests. Here is found a treatise directly arguing for limited papal power derived from the popular sovereignty of the people. This is a far cry from the papal supremacy model that was articulated by several popes of the thirteenth century and reaffirmed in the mid-nineteenth century by Pius IX with his closely scripted First Vatican Council.

13.3. William of Ockham on Law

William of Ockham was born in Surrey in the last decade of the thirteenth century. Like Scotus, he entered the Franciscan order and eventually studied at Oxford. Much of his life was not that of the tranquil scholar. Involved in an ecclesiastical skirmish with Pope John XXII, Ockham fled to Germany and eventually was subjected to the censure of excommunication. Legend has it that he suffered and died in 1349 from the plague that ravaged Western Europe in the middle of the fourteenth century.

In the history of philosophy, Ockham traditionally is portrayed as a fourteenth-century empiricist and nominalist. Empiricism is the view in epistemology asserting that all knowledge is based on sense experience. Nominalism denies the possibility of essential properties or natural kinds existing outside the human mind. Some historians have even suggested that Ockham was fundamentally a late medieval precursor of the empiricist philosopher David Hume (e.g., Moody 1975b, 419). Recent scholarship has tempered this more radical interpretation of Ockham's role in the history of philosophy.

Ockham appears to have worried that the incorporation of Aristotelian metaphysics into Christian theology in the manner articulated and defended by Aquinas created theological impurities and conceptual muddles. According to Ockham, this Aristotelianism limits two claims that are important for Ockham's theology: divine freedom and divine omnipotence. Given Ockham's empiricist worries about rationalist metaphysics, he disregarded an Aristotelian theory of natural kinds. He also appears to have rejected the classical theory of divine ideas, which asserts that the ideas in the divine mind are archetypes, after which the essences of individual things in the created world are patterned or copied. Hence, it is no surprise that Ockham's development of natural law theory, with no natural kind theory and no account of divine ideas, would be in some rudimentary sense "command based" as opposed to "reason based." The concept of right reason functions differently in Ockham's moral and political theory than it did in Aquinas'. While appropriating a form of right reason, nonetheless Ockham adopts a divine prescriptivism in which the ultimate philosophical justification for a moral prescription is that God wills the action. A form of voluntarism thus takes hold in Ockham's philosophy. Human dignity, for instance, is based on the ability of a human person to be a free agent. The justification that "Act *x* is right" is dependent foundationally on the fact that God so wills this to be the case. (For Aquinas, in contrast, "Act *x* is right" because it is in accord with human nature.) In *Reportatio*,[10] Ockham writes, "By the very fact that God wills something, it is right for it to be done" (IV.q.9.E–F). While one can find such examples of the role of the will in early medi-

[10] *Reportatio* is a written record by persons who attended the lectures that Ockham gave on the last three books of the *Sentences* of Peter Lombard.

eval philosophy, especially the work of Augustine, nonetheless it is in Ockham where divine voluntarism becomes significant.

Ockham does not accept the account put forward by Aquinas that God's commandments must be in accord with human nature as established in the divine idea of the human essence. Ockham argues: "Obligation does not fall on God, since God is not under any obligation to do anything" (*Rep.* III.q.5.H). In some ways, Ockham appears to be a modified legal positivist in his theory of morality and law, and he is willing to extend this voluntarism. He notes, in opposition even to Scotus, that God could command a human person to hate him. The present moral order is dependent ultimately on the will of God. Hence, God could have, had he so chosen, promulgated a different set of commandments. As Copleston once noted, Ockham, in placing emphasis on a divine command theory, preserved two key theological claims:

> Ockham was not concerned with promoting disbelief in the moral law; he was concerned with [1] exalting the divine freedom and omnipotence and [2] drawing what he considered to be logical consequences of the divine omnipotence. (Copleston 1961, 133)

It is important to lay bare how Ockham develops the "logical consequences of the divine omnipotence." While it is problematic to argue that Ockham's position on divine command theory is reducible to Justinian's classic formulation of legal positivism as found in his *Institutes*—"What pleases the prince has the force of law" (1.2.6)—nonetheless, the exact role that the divine will plays in this theory requires detailed elucidation.

One perspicuous way to delineate the difference between Aquinas and Ockham on the issue of God's role in determining moral maxims is to consider the question that Socrates put to Euthyphro: Is something good because the gods love it, or do the gods love it because it is good? That is, does the act of divine love—or divine willing—entail that an act is right, or is the act right because it corresponds to another standard that determines the goodness or rightness of the act?[11] Ockham endorses the first half of the disjunct, while Aquinas accepts the second half. For Aquinas, then, an act is right and can be the prescriptive content of a divine command because it is in accord with the content of human nature existing in the mind of God as a divine idea. For Ockham, to the contrary, the very act of God commanding renders the

[11] This is what Veatch and Rautenberg 1991, 828, often call the "Euthyphro Principle." They use this methodological principle to determine whether a philosopher argues for a strong sense of natural law based on a "thick" theory of human nature or a weaker sense of natural law based on either a good-reasons account or a noncognitivist position. A good-reasons account attempts to justify a moral argument by means of consistency of propositions. There is not an attempt to ground the argument in any fact of reality. A noncognitivist position, for example, emotivism, holds that a moral claim is nothing more than the expression of an emotion in what might be considered a moral situation; as such, these sorts of claims have no truth value.

act right. Aquinas' account is based upon a realist ontology of essences, while Ockham's account is consistent with a nominalist denial of essential properties. This is one ontological difference between a voluntarist and an intellectualist. An intellectualist also holds that the use of reason plays the predominant role, while a voluntarist holds that the will has precedence over reason. It appears that for Ockham the possibility of deriving a moral theory based sufficiently on ethical naturalism, and thus divorced from theological propositions, is beyond the pale of human reason. However, in his *Commentary on the Sentences*, Ockham writes: "By the very fact that the divine will commands this, right reason says that it is to be willed (by human persons)" (*In I Sent.* d.41, q.1.K). He further writes that "every will is right through its conformity with right reason." Of course, the question demanding a response is "How does one offer an analysis of 'right reason' in passages like this one in the texts of Ockham?"

Recent discussion on the political theory and the natural rights theory of William of Ockham draws attention to the role of "right reason" in Ockham's elucidation of the foundation of moral theory and a theory of rights (Tierney 1997; see also Section 13.4 below for further discussion). The argument suggests that the use of right reason by Ockham tempers what earlier scholars had understood as the radical voluntarism attributed to Ockham's foundation for moral theory. Hence, recent scholarship indicates that Ockham was not the extreme voluntarist that several twentieth-century historians of philosophy have suggested (including Copleston 1974, 253; Bourke 1968, 104–95; Maurer 1962, 285–6). In the passage from the *Commentary on the Sentences* noted above, Ockham argues that right reason is determined when the intellect understands what God wills. This would differ from Aquinas, who argued that reason is right only when it knows the essential properties of things in the world.[12] Attempts to understand the role that right reason plays in Ockham's account of moral theory need to take into account how Ockham differs from Aquinas in this regard. Even with this account of right reason, it appears that voluntarism is still paramount in Ockham's analysis.[13]

There are several difficult issues involved in Ockham's interpretation of natural law: the role of right reason, the role of the will, the role of human nature or human essence, and the role of final cause in a human essence. All of these issues are conflated in most discussions of Ockham on natural law. As we have seen, Ockham differs from Aquinas in that Ockham offers a limited use

[12] This is what Aquinas means by truth—a correspondence of idea and thing. In *Summa Theologiae*, Aquinas discusses the concept of truth in the following way: "Truth is defined by the conformity [*adequatio*] of mind and thing. Thus, to know this conformity is to know truth" (*STh* Ia.16.a.4).

[13] Adams 1999 may be the best overall account of both recent work and more traditional analyses on the relation between nature and moral theory in Ockham. In the end, Adams indicates how the role of the will is central to Ockham's analysis of moral and political theory.

of right reason. He posits the will as an unlimited power that leads to what Adams calls a "liberty of indifference," which she describes as "[t]he notion that created willpower is power to will, to nill, or to do nothing with respect to any object" (Adams 1999, 262 and 245). He has a nominalist analysis of human nature and dismisses a role for final cause—that is, that there is a natural end that determines proper function—in his account of human nature. In contemporary philosophy, Ockham's use of right reason is at least analogous to if not coextensive with what twentieth-century philosophers called "a good-reasons" theory of moral justification.[14] With the good-reasons philosophers, what is required is consistency of application and not reference to natural kind properties external to the mind.[15]

The will is prominent in Ockham's theory. He rejects Aquinas' intellectualist position because he thinks that that position limits the will and subjects willing to the requirements of the intellect. In Aquinas' moral theory, both the practical reason and the will are inclined "naturally" to the good. The first principle of practical reason for Aquinas is "Good is to be done and pursued and evil avoided" (*STh* IaIIae.94.a.2). The will is a rational appetite that always undertakes actions under the guise of what is good, and this cognitive content depends on both speculative and practical reason. Ockham denies that such limits can be placed upon the will by reason (see Adams 1999).[16]

Ockham's view of law, while part of the natural law tradition, differs from that proposed by Aquinas, who adopted a stronger version of Aristotelian naturalism. Ockham's emphasis on voluntarism together with right reason develops a less stringent voluntarism than what many critics once attributed to him. Nonetheless, like Bacon before him, Ockham had theological concerns that directed his philosophical engagement. Ockham's disputes over the nature of the Franciscan vow of poverty that led to his work served as a harbinger of

[14] Coleman (2000, vol. 2: 190) writes, "Ockham's emphasis on rationally guided choice is central to what has come to be called his voluntarism [...]. Right reason is an integral requirement of virtue and hence agents must intend to aim at what is most objectively rational." However, "what is most objectively rational" is similar structurally to the concept of rational consistency proposed on a good-reasons theory; it is not the right reason of an essentialist natural law position.

[15] McInerny 1998 calls this sort of theory "natural law theory without nature," where "nature" refers to a dispositional account of human essence.

[16] For a discussion of the limitations of such a strongly voluntarist good-reasons theory, see Lisska 1996, chap. 3, and Veatch 1985. Warnock 1967 offers an analysis of the good-reasons approach: Cruelty is not wrong because it is wrong, but because we decide that it is wrong. Warnock objects to this approach and writes: "[N]ot only [...] [does the good-reasons approach hold that it is] for us to decide what our moral opinions are, but also that it is for us to decide what to take as grounds for or against any moral opinion. We are not only, as it were, free to decide on the evidence, but also free to decide what evidence is" (Warnock 1967, 47). Warnock's objection to the good-reasons approach is that it has no referent to reality on which to ground a moral judgment. It is unclear whether Ockham ever gets beyond Warnock's objection.

the important subjective theory of human rights, which will be discussed in the following section.

13.4. Ockham and Natural Rights[17]

William of Ockham had an unusual career. As a young scholar and teacher he was a brilliantly innovative philosopher and theologian, but he devoted the whole latter part of his life to writing on issues of law and political thought. In his philosophical teaching Ockham was a nominalist and a voluntarist. He held that, in the external world, nothing actually existed except individual entities; the general terms that humans apply to collections of like objects were only mental constructs. As a voluntarist Ockham emphasized the absolute freedom and omnipotent will of God, as well as human free will. His characteristic teaching was that the whole universe, including the universe of moral values, existed as it did simply because God willed that it be so. Everything was contingent. If God had so willed, he could have created some other world in which it would be virtuous to steal and lie. These considerations did not, however, lead Ockham to a skeptical or relativist theory of morality. Precisely because the human will could choose good or evil it needed a directing rule to guide it; this rule, Ockham held, was right reason. As a Christian and a Franciscan Ockham knew that God loved this world that he had chosen to make and that he willed the good of humanity. Ockham thought that right reason, reflecting on human experience, could discern moral norms in accordance with that end.

A major problem in addressing Ockham's work is to determine the relationship between his abstract philosophical positions and his practical political conclusions. Scholars have never agreed about this. Some hold that Ockham's later writing was essentially an extrapolation into the political sphere of his underlying philosophical premises; others see little significant relationship between the two sides of Ockham's thought. Arguing for the former view, Villey (1975, 199–272, especially 228, 261) emphasizes Ockham's teaching on natural rights. He maintains that Ockham instituted a semantic revolution when he defined the word *ius* as a subjective right, that is, as a power or faculty inhering in individual persons. Villey also maintains that metaphysics always precedes jurisprudence, so that Ockham's nominalist philosophy naturally led on to an individualistic theory of law and politics.

Villey's argument is appealing but it is open to various objections. Some critics have argued that in principle political conclusions cannot be derived from metaphysical premises (Zuckerman 1973). Indeed, it is quite possible to start out from nominalist and voluntarist premises and arrive at political con-

[17] The views of Ockham considered in this section are discussed more fully, with detailed references to the relevant texts in Ockham's works, in Tierney 1997.

clusions quite different from those of Ockham, as Thomas Hobbes (1588–1679) did centuries later. Ockham himself did not appeal to his philosophical doctrines in his political writings, but relied almost entirely on citations of scripture and canon law. Moreover, recent research has shown that the understanding of *ius* as a subjective faculty or power was quite common in earlier canonistic writings. It remains true, though, that the individualist strain in Ockham's political writings was entirely congruent with his philosophical principles even if not formally derived from them; in considering his work, it is one mind we have to deal with rather than two. Still, it seems clear that the actual content of Ockham's juridical and political thought was shaped primarily by the circumstances of the controversies in which he became involved.

Ockham's involvement in church politics came about as follows. In 1324 he was summoned from Oxford to the papal curia, then resident at Avignon, and there was accused of various doctrinal errors. While Ockham was in Avignon a bitter dispute broke out between Pope John XXII and the leaders of Ockham's Franciscan order. The Franciscans claimed that they lived—and should live—in absolute poverty, having renounced all ownership and all right of use related to material property; whatever they used they held by permission or license of an owner, not by any right of their own. Moreover, the friars claimed that, in living like this, they were faithfully imitating the perfect evangelical way of life instituted by Christ and the first apostles. Pope John XXII apparently found this doctrine subversive. He denounced the Franciscan position in a series of bulls, and in 1323 promulgated a formal dogmatic decree stating that henceforth it would be heretical to maintain that Christ and the apostles had nothing or that they had no rights in the things that they did have (*Corpus Iuris Canonici* 2: col. 1229). The pope's language ensured that the concept of a right would be at the center of the subsequent dispute.

Eventually nearly all the Franciscans reluctantly accepted the pope's decrees, but the minister-general of the order, Michael of Cesena, and a small group of adherents including Ockham, refused to do so. In 1328 they escaped from Avignon, denounced John XXII as a heretic, and took refuge at the court of the emperor Ludwig of Bavaria. Ludwig had his own quarrel with the pope and he welcomed the dissident Franciscans as allies.[18]

One of John XXII's arguments against the Franciscans asserted that there could be no licit use of anything without a right of using; to use without a right was simply to use unjustly. Ockham first employed the concept of a natural right in responding to this argument. His counterargument turned on a distinction between positive and natural rights. The kind of right that the friars had given up, Ockham argued, was every positive or legal right, every right for which one could sue in court. But, Ockham continued, there also existed an

[18] Ludwig was elected by a majority of the German princes, but the pope refused to recognize the election as valid and excommunicated Ludwig in 1324.

inalienable natural right of using things. No one, not even a Franciscan, could renounce this right; to do so would be tantamount to suicide, since the use of things was necessary to sustain life. According to Ockham, this natural right justified the Franciscan use of property without any ownership or legal right of use. "The Friars Minor have no positive right," Ockham writes, "but they do have a right, namely a natural right" (*Opera Politica*, vol. 2: 561).

To explain this further, Ockham turned to an old doctrine of the canonists. They had held that by natural law all things were common and that the natural right grounded in this natural law could still be exercised in case of extreme necessity. Ockham, however, had to explain how the friars could avail themselves of a natural right in their day-to-day living when they were not in a state of extreme need, so he added a refinement of his own. The natural right of common use could not be wholly abolished, he noted, but its exercise had been restricted by the human laws instituting private property; the ownership of property by one person was an impediment to its use by another. But, if an owner granted to another a license or permission to use his property, the impediment was removed. The license did not confer any new right; it merely allowed the exercise of a pre-existing natural right. And so, Ockham concluded, the friars could use property by natural right even outside the case of extreme necessity (*Opera Politica*, vol. 2: 578).

Ockham introduced the idea of a natural right into his work essentially as a debating tactic to respond to an argument of John XXII. But, as his work broadened into a more general critique of papal power, he evidently realized that the idea could have much broader implications. In his later works Ockham, like John Locke (1632–1704) in a later age, persistently used the idea of natural rights to attack the doctrine of divine right absolutism, though in Ockham's case it was papal absolutism rather than royal absolutism that was combated.

Ockham was especially concerned to refute the arguments of extreme papalist theologians who held that all *dominium*, that is, all rightful rulership and all rights of ownership, were derived from the pope as vicar of God. Ockham's response to such claims is set out most clearly and succinctly in a work appropriately called *A Short Discourse*, which begins with a robust assertion that the abuse of papal power is a threat to "the rights and liberties given by God and nature" (*A Short Discourse*, 3). Ockham goes on to argue that licit government and rights of property are not derived from the pope but from human reason. He explains that the power initially given by God to the human race in the person of Adam should be understood as "the power [...] that reason pronounces to be necessary, expedient, fit, or useful, not only for living but for living well" (ibid., 90). But, Ockham continues, right reason shows that among fallen men the institutions of private property and government are necessary for living well. Accordingly, individual property was instituted by human laws, and imperial power was established "through men voluntarily subjecting themselves to an emperor" (ibid., 91, 93, 117). Such power does not come from the pope. It follows that rulers and others have rights that the pope is bound to respect.

Extreme papalists held that the pope's power was limited only by the express commands of divine and natural law. (Even they agreed that the pope could not command someone to commit adultery, incest, or murder.) But Ockham attacked this view. He holds that papal power is also limited by the rights of the faithful. In arguing for this, Ockham develops a novel synthesis of the old idea of Christian liberty with a canonistic doctrine asserting that no one can be deprived of a right "without fault or cause." He quotes the teaching of St. James that the law of the gospel is "a law of perfect liberty," and the words of St. Paul that "[w]here the spirit of the Lord is, there is freedom." But, Ockham argues, if the pope has the power to do anything not expressly forbidden by divine and natural law the Christian people will be reduced to a state of horrendous servitude, for this is exactly the kind of power that a master has over a slave. The pope would be able to deprive kings of their power and take others' goods just as a master can take anything from his slave—and all this without fault or cause. But this is absurd, Ockham insists (ibid., 22–4). Papal power was given for the common good, not for the pope's own advantage (ibid., 26). The pope can do anything necessary to sustain the faith or the common good, but only while "saving the rights and liberties of others" (ibid., 62).

In another argument, Ockham emphasizes the liberties granted by God and nature. He has in mind here the freedom to choose a way of life, for example, to take a vow of virginity, enter a religious order, or undertake a fast. Such decisions were certainly not contrary to divine or natural law, but the pope had no power to command such things; they had to be undertaken freely (ibid., 54–5). Ockham is concerned here to defend a right understood as a sphere of individual moral autonomy, which is outside the scope of government control.

Ockham was primarily concerned to attack papal tyranny and defend the rights of the emperor, but he did note that imperial power also has limitations. Commenting on a famous text of Roman law asserting that what pleased the emperor had the force of law, Ockham explains that it should be understood to mean what pleased him "reasonably and justly and for the common good" (*Dialogus in Monarchia S. Romani Imperii*, 2: 924). Ockham often mentions the common good alongside his emphasis on natural rights. He does not regard the two things as normally opposed to one another; rather, he holds that the private good of each individual redounds to the common good of all (ibid.). Ockham acknowledges that in case of urgent necessity or extreme peril the common good might override private rights. But even here there is a final reservation. If the ruler's command is just and useful it is to be obeyed; if it is unjust and useless it is to be resisted. In the last resort, it is left to the individual conscience to resist or obey (*Opera Politica*, vol. 1: 152).

Ockham's ideas exercised a continuing influence—often unacknowledged—in the ensuing centuries. McGrade (1982, 745) observes that, if a history of political Ockhamism could be written, it would include "Peter of Ailly and John Gerson in the fifteenth century, James Almain and John Major in the sixteenth, and very likely a chapter on Locke."

13.5. The Beginning Stages of Absolutism

In the fourteenth century, there arose a tendency to appeal to the insights of earlier natural law theory in order to justify what might be called "royal absolutism." Accordingly, some of the issues central to jurisprudence became part of the discussions concerning political power. A new group of legal thinkers known as "the commentators" emerged on the scene (Zane 1998, 198). These students of the law began writing comments on legal problems rather than limiting themselves to the theoretical questions regarding the justification of law. In particular, the commentators attempted to resolve legal difficulties that arose in the emerging city-states, where local laws often were not consistent with one another across territorial boundaries.

Bartolus of Sassoferrato (1314–1357) was "the great man of this school of Commentators" (Zane 1998, 199). Writing in the context of the Italian city-states, Bartolus asserted rather boldly that the ruler is not obliged to follow the ordinary laws of the nation or the city-state. Nonetheless, it is "equitable" for the ruler to abide voluntarily by the dictates of the positive law. Despite this qualifier, it appears that Bartolus put the ruler on a pedestal beyond the requirements of the legal system. This appears to be a harbinger of the later legal positivist theory of jurisprudence. Bartolus argued that members of a community can formulate written laws; this makes the state itself a sovereign, and the state itself is in some way reducible to the sovereign himself (*civitas sibi princeps*).

Some historians of political theory claim that Bartolus developed a modern concept of property rights, though others argue against this interpretation (e.g., Brett 1997, 22).[19] Bartolus also discussed issues common to natural right (*ius naturale*) and the law of nations (*ius gentium*), and argued that natural right was common to all animals. Since only rational beings can be morally obligated and nonhuman animals lack rationality, natural right could not be the source of or justification for a theory of obligation. Next, Bartolus divided the law of nations into two categories:

[19] Brett 1997, 204, argues, however, that Bartolus importantly influenced later philosophers of law, especially the Spanish jurist Fernando Vazquez (b. 1512); Vazquez argues for an original absolute natural liberty. In fact, Vazquez argues that *dominium* is "a natural faculty [*naturalis facultas*] that permits someone to do something, unless this action is prohibited through force or by law" (Tuck 1979, 51).

It should be known that the *ius gentium* is two-fold. The first category comes through natural reason, without any agreement, such as that a free person should keep faith or promises, etc. And under this primitive *ius gentium* the free status of a slave was not destroyed, indeed all men were free [...]. The other *ius gentium* was what all *gentes* used by agreement, not following natural reason [...] such as wars, imprisonment, servitude and distinct *dominium*. (Tuck 1979, 35, n. 5)

Bartolus' account of rights contained the seeds of a theory of absolute liberty, which the Spanish Dominicans of early modern scholasticism would develop (see Chapter 14 of this volume).

Another political theorist in this era of early absolutism is Lucas de Penna (1320–1390). Lucas claimed that the justification for any prince's rule was founded upon divine authority. It follows, so Lucas suggests in his *Corpus Iuris*, that the ruler answers only to God. The members of the community have no recourse to the legal utterances of the person in power. Whatever law might be, its foundation is not reducible to the will of the persons in the society, however such a general will might be construed. This legal theory appears to be a form of divine prescriptivism, yet the ruler in turn appears to have a privileged awareness of what counts for the divine law. An unjust law is one that goes contrary to the divine law, and its obligatory force is thus removed. It is unclear how any rationally determined set of moral concepts could apply to a set of rules, although such language appears in the discussions.

The seeds of what later developed as legal positivism, especially in the writings of Jean Bodin (1530–1596) and John Austin (1790–1859), seem all too apparent in these discussions by the royal absolutists of the fourteenth century. In his *Six Books of the Commonwealth*, Bodin writes that the "law is nothing else than the command of the sovereign in his exercise of sovereign power" (I.5). Austin (1832, V note) is famous for his claim that "the law is one thing; its merit or demerit is another." Both Bodin and Austin adopt a form of command theory of law, which is rooted in the voluntarism first articulated by Ockham in the early-fourteenth century. This Bodin-Austin position is rightly characterized as one of "unlimited sovereignty" of the law. The philosophical problems common to legal positivism would apply equally, it would seem, to these theories of royal absolutism.

13.6. Conclusion

Several changes occur in natural law theory during this period, which contrast with natural law as articulated by Aquinas. First, there is the emergence of a strong voluntarist tradition, especially in the writings of the Franciscan philosophers. Scotus and Ockham, to varying degrees, insist that in understanding the human condition, the will must be considered as superior to the intellect. Beginning with Bacon, there is less optimism about determining the content of human nature on which a theory of natural law might be constructed. This was also applied to a human understanding, as far as possible, of God. God was now seen as above all limits. Ockham's "liberty of indifference" begins to play a pivotal role here. The will is determined by nothing outside of itself, especially not by the intellect. Hence, at an ultimate level of explanation, the divine will becomes paramount. The fourteenth century witnessed the rise of absolutism with Bartolus' and Lucas' further emphasis on the role of the will, thus extending the voluntarist tradition. This voluntarism is again emphasized in the early-nineteenth century with the rise of legal positivism in the writings of legal theorists such as John Austin (see Volume 8, Chapter 6 of this Treatise for further discussion).

Ockham and Aquinas differ also over the nature of society and the person's place in society. For Aquinas, following Aristotle, human beings are by nature social beings; hence, the development of social forms of community is a natural occurrence among humans. For Ockham, to the contrary, the need for a society and its corresponding rules began only after the Fall of Adam with original sin. Hence, prior to the Fall there was no need for human society. The same holds for private property. John of Paris, following Aquinas, argued that private property is fundamental for humans working in the world. Ockham, on the other hand, held that private property came about only after the Fall under the auspices of positive law. Where Aquinas attributed moral traits to human nature as human nature, Ockham distinguished human persons prior to the Fall from how they existed following original sin.

The groundbreaking work of Tierney on the role of the origin of subjective human rights, especially in the writings of Ockham, has influenced a general reconsideration of the history of rights theory. Ockham's analytic consideration of the right to property sets the stage for the development of what came to be known as subjective human rights. This subjective human right, which is a power or ability possessed by a human person, goes beyond Aquinas' view of right as the "just thing."

In the sixteenth century, the role of the intellectualist tradition received a revived stimulus with the advent of early modern Scholasticism with the Dominican and Jesuit jurisprudence writers at Salamanca. The intellectualist tradition rooted in Aquinas has seen a renewed interest in the twentieth century with the writings of John Finnis. The intellectualist tradition of the late-thirteenth century and the voluntarist tradition of the early-fourteenth century have clearly influenced later developments in the history of jurisprudence.

Like Joseph's coat of many colors, the theory of natural law found in the writings of philosophers in the Middle Ages is far from a seamless web. Nonetheless, the importance of reason, the discussion of the human good, the centrality of the human person and human needs, and the development of a theory of human rights all suggest the importance of these philosophers and their arguments in coming to terms with the history of jurisprudence.

Further Reading

Coleman 2000, vol. 2, provides an excellent introduction to political thought from the Middle Ages to the Renaissance. Following an overview of medieval political ideas and medieval society, she has valuable chapters on Aquinas, John of Paris, Marsilius of Padua, and Ockham, concluding with a chapter discussion of the Italian Renaissance, arguing for the dependence of Machiavelli on his medieval predecessors. Canning 1996 is another valuable introduction of medieval political thought. Black 1992 also surveys political thought from 1250 to 1450. Kretzmann, Kenny, and Pinborg 1982 contains essays by leading scholars on the entire period, some of which focus on political and legal philosophy. A companion volume by McGrade, Kilcullen, and Kempshall 2001 provides excellent translations of important texts by philosophers of the thirteenth and fourteenth centuries. Burns 1988 also contains valuable material, including several chapters devoted to legal issues. Tierney 1955 is an informative account of the relationship between canon law and the conciliar movement. Tierney 1982 is also a valuable discussion of legal and constitutional thought from 1150 to 1650.

Excellent collections of translations of and commentary of Duns Scotus include those of Wolter (1975; 1987 and 1997). The recent work by Cross 1999 is a readable introduction to Scotus. Cross 1998 also offers a sustained analysis of Scotus' physics and metaphysics. Lee 1982, 1985, and 1997 provide comparative analyses of moral theory in Aquinas and Scotus. Wolter (1993) was special editor of an issue of *American Catholic Philosophical Quarterly* devoted to Scotus.

The translation of Marsilius of Padua's *Defender of the Peace* (*Defensor Pacis*) by Gewirth along with a critical introduction, helped to reestablish Marsilius as a major political and legal thinker. Nederman 1995 is a valuable study of Marsilius' secular political theory.

Ockham's *Letter to the Friars Minor* and other political writings are translated by McGrade and Kilcullen. Boehner 1958 is a collection of essays on Ockham by a premier twentieth-century scholar, while Adams 1987 may be the best recent general study of Ockham. Spade 1999 is a valuable collection of essays on Ockham, including essays by Adams, McGrade, and Kilcullen dealing with Ockham's moral and political theory and the tensions between intellectualism and voluntarism. McGrade 1974 is a good introduction to Ockham's political and legal theory. On Ockham's political theory, Coleman 2000 is always instructive; her extensive writings (cited in her bibliography) on Ockham and the development of rights theory are also very illuminating. On Ockham and the study of the origin and development of subjective natural rights theory, Tierney 1997 is an exceptional study of the development of natural rights, especially the discussion on Ockham; Tierney also questions whether Ockham was a radical voluntarist. Pennington 1998 offers a reflective account of Tierney's work. Brett 1997 is a compendious study of the evolution of rights theory in the late Middle Ages; in addition to her discussion of Scotus and Ockham, Brett's analysis of fifteenth-century Thomism, especially the early modern scholasticism at Salamanca, is informative and useful. Tuck 1979 is an earlier work that is a wide-ranging and readable discussion of issues in the development of rights theory. Skinner 1990 is a thorough discussion of this period of political philosophy and rights theory. Schmitt and Skinner 1990 is a general collection of essays on Renaissance philosophy from 1400 onward.

Chapter 14

LATER SCHOLASTIC PHILOSOPHY OF LAW

by Annabel Brett[1]

14.1. Introduction

In this chapter we are concerned with the movement known, in its initial phase, as the "School of Salamanca" after the university initially at its center, and subsequently more broadly as the "second scholastic" in recognition of its spread beyond the University of Salamanca to cover the entirety of Counter-Reformation Europe and the new universities of the Spanish dominions in the New World. Chronologically, it extends from the second decade of the sixteenth century to about the third quarter of the seventeenth.[2] The term "second" refers to the perceived re-foundation of scholastic theology in the wake of the Reformation, a "renewal" based on the works of Thomas Aquinas (ca. 1226–1274) after the prevalence, in the later medieval period, of nominalist and Scotist approaches that followed the work of William of Ockham (1280–1347) and Johannes Duns Scotus (1274–1347), respectively. These traditional historiographical characterizations are not entirely apt, though. More recent scholarship shows how much continuity there was between pre- and post-Reformation scholasticism, and questions the trope of the "decadence" of late-medieval nominalism which dominates the literature on these thinkers from the first half of the twentieth century as well as the degree of their allegiance to the teachings of Aquinas. Nevertheless, there is no doubt that, in self-understanding and literary production, sixteenth- and seventeenth-century scholastic theologians differed from their predecessors, and that the adoption of Aquinas's works—especially, the *Summa Theologiae*—as the central point of reference was a key aspect of this difference. This of itself pushed the question of law into the foreground, given Aquinas's extensive treatment of law in the *Prima Secundae* of the *Summa*, but there are also contextual factors explaining both the turn to Aquinas and the interest in the subject of law.

The early sixteenth century was a ferment of new intellectual movements and ideas. For at least a century, humanism had been challenging scholastic practices of education and scholarship with its alternative pedagogy centered around mastery of the classical languages and literature, and the related studies

[1] All translations are by the author unless otherwise indicated.

[2] There are interesting developments within eighteenth-century scholasticism, but the political circumstances had dramatically changed and so had the intellectual challenges that generated the particular movement with which we are concerned, to be replaced by new ones demanding a different response.

of philology, rhetoric, and history. In the figure, especially, of Desiderius Erasmus (1466–1536), humanist scholarship began to have an impact on the traditionally scholastic study of theology. Erasmus used his philology to publish, in 1516, a new translation of the New Testament from the Greek, challenging the authority of the Vulgate version sanctioned by the Church. He also argued for a more interior understanding of spirituality, apparently reducing the importance of ecclesiastical rites and ceremonies. Other humanist scholars were involved in growing calls for Church reform and criticism of the contemporary papacy and its practices. These humanist developments were shortly followed by what would turn out to be a far more momentous challenge, namely, Martin Luther's nailing of his ninety-five theses to the door of the Church of All Saints in Wittenberg in October 1517. Luther's original criticisms, which can be seen as part of the call for Church reform, hardened into theological opposition and initiated the movement we now know as the Reformation. Two central, and related, aspects of Luther's teaching were his appeal to "scripture alone" (*sola scriptura*) in understanding the Word of God, and his denial of the traditional authority of the Church, especially that of the Pope. The challenge to scholastic theologians from both humanism and Lutheranism was clear: to defend a certain kind of study of theology as well as a certain kind of understanding of the Church.

These intellectual developments were intimately connected with far-reaching, indeed, world-changing, political developments. In 1516 Charles, the Habsburg archduke of Burgundy and the Low Countries, acceded to the thrones of Aragon and Castile, and in 1519 was elected Holy Roman Emperor. He thus became the Emperor Charles V, ruler of a composite empire that stretched from the far east to the far west of Europe, and further west still to Spain's nascent dominions in the New World. Salamanca, the principal theological university of Spain, grew enormously in influence and prestige as a result. The Spanish crown had a well established practice of consulting the theologians of Salamanca for authorization (and thus legitimation) of royal policy, and those theologians became involved in the intellectual politics of Charles V and the Counter-Reformation: his fight, as Emperor, against the opposition, both political and religious, of those German princes who had adopted the Lutheran faith; and his uneasy relations with the papacy at Rome, sacked by his troops in 1527, including his efforts to force the pope to call a new general council to settle doctrinal issues in the wake of the Reformation, efforts that were finally successful as the Council of Trent convened in 1545. Their eyes were turned west as well as east, however, toward America and the issues of conscience raised by the Spanish treatment of the native Amerindian populations. The legitimacy of political authority in general, the capacity to make law, authority within the church, the justification of war and conquest—all of these issues were on the agenda for the leading theologians of Spain, and explain the distinctive political cast of the School of Salamanca. Equally on the agenda was a strengthening of scholastic intellectual practice to secure the theology of Catholic universities against challenges that came, initially, from outside the universities, but increasingly from the new Lutheran and subsequently Calvinist universities, training their own academic theologians as part of their own intellectual and political strategies.

The turn to Aquinas's *Summa* was a key element of both enterprises. Long the authoritative textbook within the schools of the Dominican Order, the Salamanca theologians institutionalized it as the basis for teaching theology in the universities; their lectures upon it equally institutionalized commentary on the *Summa* as an academic genre. At the same time, the systematic expositions of law and justice found in that work provided the basis for their response to the pressing political and ecclesiological questions in which they found themselves involved. The foundation of the Society of Jesus in 1545 brought a new Order onto the scene, one dedicated to the cultural politics of Counter-Reform, with education a central aspect of its mission. As the century wore on, Jesuits and Dominicans would come into conflict over the interpretation of Aquinas, particularly on the question of free will, and the Society of Jesus itself would disagree internally on how much interpretative freedom was to be allowed its members with respect to his teachings. Nevertheless, the *Summa* continued to be the fundamental reference point for Jesuit as well as Dominican theologians, and commentary upon it one of their central intellectual activities.

For our purposes, the most important sections of the *Summa* are QQ. 90–108 of the *Prima Secundae* (the "treatise" on law) and QQ. 57–66 of the *Secunda Secundae* (the "treatise" on justice and right). Often, commentaries upon these sections were published as separate, free-standing works, under the titles *De Legibus* and *De Iustitia et Iure*, respectively, but they could equally form part of a commentary on the entire *Summa*. This, again, might explicitly be labelled as such, but could also, in the seventeenth century, be presented rather as a *Cursus Theologicus*, offering a course of instruction in theology organized around the *Summa*. As the variety of formats already suggests, "commentary" here should be understood in a broad sense. Aquinas's work is divided into "questions," but these turn out to be more in the way of broad headings (e.g., *Prima Secundae,* Q. 96, "On human law"). They then subdivide into a series of articles which actually take the form of questions (e.g., especially significant for us, *Prima Secundae,* Q. 96, a. 4, "Does human law impose a necessity in the court of conscience?"). Some later scholastic commentaries stay with Aquinas's own questions and offer interpretative commentary upon them, although even here there is a marked tendency to open up the discussion beyond the terms in which it had originally been framed. This departure from the original questions is made explicit in those commentaries which formally introduce new questions of their own, and either alter the order of the questions or run several of them together to create a new subject heading. Increasingly in the Jesuit literature, these new treatments are termed "disputations," full-blown, freestanding treatments of a subject that are prompted by Aquinas's text, but are no longer restricted either to his terms or to his conclusions. Again, sometimes the original passages of the *Summa* are reproduced in full, but sometimes the author simply offers a summary before turning to his own exposition. Finally, some works are organized into books or tractates that have no prompt at all in the *Summa*, and are a function of the author's independent understanding of the proper organization of the material. One might therefore ask whether "commentary," even in a very broad sense, is still an apt term for these productions. I retain it because these texts almost entirely originate in lecturing activity on the *Summa* as the "set text" in theology, and continue to be conditioned by Aquinas's questions even when they depart from him radically both in form and content.

Related to this principal academic genre are various others that are informed by it and inform it in their turn. The later middle ages had seen the development of a genre known as *Summae Confessorum*, "Summaries for confessors," which are handbooks of practical moral theology designed to assist the confessor in judging in the court of conscience. They are heavily legalistic, involving constant reference especially to canon, but also to Roman, law. While the genre did not survive in its late-medieval form, in which topics are treated in alphabetical order, a vast literature on cases of conscience continued to flourish. While these are works of casuistry, geared to the particular, they are still indebted to the broader theology of law being developed in the context of commenting on the *Summa*; conversely, those commentaries are themselves pervaded by the same interleaving of theology and law that characterizes the literature on cases of conscience. That literature had since its late-medieval inception been deeply concerned with the morality of economic transactions, and this aspect again flourished in the period with which we are concerned, with a huge number of works, both in Latin and in the vernacular, that are in some form *de contractibus* ("concerning contracts"). In turn, this preoccupation also marks, especially, the commentaries *De Iustitia et Iure*, which are "academic" in the sense that they stem from curricular activity and consider questions of right at a theoretical level, but which are also deeply invested in questions of practical morality and conscience generated by the complex economic world around them. The moral authority of the confessor combined with the ubiquity of such dilemmas ensured that these works had a diffusion in society far beyond the confines of the university.

Another dimension of the extra-curricular engagement of the academic literature is its relationship to "controversial" theology, that is, the teaching and literature generated by the demand to respond to "the heretics of our time." Much of this literature concerns questions of grace and free will, but it is important that the "controversies" had a strong political dimension as well. On the question of law, the works of the entire movement are strongly marked by the rebuttal of the view of law that they attribute to Luther, that is, that no human law is binding in the court of conscience insofar as it is *human* law, by which they mean law that is neither natural nor divine. In the early stages, the critique of the Lutheran position centered on his repudiation of canon law, the human law of the church. However, this critique soon extended to include civil law, the law of the political commonwealth, and led some commentators on the *Summa* to insert a question on the necessity of human law purely directed against "the heretics." Almost all of them, in any case, vastly expand Aquinas's question on obligation in conscience. The implication that Lutheran teaching was antinomian as far as this world is concerned was highly opportunistic, despite some of Luther's more vitriolic pronouncements against the laws of popes and emperors. At a deeper level, though, they were taking issue with the Lutheran conception not primarily of human law but of the human authority to legislate. Luther denied any law-making authority to the Church, a position that Catholic theologians regarded as entirely unacceptable and contrary to the divinely instituted position of the pope. By contrast, for Luther the secular magistrate had, indeed, the authority to make law, but the magistrate was conceived as the vice-regent of God, with the source of his authority divine. Thus, at least as far as Catholic theologians understood him, the obligation in conscience to obey his law reduced to the obligation to obey God's law, and they regarded this as undermining both human political power and human law. While insisting as strongly as Luther on Paul's dictum in the Epistle to the Romans that "the powers that be are ordained of God," they sought to establish a human source of political authority that could ground the obligation in conscience to obey human law *as human law*.

Their way of thinking about law was thus embedded in a distinctive political philosophy and theology, one that was, precisely, highly "controversial" not merely in its ecclesiological dimension but in its secular dimension, too. As such, it reached out of the academy and into the political arena. Perhaps the most spectacular example is the early-seventeenth-century controversy around the Oath of Allegiance that James I of England demanded from his Catholic subjects following the Gunpowder Plot of 1605. Two prominent voices against the Oath were the Jesuits Robert Bellarmine (1542–1621) and Francisco Suárez (1548–1617), both academic theologians who nevertheless stepped out of their teaching roles to intervene in the inflamed polemics of the time. Bellarmine held the Chair of Controversies at the Jesuit Collegio Romano in Rome between 1576 and 1590, and wrote a multi-volume work on the entire range of controversies in the academic form of "disputations": the *Disputationes de Controversiis Fidei Adversus Huius Temporis Haereticos*, including the tractate *De Laicis* (*On the Laity*), which presents the basis of his political philosophy. He also wrote, pseudonymously as was common in such polemics, the *Responsio Matthaei Torti* to the writings of the King. Suárez wrote both an academic treatise on the laws, *De Legibus ac Deo Legislatore* (1612), and a specific piece of controversial theology, *Defensio Fidei* (1613), against James in the same dispute, which drew on his academic political philosophy in a polemical context. It would be a misguided interpretation simply to reduce the academic works to the polemical; an intense engagement with Catholic intellectual traditions and writers is as much a feature of the works as the engagement with "the heretics," and some authors prefer just to refer their readers to the existing controversial literature, saving their intellectual energies for the more theoretical points that interest them. Nevertheless, the political inflection of this conception of law represents another way in which it reaches beyond the academy, and was read by a broader reading public both Catholic and Protestant. Just to take one example, Englishman Sir Robert Filmer opened his political treatise *Patriarcha* with a denunciation of Bellarmine and Suárez, and indeed all the doctors of the schools, for their pernicious teachings on political authority.

Late-scholastic philosophy of law, then, was not an isolated theoretical subject, but part of a practical moral theology for the entirety of life within a Christian commonwealth, including the treacherous question of political obligation. Nevertheless, precisely because the issues were so contested, the movement generated an exceptionally rich meditation on the specific question of law, with basic areas of agreement varied by intense disagreement at critical points. We shall examine this vast literary production, and the theoretical issues and shifts within it, by concentrating on five major authors. The first two are Dominican, and belong to the first generation of the "School of Salamanca." The second three are Jesuit, all writing around the turn of the seventeenth century. It is not that Dominican authors stopped writing about law, to be superseded entirely by Jesuits; nor that Dominican and Jesuit thought are discontinuous; quite the contrary, the initial Dominican writings were enormously influential for Jesuit authors. It is true, though, that the major classics of the seventeenth century were written by Jesuits and not by Dominicans, and also that we can see certain changes of emphasis and approach even given the continuity involved—enough, at any rate, to justify a broad division into two sections on grounds that are both chronological and substantive.

14.2. Dominican Scholastics: Francisco de Vitoria and Domingo de Soto

The beginnings of the School of Salamanca are traditionally associated with the figure of Francisco de Vitoria (1483–1548), a Dominican friar educated in Paris, who returned to Spain and took up the Prima Chair in theology at the University of Salamanca in 1526 and revolutionized teaching there by basing his lectures on Aquinas's *Summa*. Arguably no less important for the subsequent fortunes of the movement, however, was Vitoria's fellow Dominican and close colleague, Domingo de Soto (1495–1560), who likewise studied in Paris but taught philosophy at the University of Alcalá before taking up the Vespers Chair in theology at Salamanca in 1532, succeeding to the Prima Chair in 1552. Together they permanently changed the way in which moral theology was taught at Catholic universities and initiated the new intellectual style in which we are interested. This is not to say that they were the originators of all of its features. The complete commentary on the *Summa* by Dominican Tommaso de Vio (1469–1534), Cardinal Cajetan, published between 1515 and 1519, was a critically important resource for them, as was Dominican Silvestro da Prierio Mazzolini's (1456–1527) *Summa Summarum* of 1518. They were also decisively influenced, on the crucial question of civil and ecclesiastical power, by the debate between Cajetan and Jacques Almain (d. 1515) of the Sorbonne generated by the disputed legitimacy of the council of Pisa in 1511.[3] However, they shaped these resources into a distinctive philosophy conditioned by their distinctive understanding of theology.[4] That understanding was developed in response to three competing intellectual trends. The first is what they saw as the degeneration of scholastic theology into logical and metaphysical subtleties at the expense of the word of God and to the detriment of its true role in society. They shared this critique of the late-medieval nominalist tradition with the humanists, especially Erasmus. In response to him, however, they were, secondly, concerned to argue that philology, which they reductively described as "grammar," was not the answer. The key to restoring theology lay in a proper balance between scripture and reason, which, in the third place, served as the basis of their response to Lutheranism and *sola scriptura*. They did not entirely reject humanist learning, and they insisted on the centrality of revelation to theology and the concomitant necessity of a thorough reading of Scripture. However, the theologian, for them, must also be a reasoner, using the reason that is natural to him as a human being both to decide between competing interpretations of scripture and to draw from it conclusions for the conduct of human life, which itself must involve natural reason.

14.2.1. Natural Reason and Political Resonance

Vitoria and Soto connected this interpretation of the proper role of reason in theology with the Thomist formula "grace does not take away nature but perfects it." Thus Vitoria writes, in his commentary on the first question of the *Summa*, that "since under the law of nature it would have been praiseworthy to terminate questions with natural reasons, it ought not now"—that is, under the law of grace—"to be a source of censure" (*Comm. STh*, Ia.1.a.8, in Pozo 1962, 113). Likewise, Soto, in the programmatic preface to *De Natura et Gratia*, addressed to the fathers of the Council of Trent, asserts that "man is a rational animal, who for that reason enjoys no force nor means for the investigation of truth, and its deduction from its causes, greater than discursive reasoning [...] [F]aith does not (as they boast) oppose nature, but certainly

[3] The texts are given, with an excellent introduction, in Burns and Izbicki 1997.
[4] See, for the following, Brett 2000, Langella 2007, and Belda Plans 2000.

perfects it" (fo. 3). That Thomist formula was used by Aquinas himself, and by Vitoria and Soto after him, to vindicate the space of natural reason and natural law in human life more generally. There is, then, a very tight link between this defense of the use of reason in theology and the characteristic focus of Vitoria, Soto, and the entire first generation of the School of Salamanca on moral theology: specifically, a broadly neo-Thomist moral theology based on natural practical reason and its principles, the natural law. We shall see below how this connection operates more concretely.

Meanwhile, the same stance allows them to vindicate the usefulness of scholastic theology, likewise against the taunts of both Erasmus and "the heretics." "It is scholastics alone," states Soto in the same place, "who discuss and treat of those things that pertain to laws, to virtue and vice, to human duties, contracts, and necessities—all of which are most necessary to be understood in the Christian commonwealth." Scholastic theology is a kind of civil reasoning, an architectonic discourse that mediates between the different and more particular civil discourses through and in which the political life of the commonwealth is lived. As such, it must be able to speak the language of people outside the academy: Vitoria insisted that scholastic theologians must use plain speech and strive for the least complicated explanatory terms. This accounts for his objection to metaphysics in inappropriate places: "Cajetan goes all metaphysical here, I've no idea what he means," he famously remarked at the opening to his commentary on the *Secunda Secundae*.[5] Despite his opposition to littering theology with metaphysical technicalities, however, his vindication of the use of reason in theology is explicitly also a vindication of the use of *philosophy*. Thus he asserts clearly that it "is impious and heretical to say—as these new heretics do say—that it is the work of the devil to use natural reasons and those of philosophers in theology" (*Comm STh*, Ia.1.a.8, in Pozo 1962, 113). And in the preface to *De Natura et Gratia* quoted above, Soto continues by saying, "It is philosophy, in great part, which supplies the reasons for these" (fo. 3). However, it is not merely moral philosophy that interests them. As we shall see more fully below, natural necessitation is a crucial background condition both to the exercise of human reason and to the exercise of human freedom, and thus natural philosophy, the study of natural causality, plays a critical role in a moral theology premised on the operation of human reason.

As noted above, Vitoria's and Soto's linking of the stature of scholastic theology to its role outside the schools reflected not only the intellectual controversies of the early sixteenth century, but also a native Spanish political tradition of legitimating royal policy through theological sanction (see Pagden 1982, chap. 1). Beginning with Ferdinand and Isabella, *los reyes católicos* ("the Catholic monarchs"), and continuing into the reigns of Charles V and Philip II, the crown called upon its leading theologians to debate and confirm the

[5] Quoted in Villoslada 1938, 116, n. 13.

theological acceptability of its activities. The most famous moment was perhaps the celebrated Junta of Valladolid of 1550–1551, called to discuss the legitimacy of conquest of the Indies, in which Soto participated. Both Soto and Vitoria saw it as entirely their role to comment *theologically* on current Spanish affairs, anything from the justice of the *alcabala* (the Spanish sales tax) to poor law reform to the actions of the *conquistadores*: "theologically" meaning, as we have seen, by appeal to plain-spoken reason as well as to scriptural authority. This gave their writings a critical edge not always pleasing to their superiors, either religious or civil. "By what right," demanded Soto in his early lecture on *dominium* ("dominion") of 1532, "do we retain the overseas empire that has just been discovered? For my part, I really don't know."[6]

In this complex political, intellectual, and cultural context it becomes clear, then, why the understanding of law is so central to their theological enterprise and why they thought that as theologians they were the most competent to handle the subject. While canon and civil lawyers work from the letter of human law, the theologian alone can relate human law ultimately back to God, whether this be directly or "through nature" (a key locution, as we shall see). Moreover, as Vitoria argues in his lecture *On the American Indians* (1539), the determination of that question "does not belong to lawyers, or at least not only to them, because since those barbarians, as I shall go on to argue, are not subject to human justice [*ius*], their affairs cannot be examined through human laws, but divine laws, in which lawyers are not sufficiently expert [...]" (*De Ind.*, in Pagden and Lawrance 1992, 238).[7] Here we see the critical symbiosis between their renewal of moral theology and the circumstances of the Indies: the conquest shored up the authority of these theologians even while it made distinct demands on their legal philosophy. However, neither Vitoria nor Soto ever intended their appeal beyond human law to undermine it; quite to the contrary, in their eyes it is only theology that can adequately support the authority of human law by showing that it obliges in conscience. In his defense of scholastic theology against its denigration at the hands of Luther, Soto gives this as a key example: "from Romans 13, 'let every soul be subject to the higher powers' [...] [scholastic] doctors infer: therefore princes can oblige in the court of conscience. That conclusion [...] is purely theological: and therefore that science [sc. theology] is not superfluous, as they [the heretics] shamelessly say, but is necessary for life according to the divine precepts and rules" (*Comm. STh.* Ia.1.a.1, in Pozo 1962, 150).

[6] Soto's lecture is edited in Brufau Prats 1988; for the School in relation to the conquest of America, see also Brufau Prats 1988, Pagden 1982, and Lupher 2006.

[7] The Latin can be found in the parallel-text Latin-German edition, Horst et al. 1995–1997.

14.2.2. Reason, Will, and Obligation

With some sense of the general place of law in their thinking, we can now turn to the more specific elements of their account. For Vitoria and Soto, as for Aquinas, God and his law are the anchor of the entire legal system; consistently with their theological approach, this must be a conception of divine law that allows for the cooperation of natural human reason. However, the two theologians handle this key relationship in rather different ways. Commenting on Aquinas's definition of law as a rule and measure of human action, both agree with him that it must therefore be *aliquid rationis*, that is, something that belongs to reason, rather than an act of will (Aquinas, *STh.* Ia.2.a.e, 90.a.1).[8] In Aquinas's text, a law is characterized as a rule because it is something that obliges; reason is the rule because it belongs to reason to order things toward an end (*ordinare ad finem*). In their commentary on this passage, both Soto and Vitoria underline, far more strongly than Aquinas, the aspect of obligation. As Soto says, "it is a property of law both that it is a rule, and that it is a precept that obliges." Obligation is the function of an act of *imperium* ("command"), which, as Aquinas himself had said earlier in the *Prima Secundae* (17.a.1), is an act of reason. Thus, while saying nothing that cannot be found, in some way, in Aquinas, the two Salamancan professors effectively reground his intellectualism primarily in the capacity to oblige, and it is on this basis that they combat the voluntarist thesis that law is an act of will. As Vitoria writes, "if the pope should pass a law: It is my will, that Christians fast, that act is not a law, because it does not oblige, however much he wills, unless he commands." A key example for both of them, going back to twelfth-century theologian Peter Lombard (1095–1160), is the story of Abraham and Isaac (*Sentences* I, dist. 45, caps. 5–7). God's will was not, in fact, for Isaac to be sacrificed; however, that will had nothing to do with Abraham's obligation, as a result of God's command, to sacrifice Isaac. God's will in the sense of *voluntas beneplaciti* ("his will for what happens in the world") shall be done, but it does not oblige and it is not law.

At this point, however, Vitoria shows himself more sympathetic than Soto to some sort of modified voluntarist thesis. There is another way in which we talk of God's will, his *voluntas signi* ("the will that he signifies to mankind in his requirements and prohibitions"). This is not "properly" his will, but it is still his will in some sense, and Vitoria brings in another *quaestio* of the *Prima Secundae* (19.a.9) in which Aquinas argues that, for the human will to be good, it must conform to the divine will as its measure. "And," Vitoria goes on, "if

[8] Vitoria, *De Lege,* in Stüben 2010, [3]–6; Pagden and Lawrance 1992, 155–6; Soto, *De Iust. et Iure* I.1.a.1. Soto is the more pugnaciously intellectualist of the two, combating as he is the rival voluntarist definition of the Franciscan theologian Alfonso de Castro (1495–1588) in his *De Potestate Legis Poenalis* (*On the Power of Penal Law*), published at Salamanca in 1550 after Vitoria was dead.

it is a measure, then it is a rule. And if a rule, then a law. *Ergo*, [...] It does not therefore seem inappropriate to concede, that the divine will is law and also the divine reason." These passages, dating from 1533–1534, are consistent with his earlier lecture *On Civil Power* (1528), in which Vitoria handles the differences between divine and human law, holding that "in the case of divine law, for it to be just and in consequence obligatory, the will of the legislator is enough, since will stands in place of reason," and that "the entire goodness of the human will [...] results from conformity with the divine will and law [...] which is the rule of all human actions" (in Pagden and Lawrance 1992, 34; Horst et al. 1995–1997, vol. 1, 146).[9] They are also consistent with his lecture *On That to Which Man Is Obliged, When First He Comes to the Use of Reason* (1535), in which Vitoria insists that there is no sin where there is no obligation, and no obligation where there is no law, and no law where there is no superior; moral evil is necessarily a contravention of divine law, and moral goodness depends on divine authority, because God can make even something *per se* morally evil, like killing the innocent, not so (see Vitoria in Horst et al. 1995–1997, vol. 2, 158–60). One of his references here is again Q. 19 of the *Prima Secundae*, this time a. 4, in which Aquinas argues that the goodness of the human will depends on *eternal* law. Significantly, however, Vitoria substitutes the term *lex divina* ("divine law") for Aquinas's *lex aeterna* ("eternal law"). There is thus no difference in his terminology here between what was for Aquinas God's overarching directive rationale for all his creation, that is, eternal law, and divine positive law, the law of revelation. The reasoning behind this, but at the same time his uneasiness with the Thomist conception of eternal law, becomes clear in Vitoria's very brief commentary on *Prima Secundae*, Q. 93, a. 3: "There is a doubt over how divine positive law derives from eternal law. Cajetan's understanding here seems to be that by eternal law we should understand only natural law. But as far as I can grasp it, by eternal law St. Thomas means absolutely every divine law" (Vitoria, *De Lege*, in Stüben 2010, 32; Pagden and Lawrance 1992, 168). The contrast with Soto will become clear below.

Meanwhile, though, Vitoria is very careful to distinguish his position from that of the *moderni*, or *nominales*, by which he means the late-medieval nominalist school arising from the work of William of Ockham, and which he associates with the position that God is under no necessity whatsoever in his commandments.[10] Questioning and responding to Aquinas's assertion that all human law is derived from natural law, Vitoria argues in *De Lege* (95.a.2) that, even though we need seek no other rationale for divine law than the divine will, nevertheless divine law too depends on natural law, because "God disposes all things sweetly" (Wisdom 8,1) (see Vitoria, *De Lege*, in Stüben

[9] For a strong argument as to the significance of these passages, and for the centrality of obligation to Vitoria's conception of law, marking a departure from Aquinas, see Stiening 2011.

[10] See Chapter 13 of this volume, 321–6.

2010, 44; Pagden and Lawrance 1992, 173).[11] God's law is an order, not a pure play of will. Again, defending the role of reason in theology in his commentary on the first question of the *Summa*, Vitoria insists that there must be some things that are necessary even while we concede that God's *potentia absoluta* ("absolute power") is unlimited and totally free. For to stress the free operation of God to the extent that everything becomes contingent is to deny any place for human reason, which must operate with at least some necessary propositions. Divine law, creating a universal rule, brings with it necessity, for example, that a man must be baptized in order to be saved; it is divine providence, steering all things to their appointed ends, which is the domain of God's free will.[12]

A parallel distinction comes in Vitoria's commentary on *Prima Secundae*, Q. 100, a. 8, the celebrated question of whether God can exercise dispensation in the precepts of the Decalogue (the Ten Commandments), and if so, whether only in the "second table" (containing man's duties toward man, e.g., "Thou shalt not steal"), or even in the "first table" as well (containing man's duties toward God, e.g., "Thou shalt have no other gods before me"). Vitoria, like Aquinas, took the Decalogue to be a matter of natural law, so the question becomes one of whether God can exercise dispensation in the precepts of natural law. God certainly seemed to have done so on various occasions in the narrative of the Old Testament: Abraham and Isaac; the destruction of Sodom (surely there were many innocents among the dead); Samson destroying the temple (and so destroying himself). Here Vitoria, saving Aquinas's position that all the precepts of the Decalogue are indispensable even for God, argues that God's omnipotence involves two things: first, that he is master (*dominus*) of everything; second, that he is a legislator. Thus, in allowing innocents to be killed, there was no dispensation, because he did not use his authority as a legislator; rather, he transferred his divine *dominium* over the life and death of every mortal to a human being (or human beings), who then did not act against the law (see Vitoria, *De Lege*, in Stüben 2010, 112–4).[13] However, Vitoria also allows that Scotus's opinion—that God can dispense in the second but not the first table of the Decalogue—is *probabilis* ("approvable"), even if Aquinas's is more so.[14] Despite the clear drive to save a space for human reason in the face of divine omnipotence, then, Vitoria's negotiation between the Thomist heritage and other, late-medieval currents of thought on this issue remains tense.

[11] The text is incorrect in Stüben 2010; correct in Langella 2010, 130.

[12] The relevant passages are given, and discussed briefly, in Langella 2007, 112–4.

[13] Again, there is a certain prompt in the text of Aquinas, but no such thoroughgoing distinction between God as legislator and as master.

[14] Vitoria's wrestling with both the Scotist and the nominalist traditions in the matter of God's freedom is well discussed in Deckers 1991, 83–109.

By contrast, Soto fully embraces Aquinas's understanding of eternal law as God's practical reason (*ratio agibilium*), governing and directing the whole of his creation. It is clearly distinct (and Soto emphasizes this twice) from divine positive law, which governs only mankind in its aspect as ordered toward a supernatural as well as a natural end. It is also distinct from natural and human law. However, elaborating here upon Aquinas's view, Soto explains that it is not simply the case that there are four distinct laws, each differing in species; rather, there is a difference between eternal law and the other three, "because it is their fount and origin: not passed but passing (*non lata, sed ferens*), not imprinted but imprinting, not the participation of any other but the light of which the others are participations" (*De Iust. et Iure* I.3.a.1, and a.2, fo. 22–3). Thus, we cannot think of eternal law as simply one more standard of action (just higher than all the rest) to which we can refer our conduct. Indeed, because it is not a law that has been passed, we cannot know its content except through those other laws. In itself, it is incomprehensible to human beings (ibid., fo. 22, col. 1; fo. 23, col. 2).[15] It further differs from any legislated law in that not only free action—that is, action proceeding from reason and will—is subject to it, but also the whole realm of necessitation, from animal action to planetary motion and even to necessary truths, like three plus four equals seven. All proceed from God's reason and are governed by it. At this point, however, Soto's insistence that a law is not simply a "rule and measure" but an "obligatory precept," appears to come under strain; it is not clear how *obligation* functions with any other than free agents, nor is it clear how a precept, which requires speech (as Soto argues in his opening question, as part of his demonstration that law is a matter of reason not will), can be given to things that cannot comprehend, let alone to a mathematical truth. As we shall see below, opponents used these arguments and more to attack eternal law as the weak point of the Thomist system.

Meanwhile, Soto in the course of this *quaestio* also poses the question of whether God's own will is subject to eternal law, since God's will is rational and eternal law is reason. He answers, entirely as Aquinas had done, that in itself, God's will is not subject to, but rather identical to, eternal law; it is not rational, but rather reason itself (Aquinas, *ST* Ia.2.ae, 93.a.4, ad 1). However, in relation to God's creatures, it is indeed rational, and therefore (though neither Aquinas nor Soto spells this out in so many words) subject to eternal law. Soto thus touches on the controversy with the nominalists of whether the freedom of God's will can be limited in any way, and whether God, of his absolute power, can override his own law. Soto too, like Vitoria, directly tackles the issue in

[15] Soto's characterization of eternal law has, I think, something in common with Pauline Westerman's analysis of it as God's "style": we can only recognize a style through its being the style *of other things*; it is not itself such a thing (see Westerman 1997, chap. 1. See also Scattola 2001, 35–6, and Todescan 1973, 228–32).

commenting on Q. 100, a. 8 (Soto, *De Iust. et Iure* II.3.8, fo. 114–20). Here we find him, as already suggested, more strongly intellectualist than Vitoria, not only against Ockham (on whom they both agree), but also against Scotus. In Soto's eyes, for God to dispense in the second table of the Decalogue is equally as self-contradictory as for him to dispense in the first. His first argument is to show that the commandments of the second table involve duties to God just as much as those of the first. His second is to counter another argument of Scotus, to the effect that "if the precepts of the second table were not dispensable, it would follow that God necessarily willed something outside himself." Soto responds that God can will things outside himself in two ways. In one way, he can will their very existence; this is entirely non-necessitated, since he can will them out of existence at any point. In another, he can will the connections between them; here "philosophers must admit that God wills some things necessarily," for example, that three plus four equals seven. Thus, "thou shalt not kill," or steal, or commit adultery, are necessary objects of divine will; God cannot command the contrary, nor permit them to happen justly (ibid., fo. 117, col. 1; fo. 118, col. 2). To explain the various remarkable happenings of the Old Testament, Soto appeals to the same distinction as Vitoria, between God as *legislator* and God as *dominus*, as the indisputable solution to the problem. However, his own qualifications show that this is not quite such a good solution: Soto insists that even when God was exercising his *dominium*, he did not use his "absolute power" as such, but acted as a just judge and so as to "dispose all things sweetly"—the same quotation to which Vitoria had appealed.

In both authors, then, despite their differences, there is a close link between their vindication of the stability of God's law, which involves some degree of divine necessitation, and their conception of theology as allowing a space for human reason and for philosophy. We now turn to look at the intersection between human reason and divine government which is constituted by natural law.

14.2.3. Reason and Natural Law

Aquinas famously defined natural law as the participation of eternal law in a rational creature (*ST* Ia.2.ae, 92, a.2). It is that through which man involves himself in his own direction by sharing rationally in God's direction of him. Since Vitoria, as we have seen, appealed to a more general conception of "divine" rather than "eternal" law, it is not surprising that, in his commentary on Q. 94 of the *Prima Secundae*, the language of participation is absent. Nevertheless, he shares the basic thesis that God communicates his law both through nature and through revelation, and his main concern here is to vindicate the former mode, that is, to establish the natural knowability of the precepts of natural law independent of revelation (*De Lege* 94.a.2). In Vitoria's handling, Aquinas's link between the natural inclinations of mankind and the precepts of natural law is central to this enterprise. Aquinas had suggested that everything to which man naturally inclines, must be naturally good, and therefore man, commanded by the very nature of practical reason to pursue the good, understands what goods he must pursue from his own inclinations (*ST* Ia.2.ae, 94.a.2). Vitoria concurs, but not before allowing that, according to some, the derivation of precepts from inclinations is invalid. His answer is to ask in what other way man can *naturally* know what he is to do. He rejects any notion that natural law is innate in us in the sense of born with us (*De Lege* 94.a.1).[16] It is something that we work out as we come to the use of reason, that is, as we become fully moral agents: the two are inextricably intertwined. Thus, children and those who never achieve the use of reason cannot direct themselves according to natural law. The case is very different for the American Indians, though, who must, in Vitoria's understanding, have moral agency even without revelation.[17] And thus he defends Aquinas's sequence of reasoning, adding that, if we cannot be confident of our inclinations, we cannot be confident of God, since those inclinations were implanted in us by God. As in Aquinas, then, practical reason, that which lifts human beings into moral agency and moral responsibility, operates within a framework of natural necessitation, the kind of necessitation to which all creation is subject. Crucially, however, and as for Aristotle, this is not purely material necessitation, but what is demanded by the ends that all things have and toward which their natural inclinations incline. Vitoria gives an extended account of the teleological universe of Aristotelian natural philosophy in his lecture *On Civil Power* (in Pagden and Lawrance 1992, 4–10).[18]

The world of Aristotelian natural science receives equal emphasis in Soto's account of natural law, which keeps up a kind of second-level dialogue with natural philosophers, whom the theologian must satisfy but whose procedures he himself sometimes adopts. Thus, in the first article, "the student of philosophy" objects to the idea of innate *species*, which would be contrary to the Aristotelian principle that all *species* are acquired through experience; Soto responds that the precepts of the law of nature are not innate in that way (*De Iust. et Iure* I.4.a.1, fo. 29–30). In establishing that we can nevertheless have natural knowledge of them, Aquinas's appeal to the inclinations is as important to Soto as to Vitoria, but in a different way. For Vitoria, as we have seen, the trustworthiness of our natural inclinations guarantees our natural ability to know God's law; in effect, by vindicating the validity of Aquinas's reasoning from inclination to law, he is vindicating the validity of every man's. For Soto,

[16] In Stüben 2010, 36, Pagden and Lawrance 1992, 169: "Natural law is not so-called because it is in us from birth, for children do not have natural law nor the disposition [for it], but because from the inclination of nature we judge those things that are right."

[17] See Vitoria, *On That to Which Man Is Obliged*, passim.

[18] See the discussion in Deckers 1991, 110–43.

however, the gap between natural precept and natural inclination narrows to a vanishing point. Just as we instinctively tend toward certain ends, so we instinctively know that we should tend toward them: natural law is promulgated "by instinct" (ibid., I.1.a.4, fo. 16, col. 1).[19] The crucial point here is the immediacy of our grasp of the fundamental precepts of natural law. They are not innate, but they are nevertheless known immediately to practical reason, without any further discursive process of thought. This makes the list of precepts of natural law very short and basic: Soto explicitly gives as examples only two: "Do not to another what you would not have done to yourself" and "Life is to be lived together tranquilly and peacefully." He describes these precepts as *semina*, seeds implanted in the nature of our reason that enable us to carry out the further reasoning that is necessary for achieving our ends.[20] They do not bear fruit without further cultivation by human reason. This is so to the extent that Soto hesitates over whether to include the Decalogue in natural law, something almost universally taken for granted at the time (and assumed by Vitoria, as we have seen), or whether to make it instead part of the *ius gentium* ("law of nations"). Soto clearly believes that "thou shalt not kill," for example, is not known by instinct, but by discursive reasoning—even if its proximity to natural law means that it either should be, or is usually taken to be (Soto hesitates here), part of it (ibid., I.5.a.1, a.5).[21]

For both Soto and Vitoria, then, as indeed for Aquinas, natural law lies at the intersection between the end-directed nature given to human beings by God, and their ability to direct themselves to that end. The necessitated character of the natural inclinations is the crucial background condition for the operation of natural human reason and freedom. Equally, though, as for Aquinas, natural law provides insufficient direction. This is partly because after the Fall, humans' ultimate end, eternal beatitude, surpasses their natural means to achieve it, necessitating divine positive law in the form of the "old law" of Moses and the "new law" of Christ. Vitoria's commentary on the laws contains some quite lengthy questions on the first—for example, as we have seen, whether God can dispense in the precepts of the Decalogue—but almost nothing on the second. Vitoria apparently believes that he has little to add. (Characteristically, the only matter which receives extended attention here is one thrown into question by the Lutherans, of whether the authority to determine the faith lies in the Church or in Holy Scripture.) Soto's commentary (*De*

[19] I have discussed Soto's account of natural law in Brett 1997, chap. 4.

[20] Soto, *De Iust. et Iure* I.5.a.1, fo. 38, col. 1: "[T]he quality and nature of reason is discursive: and therefore a wise God and a knowing nature planted within us only seeds, which with the cultivation of reason would come to bear fruit."

[21] There is support for Soto's placing of the Decalogue under the *ius gentium* in Aquinas himself, *STh.* Ia.2.ae, 95.a.2, in which Aquinas argues that "thou shalt not kill" (*non esse occidendum*) is a conclusion from the natural law principle "thou shalt do evil to no one" (*nulli esse malum faciendum*).

Iust. Et Iure II), though fuller, has much the same balance. The "new law" is fundamentally a matter of faith and the sacraments, which Aquinas had handled extensively not in the *Prima Secundae* but in the *Pars Tertia* of the *Summa*. Neither Vitoria nor Soto wrote a commentary on the *Pars Tertia*, although Soto did write a commentary on Book IV of Peter Lombard's *Sentences*, which is devoted to the sacraments. Here, tackling the sacrament of penance, he deliberately refuses to engage in the kind of juridical treatment the subject had received in the late-medieval nominalist tradition. Thus, although Vitoria and Soto, like Aquinas, include the law of Christ within the field of law, it does not demand—and (for Soto, at least) it would be inappropriate to deploy—the kind of juridical-philosophical theology that the other types of law call forth, and which is their central intellectual enterprise.

14.2.4. Human Law: The Law of Nations

By far the greatest weight of their discussion falls, then, on the other kind of supplementation of natural law: human law. Although natural law provides the basic orientation for practical reason, it is inadequate to the complex demands of human society. Why? Aquinas's answer in *Prima Secundae*, Q. 95, closely relying on Book X of Aristotle's *Nicomachean Ethics*, was framed in terms of the necessity for coercion: natural law does not carry coercive sanctions, but some people cannot be brought to act reasonably without them.[22] In *De Regno*, however, Aquinas's answer to the question why man does not live purely by natural law is his nature as a "social and political animal" who must live together with others; indeed, natural law itself contains the precept to live sociably.[23] This, however, requires common direction to the common good, and for this reason the commonwealth is formed and its ruler and legislator established. In Q. 92 of the *Prima Secundae*, Aquinas accordingly stressed that law must be legislated for the common good: it is not in itself a form of personal moral direction. To the question of whether, then, law has any capacity to make men morally good, his answer was nuanced, relying on Aristotle's distinction between the good citizen and the good man (Aristotle *Pol.* III.4–5). If law is properly framed "according to divine justice," then it will certainly "make men good"; if not, it will make good citizens but not good men. Ideally, there ought to be a positive interaction between laws framed for the common good and for individual moral good; the coercive force of the law should function both ways.

Vitoria and Soto retain many of these basic Thomist motifs, but they have a far more complex picture of the field of human law, including a sophisticated conception of the interplay between two different features of the juridical universe—law and right—and, relatedly, a hugely expanded place for the

[22] See the discussion in Chapter 4 of this volume, 88–9.
[23] Dyson 2002, 5–6.

ius gentium ("law of nations"). Moreover, within "human law" they centrally include ecclesiastical law, of which there is no mention in Aquinas's handling of law in the *Prima Secundae*. This affects their discussion in two ways. First, their understanding of the obligation of human law as a whole is marked by their appreciation of and familiarity with canon law, as well as its related casuistry of conscience, the genre of *Summae Confessorum* noted above in Section 14.1. They will frequently choose an example from ecclesiastical law to illustrate general points that apply to any kind of positive human ordinance, and they are deeply indebted to distinguished contemporary canon lawyers such as Martín de Azpilcueta (1493–1586) and Diego de Covarruvias (1512–1577). Second, it is also a central aspect of their Counter-Reformation political theology. For Vitoria and Soto, the pope is a human legislator, equally as is the prince: civil law and the law of the church together govern the lives of citizens of the Christian commonwealth. Against Luther, who burned books of canon law as "diabolical" and who appeared to them to be arguing that the law of princes does not oblige except as a function of divine law, they want to save the "human" character of both, albeit in different ways, and to argue that nevertheless both types of law carry an obligation in conscience to obey them *as human laws*. It is in this context that they discuss the interplay between the law and the good of the individual.

To begin with the relationship between law and right, it is one of the markers of Vitoria's and Soto's legal philosophy that they imported, and embedded, a "subjective" notion of right—right as what "I have"—from the late-medieval nominalist tradition into a basically Thomist structure of law.[24] Aquinas had worked with an "objective" conception, inherited from Aristotle, of right as "the right thing," "what is just," which is the object of the virtue of justice. This "right thing" is right between two persons; it is not subjectively held by one or the other. Of the relationship of this right, this *ius*, to law, Aquinas had only said in the *Summa*'s *Secunda Secundae* that law is in some sense the basis, ground, or rationale (*ratio*) of right (57.a.1, 2).[25] Soto took up this hint by understanding laws as the "rules" (*regulae*) of justice, and placing his discussion of laws at the start of a work whose overall subject is "justice and right" (*De Iust. et Iure*, proem, sec. 2). However, it does not follow that right, for him, is derived from law in any simple sense, or can be reduced to it; as we shall see in the context of the *ius gentium*, establishing right requires its own distinctive mode of reasoning.[26] Soto begins his discussion of right with the "objec-

[24] See the differing accounts in Tuck 1979; Brett 1997; and Tierney 1997. Tierney gives much greater weight to the medieval canonists (compare the discussion in Chapter 10 of this volume, Section 5) in the origins of subjective rights. Some trace the notion back to the ancient Greeks and Romans; see Chapters 4 and 6 of this volume, Sections 8 and 6, respectively; and Garnsey 2007.

[25] See Finnis 1998, 135; and, in relation to Vitoria, Tierney 1997, 259.

[26] Scattola 2010, 347–9, stresses the structuring role of justice as a virtue in Soto's handling of law and right. Justice requires both a principle of order (law) and the concrete relations of right

tive" sense, but he soon moves to define it subjectively in terms of a "faculty" or "power" of the individual, which he glossed as a "facility"—something which gives an individual the juridical availability of something else. Moreover, he made *dominium*, the right of "ownership" or "lordship" over other things and other persons, the central object of "commutative justice" (the justice of exchange).[27] For his part, Vitoria took a different path from Soto, by understanding "law is the rationale of right" in a permissive sense: right is what is licit, what there is a licence for, under the law (*quod lege licet*). Equally with Soto, however, he understood this area of licence subjectively, as a power or faculty of the individual, and he further equated right conceived in this way with *dominium* taken in a broad sense.[28]

For Vitoria and Soto, then, human beings as the subjects of law are also equipped with individual rights. Some of these are natural; both of them conceive of a natural right of self-preservation and of self-defense, and both of them understand human beings to have natural *dominium* over some things, principally their own actions—this is liberty—and over the other creatures of the earth. While those natural rights that are the immediate corollary of natural law—principally, the right of self-preservation and self-defense, but also the right of matrimony, and others—cannot be altered, they hold that natural *dominium* both can and must be changed. To this extent they agree with Aquinas, who had insisted that the introduction of private property was both necessary and not contrary to natural law, and thus a part of the *ius gentium*. However, they encountered problems with his account of this domain of law. In Q. 95 of the *Prima Secundae*, Aquinas had placed the *ius gentium* within human, not natural, law; for him, it is the kind of human law that is derived from natural law as conclusions from principles. Although it is a positive law (a. 4), it is not contained in human law "as solely laid down by law" (*tanquam sola lege posita*); it has "something of force" (*aliquid vigoris*) from natural law (a. 2). By contrast, in Q. 57 of the *Secunda Secundae*, Aquinas had placed the *ius gentium* under natural, not positive, right; it is natural not in an "absolute" or unqualified sense, but by a form of comparison (a. 3), which is the work of human reason. The relationship between the two dichotomies (natural/human, natural/positive) is unclear.[29] Nevertheless, what is clear is that both the *ius gentium* as law and the *ius gentium* as right are constituted by the operation of human reason, working from natural principles either deductively or inferentially.

in which the order is realized; the two are distinct but mutually dependent, so that neither collapses into the other (ibid., 361–2).

[27] Soto, *De Iust. et Iure*, proem, IV: *dominium* is the foundation of all of the relationships that commutative justice regulates, and all offenses against commutative justice are violations or corruptions of *dominium*.

[28] Vitoria, *Comm. STh.* III.62.a.1, in Beltrán de Heredia 1934; discussed in Tierney 1997, chap. 11, and Brett 1997, chap. 4.

[29] See, however, the excellent discussion in Murphy 2005, chap. 2.

Soto, in essence, takes over this perspective. The *ius gentium*, both in the sense of law and in the sense of right, is constituted by natural reason working from the principles of natural law, or the fundamentals of natural right, to distinct conclusions and new rights that can nevertheless be traced back by a direct chain of reasoning to their source (*De Iust. et Iure* I.5.a.2, a.4; III.1.a.3). However, this makes it, both as law and as right, positive, not natural. As we have seen, for Soto what marks the natural in both law and right is being apprehended immediately, without any discursive reasoning. By contrast, the *ius gentium* is constituted precisely by this activity. In the case of the *law* of nations, this is reasoning that Soto calls both deductive and inferential, and proceeds by syllogism. For example: "Let us lay down that natural principle: Human life is to be maintained and fostered in peace and tranquillity. From there, assuming a second premise, that corrupt nature, living in common, would neither cultivate the fields diligently, nor live in peace, the nations inferred that possessions must be divided" *(De Iust. et Iure* I.5.a.2, a.4, fo. 44–5). In the case of the *right* of nations, this is reasoning that Soto describes as *collativa*, from *conferre*, which involves bringing things together: "to judge of things in order towards an end and under certain circumstances does not belong to all animals, but peculiarly to man in virtue of his reason, whose office it is to bring one thing together with another" (ibid., III.1.a.3). The *ius gentium* in both senses, then, is properly *human*, the result of the discursive ratiocination that, as Soto stresses again and again and in different contexts, is the distinctive marker of *human* reason. A key word in its elucidation is *circumstantiae* (ibid., I.5.a.1, fo. 38, col. 1). The prompt for the further activity of human reasoning is the circumstances of time and place in which human beings find themselves—most prominently, life after the Fall, a life of labor and the loss of innocence. The critical point about the discursive reasoning to which they give rise is that, both in the case of law and of right, Soto stresses that it is done by individual human beings by themselves: establishing the *ius gentium* does not require humans to gather together in one body, nor does it require a prince (ibid., I.5.a.4, fo. 45, col. 1; III.1.a.3; IV.3.a.1). There is no world power or world legislator; there is simply a consensus of the nations, the *gentes*, in the sense of "all people" and therefore of "all peoples."

Turning now to Vitoria, a surprising feature of his work is that he has nothing at all to say about the *ius gentium* in his commentary on *Prima Secundae*, Q. 90ff., that is, the questions on law. He remarks briefly at the relevant question, Q. 95, a. 4, only that Aquinas seems to contradict himself on the subject. In his commentaries on the *Summa*, it figures only—but then very extensively—in *Secunda Secundae*, Q. 57ff., the questions on right. Here, Vitoria, like Soto, follows Aquinas in seeing the *ius gentium* as a function of natural reason, but departs from him in understanding it as a kind of positive right, based on agreement (Vitoria, *Comm. STh.*, III.57.a.3, nn. 1–5).[30] The universal character

[30] See the discussion in Deckers 1991, 358–65.

of that agreement means that it retains a close proximity to natural law, both in being a result of natural reasoning processes and in functioning to protect the operation of natural law. Nevertheless, it has a human source in "the consensus of all peoples and nations" or "of the whole world" (ibid., 57.a.3, nn. 4 and 5). Vitoria shares with Soto the perspective that the *ius gentium* in the sense of right is centrally about the division of *dominium*. Like Soto, again, Vitoria is equally clear that this does not need a prince: divisibility is contained within the very concept of *dominium*. It can be done, and in all likelihood was originally done, by consent between parties, either tacit or explicit (ibid., 62.a.1, nn. 21–3).[31] Going by the commentary on the *Summa* alone, then, it could seem as if the *ius gentium* simply collapses into a series of relations of right, which (as we have seen) Vitoria analyzes as relations of *dominium* in a broad sense. However, in *On Civil Power*, Vitoria argues that it is not the case that the *ius gentium* has its force purely from human agreement, *ex pacto et condicto*; it also has the force of law, *vim legis*. But, in contrast to Soto, asserting that it has the force of law involves crediting the whole human race with *potestas*, "as if it were a commonwealth." The *as if* is important here: Vitoria is not saying that there *is* one world-commonwealth. What he is saying is rather that the *legislative* force of the *ius gentium* cannot be thought about without thinking in terms of a united body that is the locus of quasi-political power (see *De Pot. Civ.*, in Pagden and Lawrance 1992, 40; see also Wagner 2011).

Despite their differences, Vitoria and Soto together radically reposition Aquinas's *ius gentium* so that it becomes not simply a first mode of the concretization of natural law and right, but a global system of justice governing all relations between individuals and peoples that involve some claim to ownership or lordship (*dominium* in both senses). It is temporally or historically situated following the Fall, but, although human wickedness does play a role in its genesis, it has far more to do with the circumstances of necessity, the need to cultivate the earth, and, in parallel, to spread out over it: it is a law of dispersion and settlement. In the background of this understanding is Augustine's influential account, whereby the progeny of the three sons of Noah founded the *gentes* or the *nationes*, "and by their increase filled even the islands" (*CD* XVI.3 and 6)[32]; or, again, one of Vitoria's central examples is the case of Abraham and Lot, agreeing to go their separate ways and thus tacitly dividing *dominium*. The *ius gentium* thus has for its field the whole surface of

[31] Here Vitoria suggests (after canvassing various other options) that the most likely way in which this division occurred was by a process of virtual consent: "not with a clear and formal consent, but a kind of interpretative consent, so that some began to cultivate certain lands and others, others; and from the use of those things it came about that one man would be content with the lands that he had occupied, and another with others, so that none occupied the lands of another." This is what happened between Lot and Abraham, who thus become the model for the settlement of the globe.

[32] See my discussion in Brett 2011, chap. 8.

the globe, created at a moment in human history when human life required the establishment of rules for mutually inhabiting that space. The *ius gentium* accordingly regulates not merely what people own, but what they do not own, for example, routes of travel between places. This is the basis for Vitoria's notorious *ius communicandi* ("right of travel and intercommunication"), which is one of the rights by which he justifies the Spanish presence in the Indies: "in the beginning of the world, when everything was in common, everyone was allowed to visit and travel through any land he wished. This right was clearly not taken away by the division of property: it was never the intention of the nations to prevent men's free mutual intercourse with one another by this division. Certainly it would have been thought inhuman in the time of Noah" (*De Ind.* 3.a.1, in Pagden and Lawrance 1992, 278). The *ius gentium*, finally, regulates all exchanges of things that are owned, and it regulates all violations of right for which there is no other redress. Thus, in the final analysis, it also regulates war. It is a global system of *dominium* and of the justice which takes *dominium* for its object (see Koskenniemi 2011).

14.2.5. Human Law: Civil and Ecclesiastical Law

We turn now, finally, to the other kind of human law, that which governs a "perfect" or self-sufficient community, a *respublica*, be it civil or ecclesiastical: for the church is equally a "perfect" community, even if it is not to be thought of as simply one among the others. ("It should not be imagined," states Vitoria in *On the Power of the Church*, "that civil and spiritual power are like two different and separate commonwealths, such as France and England."[33]) The church has its origin in divine law; its power is primarily spiritual, and is held by the pope as the vicar of Christ. Nevertheless, the law of that church does not reduce to divine law: it contains many precepts, for example, concerning fasting in Lent, which are to a spiritual end but of human origin, and thus part of human law. Civil power, on the other hand, originates from natural law. If the *ius gentium* has its genesis in the separation and dispersion of the *gentes*, the *ius civile* has its origin in a contrasting moment of coalition. Vitoria and Soto both hold that a "scattered" life is not enough for human beings to achieve their natural "end," a life where bodily needs are provided for and in which the "felicity" of natural moral goodness is achieved. Drawing closely on the account provided in Aquinas's *De Regno*, concerning the needs of human nature, they sketch how a life in community with others is the necessary condition for this, a community that requires directing to the common good if it is not to disintegrate. This, in turn, necessitates power, civil or political, which may be held either by the community itself or its representatives, or by a prince or king chosen by the commonwealth. Political power, then, as dis-

[33] Relection I, in Pagden and Lawrance 1992, 90.

tinct from ecclesiastical power, is a function of the demands of natural inclination and natural law; it is equally from God, but from "God through nature," in Soto's formulation (*De Iust. et Iure* IV.4.a.1, 6.a.4).[34] In either case, power is conceived teleologically, as "for" an end and as directing to that end (see Senellart 1995; Brett 2011, chap. 5). The end of spiritual power is the ultimate good, supernatural beatitude, and its laws are there to help human beings attain that end. The end of civil power is the common good of all of the members of the political community. Vitoria and Soto are as aware as Aquinas of the complexity of legislating for the common good: the law must be suitable to time and place, it must be "possible" in the sense of not imposing too great a burden on the people, and there must be a place for equity if the letter of the law goes against the end for which all law is passed.

Vitoria and Soto uphold the principle, which they also take from Aquinas, that human law in this sense must ultimately be "derived" from natural law just as is the *ius gentium*, but in a different way: not by deduction, but by specific "determinations" suited to the particular community in question. Both theologians feel the need, however, to give a more precise sense to Aquinas's term "determination." Going beyond his text, then, here they argue that what human law does is to change the moral character of an act. Thus, in Soto's words, "the second kind of derivation is a new constitution of an act in the genus of virtue. For by natural law it was not a virtue to kill a robber or a heretic: for natural law only dictated they be punished: but human law made their killing into a virtue" (*De Iust. et Iure* I.5.a.2).[35] The case is similar for abstaining from meat or keeping certain days sacred. Vitoria too gives the example of fasting, made into a virtue by human law, but "so that we do not just give an example from ecclesiastical laws, to buy a magistracy with money is ambitious, because it is forbidden in human law" (*De Pot. Civ.* para. 16, in Pagden and Lawrance 1992, 35). A human law, then, whether ecclesiastical or civil, will, if it is just, oblige not simply to a penalty—*ad poenam*—but to guilt—*ad culpam*: it is morally wrong, a sin, to transgress it.[36] Vitoria directly compares human law with divine law in this respect (ibid.), and both he and Soto appeal to the famous chapter of Paul's letter to the Romans, chapter 13, "the powers that

[34] Notoriously, Vitoria, while seeming to share the same understanding, says at one point in *On Civil Power* that the power of kings (as opposed to any other form of government) is not from the commonwealth but from God himself. See the Introduction in Pagden and Lawrance 1992, xix–xx; more generally on Soto and Vitoria, see Brett 1997, chap. 4.

[35] There is no irony here, of course.

[36] Both Vitoria and Soto reject the notion of a "purely penal" law, that is, a law which imposes a penalty (Vitoria's example is "he who cuts wood on the mountain shall pay 100 gold pieces") but does not involve any moral fault or guilt (*culpa*); Vitoria, briefly, at *De Lege* 96.a.4; Soto, at much greater length, and again in tacit opposition to Alfonso de Castro, *De Iust. et Iure* I.6.a.5. For both of them, the penalty is attached, and has its justification, only because of the moral necessity involved in the prohibition.

be are ordained of God," to support the conclusion that human law obliges in conscience (ibid., par. 15, in Pagden and Lawrance 1992, 33).[37] As stated briefly above in Section 14.1, the anti-Lutheran resonance of their reading of Romans 13 applies, in their hands, mostly to Luther's denial of authority to legislate within the Church. In their rebuttal of the parallel thesis for civil power, they are more concerned with the views of two previous Catholic theologians, Gerson (1363–1429) and Almain, both of whom had argued that civil law had no power to bind in conscience of itself: the obligation in conscience to obey it was only a precipitate of the obligation to obey divine law or natural law.[38] For the two Dominicans, by contrast, the authority to make law and the property of that law of being binding in conscience are indissolubly connected, and belong to both church and commonwealth, ecclesiastical and civil law, of their nature as such.

To obey human law, then, is not merely prudential, for the sake of avoiding a penalty. Rather, it is an act of virtue, in two senses: first, the virtue of obedience involved in fulfilling a duty in conscience; second, the virtue of doing something that has been made virtuous by human law. It is, then, a central part of the moral life of an individual, the "living well," the good life, which in Aristotelian thought is the "end" of human life together. As we have seen, the powers that be do not simply exist; they exist "for" something, for the human good. Their laws, therefore, function to "make men good," as Vitoria and Soto insist in their commentaries on *Prima Secundae*, Q. 92, a. 1, Aquinas's question "whether the effect of the law is to make men good." Here, both Vitoria and Soto are primarily concerned with civil law, and argue that the commonwealth and its law are not there just to provide for the conveniences of life or to supply human wants. Vitoria deliberately rejects the perspective of those who say that the laws are "like artificers, who do not aim at moral goodness, but at an artificial goodness"; on the contrary, he insists, "the intention of the king is without doubt to make men good absolutely speaking and to direct them to virtue" (*De Lege* 92.a.1, in Stüben 2010, 28; Pagden and Lawrance 1992, 165–6). Soto equally argues that "all civil laws [...] are to be instituted for the good of the soul, in which our felicity is in question [...] . For by the reason that man is born to felicity, by that same reason he is a civil animal" (*De Iust. Et Iure* I.2.a.1). The common good of the whole community is not, then, simply a technical matter of ensuring that collective life runs smoothly; it involves the moral good of living virtuously, which for both Dominicans—as for Aquinas and for Aristotle himself—is that in which human "felicity" or happiness consists. In a sharp divergence between the two theologians, however, Vitoria

[37] See Vitoria, *De Lege* 96.a.4; Soto, *De Iust. et Iure* I.6.a.4.

[38] The best discussion of this position is in Vereecke 1957. Both Gerson and Almain had worked in Paris, and Vitoria and Soto would have become very aware of their teachings during their years studying there.

distinguishes between "eternal" and "human" felicity, with the latter alone being the end of the civil power. Soto insists, by contrast, that the civil power too aims at supernatural well-being. In making this argument, Soto appeals again to Romans 13 that all power is of God; therefore, all laws, even those of princes, should be referred back to God. Vitoria uses the same text to support the more general argument that all human laws should be made for the sake of *felicitas*, whether natural or eternal: "And this is proved on the authority of Holy Scripture, Romans 13, 1: 'Let every soul be subject to the higher powers. For there is no power but of God.' Therefore its end too is of God. And: 'Whosoever resists the power, resists the ordinance of God.' But if the laws achieve nothing other than natural convenience, why then would he who resists the king resist the ordinance of God?" The true reading of Romans 13 depends on the understanding that the commonwealth is directly positioned within the moral teleology of human life.

In their different ways, then, for both Vitoria and Soto the moral dimension of obeying human law is part of the concept of human law and human legislative power itself, and is—at the same time—inseparable from its place within a divinely ordained structure of government, obedience to which is spiritually enjoined. It has its place within a distinctive and powerful vision of the Christian commonwealth, drawing upon centuries of Dominican (and other) thought, but they situate it now within a global order and defend it against the very different conception of human political and spiritual life advanced by their Lutheran adversaries. It is, to that extent, a Counter-Reformation theology—but also philosophy, in the way that we have seen, of law; in outline, it continued to form the backbone of Catholic thinking about law at least until the middle of the next century. As we have also seen, though, its distinctive shape owes a great deal to the specific circumstances of the first half of the sixteenth century. We now turn to consider the later development of this school, in the wake of the Council of Trent.

14.3. Jesuit Scholastics: Francisco Suárez, Gabriel Vázquez, and Juan de Salas

The years following the Council of Trent were marked by the hardening of the Counter-Reformation controversial effort against "the heretics," by the changing role of Spain in European politics, including vis-à-vis the papacy, and by changes, not unrelated, within the politics of the religious orders—especially the advent of the Society of Jesus to its position both of political influence and of intellectual prominence. The three authors we shall be considering in this section represent the "golden generation" of Jesuit theologians writing on law. The most famous of them is undoubtedly Suárez, whose work *On the Laws and God the Lawgiver* (*De Legibus ac Deo Legislatore*) of 1612 was read all over Europe, both Catholic and Protestant, and became the central point of reference for later scholastics thinking about the subject. A close associate of his, Juan de Salas (1553–1612), wrote a near-contemporaneous work *On the Laws* (*De Legibus*), published in 1611, which is clearly in dialogue (and sometimes in disagreement) with some key Suarezian ideas. In many respects both Suárez and Salas were responding, the latter more positively, the former almost entirely negatively, to the work of Gabriel Vázquez (1549–1604), whose "disputations" on the subject of law (first published at Alcalá in 1598) are in important ways the most innovative and challenging of all. A glance at the intellectual formation of these three Jesuit writers shows how much the world had changed since the beginning of the sixteenth century, when Vitoria and Soto had studied at Paris as the undoubted European center of gravity in theology. Educated, instead, in the Jesuit colleges and the universities of Spain, Suárez, Salas, and Vázquez each had a period at the Collegio Romano in Rome, the most celebrated college of the Society of Jesus, before returning to resume university teaching careers in the Iberian peninsula (at Coimbra, Salamanca, and Alcalá, respectively). They thus represent a new kind of Counter-Reformation academic internationalism, and their work is marked by great confidence and independence, including vis-à-vis the authority of Aquinas. Scholars differ on how to assess both the nature and the extent of their distance from him on the nature of law, a distance that is often characterized pejoratively.[39] It is not the purpose of the following sections to offer any such overall account, but rather to highlight certain distinctive aspects of the way these three Jesuits think about law, in relation to their Dominican predecessors as much as to Aquinas.

14.3.1. Reason, Will, and Legal Obligation

We begin our discussion with Vázquez, whose work is the earliest of the three, and with the question of whether law is an act of intellect or of will. Vázquez starts out by endorsing the position that we found in Vitoria and Soto: that law, as an act of *imperium* ("command"), is an act of intellect. For him as for them, the *nuda voluntas* ("bare will") of a superior does not of itself oblige, and is therefore not law. Vázquez adds the qualification, however, that a preceding act of will must nonetheless be involved in legislation: an act of *electio* ("choice"), a will for his subjects to do one thing rather than another. What a law does is to command subjects to do the will of the superior; thus, without any such act of will, there can be no law, even if that act of will is not *itself* law (*Comm. STh.* disp. 105 [recte 150], cap. 3, fo. 4–50). It might be argued, then, that for all of his apparent allegiance to the intellectualist position, his thesis that an act of command is unintelligible without an act of will in effect concedes the voluntarist position on law.[40] For Vázquez, as for Vitoria and Soto, the issue turns on the force of obligation that is distinctive to law. Vázquez

[39] See, e.g., Finnis 1980; Todescan 1973.
[40] Höpfl 2004, chap. 11, speaks of the "voluntarist collapse" in Jesuit theories of law.

makes this plain in his reply to "certain more recent writers," who say that law is an act of the intellect in the sense of a *iudicium* ("judgment"), not command: "they prove it, because law is a rule, but the act that proposes to subjects the will of a superior is not a rule, but rather the putting-forward, and explanation of a rule: therefore that act (they say) is not law [...]" (ibid., cap. 4, fo. 6, col. 1). These "certain" authors clearly base their argument on Aquinas's statement that a law is *aliquid rationis*, something that belongs to reason, because it is "a rule and a measure" (*STh.* Ia.2.ae.90.a.1), and use it to overturn the consensus of opinion (itself based on Aquinas's text) that law is an act of command.[41] To Vázquez, this is "frivolous," because in his opinion it is clear to everyone that a judgment on its own is not a law. In effect, merely to rely on the term "rule" to save the intellectualist position does not solve the issue.

So far, Vázquez has been working with a set of issues familiar from our discussion of Vitoria and Soto, even if his solution is not the same. He now makes a move, however, that distances him radically from his Dominican predecessors. He stipulates that the definition of law as an act of command, situated in the intellect but dependent upon a precedent act of will, is only applicable to positive law, whether divine or human. The same definition cannot be offered for natural law, and the reason is that natural law commands or prohibits things that are good or bad in themselves, independently of any will, even that of God. If we now ask what constitutes this goodness and badness that are independent of any act of will, the answer lies in the conformity or otherwise of certain actions or objects to rational nature. It is rational nature itself that is, therefore, natural law; and, since created rational nature proceeds from God, this must be so in God as well as in the rational creature. Vázquez allows that, in a secondary sense, we can speak of natural law as an act of the intellect, an act of command, at least in God, since God does command us to do what is good and prohibit us from doing what is bad. However, in us, the act of the intellect involved in natural law is not command, but judgment: "for we do not impose upon ourselves the command of not killing; or even if we did, it is not this that makes killing a sin; rather we judge, led by natural reason and light, that this, or that, is a sin [...]" (*Comm. STh* disp. 105 [recte 150], cap. 3, fo. 5, col. 2). In sum, then, the element of will involved in the notion of command—even if command is in itself an act of intellect—rules out a single definition of law that will cover both natural and positive law, or rather, that "the term 'law' is not as appropriate to natural as to positive law, whether the word [*lex*] is derived from 'reading' [*legendo*] from something written, or from 'choosing'

[41] Aquinas, *STh.* Ia.2.ae.90.a.1, sed contra: "to command is an act of reason" (*imperare est rationis*), and ad 3: "from the fact that someone has a will for an end, reason commands (*imperat*) in respect of those things that have regard for that end." Notice that the motive force that Aquinas here gives the will is not so very far from Vázquez's own position; certainly he could claim that Aquinas's words support his own.

[*eligendo*]; because natural law is neither read in something written, nor constituted by an act of will in any choice, even of God; but necessarily is so of its own nature. It is therefore better called right (*ius*), because it is the rule of the just and the unjust." In the case of natural law, then, Vázquez holds on to the Thomist notion of law as a "rule" (*regula*), but precisely the character of rational nature as a rule means that it is not very appropriately called natural *law*. Rather, it is "something prior" to any law.

It is typical of Vázquez's originality and audacity—and courage—that only five folios into the subject of law he has overturned much of the entire Thomist system. First, he has denied Aquinas's premise that a single definition of law, as a "rule and measure of actions," will cover all types of law. Second, although Vázquez has kept natural law as "the rule of human actions," the "rule of the just and the unjust," and therefore its place within the hierarchy of laws, he has entirely changed its character. As we have seen, for Aquinas it is human practical reason, working from the natural inclinations of human beings, which generates the precepts of natural law. For Vázquez, however, not only is natural law not primarily a series of precepts, but rational nature itself; in addition, rational nature has nothing to do with natural inclinations. It is the same in God, who has no natural inclinations, as in man.[42] The whole world of Aristotelian natural teleology, natures created by God with ends and with inclinations toward them, and of man as a rational participant in this government, is absent. Non-rational nature has no normative force or even contribution to normative force; it is outside the world of law. This perspective governs Vázquez's treatment of eternal law as well. Having summarized Aquinas's argument, he continues by listing the difficulties with its being counted as *law*: "First, because this law is not an *imperium* in the mind of God [...] . Secondly because it is not promulgated [...] . Thirdly and finally because rationals and irrationals and inanimates are subject to this law [...] but law cannot be imposed on things that have no sense, or no reason." The Thomists "labor not a little" to defend this conception, but in vain. Vázquez is happy to grant some sense of eternal law, as an idea in God's mind, a rule of everything that happens, but this is not law in the same sense. When Scripture says, in Proverbs 8, "And he laid a law upon the waters," this was, according to Vázquez, "nothing other than the very nature of the waters, which God created with this inclination natural to them" (*Comm. STh.* 91.a.1).

If we now turn to Juan de Salas, we find him sympathetic to Vázquez in many respects, although not entirely agreeing with him. Salas has an explicit critique in *Tractatus de Legibus* of Aquinas's definition of law as a rule or measure, because this covers many things that are not the same at all: the rules of a trade, for example, or the natural inclinations of irrational creatures (*Tract.*

[42] The contrast between Aquinas and Vázquez on "rational nature" is well brought out in Westerman 1997, chap. 2.

XIII, disp. 1.iii, fo. 5). However, the "rule" by which God governs these latter is not properly law, because it represents "natural" rather than "moral" obligation. The contrast that Salas here invokes between the "natural" and the "moral" requires a little elucidation. It is based upon a conception of the freedom of the will forcefully articulated by his fellow Jesuit Luis de Molina (1536–1600), whose *Concordance of Freewill with the Gifts of Divine Grace* (1588) caused controversy for the degree of liberty it accorded the human will.[43] In this conception, the will must be free in the sense of not subject to any necessitation whatsoever. Necessitation characterizes the realm of natural phenomena and natural activity. The operation of free will, however, generates a world of moral, as opposed to natural, phenomena and agency: a thing, or an action, is moral rather than natural in relation to a free act of the will. For Salas here, then, irrational creatures, being incapable of free will, can only be naturally necessitated rather than morally obliged. However, Salas is unwilling to give up entirely on the notion of eternal law in the proper sense of law. He therefore asserts that there are two eternal laws in God: one, not properly a law, by which he governs irrational creatures; another, properly a law and properly obliging, by which he governs rational creatures (*Tract.* XIII, disp. 4.i, fo. 63). To the question of how this is promulgated, he responds that it is not promulgated formally but "virtually," and this is possible because "God's eternal law does not oblige except through the mediation of temporal law, be it natural or positive"; therefore, God's eternal decree that these other laws should exist and be promulgated constitutes a virtual, and eternal, promulgation of the eternal law (ibid., disp. 2.i, fo. 32, col. 2).

On the question of whether law is an act of the will or the intellect, Salas's first conclusion, at the most general level, is that law, being something of its nature as such that stems from rational nature, must be something that "pertains to reason" (ibid., disp. 1.vi, fo. 10, col. 2). Beyond this, however, he, like Vázquez, feels compelled to answer the question differently in the cases of natural and of positive law. Like Vázquez, Salas argues that the latter essentially involves an act of will on the part of a superior, but in a different way. Vázquez had argued that the relevant will was an act of choice preceding the act of command which is situated in the intellect and is properly law. Salas argues, by contrast, that the relevant will is a will to oblige subjects, which must be externally expressed in some form. (This makes him sympathetic to—though not entirely in agreement with—the view that law is neither an act of the will nor of the intellect, but a kind of "sign" in writing or other medium.) Taking this view, it is wrong to place positive law in an act of command as opposed to an act of judgment, as if this made the relevant difference: command is neither necessary nor sufficient for obligation, and hence for law (ibid., fo. 14–5).

[43] See Schmutz 2001 for an excellent account of Molina's theory.

The case is different for natural law, which is only "a concept, or elicited act of our intellect, dictating that something is dissonant, or inappropriate, and shameful to rational nature; or necessary, and altogether to be done, if one would behave honourably" (ibid., fo. 10, col. 2). To do something that does not conform to this dictate is a sin, and sin betokens that a law has been transgressed; thus the dictate is itself a law. Salas agrees with Vázquez in removing any trace of an act of will on the part of a superior from natural law: clearly not a temporal prince, since we are obliged by natural law entirely independently of whatever any such prince may command, but not God either. Against the position that *all* law must involve an act of will on the part of a superior, willing to oblige us, and therefore that natural law does not oblige without the will of God, Salas counters, "firstly because if *per impossibile* there were man in the world, but not God, it would be wrong to lie: therefore contrary to some law; but there would be no will of God: therefore natural law does not include the will of God." Salas then introduces some of the same considerations that we saw govern Vitoria's, and especially Soto's, discussions of God's law, but to the opposite effect. Thus, supposing such a will of God to oblige us, either it is necessitated or it is free. If free, then he could have willed not to oblige us; indeed, he could do so now: "and thus he could dispense in every precept of natural law, indeed, abrogate it entirely, and render licit all acts and omissions, even the hatred of God" (ibid., fo. 11, col. 2). All of this is entirely false, but on the other hand, it is, in the first place, absurd to suppose any necessitated will of God in respect of his creatures; moreover, in the second, the will to oblige *must* be a free will for the resulting obligation to have the quality of being "moral." Salas says that if he had to posit one or the other will of God, he would rather go with the nominalists, including Ockham, and make it entirely free, than go with "not a few more recent" writers—including Soto, as we have seen—and say that God necessarily wills to oblige us to things that are in themselves good (ibid., disp. 5.iv, fo. 10, col. 2). The entire issue is avoided, though, by taking divine will out of the obligation of natural law altogether.

Salas thereby gives himself the problem, however, of accounting for natural law's capacity to oblige. Vázquez's very radical solution, as we saw, was to make natural law rational nature itself, and thus to deny that natural law, at least in its primary sense, obliges at all: it is a rule or standard, what is right (*ius*) rather than a law. Salas shares his conception of "rational nature," as well as his implicit dismissal of the role of natural inclinations in natural law, which he makes explicit in a direct critique of Aquinas: "any command which is founded purely upon reason without any positive or arbitrary law should be called natural, whether it commands things that are in accordance with natural inclination, or not" (ibid., disp. 2.ii, fo. 35). However, Salas does not want to follow Vázquez entirely in positing that rational nature just is natural law. He allows that rational nature can metaphorically be called natural law, insofar as rules and precepts of action can be derived from it: "But I only deny, that it is properly law: since a law, properly speaking, is a form of command: but rational nature [...] is not a command: therefore not a law" (ibid., disp. 1.vi, fo. 10, col. 2). (Vázquez had in fact acknowledged this as we have seen.) For Salas, natural law, more traditionally, is rather a dictate of the intellect. To save the obligatory character of this dictate, Salas has recourse to an old distinction, between *lex imperans* ("law that commands," which always requires the will of a superior) and *lex indicans* ("law which shows what is to be done"), reason and natural law being of the second type. He insists nevertheless that in a broader sense "*lex indicans* is truly a precept, and a command, insofar as it is a rule that is necessarily to be followed, if a deed would be righteous, or insofar as it has the power of obliging" (ibid., fo. 14, col. 1). The rules that have to be obeyed in any skill, he argues, are called "precepts," and similarly those that have to be obeyed in the domain of morals. This seems equivalent, though, to arguing for a different sense of "obligation" from that imposed by positive law, and Salas never directly articulates such a conception; it seems, moreover, to go directly against the spirit of his critique of "rule" as a definition of law.

By contrast with both Vázquez and Salas, Suárez makes a determined attempt to salvage a single concept of law to cover all four laws of the Thomist account. He shares the view that law is exclusively the preserve of rational creatures. The grounds for this lie, however, more in the consequences of possessing reason than in reason itself; that is, they lie in the freedom to which it gives rise and in the government which this then necessitates: "talking about law in the proper sense [...] it can only be for the sake of the rational creature: for law is not imposed except on a free nature, nor does it have for its subject-matter any acts other than free acts." Suárez also holds that "a creature possessed of intellect, of the very fact that it is a creature, has a superior to whose providence and ordination it is subject; and because it is possessed of intellect, it is capable of moral government, which comes about through *imperium*" (*Leg.* I, cap. 3, nn. 2–3). For Suárez, this view of law as an essential part of the moral government of free individuals involves abandoning the Thomist position that law is essentially an act of the intellect. He agrees with Vitoria and Soto that what law does is to change the moral character of a particular action, so that such-and-such is now *morally* necessary where before it was not; as for Salas, a moral (as opposed to a natural) necessity is precisely an obligation. However, this power to oblige, he argues, is in the will and not in the intellect, "for the intellect can only point out the necessity, which is in the object itself; and which if it is not in the object, cannot give it to it; but the will confers a necessity, which was not before in the object and, for example in the case of justice, makes something worth this much or that much, and in the case of the other virtues, that here and now it is necessary to perform some deed, which otherwise was not of itself necessary" (ibid., cap. 5). All law, therefore, involves an act of will on the part of a superior: not directly the will for such-and-such an action—for, just as in Vitoria and Soto, such a will has no capacity to oblige—but the will to oblige subjects to perform that action, which is not the same thing (ibid., cap. 4, nn. 8–9).

Again, and in a way that will now be familiar, for Suárez this puts paid to the Thomist conception of eternal law as governing all nature: for irrational and inanimate creatures "effect their motions not freely, but of the necessity of nature." As a result they are not and cannot be subject to law in the proper sense of the term, "because the property of law is to impose a bond and a moral obligation; but only intellectual beings are capable of this, and even they, not in all their actions, but only in those that they do freely; for all moral being depends upon freedom" (ibid., II, cap. 2, nn. 10–1).[44] However, it gives Suárez a problem with natural law, for he concedes that what natural law commands and forbids is intrinsically good and intrinsically evil. That is, the "moral necessity" appears to be already in its objects, independently of any act of will. Moreover, this goodness and badness is accessible to natural reason, making the precepts of natural law "dictates of natural reason." Suárez thus accepts much of the intellectualist position as developed in the other two Jesuits; he was not so direct in his rejection of the inclinations as a basis for the commands of natural law, but he made it plain that Aquinas's categorization of the precepts of natural law is only one among several, and he put it last with the qualification that we are not to think of these inclinations as "purely natural" but as "determined and elevated" by reason (*Leg.* II, cap. 8, nn. 3–4).

Nevertheless, Suárez is unwilling to allow that natural law is either not a law at all, properly speaking, or a law in a different sense, a *lex indicans* rather than a *lex imperans*. He equally rejects the Ockhamist position that natural law exists wholly as a command of the divine will, which can therefore be abrogated at God's will. He therefore chooses what he describes as a middle way—"and this I take to be the opinion of Saint Thomas and the common opinion of theologians"—that, on the one hand, "natural law does not simply indicate the bad and the good, but contains in addition its own prohibition of the bad and command of the good."[45] On the other hand, however, "this will of God, this prohibition or command does not constitute the entire rationale of the goodness and badness which lies in the observation or the transgression of the natural law, but presupposes that there is in those actions a certain necessary righteousness or disgrace, and joins onto them the special obligation of divine law." On the related question of whether God can dispense in the precepts of natural law, Suárez takes a position close to Soto's, although his authority is Cardinal Cajetan's commentary on the same locus, *Prima Secundae*, Q. 100, a. 8: that God did not necessarily will to create rational nature, but that once

[44] See Westerman 1997, chap. 3; Breiskorn 2001, 2010; Courtine 1999, chap. 4.

[45] One of Suárez's authorities for this assertion is Vitoria's lecture *On That to Which Man Is Obliged*, which we noted above in Section 14.2.2, when examining the voluntarist elements of Vitoria's theory.

having freely willed it, he then necessarily willed to prohibit things that were not consonant with that nature; to do otherwise would have been a failure of divine providence, and not consistent with his goodness (*Leg.* II, cap. 6, nn. 1–4, 7, 11, 23). It is, in general, a modified voluntarism quite similar to that of Vitoria, and with the same uneasiness—highlighted by Salas, none too kindly describing the argument from providence as "laughable": "for God, to save men from sinning and meriting eternal or temporal punishment, could have abstained from that prohibition, and in doing so would have proceeded most wisely, and provided for our good in the best possible way" (Salas, *Tract.* XIII, disp. 5.iv, fo. 76).

To sum up, then, all three of these authors seek to accommodate both the idea that natural law is a "commanding" law, comprising precepts which impose a moral obligation, and at the same time the idea that it is not simply a series of commands, but is intrinsically connected to and necessary for human nature understood as rational nature. Salas dismisses Suarez's resolution of the problem, and yet, as we have seen, cannot himself solve it without implicitly appealing to a different sense of obligation from that which he had defended in discussing the nature of law in general. Vázquez's solution was to locate the commanding aspect of natural law solely in God's intellect rather than in our own, and to argue that this aspect is in any case only a secondary sense of natural law; in its primary sense, natural law is simply rational nature itself, properly a *ius* rather than a *lex*. But his sacrifice of natural law as a law that primarily commands us to do good and avoid evil was unacceptable to either of the other two.

14.3.2. Human Law and the Law of Nations

Turning now from natural to human law, we begin with the *ius gentium*, which is the source of more innovative thinking from all three of these authors.[46] Vázquez, once again, is the most original. With characteristic intellectual enterprise, Vázquez handled the question of the relationship between natural law and the law of nations by stepping out of the confines of the Thomist debate entirely and looking instead to the French humanist jurist François Connan (1508–1551), who had distinguished between a kind of *ius* (law, or right; Connan does not make a sharp distinction) that is concerned with the immutable rules of fair and honest conduct and a kind of *ius* that is concerned instead with utility. Connan suggested that the former was the *ius naturale*, the latter the *ius gentium*. Vázquez equates the first to his own understanding of natural *ius* as nothing other than human nature itself, which, as we have seen, is the primary rule of the just and the unjust. The second, though, "is that which is

[46] The following account of human law is taken, with modifications, from Brett 2011, chaps. 3 and 6.

not the rule of the just and the unjust, virtue and sin, nor does it command anything in such a way that the contrary is a sin, but simply concedes a free faculty of using a thing as useful, or even as honorable: but in such a way that not to use it, or to use something else, is not morally wrong" (*Comm. STh.* disp. 157, cap. 3, fo. 53). The *ius gentium*, then, is not *ius* in the sense of a law, but only in the sense of "a licence or faculty," "for this is one of the significations of *ius*" (ibid.). Thus, "the *ius gentium* is solely a law of permission and utility" (ibid., fo. 54). Vázquez's creative fusion of a scholastic and a legal-humanist inheritance produced a startlingly novel and, to contemporaries, threatening account of the *ius gentium*: that the law of nations is not a separate legislative domain, but a zone of permission accommodated within natural law, a series of rights but not obligations. No one is legally obliged to go to war, for example, under the *ius gentium*; they only *may* do so, but if they do, then natural law dictates that no one should be killed without just cause, just as it dictates that no individual man should kill another without due cause. The only *law* governing relations between commonwealths is natural law.

Both Suárez and Salas engage in an extensive polemic against this way of thinking.[47] Neither of them will accept that the *ius gentium* is purely permissive. Both insist that the *ius gentium* is properly a law, but what kind of law? We have already seen how Vitoria and Soto had begun to insist on the positivity of the *ius gentium*, without abandoning the idea that it is in some sense an exercise of natural reason. In the context of clearing up Aquinas's confusing statements, the upshot of their work had been to preserve the idea that the *ius gentium* is constituted by a process of natural reasoning, but nevertheless to distinguish it more decidedly from natural law by arguing that its status as law was a function of human consensus, not nature, and that therefore it was positive rather than natural law. By contrast, Salas and Suárez differ with Vitoria and Soto in holding that the positivity of the *ius gentium* entails that it *cannot* be the product of natural reason. Suárez explained the nub of the matter in the second book of his *De Legibus* (caps. 17 and 19). The law of nations cannot be an exercise of natural reason, because if it were, it would be natural law; again, this cannot be the correct position to take, because the *ius gentium* involves things that are not intrinsically necessary to rational human nature, such as the division of property, servitudes, the practice of warfare, and other such things (ibid., cap. 17, n. 8). The conclusion must be, then, that the *ius gentium* as distinct from natural law cannot contain *any* precepts that are intrinsically necessary to a rational creature and thus discoverable by natural reason alone (ibid., n. 9). The source of the substantive content of the *ius gentium*, the basis for positive consensus, is not natural reason but customary *usage*.[48]

[47] There is a brief treatment of the contrast with Vázquez in Doyle 1999; see also Kremer 2008, 127–30.

[48] E.g., the immunity of ambassadors: Suárez, *Leg.* II, cap. 19, n. 7. See Tierney 2007.

Given that the *ius gentium*, for both of these authors, is positive law, the question arises as to who is its legislator. Here, Salas and Suárez both kept elements of Vitoria's conception of a world community that is lacking in Soto, for whom the reasoning involved in the *ius gentium* can be done by individuals alone. For Salas, the legislator is "all the nations" (*omnes gentes*): "it is called the law of nations not precisely because all nations use it, but because they use it *as its authors*" (*Tract.* XIII, disp. 2.iii, fo. 39; emphasis added). Salas makes it clear that they are not its authors as single nations, but as forming one community: "For all nations, insofar as they make up one community of the whole human race, can oblige individuals to those things that are useful to the whole human race" (ibid.). However, this same passage makes it clear that the *ius gentium* is still, for Salas, a law governing individuals, just as it was for Soto. By contrast, it is Suárez's well recognized innovation to have made a distinction between two senses of the *ius gentium*: one is "the law that all peoples and the various nations [*omnes populi et gentes variae*] ought to keep between themselves," and the other is "the law that individual cities, or kingdoms observe within themselves," but in which nevertheless all or almost all cities and kingdoms coincide (*Leg.* II, cap. 19, n. 8). The former is properly the law of nations; the latter is a kind of universal civil law. Suárez goes on to give the reason for the existence of the *ius gentium* in its proper sense. It lies in the fact that the human race "always has some kind of unity, not simply of a species, but also a quasi-political and moral unity [...] . So that even if every perfected city, commonwealth or kingdom, is in itself a perfect community, and being made up of its own members, nevertheless each of them is also a member in some sense of this universal community" (ibid., n. 9). Thus, despite the similarities in language to Salas—and indeed to Vitoria—on the unity of the whole human race, Suárez differed profoundly in perceiving the universal community to be made up not simply of individual human beings, nor even of *gentes*, but of commonwealths. The *ius gentium* properly speaking, then, is a law between commonwealths, not individuals, marking a decisive change in the older conception and coming closer to the modern understanding—although, historically speaking, that understanding is (perhaps paradoxically) more likely to be rooted ultimately in Thomas Hobbes's conception of natural law.[49]

14.3.3. Human Law: Civil and Ecclesiastical Law

It remains to discuss human law in the sense of civil and ecclesiastical law. Here, by contrast with Vitoria and Soto, the thought of the three Jesuit theologians we have been studying is marked by a decisive trend to see the "end," or the common good, of the civil commonwealth and its law in terms of peaceable coexistence rather than directly in terms of the individual moral good

[49] See Schröder 2000.

(which Vitoria and Soto had still viewed, in Aristotelian terms, as an important part of its rationale). As we saw, "felicity" is twofold, natural and supernatural, and Vitoria and Soto differed in that Soto had posited the latter as the "end" of the civil commonwealth as well as of the church. Vázquez, Suárez, and Salas agree strongly with Vitoria that the civil commonwealth must be confined to the natural end. Suárez articulated this position by drawing expressly on the theology of "pure nature" that had begun to be developed by both Dominican and Jesuit authors in resolving the controversial question of the freedom of the human will in relation to the operation of divine grace. The original idea was hypothetically to skim off the supernatural aspects of the actual condition (*status*) of mankind in order better to understand the potentials of human nature alone. Suárez, however, appeared to take this one step further and to think of human nature in *any* condition as "purely natural." Thus, in his treatise on the ultimate end of human life, Suárez argued that there is no natural appetite in man for his supernatural end because there is no natural potential for that end. "Purely naturally"—that is, *naturally*—man is ordered only toward the end of natural felicity; his being ordered toward supernatural felicity is something *added* to that nature.[50] Suárez used this theological stance to argue that political power is "simply natural" (*mere naturalis*), and therefore does not and cannot have for its end the supernatural felicity of the future life, except by some extrinsic relation (*Leg.* III, cap. 11, nn. 4–5). Neither does it have for its end the spiritual felicity of this life, because that felicity is a disposition intrinsically ordered to future, supernatural felicity, and therefore equally falls outside the scope of civil power (ibid., n. 6). Finally, however, Suárez departed from Vitoria's position as well as Soto's in arguing that "the civil legislative power, even considered purely naturally, does not have for its intrinsic and *per se* intended end the natural felicity of the future life, and not even the proper felicity of the present life insofar as it pertains to individual men in their aspects as particular persons. Its end is rather the natural felicity of the perfect human community of which it is charged with the care, and of individual men in their aspect as members of such a city, that they might live in it in peace and justice, with a sufficiency of those goods that relate to the preservation and comfort of bodily life" (ibid., n. 7). The city figures in this sense as a necessary condition of individual human felicity rather than the intrinsic locus of it.

Neither Salas nor Vázquez in their commentaries on the law explicitly deploy the theology of "pure nature" to elucidate the function of civil power and of the commonwealth more generally. However, they do share the thesis that for Suárez was the corollary of the "purely natural" understanding, which is

[50] The classic studies of *pura natura* are de Lubac 1945 and 1965. It remains, however, a deeply contested concept, and its history no less so; the 2001, vol. 101, issue of the *Revue Thomiste* is devoted to this subject. The political ramifications of de Lubac's understanding of *pura natura* in Suárez are pursued in Courtine 1999, chap. 2.

that civil power is fundamentally concerned not with the internal acts of its subjects—acts of intellect and of will—but rather with their external actions. There was support for this position in the rationale that Aquinas had offered, in his treatment of laws in the *Prima Secundae*, for the necessity of divine law: human judgment can only concern exterior motions, and thus a divine law and a divine judge are necessary to regulate their interior acts (*STh.* Ia.2.ae.91.a.4). Soto had repeated this view in the introduction to his treatment of divine positive law, but it is not remotely central to his exposition of human positive law, nor does it affect his conclusion concerning the "end" of that law. By contrast, it is a key theme for Suárez, for whom political "community" involves only external acts (*Leg.* III, cap. 13, n. 3); for Salas, who held that "civil power is external, and is ordained for the sake of ruling an external community" (*Tract.* disp. 9.1, fo. 195, col. 2); and for Vázquez, who argued that "law is the command of a superior, to which subjects are bound to conform according to their own mode; and therefore since it is peculiar to man among rational creatures to be corporeal, it is in corporeal, and external matters that he must conform to his superiors [...] not in internal, in which he shares with the angels" (*Comm. STh.* disp. 160, cap. 2, fo. 71, col. 1).

All of these authors, however, add a qualification on "external" acts. By their own arguments, law can only fall on moral acts, that is, acts that are the result of choice, an internal act of free will. As Suárez said, an external human act "cannot take place without an internal, for the external act has its quality as human and moral from the internal act as from its moral form [...] just as a human being is made up of body and soul" (*Leg.* III, cap. 13, n. 1). How then to save the principal thesis of the externality of the city and its law? It was Vázquez who supplied the answer, which is that *indirectly* the human law must, and does, command those acts of will that are involved in external acts, though it has no need to, and cannot, command purely internal acts (*Comm. STh.* disp., 160, cap. 3).[51] This concession, however, entails that in fact the law of the commonwealth does intervene in, and shape, the individual's moral life, and thus affects his "natural felicity," at least, if not his spiritual. Thus Vázquez wrote that it is not the case, as some think, that civil laws make men good only in an external sense: "laws which are properly laws, even if you include civil laws, when they are observed from the desire for virtue, make man virtuous not only externally, but also internally, and good in terms of true virtue, at least moral virtue" (ibid., 92.a.1, fo. 16–7). Likewise, Suárez admitted that his thesis of the "end" of the city gave some plausibility to the view that the only virtue the civil law demanded of its citizens was that of justice, the virtue that governs our external relations with others (*Leg.* III, cap. 12, n. 3). However, he insisted that this plausibility was specious: securing the external end of the city de-

[51] Cf. Salas, *Tract.* disp. 9.1, fo. 196, col. 2; Suárez, *Leg.* III, cap. 13, n. 9 (who, however, does not cite Vázquez directly). For Vázquez's position in more detail, see Vereecke 1957, chap. 5.

mands all of the virtues, and "the civil laws intend to make good men, because they cannot otherwise make good citizens" (ibid., n. 8).

All three authors, then, secure in some sense the Aristotelian thesis that the laws "make men good," but it is only indirectly rather than directly, as in Vitoria and Soto. This may account for the subtly different way in which they argue for the obligation in conscience of human law. They entirely agree with the two Dominicans that to hold the contrary is to concur with "the heretics" in taking away any true power of legislating from both ecclesiastical and civil power, "for [the heretics] do not deny," as Vázquez wrote, "that princes can lay down certain ordinances for the good state and government of the commonwealth; but they deny, that they can oblige the consciences of subjects with them" (*Comm. STh.* disp. 158, cap. 2, fo. 61, col. 1). However, while Romans 13 is still important to them in establishing the contrary, it does not have the resonance that it did for their Dominican predecessors. Instead, they use another argument that we do not find in Vitoria and Soto, which is the command of natural law to obey superiors. The two Dominicans certainly accept, from Aquinas, that there is a natural law command to live in society with others, and from this follows the establishment of civil power and its laws; in addition, those laws must be derived from natural law by way of "determination." However, they never think of the obligation to obey human law as directly grounded on a specific natural law precept to obey superiors. By contrast, this is a central theme in all three of these Jesuits. Thus, Vázquez defends the power of human law to oblige in conscience of itself: the obligation "does not arise wholly from natural law, without the addition of a command and order of the prince"; nevertheless, "when St Thomas said that laws laid down by men, derived in the second way [sc. by way of 'determination' rather than 'deduction'], oblige only from the will of the prince, all he was doing was assigning the principle of obliging in this matter as opposed to another; he does not exclude the universal principle of natural law, i.e., that superiors are to be obeyed, on which as upon its foundation the obligation of human law rests" (ibid., disp. 154, cap. 3, fo. 41, col. 2). Salas, combating Gerson's thesis, vigorously argues against the idea that the obligation of human law depends on that of divine law, appealing to the same intellectualist account that we saw him develop above in the context of natural law. Human law would oblige in conscience even if there were no divine law, because the dictate of reason would still constitute law, and would bind in conscience; therefore, so too would human laws, because reason would dictate that they should be obeyed. As it happens, God does in fact command that we obey our superiors and their laws, but he does not need to in order for them to be binding. This position, however, entails that human laws do not oblige independently of natural law, and specifically a natural law command to obey human superiors and human laws (*Tract.* disp. 10.1, fo. 219, col. 2). Suárez, finally, argues from both the divine law and the natural law precept to obey the just laws of legitimate superiors.

All three of these authors, then, just like Vitoria and Soto, feel the need to firm up Aquinas's second mode of derivation of human law from natural law, the mode of "determination," in order to account for its capacity to oblige in conscience. They do so, however, not by insisting on the moral creativity of human law, backed up by a reading of Romans 13 that associates it directly with the moral "end" of the commonwealth. Rather, they combat the possible moral shakiness of "determination" by grounding it more firmly in the obligation of a higher law. Suárez, at least, is well aware of the danger inherent in this strategy: that it threatens to reduce the obligation of civil law to that of divine or natural law, ceding the position of Gerson and "the heretics" and depriving the prince of any real power of his own. Suárez argues that this does not, in fact, follow, because the civil law is the *proximate* cause of the obligation, which would not exist without it and which can therefore be said simply to be speaking about an obligation of civil law (*Leg.* III.21, n. 7). He does not leave the matter there, moreover, but adds the more traditional argument from Romans 13 and also an argument from the impossibility of moral government without obligation in conscience. His uneasy text shows the fine line that these authors are treading in their appeal to either divine or natural law in this context, threatening to undermine the whole sphere of human power and law—the Christian commonwealth—which it had been the concern of this movement from the beginning to uphold and defend. On the one hand looms the Charybdis of divine right theories of kingship, on the other the Scylla of a purely natural law theory of the commonwealth. Either way, the distinctive voice and authority of the scholastic theologian are—and would be—lost.

14.4. Conclusion

As noted above in Section 14.1, later scholastic philosophy of law cannot be detached from the broader political and theological enterprise to which all members of the movement, in their different ways, were essentially committed. Nevertheless, it *is* a philosophy; and what I hope to have shown is some of the extraordinary quality of the philosophical thinking involved, as members of the movement wrestled with fundamental questions left insufficiently clear by Aquinas's text: What *is* it to think of law as "a rule and a measure"? How does this square with the demand that the law oblige? Can there be one single sense of "law" to cover all of the "rules" by which human beings are governed? How can a law be "natural"? Assuming that there is a natural law, what precisely is its relationship to positive law? What accounts for our duty to obey positive law? This is not to say that their thinking does not have its limits. The intense discussion between different authors can take place on ground that is very narrow indeed. For example, the interminable disputes over whether law is an act of will or of the intellect, and precisely which act of the will or the intellect that might be, effectively exclude the possibility that it might not be an act of the will or the intellect at all. Alternatives are considered, for example, as we have seen, by Salas in thinking about the written quality of positive law, but they are all pulled back into the dominant psychological model of legislation. That model depends itself on a philosophy and theology of agency, both human and divine, in which the "acts" of reason and will are the markers of any "act" that is to be counted as such. This philosophy would come under serious pressure as the seventeenth century wore on, and into the eighteenth, challenging at the same time the philosophy of law that it underpinned.[52] However, that does not detract from either the interest or the quality of the legal thinking involved. Indeed, precisely because they do not think as we do, the limits of their thought invite us to consider the limits of our own.[53]

Further Reading

The most extensive recent study of the initial School of Salamanca, with lengthy chapters on both Vitoria and Soto, and a rich bibliography, is Belda Plans 2000. For the Jesuit period of the movement, Höpfl 2004 is outstanding. The older study by Hamilton (1963) is still valuable; Skinner 1978, vol. 2 contains an excellent general overview of "The revival of Thomism." Pagden (1982) discusses the School in the context of Spain and the politics of the Spanish Crown in America. For biographical and bibliographical information on all authors of the second scholastic, the reader should consult the excellent and indispensable website edited by Schmutz (2008).

Regarding the individual theorists here discussed, the best study of Vitoria's legal philosophy is Deckers 1991; an excellent recent collection of essays is Bunge et al. 2011. There is, to my knowledge, no recent monograph devoted entirely to Soto; Carro 1967 is seriously outdated. I discuss Vitoria and Soto in Brett 1997 (chap. 4). Of the three Jesuit authors here discussed, there is no monograph, to my knowledge, on Salas, despite his recognized importance. An excellent treatment of Vázquez's legal theory is Vereecke 1957. Recent collections of articles on Suárez, with contributions on the subject of his legal philosophy, include Doyle 2010, Schwartz 2012, Hill and Lagerlund 2012, and Bach et al. 2013. I discuss aspects of Jesuit theories of political power and law in Brett 2011 (passim). Tierney 1997 has chapters on both Vitoria and Suárez.

Contextual background for the studies of Vitoria and Soto in Paris can be found in two older but still indispensable studies, Villoslada 1938 and Bataillon 1991. The broader background of the Reformation is discussed in Skinner 1978, vol. 2, and an excellent account of Lutheran legal theory is provided in

[52] This point is made in Pink 2009.

[53] I would like to thank the editors of this volume for their perceptive and helpful comments and suggestions, which have greatly improved the chapter, and Ben Slingo for many enjoyable conversations on the subject.

Witte 2002. For the later period, Worcester 2008 and Bamji et al. 2013 are collections that give overviews of the cultural and political environment of Jesuits and of the Counter-Reformation more broadly. Broggio 2009 is excellent on the academic and political milieu of the Society of Jesus around the turn of the seventeenth century; Tutino 2010 is equally excellent on the theology and politics surrounding the Oath of Allegiance controversy.

Epilogue

THE LEGACY OF ANCIENT AND MEDIEVAL LEGAL THOUGHT FOR MODERN LEGAL PHILOSOPHY

by Carrie-Ann Biondi

Many currents from ancient and medieval legal thought still direct the flow of conversation in modern legal philosophy. Recent centuries have deepened and developed in more sophisticated ways legal concepts and controversies that had their origins in ancient Greece, Rome, and the Near East and became transmuted during the medieval period through the influence of the Abrahamic faiths. A brief survey of some central legal concepts discussed in this volume—such as natural or divine law versus positive law, reason and rule of law, equity, and cosmopolitan universal law—reveals a historical current that has continued through modern and contemporary legal philosophy.

The dramatically depicted tension between Antigone's higher law and Creon's positive law (see Chapter 1 of this volume) that only sharpened in the repeated confrontations between Socrates and various Sophists (see Chapters 2 and 3 of this volume), continued to play out most prominently in twentieth-century debates between legal positivists and moral realists. Located at the heart of the decades-long exchange between preeminent legal positivists H. L. A. Hart (1907–1992), Hans Kelsen (1881–1973), and Joseph Raz (b. 1939) and their critics—such as John Finnis (b. 1940), Lon Fuller (1902–1978), and Ronald Dworkin (1931–2013)—are the "separability thesis" and the source of law's authority.

The separability thesis separates claims about the moral evaluation of law from claims about its legal validity. Laws are valid if they "were enacted in proper form, clear in meaning, and satisfied all the acknowledged criteria of validity of a system," and as valid they must be obeyed, even if they are judged by individuals to be "morally iniquitous" (Hart 1961, 203). Picking and choosing which laws to obey or reject on moral grounds—which is how positivists view the implications of natural law theory—would create enormous social and political upheaval. Hart is influenced here by Thomas Hobbes (1588–1679), Jeremy Bentham (1748–1832), and John Austin (1790–1859), who all share a deep fear of anarchy. Glimmers of legal positivism are present throughout the history of legal thought, but it did not garner a strong intellectual foothold until modern legal philosophy, when prominent and influential thinkers theorized about the modern state. Legal positivism thus grew apace with the rise and crystallization of the Westphalian state system and the dominance of territorially large, multicultural states.[1]

[1] See Volume 8, Chapter 6 of this Treatise, esp. 174.

Carving out a morally tolerant legal space in these political entities facilitated the popularity of John Stuart Mill's (1806–1873) "harm principle" that requires individuals to be left alone unless their actions would cause harm to others (see Mill 1985, chap. 1). The harm principle, famously explored in Joel Feinberg's landmark *Harm to Others* (Feinberg 1984), has been a linchpin of Western legal and political thought for over 150 years.[2]

The source of legal authority also divides legal positivists and their moralist critics. Positivists anchor authority in the sovereignty of law *per se*, while moralists locate it in some higher-level normative principles, be it universal morality, abstract principles of political morality, or religious ethics. This issue is deeply connected to the medieval conflict between Thomas Aquinas's (ca. 1226–1274) intellectualism and William of Ockham's (1280–1347) voluntarist critique of Aquinas, which later influenced Jean Bodin (1530–1546) (see Chapter 13 of this volume). Intellectualism holds that the authority of law resides in its being consonant with a higher moral law, which is apprehended and justified by reason. Voluntarism holds, instead, that legal authority flows from a sovereign's will, whether that sovereign is God, a king, or the people. This debate arises prominently in sixteenth-century scholastic debates among Dominicans and Jesuits over the proper role of reason and will in law's authority (see Chapter 14 of this volume), and again in muted form in the rival political philosophies of Thomas Hobbes and John Locke (1632–1704) (see Chapter 8, 217–8, and Chapter 5, 130, respectively, in this volume). The positivist jurisprudence of John Austin follows directly on Hobbes's and Bentham's "command theory" of law, which explained that the commands issued by a sovereign correlatively oblige citizens to obey the law.[3] H. L. A. Hart criticizes but then develops Austin's insight about commands in the direction of authority as distinct from mere power.[4] Raz (1986, chap. 2) further develops the will theory by introducing "content-independent reasons" and explains how law as such provides "authoritative reasons" (Raz 1979) for obedience.[5]

Various moral (especially natural law) theorists have responded to the positivists' emphasis on legal validity and the authority of law *per se* with a call for legal legitimacy on grounds of justice and morality apprehended through reason. Broadly speaking, there are two types of natural law theory in conflict with legal positivism: substantive natural law (held by Aquinas and Finnis; see Chapter 12 of this volume) and procedural natural law (held by John Duns

[2] See Riley in Volume 10, Chapter 15 of this Treatise for further discussion of Mill's philosophy of law, and Feinberg (1984, 5) for the compatibility of his theory with legal positivism.

[3] See Austin 1967. See Riley in Volume 10, Chapter 3 of this Treatise on the legal philosophy of Hobbes; and Lobban in Volume 8, Chapter 6 of this Treatise on the legal theories of Bentham and Austin.

[4] See Hart 1961. See Postema in Volume 11, Chapter 7 of this Treatise on Hart's critical positivism.

[5] See Postema in Volume 11, Chapter 8 of this Treatise on Raz's theory of law.

Scotus [1266–1308] and Fuller; see Chapter 13 of this volume). Substantive theories aim directly at promoting certain values and guiding a citizenry toward the good in relation to a specific set of moral principles, while procedural natural law theories aim at devising morally just legal processes consistently with natural law. As a procedural natural law theorist, Fuller maintains that for something to count as law, it must meet eight "desiderata" (e.g., being publicly promulgated, not retroactive, etc.), which comprise "the internal morality of law" limiting "the kinds of substantive aims that may be achieved through legal rules" (Fuller 1964, 4, 38–9).[6] These eight desiderata are compatible with various different substantive moral theories, such as Thomism or Aristotelian eudaimonism. Substantive types of natural law can be sub-divided further between theistic and naturalistic theories, though most modern natural law theories have been naturalistic rather than theistic (with the exception of neo-scholastic theories, such as those of Jacques Maritain [1882–1973] and Yves Simon [1903–1961]). Aquinas deliberately fuses Aristotelian natural teleology with Catholic theology (see Chapter 12 of this volume), and both Aristotle and Aquinas have inspired many early modern natural law theorists, including Hugo Grotius (1583–1645), Samuel Pufendorf (1632–1694), Gottfried Leibniz (1646–1716), and Christian Wolff (1769–1754).[7] The influence is even more direct in recent natural law theorists such as John Finnis (1980).[8] According to Finnis, we must look to what is good for human beings in order to create a legal system that addresses law's genuine purpose. Among the "basic goods" of human life that law should facilitate are life, knowledge, play, aesthetic experience, friendship/sociability, practical reasonableness, and "religion" (Finnis 1980, chaps. 1 and 4). Natural law theorists of all varieties appeal to moral principles in order to drive a wedge between immoral positive laws and obligation, citing a "higher" moral authority as the justification for civil disobedience. They thus resist Bentham's dictum "to obey punctually; to censure freely" (Bentham 1838, 230)—they censure freely, to be sure, but obey punctually only if the injustice falls beneath a morally specified threshold. It should be noted that the legal validity/legitimacy split is a somewhat exaggerated dichotomy. Many of the legal philosophers discussed here wrestle (with varying degrees of success) with integrating concerns of stability and justice in legal systems.

While not a self-identified natural law theorist, Dworkin has been one of legal positivism's sharpest critics. His distinctive "interpretivist" approach to adjudication calls in "hard cases" for judges to draw upon the "best interpreta-

[6] See Postema in Volume 11, Chapter 4 of this Treatise for Fuller's theory of law.

[7] See Scattola in Volume 9, Chapter 1, 15–41 of this Treatise for an overview of modern European natural law philosophers; and see also Riley in Volume 10, Chapters. 2, 5, and 6 of this Treatise for fuller discussion of Grotius, Pufendorf, and Leibniz.

[8] See Postema in Volume 11, Chapter 12, 547–62 of this Treatise on the legal theory of Finnis.

tion" of "principles of political morality," which he argues constitute an important part of a state's legal system that is wider than positive law (Dworkin 1977, 1986). Dworkin holds that law properly embodies integrity as a substantive value of political morality, which explains why governmental directives have normative force. What Dworkin shares with natural law theorists is their dissatisfaction with settling for the authority of the positive law by itself, as well as their reliance on reason to make moral determinations that ensure that legal systems move toward moral goodness and satisfy the requirements of justice.[9]

The role of reason in law as a bulwark against majoritarian prejudices or the whims of dictators derives from the "rational order" or "right reason" of ancient Greek thought (see Chapters 2–5 of this volume). Historically, this "appeal to reason" arose in resurgent form in late scholastic and early modern resistance to royal absolutism (see Chapters 11–14 of this volume). To have a "government of laws rather than men" has thus been a long-standing beacon of hope, pervading modern legal thought from John Locke's *Second Treatise of Government* (Locke 1980) to James Madison's *Federalist* 49 (Hamilton et al. 1961) to John Rawls's (1921–2002) repeated insistence on "public reason" (Rawls 1993, 1999). Although Locke has a relatively sanguine view of man in the "state of nature," like Aristotle, he acknowledges that even rational beings require law, for "men being biassed by their interest, as well as ignorant for want of study of [the law of nature], are not apt to allow of it as a law binding to them in the application of it to their particular cases" (Locke 1980, 66). Hence, there is a need for an established and impartially administered rule of law. The kinds of rules that can be adopted, Rawls (1993, xv–xvii) argues, are those that meet the conditions of "public reason" by being found fair and reasonable to "free and equal" citizens who hold various "comprehensive doctrines" of the good. Regardless of the type of constraint on the actions of fellow citizens and ruling politicians alike—whether structural checks and balances or rules concerning reason-giving—the aim of mitigating the pernicious effects of private "passions" through a government of "reason" (Hamilton et al. 1961, 317) remains a perennial one.[10]

Whereas the rule of law captures the generalities that largely hold for the great majority of human social life, it takes a combination of reason, experience, and wisdom for a judge or other legal adjudicator to be equitable when unusual circumstances require it. Aristotle's virtue of equity (*epieikeia*) (see Chapter 4 of this volume), which allows a judge to make a just determination contrary to the letter of the law so as to compensate for the defect of law's necessary universality, reappears later in the work of John Fortescue (ca. 1395–

[9] See Postema in Volume 11, Chapter 9 of this Treatise on Dworkin's theory of law.

[10] See Lobban in Volume 8, Chapter 5 of this Treatise on the Federalist theory of law and its influence on early American jurisprudence and judicial practice.

1479) and Christopher St. German (1460–1541). Fortescue argues on natural law grounds that the king must render equity if his legislation is fully to live up to the principles of natural justice. St. German defends the existence of British courts of equity known as the Court of Chancery, which developed in order to handle unusual and pressing circumstances in a flexible and just way (see Lobban in Volume 8, Chapter 1 of this Treatise). In his procedural natural law theory, Fuller (1964, 64, 94) harks back to Aristotle's appreciation for the need for both general rules in law and to context-sensitive judgment for cases in which justice would not best be served by too rigid or mechanical an adherence to rule of law.[11]

Many legal theorists—both ancient and modern—have argued in terms of *legal systems*. Even those defending some version of natural or divine law typically see universalistic moral law as allowing for the sovereignty of distinct states with their own systems of positive law. This is the "law of nations" or "law of peoples" (*ius gentium*) systematized in Roman law (see Chapters 6 and 10 of this volume) and developed further by later scholastics (see Chapter 14 of this volume). The law of nations is what all people observe regardless of citizenship and is compatible with natural law, regulating practices concerning property, treaties, and warfare.[12] Such practices became the backbone of the relatively recent field of "international law," whose origin is attributed to Bentham's introduction of the phrase in his 1789 *The Introduction to the Principles of Morals and Legislation* (Bobbitt 1996, 96). Shortly thereafter in 1795, Immanuel Kant (1724–1804) published *Perpetual Peace* (Kant 1983), in which he defended the state sovereignty aspect of the law of nations, maintaining that each state is independent from all others and hence accountable only to its own citizens and that states are not justified in interfering in other states' internal affairs. He did so on the ground that a world government would lead to "a universal monarchy" and cause a "peace that despotism (in the graveyard of freedom) brings about by vitiating all powers" (ibid., 125). Although there exists war between states in a Westphalian system, this is far preferable to a world where one power could dominate in the absence of a structure of international checks and balances that can stave off such despotism. Rawls (1999, 36, 86–87) echoes Kant's call for strong international cooperation for rational mutual benefit and also resists the lure of world government so as to achieve that aim.

There is a fine line, though, between the law of peoples and universal principles, as anyone who is familiar with the fragile workings of the United Na-

[11] Roger Shiner (1994) has a lucid discussion of Aristotelian equity, which he subtly applies to the heated contemporary debate between Hart and Dworkin in an effort to avoid the drawbacks of both approaches.

[12] The origin of modern international law is usually traced back to Grotius, for which see Riley in Volume 10, Chapter 2, 12, of this Treatise, where he describes international law as "a modernized version of the Roman *ius gentium*."

tions can attest to. Theorists like Kant and Rawls may hold the line against a global state, but others have pressed universalistic principles of morality or justice in the direction of cosmopolitanism as first envisioned by the Cynics (see Chapter 5 of this volume). From various nineteenth-century labor movements to contemporary transnational global justice movements, groups now exist that fight for the recognition and enforcement of universal human dignity or rights through humanitarian intervention and an international criminal court and who challenge the state sovereignty principle that lies at the center of the law of nations.[13] Zeno of Citium (ca. 334–ca. 262 B.C.), who followed Diogenes of Sinope (ca. 412–ca. 324 B.C.) in regarding himself as a "citizen of the world," might very well feel at home in this most contemporary of conversations about international law (see Chapter 2 of this volume).

Ancient and medieval legal thought clearly have had a lasting impact on modern and contemporary philosophy of law. Whether the influence is by means of direct inspiration, such as natural law or the Aristotelian virtue of equity, or through more indirect and general concerns with the nature and normativity of law and with the role of the rule of law in keeping human passions in check, historical sources in legal thought remain relevant to the theory and practice of the legal, political, and social institutions of the present day.

Further Reading

Dennis Patterson provides a valuable and concise series of chapters on various areas of law, schools of thought, and specific issues in contemporary philosophy of law that are also historically informed (see Coleman and Leiter 1996). See also generally Lobban in Volume 8, Riley in Volume 10, and Postema in Volume 11 of this Treatise for extensive discussions of how ancient through scholastic legal thought influenced modern and contemporary Western legal philosophy.

One of the touchstones of contemporary natural law theory is Finnis 1980, but see also Fuller 1964, Ralph McInerny 1992, Germain Grisez 1965, Henry Veatch 1985 and 1990, and Jacques Maritain 1951. See Brian Bix 1996 for an excellent survey of historical and contemporary natural law theory; Bix also places Dworkin's interpretivist theory on the natural law side of the natural law/legal positivism debate.

Hart 1961 looms as the towering figure in contemporary legal positivism. Coleman and Leiter 1996 provide a concise summary of the tenets of positivism, situate Hart within the historical trajectory of this school of legal thought, and compare and contrast Hart's theory with the legal positivism of thinkers such as Kelsen 1967 and Raz 1979 and 1986. Postema, in Volume 11, Chapters 7–9, 12 of this Treatise, offers nuanced expositions of Hart's legal positivism,

[13] See Osiander 2001 for discussion of resistance to the state sovereignty principle.

its extension and application, and significant critiques raised against his approach by various natural law and moral realist theorists.

Bentham 1988 introduced the phrase "international law" as a way of theorizing what historically has been called "the law of nations," and Kant 1983 developed it in a more sophisticated philosophical way. Since then, work in the field of international law has grown tremendously, especially since the founding of the United Nations in 1945 in replacement of the League of Nations. Steiner and Alston 2000 collect together in nearly 1,500 pages a vast amount of material pertaining to the history, documents, issues, and controversies involved in international law with a special focus on human rights.

BIBLIOGRAPHY

Compiled with the assistance of Mahesh Ananth

Note that in the text, except where otherwise indicated, quotations from the Hebrew Bible (or Old Testament) are taken from *Tanakh: The Holy Scriptures*. Philadelphia, PA: The Jewish Publication Society, 1985; the quotations from The New Testament and from Apocrypha are taken from *The Revised English Bible*. Oxford: Oxford University Press, 1989; and quotations from the Quran are taken from *The Holy Qur'an: Text, Translation and Commentary*, Abdullah Yusuf Ali (Beirut: Dar al-'Arabiyya li-al-Ṭiba'a wa al-Nashr wa al-Tawzi', 1963).

Adams, Marilyn McCord. 1987. *William Ockham*. 2 Vols. Notre Dame, IN: University of Notre Dame Press.

———. 1999. Ockham on Will, Nature, and Morality. In *The Cambridge Companion to Ockham*. Ed. Paul Vincent Spade, 245–72. Cambridge: Cambridge University Press.

Adler, Mortimer. 1990. A Sound Moral Philosophy. In *Reforming Education: The Opening of the American Mind*. Ed. Geraldine Van Doren, 254–62. New York, NY: Macmillan.

Aeschylus. *Eumenides*. Trans. Richmond Lattimore. In *Aeschylus I*. Ed. David Grene and Richmond Lattimore, 151–90. New York, NY: Random House, 1942.

Aesop. *Fables*. In *Early Greek Political Thought from Homer to the Sophists*. Trans. Michael Gagarin and Paul Woodruff, 145–9. Cambridge: Cambridge University Press, 1995.

Alcinous. *Didaskalikos*. In *Alcinous. The Handbook of Platonism*. Trans. John Dillon. Oxford: Clarendon Press, 1997. (*Alcinoos: Enseignement des doctrines de Platon*. Ed. John Whittaker, trans. P. Louis. Paris: Budé, 1990.)

Aldama, J. A. 1938. Luis de Molina S.J. De spe: Comentario a la 2a 2ae, 17–22. *Archivo teologico Granadino* 1: 111–212.

Alden, Dauril. 1996. *The Making of an Enterprise: The Society of Jesus in Portugal, Its Empire and Beyond 1540–1750*. Stanford, CA: Stanford University Press.

Alexander of Hales. *Summa Fratris Alexandri*. In *Alexander of Hales: Summa Theologica, III*. Trans. Father of the College of St. Bonaventure. Quaracchi: Collegium S. Bonaventurae, 1948.

Alfarabi. *Attainment of Happiness*. In *Alfarabi's Philosophy of Plato and Aristotle*. Trans. Muhsin Mahdi, 11–50. Ithaca, NY: Cornell University Press, 2002.

———. *Book of Religion*. In *Alfarabi, The Political Writings: "Selected Aphorisms" and Other Texts*. Trans. and annot. Charles E. Butterworth, 85–113. Ithaca, NY: Cornell University Press, 2001. (Arabic text in *Kitāb al-Milla wa Nuṣūṣ Ukhrā*, edited, with an introduction and notes, by Muhsin Mahdi. Beirut: Dār al-Mashriq, 1968.)

———. *Enumeration of the Sciences*. In *Alfarabi, The Political Writings: "Selected Aphorisms" and Other Texts*. Trans. and annot. Charles E. Butterworth, 69–84. Ithaca, NY: Cornell University Press, 2001.

———. *L'Harmonie Entre les Opinions de Platon et d'Aristote*. Ed. and trans. Fauzi Mitri Najjar and Dominique Mallet. Damascus: Institut Français de Damas, 1999.

———. *Philosophy of Aristotle*. In *Alfarabi's Philosophy of Plato and Aristotle*. Trans. Muhsin Mahdi, 69–130. Ithaca, NY: Cornell University Press, 2002.

———. *Philosophy of Plato*. In *Alfarabi's Philosophy of Plato and Aristotle*. Trans. Muhsin Mahdi, 51–67. Ithaca, NY: Cornell University Press, 2002.

———. *Political Regime*. In *Alfarabi, The Political Writings: "Political Regime" and Other

Texts. Trans. and annot. Charles E. Butterworth. Ithaca, NY: Cornell University Press, forthcoming.

———. *Principles of the Opinions of the Inhabitants of the Virtuous City*. In *Al-Farabi on the Perfect State: Abū Naṣr al-Fārābī's Mabādi' Ārā' Ahl al-Madīna al-Fāḍila*. Revised text. Ed. and trans. Richard Walzer. Oxford: Clarendon, 1985.

———. *Selected Aphorisms*. In *Alfarabi, The Political Writings: "Selected Aphorisms" and Other Texts*. Trans. and annot. Charles E. Butterworth, 1–67. Ithaca, NY: Cornell University Press, 2001. (Arabic text in *Fuṣūl Muntaza'a* [Selected Aphorisms]. Ed. and introd. Fauzi M. Najjar. Beirut: Dār al-Mashriq, 1971.)

———. *Summary of Plato's Laws*. In *Alfarabi, The Political Writings: "Political Regime" and Other Texts*. Trans. and annot. Charles E. Butterworth. Ithaca, NY: Cornell University Press, forthcoming. [Arabic text in *Le Sommaire du Livre des "Lois" de Platon (Jawāmi' Kitāb al-Nawāmis li-Aflāṭūn)* by Abū Naṣr al-Fārābī. Ed. and intro. Thérèse-Anne Druart. *Bulletin d'Études Orientales* 50 (1998): 109–55.]

Algra, Keimpe, Jonathan Barnes, Jaap Mansfeld, and Malcolm Schofield. 2000. *The Cambridge History of Hellenistic Philosophy*. Cambridge: Cambridge University Press.

Allen, R. E. 1980. *Socrates and Legal Obligation*. Minneapolis, MN: University of Minnesota Press.

Álvarez, Mariano. 2000. La omnipotencia de Dios y el principio de contradicción en Francisco Suárez. In *Potentia Dei. L'omnipotencia divina nel pensiero dei secoli XVI e XVII*. Ed. Guido Canzani et al., 173–93. Milan: Franco Angeli.

Ambrose of Milan. *De Jacob and Vita Beata*. *PL* vol. 14.25.

———. *De Officiis Ministrorum*. In *Ambrose. De Officiis*. Ed. and trans. Ivor J. Davidson. Oxford: Oxford University Press, 2001.

———. *Epistles*. In *The Letters of S. Ambrose, Bishop of Milan*. Translated with Notes and Indices. Oxford: James Parker, 1881.

Ambrosiaster. *Expositions of Romans (In Epistulam ad Romanos)*. In *Commentarius in Epistulas Paulinas*. Ed. Heinrich Josef Vogels. Vienna: Hoelder-Pichler-Tempsky, *CSEL* vol. 81.1.

Andrés, M. 1976. *La teólogía española en el siglo XVI*. Madrid: BAC.

Annas, Julia. 1981. *An Introduction to Plato's Republic*. Oxford: Clarendon.

———. 1989. Cicero on Stoic Moral Philosophy and Private Property. In *Philosophy Togata: Essays on Philosophy and Roman Society*. Ed. Miriam Griffin and Jonathan Barnes, 151–73. Oxford: Clarendon.

———. 1993. *The Morality of Happiness*. Oxford: Oxford University Press.

Anscombe, Elizabeth. 1958. Modern Moral Philosophy. *Philosophy* 33: 1–19.

Anselmo, B. 1943. Gli elementi di una giusta pace nella dottrina di Ludovico Molina S.J. *Civiltà Cattolica* 4: 307–16.

Antiphon. Truth. In *Early Greek Political Thought from Homer to the Sophists*. Ed. Michael Gagarin and Paul Woodruff, 244–7. Cambridge: Cambridge University Press, 1995.

Aristotle. *Analytica Priora (Prior Analytics)*. Trans. A. J. Jenkinson. In *The Complete Works of Aristotle*. Ed. Jonathan Barnes, 39–113. Princeton, NJ: Princeton University Press, 1984.

———. *Athênaiôn Politeia (Constitution of Athens)*. Trans. F. G. Kenyon. In *The Complete Works of Aristotle*. Ed. Jonathan Barnes, 2341–83. Princeton, NJ: Princeton University Press, 1984. (*Aristotle. Constitution of Athens and Related Texts*. Ed. and trans. Kurt von Fritz and Ernst Kapp. New York, NY: Hafner, 1950. *Aristotle. Constitution of the Athenians*. Ed. and trans. P. J. Rhodes. Harmondswoth: Penguin, 1984.)

———. *De Anima (On the Soul)*. Trans. J. A. Smith. In Aristotle, *The Complete Works of Aristotle*. Ed. Jonathan Barnes, 641–92. Princeton, NJ: Princeton University Press, 1984.

———. *De Caelo (On the Heavens)*. Trans. J. A. Stocks. In *The Complete Works of Aristotle*. Ed. Jonathan Barnes, 447–511. Princeton, NJ: Princeton University Press, 1984.

———. *De Generatione Animalium (Generation of Animals)*. Trans. A. Platt. In *The Complete Works of Aristotle*. Ed. Jonathan Barnes, 1111–218. Princeton, NJ: Princeton University Press, 1984.

———. *De Motu Animalium (Movement of Animals)*. Trans. A. S. L. Farquharson. In *The Complete Works of Aristotle*. Ed. Jonathan Barnes, 1087–96. Princeton, NJ: Princeton University Press, 1984.

———. *De Partibus Animalium (Parts of Animals)*. Trans. W. Ogle. In *The Complete Works of Aristotle*. Ed. Jonathan Barnes, 994–1086. Princeton, NJ: Princeton University Press, 1984.

———. *Eudemian Ethics*. Trans. J. Solomon. In *The Complete Works of Aristotle*. Ed. Jonathan Barnes, 1922–81. Princeton, NJ: Princeton University Press, 1984.

———. *Magna Moralia*. Trans. St. G. Stock. In *The Complete Works of Aristotle*. Ed. Jonathan Barnes, 1868–921. Princeton, NJ: Princeton University Press, 1984.

———. *Metaphysics*. Trans. W. D. Ross. In *The Complete Works of Aristotle*. Ed. Jonathan Barnes, 1552–728. Princeton, NJ: Princeton University Press, 1984.

———. *Nicomachean Ethics*. Trans. W. D. Ross, rev. J. O. Urmson. In *The Complete Works of Aristotle*. Ed. Jonathan Barnes, 1729–867. Princeton, NJ: Princeton University Press, 1984.

———. *Physics*. Trans. R. P. Hardie and R. K. Gaye. In *The Complete Works of Aristotle*. Ed. Jonathan Barnes, 315–446. Princeton, NJ: Princeton University Press, 1984.

———. *Politics*. Trans. B. Jowett. In *The Complete Works of Aristotle*. Ed. Jonathan Barnes, 1986–2129. Princeton, NJ: Princeton University Press, 1984. (*The Politics of Aristotle*. Trans. and ed. E. Barker, rev. R. F. Stalley. Oxford: Oxford University Press, 1995. *Aristotle Politics Books I and II*. Trans. and ed. Trevor Saunders. New York, NY: Oxford University Press, 1995. *Aristotle. Politics: Books III and IV*. Trans. and Ed. Richard Robinson. Oxford: Clarendon, 1995. *Aristotle. Politics Books V and VI*. Trans. and Ed. David Keyt. Oxford: Clarendon, 1999. *Aristotle. Politics Books VII and VIII*. Ed. and trans. Richard Kraut. Oxford: Clarendon, 1997. *The Politics of Aristotle, 4 vols*. Ed. W. L. Newman. Oxford: Clarendon, 1887–1902.)

———. *Problemata (Problems)*. Trans. E. S. Forster. In *The Complete Works of Aristotle*. Ed. Jonathan Barnes, 319–1527. Princeton, NJ: Princeton University Press, 1984.

———. *Rhetoric*. Trans. W. Rhys Roberts. In *The Complete Works of Aristotle*. Ed. Jonathan Barnes, 2152–269. Princeton, NJ: Princeton University Press, 1984. (*Arisṭūṭālīs, al-Khaṭāba, al-Tarjama, al-ʿArabiyya al-Qadīma (Aristotle, Rhetoric, The Old Arabic Translation)*. Ed. ʿAbd al-Raḥmān Badawī Cairo: Maktabat al-Nahḍa al-Miṣriyya, 1959.)

——— (pseudo). *Rhetoric to Alexander*. Trans. E. S. Forster. In *The Complete Works of Aristotle*. Ed. Jonathan Barnes, 2270–315. Princeton, NJ: Princeton University Press, 1984.

———. *Sophistici Elenchi (Sophistical Refutations)*. Trans. W. A. Pickard-Cambridge. In *The Complete Works of Aristotle*. Ed. Jonathan Barnes, 278–314. Princeton, NJ: Princeton University Press, 1984.

——— (pseudo). *To Alexander on Kingship*. Trans. S. M. Stern, in *Aristotle on the World State*. London: Bruno Cassirer, 1968.

———. *Topics*. Trans. W. A. Pickard-Cambridge. In *The Complete Works of Aristotle*. Ed. Jonathan Barnes, 167–277. Princeton, NJ: Princeton University Press, 1984.

Arnaoutoglou, Ilias. 1998. *Ancient Greek Laws: A Sourcebook*. London and New York, NY: Routledge.

Assmann, Jan. 1996. *Maʿat: Gerechtigkeit und Unsterblichkeit im Alten Ägypten*. Munich: Carl Hanser.

———. 1997. *Moses the Egyptian: the Memory of Egypt in Western Monotheism*. Cambridge, MA: Harvard University Press.

———. 2002. *The Mind of Egypt*. Trans. A. Jenkins. New York, NY: Henry Holt Metropolitan.

Assmann, Jan, Bernd Janowski, and Michael Welker, eds. 1998. *Gerechtigkeit: Richten und Retten in der abendländischen Tradition und ihren altorientalischen Ursprüngen*. Munich: Wilhelm Fink.

Astrain, Antonio. 1902–1925. *Historia de la Compañia de Jesús en la Asistencia de España*. Madrid: Sucesores de Rivadeneryra.

Athenaeus. *Deipnosophistae*. In *The Deipnosophists*. Trans. Charles Burton Gulick, 7 vols. Cambridge, MA: Harvard University Press, 1927–1941.

Atkins, E. M., and R. J. Dodaro, eds. 2001. *Augustine: Political Writings*. Cambridge: Cambridge University Press.
Atkins, Margaret. 2000. Cicero. In *The Cambridge History of Greek and Roman Political Thought*. Ed. Christopher Rowe and Malcolm Schofield, 477–516. Cambridge: Cambridge University Press.
Augustine of Hippo. *Confessionum Libri Tredecim*. In *Confessions*. Trans. Henry Chadwick. Oxford: Oxford University Press, 1991.
———. *Contra Academicos*. In *Against the Academics*. Trans. Peter King. Indianapolis, IN: Hackett, 1995.
———. *Contra Faustum Manichaeum* (*Against Faustus the Manichean*). Trans. R. Stothert. In *A Select Library of the Nicene and Post-Nicene Fathers of the Christian Church*, vol. 4. Ed. P. Schaff, 151–345. New York, NY: The Christian Literature Co., 1886–1888.
———. De *Bono Conjugali* (On the Good Marriage). *PL* vol. 40.20.
———. *De Civitate Dei*. In *The City of God against the Pagans*. Trans. R. W. Dyson. Cambridge: Cambridge University Press, 1998.
———. *De Diversis Quaestionibus*. *PL* vol. 40.2.
———. *De Libero Arbitrio*. In *On Free Choice of the Will*. Trans. T. Williams. Indianapolis, IN: Hackett, 1993.
———. *De Opere Monachorum*. *PL* vol. 40.27.
———. *De Praedestinatione Sanctorum* (*On the Predestinations of Saints*). Trans. R. E. Wallis. In *Basic Writings of Saint Augustine*. Ed. W. Oates, vol. 1, 775–817. New York, NY: Random House, 1948.
———. *De Trinitate*. In *The Trinity*. Trans. Stephen McKenna. Washington, DC: Catholic University of America, 1963.
———. *De Vera Religione* (*On True Religion*). In *Augustine: Earlier Writings*. Trans. J. H. S. Burleigh, 218–83. London: SCM Press, 1953.
———. *Enarratione in Psalmos*. *PL* vol. 36.11 and 37.11.
———. *Epistolae*. *PL* vol. 33.9.
———. *In Ioannis Evangelium Tractatus*. In *Homilies on the Gospel of John*. Trans. J. W. Rettig. Washington, DC: Catholic University of America, 1988–1995.
———. *Sermones*. *PL* vol. 46.13 and 47.12.
———. *Soliloquia* (*Soliloquies*). Trans. C. C. Starbuck. In *Basic Writings of Saint Augustine*. Ed. W. Oates, vol. 1, 257–97. New York, NY: Random House, 1948.
Austin, John. 1832. *The Province of Jurisprudence Determined and the Uses of Jurisprudence*. London: John Murray.
Avalos, Hector. 1995. Legal and Social Institutions in Canaan and Ancient Israel. In *Civilizations of the Ancient Near East*. Ed. Jack M. Sasson, 615–31. New York, NY: Simon & Schuster Macmillan.
Averroes (Ibn Rushd). *Averroes' Commentary on Plato's Republic*. Trans. E. I. J. Rosenthal. Cambridge: Cambridge University Press, 1956. (*Averroes on Plato's Republic*. Trans. Ralph Lerner. 1974. Ithaca, NY: Cornell University Press, 1974.)
———. *The Book of the Decisive Treatise, Determining the Connection Between the Law and Wisdom and Epistle Dedicatory*. Trans. Charles E. Butterworth. Provo, UT: Brigham Young University Press, 2001.
———. *Bidāyat al-Mujtahid wa Nihāyat al-Muqtaṣid* (*The Legal Interpreter's Beginning and the Mediator's Ending*). Ed. 'Abd al-Ḥalīm Muḥammad 'Abd al-Ḥalīm and 'Abd al-Raḥmān Ḥasan Maḥmūd. Cairo: Dār al-Kutub al-Ḥadītha, 1975.
———. *Averroès, Commentaire Moyen à la Rhétorique d'Aristote, Édition critique du texte arabe et traduction française*. 3 Vols. Ed. and trans. Maroun Aouad. Paris: Vrin, 2002.
Avicenna (Ibn Sīnā). *La Métaphysique* (*al-Ilāhiyyāt*). 3 Vols. Trans. George Chehata Anawati. Montreal: Institut d'Études Médiévales, 1952.
———. *Risāla fī Aqsām al-'Ulūm al-'Aqliyya* (*Epistle on the Division of the Intellectual Sciences*). In *Tis' Rasā'il* (*Nine Epistles*), 104–18. Cairo: publisher unlisted, 1908.

———. *Kitāb al-Shifā', al-Ilāhiyyāt* (*Book of Healing: Metaphysics*). Ed. al-Ab Qanawātī and Sa'īd Zāyid. Cairo: al-Hai'a al-'Āmma li Shu'ūn al-Maṭ ābi' al-Amīriyya, 1960.

———. *Kitāb al-Shifā', al-Ṭabī'iyyāt, al-Nafs* (*Book of Healing, Physical [Sciences], The Soul*). Ed. al-Ab al-Duktūr Gūrg al-Qanawātī and Sa'īd Zāyid. Cairo: al-Hai'a al-Miṣriyya al-'Āmma li-al-Kitāb, 1975.

Axelrod, Robert. 1985. *The Evolution of Cooperation*. New York, NY: Basic.

Ayers, Michael. 1981. Locke versus Aristotle on Natural Kinds. *The Journal of Philosophy* 78/5: 247–72.

Badawī, 'Abd al-Raḥmān, ed. 1959. *Arisṭūṭālīs, al-Khaṭāba, al-Tarjama al-'Arabiyya al-Qadīma* (*Aristotle, Rhetoric, The Old Arabic Translation*). Cairo: Maktabat al-Nahḍa al-Miṣriyya.

Bach, Oliver, et al., eds. 2013. *"Auctoritas Omnium Legum": Francisco Suárez' De Legibus Zwischen Theologie, Philosophie, und Jurisprudenz*. Stuttgart, Bad Canstatt: Frommann-Holzboog.

Bagnall, R. 1987. Church, State and Divorce in Late Roman Egypt. In *Florilegium Columbianum: Essays in Honour of P.O. Kristeller.* Ed. K.L. Selig and R. Somerville, 41–61. New York, NY: Italica.

Bainton, Ronald, H. 1930. The Immoralities of the Patriarchs According to the Exegesis of the Late Middle Ages and Reformation. *Harvard Theological Review* 23: 39–49.

Bamji, Alexander, et al., eds. 2013. *The Ashgate Research Companion to the Counter-Reformation*. Aldershot: Ashate.

Banateanu, Anne. 2001. *La Théorie Stoïcienne de l'amitié: Essai de Reconstruction*. Fribourg: Cerf, Editions Universitaires de Fribourg.

Barker, Ernest. 1918. *Greek Political Theory*. London: Methuen.

———. 1931. The Life of Aristotle and the Composition and Structure of the Politics. *Classical Review* 45: 162–72.

———. 1946. *The Politics of Aristotle*. Oxford: Oxford University Press.

———. 1959. *The Political Thought of Plato and Aristotle*. New York, NY: Dover.

Barnes, Jonathan, ed. 1984. *The Complete Works of Aristotle: The Revised Oxford Translation*. Princeton, NJ: Princeton University Press.

Barnes, Timothy D. 1981. *Constantine and Eusebius*. Cambridge, MA: Harvard University Press.

Barnett, Randy. 1998. *The Structure of Liberty: Justice and the Rule of Law*. Oxford: Oxford University Press.

Bataillon, Marcel. 1991. *Érasme et l'Espagne*. 3rd. ed. Geneva: Droz.

Bauman, Richard A. 1971. *Lawyers in Roman Republican Politics: A Study of Roman Jurists in their Political Setting, 316–82 B.C.* Munich: Beck.

———. 2000. *Human Rights in Ancient Rome*. London: Routledge.

Bava Mesia. In *Tractate Bava Mesia*. Trans. Jacob Neusner. Atlanta, GA: Scholars, 1990.

Belda Plans, Juan. 2000. *La Escuela de Salamanca y la renovacíon de la teología en el siglo XVI*. Madrid: BAC maior.

Beltrán de Heredia, Vicente. 1931a. El maestro Domingo (Francisco) de Soto en la Universidad de Alcalá. *Ciencia tomista* 43: 357–573.

———. 1931b. El maestro Domingo (Francisco) de Soto en la Universidad de Alcalá. *Ciencia tomista* 44: 28–51.

———. 1932. El maestro Domingo de Soto en la controversia de Las Casas con Sepúlveda. *Ciencia tomista* 45: 35–49.

———. 1934. *Francisco de Vitoria: Comentarios a la Secunda Secundae de Santo Tomás*. 6 vols. Salamanca: Editorial San Esteban.

———. 1938. El maestro Domingo de Soto, Catedrático de Vísperas en la Universidad de Salamanca. *Ciencia tomista* 57: 38–67, 281–302.

———. 1960. *Domingo de Soto: Estudio Biográfico Documentado*. Salamanca: Biblioteca de teologos espanoles.

Bentham, Jeremy. 1838. A Fragment on Government. In *The Works of Jeremy Bentham*. Ed. John Bowring. Edinburgh: Stevenson and Co.

———. 1843. *Anarchical Fallacies*. Edinburgh: Bowring.
———. 1988. *Introduction to the Principles of Morals and Legislation*. Amherst, NY: Prometheus Press.
Berman, Harold J. 1983. *Law and Revolution. The Formation of the Western Legal Tradition*. Cambridge, MA: Harvard University Press.
Bernal, Martin. 1987. *Black Athena. Vol. 1: The Fabrication of Ancient Greece 1785–1985*. Brunswick, NJ: Rutgers University Press.
Bernard of Chartres. *Commentary on the Timaeus*. In *The Glosae Super Platonem of Bernard of Chartres*. Ed. Paul E. Dutton. Toronto: Pontifical Institute of Mediaeval Studies, 1991.
Bett, Richard. 2012. Did the Stoics Invent Human Rights? In *Oxford Studies in Ancient Philosophy, Supplementary Volume*. Ed. Rachana Kamtekar, 149–69. Oxford: Oxford University Press.
Beuchot, Mauricio. 1996. *Historia de la filosofia en el Mexico Colonial*. Barcelona: Herder.
Birks, P., ed. 1989. *New Perspectives in the Roman Law of Property*. Oxford: Clarendon.
Birley, Anthony Richard. 1966. *Marcus Aurelius*. London: Eyre & Spottiswoode.
———. 1987. *Marcus Aurelius: A Biography*. New Haven, CT: Yale University Press.
Bix, Brian. 1996. Natural Law Theory. In *A Companion to Philosophy of Law and Legal Theory*. Ed. Dennis Patterson, 223–40. Malden, MA: Blackwell Publishers.
Black, Antony. 1992. *Political Thought in Europe, 1250–1450*. Cambridge: Cambridge University Press.
———. 2001. *The History of Islamic Political Thought: From the Prophet to the Present*. Edinburgh: Edinburgh University Press.
Blum, Paul Richard. 1998. *Philosophenphilosophie und Schulphilosophie: Typen des Philosophierens in der Neuzeit*. Stuttgart: Franz Steiner.
Bobbitt, Philip. 1996. Public International Law. In *A Companion to Philosophy of Law and Legal Theory*. Ed. Dennis Patterson, 96–112. Malden, MA: Blackwell Publishers.
Bobonich, Christopher. 1992. Persuasion, Compulsion and Freedom in Plato's *Laws*. *Classical Quarterly* 41: 365–88.
———. 1994. Akrasia and Agency in Plato's *Laws* and *Republic*. *Archiv fur Geschichte der Philosophie* 76: 3–36.
———. 1995. The Virtues of Ordinary People in Plato's *Statesman*. In *Reading the Statesman: Proceedings of III Symposium Platonicum*. Ed. Christopher Rowe, 313–29. *Sankt Augustin: Acadamia*.
———. 2002. *Utopia Recast: Plato's Later Political Philosophy*. Oxford: Oxford University Press.
Bobzien, Susanne. 1998. *Determinism and Freedom in Stoic Philosophy*. Oxford: Oxford University Press.
Bodin, Jean. *Six Books of the Commonwealth* (*Les Six Livres de la Republique*). In *The Six Books of a Commonweale*. Ed. K. D. McRae. Cambridge, MA: Harvard University Press, 1962. (Partial trans. *Jean Bodin. On Sovereignty: Four Chapters from the Six Books of the Commonwealth*. Ed. and trans. Julian H. Franklin. Cambridge: Cambridge University Press, 1992.)
Boecker, Hans Jochen. 1980. *Law and the Administration of Justice in the Old Testament*. Minneapolis, MN: Augusburg Publishing House.
Boegehold, Alan L. et al. 1995. *The Lawcourts at Athens: Sites, Buildings, Equipment, Procedure, and Testimonia*. Princeton, NJ: The American School of Classical Studies at Athens.
Boegehold, Alan L., and Adele C. Scafuro, eds. 1994. *Athenian Identity and Civic Ideology*. Baltimore, MD: The Johns Hopkins University Press.
Boehner, Philotheus. 1958. *Collected Articles on Ockham*. Ed. Eligius M. Buytaert. St. Bonaventure, NY: The Franciscan Institute.
Bonner, Gerald. 1986. *St. Augustine of Hippo, Life and Controversies*. 2nd. ed. Norwich: Canterbury.
Borkowski, Andrew, and Paul du Plessis. 2005. *Textbook on Roman Law*. 3d ed. Oxford: Oxford University Press.
Boureau, A. 1992. Droit et Théologie au XIIIe Siècle. *Annales ESC* 47.6: 1113–25.

Bourke, Vernon. 1960. *The Pocket Aquinas*. New York, NY: Washington Square Press.
———. 1968. *History of Ethics*. Garden City, NY: Doubleday and Company.
Bowe, Gabriel. 1955. *The Origins of Political Authority: an Essay in Catholic Political Philosophy*. Dublin: Clonmore and Reynolds.
Bowman, Alan K. 1989. *Egypt After the Pharaohs: 322 B.C.–A.D. 642: From Alexander to the Arab Conquest*. Berkeley, CA: University of California Press.
Brandwood, Leonard. 1990. *The Chronology of Plato's Dialogues*. Cambridge: Cambridge University Press.
———. 1992. Stylometry and Chronology. In *The Cambridge Companion to Plato*. Ed. Richard Kraut, 90–120. Cambridge: Cambridge University Press.
Branham, R. Bracht, and Marie-Odile Goulet-Cazé. 1996. *The Cynics: The Cynic Movement in Antiquity and Its Legacy*. Berkeley, CA: University of California Press.
Breasted, James. 1906–1907. *Ancient Records of Egypt*. Chicago, IL: University of Chicago Press.
Brett, Annabel. 1997. *Liberty, Right and Nature: Individual Rights in Later Scholastic Thought*. Cambridge: Cambridge University Press.
———. 2000. Authority, Reason, and the Self-Definition of Theologians in the Spanish "Second Scholastic." In *Forms of the Medieval in the Renaissance*. Ed. George Tucker, 63–90. Charlottesville, VA: Rookwood Press.
———. 2011. *Changes of State: Nature and the Limits of the City in Early Modern Natural Law*. Princeton, NJ: Princeton University Press.
Brewer, Douglas J., and Emily Teeter. 1999. *Egypt and the Egyptians*. Cambridge: Cambridge University Press.
Briant, Pierre. 2002. *From Cyrus to Alexander: A History of the Persian Empire*. Trans. P. T. Daniels. Winona Lake, IN: Eisenbrauns.
Brickhouse, Thomas C., and Nicholas D. Smith. 1989. *Socrates on Trial*. Princeton, NJ: Princeton University Press.
———. 1994. *Plato's Socrates*. New York, NY: Oxford University Press.
———. 2000. *The Philosophy of Socrates*. Boulder, CO: Westview Press.
———. 2002. *The Trial and Execution of Socrates: Sources and Controversies*. Oxford: Oxford University Press.
Breiskorn, Norbert. 2001. Lex Aeterna. In *Die Ordnung der Praxis*. Ed. Grunert and Seelmann, 49–73. Tubingen: Niemeyer.
———. 2010. Lex and Ius bei Francisco Suarez. In *Lex und Ius*. Ed. Fidora et al., 429–64. Stuttgart-Bad Canstatt: Frommann-Holzboog.
Broggio, Paolo. 2009. *La Teologia e la Politica*. Florence: Olschki.
Brower, Jeffrey, and Kevin Guilfoyle. 2004. *The Cambridge Companion to Abelard*. Cambridge: Cambridge University Press.
Brown, Eric. 2009. The Emergence of Natural Law and the Cosmopolis. In *The Cambridge Companion to American Political Thought*. Ed. Stephen Salkever, 331–63. New York, NY: Cambridge University Press.
Brown, Peter. 1967. *Augustine of Hippo, A Biography*. London: Faber.
———. 1972. *Religion and Society in the Age of St. Augustine*. London: Faber.
———. 1989. *The Body and Society: Men, Women and Sexual Renunciation in Early Christianity*. London: Faber.
Browning, Robert. 1971. *Justinian and Theodora*. Washington, DC: Praeger.
Brufau Prats, Jaime. 1988. *La Escuela de Salamanca ante el Descubrimiento del Nuevo Mundo*. Salamanca: Editorial San Esteban.
———, ed. 2000. *Domingo de Soto: Relecciones y Opúsculas*. Salamanca: Editorial San Esteban.
Brundage, James A. 1995. *Medieval Canon Law*. London: Longman.
Buckland, W. W. 1931. *The Main Institutions of Roman Law*. Cambridge: Cambridge University Press.
———. 1939. *Studies in the Glossators of the Roman Law*. Cambridge: Cambridge University Press.

Buckland, W. W., and Peter G. Stein. 1975. *Textbook of Roman Law from Augustus to Justinian*. 3rd ed. Cambridge: Cambridge University Press.
Bunge, Kirsten, et al., eds. 2011. *Die Normativität des Rechts bie Francisco de Vitoria*. Stuttgart-Bad Canstatt: Frommann-Holzboog.
Bürge, Alfons. 1999. *Römisches Privatrecht: Rechtsdenken und Gesellschaftliche Verankerung; eine Einführung*. Darmstadt: Wissenschaftliche Buchgesellschaft.
Burns, J. H, ed. 1988. *The Cambridge History of Medieval Political Thought c. 350–c. 1450*. Cambridge: Cambridge University Press.
Burns, J. P. 1980. *The Development of Augustine's Doctrine of Operative Grace*. Paris: Etudes Augustiniennes.
Burns, John, and Thomas Izbicki, eds. 1997. *Conciliarism and Papalism*. Cambridge: Cambridge University Press.
Burns, Tony. 1998. Aristotle and Natural Law. *History of Political Thought* 19: 142–66.
———. 2011. *Aristotle and Natural Law*. London: Continuum.
Burnyeat, M. F. 1984. The Sceptic in His Place and Time. In *Philosophy in History*. Ed. R. Rorty, J. B. Schneewind and Q. Skinner, 225–54. Cambridge: Cambridge University Press.
Butterworth, Charles E. 2000. The Political Teaching of Avicenna. *Topoi* 19: 35–44.
Calcidius. *Platonis Timaeus (Commentary on Plato's Timaeus)*. Ed. J. H. Waszink. London: Warburg Institute, 1962. (*Timaeus*. A Calcidio translatus commentarioque instructus [editio altera]. Ed. J. H. Waszink. London and Leiden; Warburg Institute and Brill, 1975.)
Canning, Joseph. 1996. *A History of Medieval Political Thought, 300–1450*. New York, NY: Routledge.
Carey, Christopher. 1996. *Nomos* in Athenian Rhetoric and Oratory. *Journal of Hellenic Studies* 116: 33–46.
———. 1997. *Trials from Classical Athens*. New York, NY: Routledge.
Carlyle, R. W., and A. J. A. Carlyle. 1936. *History of Mediaeval Political Theory in the West*. New York, NY: Barnes and Noble.
Carro, Venancio, ed. 1967. *Domingo de Soto y su Doctrina Juridical*. Madrid: CISC.
———. 1950. *La Controversias Teólogico-Juristas en el Siglo XVI*. Salamanca: Universidad Salamanca.
———. 1966. *Los Postulados Teológico-Jurídicos de Bartolomé de las Casas. Sus Aciertos, sus Olvidos y sus Fallas, ante los Maestros Franciso de Vitoria y Domingo de Soto*. Seville: Escuela de Estudios Hispanoamericanos/CSIC.
Cartledge, Paul. 1997. Introduction to *Hiero*. In Xenophon, *Hiero the Tyrant and Other Treatises*. Trans. Robin Waterfield, vii–xx, 3–6. London: Penguin.
Cartledge, Paul, and Matt Edge. 2009. "Rights," Individuals, and Communities in Ancient Greece. In *A Companion to Greek and Roman Political Thought*. Ed. Ryan K. Balot, 149–63. Oxford: Blackwell.
Cartledge, Paul, Paul Millett, and Stephen Todd. 1990. *Nomos: Essays in Athenian Law, Politics, and Society*. Cambridge: Cambridge University Press.
Charlton, David. 1988. *Weakness of Will*. Oxford: Basil Blackwell.
Cherniss, H. 1957. The Relation of the *Timaeus* to Plato's Later Dialogues. *American Journal of Philology* 78: 225–66.
Christ, Matthew R. 1998. *The Litigious Athenian*. Baltimore, MD: Johns Hopkins University Press.
Chroust, Anton-Hermann. 1946. The Philosophy of Law from St. Augustine to St. Thomas Aquinas. *The New Scholasticism* 20: 26–71.
Cicero. *De Finibus*. In *On Moral Ends*. Ed. Julia Annas, trans. Raphael Woolf. Cambridge: Cambridge University Press, 2001. (*M. Tulli Ciceronis De Finibus Bonorum et Malorum*. Ed. L. D. Reynolds. Oxford: Oxford University Press, 1998.)
———. *De Inventione* (*On Invention*). In *Cicero II*. Trans. H. M. Hubbell, 1–346. Cambridge, MA: Harvard University Press, 1949.
———. *De Legibus* (*On the Laws*). In *Cicero. On the Commonwealth and On the Laws*. Ed. and

trans. James E. G. Zetzel, 105–75. Cambridge: Cambridge University Press, 1999. (*M. Tulli Ciceronis De Legibus*. Ed. Konrat Ziegler, rev. W. Goerler. Freiburg: Ploetz, 1979.)
———. *De Natura Deorum*. Ed. and trans. H. Rackham. Cambridge, MA: Harvard University Press, 1933.
———. *De Officiis*. In *Cicero. On Duties*. Ed. and trans. M. T. Griffin and E. M. Atkins. New York, NY: Cambridge University Press, 1991. (*M. Tulli Ciceronis De Officiis*. Ed. Michael Winterbottom. Oxford: Oxford University Press, 1994.)
———. *De Re Publica* (*On the Commonwealth*). In *Cicero. On the Commonwealth and On the Laws*. Ed. and trans. James E. G. Zetzel, 1–103. Cambridge: Cambridge University Press, 1999. (*M. Tulli Ciceronis De Re Publica*. Ed. C. Ziegler. Leipzig: Teubner, 1969.)
———. *Letters to Atticus*. Trans. E. O. Winstedt. Cambridge, MA: Harvard University Press, 1962–1967. (Trans. D. R. Shackleton Bailey. Harmondsworth: Penguin, 1978.)
———. *Tusculan Disputations*. Trans. J. E. King. Cambridge, MA: Harvard University Press, 1927.
Clanchy, Michael T. 1996. *Abelard: A Medieval Life*. Oxford: Blackwell.
Clark, Gillian. 1993. *Women in Late Antiquity, Pagan and Christian Lifestyles*. Oxford: Oxford University Press.
Clement of Alexander. *Stromateis*. In *Clemens Alexandrinus. Stromata*. 3 vols. Ed. Otto Stahlin and Ludwig Fruchtel. Berlin: Akademie Verlag, 1970. (Stoic fragments drawn from this work are contained in *Stoicorum Veterum Fragmenta*. 4 vols. Ed. J. von Arnim. Leipzig: Teubner, 1924.)
Cohen, Abraham. 1995. *Everyman's Talmud: The Major Teachings of the Rabbinic Sages*. New York, NY: Schocken.
Cohen, David. 1991. *Law, Sexuality and Society: The Enforcement of Morals in Classical Athens*. Cambridge: Cambridge University Press.
———. 1995. *Law, Violence and Community in Classical Athens*. Cambridge: Cambridge University Press.
Cohen, Edward E. 2000. *The Athenian Nation*. Princeton, NJ: Princeton University Press.
Coing, Helmut, ed. 1973. *Handbuch der Quellen und Literatur der Neueren Europäischen Privatrechtsgeschichte. I. Mittelalter (1100–1500). Die Gelehrten Rechte und die Gesetzgebung*. Munich: Beck.
Colaiaco, James A. 2001. *Socrates against Athens: Philosophy on Trial*. London: Routledge.
Coleman, Janet. 1992. *Ancient and Medieval Memories. Studies in the Reconstruction of the Past*. Cambridge: Cambridge University Press.
———. 1994. The Christian Platonism of St Augustine. In *Platonism and the English Imagination*. Ed. Anna Baldwin and Sarah Hutton, 27–37. Cambridge: Cambridge University Press.
———. 2000. *A History of Political Thought from Ancient Greece to Early Christianity*. 2 Vols. Oxford: Blackwell.
Coleman, Jules, and Brian Leiter. 1996. Legal Positivism. In *A Companion to Philosophy of Law and Legal Theory*. Ed. Dennis Patterson, 241–60. Malden, MA: Blackwell Publishers.
Colish, Marcia. 1985. *The Stoic Tradition from Antiquity to the Early Medieval Ages*. Leiden: Brill.
Connolly, William E. 1993. *The Augustinian Imperative: A Reflection on the Politics of Morality*. London: Verso.
Cooper, John. 1999. Notes on Xenophon's Socrates. In *Reason and Emotion: Essays on Ancient Moral Psychology and Ethical Theory*. Ed. John Cooper, 3–28. Princeton, NJ: Princeton University Press.
Cooper, John, and J. F. Procopé. 1995. *Seneca. Moral and Political Essays*. New York, NY: Cambridge University Press.
Copleston, Frederick. 1957. *A History of Philosophy. Vol. 2: Medieval Philosophy*. Westminster: Newman.
———. 1961. *Medieval Philosophy*. New York, NY: Harper.
———. 1965. Copleston and Bertrand Russell. 1948 BBC Third Programme Debate: The Existence of God. In *A Modern Introduction to Philosophy*. Rev. ed. Ed. Paul Edwards and Arthur Pap, 474–81. New York, NY: The Free Press.

———. 1974. *A History of Medieval Philosophy*. New York, NY: Harper and Row.
Corbin, Henri. 1964. *Histoire de la Philosophie Islamique: 1. Des Origines jusqu'à la Mort d'Averroës (1198)*. Avec Seyyed Hosseïn Nasr et Osman Yahya. Paris: Gallimard.
Coulson, Noel James. 1964. *A History of Islamic Law*. Edinburgh: University Press.
Courtine, Jean-François. 1999. *Nature et Empire de la Loi. Études Suaréziennes*. Paris: Vrin-EHESS.
Courtois, C. 1985. *Les Vandales et L'Afrique*. Paris: Presses Universitaires de France.
Covell, Charles. 1992. *The Defence of Natural Law*. New York, NY: Macmillan.
Cranfield, C. E. B. 1970. St. Paul and the Law. In *New Testament Issues*. Ed. Richard A. Batey, 148–72. New York, NY: Harper & Row.
Crawford, M. H. 1996. *Roman Statutes*. London: Institute of Classical Studies, School of Advanced Study, University of London.
Cristiani, Marta. 1976. La Notion de Loi dans le "De Praedestinatione" de Jean Scot. *Studi Medievali* 17.1: 81–114.
Critias [?]. *Sisyphus Fragment*. In *Early Greek Political Thought from Homer to the Sophists*. Ed. Michael Gagarin and Paul Woodruff, 260–2. Cambridge: Cambridge University Press, 1995.
Crook, John. 1967. *Law and Life of Rome*. Cambridge: Cambridge University Press.
Cross, Richard. 1998. *The Physics of Duns Scotus: The Scientific Context of a Theological Vision*. Oxford: Oxford University Press.
———. 1999. *Duns Scotus*. New York, NY: Oxford University Press.
Crowe, Michael B. 1977. *The Changing Profile of Natural Law*. The Hague: Nijohoff.
Curren, Randall R. 2000. *Aristotle on the Necessity of Public Education*. Lanham, MD: Rowman & Littlefield.
Daube, David. 1969. *Roman Law: Linguistic, Social, and Philosophical Aspects*. Edinburgh: Edinburgh University Press.
———. 1981. *Ancient Jewish Law*. Leiden: Brill.
Davidson, Ivor J. 2001. *Ambrose. De Officiis*. Oxford: Oxford University Press.
Deckers, Daniel. 1991. *Gerechtigkeit und Recht. Eine Historisch-Kritische Untersuchung der Gerechtigkeitslehre des Francisco de Vitoria (1483–1546)*. Freiburg: Universitätverlag.
Decleva Caizzi, Fernanda. 1996. Pirroniani ed Accademici nel III secolo a.C. In *Aspects de la Philosophie Hellénistique*. Fondation Hardt. Entretiens sur l'antiquité classique 32: 147–83.
DeFilippo, Joseph G., and Philip T. Mitsis. 1994. Socrates and Stoic Natural Law. In *The Socratic Movement*. Ed. Paul A. Vander Waerdt, 252–71. Ithaca, NY: Cornell University Press.
De Gandillac, Maurice. 1975. Intention et Loi dans l'Ethique d'Abélard. In *Pierre Abélard, Pierre le Vénérable*. Ed. Centre national de la recherche scientifique, 585–608. Paris: CNRS.
De Lubac, Henri. 1946. *Surnaturel: Études Historiques*. Paris: Aubier.
———. 1965. *Augustinisme et Théologie Moderne*. Paris: Aubier.
Demos, Raphael. 1964. A Fallacy in Plato's *Republic*? *Philosophical Review* 73: 395–98.
Demosthenes. *Against Aphobus* (Orations 27–29). In *Demosthenes IV*. Ed. and trans. A. T. Murray, 1–123. Cambridge, MA: Harvard University Press, 1936.
———. *Against Leptines* (Oration 20). In *Demosthenes I*. Ed. and trans. J. H. Vince, 485–603. Cambridge, MA: Harvard University Press, 1930.
———. *Against Timocrates*. (Oration 24). In *Demosthenes III*. Ed. and trans. J. H. Vince, 370–511. Cambridge, MA: Harvard University Press, 1935.
D'Entreves, Alexander P. 1970. *Natural Law*. 2nd. rev. ed. London: Hutchinson.
De Romilly, J. 1971. *The Law in Greek Thought*. Paris: Les Belles Lettres.
———. 1991. *The Great Sophists in Periclean Athens*. Oxford: Oxford University Press.
Derrett, J. Duncan M. 1970. *Law in the New Testament*. London: Darton, Longman, and Todd.
De Salvo, L. 1993. Nolo Munera Ista (Aug. Sermo 355,3): Eredità e Donazioni in Agostino. *Atti dell' Accademia Romanistica Costantiniana IX, 1989, convegno internazionale*: 139–86.
Dewan, Lawrence. 2002. Jean Porter on Natural Law: Thomistic Notes. *The Thomist* 66: 275–309.
Díez-Alegría, José M. 1951. *El Desarrollo de la Doctrina de la ley Naturale en Luis de Molina y en*

los Maestros de la Universidad de Évora de 1565 a 1591: Estudio Histórico y Textos Inéditos. Barcelona: Consejo superior de investigaciones científicas.

Dillon, John. 1977. *The Middle Platonists: A Study of Platonism 80 B.C. to A.D. 220.* Ithaca, NY: Cornell University Press.

Dio Chrysostom. *Orationes.* In *Dio Chrysostom.* Trans. J. W. Cohoon. Cambridge, MA: Harvard University Press, 1971–1986.

Diogenes Laertius. *Vitae Philosophorum* (*Lives of the Philosophers*). In *Diogenes Laertius I and II.* Trans. R. D. Hicks. Cambridge, MA: Harvard University Press, 1925.

Diogenes of Oenoanda. *Fragments.* In *Diogenes Oenoandensis.* Ed. C. W. Chilton. Leipzig: Teubner, 1967.

Dod, Bernard G. 1982. Aristoteles Latinus. In *The Cambridge History of Later Medieval Philosophy. From the Rediscovery of Aristotle to the Disintegration of Scholasticism, 1100–1600.* Ed. Norman Kretzmann, Anthony Kenny, and Jan Pinborg, 45–79. Cambridge: Cambridge University Press.

Dodd, C. H. 1953. *New Testament Studies.* Manchester: University of Manchester Press.

Dodds, E. R. 1959. *Plato. Gorgias.* Oxford: Oxford University Press.

Donagan, Alan. 1982. Thomas Aquinas on Human Action. In *The Cambridge History of Later Medieval Philosophy.* Ed. Norman Kretzmann, Anthony Kenny, and Jan Pinborg, 642–54. Cambridge: Cambridge University Press.

Doyle, John P. 1991–1992. Francisco Suárez: On Preaching the Gospel to People Like the American Indians. *Fordham International Law Journal* 15: 879–951.

———. 1999. Francisco Suárez on the Law of Nations. In *Religion and International Law.* Ed. Mark W. Janis and Carolyn Evans, 103–20. The Hague-London: Nijhoff.

———. 2001. Francisco Suárez SJ on Human Rights. In *Menschenrechte: Rechte und Pflichten in Ost und West,* Band 9. Ed. Konrad Wegmann, 105–32. Münster: LIT.

———. 2010. *Collected Studies on Francisco Suarez.* Ed. Victor M. Salas. Leuven: Leuven University Press.

Driver, Godfrey Rolles, and John C. Miles, eds. and trans. 1935. *The Assyrian Laws.* Oxford: Clarendon Press.

———, eds. and trans. 1960. *The Babylonian Laws.* Oxford: Clarendon.

Driver, S. R. 1902. *A Critical and Exegetical Commentary to Deuteronomy.* 3rd. ed. Edinburgh: T & T Clark.

Dronke, Peter. 1988. *A History of Twelfth-Century Western Philosophy.* Cambridge: Cambridge University Press.

Düll, Rudolf. 1972. Seneca Iurisconsultus. In *Aufstieg und Niedergang der Römischen Welt.* Ed. Hildegard Temporini and Wolfgang Haase, II 15: 365–380. Berlin: de Gruyter.

Dumont, Paul. 1936. *Liberté Humaine et Concours Divin d'après Suárez.* Paris: Beauchesne.

Duns Scotus, John. *God and Creatures; the Quodlibetal Questions.* Trans. with introd., notes, and glossary by Felix Alluntis and Allan B. Wolter. Princeton, NJ: Princeton University Press, 1975.

———. *Ordinatio* III and IV. In *On the Will and Morality.* Trans. Allan B. Wolter. Ed. William A. Frank. Washington, DC: Catholic University of America Press, 1997.

———. *Philosophical Writings.* Trans. with introd. Allan B. Wolter. Indianapolis, IN: Hackett Pub. Co., 1987.

———. *Reportatio Parisiensis.* In *Opera Omnia. Editio nova iuxta editionem Waddingi XII tomos continentem.* Ed. L. Wadding, vol. 11. Paris: L. Vives, 1891.

Dutton, Paul E., ed. 1991. *The Glosae Super Platonem of Bernard of Chartres.* Toronto: Pontifical Institute of Mediaeval Studies.

Dvornik, Francis. 1966. *Early Christian and Byzantine Political Philosophy*, 2 vols. Washington, DC: Dumbarton Oaks Center for Byzantine Studies.

Dworkin, Ronald. 1977. *Taking Rights Seriously.* Cambridge, MA: Harvard University Press.

———. 1986. *Law's Empire.* Cambridge, MA: Harvard University Press.

Dyke, Andrew R. 2004. *A Commentary on Cicero, De Legibus.* Ann Arbor, MI: University of Michigan Press.

Dyson, R. W., ed. 2002. *Aquinas: Political Writings*. Cambridge: Cambridge University Press.
Eder, Walter. 1991. Who Rules? Power and Participation in Athens and Rome. In *City-States in Classical Antiquity and Medieval Italy*. Ed. Anthony Molho, Kurt Raaflaub, and Julia Emlen, 169–96. Ann Arbor, MI: University of Michigan Press.
Eissfeldt, O. 1975a. The Hebrew Kingdom. In *The Cambridge Ancient History*. Vol. 2. Pt. 2. Ed. I. E. S. Edwards, C. J. Gladd, N. G. L. Hammond, and E. Sollberger, 537–605. Cambridge: Cambridge University Press.
———. 1975b. Palestine in the Time of the Nineteenth Century. In *The Cambridge Ancient History*. Vol. 2, Pt. 2. Ed. I. E. S. Edwards, C. J. Gladd, N. G. L. Hammond, and E. Sollberger, 307–37. Cambridge: Cambridge University Press.
Elon, Menachem. 1994. *Jewish Law: History, Sources, Principles*, 4 vols. Trans. Bernard Auerbach and Melvin J. Sykes. Philadelphia, PA: Jewish Publication Society of America.
Elster, Marianne. 2003. *Die Gestze der Mittleren Römischen Republik: Text und Kommentar*. Darmstadt: Wissenschaftliche Buchgesellschaft.
Engberg-Pedersen, Troels. 1990. Stoic Philosophy and the Concept of the Person. In *The Person and the Human Mind. Issues in Ancient and Modern Philosophy*. Ed. Christopher Gill, 109–35. Oxford: Clarendon.
Epictetus. *Dissertationes* (*Discourses*). In *Epictetus. The Discourses as Reported by Arrian, and Fragments*. Ed. and trans. W. A. Oldfather, 2 vols. Cambridge, MA: Harvard University Press, 1925.
———. *Enchiridion* (*Handbook*). In *Epictetus. The Discourses as Reported by Arrian, and Fragments*. Ed. and trans. W. A. Oldfather, vol. 2, 479–537. Cambridge, MA: Harvard University Press, 1925.
Epicurus. *De Natura* (*On Nature*). In *Epicuro: Opere*. 2nd ed. Ed. Graziano Arrighetti, 119–37. Turin: Giulio Einaudi Editore, 1973. (In *The Epicurus Reader*. Trans. and ed. Brad Inwood and L. P. Gerson, 75–7. Indianapolis, IN: Hackett, 1994.)
———. *Kuriai Doxai* (*Key Doctrines*). In *Epicuro: Opere*. 2nd ed. Ed. Graziano Arrighetti, 119–37. Turin: Giulio Einaudi Editore, 1973. (In *The Epicurus Reader*. Trans. and ed. Brad Inwood and L. P. Gerson, 32–6. Indianapolis, IN: Hackett, 1994.)
———. *Sententiae Vaticanae* (*Vatican Sayings*). In *Epicuro: Opere*. 2nd ed. Ed. Graziano Arrighetti, 139–57. Turin: Giulio Einaudi Editore, 1973. (In *The Epicurus Reader*. Trans. and ed. Brad Inwood and L. P. Gerson, 36–40. Indianapolis, IN: Hackett, 1994.)
Erskine, Andrew. 1990. *The Hellenistic Stoa: Political Thought and Action*. Ithaca, NY: Cornell University Press.
Espinel, J. L. 1978. *San Estebán de Salamanca, Historia y Gúia, Siglos XIII–XX*. Salamanca: Editorial San Estebán.
Euripides. *Bacchae*. Trans. Paul Woodruff. Indianapolis, IN: Hackett, 1998.
———. *Ion*. Trans. Ronald Frederick Willetts. In *Euripides II*. Ed. David Grene and Richmond Lattimore, 265–348. New York, NY: Random House, 1958. (Partial trans. in *Early Greek Political Thought from Homer to the Sophists*. Ed. Michael Gagarin and Paul Woodruff, 67–8. Cambridge: Cambridge University Press, 1995.)
———. *The Suppliant Women*. Trans. Frank William Jones. In *The Complete Greek Tragedies*, vol. 6: *Euripides II*. Ed. David Grene and Richmond Lattimore, 405–50. New York, NY: Random House, 1958. (Partial trans. in *Early Greek Political Thought from Homer to the Sophists*. Ed. Michael Gagarin and Paul Woodruff, 62–5. Cambridge: Cambridge University Press, 1995.)
Eusebius. *Ecclesiastical History*. In *Eusebius. The History of the Church*. Trans. G. A. Williamson. Harmondsworth: Penguin, 1965.
———. *Life of Constantine*. In *Eusebius' Life of Constantine*. Trans. Averil Cameron. Oxford: Oxford University Press, 1999.
Evans, Gillian. 1982. *Augustine on Evil*. Cambridge: Cambridge University Press.
Faruki, Kemal A. 1971. *The Evolution of Islamic Constitutional Theory and Practice From 610 to 1926*. Karachi: National Publishing House Ltd.

Fassò, Guido. 2001. *Storia della filosofia del diritto*, vol. 2. Rome-Bari: Laterza.
Father of the College of St. Bonaventure, trans. 1948. *Alexander of Hales: Summa Theologica, III*. Quaracchi: Collegium S. Bonaventurae.
Feinberg, Joel. 1984. *Harm to Others*. New York, NY: Oxford University Press.
Fernández, Clemente, ed. 1986. *Los Filósofos Escolásticos de los Siglos XVI y XVII. Seleccíon de texts*. Madrid: Bac.
Fernández Castaneda, Jaime. 1968. Right Reason in Francisco Suárez. *Modern Schoolman* 45: 105–22.
Fernández-Santamaria, J. A. 1977. *The State, War and Peace: Spanish Political Thought in the Renaissance 1516–1559*. Cambridge: Cambridge University Press.
———. 1998. *The Theatre of Man: J. L. Vives on Society*. Philadelphia, PA: Transactions of the American Philosophical Society.
Ferrary, J.-L. 1995. The Statesman and the Law in the Political Philosophy of Cicero. In *Justice and Generosity: Studies in Hellenistic Social and Political Philosophy*. Ed. André Laks and Malcolm Schofield, 48–73. Cambridge: Cambridge University Press.
Fichter, Joseph. 1940. *Man of Spain, Francis Suárez*. New York, NY: Macmillan.
Fidora, Alexander, et al., eds. 2010. *Lex und Ius*. Stuttgart-Bad Canstatt: Frommann-Holzboog.
Finnis, John. 1980. *Natural Law and Natural Rights*. Oxford: Oxford University Press.
———. 1982. *Natural Law and Natural Rights*. Oxford: Oxford University Press. (Corrected edition.)
———. 1983. *Fundamentals of Ethics*. Oxford: Oxford University Press.
———. 1998. *Aquinas: Moral, Political, and Legal Theory*. Oxford: Oxford University Press.
Fitzmyer, Joseph A. 1981. *To Advance the Gospel: New Testament Studies*. New York, NY: Crossroad.
———. 1993. *Romans: A New Translation with Introduction and Commentary*. New York, NY: Doubleday.
Flach, Dieter. 1994. *Die Gesetze der Frühen Römischen Republik: Text und Kommentar*. Darmstadt: Wissenschaftliche Buchgesellschaft.
Foot, Philippa. 1978. *Virtues and Vices and Other Essays in Moral Philosophy*. Berkeley, CA: The University of California Press.
Fornara, Charles W. 1977. *Archaic Times to the End of the Peloponnesian War*. Baltimore, MD: Johns Hopkins University Press.
Fortenbaugh, William W. 1993. Theophrastus on Law, Virtue, and the Particular Situation. In *Nomodeiktes: Greek Studies in Honor of Martin Ostwald*. Ed. Ralph M. Rosen and Joseph Farrell, 447–58. Ann Arbor, MI: University of Michigan Press.
Fortenbaugh, William W., and Eckart Schutrümpf, eds. 2000. *Demetrius and Phalerum: Text, Translation, and Discussion*. New Brunswick, NJ: Transaction.
———. 2001. *Dicaearchus of Messana: Text, Translation, and Discussion*. New Brunswick, NJ: Transaction.
Fortenbaugh, William W., P. M. Huby, R. W. Sharples, and D. Gutas, eds. 1992. *Theophrastus of Eresus: Sources for His Life, Writings, Thought and Influence*. Leiden: E. J. Brill.
Foucault, Michel. 1985. *The History of Sexuality. Volume 1: The Use of Pleasure*. Trans. Robert Hurley. New York, NY: Pantheon.
———. 1986. *The History of Sexuality. Volume 2: The Care of the Self*. Trans. Robert Hurley. New York, NY: Pantheon.
Fox, Robin Lane. 1986. *Pagans and Christians in the Mediterranean World: From the Second Century AD to the Conversion of Constantine*. Harmondsworth: Penguin.
Foxhall, L., and A. D. E. Lewis, eds. 1996. *Greek Law in Its Political Setting: Justifications not Justice*. Oxford: Clarendon.
Fraga, Iribarne. 1947. *Luis de Molina y el Derecho de la Guerra*. Madrid: CISC.
Frankfort, Henri, John Albert Wilson, Thorkild Jacobsen, and William Andrew Irwin. 1946. *The Intellectual Adventure of Ancient Man: An Essay on Speculative Thought in the Ancient Near East*. Chicago, IL: University of Chicago Press.

Freddoso, Alfred J. 1988. *Luis de Molina: On Divine Foreknowledge*. Ithaca, NY: Cornell University Press.
Friedberg, Emil, ed. 1879. *Corpus Juris Canonici*. Leipzig: Tauchnitz.
Friedrich, Carl J. 1958. *The Philosophy of Law in Historical Perspective*. Chicago, IL: University of Chicago Press.
Frier, Bruce W. 1985. *The Rise of the Roman Jurists: Studies in Cicero's Pro Caecina*. Princeton, NJ: Princeton University Press.
Fuller, Lon. 1964. *The Morality of Law*. New Haven, CT: Yale University Press.
Gagarin, Michael. 1986. *Early Greek Law*. Berkeley, CA: University of California Press.
———. 2000. The Legislation of Demetrius of Phalerum and the Transformation of Athenian Law. In *Demetrius of Phalerum: Text, Translation and Discussion*. Ed. William W. Fortenbaugh and Eckart Schütrumpf, 347–66. New Brunswick, NJ: Transaction.
———. 2002. *Antiphon the Athenian: Oratory, Law, and Justice in the Age of the Sophists*. Austin, TX: University of Texas Press.
Gagarin, Michael, and Douglas MacDowell. 1998. *Antiphon and Andocides*. Austin, TX: University of Texas Press.
Gagarin, Michael, and Paul Woodruff, eds. 1995. *Early Greek Political Thought from Homer to the Sophists*. Cambridge: Cambridge University Press.
Gagnér, S. 1960. *Studien zur Geschichte der Gesetztgebung*. Stockholm: Göteborg.
Gaius. *Institutes*. In *The Institutes of Gaius*. Ed. and trans. W. M. Gordon and O. F. Robinson. Ithaca, NY: Cornell University Press, 1998.
Garnsey, Peter. 2007. *Thinking about Property: From Antiquity to the Age of Revolution*. Cambridge: Cambridge University Press.
Gaskin, Richard. 1994. Molina on Divine Foreknowledge and the Principle of Bivalence. *Journal of the History of Philosophy* 32: 551–71.
Gaudemet, Jean. 1957. *La Formation du Droit Séculier et du Droit de l'Eglise aux IVe et Ve Siècles*. Paris: Sirey.
———. 1958. *L'Église dans l'Empire Romain (IVe–Ve S.)*. Paris: Sirey.
———. 1983. Les Constitutions Constantiniennes du Code Theodosien. *Atti dell'Accademia Romanistica Costantiniana V, 1981, convegno internazionale*. (Università degli studi di Perugia, Facoltà di Giurisprudenza), 136–55.
———. 1993. *Les Sources du Droit Canonique, VIIIe–XXe Siècle*. Paris: Editions du Cerf.
Gauthier, R-A. 1959. *La Morale d'Aristote*. Paris: Presses Universitaires de France.
Gellius, Aulus. *Attic Nights* (*Noctes Atticae*). Trans. John C. Rolfe, 3 vols. Cambridge, MA: Harvard University Press, 1960. (1st ed. 1927.)
George, Robert, ed. 1992. Natural Law and Human Nature. In *Natural Law Theory: Contemporary Essays*. Ed. Robert George, 31–41. Oxford: Oxford University Press.
———. 1993. *Making Men Moral*. Oxford: Oxford University Press.
———. 1999. *In Defense of Natural Law*. Oxford: Clarendon.
Getino, Luis Alonso. 1930. *El Maestro Fray Francisco de Vitoria. Su Vida, su Doctrina e Influencia*. Madrid: Imperenta Catolica.
Getty, M. M. 1931. *The Life of the North Africans as Revealed in the Sermons of Saint Augustine*. Washington, DC: The Catholic University of America.
Gewirth, Alan, ed. and trans. 1951–1956. *Marsilius of Padua, The Defender of Peace*, 2 vols. New York, NY: Columbia University Press.
Giacon, Carlo. 1944. *La Seconda Scholastica*. Vol. 1. Milan: Bocca.
———. 1956. *La Seconda Scholastica*. Vol. 2. Milan: Bocca.
Gibb, Hamilton A. R. 1955. *Mohammedanism, An Historical Survey*. New York, NY: New American Library.
Gilby, Thomas, ed. and trans. 1964–1980. Thomas Aquinas, *Summa Theologiae*, 60 vols. New Blackfriars Edition. New York, NY: McGraw-Hill Book Company.
Gill, Christopher. 1995. Rethinking Constitutionalism in *Statesman* 291–303. In *Reading the Statesman: Proceedings of III Symposium Platonicum*. Ed. Christopher Rowe, 292–305. Sankt Augustin: Academia.

Ginzberg, Louis. 1941. *A Commentary on the Palestinian Talmud*. New York, NY: Jewish Theological Seminary.
Glauche, Gunter. 1970. *Schüllekture im Mittelalter. Entstehung und Wandlungen des Lektürekanons bis 1200 nach der Quellen Dargestellt*. Munich: Arbeo.
Glucker, J. 1988. Cicero's Philosophical Affiliations. In *The Question of Eclecticism: Studies in Later Greek Philosophy*. Ed. J. M. Dillon and A. A. Long, 34–69. Berkeley, CA: University of California.
Golding, Martin. 1974. Aquinas and Some Contemporary Natural Law Theories. *Proceedings of the American Catholic Philosophical Association* 48: 254–64.
Gómez-Camacho, Francisco. 1985. Luis de Molina y la Metodología de la Ley Natural. *Miscelánea Comillas* 43: 155–94, 437–63.
Goodblatt, D. 1971. The Babylonian Talmud. In *Aufstieg und Niedergang der Römischen Welt*. Ed. Wolfgang Haase, II.19.2: 257–336. Berlin: De Gruyter.
Goodenough, E. R. 1933. Philo's Exposition of the Law and His *De Vita Mosis*. *Harvard Theological Review* 26: 109–25.
———. 1940. *Introduction to Philo Judaeus*. New Haven, CT: Yale University Press.
Gordley, James R. 1999. Tort Law in the Aristotelian Tradition. In *Aristoteles: El Pensamiento Político y Jurídico*. Ed. Salvador Rus Rufino, 71–97. León and Seville: University of León and University of Seville.
Gordon, W. M., and O. F. Robinson. 1988. *The Institutes of Gaius*. Ithaca, NY: Cornell University Press.
Gorgias. *Funeral Oration* (fragments). In *Early Greek Political Thought from Homer to the Sophists*. Ed. Michael Gagarin and Paul Woodruff, 202–3. Cambridge: Cambridge University Press, 1995.
Gottschalk, Hans B. 2000. Demetrius of Phalerum: A Politician Among Philosophers and a Philosopher Among Politicians. In *Demetrius of Phalerum: Text, Translation and Discussion*. Ed. William W. Fortenbaugh and Eckart Schütrumpf, 367–80. New Brunswick, NJ: Transaction.
Goulet-Cazé, Marie-Odile. 1982. Un Syllogisme Stoïcien sur la Loi dans la Doxographie de Diogène le Cynique—a propos de Diogène Laërce. VI 72. *Rheinisches Museum* 125: 214–40.
———. 1996. Who Was the First Dog? In *The Cynics: The Cynic Movement in Antiquity and Its Legacy*. Ed. R. Bracht Branham and Marie-Odile Goulet-Cazé. Berkeley, CA: University of California Press.
Gracia, Jorge. 1991. Francisco Suárez. Special Issue. *American Catholic Philosophical Quarterly* 65: 3.
Gratian. *Decretum*. In *Gratian. The Treatise on Laws (Decretum DD. 1–20)*. Trans. Augustine Thompson; with Ordinary gloss, trans. James Gordley; introd. Katherine Christensen. Washington, DC: Catholic University of America Press, 1993.
Greengus, Samuel. 1995. Legal and Social Institutions of Ancient Mesopotamia. In *Civilizations of the Ancient Near East*. Ed. Jack M. Sasson, 469–84. New York, NY: Scribner.
Greenstein, Edward L. 1984. Biblical Law. In *Back to the Sources*. Ed. Barry W. Holtz, 83–104. New York, NY: Summit.
Griffin, M. T. 1976. *Seneca: A Philosopher in Politics*. Oxford: Clarendon.
Griffin, M. T., and Jonathan Barnes, eds. 1989. *Philosophy Togata: Essays on Philosophy and Roman Society*. Oxford: Clarendon.
———, eds. 1997. *Philosophy Togata II: Plato and Aristotle at Rome*. Oxford: Clarendon.
Grimaldi, W. M. A. 1980. *Aristotle, Rhetoric I, A Commentary*. New York, NY: Fordham University Press.
Grisez, Germain. 1965. The First Principle of Practical Reason. *Natural Law Forum* 10: 168–96.
Grubbs, Judith Evans. 1993. Constantine and Imperial Legislation on the Family. In *The Theodosian Code*. Ed. J. Harries and I. Wood, 120–42. Ithaca, NY: Cornell University Press.
Gruen, Erich S. 1993. The Polis in the Hellenistic World. In *Nomodeiktes: Greek Studies in Honor of Martin Ostwald*. Ed. Ralph M. Rosen and Joseph Farrell, 339–54. Ann Arbor, MI: University of Michigan Press.

Grundert, Frank, and Kurt Seelmann, eds. 2001. *Die Ordnung der Praxis. Neue Studien zur Spanischen Spätscholastik*. Tübingen: Niemeyer.
Gurney, O. R. 1990. *The Hittites*. 2nd ed. Harmondsworth: Penguin.
Guthrie, W. K. C. 1975. *History of Greek Philosophy: 4*. Cambridge: Cambridge University Press.
———. 1978. *History of Greek Philosophy: 5*. Cambridge: Cambridge University Press.
Haakonssen, Knud. 1996. *Natural Law and Moral Philosophy: From Grotius to the Scottish Enlightenment*. Cambridge: Cambridge University Press.
Hahm, David E. 1995. Polybius' Applied Political Theory. In *Justice and Generosity: Studies in Hellenistic Social and Political Philosophy. Proceedings of the Sixth Symposium Hellenisticum*. Ed. André Laks and Malcolm Schofield, 7–47. Cambridge: Cambridge University Press.
Haldon, J. F. 1997. *Byzantium in the Seventh Century*. Cambridge: Cambridge University Press.
Hall, Robert W. 1981. *Plato*. London: Allen & Unwin.
Hamburger, Max. 1951. *Morals and Law: The Growth of Aristotle's Legal Theory*. New Haven, CT: Yale University Press.
Hamilton, Alexander, James Madison, and John Jay. 1961. *The Federalist Papers*. Ed. Clinton Rossiter. New York, NY: New American Library.
Hamilton, Bernice. 1963. *Political Thought in Sixteenth Century Spain. A Study of the Political Ideas of Vitoria, De Soto, Suárez and Molina*. Oxford: Clarendon.
Hanke, Lewis. 1951. *Bartolomé de las Casas: An Interpretation of His Life and Writings*. The Hague: Nijhoff.
———. 1970. *Aristotle and the American Indians: A Study in Race Relations in the Modern World*. Bloomington, IN: Indiana University Press.
Hankins, James. 1996. Humanism and the Origins of Modern Political Thought. In *The Cambridge Companion to Renaissance Humanism*. Ed. Jill Kraye, 118–41. Cambridge: Cambridge University Press.
Hansen, Mogens Herman. 1996. The Ancient Athenian and the Modern Liberal View of Liberty as a Democratic Ideal. In *Demokratia*. Ed. J. Ober and C. Edrick, 91–104. Princeton, NJ: Princeton University Press.
Hardie, W. F. R. 1980. *Aristotle's Ethical Theory*. 2nd. ed. New York, NY: Oxford University Press.
Harries, Jill. 1999. *Law and Empire in Late Antiquity*. Cambridge: Cambridge University Press.
Harries, Jill, and Ian Wood. 1993. *The Theodosian Code*. Ithaca, NY: Cornell University Press.
Harris, C. S. R. 1937. Duns Scotus, John. In *Encyclopedia of the Social Sciences*. vol. 3. Ed. Edwin Robert Anderson Seligman and Alvin Saunders Johnson, 282ff. New York, NY: Macmillan.
Harrison, A. R. W. 1998. *The Law of Athens*. Indianapolis, IN: Hackett. (1st ed. 1968–1971.)
Hart, H. L. A. 1961. *The Concept of Law*. Oxford: Oxford University Press.
Harte, Verity. 1999. Conflicting Values in Plato's *Crito*. *Archiv für Geschichte der Philosophie* 81: 117–47.
Haskins, Charles Homer. 1927. *The Renaissance of the Twelfth Century*. Cambridge, MA: Harvard University Press.
Hayek, Friedrich A. 1973. *Law, Legislation, and Liberty, Volume I: Rules and Order*. Chicago, IL: University of Chicago Press.
Hegel, Georg Wilhelm Friedrich. 1930. *Grundlinien der Philosophie des Rechts*. Ed. Georg Lasson. Leipzig: Felix Meiner.
———. 1991. *Elements of the Philosophy of Right*. Ed. Allen W. Wood. Trans. H. B. Nisbet. Cambridge: Cambridge University Press.
Heinaman, Sara, and Martina Reuter, eds. 2009. *Psychology and Philosophy*. Dordrecht: Springer.
Herodotus. *History*. In *Herodotus The History*. Trans. David Grene. Chicago, IL: University of Chicago Press, 1988. (Partial trans. in *Early Greek Political Thought from Homer to the Sophists*. Trans. Michael Gagarin and Paul Woodruff, 77–85. Cambridge University Press, 1995.)
Herrin, Judith 1987. *The Formation of Christendom*. Princeton: Princeton University Press.
Herrmann, Frank R., and Brownlow M. Speer. 1994. Facing the Accuser: Ancient and Medi-

eval Precursors of the Confrontation Clause. *Virginia Journal of International Law.* 34:3, 481–552.

Hesiod. *Fragments.* In *Fragmenta Hesiodea.* Ed. Reinhold Merkelbach and Martin L. West. Oxford: Clarendon, 1967.

———. *Theogony.* In *Hesiod. The Homeric Hymns and Homerica.* Ed. Hugh G. Evelyn-White, 78–155. Cambridge, MA: Harvard University Press, 1914. (*Hesiodi Theogonia Opera et Dies Scutum.* Ed. Friedrich Solmsen, 5–48. Oxford: Oxford University Press, 1970. Partial trans. in *Early Greek Political Thought from Homer to the Sophists.* Ed. Michael Gagarin and Paul Woodruff, 9–20. Cambridge: Cambridge University Press, 1995.)

———. *Works and Days.* In *Hesiod. The Homeric Hymns and Homerica.* Ed. Hugh G. Evelyn-White, 2–65. Cambridge, MA: Harvard University Press, 1914. (*Hesiodi Theogonia Opera et Dies Scutum.* Ed. Friedrich Solmsen, 49–85. Oxford: Oxford University Press, 1970. Partial trans. in *Early Greek Political Thought from Homer to the Sophists.* Ed. Michael Gagarin and Paul Woodruff, 9–20. Cambridge: Cambridge University Press, 1995.)

Hilary of Poitiers. *Tractatus on Psalms.* In *Sancti Hilarii Pictaviensis Episcopi Tractatus super Psalmos.* Ed. J. Doignon. Turnholti: Brepols, 1997.

Hill, Benjamin, and Henrik Lagerlund, eds. 2012. *The Philosophy of Francisco Suárez.* Oxford: Oxford University Press.

Hippocrates. *Airs, Waters, Places.* In *Hippocrates I.* Ed. and trans. W. H. S. Jones, 65–137, 224–419. Cambridge, MA: Harvard University Press, 1931. (Partial trans. in *Early Greek Political Thought from Homer to the Sophists.* Ed. Michael Gagarin and Paul Woodruff, 164–6. Cambridge: Cambridge University Press, 1995.)

———. *De Victu (Regimen).* In *Hippocrates IV.* Ed. and trans. W. H. S. Jones, 224–419. Cambridge, MA: Harvard University Press, 1931.

Hittinger, Russell. 1993. Natural Law and Virtue. In *Natural Law Theory: Contemporary Essays.* Ed. Robert George, 42–70. Oxford: Oxford University Press.

Hobbes, Thomas. 1985. *Leviathan.* Ed. C. B. Macpherson. New York: Penguin Classics.

Hochberg, Herbert. 2001. The Radical Hylomorphism of Bergmann's Aristotelian Metaphysics and the Ontology of Relations. *The Modern Schoolman* 78: 257–88.

Hochstrasser, T. J. 2000. *Natural Law Theories in the Early Enlightenment.* Cambridge: Cambridge University Press.

Hodgson, Marshall G. S. 1974. *The Venture of Islam: Conscience and History in a World Civilization.* Chicago, IL: University of Chicago Press.

Hoffner, Harry A. Jr. 1997. *The Laws of the Hittites: A Critical Edition.* Leiden: Brill.

Hohfeld, Wesley N. 1923. *Fundamental Legal Conceptions as Applied in Judicial Reasoning.* New Haven, CT: Yale University Press.

Homer. *Iliad.* Trans. A. T. Murray; rev. William E. Wyatt, 2 vols. Cambridge, MA: Harvard University Press, 1999. (Partial trans. in *Early Greek Political Thought from Homer to the Sophists.* Ed. Michael Gagarin and Paul Woodruff, 3–7. Cambridge: Cambridge University Press, 1995.)

Honoré, Tony. 1962. *Gaius.* Oxford: Clarendon.

———. 1978. *Tribonian.* London: Duckworth.

———. 1981. *Emperors and Lawyers.* London: Duckworth.

———. 1982. *Ulpian.* Oxford: Oxford University Press.

———. 1994. *Emperors and Lawyers.* 2nd ed. Oxford: Oxford University Press.

Höpfl, Harro. 2004. *Jesuit Political Thought.* Cambridge: Cambridge University Press.

Horsley, R. A. 1978. The Law of Nature in Philo and Cicero. *Harvard Theological Review* 71: 35–59.

Horst, Ulrich, et al. eds. 1995–1997. *Francisco de Vitoria*: Vorlesungen, 2 vols. Stuttgart: Kohlhammer.

Hostiensis. 1581. *Super Sexto Decretalibus.* Venice. Reprint by Turin in 1965.

Hourani, Albert. 1991. *A History of the Arab Peoples.* Cambridge, MA: Harvard University Press.

Hume, David. 1751. *Enquiry Concerning the Principles of Morals.* London: A. Millar.

Humfress, Caroline. 2005. Law and Practice in the Age of Justinian. In *The Age of Justinian*. Ed. Michael Maas, 161–84. Cambridge: Cambridge University Press.

Hunt, D. 1993. Christianising the Roman Empire. In *The Theodosian Code, Studies in the Imperial Law of Late Antiquity*. Ed. J. Harries and I. Wood, 143–60. London: Duckworth.

Ibn Taimiyya, Takī al-Dīn Ahmad. *Ibn Taimiyya, Against the Greek Logicians*. Trans. Wael B. Hallaq. Oxford: Clarendon, 1993.

———. *Mukhtaṣar Naṣīḥat Ahl al-Īmān fī al-Radd 'alā Manṭiq al-Yūnān* (*Abridgement of the Counsel to the People of the Faith Concerning the Response to the Logic of the Greeks*). In *Majmū' Fatāwī Shaikh al-Islām Aḥmad ibn Taimiyya* (*Collection of the Legal Opinions of the Islamic Eminence, Ahmad Ibn Taimiyya*), vol. 9. Ed. 'Abd al-Raḥmān ibn Muḥammad ibn Qāsim al-'Āṣīmī and Muḥammad ibn 'Abd al-Raḥmān ibn Qāsim al-'Āṣīmī, 82–255. Rabāṭ: Maktabat al-Ma'ārif, 1961.

Ierodiakonou, Katerina, ed. 1999. *Topics in Stoic Philosophy*. New York, NY: Oxford University Press.

Ingham, Mary Elizabeth. 1993. Scotus and the Moral Order. In *Duns Scotus*. Special Issue. *American Catholic Philosophical Quarterly* 67: 127–50.

Inwood, Brad. 1985. *Ethics and Human Action in Early Stoicism*. Oxford: Oxford University Press.

———. 1986. Goal and Target in Stoicism. *Journal of Philosophy* 83: 547–56.

———. 1995. Seneca in His Philosophical Milieu. *Harvard Studies in Classical Philology* 97: 63–76.

———. 1996. L'*oikeiôsis* sociale chez Epictète. In *Polyhistor: Studies in the History and Historiography of Ancient Philosophy*. Ed. K. Algra, P. van der Horst, and D. Runia, 243–64. Leiden: Brill.

———. 1999. Rules and Reasoning in Stoic Ethics. In *Topics in Stoic Philosophy*. Ed. Katerina Ierodiakonou, 95–127. Oxford: Oxford University Press.

———. 2003. Natural Law in Seneca. In *The Studia Philonica Annual* 15. Ed. David T. Runia, Gregory E. Sterling, and Hindy Najman, 81–99. Providence, RI: Brown University.

———. 2004. Moral Judgment in Seneca. In *Stoicism: Traditions and Transformations, Proceedings of the Second Loemker Conference*. Ed. J. Zupko and S. K. Strange. Cambridge: Cambridge University Press.

Inwood, Brad, and L. P. Gerson, eds. and trans. 1994. *The Epicurus Reader: Selected Writings and Testimonia*. Indianapolis, IN: Hackett.

Irenaeus of Lyons. *Against the Heresies* (*Adversus Haereses*). Trans. Dominic J. Unger, rev. John J. Dillon. New York, NY: Paulist Press, 1992.

Irwin, Terence H. 1975. *Plato. Gorgias*. Oxford: Oxford University Press.

———. 1985. Moral Science and Political Theory in Aristotle. In *Crux: Essays in Greek History Presented to G. E. M. de. Ste. Croix on his 75th Birthday*. Ed. Paul A. Cartledge and F. D. Harvey, 150–68. London: Duckworth.

———. 1992. Socrates the Epicurean. In *Essays on the Philosophy of Socrates*. Ed. Hugh H. Benson, 198–219. Oxford: Oxford University Press.

———. 1997. *Plato's Ethics*. Oxford: Oxford University Press.

Isidore. *Etymologies*. In *From Irenaeus to Grotius: A Sourcebook in Christian Political Thought*. Ed. Oliver O'Donovan and Joan Lockwood O'Donovan, 209–11. Grand Rapids, MI: Eerdmans, 1999.

———. *Sentences*. In *From Irenaeus to Grotius: A Sourcebook in Christian Political Thought*. Ed. Oliver O'Donovan and Joan Lockwood O'Donovan. Grand Rapids, MI: Eerdmans, 1999.

Jacobsen, Thorkild. 1946. Mesopotamia. In *The Intellectual Adventure of Ancient Man: An Essay on Speculative Thought in the Ancient Near East*. Ed. Henri Frankfort et al., 125–202. Chicago, IL: University of Chicago Press.

Jasnow, Richard. 2003. Egypt: Middle Kingdom and Second Intermediate Period. In *A History of Ancient Near Eastern Law*. Ed. Raymond Westbrook, 255–88. Leiden: Brill.

Jeffery, L. H. 1961. *The Local Scripts of Archaic Greece*. Oxford: Oxford University Press.

Jerome (Hieronymus Stridonensis). *Epistolae*. *PL* vol. 22.18.
John of Paris. *On Royal and Papal Power* (*De Potestate Regia et Papali*). In *John of Paris on Royal and Papal Power*. Trans. A. P. Monahan. New York, NY: Columbia University Press, 1974.
John Scottus Eriugena. *On Divine Predestination* (*De Divina Praedestinatione Liber*). Ed. Goulven Madec. Turnhout: Brepols, 1978.
Johnson, Allan Chester, Paul Robinson Coleman-Norton, and Frank Card Bourne. 1961. *Ancient Roman Statutes: A Translation, with Introduction, Commentary, Glossary, and Index*. Austin, TX: University of Texas Press.
Johnston, David. 1999. *Roman Law in Context*. Cambridge: Cambridge University Press.
———. 2000. The Jurists. In *The Cambridge History of Greek and Roman Political Thought*. Ed. Christopher Rowe and Malcolm Schofield, 635–60. Cambridge: Cambridge University Press.
Johnstone, Steven. 1999. *Disputes and Democracy: The Consequences of Litigation in Ancient Athens*. Austin, TX: University of Texas Press.
Jolowicz, H. F. and Barry Nicholas. 1972. *Historical Introduction to the Study of Roman Law*. 3rd ed. Cambridge: Cambridge University Press.
Jordan, Mark D. 1993. Theology and Philosophy. In *The Cambridge Companion to Aquinas*. Ed. Norman Kretzmann and Eleonore Stump, 232–51. Cambridge: Cambridge University Press.
Josephus. *Jewish Antiquities*. In *The Works of Josephus*. Trans. William Whiston, 27–542. Peabody, MA: Hendrickson, 1987.
Justin Martyr. *Dialogue with Trypho*. Trans. Thomas B. Falls; rev. Thomas P. Halton; ed. Michael Slusser. Washington, DC: Catholic University of America Press, 2003.
Justinian. *Code*. In *Corpus Iuris Civilis*. Ed. Paul Krueger, Rudolf Schoell, and Wilhelm Kroll. Berlin: Weidmann, 1970–1973. (*The Civil Law*. Trans. S. P. Scott. Cincinnati, OH: The Central Trust Company, 1932.)
———. *Corpus Iuris Civilis*. Ed. Paul Krueger, Rudolf Schoell, and Wilhelm Kroll. Berlin: Weidmann, 1970–1973.
———. *Digest*. In *Corpus Iuris Civilis*. Ed. Paul Krueger, Rudolf Schoell, and Wilhelm Kroll. Berlin: Weidmann, 1970–1973. (*The Digest of Justinian*. Ed. and trans. Alan Watson. Philadelphia, PA: University of Pennsylvania Press, 1985. *The Digest of Justinian*. 2 vols. Ed. and trans. Alan Watson. Philadelphia, PA: University of Pennsylvania Press, 1998.)
———. *Institutes*. In *Corpus Iuris Civilis*. Ed. Paul Krueger, Rudolf Schoell, and Wilhelm Kroll. Berlin: Weidmann, 1970–1973. (*Justinian's Institutes*. Trans. Peter Birks and Grant McLeod. Ithaca, NY: Cornell University Press, 1987.)
———. *Novels*. In *Corpus Iuris Civilis*. Ed. Paul Krueger, Rudolf Schoell, and Wilhelm Kroll. Berlin: Weidmann, 1970–1973. (*The Civil Law*. Trans. S. P. Scott. Cincinnati, OH: The Central Trust Company, 1932.)
Kahn, Charles. 1981a. Did Plato Write Socratic Dialogues? *Classical Quarterly* 31: 305–20.
———. 1981b. The Origin of Social Contract Theory in the Fifth Century BC. In *The Sophists and Their Legacy*. Ed. G. B. Kerferd, 92–108. Wiesbaden: Steiner.
———. 1988. Discovering the Will: From Aristotle to Augustine. In *The Question of Eclecticism: Studies in Later Greek Philosophy*. Ed. J. M. Dillon and A. A. Long, 234–59. Berkeley, CA: University of California Press.
———. 1995. The Place of the *Statesman* in Plato's Later Work. In *Reading the Statesman: Proceedings of III Symposium Platonicum*. Ed. Christopher Rowe, 49–60. Sankt Augustin: Academia.
———. 1996. *Plato and the Socratic Dialogue*. Cambridge: Cambridge University Press.
———. 1997. Greek Religion and Philosophy in the Sisyphus Fragment. *Phronesis* 42: 247–62.
Kant, Immanuel. 1983. *Perpetual Peace and Other Essays*. Trans. Ted Humphrey. Indianapolis, IN: Hackett Publishing Company.
Kaser, Max. 1996. *Das Römische Zivilprozessrecht*. 2nd ed. Munich: Beck.
Kazhdan, Alexander P., and Alice-Mary Talbot, eds. 1991. *The Oxford Dictionary of Byzantium*. Oxford: Oxford University Press.
Kelly, John M. 1992. *A Short History of Western Legal Theory*. Oxford: Clarendon.

Kelsen, Hans. 1957. Aristotle's Doctrine of Justice. In *What Is Justice?* Ed. Hans Kelsen, 110–36. Berkeley, CA: University of California Press.
———. 1967. *Pure Theory of Law*. 2d ed. Trans. Max Knight. Berkeley, CA: University of California Press.
Kenny, Anthony. 1975. *Will, Freedom, and Power.* Oxford: Oxford University Press.
———. 1993. *Aquinas on Mind*. London: Routledge.
———. 2001, October 5. Aquinas and the Appearances of Bread. Review of Milbank and Pickstock. *Times Literary Supplement* 5140: 14.
Kent, Bonnie. 2001. Augustine's Ethics. In *The Cambridge Companion to Augustine*. Ed. E. Stump and N. Kretzmann, 205–33. Cambridge: Cambridge University Press.
Kerferd, G. B. 1982. *The Sophistic Movement*. Cambridge: Cambridge University Press.
Keyt, David. 1991. Aristotle's Theory of Distributive Justice. In *A Companion to Aristotle's Politics*. Ed. David Keyt and Fred D. Miller, Jr., 239–78. Oxford: Blackwell.
———. 1999. *Aristotle. Politics. Books V and VI. Trans. with commentary*. Oxford: Clarendon.
Keyt, David, and Fred D. Miller, Jr., eds. 1991. *A Companion to Aristotle's Politics*. Oxford: Blackwell.
Kidd, Ian G. 1979. Moral Actions and Moral Rules in Stoic Ethics. In *The Stoics*. Ed. John M. Rist, 247–58. Berkeley, CA: University of California Press.
Kilcullen, John. 1997. The Political Writings. In *The Cambridge Companion to Ockham*. Ed. Paul Vincent Spade, 302–25. Cambridge: Cambridge University Press.
King, Martin Luther, Jr. 1963. A Letter from a Birmingham Jail, June 12, 1963. *The Christian Century* 80: 767–73.
King, P. D. 1988. The Barbarian Kings. In *The Cambridge History of Medieval Political Thought: c. 350–c. 1450*. Ed. J. H. Burns, 123–53. Cambridge: Cambridge University Press.
Kleinhappl, Johann. 1932. Die Eigentumslehre Ludwig Molinas. *Zeitschrift für Katholische Theologie* 52: 46–66.
———. 1935. *Der Staat bei Ludwig Molina*. Innsbruck: F. Rauch.
Klosko, George. 1986. *The Development of Plato's Political Theory*. London: Methuen.
———. 1988. The Nocturnal Council in Plato's Laws. *Political Studies* 36: 74–88.
Knebel, Sven. 2000. *Wille, Würfel und Wahrscheinlichkeit. Das System der Moralischen Notwendigkeit in der Jesuitenscholastik 1550–1700*. Hamburg: Meiner.
Köhler, Ludwig. 1956. *Hebrew Man*. Trans. P. R. Ackroyd. New York, NY: Abingdon.
Koskenniemi, Martti. 2011. Empire and International Law: The Real Spanish Contribution. *University of Toronto Law Journal* 61(1): 1–36.
Kramer, Samuael Noah. 1963. *The Sumerians: Their History, Culture, and Character*. Chicago, IL: University of Chicago Press.
Kraut, Richard. 1984. *Socrates and the State*. Princeton, NJ: Princeton University Press.
———, ed. 1992. *The Cambridge Companion to Plato*. Cambridge: Cambridge University Press.
———. 2002. *Aristotle: Political Philosophy*. Oxford: Oxford University Press.
Kremer, Markus. 2008. *Den Frieden Verantworten: Politische Ethik bei Francisco Suárez (1548–1617)*. Stuttgart: Kohlhammer.
Kretzmann, Norman, Anthony Kenny, and Jan Pinborg, eds. 1982. *The Cambridge History of Later Medieval Philosophy*. Cambridge: Cambridge University Press.
Kripke, Saul. 1971. Identity and Necessity. In *Identity and Individuation*. Ed. Milton K. Muniz, 135–64. New York, NY: New York University Press.
Kruchten, Jean-Marie. 2001. Law. In *The Oxford Encyclopedia of Ancient Egypt*. Vol. 2. Ed. Donald B. Redford, 277–82. Oxford: Oxford University Press.
Kuttner, Stephan. 1935. Sur les Origines du Terme "Droit Positif." *Revue Historique de Droit Français et Etranger* 15: 728–40.
———. 1936. *Kanonistische Schuldlehre von Gratian bis auf die Dekretalen Gregors IX*. Vatican City: Biblioteca Apostolica Vaticana.
———. 1982. The Revival of Jurisprudence. In *Renaissance and Renewal in the Twelfth Century*. Ed R. L. Benson and G. Constable, 299–323. Oxford: Oxford University Press.

Lacerte, Henry. 1964. *The Nature of Canon Law According to Suárez*. Ottawa: University of Ottawa Press.
Lactantius. *De Mortibus Persecutorum (On the Deaths of the Persecutors)*. Ed. and trans. J. L. Creed. Oxford: Clarendon, 1984.
———. *Divine Institutes (Institutiones)*. Trans. Anthony Bowen and Peter Garnsey. Liverpool: Liverpool University Press, 2003.
Laks, André. 1991a. Legislation and Demiurgy: On the Relation between Plato's Republic and Laws. *Classical Antiquity* 9: 209–29.
———. 1991b. L'Utopie Législative de Platon. *Revue Philosophique* 4: 417–28.
———. 1995. Prodige et Méditation: Esquisse d'une Lecture des *Lois*. In *D'une Cité Possible. Sur les* Lois *de Platon*. Ed. J-F. Balaude, 11–28. Paris: Universite Paris X-Nanterre.
———. 2000. *The Laws*. In *The Cambridge History of Greek and Roman Political Thought*. Ed. Christopher Rowe and Martin Schofield, 258–92. Cambridge: Cambridge University Press.
Laks, André, and Malcolm Schofield, eds. 1995. *Justice and Generosity. Studies in Hellenistic Social and Political Philosophy*. Cambridge: Cambridge University Press.
Lamadrid, R. S. de. 1939. Luis de Molina S.I. – *De Bello*: Commentario a Ia 2.2, Q. 40. *Archivo Teológico Granadino* 1: 155–231.
Lambton, Ann K. S. 1981. *State and Government in Medieval Islam: An Introduction to the Study of Islamic Political Theory: The Jurists*. Oxford: Oxford University Press.
Lanata, Giuliana. 1984. *Legislazione e Natura nelle Novelle Giustinianee*. Naples: Edizioni Scientifiche Italiane.
Landgraf, Artur Michael. 1973. *Introduction à l'histoire de la littérature théologique de la scolastique naissante*. Trans. Louis-B. Geiger. Montreal: Institut d'études médiévales, 1973. (Orig. *Einführung in die Geschichte der theologischen Literatur der Frühscholastik unter dem Gesichtspuhkte der Schulenbildung*. Regensburg: Gregorius, 1948.)
Lane, Melissa. 1995. A New Angle on Utopia: The Political Theory of the *Statesman*. In *Reading the Statesman: Proceedings of III Symposium Platonicum*. Ed. Christopher Rowe, 276–91. Sankt Augustin: Academia.
———. 1998. *Method and Politics in Plato's Statesman*. Cambridge: Cambridge University Press.
———. 2000. Socrates and Plato: An Introduction. In *The Cambridge History of Greek and Roman Political Thought*. Ed. Christopher Rowe and Martin Schofield, 155–63. Cambridge: Cambridge University Press.
Langella, Simona. 2007. *Teologia e Legge Naturale: Studio Sulle Lezioni di Francisco de Vitoria*. Genova: Glauco Brigati.
———, ed. 2010. *Francisco de Vitoria: De Legibus*. Salamanca: Ediciones Universidad Salamanca.
Las Casas, Bartolomeo De. *De Regia Potestae o Derecho de Autodeterminación*. Ed. L. Perena. Madrid: CSIC, 1969.
———. *Del Úncio Modo de Atraer*. In *Del Úncio Modo de Atraer a Todos los Pueblos a la Verdadera Religion*. Ed. A. Millaers Carlo. Mexico City: FCE, 1942.
———. *Tratados*. Ed. L. Hanke, J. Tudela, and A. Millaers Carlo, 2 Vols. Mexico City: FCE, 1965.
Le Bras, G. C. Lefebvre, and J. Rambaud. 1965. *Histoire du Droit et des Institutions de l'Église en Occident. VII. L'Âge Classique, 1140–1378. Sources et Théorie du Droit*. Paris: Sirey.
Lee, Patrick. 1982. Aquinas and Scotus on Liberty and Natural Law. *Proceedings of the American Catholic Philosophical Association* 56: 70–8.
———. 1985. The Relation between Intellect and Will in Free Choice according to Aquinas and Scotus. *The Thomist* 49: 321–42.
———. 1997. Is Thomas's Natural Law Theory Naturalist? *American Catholic Philosophical Quarterly* 71: 567–87.
Lefkowitz, Mary. 1996. *Not Out of Africa: How Afrocentrism Became an Excuse to Teach Myth as History*. New York, NY: Basic Books.
Legnano, Giovanni de. *De Bello, De Represaliis, et De Duello*. Ed. Thomas Erskine Holland. Washington, DC: Oxford University Press, 1917.

Lenel, O. 1889. *Palingenesia Iuris Civilis*. Leipzig: Tauchniz.
Leoni, Bruno. 1991. *Freedom and the Law*. 3rd ed. Indianapolis, IN: Liberty Fund.
Lerner, Ralph, and Mushin Mahdi. 1963. *Medieval Political Philosophy: A Sourcebook*. Glencoe, IL: Free Press of Glencoe.
Levy, Ernst. 1949. Natural Law in Roman Thought. *Studia et Documenta Historias et Juris* 15: 1–23.
———. 1951. *West Roman Vulgar Law: The Law of Property*. Philadelphia, PA: American Philosophical Society.
Lewis, Bernard. *The Arabs in History*. 1960. New York, NY: Harper & Row.
Lewittes, Mendell. 1987. *Principles and Development of Jewish Law: The Concepts and History of Rabbinic Jurisprudence from its Inception to Modern Times*. New York, NY: Bloch.
Lewy, Guenter. 1960. *A Study of the Political Philosophy of Juan de Mariana SJ*. Geneva: Droz.
Lichtheim, Miriam. 1973. *Ancient Egyptian Literature*. Vol. 1. Berkeley, CA: University of California Press.
———. 1976. *Ancient Egyptian Literature*. Vol. 2. Berkeley, CA: University of California Press.
———. 1980. *Ancient Egyptian Literature*. Vol. 3. Berkeley, CA: University of California Press.
Liebs, Detlef. 2000. Roman Law. In *The Cambridge Ancient History*. Ed. Averil Cameron, Bryan Ward-Perkins, and Michael Whitby. Vol. 14: 238–59. 2nd ed. Cambridge: Cambridge University Press.
Lintott, Andrew. 1997. The Theory of the Mixed Constitution at Rome. In *Philosophia Togata II: Plato and Aristotle at Rome*. Ed. Jonathan Barnes and Miriam Griffin, 70–86. Oxford: Clarendon.
Lisska, Anthony J. 1991. Finnis and Veatch on Natural Law in Aristotle and Aquinas. *The American Journal of Jurisprudence* 36: 55–71.
———. 1996. *Aquinas's Theory of Natural Law: An Analytic Reconstruction*. Oxford: Clarendon.
———. Forthcoming. Thomas Aquinas on *Phantasia*: Rooted in but Transcending Aristotle's *De Anima*. In *Aquinas's Sources*. Ed. Timothy L. Smith. South Bend, IN: St. Augustine.
Livy. *The Rise of Rome (Ab Urbe Condita)*. Trans. T. J. Jones. Oxford: Oxford University Press, 1998.
Locke, John. 1980. *Second Treatise of Government*. Ed. C. B. Macpherson. Indianapolis, IN: Hackett Publishing Company.
Long, Anthony A. 1996. The Socratic Tradition: Diogenes, Crates, and Hellenistic Ethics. In *The Cynics: The Cynic Movement in Antiquity and Its Legacy*. Ed. R. Bracht Branham and Marie-Odile Goulet-Cazé, 28–46. Oxford: Clarendon.
———. 2002. *Epictetus: A Stoic and Socratic Guide to Life*. Oxford: Oxford University Press.
———. 2006. Stoic Philosophers on Persons, Property-Ownership, and Community. In *From Epicurus to Epictetus: Studies in Hellenistic and Roman Philosophy*, 335–59. Oxford: Oxford University Press.
Long, Anthony A. and D. N. Sedley. 1987. *The Hellenistic Philosophers: Translations of the Principal Sources with Philosophical Commentary, vol. 1*. New York, NY: Cambridge University Press.
Long, Roderick T. 1996. Aristotle's Conception of Freedom. *Review of Metaphysics* 49: 775–802.
———. 2000. *Reason and Value: Aristotle versus Rand*. Poughkeepsie: Objectivist Center.
———. Unpublished Manuscript. *Passionate Amnesia: Xenophon's Solution to the Socratic Paradox*.
Lorton, David. 1995. Legal and Social Institutions of Pharaonic Egypt. In *Civilizations of the Near East*. Ed. Jack. M. Sasson, 345–62. New York, NY: Simon & Schuster Macmillan.
Lottin, Odon. 1924. Le Droit Naturel Chez Saint Thomas d'Aquin et ses Prédécesseurs, I. *Ephemerides Theologicae Lovanienses* 1: 369–88.
———. 1948. *Psychologie et Morale aux XIIe et XIIIe Siècles. II. Problèmes de Morale*. Gembloux: Duculot.
Lucretius. *De Rerum Natura (On the Nature of Things)*. Trans. Martin Ferguson Smith. Indianapolis, IN: Hackett, 2001.

Lupher, David. 2006. *Romans in a New World: Classical Models in Sixteenth-Century Spanish America*. Ann Arbor, MI: University of Michigan Press.
Luscombe, David E. 1970. *The School of Peter Abelard*. Cambridge: Cambridge University Press.
———. 1982. Natural Morality and Natural Law. In *The Cambridge History of Later Medieval Philosophy. From the Rediscovery of Aristotle to the Disintegration of Scholasticism, 1100–1600*. Ed. Norman Kretzmann, Anthony Kenny, and Jan Pinborg, 705–19. Cambridge: Cambridge University Press.
Luther, Martin. 1961. *Lectures on Romans*. Philadelphia, PA: Westminster Press.
Lynch, John. 1972. *Aristotle's School: A Study of a Greek Educational Institution*. Berkeley, CA: University of California Press.
———. 1981. *Spain under the Habsburgs. Volume One: Empire and Absolutism, 1516–1598*. 2nd. ed. Oxford: Basil Blackwell.
Lyon, B. 1980. *A Constitutional and Legal History of Medieval England*. 2nd. ed. New York, NY: Norton.
Lysias. *Funeral Oration* (Oration 2). In *Lysias*. Trans. S. C. Todd, 25–41. Austin, TX: University of Texas Press, 2000.
Maas, Michael. 1986. Roman History and Christian Ideology in Justinianic Reform Legislation. *Dumbarton Oaks Papers* 40: 17–31.
———. ed. 2005. *The Age of Justinian*. Cambridge: Cambridge University Press.
MacCormack, Geoffrey. 1998. Sources. In *A Companion to Justinian's Institutes*. Ed. Ernest Metzger, 1–17. Ithaca, NY: Cornell University Press.
MacDowell, Douglas M. 1978. *The Law in Classical Athens*. Ithaca, NY: Cornell University Press.
MacIntyre, Alasdair. 1981. *After Virtue*. Notre Dame, IN: University of Notre Dame Press.
———. 1984. *After Virtue*. 2nd ed. Notre Dame, IN: University of Notre Dame Press.
———. 1988. *Whose Justice, Which Rationality?* Notre Dame, IN: University of Notre Dame Press.
———. 1990. *Three Rival Versions of Moral Enquiry*. Notre Dame, IN: University of Notre Dame Press.
MacKendrick, Paul Lachlan, and Karen Lee Singh. 1989. *The Philosophical Books of Cicero*. London: Duckworth.
Mackenzie, M. M. 1981. *Plato on Punishment*. Berkeley, CA: University of California Press.
Maclean, Ian. 1992. *Interpretation and Meaning in the Renaissance: The Case of Law*. Cambridge: Cambridge University Press.
Maguire, J. P. 1947. Plato's Theory of Natural Law. *Yale Classical Studies* 10: 151–78.
Mahdi, Muhsin. 2001. *Alfarabi and the Foundation of Islamic Political Philosophy*. Chicago, IL: University of Chicago Press.
Maimonides. *Eight Chapters*. In *Ethical Writings of Maimonides*. Trans. Raymond L. Weiss and Charles E. Butterworth. New York, NY: NYU Press, 1975.
———. *The Guide of the Perplexed*. Trans. Shlomo Pines. Chicago, IL: University of Chicago Press, 1963. (Arabic text: *Maimonides. Dalālat al-Ḥā'irīn* [*Guide of the Perplexed*]. Ed. Ḥusayn Atāy. Ankara: Ankara Üniversitesi Basimevi, 1974.)
———. *Treatise on the Art of Logic*. In *Ethical Writings of Maimonides*. Trans. Raymond L. Weiss and Charles E. Butterworth. New York, NY: New York University Press, 1975.
Maine, Henry Sumner. 1861. *Ancient Law: Its Connection with the Early History of Society and Its Relation to Modern Ideas*. London: J. Murray.
Maravall, José Antonio. 1960. *Carlos V y el Pensamiento Politico del Renacimiento*. Madrid: Instituto de Estudios Politicus.
Marcian. *Institutes* (*Institutiones*). In *Stoicorum Veterum Fragmenta*. Ed. J. von Arnim, vol. 3, 314. Leipzig: Leipzig, 1921–1924. (Partial trans. in *The Hellenistic Philosophers: Translations of the Principal Sources with Philosophical Commentary*, vol. 1, 432. Ed. and trans. Anthony A. Long and D. N. Sedley. New York, NY: Cambridge University Press, 1987.)
Marcus Aurelius Antoninus. *Meditations*. In *Marcus Aurelius*. Ed. and trans. C. R. Haines. Cambridge, MA: Harvard University Press, 1916.

Marenbon, John A. 1987. *Later Medieval Philosophy (1150–1350): An Introduction*. London: Routledge.
———. 1988. *Early Medieval Philosophy (480–1150): An Introduction*. 2nd ed. London: Routledge.
———. 1990. John Scottus and Carolingian Theology: From the *De Praedestinatione*, Its Background and Its Critics, to the *Periphyseon*. In *Charles the Bald: Court and Kingdom*. Ed. M. Gibson and J. Nelson, 303–25. Aldershot: Variorum.
———. 1992. Abelard's Concept of Natural Law. In *Mensch und Natur im Mittelalter*. Ed. A. Zimmermann and A. Speer. Vol. 2: 609–21. Berlin: De Gruyter.
———. 1996. *The Philosophy of Peter Abelard*. Cambridge: Cambridge University Press.
———, ed. 1997. *The Routledge History of Philosophy. III. Medieval Philosophy*. London: Routledge.
Marenbon, John A., and Giovanni Orlandi, eds. and trans. 2001. *Peter Abelard, Collationes*. Oxford: Clarendon and New York, NY: Oxford University Press.
Maritain, Jacques. 1951. *Man and the State*. Chicago, IL: University of Chicago Press.
Markus, Robert A. 1970. *Saeculum: History and Society in the Theology of St. Augustine*. Cambridge: Cambridge University Press.
———, ed. 1972. *Augustine: A Collection of Critical Essays*. Garden City, NY: Anchor.
———. 1988. The Latin Fathers. In *The Cambridge History of Medieval Political Thought: c. 350–c. 1450*. Ed. J. H. Burns, 99–122. Cambridge: Cambridge University Press.
———. 1990. *The End of Ancient Christianity*. Cambridge: Cambridge University Press.
Marsilius of Padua. *The Defender of the Peace (Defensor Pacis)*. In *Marsilius of Padua, The Defender of Peace*. Trans. and intro. Alan Gewirth. Afterward and bibliography by Cary J. Nederman. New York, NY: Columbia University Press, 2001.
Martin, W. C. 1974. The Bible and Natural Law. *Restoration Quarterly* 17: 193–221.
Martyn, J. Louis. 1997. *Galatians (Anchor Bible)*. New York, NY: Doubleday.
Marx, A., ed. 1935. Ibn Maimūn, Mūsā (Maimonides): "Letter to Samuel Ibn Tibbon." *Jewish Quarterly Review* N.S. 25 4: 371–428.
Mateos, Francisco. 1960. El Padre Luis de Molina y la Trata de Negros. *Estudios Eclesiásticos* 35: 209–67.
Mattha, Girgis. 1975. *The Demotic Legal Code of Hermopolis*. Le Caire: Institut français d'archéologie orientale du Caire.
Matthews, John. 1993. The Making of the Text. In *The Theodosian Code*. Ed. J. Harris and I. Wood, 19–44. Ithaca, NY: Cornell University Press.
———. 2000. *Laying Down the Law, A Study of the Theodosian Code*. New Haven, CT: Yale University Press.
Maurach, Gregor. 1991. *Seneca: Leben und Werk*. Darmstadt: Wissenschaftliche Buchgesellschaft.
Maurer, Armand A. 1962. *Medieval Philosophy*. New York, NY: Random House.
May, William E. 1984. The Natural Law Doctrine of Francis Suárez. *New Scholasticism* 58: 409–23.
McGrade, Arthur Stephen. 1974. *The Political Thought of William of Ockham*. London: Cambridge University Press.
———. 1982. Rights, Natural Rights, and the Philosophy of Law. In *The Cambridge History of Later Medieval Philosophy*. Ed. Norman Kretzman, et al., 738–56. Cambridge: Cambridge University Press.
McGrade, Arthur Stephen, John Kilcullen, and Matthew Kempshall, eds. 2001. *The Cambridge Translations of Medieval Philosophical Texts*, Vol. 2: *Ethics and Political Philosophy*. Cambridge: Cambridge University Press.
McInerny, Ralph. 1992. *Aquinas on Human Action: A Theory of Practice*. Washington, DC: Catholic University of America Press.
———. 1998. Review of Lisska: *Aquinas's Theory of Natural Law*. *The Medieval Review*. On-line at: http://www.hti.umich.edu/t/tmr/ (TMR ID: 98.01.10). Kalamazoo, MI: The Medieval Institute.

McKenzie, J. L. 1964. Natural Law in the New Testament. *Biblical Research* 9: 3–13.
McNabb, Vincent. 1929. St. Thomas Aquinas and Law. *Blackfriars* 10: 1047–1067.
Meeks, Wayne A, ed. 1972. *The Writings of St. Paul*. New York, NY: Norton.
Meiggs, Russell, and David Lewis. 1988. *Selection of Greek Historical Inscriptions to the End of the Fifth Century B.C.* Revised Edition. Oxford: Oxford University Press.
Méleze-Modrzejewski, Joseph. 1995. Law and Justice in Ptolemaic Egypt. In *Legal Documents of the Hellenistic World*. Ed. Markham J. Geller, Herwig Maehler, and A. D. E. Lewis, 1–19. London: The Warburg Institute, University of London.
Mews, Constant J. 1986. The *Sententie* of Peter Abelard. *Recherches de Théologie Ancienne et Médiévale* 53: 130–84.
Milbank, John, and Catherine Pickstock. 1999. *Truth in Aquinas*. London: Routledge.
Mill, John Stuart. 1985. *On Liberty*. New York, NY: Penguin Classics.
Miller, D. L. Carey. 1998. Property. In *A Companion to Justinian's Institutes*. Ed. Ernest Metzger, 42–79. Ithaca, NY: Cornell University Press.
Miller, Eugene F. 1979. Prudence and the Rule of Law. *American Journal of Jurisprudence* 24: 181–206.
Miller, Fred D. Jr. 1991. Aristotle on Natural Law and Justice. In *A Companion to Aristotle's Politics*. Ed. David Keyt and Fred D. Miller, Jr., 279–306. Oxford: Blackwell.
———. 2009. Origins of Rights in Ancient Greek Political Thought. In *The Cambridge Companion to Ancient Political Thought*. Ed. Stephen Salkever, 301–30. New York, NY: Cambridge University Press.
———. 1995. *Nature, Justice, and Rights in Aristotle's Politics*. Oxford: Clarendon.
Milsom, S. F. C. 1981. *Historical Foundations of the Common Law*. 2nd. ed. London: Butterworths.
Mishnah. In *The Mishnah: A New Translation*. Ed. Jacob Neusner. New Haven, CT: Yale University Press, 1987.
Mitchell, T. C. 1991. Judah Until the Fall of Jerusalem (*c*.700–586 B. C.). In *The Cambridge Ancient History*. Ed. John Boardman et al. Vol. 3, part. 2: 371–409. Cambridge: Cambridge University Press.
Mitsis, Phillip. 1988. *Epicurus' Ethical Theory: The Pleasures of Invulnerability*. Ithaca, NY: Cornell University Press.
———. 1993. Seneca on Reason, Rules and Moral Development. In *Passions & Perceptions*. Ed. Jacques Brunschwig and Martha C. Nussbaum, 285–312. Cambridge: Cambridge University Press.
———. 1994. Natural Law and Natural Right in Post-Aristotelian Philosophy: The Stoics and Their Critics. In *Aufstieg und Niedergang der Römischen Welt*. Ed. Wolfgang Haase, II 36.7: 4812–50. Berlin: W. de Gruyter.
———. 1999. The Stoic Origin of Natural Rights. In *Topics in Stoic Philosophy*. Ed. Katerina Ierodiakonou, 153–77. Oxford: Oxford University Press.
———. 2003. The Stoics and Aquinas on Virtue and Natural Law. In *The Studia Philonica Annual* 15. Ed. David T. Runia, Gregory E. Sterling, and Hindy Najman, 35–53. Providence, RI: Brown University.
———. 2011. Hellenistic Political Theory. In *The Oxford Handbook of Political Philosophy*. Ed. George Klosko, 120–41. Oxford: Oxford University Press.
Moles, John L. 1995. The Cynics and Politics. In *Justice and Generosity: Studies in Hellenistic Social and Political Philosophy. Proceedings of the Sixth Symposium Hellenisticum*. Ed. André Laks and Malcolm Schofield, 129–60. Cambridge: Cambridge University Press.
———. 1996. Cynic Cosmopolitanism. In *The Cynics: The Cynic Movement in Antiquity and Its Legacy*. Ed. R. Bracht Branham and Marie-Odile Goulet-Cazé, 121–35. Oxford: Clarendon.
Molina, Luis de. *Concordia Liberi Arbitrii cum Gratiae Donis, Divinia Praescientia, Providential, Praedestionatione, et Reprobatione, ad non Nullus Primae Partris D. Thomae Articulos*. Paris: P. Lethielleux, 1876.
———. *De Iure et Iustitia*. Vols. 1–2: Moguntiae, 1602; vol. 3: Antwerp, 1615; vol. 4: Cologne, 1614; vol. 5, Antwerp, 1609.

Mommsen, Theodor and Paul M. Meyer. 2002–2005. *Codex Theodosianus*. 3 vols. Hildesheim: Olms.
Moody, Ernest A. 1975a. *Studies in Medieval Philosophy, Science and Logic: Collected Papers: 1933–1969*. Berkeley, CA: University of California Press.
———. 1975b. William of Ockham. In *Studies in Medieval Philosophy, Science and Logic: Collected Papers: 1933–1969*. Ed. Ernest A. Moody, 409–39. Berkeley, CA: University of California Press.
Moore, G. E. 1903. *Principia Ethica*. Cambridge: Cambridge University Press.
Moore, G. F. 1927–1930. *Judaism in the First Centuries of the Christian Era. The Age of the Tannaim*. Cambridge, MA: Harvard University Press.
Morrison, Donald. 1987. On Professor Vlastos's Xenophon. *Ancient Philosophy* 7: 9–22.
———, ed. 1988. *Bibliography of Editions, Translations, and Commentary on Xenophon's Socratic Writings, 1600–Present*. Pittsburgh, PA: Mathesis.
———. 1995. Xenophon's Socrates on the Just and the Lawful. *Ancient Philosophy* 15: 329–47.
Morrow, Glenn. 1941. Plato and the Rule of Law. *Philosophical Review* 50: 105–26.
———. 1993. *Plato's Cretan City*. 2nd ed. Princeton, NJ: Princeton University Press.
Moser, Simon. 1952. Platons Begriff des Gesetzes. *Österreichesches Zeitschift für öffentliches Recht* NF 5: 135–58.
Muirhead, James. 1880. *The Institutes of Gaius and Rules of Ulpian*. Edinburgh: T & T Clark.
Mullaney, Thomas U. 1950. *Suárez on Human Freedom*. Baltimore, MD: Carroll.
Müller, Wolfgang P. 1990. The Recovery of Justinian's Digest in the Middle Ages. *Bulletin of Medieval Canon Law* 20: 1–29.
Murphy, Jeffrie G., and Jules L. Coleman. 1990. *Philosophy of Law: An Introduction to Jurisprudence*. Boulder, CO: Westview.
Murphy, Jeffrie G. 2005. *The Philosophy of Positive Law*. New Haven, CT; Yale University Press.
Najjar, Fawzi Mitri, and Domonique Mallet, ed. and trans. 1999. *L'Harmonie entre les Opinions de Platon et d'Aristote/Al Farabi*. Damas: Institut Français de Damas.
Najman, Hindy. 1999. The Law of Nature and the Authority of Mosaic Law. *The Studia Philonica Annual* 11. Ed. David T. Runia and Gregory E. Sterling. Atlanta, GA: Scholars Press.
———. 2003. A Written Copy of the Law of Nature: An Unthinkable Paradox? In *The Studia Philonica Annual* 15. Ed. David T. Runia, Gregory E. Sterling, and Hindy Najman, 54–63. Providence, RI: Brown University.
Nederman, Cary J. 1995. *Community and Consent: The Secular Political Theory of Marsiglio of Padua's Defensor Pacis*. Lanham, MD: Rowman & Littlefield.
Nelson, Everett J. 1967, October. The Metaphysical Presuppositions of Induction. In *Proceedings and Addresses of the American Philosophical Association* 40: 19–33. Yellow Springs, OH: The Antioch Press.
Nemesius. *De Natura Hominis (On the Nature of Man)*. In *Cyril of Jerusalem and Nemesius of Emesa*. Trans. William Telfer. Philadelphia, PA: Westminster, 1955.
Neufeld, E., trans. 1951. *The Hittite Laws*. London: Luzac.
Neusner, Jacob, ed. 1981. *The Study of Ancient Judaism*. New York, NY: Ktav.
———, ed. 1992. *The Study of Ancient Judaism*. Atlanta, GA: Scholars Press.
New Catholic Edition of the Holy Bible. New York, NY: Catholic Book Pub. Co., 1954.
Newman, W. L. 1887–1902. *The Politics of Aristotle*. Oxford: Clarendon.
Nicholas, Barry. 1962. *An Introduction to Roman Law*. Oxford: Clarendon.
Nicol, D. M. 1988. Byzantine Political Thought. In *The Cambridge History of Medieval Political Thought c. 350–c.1450*. Ed. J. H. Burns, 51–79. Cambridge: Cambridge University Press.
Nims, C. F. 1948. The Term *Hp*, "Law, Right," in Demotic. *Journal of Near Eastern Studies* 7: 243–60.
Noonan, John T. 1977. Who was Rolandus? In *Law, Church, and Society. Essays in Honour of Stephan Kuttner*. Ed. K. Pennington and R. Sommerville, 21–48. Philadelphia, PA: University of Pennsylvania Press.
———. 1979. Gratian Slept Here: The Changing Identity of the Father of the Systematic Study of Canon Law. *Traditio*: 145–72.

Noreña, Carlos. 1973. *Studies in Spanish Renaissance Thought*. The Hague: Nijhoff.
Noth, M. 1984. *The Laws in the Pentateuch*. London: SCM.
Nussbaum, Martha C. 1993. Non-Relative Virtues. In *The Quality of Life*. Ed. Martha Nussbaum and Amartya Sen, 242–69. Oxford: Oxford University Press.
———. 1994. *The Therapy of Desire: Theory and Practice in Hellenistic Ethics*. Princeton, NJ: Princeton University Press.
Obbink, Dirk. 1999. The Stoic Sage in the Cosmic City. In *Topics in Stoic Philosophy*. Ed. Katerina Ierodiakonou, 178–95. Oxford: Clarendon.
Ober, Josiah. 1989. *Mass and Elite in Democratic Athens: Rhetoric, Ideology, and the Power of the People*. Princeton, NJ: Princeton University Press.
———. 2000a. Aristotle's Natural Democracy. In *Aristotle's Politics: Critical Essays*. Ed. Richard Kraut and Stephen Skultety, 223–43. Lanham, MD: Rowman and Littlefield.
———. 2000b. Quasi-Rights: Participatory Citizenship and Negative Liberties in Democratic Athens. *Social Philosophy and Policy* 17: 27–61.
O'Connor, D. J. 1967. *Aquinas and Natural Law*. London: Macmillan.
O'Daly, Gerard. 1989. Predestination and Freedom in Augustine's Ethics. In *The Philosophy in Christianity*. Ed. G. Vesey, 85–97. Cambridge: Cambridge University Press.
O'Donovan, Oliver, and Joan Lockwood O'Donovan, eds. 1999. *From Irenaeus to Grotius: A Sourcebook in Christian Political Thought*. Grand Rapids, MI: Eerdmans.
Oliveria Dias, José de. 1954. En Torno do Duelo Fonseca-Molina: Uma Argumentação Suicida. *Verbum* 11: 37–63.
———. 1955. Fonseca e Molina: Os Ultimos Ecos dum Litigio Plurissecular. *Revista Portuguesa de Filosofia* 11: 54–67.
Olmstead, A. T. 1948. *History of the Persian Empire*. Chicago, IL: University of Chicago Press.
O'Malley, John W. 1994. *The First Jesuits*. Cambridge, MA: Harvard University Press.
O'Meara, Thomas. 1992. The Dominican School of Salamanca and the Spanish Conquest of America: Some Bibliographical Notes. *The Thomist* 56: 555–82.
———. 1994. The School of Thomism at Salamanca and the Presence of Grace in the Americas. *Angelicum* 71: 321–70.
Oppenheim, A. Leo. 1977. *Ancient Mesopotamia: Portrait of a Dead Civilization*. Revised edition. Chicago, IL: University of Chicago Press.
Origen. *Contra Celsum* (*Against Celsus*). Trans. Henry Chadwick. Cambridge: Cambridge University Press, 1953.
Osiander, Andreas. 2001. Sovereignty, International Relations, and the Westphalian Myth. *International Organization* 55: 251–87.
Ostwald, Martin. 1969. *Nomos and the Beginnings of the Athenian Democracy*. Oxford: Oxford University Press.
———. 1973. Was There a Concept of *Agraphos Nomos* in Classical Greece? In *Exegesis and Argument*. Ed. N. E. Lee, A. P. D. Mourelatos, and R. M. Rorty, 70–104. Assen: Van Gorcum.
———. 1986. *From Popular Sovereignty to the Sovereignty of Law*. Berkeley, CA: University of California Press.
———. 1990. *Nomos* and *Phusis* in Antiphon's *Peri Alêtheias*. In *Cabinets of the Muses; Essays on Classical and Comparative Literature in Honor of Thomas G. Rosenmeyer*. Ed. Mark Griffith and Donald J. Mastronarde, 293–306. Atlanta, GA: Scholars.
———. 1996. Shares and Rights: "Citizenship" Greek Style and American Style. In *Demokratia*. Ed. J. Ober and C. Edrick, 49–61. Princeton, NJ: Princeton University Press.
Owen, G. E. L. 1953. The Place of the *Timaeus* in Plato's Dialogues. *Classical Quarterly* 3: 79–95.
Owens, Joseph. 1993. Aristotle and Aquinas. In *The Cambridge Companion to Aquinas*. Ed. Norman Kretzmann and Eleonore Stump, 38–59. Cambridge: Cambridge University Press.
Pagden, Anthony. 1982. *The Fall of Natural Man*. Cambridge: Cambridge University Press.
Pagden, Anthony, and Jeremy Lawrance, eds. 1992. Vitoria: Political Writings. Cambridge: Cambridge University Press.

Patrick, Dale. 1985. *Old Testament Law*. Atlanta, GA: John Knox.
Pazdernik, Charles. 2005. Justinianic Ideology and the Power of the Past. In *The Age of Justinian*. Ed. Michael Maas, 185–212. Cambridge: Cambridge University Press.
Pegis, Anton C. 1939. Molina and Human Liberty. In *Jesuit Thinkers of the Renaissance*. Ed. Gerard Smith, 75–130. Milwaukee, WI: Marquette University Press.
Pelikan, Jaroslav. 1971–1978. *The Christian Tradition*. Chicago, IL: University of Chicago Press.
Pennington, Kenneth. 1998. The History of Rights in Western Thought. *Emory Law Journal* 47: 237–52.
Pereña, Luciano, ed. 1971-1980. *Francisco Suárez: De Legibus ac Deo Legislatore*, 6 vols. Madrid: CSIC.
Pereña Vicente, L. 1954. *La Universidad de Salamanca, Forja del Pensamiento Politico en el Siglo XVI*. Salamanca: Universidad de Salamanca.
Pérez Beneyto, J. 1949. *Los Origenes de la Ciencia Politica en España*. Madrid: Instituto de Estudios Politicos.
Pérez Fernández, I. 1984. *Fray Bartolomé de Las Casas*. Caleruega: OPE.
Pérez Modesto, Lewis. 1994. *The Common Good as a Fundamental Principle of the Law According to Suárez*. Rome: Gregorian University.
Perreau-Saussine, Amanda, and Jeffrie Murphy, eds. 2007. *The Nature of Customary Law*. Cambridge: Cambridge University Press.
Peter Abelard. *Collationes*. Ed. and trans. John A. Marenbon and Giovanni Orlandi. Oxford: Clarendon and New York, NY: Oxford University Press, 2001.
———. *Commentary on Romans*. In *Peter Abelard. Opera Theologica I*. Ed. E. Buytaert. Turnhout: Brepols, 1969.
———. *Problemata Heloissae*. *PL* 78, col. 677–730.
———. *Scito Teipsum*. In *Peter Abelard. Opera Theologica IV*. Ed. R. M. Ilgner. Turnhout: Brepols, 2001. (*Peter Abelard's Ethics*. Ed. David E. Luscombe. Oxford: Oxford University Press, 1971.)
———. *Theologia Christiana*. In *Petri Abaelardi Opera Theologica II*. Ed. E. M. Buytaert, 69–372. Turnhout: Brepols, 1969. (*Corpus Christianorum, Continuatio Mediaevalis* 12.)
Peters, Rudolph, ed. and trans. 1977. *Jihad in Mediaeval and Modern Islam: The Chapter on Jihad from Averroes' Legal Handbook "Bidāyat al-Mudjtahid" and The Treatise "Koran and Fighting" by the Late Shaykh al-Azhar, Maḥmūd Shaltūt*. Leiden: E. J. Brill.
Pharr, Clyde. 1952. *The Theodosian Code*. Princeton, NJ: Princeton University Press.
Phillips, Anthony. 1970. *Ancient Israel's Criminal Law: A New Approach to the Decalogue*. New York, NY: Shocken.
Phillips, David D. 2013. *The Law of Ancient Athens*. Ann Arbor, MI: University of Michigan Press.
Philo. *De Opificio Mundi* (*On the Creation*). In *The Complete Works of Philo: Complete and Unabridged*. Trans. C. D. Yonge, 3–24. Peabody, MA: Hendrickson, 1993.
———. *De Specialibus Legibus* (*On the Special Laws*). In *The Complete Works of Philo: Complete and Unabridged*. Trans. C. D. Yonge, 534–639. Peabody, MA: Hendrickson, 1993.
———. *De Vita Mosis* (*On the Life of Moses*). In *The Complete Works of Philo: Complete and Unabridged*. Trans. C. D. Yonge, 459–517. Peabody, MA: Hendrickson, 1993.
———. *Legum Allegoriae* (*Allegorical Interpretation*). In *The Complete Works of Philo: Complete and Unabridged*. Trans. C. D. Yonge, 25–79. Peabody, MA: Hendrickson, 1993.
———. *Quod Omnis Probus Liber Sit* (*Every Good Man Is Free*). In *The Complete Works of Philo: Complete and Unabridged*. Trans. C. D. Yonge, 682–97. Peabody, MA: Hendrickson, 1993.
Philodemus of Gadara. *Academicorum Index* (*History of Philosophers*). In *Filodemo: Storia dei Filosofi: Platone e l'Academia Storia dei Filosofi (PHerc. 1021 e 164)*. Ed. Tiziano Dorandi. Naples: Bibliopolis, 1991.
———. *Index Stoicorum* (*On the Stoics*). In *Index Stoicorum Herculanensis*. Ed. Augustus Traversa. Genoa: Instituto di filologia classica, 1952.
Photius. *Bibliotheca* (*Library*). In *Photius. Bibliothèque*. Ed. and trans. René Henry, 9 vols. Paris:

Société d'Édition Les Belles Lettres, 1959–1977. (*Photius' Bibliotheca: A Selection Translated with Notes*. Trans. N. G. Wilson. 1994.)

Pickstock, Catherine. 2000. Imitating God: The Truth of Things According to Thomas Aquinas. The 1999 Aquinas Lecture. *New Blackfriars* 81: 308–26.

Pieler, Peter E. 1978. Byzantinische Reichsliteratur. In *Die Hochsprachliche Profane Literatur der Byzantiner*. Ed. Herbert Hunger. Vol. 2: 341–480. Munich: Beck.

Pindar. *Fragments*. In *Pindar II*. Trans. William H. Race, 221–413. Cambridge: Harvard University Press, 1997. (Partial trans. in *Early Greek Political Thought from Homer to the Sophists*. Ed. Michael Gagarin and Paul Woodruff, 40–1. Cambridge: Cambridge University Press, 1995.)

Pink, Thomas. 2009. Natural Law and the Theory of Moral Obligation. In *Psychology and Philosophy*. Ed. Sara Heinaman and Martina Reuter, 97–114. Dordrecht: Springer.

Plato [?]. *Alcibiades*. Trans. D. S. Hutchinson. In *Plato: Complete Works*. Ed. John M. Cooper, 557–95. Indianapolis, IN: Hackett, 1997.

———. *Apology*. Trans. G. M. A. Grube. In *Plato: Complete Works*. Ed. John M. Cooper, 17–36. Indianapolis, IN: Hackett, 1997.

———. *Clitophon*. Trans. Francisco J. Gonzalez. In *Plato: Complete Works*. Ed. John M. Cooper, 965–70. Indianapolis, IN: Hackett, 1997.

———. *Cratylus*. Trans. C. D. C. Reeve. In *Plato: Complete Works*. Ed. John M. Cooper, 101–56. Indianapolis, IN: Hackett, 1997.

———. *Crito*. Trans. G. M. A. Grube. In *Plato: Complete Works*. Ed. John M. Cooper, 37–48. Indianapolis, IN: Hackett, 1997.

——— (pseudo). *Eryxias*. Trans. Mark Joyal. Ed. John M. Cooper, 1718–33. Indianapolis, IN: Hackett, 1997.

———. *Euthydemus*. Trans. Rosamond Kent Sprague. In *Plato: Complete Works*. Ed. John M. Cooper, 708–43. Indianapolis, IN: Hackett, 1997.

———. *Euthyphro*. Trans. G. M. A. Grube. In *Plato: Complete Works*. Ed. John M. Cooper, 1–16. Indianapolis, IN: Hackett, 1997.

———. *Gorgias*. Trans. Donald J. Zeyl. In *Plato: Complete Works*. Ed. John M. Cooper, 791–869. Indianapolis, IN: Hackett, 1997. (*The Gorgias*. In *Early Greek Political Thought from Homer to the Sophists*. Ed. Michael Gagarin and Paul Woodruff. Cambridge: Cambridge University Press, 1995. *Plato, Gorgias*. Trans. Terence H. Irwin. Oxford: Oxford University Press, 1979.)

——— [?]. *Hipparchus*. Trans. Nicholas D. Smith. In *Plato: Complete Works*. Ed. John M. Cooper, 609–17. Indianapolis, IN: Hackett, 1997.

———. *Hippias Major* (*Greater Hippias*). Trans. Paul Woodruff. In *Plato: Complete Works*. Ed. John M. Cooper, 898–921. Indianapolis, IN: Hackett, 1997.

———. *Laws*. Trans. Trevor J. Saunders. In *Plato: Complete Works*. Ed. John M. Cooper, 1318–1616. Indianapolis, IN: Hackett, 1997. (*The Laws of Plato*. Trans Thomas L. Pangle. New York, NY: Basic, 1980. *Plato, Laws*. Trans. R. G. Bury. Cambridge, MA: Harvard University Press, 1926.)

———. *Letters*. Trans. Glenn R. Morrow. In *Plato: Complete Works*. Ed. John M. Cooper, 1634–76. Indianapolis, IN: Hackett, 1997.

——— (pseudo). *Minos*. Trans. Malcom Schofield. In *Plato: Complete Works*. Ed. John M. Cooper, 1307–17. Indianapolis, IN: Hackett, 1997.

——— (pseudo). *On Justice*. Trans. Andrew S. Becker. In *Plato: Complete Works*. Ed. John M. Cooper, 1687–93. Indianapolis, IN: Hackett, 1997.

———. *Phaedo*. Trans. G. M. A. Grube. In *Plato: Complete Works*. Ed. John M. Cooper, 49–100. Indianapolis, IN: Hackett, 1997.

———. *Politicus* (*Statesman*). Trans. C. J. Rowe. In *Plato: Complete Works*. Ed. John M. Cooper, 294–358. Indianapolis, IN: Hackett, 1997.

———. *Protagoras*. Trans. Stanley Lombardo and Karen Bell. In *Plato: Complete Works*. Ed. John M. Cooper, 746–90. Indianapolis, IN: Hackett, 1997. (*Protagoras*. Trans. C. C. W. Taylor. Oxford: Clarendon, 1976. In *Early Greek Political Thought from Homer to the Sophists*. Partial trans. Michael Gagarin and Paul Woodruff, 173–85. Cambridge: Cambridge University Press, 1995.)

———. *Republic.* Trans. G. M. A. Grube, rev. C. D. C. Reeve. In *Plato: Complete Works.* Ed. John M. Cooper, 971–1223. Indianapolis, IN: Hackett, 1997. (*The Republic of Plato.* Trans. Allan Bloom. New York, NY: Basic, 1968.)

———. *Timaeus.* Trans. Donald J. Zeyl. In *Plato: Complete Works.* Ed. John M. Cooper, 1224–91. Indianapolis, IN: Hackett, 1997.

Plautus. *Bacchides.* Trans. Douglass Parker. In *Plautus and Terence. Five Comedies.* Ed. Deena Berg and Douglass Parker, 185–294. Indianapolis, IN: Hackett, 1999.

Plescia, Joseph. 1995. *The Bill of Rights and Roman Law.* Bethesda, MD: Austin & Winfield.

Plotinus. *Enneads.* Trans. A. H. Armstrong, 7 vols. Cambridge, MA: Harvard University Press, 1966–1988.

Plutarch. *Contra Epicuri Beatitudinem* (*Against Epicurean Happiness*). In *Plutarch Moralia 14.* Trans. Benedict Einarson and Phillip H. De Lacy, 2–149. Cambridge, MA: Harvard University Press, 1967.

———. *De Alexandri Magni Fortuna aut Virtute* (*On the Luck or Virtue of Alexander*). In *Plutarch Moralia 4.* Trans. Frank Cole Babbitt, 380–487. Cambridge, MA: Harvard University Press, 1936.

——— (pseudo). *De Fato* (*On Fate*). In *Plutarch Moralia 7.* Trans. Phillip H. De Lacy and Benedict Einarson, 303–59. Cambridge, MA: Harvard University Press, 1959.

———. *De Stoicis Repugnantiis* (*On Stoic Self-Contradictions*). In *Plutarch Moralia 13, Part 1.* Trans. Harold Cherniss, 367–603. Cambridge, MA: Harvard University Press, 1976.

———. *Life of Lycurgus.* In *Plutarch Lives 1.* Trans. Bernadotte Perrin, 203–303. Cambridge, MA: Harvard University Press, 1914.

———. *Life of Solon.* In *Plutarch Lives 1.* Trans. Bernadotte Perrin, 403–99. Cambridge, MA: Harvard University Press, 1914.

Pollock, Sir Frederick Bart, and Frederic W. Maitland. 1923. *The History of English Law before the Time of Edward I.* 2nd. ed. Cambridge: Cambridge University Press.

Polybius. *The Histories.* Trans. W. R. Paton, 6 vols. Cambridge, MA: Harvard University Press, 1922–1927.

Porphyry. *On Abstinence* (*De Abstinentia*). In *Porphyry. On Abstinence from Killing Animals.* Trans. Gillian Clark. Ithaca, NY: Cornell University Press, 2000.

Porter, Jean. 1999. *Natural and Divine Law.* Grand Rapids, MI: William B. Eerdmans.

Post, Gaines. 1973. Ancient Roman Ideas of Law. In *Dictionary of the History of Ideas.* Ed. Philip Wiener, 685–90. New York, NY: Scribner.

Postgate, J. N. 1992. *Early Mesopotamia: Society and Economy at the Dawn of History.* London: Routledge.

Potts, Timothy. 1982. Conscience. In *The Cambridge History of Later Medieval Philosophy. From the Rediscovery of Aristotle to the Disintegration of Scholasticism, 1100–1600.* Ed. Norman Kretzmann, Anthony Kenny, and Jan Pinborg, 687–704. Cambridge: Cambridge University Press.

Powell, J. G. F., ed. 1995. *Cicero the Philosopher: Twelve Papers.* Oxford and New York, NY: Clarendon.

Pozo, Cándido. 1962. *Fuentes para la Historia del Método Teologico en la Escuela de Salamanca.* Granada: Facultad de Teología.

Pritchard, James B., ed. 1958. *The Ancient Near East.* Princeton, NJ: Princeton University Press.

———. 1975. *The Ancient Near East, Volume 2: A New Anthology of Texts and Pictures.* Princeton, NJ: Princeton University Press.

Pugliese, Giovanni. 1954. "Res Corporales," "Res Incorporales" e il Problema del Diritto Soggettivo. In *Studi in Onore di Vincenzo Arangio-Ruiz,* 223–60. Naples: Jovene.

Queralt, Antonio. 1975. Libertad Humana en Luis de Molina. *Archivo teológico Granadino* 38: 5–155.

———. 1976. Libertad Humana en Luis de Molina: Sus Elementos Constitutivos y Posibilidades en un Orden Natural. *Archivo teológico Granadino* 39: 5–100.

Quinto, Riccardo. 2001. *Scholastica. Storia di un Concetto.* Padua: Il Poligrafo.

Raaflaub, Kurt A. 2000. Poets, Lawgivers, and the Beginnings of Political Reflection in Archaic Greece. In *The Cambridge History of Greek and Roman Political Thought*. Ed. Christopher Rowe and Martin Schofield, 23–57. Cambridge: Cambridge University Press.
Rabeneck, Joannes. 1950a. De Vita et Scriptis Ludovici Molina. *Archivum Historicum Societatis Jesu* 19: 75–145.
———. 1950b. Quis Prior Proposuerit Doctrinam de Scientia Media, Fonseca an Molina. *Archivum Historicum Societatis Jesu* 19: 141–5.
Rahman, Fazlur. 1968. *Islam*. New York, NY: Doubleday.
Ramos, D. Lisson. 1972. La Ley Natural en Domingo de Soto. *Persona y Derecho* 2: 605–26.
———. 1976. *La Ley Ségun Domingo de Soto*. Pamplona: Eunsa.
Rashdall, Hastings. 1936. *The Universities of Europe in the Middle Ages*. Rev. F. M. Powicke and A. B. Emden. 3 vols. Oxford: Oxford University Press.
Rawls, John. 1955. Two Concepts of Rules. *The Philosophical Review* 64: 3–13.
———. 1971. *A Theory of Justice*. Cambridge, MA: Harvard University Press.
———. 1993. *Political Liberalism*. New York, NY: Columbia University Press.
———. 1999. *The Law of Peoples*. Cambridge, MA: Harvard University Press.
Rawson, Elizabeth. 1975. *Cicero: A Portrait*. London: Allen Lane.
Raz, Joseph. 1979. *The Authority of Law*. New York, NY: Oxford University Press.
———. 1986. *The Morality of Freedom*. New York, NY: Oxford University Press.
Reeve, C. D. C. 1989. *Socrates in the Apology*. Indianapolis, IN: Hackett.
Reid, Charles J. Jr. 1991. The Canonistic Contribution to the Western Rights Tradition: An Historical Inquiry. *Boston College Law Review* 33: 59–72.
———. 1996. Thirteenth-Century Canon Law and Rights: The Word *ius* and Its Range of Subjective Meanings. *Studia Canonica* 30: 312–31.
———. 1998. Roots of a Democratic Church Polity in the History of Canon Law: The Case of Elections in the Church. *Proceedings of the Canon Law Society of America* 60: 154–5.
———. 2002. "So It Will Be Found that the Right of Women in Many Cases Is of Diminished Condition": Rights and the Legal Equality of Men and Women in the Twelfth- and Thirteenth-Century Canon Law. *Loyola (Los Angeles) Law Review* 35: 499–511.
Rhodes, P. J. 1981. *A Commentary on the Aristotelian Athenaion Politeia*. Oxford: Clarendon.
Richardson, M. E. J. 2000. *Hammurabi's Code: Text, Translation and Glossary*. Sheffield: Sheffield Academic Press.
Richardson, P., and S. Westerholm. 1991. *Law and Religious Communities in the Roman Period: The Debate over Torah and Nomos in Postbiblical Judaism and Early Christianity*. Waterloo: Laurier.
Riggsby, Andres M. 2010. *Roman Law and the Legal World of the Romans*. Cambridge: Cambridge University Press.
Rist, J. M. 1969. Augustine on Free Will and Predestination. *Journal of Theological Studies* 20: 420–47.
———, ed. 1979. *The Stoics*. Berkeley, CA: University of California Press.
———. 1994. *Augustine, Ancient Thought Baptized*. Cambridge: Cambridge University Press.
Ritchie, David G. 1895. *Natural Rights: A Criticism of Some Political and Ethical Conceptions*. London: S. Sonnenschein.
Robinson, O. F. 1997. *The Sources of Roman Law: Problems and Methods for Ancient Historians*. London: Routledge.
Robinson, T. H., and O. F. Oesterly. 1937. *Hebrew Religion. Its Origin and Development*. 2nd ed. New York, NY: Macmillan.
Rommen, Heindrich. 1926. *Die Staatslehre des Franz Suárez*. Münchengladbach: Volksvereins.
Roth, Martha T. 1997. *Law Collections from Mesopotamia and Asia Minor*. 2nd. ed. Atlanta, GA: Scholars.
Rowe, Christopher, ed. and trans. 1995a. *Plato's* Statesman. Warminster: Aris and Phillips.
———, ed. 1995b. *Reading the Statesman: Proceedings of III Symposium Platonicum*. Sankt Augustin: Academia.

———. 2000. The *Politicus* and Other Dialogues. In *The Cambridge History of Greek and Roman Political Thought*. Ed. Christopher Rowe and Martin Schofield, 233–57. Cambridge: Cambridge University Press.
Rowe, Christopher, and Martin Schofield. 2000. *The Cambridge History of Greek and Roman Political Thought*. Cambridge: Cambridge University Press.
Rudebusch, George. 1999. *Socrates, Pleasure, and Value*. Oxford: Oxford University Press.
Rufinus. *De Summa Decretorum*. In *Die "Summa Decretorum" des Magister Rufinus*. Ed. H. Singer. Paderborn: Schöningh, 1902.
Runia, David T. 2001. *Philo of Alexandria. On the Creation of the Cosmos According to Moses*. Introduction, translation, and commentary. Leiden: Brill.
Russell, Frederick H. 1976. Innocent IV's Proposal to Limit Warfare. In *Proceedings of the Fourth International Congress of Medieval Canon Law*. Ed. Stephan Kuttner, 386–88. Vatican: Biblioteca Vaticana.
Rutherford, R. B. 1989. *The Meditations of Marcus Aurelius: A Study*. Oxford: Clarendon.
Ryan, Alan. 1985. Utility and Ownership. In *Utility and Rights*. Ed. R. G. Frey, 175–95. Oxford: Blackwell.
Ryan, Columba. 1965. The Traditional Concept of Natural Law. In *Light on the Natural Law*. Ed. Iltud Evans. 13–37. Baltimore, MD: Helicon.
Sachs, David. 1963. A Fallacy in Plato's *Republic*. *Philosophical Review* 72: 141–58.
Saggs, H. W. F. 1968. *The Greatness That Was Babylon; A Sketch of the Ancient Civilization of the Tigris-Euphrates Valley*. New York, NY: Mentor.
———. 1989. *Civilization Before Greece and Rome*. New Haven, CT: Yale University Press.
Saller, Richard P. 1994. *Patriarchy, Property and Death in the Roman Family*. Cambridge: Cambridge University Press.
Sanders, E. P. 1977. *Paul and Palestinian Judaism*. Philadelphia, PA: Fortress.
———. 1983. *Paul, the Law, and the Jewish People*. Philadelphia, PA: Fortress.
Santas, Gerasimos. 1979. *Socrates: Philosophy in Plato's Early Dialogues*. London: Routledge & K. Paul.
———. 2001. *Goodness and Justice: Plato, Aristotle, and the Moderns*. Malden: Blackwell.
Sarraf, Joseph. 1984. *La Notion du Droit d'après les Anciens Égyptiens*, vol. 10. Vatican City: Libreria Editrice Vaticana.
Saunders, Trevor J. 1970. *Plato. The Laws*. Trans. with intro. Harmondsworth: Penguin.
———. 1981. Protagoras and Plato on Punishment. In *The Sophists and Their Legacy*. Ed. G. B. Kerferd, 129–41. Wiesbaden: Steiner.
———. 1991. *Plato's Penal Code*. Oxford: Oxford University Press.
———. 1992. Plato's Later Political Thought. In *The Cambridge Companion to Plato*. Ed. Richard Kraut, 464–92. Cambridge: Cambridge University Press.
Saunders, Trevor J. and Luc Brisson. 2000. *Bibliography on Plato's Laws*. Sankt Augustin: Academia.
Scattola, Merio. 2001. Naturrecht als Rechts Theorie. In *Die Ordnung der Praxis*. Ed. Frank Grunen and Kurt Seelmann, 21–48. Tübingen: Niemeyer.
———. 2010. Die Weiche Ordnung—Recht und Gesetz in der Naturrechtslehre des Domingo de Soto. In *Lex und Ius*. Ed. Fidora et al., 333–68. Stuttgart-Bad Canstatt: Frommann-Holzboog.
Schacht, Joseph. 1964. *An Introduction to Islamic Law*. Oxford: Clarendon.
Schäfer, Peter. 2003. *The History of the Jews in the Greco-Roman World*. London: Routledge.
Scheltema, H. J. 1967. Byzantine Law. In *The Cambridge Medieval History*, Vol. 4, pt. 2. 2nd ed. Ed. J. M. Hussey, 55–77. Cambridge: Cambridge University Press.
Schmitt, Charles B., and Quentin Skinner, eds. 1990. *The Cambridge History of Renaissance Philosophy*. Cambridge: Cambridge University Press.
Schmutz, Jacob. 2001. La Doctrine Medievale des Causes et la Theologie de la Nature Pure (XIII–XVII Siècles). *Revue Thomiste* 101: 217–64.
———. 2002. L'Heritage des Subtils. Cartographie du Scotisme de l'Age Classique. *Les Études Philosophiques* 1: 52–81.

———. 2008. *Scholasticon*. http://www.scholasticon.fr/.
Schofield, Malcolm. 1991. *The Stoic Idea of the City*. Cambridge: Cambridge University Press.
———. 1995. Two Stoic Approaches to Justice. In *Justice and Generosity: Studies in Hellenistic Social and Political Philosophy. Proceedings of the Sixth Symposium Hellenisticum*. Ed. André Laks and Malcolm Schofield, 191–212. Cambridge: Cambridge University Press.
———. 1999a. The Disappearing Philosopher King. In *Saving the City: Philosopher-Kings and Other Classical Paradigms*. Ed. Malcolm Schofield, 31–50. London: Routledge.
———. 1999b. Social and Political Thought. In *The Cambridge History of Hellenistic Philosophy*. Ed. Keimpe Algra et al., 739–70. Cambridge: Cambridge University Press.
———. 2000a. Approaching the *Republic*. In *The Cambridge History of Greek and Roman Political Thought*. Ed. Christopher Rowe and Martin Schofield, 190–232. Cambridge: Cambridge University Press.
———. 2000b. Epilogue. 2. Augustine. In *The Cambridge History of Greek and Roman Political Thought*. Ed. Christopher Rowe and Malcolm Schofield, 665–71. Cambridge: Cambridge University Press.
———. 2000c. Plato and Practical Politics. In *The Cambridge History of Greek and Roman Political Thought*. Ed. Christopher Rowe and Martin Schofield, 293–302. Cambridge: Cambridge University Press.
Schofield, Malcolm, and Gisela Striker, eds. 1986. *The Norms of Nature: Studies in Hellenistic Ethics*. Cambridge: Cambridge University Press.
Schrimpf, Gangolf. 1982. Der Beitrag des Johannes Scottus Eriugena zum Prädestinationsstreit. In *Die Iren und Europa im frühen Mittelalter*. Ed. Hienx Löwe, 819–65. Stuttgart: Klett-Cotta.
Schröder, Jan. 2000. Die Entstehumg des Modernen Völkerrechtsbegriffs im Naturrecht der Frühen Neuzeit. *Jahrbuch für Recht und Ethik* 8: 47–71.
Schroeder, Donald N. 1981. Aristotle on Law. *Polis* 4: 17–31.
Schulz, Fritz. 1967. *History of Roman Legal Science*. Oxford: Oxford University Press.
———. 1992. *Classical Roman Law*. Aalen: Scientia.
Schwartz, Daniel, ed. 2012. *Interpreting Suárez: Critical Essays*. Cambridge: Cambridge University Press.
Schwartz, Seth. 2001. *Imperialism, 200 B. C. E. to 640 C. E.* Princeton, NJ: Princeton University Press.
Schwenk, Cynthia J. 1985. *Athens in the Age of Alexander: the Dated laws and Decrees of "The Lykourgan Era" 338–322 B.C.* Chicago, IL: Ares.
Scorraille, Raoul de. 1911–1913. *François Saurez de la Compagnie de Jésus: D'après ses Lettres, ses Autres Ecrits Inédits et un Grand Nombre des Documents Nouveaux*. Paris: P. Lethielleux.
Scott, James Brown.1934. *The Spanish Origin of International Law. Francisco Vitoria and his Law of Nations*. Oxford: Clarendon.
Sedley, David N. 1983. The Motivation of Greek Scepticism. In *The Skeptical Tradition*. Ed. Myles F. Burnyeat, 9–30. Berkeley, CA: University of California Press.
Seeck, Otto. 1919. *Regesten der Kaiser und Papste für die Jahre 311 bis 476 n. Chr. Vorarbeit zu einer Prosopographie der christlichen Kaiserzeit*. Stuttgart: Metzler.
Seelmann, Kurt. 1979. *Die Lehre des Fernando Vázquez de Menchaca vom "Dominium"*. Cologne: Graz.
Segal, M. H. 1967. *The Pentateuch: Its Composition and Its Authorship*. Jerusalem: Magnes, Hebrew University.
Seidl, Erwin. 1942. Law. In *The Legacy of Egypt*. Ed. S. R. K. Glanville, 198–217. Oxford: Clarendon.
Seneca. *De Beneficiis* (*On Favours*). In *Seneca. Moral and Political Essays*. Ed. John M. Cooper; trans. J. F. Procopé, 181–308. New York, NY: Cambridge University Press, 1995.
———. *De Brevitate Vitae* (*On the Shortness of Life*). In *Seneca. Moral Essays*. Trans. John W. Basore, vol. 2, 286–355. Cambridge, MA: Harvard University Press, 1932.
———. *De Clementia* (*On Mercy*). In *Seneca. Moral and Political Essays*. Ed. John M. Cooper; trans. J. F. Procopé, 117–64. New York, NY: Cambridge University Press, 1995.

———. *De Consolatione ad Helviam* (*To His Mother Helvia on Consolation*). In *Seneca. Moral Essays*. Trans. John W. Basore, vol. 2, 416–89. Cambridge, MA: Harvard University Press, 1932.
———. *De Consolatione ad Marciam* (*To Marcia on Consolation*). In *Seneca. Moral Essays*. Trans. John W. Basore, vol. 2, 2–97. Cambridge, MA: Harvard University Press, 1932.
———. *De Ira* (*On Anger*). In *Seneca. Moral and Political Essays*. Ed. John M. Cooper; trans. J. F. Procopé, 1–116. New York, NY: Cambridge University Press, 1995.
———. *De Otio* (*On Leisure*). In *Seneca. Moral Essays*. Trans. John W. Basore, vol. 2, 180–201. Cambridge, MA: Harvard University Press, 1932.
———. *De Providentia* (*On Providence*). In *Seneca. Moral Essays*. Trans. John W. Basore, vol. 1, 2–47. Cambridge, MA: Harvard University Press, 1928.
———. *De Vita Beata* (*On the Happy Life*). In *Seneca. Moral Essays*. Trans. John W. Basore, vol. 2, 198–179. Cambridge, MA: Harvard University Press, 1932.
———. *Epistulae* (*Moral Epistles*). In *Seneca. Epistles*. Trans. Richard M. Gummere, 3 vols. Cambridge, MA: Harvard University Press, 1917–1925.
———. *Naturales Quaestiones* (*Natural Questions*). Trans. T. H. Corcoran, 2 vols. Cambridge, MA: Harvard University Press, 1971–1972.
Senellart, Michel. 1995. *Les Arts de Gouverner: Du Regimen Médiéval au Concept de Gouvernement*. Paris: Seuil.
Sextus Empiricus. *Adversus Mathematicos* (*Against the Professors*). Trans. R. G. Bury. Cambridge, MA: Harvard University Press, 1949.
———. *Outlines of Pyrrhonism*. Trans. R. G. Bury. Cambridge, MA: Harvard University Press, 1933.
Shāfiʿī, Muḥammad Ibn Idrīs al-. 1961. *Islamic Jurisprudence: Shāfiʿī's Risāla*. Trans. Majid Khadduri. Baltimore, MD: Johns Hopkins Press.
Sharples, Robert W. 1998. Theophrastus as Philosopher and Aristotelian. In *Theophrastus: Reappraising the Sources*. Ed. Johannes M. van Ophuijsen and Marlein van Raalte, 267–80. New Brunswick, NJ: Transaction.
Shaw, B. 1987. The Family in Late Antiquity: The Experience of Augustine. *Past and Present* 115: 3–51.
Shellens, Salomon M. 1959. Aristotle on Natural Law. *Natural Law Forum* 4: 72–100.
Shiner, Roger. 1994. Aristotle's Theory of Equality. *Loyola of Los Angeles Law Review* 27: 1245–64.
Sigmund, Paul. 1988. *St. Thomas Aquinas: On Politics and Ethics*. New York, NY: W. W. Norton and Company.
———. 1993. Law and Politics. In *The Cambridge Companion to Aquinas*. Ed. Norman Kretzmann and Eleonore Stump, 217–31. Cambridge: Cambridge University Press.
Simon, Yves. 1965. *The Tradition of Natural Law*. Ed. Vulkan Kuic. New York, NY: Fordham University Press.
Sinkler, Georgette. 1998. Roger Bacon. In *Routledge Encyclopedia of Philosophy*. Ed. Edward Craig, vol. 1: 632–6. London: Routledge.
Sischens Recaséns, L. 1927. *La Filosofía del Derecho de Francisco Suárez, con un Estudio Previo Sobre sus Antecedentes en la Patrística y en la Escolástica*. Madrid: V. Suárez.
Skinner, Quentin. 1978. *The Foundations of Modern Political Thought*. Cambridge: Cambridge University Press.
———. 1990. Political Philosophy. In *The Cambridge History of Renaissance Philosophy*. Ed. Charles B. Schmitt and Quentin Skinner, 389–452. Cambridge: Cambridge University Press.
Smith, Gerard. 1966. *Freedom in Molina*. Chicago, IL: Loyola University Press.
Smith, J. P. M. 1960. *The Origin and History of Hebrew Law*. Chicago, IL: The University of Chicago Press.
Snell, Daniel C. 1997. *Life in the Ancient Near East 3100–322 B.C.E.* New Haven, CT: Yale University Press.
Soden, Wolfram von. 1994. *The Ancient Orient: An Introduction to the Study of the Ancient Near East*. Grand Rapids, MI: William B. Eerdmans.

Soder, Josef. 1955. *Die Idee der Völkergemeinschaft: Francisco de Vitoria und die Philosophischen Grundlagen des Völkerrechts*. Frankfurt am Main: Metzner.

———. 1973. *Franz Suárez und das Völkrecht. Grundgedanken zu Staat, Recht und Internationalen Beziehungen*. Frankfurt am Main: Metzner.

Sophocles. *Antigone*. In *Sophocles I*. Trans. Elizabeth Wyckoff. Ed. David Grene and Richmond Lattimore, 185–236. New York, NY: Random House, 1960. (Partial trans. in *Early Greek Political Thought from Homer to the Sophists*. Trans. Michael Gagarin and Paul Woodruff, 50–2. Cambridge: Cambridge University Press, 1995.)

———. *Oedipus Tyrannus*. In *Sophocles I*. Trans. Elizabeth Wyckoff. Ed. David Grene and Richmond Lattimore, 15–90. New York, NY: Random House, 1960.

———. *Tereus* (fragment). In *Sophocles Fragments*. Trans. Hugh Lloyd Jones, 291–301. Cambridge, MA: Harvard University Press, 1996. (Partial trans. in *Early Greek Political Thought from Homer to the Sophists*. Trans. Michael Gagarin and Paul Woodruff, 56–7. Cambridge: Cambridge University Press, 1995.)

Sorabji, Richard. 1993. *Animal Minds and Human Morals: The Origins of the Western Debate*. Ithaca, NY: Cornell University Press.

Soto, Domingo de. *De Iustitia et Iure Libri Decem* (*On Justice and the Law*). Salamanca: Apud Ioannem Baptistam Terranoua, 1569. (In *De la Justicia y del Derecho en Diez Libros*. Trans. Marcelino González Ordóñez. Madrid: Sección Teólogos Juristas, Instituto de Estudios Políticos, 1967–1968.)

Southern, Richard W. 1995. *Scholastic Humanism and the Unification of Europe. I. Foundations*. Oxford: Blackwell.

———. 2001. *Scholastic Humanism and the Unification of Europe. II. The Heroic Age*. Oxford: Blackwell.

Spade, Paul Vincent, ed. 1999. *The Cambridge Companion to Ockham*. Cambridge: Cambridge University Press.

Stalley, R. F. 1983. *An Introduction to Plato's Laws*. Oxford: Blackwell.

———. 1994. Persuasion in Plato's *Laws*. *History of Political Thought* 15: 157–77.

———. 1995a. Punishment in Plato's *Laws*. *History of Political Thought* 16: 469–87.

———. 1995b. Punishment in Plato's *Protagoras*. *Phronesis* 40: 1–19.

———. 1996. Punishment and the Physiology of the *Timaeus*. *Classical Quarterly* 46: 357–70.

Stamm, J. J., and M. E. Andrew. 1967. *The Ten Commandments in Recent Research*. Naperville, IL: A. R. Allenson.

Ste. Croix, G. E. M. de. 1981. *The Class Struggle in the Ancient Greek World*. 2nd. ed. London: Duckworth.

Stegmüller, Friedrich. 1934. *Francisco de Vitoria y la Doctrina de la Gracia en la Escuela Salamanca*. Balmes: Barcelona.

———. 1935. *Geschichte des Molinismus*. Münster: Aschendorffschen Verlagsbuchhandlung.

Stein, Peter. 1988. *The Character and Influence of the Roman Civil Law: Historical Essays*. London and Rocheverte: Hambledon.

———. 1999. *Roman Law in European History*. Cambridge: Cambridge University Press.

Steiner, Hillel, and Philip Alston, eds. 2000. *International Human Rights in Context*. 2d ed. New York, NY: Oxford University Press.

Steinwenter, Artur. 1946. *NOMOS EMPSYCHOS*. Zur Geschichte einer politischen Theorie. *Anzeiger der Akademie der Wissenschaften in Wien. Philosophisch-Historische Klasse* 83: 250–68.

Stenton, Dorothy M. 1964. *English Justice between the Norman Conquest and the Great Charter, 1066–1215*. Philadelphia, PA: The American Philosophical Society.

Stern, S. M. 1968. *Aristotle on the World State*. London: Bruno Cassirer.

Stiening, Gideon. 2011. Quantitas Obligationis: Zum Verpflichtungsbegriff bei Vitoria—Mit Einem Ausblick auf Kant. In *Die Normativität des Rechts bei Francisco de Vitoria*. Ed. Bunge et al., 123–45. Stuttgart-Bad Canstatt: Frommann-Holzboog.

Stobaeus. *Eclogues*. In *Ioannis Stobaei Anthologium*. Ed. Curt Wachsmuth and Otto Hense, 5 vols. Berlin: Weidmann, 1884–1923.

Strack, Hermann Leberecht, and Günter Stemberger. 1992. *Introduction to the Talmud and Midrash*. Trans. Markus Bockmuehl. Minneapolis, MN: Fortress. (Revised Edition.)
Strauss, Leo. 1935. *Philosophie und Gesetz: Beiträge zum Verständnis Maimunis und seiner Vorläufer*. Berlin: Schocken. (New edition in: *Leo Strauss: Gesammelte Schriften. Philosophie und Gesetz: Frühe Schriften*. Ed. Heinrich Meier with Wiebke Meier. Stuttgart: J. B. Metzler, 1997. Vol. 2. English trans. in *Philosophy and Law: Contributions to the Understanding of Maimonides and His Predecessors*. Trans. E. Adler. Albany, NY: State University of New York Press, 1995.)
———. 1936a. Eine Vermisste Schrift Farabis. *Monatsschrift für Geschichte und Wissenschaft des Judentums* 80: 96–106.
———. 1936b. Quelques Remarques sur la Science Politique de Maïmonide et de Farabi. *Revue des Études Juives* 100: 1–37.
———. 1945. Farabi's Plato. In *Louis Ginsberg Jubilee Volume on the Occasion of His Seventieth Birthday*. American Academy for Jewish Research, 357–93. New York, NY: American Academy for Jewish Research.
———. 1952. *Persecution and the Art of Writing*. Glencoe, IL: The Free Press of Glencoe.
———. 1953. *Natural Right and History*. Chicago, IL: University of Chicago Press.
———. 1972. *Xenophon's Socratic Discourse: An Interpretation of the Oeconomicus*. Ithaca, NY: Cornell University Press.
Striker, Gisela. 1983. The Role of Oiekeiosis in Stoic Ethics. In *Oxford Studies in Ancient Philosophy 1*, 145–67. New York, NY: Oxford University Press.
———. 1996a. *Essays on Hellenistic Epistemology and Ethics*. Cambridge: Cambridge University Press.
———. 1996b. Origins of the Concept of Natural Law. In *Essays on Hellenistic Epistemology and Ethics*. Ed. Gisela Striker, 209–20. Cambridge: Cambridge University Press.
Stüben, Joachim, ed. 2010. *Francisco de Vitoria: De Lege: Über das Gesetz*. Stuttgart-Bad Canstatt: Frommann-Holzboog.
Stump, Eleonore. 2001. Augustine on Free Will. In *The Cambridge Companion to Augustine*. Ed. Eleonore Stump and Norman Kretzmann, 124–47. Cambridge: Cambridge University Press.
Stump, Eleonore, and Norman Kretzman, eds. 2001. *The Cambridge Companion to Augustine*. Cambridge: Cambridge University Press.
Suárez, Francisco. *Defensio Fidei Catholicae*. In *Francisco Suárez: Opera Omnia*. Ed. Carlos. Berton. Paris: Vivés, 1856–1866 and Supp. 1878.
———. *De Legibus sue de Deo Legislatore. In Francisco Suárez: Opera Omnia*. Ed. Carlos Berton. Vol. 5. Paris: Vivés, 1856–1866 and Supp. 1878.
Symmachus, Quintus Aurelius. *Relationes*. In *Prefect and Emperor: The Relationes of Symmachus, A.D. 384*. Trans. R. H. Barrow. Oxford: Clarendon, 1973.
Tacitus. *Annals*. Trans. John Jackson. In *Tacitus 3*. Trans. Clifford H. Moore and John Jackson, 225–643. Cambridge, MA: Harvard University Press, 1931.
———. *Dialogus de Oratoribus (Dialogue on Oratory)*. In *Tacitus. Dialogus, Agricola, and Germania*. Trans. W. Hamilton Fyfe. Oxford: Clarendon, 1908.
Tavares, Serveriano. 1955. A Questão Fonseca-Molina: Reposta a uma Crítica. *Revista Portuguesa de Filosofia* 11: 78–88.
Taylor, C. C. W. 1976. *Plato. Protagoras*. Oxford: Clarendon.
Taylor, John H. 2001. *Death and the Afterlife in Ancient Egypt*. Chicago, IL: University of Chicago Press.
Tellegen-Couperus, Olga. 1993. *A Short History of Roman Law*. London: Routledge.
Temporini, Hildegard, and Wolfgang Haase. 1972. *Aufstieg und Niedergang der Römischen Welt; Geschichte und Kultur Roms im Spiegel der Neuren Forschung*. Berlin: de Gruyter.
Tertullian. *Against Marcion. (Adversus Marcionem)*. Ed. and trans. Ernest Evans. Oxford: Clarendon, 1972. (*Adversus Marcionem*. Ed. A. Kroymann, vol. 1, 437–730. Turnhout: Corpus Christianorum Series Latina, 1954.)
———. *Against the Jews (Adversus Judaeos)*. In *The Writings of Tertullian*. Trans. S. Thelwall,

vol. 3, 201–58. Edinburgh: T&T Clark 1870. (*Adversus Judaeos.* Ed. A. Kroymann, vol. 2, 1337–98. Turnhout: Corpus Christianorum Series Latina, 1954.)
———. *On the Soul* (*De Anima*). In *The Writings of Tertullian.* Trans. Peter Holmes, vol. 2, 410–541. Edinbugh: T&T Clark 1870. (*De Anima.* Ed. J. H. Waszink, vol. 2, 779–870. Turnhout: Corpus Christianorum Series Latina, 1954.)
———. *Prescription of Heretics* (*De Praescriptione Haereticorum*). In *The Writings of Tertullian.* Trans. Peter Holmes, vol. 2, 1–54. Edinburgh: T&T Clark 1870. (*De Praescriptione Haereticorum.* Ed. A. Kroymann, vol. 70, 1–58. Vienna: Corpus Scriptorum Ecclesiasticorum Latinorum, 1942.)
Théodoridès, Aristide. 1971. The Concept of Law in Ancient Egypt. In *The Legacy of Egypt.* 2nd ed. Ed. J. R. Harris, 291–322. Oxford: Clarendon.
Thierry of Chartres. *Commentary on Cicero's On Invention.* In *The Latin Rhetorical Commentaries by Thierry of Chartres.* Ed. Karin M. Fredborg. Toronto: Pontifical Institute of Mediaeval Studies, 1988. (Studies and Texts 84.)
———. *Commentary on the Rhetoric to Herennius.* In *The Latin Rhetorical Commentaries by Thierry of Chartres.* Ed. K. M. Fredborg. Toronto: Pontifical Institute of Mediaeval Studies, 1988.
Thomas Aquinas. *Commentary on Nicomachean Ethics.* Trans. C. I. Litzinger. Chicago, IL: Regnery, 1964.
———. *De Veritate* (*Quaestiones Disputatae de Veritate*). In *Omnia Opera Sancti Thomae Aquinatis Doctoris Angelici.* Leonine Edition. Vol. 22. Rome: Polyglot Press, 1960. (Trans: *Truth.* Trans. Robert W. Mulligan et al. Indianapolis, IN: Hackett, 1994.)
———. *Letter to the Duchess of Brabant.* In *The Pocket Aquinas.* Ed. Vernon Bourke. New York, NY: Washington Square Press, 1960. (Latin text: *Epistola ad Ducissam Brabantiae.* In *Omnia Opera Sancti Thomae Aquinatis Doctoris Angelici.* Leonine Edition. Vol. 42. Rome: Polyglot Press, 1960.)
———. *On Kingship, to the King of Cyprus.* Ed. I. K. Th. Eschmann, trans. Gerald B. Phelan. Toronto: Pontifical Institute of Mediaeval Studies, 1982. (Latin text: *De Regimine Principum.* In *Omnia Opera Sancti Thomae Aquinatis Doctoris Angelici.* Leonine Edition. Vol. 42. Rome: Polyglot Press, 1960.)
———. *Summa Contra Gentiles.* In *Omnia Opera Sancti Thomae Aquinatis Doctoris Angelici.* Leonine Edition. Vols. 13–15. Rome: Polyglot Press, 1918–1930. (Translation: A.C. Pegis, et al. Notre Dame, IN: University of Notre Dame Press, 1975.)
———. *Summa Theologiae.* Latin Text and English Translation, Introductions, Notes, Appendices, and Glossaries. Ed., trans., and intro. Thomas Gilby. New Blackfriars Edition. New York, NY: McGraw Hill, 1964–1980.
Thucydides. *History.* In *Thucydides. History of the Peloponnesian War.* Trans. Charles Forster Smith, 4 vols. Cambridge, MA: Harvard University Press, 1921–1930. (Partial trans. in *Early Greek Political Thought from Homer to the Sophists.* Ed. Michael Gagarin and Paul Woodruff. Cambridge: Cambridge University Press, 1995.)
Tierney, Brian. 1955. *Foundations of the Conciliar Theory: The Contribution of the Medieval Canonists from Gratian to the Great Schism.* Cambridge: Cambridge University Press.
———. 1982. *Religion, Law and the Growth of Constitutional Thought, 1150–1650.* Cambridge: Cambridge University Press.
———. 1989. Origins of Natural Rights Language: Texts and Contexts, 1150–1250. *History of Political Thought* 10: 632–36.
———. 1992. *Ius* and Metonymy in Rufinus. In *Studia in Honorem Eminentissimi Cardinalis Alfonsi Stickler.* Ed. R. J. Castillo Lara, 549–58. Rome: LAS.
———. 1997. *The Idea of Natural Rights: Studies on Natural Rights, Natural Law and Church Law 1150–1625.* Atlanta, GA: Scholars.
———. 2007. Vitoria and Suárez on Ius Gentium, Natural Law, and Custom. In *The Nature of Customary Law.* Ed. Amanda Perreau-Saussine and Jeffrie Murphy, 101–24. Cambridge: Cambridge University Press.

Tkacz, Michael W., and Douglas Kries. 1994. *Augustine: Political Writings.* Indianapolis, IN: Hackett.
Tobin, Thomas H. 1983. *The Creation of Man: Philo and the History of Interpretation.* Washington, DC: Catholic Biblical Association of America.
Tobin, Vincent. 1987. *Ma'at* and *Dike*: Some Comparative Considerations of Egyptian and Greek Thought. *Journal of the American Research Center of Egypt* 24: 113–21.
Tod, Marcus N. 1948. *Greek Historical Inscriptions.* Oxford: Oxford University Press.
Todd, Stephen C. 1993. *The Shape of Athenian Law.* Oxford: Oxford University Press.
Todescan, Franco. 1973. *Lex, Natura, Beatitudo. Il problema della legge nella Scolastica spagnola del secolo XVI.* Padua: Cedam.
Torrell, Jean-Pierre. 1996. *Saint Thomas Aquinas: The Person and His Work.* Vol. 1. Trans. Robert Royal. Washington, DC: Catholic University of America Press.
Tracy, Stephen V. 2000. Demetrius of Phalerum: Who Was He and Who Was He Not? In *Demetrius of Phalerum: Text, Translation and Discussion.* Ed. William W. Fortenbaugh and Eckart Schütrumpf, 331–46. New Brunswick, NJ: Transaction.
Trainia, Cristina. 1999. *Feminist Ethics and Natural Law.* Washington, DC: Georgetown University Press.
Treggiari, Susan. 1991. *Roman Marriage.* Oxford: Oxford University Press.
Trentmann, John A. 1982. Scholasticism in the Seventeenth Century. In *The Cambridge History of Later Medieval Philosophy.* Ed. Norman Kretzmann, Jan Pinborg, and Anthony Kenny, 818–37. Cambridge: Cambridge University Press.
Troeltsch, Ernest. 1960. *The Social Teaching of the Christian Churches.* Trans. Olive Wyon. New York, NY: Harper.
Trueman, Carl, and R. L. Clark. 1999. *Protestant Scholasticism: Essays in Reassessment.* Carlisle: Paternoster.
Truman, Ronald W. 1999. *Spanish Treatises on Government, Society and Religion in the Time of Philip II: The "de regime principum" and Associated Traditions.* Leiden: Brill.
Trusen, Winifried. 1973. Die Gelehrte Gerichtsbarkeit der Kirche. In *Handbook der Quellen und Literatur der Neueren Europäischen Privaterechtsgeschichte.* Ed. Helmut Coing, 467–504. Munich: Beck.
Tuck, Richard. 1979. *Natural Rights Theories: Their Origin and Development.* Cambridge: Cambridge University Press.
Tucker, George, ed. 2000. *Forms of the Medieval in the Renaissance.* Charlottesville, VA: Rookwood Press.
Tugwell, Simon, trans. and ed. 1988. *Albert and Thomas: Selected Writings.* Mahwah, NJ: The Paulist Press.
Tutino, Stefania. 2010. *Empire of Souls: Robert Bellarmine and the Christian Commonwealth.* Oxford: Oxford University Press.
Twersky, Isadore. 1980. *Introduction to the Code of Maimonides (Mishneh Torah).* New Haven, CT: Yale University Press.
Tyldessley, J. A. 2000. *Judgment of the Pharaoh: Crime and Punishment in Ancient Egypt.* London: Weidenfeld and Nicolson.
Tyrtaeus. *Poems.* In *Early Greek Political Thought from Homer to the Sophists.* Ed. Michael Gagarin and Paul Woodruff, 23–4. Cambridge: Cambridge University Press, 1995.
Ullmann, Walter. 1975. *Law and Politics in the Middle Ages: An Introduction to the Sources of Medieval Political Ideas.* Ithaca, NY: Cornell University Press.
Urdanoz, Teofilo. 1960. Introducción Biográfica. In *Relecciones Teológicas.* Ed. Obras Francisco de Vitoria, 1–107. Madrid: BAC.
Van Asselt, Willem J., and Eef Dekker. 2001. *Reformation and Scholasticism: An Ecumenical Enterprise.* Grand Rapids, MI: Baker Academic.
Van Den Eynde, D. 1949. The Terms Ius Positivum and Signum Positivum in Twelfth-Century Scholasticism. *Franciscan Studies* 9: 41–9.
Van Effenterre, Henri, and Françoise Ruzé, eds. 1994–1995. *Nomima: Recueil d'Inscriptions Politiques et Juridiques de l'Archaïsme Grec.* Rome: Ecole Française de Rome.

Van Ophuijsen, Johannes M., and Marlein van Raalte, eds. 1998. *Theophrastus: Reappraising the Sources*. New Brunswick, NJ: Transaction.

Vander Waerdt, Paul A. 1994a. Philosophical Influence on Roman Jurisprudence? The Case of Stoicism and Natural Law. In *Aufstieg und Niedergang der Römischen Welt*. Ed. Wofgang Haase and Hildegard Temporini, II 36.7: 4851–900. Berlin: de Gruyter.

———, ed. 1994b. *The Socratic Movement*. Ithaca, NY: Cornell University Press.

———. 1994c. Zeno's *Republic* and the Origins of Natural Law. In *The Socratic Movement*. Ed. Paul A. Vander Waerdt, 272–308. Ithaca, NY: Cornell University Press.

———. 2003. The Original Theory of Natural Law. In *The Studia Philonica Annual* 15. Ed. David T. Runia, Gregory E. Sterling, and Hindy Najman, 17–34. Providence, RI: Brown University.

Vasunia, Phiroze. 2001. *The Gift of the Nile: Hellenizing Egypt from Aeschylus to Alexander*. Berkeley, CA: University of California Press.

Veatch, Henry B. 1971. *For an Ontology of Morals*. Evanston, IL: Northwestern University Press.

———. 1985. *Human Rights: Fact or Fancy?* Baton Rouge; LA: Louisiana State University Press.

———. 1990. *Swimming Against the Current in Contemporary Philosophy*. Washington, DC: Catholic University of America Press.

Veatch, Henry B., and Joseph Rautenberg. 1991. Does the Grisez-Finnis-Boyle Moral Philosophy Rest on a Mistake? *Review of Metaphysics* 44: 807–30.

Vereecke, Louis. 1957. *Conscience Morale et Loi Humaine Selon Gabriel Vasquez S.J.* Tournai: Desclée.

Versteeg, Russ. 2002. *Law in Ancient Egypt*. Durham, NC: Carolina Academic Press.

Vetulani, Adam. 1946–47. Gratien et le Droit Romain. *Revue Historique de Droit Français et Etranger* 24–25: 11–48.

———. 1955. Nouvelles Vues sur le Décret de Gratien. In *La Pologne au Xe Congrès International des Sciences Historiques à Rome*. Ed. Instytut Historii, 83–105. Warsaw: Państwowe Wydawnictwo Naukowe.

Villey, Michel. 1946. L'Idée du Droit Subjectif et les Systèmes Juridiques Romains. *Revue Historique de Droit* 24: 201–27.

———. 1953–1954. Les Origines de la Notion de Droit Subjectif. *Archives de Philosophie du Droit* 2: 163–87.

———. 1975. *La Formation de la Pensée Juridique Moderne*. 4th ed. Paris: Éditions Montchrestien.

———. 1983. *Le Droit et Les Droits de l'Homme*. Paris: Presses Universitaires de France.

———. 1996. Questions of Legal Logic in the History of the Philosophy of Law. In *European Legal Cultures*. Ed. Volkmar, Gessner, Armin Hoeland, and Csaba Varga, 111–5. Aldershot: Dartmouth.

Villoslada, Ricardo. 1938. *La Universidad de Paris durante los Estudios de Francisco de Vitoria*. Rome: Gregorian University.

Vitoria, Francisco de. *Comentarios a la Secunda Secundae de Santo Tomás*. Ed. Vincente Beltrán de Heredia. 6 vols. Salamanca: Universidad de Salamanca, 1932–1952.

———. *De Indis*. In *Relectiones XII in Duos Tomos Duisiae*. 2 vols. Lyon: Jacobus, Boyerius, 1557. (Trans. in *Franciscus de Vitoria De Indis et de Iure Belli Relectiones*. Ed. Ernest Nys; trans. John Pawley Bate. Washington, DC: Carnegie Institution, 1917. Partial trans. of QQ. 1–3 in *Vitoria. Political Writings*. Ed. and trans. Anthony Pagden and Jeremy Lawrance. Cambridge: Cambridge University Press, 1991.)

———. *De Matrimonio*. In *Relectiones XII in Duos Tomos Duisiae*. 2 vols. Lyon: Jacobus, Boyerius, 1557.

———. *De Potestate Civile* (*On Civil Power*). In *Relectiones XII in Duos Tomos Duisiae*. 2 vols. combined. Lyon: Jacobus, Boyerius, 1557. (In *Leçon sur le Pouvoir Politique*. Trans. Maurice Barbier. Paris: Vrin, 1980. Partial trans. of QQ. 1 and 3 in *Vitoria. Political Writings*. Ed. and trans. Anthony Pagden and Jeremy Lawrance. Cambridge: Cambridge University Press, 1991.)

———. 1991. *Political Writings*. Ed. and trans. Anthony Pagden and Jeremy Lawrance. Cambridge: Cambridge University Press.
Vivès, Juan Luis. *De Concordia et Discordia in Humano Genere*. In *Opera Omnia*. Ed. G. Mayans y Siscar, 8 vols. (*Obras Completas*. Trans. Lorenzo Riber. Madrid: Aguilar, 1947–1948.)
Vlastos, Gregory. 1971. Justice and Happiness in the *Republic*. In *The Philosophy of Socrates*. Ed. Gregory Vlastos, 111–39. London: Macmillan.
———. 1977. The Theory of Social Justice in the Polis in Plato's *Republic*. In *Interpretations of Plato: A Swarthmore Symposium*. Ed. Helen North, 1–40. Lugduni Batavorum: Brill.
———. 1988. Socrates. *Proceedings of the British Academy* 74: 89–111.
———. 1991. *Socrates: Ironist and Moral Philosopher*. Cambridge: Cambridge University Press.
Voegelin, Eric. 1956. *Israel and Revelation*. Volume 1 of *Order and History*. Baton Rouge, LA: Louisiana State University Press.
Volterra, E. 1958. Intorno ad alcune costituzioni di Costantino. *Rendiconti dell'Accademica Nazionale dei Lincei* 3–4: 61–89.
Von Fritz, Kurt, and Ernst Kapp. 1950. *Constitution of Athens and Related Texts*. New York, NY: Hafner.
Wagner, Andreas. 2011. *Francisco de Vitoria and Alberico Gentili on the Legal Character of the Global Commonwealth*. Oxford Journal of Legal Studies 31: 565–82.
Waldron, Jeremy. 1995. The Wisdom of the Multitude: Some Reflections on Book 3, Chapter 11 of Aristotle's *Politics*. *Political Theory* 23: 563–84.
Waldstein, Wolfgang. 1994. *Ius Naturale* im Nachklassischen Römischen Recht und bei Justinian. *Zeitschrift der Savigny-Stiftung für Rechtsgeschichte, Romanistische Abteilung* 111: 1–65.
Warmington, E. H. 1967. *Remains of Old Latin*. Rev. ed. Cambridge, MA: Harvard University Press.
Warnock, G. J. 1967. *Contemporary Moral Philosophy*. New York, NY: St. Martin's.
Watson, Alan. 1974. *Law Making in the Later Roman Republic*. Oxford: Oxford University Press.
———. 1975. *Rome of the XII Tables*. Princeton, NJ: Princeton University Press.
———. 1995a. *The Spirit of Roman Law*. Athens, GA: The University of Georgia Press.
———. 1995b. *Jesus and the Jews: The Pharisaic Tradition in John*. Athens, GA: University of Georgia Press.
———. 1996. *Jesus and the Law*. Athens, GA: University of Georgia Press.
Watson, G. 1971. The Natural Law and Stoicism. In *Problems in Stoicism*. Ed. Anthony A. Long, 216–38. London: Athlone.
Weimar, Peter. 1973. Die Legistische Literatur der Glossatorenzeit. In *Handbook der Quellen und Literatur der Neueren Europäischen Privaterechtsgeschichte*. Ed. Helmut Coing, 129–260. Munich: Beck.
Weinfeld, Moshe. 1991. *Deuteronomy 1–11* (Anchor Bible). New York, NY: Doubleday.
Weisheipl, J. A. 1983. *Friar Thomas D'Aquino*. 2nd Ed. Washington, DC: Catholic University of America Press.
Weiss, Rosalyn. 1998. *Socrates Dissatisfied*. New York, NY: Oxford University Press.
Weithman, Paul. 2001. Augustine's Political Philosophy. In *The Cambridge Companion to Augustine*. Ed. E. Stump and N. Kretzmann, 234–52. Cambridge: Cambridge University Press.
Westbrook, Richard. 2003a. *A History of Ancient Near Eastern Law*. Handbuch der Orientalistik 72. Leiden: E.J. Brill.
———. 2003b. Old Babylonian Period. In *A History of Ancient Near Eastern Law*. Ed. Richard Westbrook, 360–430. Leiden: E.J. Brill.
Westerman, Pauline. 1997. *The Disintegration of Natural Law Theory: Aquinas to Finnis*. Leiden: Brill.
White, Kevin, ed. 1998. *Hispanic Philosophy in the Age of Discovery*. Washington, DC: Catholic University of America Press.
Widow, Juan Antonio. 1997. The Economic Teachings of Spanish Scholastics. In *Hispanic Philosophy in the Age of Discovery*. Ed. Kevin White, 130–44. Washington, DC: Catholic University of America Press.

Wilenius, Reijo. 1963. *The Social and Political Theory of Francisco Suárez*. Helsinki: Acta Philosophica Fennica.

William of Auxerre. *Summa Aurea*. In *William of Auxerre, Summa Aurea, III, vol. 1*. Ed. J. Ribaillier. Paris: Centre National de la Recherche Scientifique, 1986.

William of Ockham. *Dialogus in Monarchia S. Romani Imperii*. In *Dialogus in Monarchia S. Romani Imperii*. Ed. M. Goldast. *Dialogus in Monarchia S. Romani Imperii*. Frankfurt: Conrad Bierman, 1614.

———. *A Letter to the Friars Minor, and Other Writings*. Ed. Arthur Stephen McGrade and John Kilcullen; trans. John Kilcullen. New York, NY: Cambridge University Press, 1995.

———. *Opera Politica*. Vol. 1. Ed. J. G. Sikes et al. Manchester: Manchester University Press, 1960. Vol. 2. Ed. R. F. Bennett and H. S. Offler. Manchester: Manchester University Press, 1963. Vol. 3. Ed. H. S. Offler. Manchester: Manchester University Press, 1966. Vol. 4. Ed. H. S. Offler. Oxford: Oxford University Press, 1997.

———. *Reportatio* = Books 2–4 of *Commentary on the Sentences* (*In Libros Sententiarum*). In *Guillelmi de Ockham Opera Philosophica et Theologica*. Ed. Gedeon Gál et al. St. Bonaventure, NY: The Franciscan Institute Press, 1967–1988.

———. *A Short Discourse on Tyrannical Government*. Ed. Arthur Stephen McGrade and trans. John Kilcullen. Cambridge: Cambridge University Press, 1992.

Williams, Thomas. 1998. The Libertarian Foundations of Scotus's Moral Philosophy. *The Thomist* 62: 193–215.

Wilson, A. N. 1997. *Paul: The Mind of the Apostle*. New York, NY: Norton.

Wilson, John A. 1946. Egypt. In *The Intellectual Adventure of Ancient Man: An Essay on Speculative Thought in the Ancient Near East*. Ed. Henri Frankfort et al., 31–93. Chicago, IL: University of Chicago Press.

Wilson, S. G. 1983. *Luke and the Law*. Cambridge: Cambridge University Press.

Wiltshire, Susan Ford. 1992. *Greece, Rome, and the Bill of Rights*. Norman, OK: University of Oklahoma Press.

Winroth, Anders. 2000. *The Making of Gratian's Decretum*. Cambridge: Cambridge University Press.

Wippel, John. 2000. *The Metaphysics of Thomas Aquinas*. Washington, DC: Catholic University of America Press.

Witte, John. 2002. *Law and Protestantism: The Legal Teachings of the Protestant Reformation*. Cambridge: Cambridge University Press.

Wolf, Armin. 1973. Die Gesetzgebung der Enstehenden Territorialstaaten. In *Handbook der Quellen und Literatur der Neueren Europäischen Privaterechtsgeschichte*. Ed. Helmut Coing, 517–800. Munich: Beck.

———. 1983. Gesetzgebung und Kodifikationen. In *Die Renaissance der Wissenschaften im 12.Jahrhundert*. Ed. Peter Weimar, 143–71. Zurich: Artemis.

Wolff, Hans Julius. 1951. *Roman Law: An Introduction*. Norman, OK: University of Oklahoma Press.

Wolter, Allan B. 1993. *Duns Scotus*. Special Issue. *American Catholic Philosophical Quarterly* 67.1.

Wolterstorff, Nicholas. 2008. *Justice: Rights and Wrongs*. Princeton, NJ: Princeton University Press.

Woodruff, Paul. 1993. *Thucydides on Justice, Power, and Human Nature*. Indianapolis, IN: Hackett Publishing Company.

Woozley, A. D. 1971. Socrates on Disobeying the Law. In *The Philosophy of Socrates: A Collection of Critical Essays*. Ed. Gregory Vlastos, 299–318. Garden City, KS: Doubleday.

———. 1979. *Law and Obedience: The Arguments of Plato's Crito*. London: Duckworth.

Wormuth, F. 1948. Aristotle on Law. In *Essays in Political Theory Presented to George H. Sabine*. M. R. Konvitz and A. E. Murphy, 45–61. Ithaca, NY: Cornell University Press.

Worcester, Thomas, ed. 2008. *The Cambridge Companion to the Jesuits*. Cambridge: Cambridge University Press.

Xenophon. *Anabasis*. Trans. Carleton L. Brownson; rev. John Dillery. Cambridge, MA: Harvard University Press, 1998.

———. *Cyropaedia* (*Education of Cyrus*). Trans. Walter Miller. Cambridge, MA: Harvard University Press, 1914.
———. *De Vectigalibus*. In *Xenophon 5*. Ed. E. C. Marchant and G. W. Bowersock. Cambridge, MA: Harvard University Press, 1968.
———. *Hiero*. Trans. E. C. Marchant. In *Xenophon 5*. Ed.. E. C. Marchant and G. W. Bowersock. Cambridge, MA: Harvard University Press, 1968.
———. *Historia Graeca* (*Hellenica*). Trans. Carleton L. Brownson, 2 vols. Cambridge, MA: Harvard University Press, 1918–1921.
——— (pseudo) = "The Old Oligarch." *The Constitution of the Athenians*. Trans. G. W. Bowersock. In *Xenophon 5*. Ed. E. C. Marchant and G. W. Bowersock. Cambridge, MA: Harvard University Press, 1968. (*Early Greek Political Thought from Homer to the Sophists*. Ed. and trans. Michael Gagarin and Paul Woodruff, 133–44. Cambridge: Cambridge University Press, 1995.)
———. *Memorabilia*. Trans. E. C. Marchant. In *Xenophon 4*. Ed. E. C. Marchant and O. J. Todd, 3–359. Cambridge, MA: Harvard University Press, 1923.
———. *Oeconomicus*. Trans. E. C. Marchant. In *Xenophon 4*. Ed. E. C. Marchant and O. J. Todd, 363–525. Cambridge, MA: Harvard University Press, 1923.
———. *Respublica Lacaedemoniorum* (*Constitution of the Lacedaemonians*). In *Xenophon 5*. Ed. E. C. Marchant and G. W. Bowersock. Cambridge, MA: Harvard University Press, 1968.
———. *Symposium*. Trans. O. J. Todd. In *Xenophon IV*. Ed. E. C. Marchant and O. J. Todd, 527–635. Cambridge, MA: Harvard University Press, 1923.
Yack, Bernard. 1990. Natural Right and Aristotle's Understanding of Justice. *Political Theory* 18: 216–37.
Yaron, Reuven. 1988. *The Laws of Eshnunna*. 2nd. rev. ed. Leiden: Brill.
Young, Frances. 2000. Christianity. In *The Cambridge History of Greek and Roman Political Thought*. Ed. Christopher Rowe and Malcolm Schofield, 635–60. Cambridge: Cambridge University Press.
Zalba, Marcelino. 1934. Molina y las Ciencias Jurídico-Morales. *Razón y Fé* 127: 530–43.
Zane, John Maxcy. 1998. *The Story of Law*. Reprint ed. Indianapolis, IN: The Liberty Fund.
Zeller, Eduard. 1903. *Die Philosophie der Griechen in Ihrer Geschichtlichen Entwicklung*. Leipzig: O. R. Reisland.
Zetzel, James. 1999. *Cicero On the Commonwealth and On the Laws*. Cambridge: Cambridge University Press.
Zohar, Noam J. 1998. Halakhah. In *Routledge Encyclopedia of Philosophy*. Ed. Edward Craig. Vol. 4: 204–7. London: Routledge.
Zuckerman, Charles. 1973. The Relationship of Theories of Universals to Theories of Church Government in the Middle Ages. *Journal of the History of Ideas* 35: 579–90.
Zuckert, Michael P. 1989. "Bringing Philosophy Down from the Heavens": Natural Right in the Roman Law. Review of Politics 51: 70–85.

INDEX OF SUBJECTS

INDEX OF NAMES

MIX
Papier aus verantwortungsvollen Quellen
Paper from responsible sources
FSC® C105338

If you have any concerns about our products,
you can contact us on
ProductSafety@springernature.com

In case Publisher is established outside the EU,
the EU authorized representative is:
Springer Nature Customer Service Center GmbH
Europaplatz 3, 69115 Heidelberg, Germany

Printed by Libri Plureos GmbH
in Hamburg, Germany